DIS–
RUPT

Filipina Women:

PROUD.
LOUD.
LEADING
WITHOUT
A DOUBT.

DIS-
RUPT

Filipina Women:

PROUD.
LOUD.
LEADING
WITHOUT
A DOUBT.

The First Book
on Leadership
by the Filipina
Women's Network

Edited by
MARIA AFRICA BEEBE
MAYA ONG ESCUDERO

 San Francisco, California

Cover Design: Lucille Tenazas, Tenazas Design/NY
Interior Design: Edwin Lozada, Carayan Press

Published by
Filipina Women's Network
San Francisco, CA 94119 USA

http://filipinawomensnetwork.org
Email: filipina@ffwn.org

Printed in the United States of America

Pinay, pinay,
saan ka pupunta?
•

Nandito na ako!

CONTENTS

CONTENTS

Leading Organizations

Transcending Boundaries

CONTENTS

Developing Next Generation Leaders

Appendices

FOREWORD

Marily Mondejar
FWN Founder and CEO

The Filipina Women's Network (FWN) is thrilled with the publication of the first book of a series on Filipina Leadership.

DISRUPT. Filipina Women: Proud. Loud. Leading Without a Doubt is a collective synthesis on Filipina women's leadership experiences as Filipina women navigated corporate cultures in the global workplace.

The book launch was the highlight of the 11th Filipina Leadership Global Summit at the Makati Shangri-La on October 5-8, 2014. The selected 37 authors including the editors are recipients of FWN's 100 Most Influential Filipina Women in the World Award™.

"This is the definitive book that will change the public's perceptions of Filipina women's capacities to lead, FWN's Pinay Power 2020 mission," said Susie Quesada, president of FWN. "The authors are from the United States, Philippines, Brazil, Canada, Japan, Poland, Singapore and United Arab Emirates."

I congratulate the FWN editorial board for guiding the authors' writings and in the daunting task of pulling all the details of the publishing process. The elegant book cover designed by Lucille Lozada Tenazas, Global FWN100 '13 and Associate Dean of Art, Media and Technology at Parsons The New School for Design, captures the authors' inspiring stories about victories over poverty, domestic violence, incarceration, discrimination and harassment which shaped their leader identity, world view, sense of self, life purpose, power and influence.

Filipina women are the ultimate global disrupters. They disrupted their lives, families and careers when they left their home country to immigrate to foreign lands and re-invent their lives.

They disrupted their organizations as they became achievers in their professional fields and broke glass ceilings. They disrupted the business landscape when they innovated products, improved or created services that impacted the lives of women.

They disrupted their communities as they became strong advocates for social issues that affected their families especially their children.

They disrupted the political world when they ran for elected office representing causes benefitting local communities or became political insiders as valued advisors of the elected officials they worked for.

Second generation leaders who were raised in bi-cultural or multi-cultural families are the true disrupters. Growing up confused, they learned to embrace eastern and western values and traditions. They challenged themselves by defining their new identities as they navigated their way in their schools and workplaces. They developed new paradigms to managing conflict and broke antiquated rules to spark thoughtful conversations that the 21st century is about embracing all things multi-cultural.

Filipina women do not back down—once they make up their minds that they will get behind a cause or an issue that will change how people live, or aim for that promotion or leadership position—they don't stop. They're tenacious. They're firm. They're forceful. And they don't give up.

I am proud to stand shoulder to shoulder with these amazing women. Indeed, I can loudly say, I am a Filipina Disrupter, leading my community without any doubt of my capacity to achieve results.

PREFACE

Cora Manese Tellez
CEO, Sterling Health Services Administration

Long ago, a group of women met in San Francisco and dreamed of a time when successful Filipina women could meet and network and find opportunities to mentor younger Filipinas. It was 1996.

Fast forward to 2014 and marvel at our progress! The power of a small group of women who took a simple idea and created a powerful network of Filipina women in the U.S. and indeed, the world, just takes my breath away!

But then again, I should not really be surprised. After all, a Filipina women's network is an idea whose time has come. I sense a palpable hunger for a forum, a publication, a vehicle for Pinays to express who we are and what we aspire to become. Yet, we all know that great ideas go nowhere if there is no action to make them happen. The story of the Filipina Women's Network (FWN) is one of execution, persistence, and passion. The hardworking Filipina leaders of FWN, led by the incomparable Marily Mondejar, deserve our thanks and congratulations for making this dream a reality.

Our awards are about more than celebrating the success of Filipina women who are adding value to the world in a special way. They are about three things: first, giving hope to younger women who are starting their careers and wondering whether success is possible for a Filipina; second, providing support to women of any age who dare to challenge the conventional views of what is possible for a Filipina, and finally, challenging Filipina women and men who are successful in their careers to give back to our communities. Let me elaborate on these three things.

First, the giving of hope to younger women. I am fortunate to be in a position to counsel Filipina women who are striving to succeed in their field. I am often asked whether being a Filipina in the U.S. has been a liability to me in my professional journey. I believe that question speaks to concerns that somehow Filipino values and customs conflict with what it takes to succeed.

On a personal note, being a Filipina has not kept me from succeeding in corporate America as an executive or as a board director of publicly traded and venture-backed companies or as an entrepreneur. On the contrary, I am grateful to my Filipino heritage for being grounded in who I am and what matters in life. I take pride in telling business colleagues that I am a Filipina. My experience says that being a Filipina is an asset, not a liability. If you don't believe me, just ask the 100 women who are honored by FWN each year.

At the same time, I am keenly aware that there are challenges to young women who want to succeed while staying true to values taught by our parents and our community. Sometimes it is difficult to balance the demands of home and family with the pressures at work; and sometimes those demands call to question the relevance of Filipino values.

Frankly, I have found that certain values work very much in our favor. For example, the cultural value of working with others, *pakikisama*, is a trait that fosters alliances and networking. *Pakikisama* speaks to the sense of community, of working towards the collective well-being of family, friends, organization, and community. After all, success is a team sport and we women are natural team-players. The Filipina Women's Network is the perfect forum for Filipina women to network and obtain support!

Young Filipina women complain that outside of the Philippines, we are subject to stereotypes: we are supposed to be shy, modest, retiring, hard-working, but not assertive; meaning, we are NOT leadership material. In my professional history, I have relished destroying those stereotypes. I began by destroying those views inside my head, as often our mental models impair us long before we go to work. When our self-image is positive, strong, and confident, there is no leadership position we cannot tackle!

The 100 women who receive these awards each year bear witness to the power of a positive self-image as a Filipina. So, to the young women just starting out on their leadership journey, take heart! You can make it! Someday, you are going to look back and recall that when we met at an FWN event, you were emerging as a future CEO or political leader or serial entrepreneur!

My second point: affirming support for women who defy conventional views of what is possible for a Filipina. I am an example of failed familial dreams. My mother, a devout Catholic, had her view of success for me, and that was, I would be a nun. She had even picked out the convent for me. Even at age ten (mother started programming expectations at an early age), I sensed I would fail as a nun, because I knew I could not honor one vow. The vow is obedience to laws and rules that don't make sense to me.

A character trait (or flaw) that has defined me is a violent allergy to being told what to do, especially when I am told to follow practices and policies that I do not agree with. I figured out that the only way I could avoid being told what to do, is to be *Number One* in any group or company. But striving for excellence and leadership puts me in significant conflict with conventional views of Filipina women, especially the ones about being obedient and not questioning authority.

I have been privileged to meet very successful men and women in my life. I have learned from successful women, in particular, that they are made, not born; that they became successful, in part, because they challenged societal views of what a woman should be, should act like, or should have by way of professional success. They are comfortable in their own skin, and with each passing year, they destroy limits to what they can achieve. These women are in our midst today.

If I were to take a poll of the most influential Filipina women in the world, I bet I would learn the following:

- They are self-confident, self-assured in their views of their capabilities, and their ability to influence others.
- They are strong and courageous, as they have broken limits set by society, by their families, and perhaps, by their own mental views of themselves and how far they can go.
- They are avid learners; and, just as important, they learn from their mistakes.
- They are risk takers; they are willing to make sacrifices to test an idea, to pursue a dream.
- They are generous in sharing what they have learned.
- Quite literally and figuratively, they hold the door open for other women.

Finally, these very successful women are the beneficiaries of support from their families, from husbands, children, parents, siblings, co-workers, and friends who believe in them. The support from others provided encouragement when times were hard, capital when it was needed, and support in tangible and intangible ways. As I said previously, success is a team sport, and successful women benefit enormously from their personal team of supporters.

This brings me to my final point: giving back. To me, success carries a powerful responsibility, and that has to do with giving back. For every successful woman, there are many more women who feel stuck in positions that are soul-destroying, and many young women who will be denied opportunities to grow. And who can we depend on to help such women if not successful Filipina women?

If you agree with me that success is a team sport, then it behooves us to support the home team. In this book are stories by women who model behavior that speaks to giving back. They have created opportunities for women through personal referrals, by providing scholarships, by mentoring, by advancing capital to young entrepreneurs, and by funding charitable organizations. These women are true heroes, as they model for us what success truly means. Like you, I celebrate these women and look to learn from them.

What will success look like if we achieve these three things: hope, courage, and giving back? The Filipina Women's Network offers us one definition of success: to double the number of global Filipina leaders by 2020. We have work to do to build a solid pipeline of emerging Filipina leaders if we are to meet this goal.

The goal is lofty, but achievable. Who could have imagined how far our network would come? Now imagine the future, and know it is only a matter of time before we double the number of global Filipina leaders. Let us begin by celebrating the achievements of women who succeeded against tough odds, women who have shattered glass ceilings, women who have stayed faithful to and appreciative of their Filipino heritage.

Let us now celebrate some of the 100 Most Influential Filipina Women in the World who are sharing their stories with you in this book!

INTRODUCTION

Maria Africa Beebe, Ph.D.

And their sister, the strange *diwata* [muse, mythical spirit] whose light remains contained. Witness she is, and weaver. If she would only speak, then she would tell you—*these stories I give you, I swear they are the truth.*

—EXCERPT FROM "DIWATA" BY BARBARA JANE REYES

This book is a collection of leadership stories by global Filipina women. These leaders were selected from the Filipina Women's Network's 100 Most Influential Filipina Women roster of 2013 and awardees from previous years. The narratives of these Filipina women include references to disruptions in their personal and professional lives when they left the Philippines, their home country, for economic, social, political, and educational opportunities while other Filipina women faced challenges growing up in foreign cultures. These Filipina women have overcome complex personal and professional challenges while living and working in multiple cultures. They have been widely recognized as they achieve success in their professional fields and local communities, successes that the Filipina Women's Network (FWN) have wanted to honor. This book is a significant step allowing Filipina women around the world to know about the accomplishments of their Filipina sisters. FWN provides a sisterhood, a network of peers for meet-ups, and lean-in circles.

These Filipina women share their experiences in navigating the complexities of life and work across cultures. Their reflections show how they were able to lead lives of commitment, disrupting the status quo while maintaining deep family relationships and adhering to Filipino cultural norms such as *pakikipagkapwa*. This term is difficult to translate as it encompasses the meaning of "being with-others," "equality," "shared identity" (Guevarra 2005), and "being in tune with other people's motives and with the self" (Saplala 2009).

Our hope is that these narratives will promote the recruitment and development of Filipina women for leadership and management positions in the corporate, government, and not-for-profit sectors. We expect these stories will provide inspiration to aspiring and emergent leaders among overseas Filipina women workers, Filipina women in the diaspora, and Filipina women in the Philippines.

The conceptual framework for this book builds on Philippine and U.S. academic scholarly works. Key concepts for the framework. include: (a) the *Kapwa* theory associated with Enriquez (1989), (b) the definition of Filipino leadership associated with Cuyegkeng and Palma-Angeles (2011), (c) the relational theory of leadership associated with Uhl-Bien (2006), (d) the flexible theory of leadership associated with Kaiser and Overfield (2010), and (e) the concept of global leadership associated with Mendenhall et al. (2013). The synthesis chapter applies Hammond's (2013) appreciative inquiry with its focus on what works and the identification of the best of what is and its assumptions that what we focus on and the language we use shape our reality.

Sociohistorical and Sociocultural Factors

Academic researchers who embarked upon "the quest for a general theory of leadership" have often concluded that the "study of leadership provides another way to ask very big questions about who we are, how we live together, and how we shape the course of history" (Ciulla 2005, 233). Understanding what is brought from the past fosters self-discovery that provides confidence for the journey to the future. Thus, we briefly summarize the socio-historical and cultural influences that have contributed to the creation of Filipina women's identities and how the intersection of these identities with their global experience has shaped their leadership.

Situating the Philippines in a global context, Abinales and Amoroso (2005) traced the development of the Philippines from its origin in pre-historical maritime Southeast Asia through the Spanish empire of galleons and Catholic missionaries, and the American century of colonialism and post-colonialism. In a 1986 speech, President Cory Aquino voiced the inner conflict of most Filipinos: "It is true that there are times when our Asian cultural antecedents clash with our Western cultural legacy and threaten to fragment our cultural identity. It is true that in many ways we are still in search of ourselves."

During pre-Spanish times, women leaders were known as *babaylan* (Mananzan 2010) and were considered warriors, teachers, healers, visionaries, and priestesses. According to San Juan (2011), Spanish colonialism can be blamed for destroying the memory of the egalitarian communal society that existed at the time of first contact: "It ushered a thoroughgoing gender differentiation with the institutionalization of private property, monogamy, and the patriarchal authority of fathers within the family" (39). With anti-colonial, anti-imperialist, and anti-martial law movements in the Philippines, women have contributed to cultural, economic, and political resurgence. (See a timeline of historical factors in Appendix D.)

In spite of attempts to repress women's role in Philippine politics, a tradition of female participation has continued (Aquino 1993). Women's political engagement in the Philippines in the 20th century included: (1) the struggle for women's suffrage that was won in 1937, one of the earliest in the Third World; (2) resistance to the 14 years of authoritarian martial law from 1972 to 1986 under President Ferdinand Marcos; (3) mobilization of popular resistance on a wide range of socio-political issues, such as the U.S. military bases in the Philippines, multinational corporations, militarization, human rights violations, the Bataan nuclear reactor, the country's huge foreign debt, prostitution, poverty, crime, and other social-economic problems; (4) organization of working women to fight for their rights and secure better conditions; and (5) promotion of alternative mechanisms of political or popular participation. More recently, Filipinos have elected two female presidents President Cory Aquino (1986-1992) and President Gloria Macapagal Arroyo (2001- 2010).

The latest Global Gender Gap Report by the World Economic Forum (2013) showed the Philippines as ranked fifth. The report stated that the inequality between men and women has narrowed, in terms of economic participation and opportunity, educational attainment, health and survival, and political empowerment. However, the report noted that economic and participation gaps remain particularly in senior positions, wages and leadership levels.

Filipina National Identity

Doronila (1989, 46-47) explained four patterns of Filipino national identity. These patterns are ethnocentrism, valuing of cultural aspects, loyalty to the national community, and commitments to the role requirements of citizenship (see Table 1 below). These patterns appear to inform the identity of Filipinas, no matter where they are in the world, and are foundational to their leadership, including their desire to give back to society.

The Global Filipina

> *Pinay, pinay saan ka pupunta? Nandito na ako.*
> Filipina, Filipina where are you going? I am now here.

In the Philippines, "Where are you going" [*Saan ka pupunta?*] is an informational greeting. The response to the greeting could be a lift of the eyebrows, a smile, pointing with the lips, a vague "There only" [*Diyan lang*], or naming a specific geographic place such as Israel, Saudi, Middle East, Canada or America. "Where are you going?" can also be an existential question: What is your greater purpose? Where is your life headed?

Filipina Destinations

Filipinos can be found in more than 200 countries and territories. The top five destinations for emigration are the U.S., Canada, Japan, Australia, and Italy. The top five destinations for labor migrants are the U.S., Canada, Australia, Saudi Arabia, and the United Arab Emirates.

The U.S. as the top destination for both emigration and labor can be attributed to the long history of the linkages between the U.S. and the Philippines. The literature suggests that many of the Filipina women emigrants to Australia and New Zealand involved marriage migration. Over 70 per cent of Overseas Filipino Workers (OFWs) are between 25 and 44 years of age. Those over 40 are mostly men, those younger than 40 are mostly women. About 60 percent of OFWs are women even though female labor participation in the

TABLE I: Four patterns of Filipino National Identity

PATTERNS	SPECIFIC ORIENTATION
A. Ethnocentrism	1. Preference for one's nationality over all others 2. Generalized pride in one's country over all others (including those that have exerted or are exerting influence and control over the country) 3. Support of nationalism prior to internationalism 4. Commitment to the goal of development through national self-reliance, with specific reference to the country's decolonization goals
B. Valuing of cultural aspects reflective of national identity	5. Valuing the special qualities of the people 6. Valuing their characteristic way of life 7. Valuing national traditions, including historical, cultural, legal 8. Valuing their cultural products, including language, art, literature
C. Loyalty to the national community beyond ethnic loyalties	9. Recognition of other ethnic groups as belonging to the Philippine national community 10. Personal acceptance of individuals who belong to these other ethnic groups 11. Recognition of cultural affinities of one's ethnic group with other ethnic groups 12. Acceptance of other ethnic groups as belonging to the Philippine national community 13. Commitment to the idea of national integration of all ethnic groups
D. Commitment to the role requirements of citizenship	14. Pride in national symbols 15. Deriving personal identity from identification with the nation 16. Commitment to the duties of citizenship (active citizenship, disengaged or passive citizenship, non-political aspects of citizenship)

Doronila 1989, 46-47

Philippines is only about 50 percent.

It is estimated that in 2012, the 10 million overseas Filipinos remitted about US $20 billion, making overseas employment an important source of Philippine export earnings and contributing between 8 and 10 percent of GDP (Scalabrini Migration Center 2013). Unofficial remittances are estimated to be 30 to 40 percent higher than the official figure (Remo 2012).

Reasons for Overseas Employment and Migration

Economics is the most important reason given by individuals for overseas employment and migration. Other reasons given for migration are marriages to nationals of other countries, to reunite with families members already working or residing abroad, to benefit from career and education opportunities, to have a higher standard of living, and to experience other cultures (Scalabrini Migration Center 2013). In some cases, women initiated migratory moves to gain autonomy or escape adverse domestic conditions in the Philippines (Bautista 2002).

In addition to the push factors from the Philippines, there is a strong pull factor for migrant workers in the more developed economies. Young and educated Filipino workers are able to replace the declining number of workers in other places, particularly doing domestic work. In general, domestic workers are employed by private households (International Labor Organization 2013). Filipina caregivers are employed worldwide for young, healthy children and families, or as housecleaners (Cheng 2003, Chin 1998, Constable 1997, Parreñas 2001, Shah et al. 2011). Choy (2003) observed that the Philippines had been transformed into "an empire of care" (3).

As of 2011, over 1.8 Filipino immigrants resided in the United States, of whom 60 percent were female (Stoney and Batalova 2013). Filipina women were more likely than other immigrant women to work as registered nurses, as other healthcare practitioners, and in allied healthcare support operations.

Reyes, in a report made to UNICEF (2008, 1), estimated that nine million or 27 percent of all Filipino youth under the age of 18 had been left behind in the Philippines by one or both parents migrating or working overseas. Although the extended family looks after the children left behind, those children experience large-scale displacement and disruptions.

Research on Filipina Leader Identity

Research on Filipina women leadership is limited. Roffey's (1999) study on effective leadership and management by Filipinas in Metro Manila-based businesses is a solid beginning. Roffey (1999) identified six competencies needed for effective leadership and management: (1) interpersonal; (2) leading by example; (3) initiating; (4) external public relations; (5) market and customer orientation; and (6) integrity and honesty. In contrast with a Western-based organization, a Filipino organization is organized "as extended family" where the leaders have "personal responsibility" for their employees," and the employees expect to be "looked after by their managers" (383). Roffey (1999) concluded that effective Filipina leaders make ethical use of kinship, including fictive kinship, and family alliance in their leadership (388).

President Cory Aquino was identified as exemplifying servant leadership based on her core virtues of integrity, spirituality, exemplary character, humility, simplicity, and courage while remaining authentic and people-centered and demonstrating grace under pressure (Udani and Grace-Molo 2012, 378). Her virtues influenced and were influenced by her spirituality, and Aquino viewed "her faith and the presidency as compatible dimensions of life" (379).

In *Defining Filipino Leadership*, Cuyegkeng and Palma-Angeles (2011, 340) noted that Filipino leaders have the vision to transform individuals and their institutions, have a good grasp of the institutional culture and structure, have good judgment for choosing teams, have the ability to introduce gradual reforms, and build trust by showing humility (340). The description of leadership by Cuyegkeng and Palma-Angeles is applicable to the 35 Filipinas who share their stories in this book.

To a large extent, Filipina American feminists, as well as academic writers use the language of deficit to describe overseas Filipinas. For example, de Jesus (2005) wrote "Haunted by the ghosts of colonization and imperialism, Pinay Power manifests common themes throughout: alienation, invisibility, trauma, healing, and resistance." Initial steps are being made to balance this negativity with assertions that overseas Filipinas, instead of being 'passive victims,' are increasingly able to 'negotiate with formidable structural forces' (Aguilar 2002, 2). Strobel noted the desire of Filipinos to give back, "our sense of wholeness and beauty and restore the harmony in the interconnected webs of life in all its forms" (2010, 3). It was in this spirit that FWN honorees shared their leadership stories.

Networking and Honoring Filipinas

Much of the focus on Filipino immigrants has been on Filipino men who were brought to America as farm laborers and Filipina women who came as brides. One of the goals of FWN is to change this narrative by highlighting the economic contributions to business and society of accomplished Filipina women. FWN originally focused on Filipina women in the United States but since 2013 has expanded its focus to Filipina women in countries worldwide. Between 2007 and 2013, FWN recognized almost 500 Filipina women as Founders and Pioneers, Innovators and Thought Leaders, Policymakers and Visionaries, Behind the Scenes Leaders, Builders, Emerging Leaders, and Aspiring Leaders.

FWN honors women of Philippine ancestry who are influencing and effecting change and making change happen in their communities, their industries, and their professions throughout the world. The honorees include CEOs of multinational corporations, entrepreneurs, philanthropists, scientists, executive directors and founders of not-for-profit agencies, senior program managers, journalists, clinical nurse specialists, and an international racecar driver. Also honored are the founders, chief executive officers, presidents, vice presidents, directors, and managing directors of large organizations, officers in the U.S. military, elected senators and representatives, cabinet rank administrators of government agencies, and senior administrators, deans, and professors in higher education.

According to FWN President Susie Quesada, the Global 100™

and those who have been previously identified as among the most influential Filipinas in the U.S. are already significantly changing public perceptions of Filipina women's capacities to lead, innovate, and influence society and the workplace.

Book Structure

Chapters 1, 2, and 3 of this book focus on the challenges faced in building and sustaining FWN and the role of FWN in giving voice to survivors of domestic violence, claiming political power, and building leadership.

Chapters 4 through 35 of this book offer the leadership stories from these women who have been recognized as leaders by their peers. Most of these women were identified by FWN as among the 100 most influential Filipina women in the world (FWN Global 100™) in 2013. Several women were among the most influential in the U.S. in 2007, the first year the awards were given. The individual narratives focus on their leadership journeys, the shaping of their Filipina leadership identities, the reach of their leadership, the circumstances of their leadership, and their reasons for leading. Each chapter includes leadership tips for aspiring next-generation leaders.

The book ends with a synthesis that identifies leadership themes based on the ways successful Filipina women practice leadership. These Fiipina women indicate their commitment to the leadership development of young and aspiring Filipina leaders by sharing their leadership tips. Building the pipeline for the next generation of leaders is central to FWN's mission: a Filipina woman leader in every sector of the economy.

Methodology

The perspectives of the FWN Global 100 were taken from three sources.

1. The October 2013 *Special Issue of the Filipina Women's Network* magazine has the responses of the Global 100 honorees to questions prepared by Marily Mondejar, FWN Founder and CEO. They were

asked to state: (a) current employment, (b) residence, (c) education, (d) first job, (e) the one person who influenced their professional career and why, (f) most difficult workplace challenge as a Filipina woman and why, (g) turning point in their professional life, (h) if they no longer lived in the Philippines, why they left, (i) Filipino custom or tradition they would like to pass on to others, (j) favorite Filipino recipe, (k) the things others would likely not guess about them, (l) favorite female fiction (s)hero, (m) book they are currently reading, (n) greatest regret, (o) life philosophy, and (p) wish for FWN. Instead of responding to these questions, several women submitted short statements that covered many of these same topics.

2. As part of the 10th Annual Filipina Leadership Summit in San Francisco in October, 2013, 32 of the FWN Global 100™ participated in the 'Time Capsule Project.' The Time Capsule Project was proposed at FWN's 4th Filipina Summit in 2006 when the Filipino community was celebrating 100 years of Filipino migration to America. Missing were the stories of the contributions of Filipina women. "Never again forget the role of Filipina women in the building of the U.S. of America," said Marily Mondejar. As part of the time capsule project, they responded to select questions relating to their (a) career path, (b) relationships that have affected careers, (c) ideal leadership qualities, (d) balancing of life and career, (e) advice to young women, (f) perceptions of the significance of leaving a legacy, and (g) definitions of success and failure. Their responses were video-taped, transcribed, and archived.

3. The book chapters contain extended stories of the experience and views of 35 Filipinas who responded to a call for abstracts to submit their reflections about leadership. A call for abstracts was sent to all of the Global FWN100™ and previous U.S. FWN100™ honorees in December 2013. The selected individual chapters were given a blind peer review. Moreover, three external readers read the entire book and made editorial and substantive comments. It is FWN's hope that the succeeding series of FWN leadership books will contain the stories and journeys of all of the awardees since 2007.

The Way Forward

Many Filipina women have taken tremendous strides in their homeland as well as in the foreign lands where they have relocated. They have exceeded high expectations. They have overturned myths about Filipina women, won over their opposition, and achieved success and honor in a diversity of fields. Their stories of creative disruption and their rise to leadership positions, accompanied by their giving back to society and femtoring next-generation leaders, deserve critical acclaim.

This book celebrates the achievement of these women using an academic conceptual framework. Their narratives include leadership tips for the next generation of leaders. The breadth and depth of the book should make it a useful resource in leadership courses around the world. Unique contributions of the book include addressing leadership issues in diaspora and cross-cultural settings, where Filipina women have demonstrated their ability to overcome barriers of gender, race, nationality, and language. The modular structure of the book also makes it easy for readers to focus on specific issues without having to follow a strict linear order.

In sum, this is not just a book about leadership successes of individuals but also a call to action to celebrate and expand the global leadership of Filipina women. The book is also a reminder to Filipina women of their responsibility to give back to society and to help create a better world. It is anticipated that future books by the FWN team will expand on this leadership discourse, delve deeper into cross-cultural frameworks, and offer new perspectives on leadership.

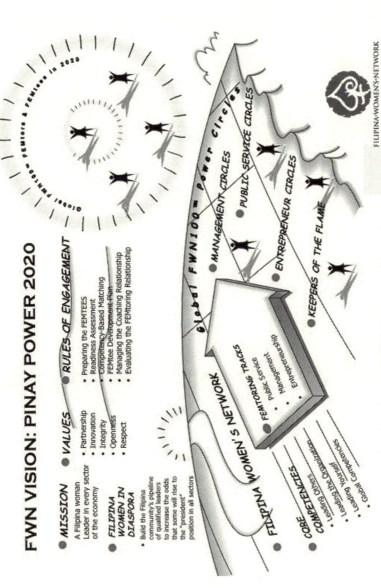

FWN VISION: PINAY POWER 2020

MISSION — A Filipina woman Leader in every sector of the economy

FILIPINA WOMEN IN DIASPORA — Build the Filipina community's pipeline of qualified leaders to increase the odds that some will rise to the "presidents" position in all sectors

VALUES
- Partnership
- Innovation
- Integrity
- Openness
- Respect

RULES OF ENGAGEMENT
- Preparing the FEMTEES
- Readiness Assessment
- Competency-Based Matching
- FEMtee Development Plan
- Managing the Coaching Relationship
- Evaluating the FEMtoring Relationship

FILIPINA WOMEN'S NETWORK

FEMTORING TRACKS
- Public Service
- Management
- Entrepreneurship

CORE COMPETENCIES
- Leading Others
- Leading Yourself
- Leading Communities
- Global Competencies

Global PWN100 Vision 4 FEMtees in 2020

Global FWN100 = Power Circles

MANAGEMENT CIRCLES · PUBLIC SERVICE CIRCLES · ENTREPRENEUR CIRCLES · KEEPERS OF THE FLAME

FILIPINA·WOMEN'S·NETWORK

"Never again forget the role of Filipina women in the building of our world's economy." – Marily Mondejar

Source: The Grove Consultants International modified to illustrate Pinay Power 2020 by Marily Mondejar.

Networking
Filipina Women Leaders

FWN and I

Marily Mondejar
Founder and CEO, Filipina Women's Network

Disruption

I was one of two Filipina women managers in Time Life Books Thailand in 1978. Bill Heinecke, a very successful American entrepreneur and the newly appointed distributor for Time Life Books Thailand, hired me to manage the product launch. He said he had been very impressed with my product knowledge when he was in Manila to observe the Philippine operations. At that time, I was just appointed the Special Projects Coordinator by the Time Life Book Division of Mondragon International. I was transitioning from sales manager for Time Life Books Quezon City. I was in an abusive marriage when I met Bill so this consulting gig was a turning point in my life. The opportunity gave me the confidence that I could support my children and myself.

I had never lived alone, especially in a foreign country. I was thrilled to have my own income, my own apartment and a promising new career. I remember one morning when Bill came to pick me up at my apartment on our way to a business meeting. In his limousine was this humungous phone attached to what I thought was a car battery. I was impressed at how he could do business in the car while his chauffeur drove us to the meeting. I learned from him how high-powered CEOs and successful entrepreneurs conduct business. He flew his own plane. He raced cars. He owned hotels and represented various American consumer goods in Thailand. Bill is famous for selling pizza in a country that did not eat cheese. He changed the eating habits of the Thai people by getting them to eat cheese. He also started the first pizza delivery service, a much-needed service given the crazy traffic jams in

Bangkok. He made ordering pizza and having it delivered to the door easy: you would call a number that was easy to remember. In fact, that was how I found him in 2010 when I was in Bangkok for business. I called the pizza number, which everyone from the taxi driver to the bellhop in my hotel knew. We had a good laugh at how I tracked him down. I learned two things from this consulting opportunity that shaped my life:

1. **Make it easy to do business with you.** I was having a challenging time trying to recruit an all-women sales force to sell English books in a non-English speaking country and I was ready to quit. I will never forget what Bill Heinecke advised: "You are a guest in this country. So behave like a guest. Learn the culture. Respect their way of life. This is a Buddhist country. Learn how they conduct business and how they treat people. Don't impose. Go with the flow." Three months later, I was exceeding expectations. We sold all the books in the inventory and we were back-ordered. We knew we had a winner. Bill ordered a Thai translation of our best-selling library. Bill was so impressed that he gave me a bonus: a trip to Hong Kong, and offered me a job, the launch of Helene Curtis in Thailand. I declined. Another mentor had advised me that my marriage came first and I went back to the Philippines to sort out my life. In 2010, Bill told me that Time Life Books, which I had helped launch, was his longest running business. I often wondered what my life would have been if I had stayed in Bangkok.

2. **Dress to Influence.** The official launch of Time Life Books Thailand was fast approaching. I started thinking about what to wear! My corporate wardrobe was conservatively simple. I always wore a jacket with a dress or a blouse and skirt combination. High heels, of course. I somehow knew that I needed to be as tall as the guys in the corporate world. My dilemma was what to wear at this important event in my career. Joan D. Manley, the first woman publisher of Time Life Books (in fact, one of the first and very few women executives of U.S. Fortune 500 companies in the early 1970s), and other important executives from America were flying to Thailand for the occasion. The country distributors in Southeast Asia were all attending. Bill who also owned the public relations firm of J. Walter Thompson was ramping

up the publicity. I got more worried when I found out that the Queen of Thailand would cut the ribbon to formally open the beautiful display of Time Life Books. The event was to be held at the elegant Oriental Hotel.

I searched books to find wardrobe advice. There was none. There was no Google at the time. There were very few women in executive positions I could turn to for advice. A fellow Filipina woman manager suggested I wear the daytime Filipina *terno* [Filipina woman's native costume with butterfly sleeves worn on formal or special occasions], She added that she would bet the Queen will wear the Thai traditional dress. I argued that it did not seem appropriate. This happened in the late 70s. *Dress for Success* written in the U.S. by John T. Molloy in 1975 had not caught on yet. There were no business clothes for sale in department stores. I even flew to Singapore and it was the same story. So I relented and called my Mom long distance and had her airship (no FedEx then) a "daytime *terno*." She knew exactly what I meant. The *terno* had light blue fabric with tiny flowers. I had never worn a *terno* in my life and I felt uncomfortable. I knew it was the wrong outfit. The 'look' in Bill's eyes that fateful morning said it all. I think he said, "What happened?" I was crushed. Then Joan Manley arrived in a beautiful dark business suit and looked powerful and in command. Then the Queen walked in with her ladies-in-waiting. They all wore daytime Chanel-type suits. I felt like someone in a country fair. I knew what I wore was wrong and it was a career-limiting *faux pas*. What saved my career was the success of the book launch.

Fast Forward to 1986. I had started my image consulting and coaching business in San Francisco. 'Dressing to Influence' was my most popular image seminar. I was coaching witnesses for courtroom appearances and depositions. My clients were doctors, professionals and executives sued for malpractice. 'Image Builds Business' and 'Corporate Savvy' workshops followed. Eventually I developed my own image strategy concept that I named *7 Aspects of Image*. Image7 was my car's license plate. Later, I developed the Image360-degree assessment to measure 'Image Required by the Job' vs. 'Image Shown by the Manager.'

Freedom and Independence

My mother used to say: "You want to be the person who signs the pay-check, not the someone who's waiting to see if you'll get one."

Not knowing anyone, I came to the U.S. to leave an abusive mar-riage, get a divorce, and start a new life. With only $200 in my pocket, the maximum dollar amount you could take out of the Philippines at that time, and chutzpah, I was determined to find success for my two young sons and myself. I never quite understood why someone who says he loves you beats you because he says he loves you. This was a secret I kept until 2005.

I crafted a plan to quickly get a job while I was waiting for my divorce to be granted. I first traveled to visit with my former class-mates and my older brother's friends in different states. I wanted to observe how people lived their day-to-day lives in other parts of the country. I loved New York the best. That was when I knew I am a city girl. I stayed with my brother's friend who had a studio apartment in Queens. I learned to take the subway. I was fascinated with her job as a computer consultant for a large corporation. She would fly to different states for consulting jobs every Monday morning and come back either Thursday afternoon or Friday. I had the apartment to myself and loved it. I walked miles to shop at the farmer's market and I learned how to cook. I decided then that one day I would have my own place.

I had never really had my own place. My apartment in Bangkok was fine but it was more like an apartment hotel. I am from a large family of 13 children (seven girls and six boys) and you can just imagine I nev-er understood the meaning of privacy. We lived in this big 'American' house in San Juan, Rizal with large bedrooms and a long driveway. An adjoining building meant for servants' quarters was turned into a print-ing and publishing facility by my parents.

I got married when I was 18, got pregnant right away, and moved out of a big house to my husband's modest home in Makati and eventually to our own place. There was no privacy for me. His grandmother and two aunts who raised him lived with us. One aunt was separated from her husband and was raising two children. The other aunt was a spin-ster (that's how we called unmarried professional women then), who had an important job, her own money, and was pretty independent.

She was a very tall woman and wore her clothes well. Her work wardrobe, in beautiful fabrics, was conservative but elegant. She worked for the Philippine Bureau of Customs and was in charge of receiving and disbursing beautiful fabrics imported to the Philippines to be manufactured into lingerie and sleepwear. She gifted me once with a long and beautiful silk nightgown, one of the items that I brought to the U.S. as it really made me feel special.

I somehow knew that my image—how I presented myself, what I wore, how I spoke, and how I looked—influenced other people's perceptions of my qualifications.

I did not know in 1980 but I was 'faking it till I made it' and found what I thought was a well-paying job. It was frustrating because I was told I was overqualified but had no local experience. My goal was to earn $1,000 a month to cover my living expenses. The two lovely ladies who had welcomed me to their home subtly hinted that I should not set my hopes too high. I did not realize that they were each earning less than $1,000 a month working at the phone company. My goal was to get a job in six months or go back to the Philippines. They said I could stay rent-free until I found a job.

Set goals. Ask. Negotiate.

I joined a women's organization, the Embarcadero Center Forum (ECF), in order to network and get job referrals. I landed a job quickly as the branch secretary for the United California Bank, which became the First Interstate Bank. The assistant manager understood my goal and saw potential in me. We negotiated a starting salary of $800 monthly and a promise to increase it to $1,000 in six months. Wow! Before I accepted the offer, I asked to continue my membership in the ECF and attend the monthly networking lunches. The assistant manager approved it and made it sweeter; she offered to pay the annual member dues and monthly meeting fees. She seemed surprised I belonged to such a prestigious women's group. ECF was my support network. I faithfully attended all their activities and volunteered for events. The ECF opened a world of sisterhood I did not know existed for me. It was then that I started thinking that there should be such a group for Filipina career women like me.

Later, I discovered that my officemates were envious of my 'perks,' which really was all about knowing how to make a business case for asking what you want, such as a salary raise. I learned that you do not succeed alone, one needs to know the right people, become an insider, or find someone who is. I understood then that you not only need a mentor but a sponsor within an organization who has the power to open doors for you to access perks, bonuses, stock options, first or business class travel, limousines, corporate apartments, memberships at private clubs and professional associations, access to sports suites, tickets to concerts, invitations to corporate events, huge salaries and bonuses.

My two lady friends could not believe I got a job in less than a month with the salary I wanted. They promptly charged me $300 a month for room and board. I learned later that I was practically paying their mortgage of $330 a month. After four months, I found a studio apartment for $160 a month and left.

I worked hard to prove to the bank's Assistant Manager that she had made the right decision in hiring me. I started running the branch like I *was* the manager. In a couple of months, I was doing commercial loans and was on first name basis with the branch's high net worth clients. The Assistant Manager and Manager signed off on my loan recommendations. My favorite client was Francis Ford Coppola who was filming *Apocalypse Now* in the Philippines. He would call me long distance to renew or increase his commercial loans as he was constantly over budget and the film needed more money. The Assistant Manager knew I had the capacity to run the branch.

Do not ever let anyone get in your way to advancement or Corporate Loyalty: what is that?

I found out about the bank's management training program. The Assistant Manager was on the Selection Committee. I told her I wanted to apply but she did not encourage me. I applied anyway. There were three of us in the branch who applied. After a series of selection interviews one of my fellow applicants was selected. I was devastated. I am very competitive. I always win.

The other applicant who was not selected was also an Asian woman. She noted that the applicant who was selected was white as well as everyone on the selection committee. At that time, I did not understand racial discrimination. I did not know that there are jobs that are not offered to certain classes of people. I went to the Assistant Manager and, thinking she would understand, shared our observation. Her response was, "I promise you, next year you will get into the management program." I replied quietly that I did not think it was fair for her to ask me to wait for another year and that she knew that I was over-qualified as a secretary. My corporate world changed at that moment.

I went across the street to Security Pacific National Bank and applied for their management program. In a couple of months I was accepted at double the pay I was receiving as bank secretary. When I resigned, the Assistant Manager at First Interstate Bank was furious. She said I betrayed her.

The bank's management training program at Security Pacific National Bank was a milestone in my career. There were 40 in our class and each of us was assigned a Management Development Officer (MDO) as a personal career coach. Her job was to help me decide which area of banking I was best suited for. We were being groomed as next generation executives for careers in banking and finance.

I did not know there were people like the MDOs whose only objective is to guide you in your career path and help you avoid career-limiting mishaps. No wonder CEOs and high-level executives become more successful and make more money every time they move to the next job. I also learned that my MDO was not my therapist. Strictly professional: only business and career problems and solutions were discussed. I knew then that this was my calling. I met many other Filipina women in this huge organization who were stuck in their jobs that did not seem to go anywhere. I started helping them by pointing them to free classes, such as those offered by the American Institute for Banking, and how to find mentors. I travelled throughout California for assignments and training.

Balancing career and home life was a challenge. I was so determined to succeed that I went back to college nights and weekends as I was raising my children. Being a single mother is no joke. I will always be grateful to my mom who allowed me to thrive while she took care of my sons. I think she was living her life through me. She raised 13 children and successfully ran a printing and publishing business. I do not think she ever had time to do anything for herself. This experience from my family life, along with my professional experiences via the Embarcadero Center Forum, would eventually lead me to found the Filipina Women's Network.

Why the Filipina Women's Network

The idea of the Filipina Women's Network (FWN) started with a lunch hosted by Cora Manese Tellez at the City Club of San Francisco in 1996. Cora wanted to meet Filipina women in management positions. At that time, Cora was herself a rising executive in the health care industry.

Cora was Vice President and Regional Manager, Hawaii Region for Kaiser Foundation Health Plan and Hospitals, and would become the first Filipina to break the 'glass ceiling' when she became the President and CEO of Health Net in 1998. The 'glass ceiling' refers to the barriers that confront women and minorities in reaching the upper echelons of corporate America. Because glass is clear, women and minorities might not, at first, even notice that a barrier is in place, which separates them from higher levels. If they try to pass through, they will quickly learn that the ceiling prevents any such rise. Cora had responsibility for Profit & Loss (P&L) for health plan operations in California, Oregon, Arizona, Connecticut, New Jersey, New York and Pennsylvania, serving 3.6 million members with revenues of $8 billion.

Virna S. Tintiangco, then a recent college graduate, assumed responsibility for continuing the group's networking "to provide a unique space for Filipina women to discuss concerns and issues related to their personal and professional lives." Virna operated the organization *ad hoc* with volunteers helping plan meetings and gatherings. They met occasionally for lunch or dinner with invited guest speakers covering topics such as growing up Filipina in the 90s, work-life balance, spirituality, mother-daughter relationships, career development and peer mentoring.

FWN *time has come*

In 1998, I was invited to speak about "Transitions: Life Planning," a favorite workshop I still offer to FWN members today. Virna announced she was moving to Oregon and was looking for someone to take over this loosely organized networking group. I met with Virna to discuss the business structure of the group. I had my own professional reasons. I recognized the challenges faced by Filipina women I had met through the years as a banker, career and image coach, organizational change consultant, and outplacement adviser. I told Virna I would continue the work with a co-chair, as my own consulting practice required a lot of travel. Victoria Urbi, who was then reviewing for the California state bar and was at the workshop, agreed to be my co-chair.

In 2001, I wrote a plan that became the blueprint for FWN and the Filipina Women's Network as a formal organization was born. I put out an eblast (the first of many!), a call to join a Steering Committee tasked to take FWN to the "next level." We met those who responded at a restaurant, and presented to them the FWN blueprint with the following goals:

- •Create a professional identity for FWN;,
- •Ensure leadership succession,
- •Provide programs that meet the professional needs of members,
- •Develop a vision of who we are and our role in the Filipino community, and
- •Create commitment to FWN's financial sustainability by charging member dues.

The original group that helped steer the FWN included Anna Bantug, Anna Villena, Judy Nipay Gee, Laarni San Juan, Tessie Zaragoza, Thelma Estrada, Victoria Urbi and myself.

We organized the FWN as a non-profit professional association, opened a bank account, conducted a needs survey, and collected member dues. We elected the founding board members and our first action

attached his very distinguished resume and invited me to meet him for dinner. He said he would show me his financial records if I would consider a relationship. Wow!

I promptly Googled 'Filipina' and was I surprised at the results. The Google search yielded 3,770,000 results. Yahoo yielded 5,530,000. Ask.com yielded 565,800. The search results listed hundreds of website links to dating and matchmaking sites, 'exotic' and 'sexy' girls, and personal ads for Filipina wives.

These sites have defined Filipina women. Perpetuation of this 'popular image' was at a 'cultural icon' level, a much-desired status for which corporations spend millions of dollars to promote their products and services (Holt 2004).

I knew then that my work was cut out for me. I needed to develop a game plan to elevate the presence and participation of Filipina women in leadership positions in corporate America, public service and the government. I felt that it is not very often we get a chance to make a difference in other people's lives. That email search was an eye-opener.

THREE. *The Vagina Monologues*

When I met Eve Ensler in 2003 at a conference in New York, she had just returned from a trip to Manila where she met the Comfort Women at a production of *The Vagina Monologues* produced by Monique Wilson. I did not know what the Comfort Women was about. Eve encouraged me to put on the show. I ordered the script and my creative juices started pumping. What I thought was going to be a funny, revealing, provocative show with a cast of only Filipina women, turned out to be the most important campaign that FWN has ever convened.

When we announced the production of Eve Ensler's *The Vagina Monologues* in 2003, FWN came under attack not only by the Filipino community but also by our own members. I was personally criticized through emails and phone calls for defaming FWN and the Filipino community, for being a bad role model, for being immoral, for daring to speak the word 'vagina' and *'puki'* [vagina]. I became known as the 'vagina lady' or the '*Puki* Lady.' We lost members. People would turn away from me at Filipino gatherings. Some would not touch me. Some of our production volunteers feared for their safety and questioned the wisdom of FWN's collaboration with Eve Ensler's V-Day, the global campaign to end violence against women and girls.

I felt very responsible for what was happening. It was difficult emotionally to separate myself from the backlash. The resistance, however, challenged me and provided an opportunity for reflection and dialogue. I was an organizational change practitioner, after all. I felt there was something deeper to the hostile reaction and that somehow we have struck a chord. Why were people so threatened by a word?

The *Vagina Monologues* is a play that highlights the tragedy and comedy about women's sexual lives. While at times funny, the play is graphic in its description and representation of women's experiences. So we decided to hold weekly home TV viewings of *The Vagina Monologues*: to learn more about the source of hostility and anger, and to alleviate any uneasiness about *pukis*. We made sure that we had an experienced facilitator to conduct the discussion after each show so that every attendee felt safe and felt their opinions were heard. What resulted was unexpected. These home viewings and weekly rehearsals became community gatherings where women shared their stories of abuse, their secrets about rape and incest, and their recipes. It became a love fest and a food fest. We called them Vagina Love Brunches.

What we thought were meetings to assuage people about doing a play about vaginas turned into a realization that Filipina women needed a safe place where they can be themselves, where they can share their secrets, their experiences and challenges with other Filipina women, and where they can feel that someone understands their struggles.

At these community gatherings, we met Filipina victims of domestic violence sharing their *hiya* [shame]. They talked about their feelings about bringing domestic violence on themselves. That it was their fault. They talked about not talking about domestic violence lest they bring *hiya* to their families.

At these community gatherings, we found that many of us still think that domestic violence only affects other communities and that it does not happen to us. That domestic violence happens only to other minority people, to poor people, to the uneducated, to the TNTs [TNT is a pop culture term for undocumented; its Tagalog translation is *Tago ng Tago*].

At these community gatherings, we sensed helplessness. No one knew where to go for help. No one was familiar with what resources were available.

At these community gatherings, we found that community agencies tasked with helping women in abusive situations lack culture and language-appropriate resources for Filipina women. Existing community agencies cannot often relate to the specific complexities that Filipinos face in abusive situations.

At these community gatherings, we learned the meaning of fear. Victims of domestic violence are afraid for themselves and for their children. Their aggressors instill such fear and isolation that victims often feel that no one will listen or help.

At these community gatherings, we heard about Claire Joyce Tempongko who was murdered by her boyfriend in front of her two young children. We heard about Marissa Corpuz and Giovannie Pico. Many stories of Filipina women still not ready to come out publicly to share their stories. I was one of these women.

At these community gatherings, we found a clear mission. Through the laughter, food, and storytelling, FWN launched the Filipina Women Against Violence Campaign. As the president of FWN then, I made it one of our organization's top priorities—help end domestic violence. Two actions we took immediately: **1) Change the verbiage**—we are survivors not victims, domestic violence is not the woman's fault; **2) Publish the V-Diaries Magazine as an anti-violence resource guide to raise awareness about the cycle of violence that permeates our culture.** The success of the campaign was achieved through coalition building. I promptly got myself appointed to the City of San Francisco's Justice and Courage Oversight Panel, which was tasked to oversee San Francisco's systemwide response to domestic violence. This panel was created because of the murder of a young Filipina woman, Claire Joyce Tempongko. Today, FWN works closely with the City of San Francisco's agencies including the offices of the Mayor, the District Attorney, Domestic Violence Victim Services, Commission on the Status of Women, the Domestic Violence Consortium and the Collaborative Against Human Trafficking. We have barely scratched the surface. There is still much work to be done.

The Truth About Leadership

There is a myth that leadership is a quality that a person is born with. There are also perceptions that only a select few can lead, that one is 'chosen' in order to succeed in a leadership role, and that managing and leading are the same. These popular myths are considered major mental barriers in leadership development.

James M. Kouzes and Barry Z. Posner, experts in leadership research, have collected more than 4,000 cases and 200,000 surveys in the last 20 years. Their research indicates that leadership is not a mystical quality, but that it is a set of behaviors that can be learned through feedback and practice. My own leadership journey was a series of 'faking it till you make it' type of blunders. You pick up the pieces when you fall. You dust off yourself and start all over again. You re-group. You re-frame. You learn from your mistakes. And when you win, you learn from your successes. You refine your abilities so you can win faster and get to your destination quicker. Leadership is a self-improvement journey. The hardest part for Filipina women is changing behaviors because often times we are dealing with cultural patterns ingrained from childhood. Many have said, "I feel I'm less authentic. I feel I'm betraying my ethnic heritage."

Kouzes and Posner further said: "Each person's journey may not have a single or final destination; it may have an initial goal and then another, and then another." Developing your leadership ability is also to grow in other areas of your life. It is a commitment to improvement and then following up with action.

The Evolving Idea of Leadership

Leadership development has been around since ancient times. It is said that Aristotle coached Alexander the Great on leadership and strategy. There is evidence that leadership development was part of ancient Egypt's master plan and that pharaohs had teams of advisers to sharpen their abilities to lead and manage their people. Sun Tzu in the *Art of War* developed competencies for military leadership and winning battles.

again instead of sharpening their abilities so they can get to the mastery level, confront the issues so they can work through what needs to be resolved to achieve common ground.

What you can do: Work differently in order to reach your goal. Embrace change. Develop better coping strategies. Develop skills and abilities. Learn how to understand complex situations. Reshape how you think. Develop a deeper understanding of your blind spots. Find ways to turn weaknesses into strengths. Let go of self-defeating habits. Understand why certain behaviors and habits have to change. Toughness and decisiveness are capacities of leadership. It is okay to leave behind cultural traditions for now because when you have a seat at the decision making table, you will find ways to incorporate it in your leadership style. Culture is our backbone and it does not leave us ever.

3. Support. Although developmental experiences stretch people and point out their strengths and weaknesses, they are most powerful when they also have an element of support. Support is most needed to help people handle the struggle and pain of leading.

Filipina women often withdraw when their leadership is questioned. Many do not have a peer network outside of their family circle. Filipina women value friendships and stay in touch with classmates from school, neighbors and extended families. This is a good start. What may be missing is the development of a circle of influential advisers outside of family and friends, people who can provide insight and strategies on how to navigate the politics of the workplace.

Filipina women should stay on course by developing their support network. Turn bosses into allies, coworkers into supporters, peers into coaches, friends into cheerleaders, professional colleagues into collaborators, coaches into confidants, mentors into sponsors. Your network is where you go for fresh air, for reassurance when you doubt your capabilities, for celebrations of victories, big and small, for a sounding board when you need to vent or be inspired. Talking with others about your struggles and receiving honest feedback so you can get back on the right path is essential in developing strong leadership and following.

Implications for the Future of
Next Generation Filipina Women Leaders

I have framed a view of leadership in terms of 'next steps' for Filipina women. If leadership development for Filipina women is an idea whose time has come, what implications are there in order to succeed? What will leadership development mean? How will it be carried out? What are the challenges? Will our Filipina women culture enhance or derail us?

Definitive answers to these questions are not in view, because no formal leadership development program unique to Filipina women has been created. What are needed now are strong supporters, funders and Filipina women coming together. We need to develop tactics of how to move toward the future. We need a transitional way to work with Filipina women who think of themselves as leaders in the traditional sense while opening up the possibility that these very same Filipina women will see themselves in a significantly different light.

FWN's Pinay Power 2020 Vision has created a way for a common direction and a mutual sense of meaning and value in preparing our next generation Filipina women leaders. We have created the FEMtor-Match™ femtoring program with Global FWN100 awardees as FEMtors™ and the Pinay Speed Femtoring at the annual Filipina Leadership Global Summit. We are learning from the publication of the first book of a leadership series, which documents the collective stories on leadership experiences of global Filipina women, and launching a U.S. and international book tour where the first group of authors reside, which will include seminars and workshops on how Filipina women lead. We are in our second year of the selection of the 100 Most Influential Filipina Women in the World, who are asked to pay forward by femtoring young Filipina women or become FEMtors™ in FEMtorMatch™ , and we are convening our 6th annual Filipina Leadership Global Summit.

Tani Gorre Cantil-Sakauye and Evelyn Dilsaver

Through the years, we have invited Filipina women who have broken through glass ceilings to share their leadership stories that we can all learn from. Their stories share similar themes with those of the contributing authors in this book—disrupting the status quo. We pass on to next generation leaders the leadership tips from the interviews of Honorable Chief Justice of California Tani Gorre Cantil-Sakauye (FWN Magazine 2007) and CEO of Charles Schwab Investments Evelyn Dilsaver (FWN Magazine 2005).

Smell the Future

The story of California Chief Justice Tani Gorre Cantil-Sakauye provides an example of how her achievement impacts other women. She is the first Asian-Filipina American and the second woman to serve as the state's chief justice. She received the Most Influential Filipina Women in the U.S. Award in 2007. In the *FWN Magazine* 2007 issue, she said, "I was raised to be gracious and respectful" but these traits seem anachronistic in a world where lawyers often win their cases by out-yelling the competition. As a trial judge, she insisted on running a genteel courtroom. Lawyers on both sides learned quickly that power trips and shouting especially at women lawyers were counterproductive in the Honorable Cantil-Sakauye's courtroom. Speaking to a group of young Filipino Americans at UC Davis entering medical school, she exclaimed, "Do you smell that? It's the torch being passed to you," as the medical students looked in confusion. Chief Tani shares strategy with Filipina women:

1. **It is important to have a goal.** You need to see yourself in that position. Project yourself into your desired future.

2. **Step out of your comfort zone.** Step up to responsibility. You do not grow from successes but from losing, struggling, learning from experience, and asserting your abilities. Your confidence will build as you go.

3. **Exposure is critical.** Influential people need to know who you are, how well you get along with others, that you are a team player, a competent professional, one who is energetic and willing to put in the time and effort. You can do this by serving in the community, chairing a committee, and planning an event. I even made my long,

hard-to-pronounce name work for me. Because of my willingness to take on responsibility and the quality of my work, in time, I stood out as "the lawyer with the long name."

4. Get your name 'in play.' You may not get the first job you apply for, or the next, but if you keep putting yourself out there, eventually, someone will bring your name up when a new opportunity arises because you have proven yourself and gotten your name in play.

5. Give up your time for something bigger than the typical goal of wanting to be rich and famous. When you give back to your community, you begin to feel rich. As you do volunteer work and hone your skills in the process, your fame will spread.

6. Persevere even if you do not look the part. They will get used to your face as the face of leadership and competence.

Chief Justice Tani explained that leadership used to look different. "The face of leadership was white, male, and older. I was a Filipina, young-looking and young, period, with a gracious manner. It did not look like a recipe for success in the legal world. But I kept at it. Now we are redefining what leadership looks like."

Top 10 Traits of an Influential Leader

In 2011, Evelyn Dilsaver, President and CEO of Charles Schwab Investments, gave the acceptance speech on behalf of the 100 Most Influential Filipina Women in the U.S. Awardees in San Francisco, California. In an interview for *FWN Magazine* (2005), Evelyn admitted that her path was not always straight and that she made lateral changes to different roles or new companies rather than simply stepping up. By doing so, Evelyn's knowledge became broader and helped her have a sense of the company and industry as a whole. To prepare for her speech, Evelyn role-modeled listening to the customer and paying attention to what they say by asking her fellow honorees for their top strategies for succeeding and becoming influential. "Like David Letterman" she said, "I've compiled the Top Ten."

1. Knowledge and competence. Knowledge is different than competence. You could be knowledgeable about a subject, but have no idea how to make it happen. Competence is knowing how to use your knowledge. Leaders have both. Leaders continue to gain knowledge and are constant learners and listeners. And they are willing to share their knowledge and skills with others.

2. Have an opinion and voice it. We all have informed opinions and have learned to voice them in a manner that is constructive, solves problems, and tells a story that influences others to believe in our cause, product or idea. We believe in ourselves and that confidence is evident and inspires others to believe.

3. Hire smarter people, build a team and let them go. While we may have started out as individual contributors, along the way we learned to lead a team. We hire people smarter than us, build a highly functioning team with a common goal or mission and get out of their way so they could do great things. We use our gifts to help others in the team grow and succeed.

4. Have a mentor but please your boss. Some of us may have had a mentor or many of them and our mentor may have been our boss. Importantly, we know that to be promoted, we had to make sure our boss was successful. Sometimes they knew what we did to help them and sometimes they didn't. I describe that as "The Wonder Bra Job" or invisible means of support.

5. Take risks. We all took risks. It might have been the job or big project that no one else wanted, traveling to other cities or countries and being away from family, moving from a staff position to one with responsibility for bringing in the sales or bottom line profit. Also, we knew when it was time to move and take on a new adventure.

6. Create a win-win situation. True leaders are respected for creating win-win situations. The "I win, you lose attitude" has no place. Sure, some make it to the top, but they are transitory and don't leave lasting legacies. Influencers bring great ideas and the right people together.

7. Show up, be present, attitude is everything. We show up on the job and not on Filipino time! We come fully prepared, with an excellent attitude, and a great sense of humor.

8. Be passionate. Would you follow someone who was not passionate about what they did? We are all passionate about our job, our product, our idea and we excite others around us to embrace and share in that passion. Our honorees are passionate and persistent!

9. Luck: where competence and timing meet. A few people are truly lucky in life. But I believe that many of us created our own luck by applying our knowledge, being observant to opportunities and willing to take a risk when we saw that opportunity.

10. Finally, and most importantly, we had parents who pushed us, created high expectations, told us we were going to college and in the case of mine, did not allow me to date until I knew how to cook for the entire family! We have husbands, significant others, children, friends, and colleagues who support us, cheer us on, pick us up when we are down, tell us the truth even if we do not want to hear it...we built trusted relationships and networks that sustained us then and continue to do so today.

Evelyn wrapped her top ten strategies for succeeding and becoming influential with the hope and expectation that many of those in the audience would be sharing this podium in the years to come and that she would be in the audience applauding the next generation of leaders when that happens.

These two amazing women represent what the Filipina Women's Network is about. I am proud and humbled to be in the company of these women.

LEADERSHIP TIPS

1. ***Work to become self-aware.*** Understand why you are the way you are. Your traits, acquired preferences, and life experiences shape your leadership style.

2. ***Develop self-confidence.*** Take on complex assignments. These difficult challenges build character.

3. ***Develop the ability to grasp a comprehensive, systemic view.*** Develop your sense of understanding of organizations and communities as complete systems, how to manage ambiguity, how to unravel the complexity of systems, how to leverage diverse frameworks in solving problems, and designing solutions.

4. ***Sharpen your capacity in understanding complex social systems.*** Learn how to deal with difficult employees and coworkers, manage conflict, interact with people from different economic situations or cultures, how to listen, honor, and work with diverse points of view.

5. ***Learn to think creatively.*** There is a need for "disruptive" thinking, getting beyond your own assumptions, reframing how people think about problems and issues, finding connections with disparate ideas, and learning to see possibilities to reach a desired conclusion.

6. ***Learn from difficulties and successes.*** Recognize when to change behaviors and attitudes from feedback, practice newly learned skills, abilities and behaviors. Seek out opportunities to sharpen new lessons.

FILIPINAS RISING

Elena Mangahas
Chairperson, Filipina Women's Network

Introduction and Memories of Violence

How did a live performance of *The Vagina Monologues* by its author, Eve Ensler in San Francisco, awaken nearly forgotten but traumatic memories from the post-war past of my life in the Philippines?

My early memory of witnessing violence against women was the male neighbors who, in anger, slapped and kicked their wives and found other ways of proving their physical power over them. It was not a one-time occurrence but seemed like an ongoing event. Being children, we walked away and played elsewhere. We could not escape the violence and would hear the alarming fall on the wood floor, the screaming, the blame, the wailing of a helpless woman. I have images of a man walking away with cigarette between his fingers leaving the home to drink with friends at a nearby *sari-sari* store [very small neighborhood convenience store store]. Once we had entered the house we played in silence because we could hear the mother crying in the next room. When the crying was over, she prepared the day's meal. Laughter among men at the store could be heard through the window.

Many of my uncles and cousins served the Philippine Army during World War II. During family gatherings they told stories of famine, malaria, and atrocities by the Japanese army such as decapitation of villagers and their own acts of heroism of gunning down the Japanese soldiers. I was amazed at how their stories and recollections back then were like video games that do not shut down. Their images of war never seemed to turn off, and in their minds they would return and re-play the events again.

These men told neither tall tales nor exaggerated *aswang* [ghoul] supernatural stories that were shared to scare young people. They were, as I realized later, men dealing with their experiences of war as if re-telling the stories provided healing. I was part of the generation that heard those stories and stored them in my mind.

San Francisco-born Filipina author Tess Uriza Holthe captured her family's own stories of war in her 2002 novel *When Elephants Dance*. The book "interweaves both the devastation of the war and the kind of mythological tales" she was told while growing up. Holthe crafted the novel because she "longed to find the fictional stories of the Philippines as told by her father and *lola* [grandmother]." She achieved the satisfaction of knowing that her book contributed to filling the void on the library shelves for this genre of literature.

I read Holthe's fictional narrative that seemed so familiar and I understood her reverent awe for the Filipino spirit of resilience. There are many of us from the post-war generation who stored these stories in our memory because our beloved elders spoke first-hand about them. It was their war, that's why my feeling is also that of reverence. I noticed the elder women stayed silent as if their stories were muted. I thought it really did not matter for a three-generation family that never reflected on the significant impact of war on the psyche. We were too busy migrating for post-war economic survival.

I was in my twenties when I personally witnessed military violence during the years following the declaration of Martial Law. The atrocities of the past were now happening during my time. I was a student at the university that staged the infamous barricade and subsequent militant protests against the Marcos dictatorship. I happen to be an active participant this time.

I discovered I was also capable of violence. I could make Molotov cocktails and hurl a desk out of a building window. I could scream and spit at a policeman's face. I was able to suppress many of these memories until the night I found myself at Eve Ensler's performance of The Vagina Monologues. There I sat between my two young daughters.

My earliest memories of violence returned with a vengeance. Yes, in addition to watching the performance of Ensler's well-crafted play, I learned new options including creating dialogues and shattering taboos for addressing violence against women. That night I pledged to make the world safer for the two young daughters. More significantly I walked away with a mission to disrupt my own silence.

The Link to the Past

The Filipina in America is never separated from her native land. Whether it is her birth and upbringing or customs and traditions handed down from one immigrant generation to another there will always be a connection to her past. The stories also provide a connection to the present and decidedly the future.

The past that traditionally has been understood through the lens of historians and anthropologists has become an area of concern to the Filipina who seeks connection to her pre-colonial history and its rich spiritual and cultural heritage. In a session during the 2007 Filipina Women's Network event recognizing the 100 Most Influential Filipinas in the U.S., Professor Leny Strobel introduced the idea of reconnecting with the spirit of the *babaylan*. Professor Stroble suggested the *babaylans* were the shamanic healer, herbalist, and folk therapist who served their community. Strobel (2010) introduced in her book *Babaylan, a model for understanding the decolonization journey of the Filipina*:

1. She understands European and American colonial history and its psychic and epistemic violence on herself and her people.

2. She understands that her presence in the U.S. is a product of this history. The narration of U.S. history as it relates to the Philippines should be understood as an imperial and colonial narrative in need of critique and revision.

3. She does archeological psychic work to uncover, discover, or re-imagine, what her Filipina indigenous memory is trying to teach or reveal to her.

4. Filipino indigenous memory reveals intuitive knowledge about who she is as an indigenous woman. Indigenous Filipino theorizing includes language-based concepts like *Kapwa* [shared humanity], *Loob* [interiority], *Damdamin* [feelings], *Diwa* [consciousness],

Dangal [honor], *Paninindigan* [stance, conviction]—that gives a decolonized Filipina a narrative that anchors her identity and her life work in Filipino values.

5. She recognizes that the framework of indigeneity and decolonization can serve as a powerful critique of modernity and its discontents.

The Struggle and the Allies in the Struggle

The Filipina's present is a myriad of engagements in socio-cultural and socio-political arena that battle head-on some of the discontents, in particular those that affect the future of Filipinas not just in America but in the diaspora: mail-order brides, globalization of domestic occupations, organized sex-trade and human trafficking, partner violence, among others.

The Filipina Women's Network (FWN) recognizes that movements to change these negative images about Filipina women while preparing to povide leadership for the future is larger than the capabilities of any one organization. It is in this context that the FWN joins the efforts of sister organizations that laid the groundwork for the effort needed to restructure an America for Filipinas. These sister organizations include GABRIELA, AF3IRM/GABNet and the MARIPOSA ALLIANCE. They have demonstrated how social activism can enhance our community of women of Philippine ancestry and can dismantle gender-based oppressions and exploitation in the mainstream community. The Filipino American Women's Network (FAWN) provides a model for battling racism especially in the workplace and for creating cultural bridges linking Filipinas to the greater community.

The FWN joined the efforts of its sister organizations in 2001 with a focus on enhancing public perceptions of Filipina women's capacities to lead. The mission is to provide leadership and development opportunities for Filipinas and build the Filipina community's pipeline of qualified leaders in industry as well as in the not-for-profit and political sectors.

FWN has begun to develop learning activities that provide its rapidly growing membership with knowledge and awareness of socio-political issues and a culture-based analysis of these issues. FWN also began to identify value-based lessons related to leadership. The time was also right to promote FWN's vision and join the international women's goal of breaking the glass ceiling and promoting political and economic empowerment.

Even while FWN and other organizations were advancing the view of Filipina Women as a strong and positive force in America and throughout the work arena, an insidious challenge to the Filipina's public and self-image lurked like a dark shadow—the prevalence of images found in search engines in the Internet portraying Filipinas as mail-order brides and an exotic human commodity.

What emerged is FWN's agenda: to disrupt the assault aimed at Filipina Women in the virtual world. The trauma experienced by some Filipinas becomes apparent as soon as organized sex trade, human trafficking, and domestic violence are put on the discussion table.

In response to and challenged by author and global activist Eve Ensler, the FWN forged a relationship with the global V-Day Movement that became 'Filipinas Against Violence.' The Filipinas Against Violence is an anti-violence educational and awareness campaign that called Filipina women to 'break the silence.' This kind of 'silence' is evident in Rosa Henson's account of her disrupted young life after she was forcibly recruited as a 'comfort woman' during World War II, her recollection is best read in Tagalog:

Sinabi ko sa aking ina ang nangyari sa akin. Umiyak siya. Masuwerte pa nga raw ako't hindi nila ako pinatay. Huwag ko raw sasabihin kahit kanino ang nangyari sa akin. Malungkot na malungkot ako. Naramdaman ko pa ang sakit sa aking kaloob-looban. Katorse pa lang ako noon; ni hindi pa nireregla. Lagi kong iniisip, bakit ba nangyari ito sa akin? Naalala ko pa ang pangi-noong maylupa na gumahasa sa nanay ko. Namana ko kaya ang kapalaran ng aking ina? (words of Rosa Henson, a Filipina Comfort Woman, translated by Joi Barrios from her book *Mula Sa Mga Pakpak ng Entablado*, 2006). I told my mother what happened to me. She cried and told me I was still lucky because they did not kill me. She advised me not to talk about the incident to anybody. But I was very sad. I could feel the pain inside me. I was fourteen and had not yet begun to menstruate. I kept thinking, why did this happen to me? I remembered the landlord who raped my mother. Did I inherit my mother's fate?

(Rosa Henson, *Comfort Woman: A Slave of Destiny* (1992)

Lola Rosa's spirit and perhaps some ancestral life-force of the *babaylan* brought Filipinas together onstage in 2004 in San Francisco for the first all-Filipina *Vagina Monologues* by Ensler. Ensler is a New Yorker who wove the voices of over 200 women into what she called the 'vagina monologues.' Staging the *Vagina Monologues* in the Filipino community in San Francisco presented a trailblaizing model in community leadership by dealing with culturally taboo topics of domestic violence and sexual assault within a culture of silence. Furthermore, it raised a sense of urgency in creating dialogues to understand the underpinnings of the little-known 'vagina economy' among Filipinas who are overseas performing artists (OPA) in other countries. The *Vagina Monologues* raised awareness that Filipina Women are included in the United Nations statistics that one of every three women of the planet will be physically or sexually abused in her lifetime.

By joining the V-Day global movement FWN members became active game-changers who can and must direct the future of their communities by working at the intersection of art, social action and politics.

The V-Day Movement makes it known that "although sources of violence seem diverse, women's responses are tragically similar." Reporting on its tenth year of anti-violence work V-Day summarizes that "the stories of the survivors illustrate their pain and strength while the themes that resonate across cultures and geographies are of indifference of authorities, the familial instinct of denial, and the lack of public outrage about the violence that millions of women experience everyday."

By the second year, 'Filipinas Against Violence' became a full-blown social justice campaign. In FWN's annual production of the *Vagina Monologues* it became known that the "casting call" is a peace work outreach and casting for the show is cathartic training for the volunteer cast and crew to become advocates for the creation of a safer environment for women and girls.

The script study begins with a *conocimiento* [knowing] session—that which provides knowledge of each other, not just by name but by profound self-evaluation of the performers' family background and relationships, values and long-held secrets. The group's conversation signals when the cast is ready to share their own stories of survival, if not of someone close to them. By this process everyone becomes involved. In theater, as in all of the arts, purpose and perspective are essential elements.

Ironically the *Vagina Monologues*, which has been translated into 42 languages including an official Tagalog version, created a new layer of controversy in the Filipino community by its daring discussion of women's sexuality. For example, the monologue 'Angry Vagina' becomes '*Galit Ang Puki*,' to the dismay of the uninitiated Filipino ears who hear it as 'Angry Cunt.'

However, beyond the criticisms on Filipinas for staging a play that uses words like '*puki*' [vagina] and '*tingil*' [clitoris] there was born an unprecedented opportunity to break lose from the shackles of the culture of '*hiya*' [shame] (when refusing to discuss the experience of assault as the root of violence), '*utang na loob*' [social debt from within] (when there was dissonance about leaving a relationship because the perpetrator has been the male) and even the oddly apologetic "*pasensya*" [please be patient with my mistake] (when the assault is by a blood relative). Those who participated in the staging of The Vagina Monologues and Usaping Puki, including four transgenders, gained a new self-image and felt connected to the broader cause of women worldwide.

At the end of every *Vagina Monologues* show the audience is invited to interact. The people—women, men, young and old—are asked to break the silence and break the shame. They are asked to stand up if any of the three statements apply to them:

1. If you have been raped or beaten or violated;

2. If you have ever known a woman who has been beaten, raped or violated or know a woman or a girl who was beaten, raped or violated;

3. If you would help break the cycle of violence, break the silence and do whatever you can do to make sure that violence will not happen to another woman or another girl.

The climactic drama is, at the end, performed by the audience. All the theater seats fold away because everyone stands up.

What has been the impact of Filipinas Against Violence after ten years beginning in 2004 until 2013?

1. FWN has taken *The Vagina Monologues* (TVM) and its translated version *Usaping Puki* to four major US cities; New York, Washington DC, Las Vegas, and repeated performances in its home base, the City of San Francisco. The shows are presented in March/April annually.

   –23 Productions of *The Vagina Monologues*
   –4 Productions of *Usaping Puki*
   –4 Productions of *A Memory, A Monologue, A Rant and A Prayer*
   –655 Volunteer Cast and Crew (after 2012 including the Asian Pacific sisters)
   –$251,805 Raised for local beneficiaries plus a 10% contribution to Global V-Day

2. FWN's Filipinas Against Violence Campaign and with the annual staging of TVM have resulted in the creation of anti-violence activists called the 'Vagina Warriors.' Vagina Warriors in the Filipino community and around the world lead their communities in increasing human understanding and social justice. They are the new activists who personify courage and conviction and are working to end violence against women in the Filipino and Asian Pacific communities. Some have experienced violence personally or witnessed it within their communities. They have dedicated themselves toward ending such violence through effective grassroots means. There have been 52 Vagina Warriors who bring dignity to countless women in their daily work.

3. The FWN has created an Anti-Violence Resource Guide named 'V-Diaries' that doubles as a TVM show playbill. The V-Diaries provides a voice for domestic violence (DV) survivors and Filipina women and girls in abusive situations and includes a resource list of domestic violence agencies, shelters, legal and counseling services, and law enforcement agencies. Articles that are useful for advocates include: How To Pack Your Getaway Bag, Why Women Stay in Abusive Relationships, Checklist for Building a Prosecutable Case, Cautions in Working with Battered Women, Technology in Stalking, and more. These articles are published annually in the Spring and are available online in the FWN V-Diaries.

4. More Filipinas from coast-to-coast are taking action by participating in

domestic violence cases court watch, petitioning for change, helping pass new laws, holding vigils, and waging domestic war to end violence against women and girls. Vagina Warriors followed the legal case of Filipina Claire Joyce Tempongko who was stabbed to death by her boyfriend in front of her children. Her killing prompted the public investigation of San Francisco's citywide response system designed to handle domestic violence. FWN also played a big role in educating the community on the impact of outdated laws and raised public awareness that violence is never a private matter.

5. The story of Filipina 'Comfort Women' was made the centerpiece during the 2008 staging and became a part of all succeeding performances thereafter. The video featuring Monique Wilson, V-Day's ground activist based in the Philippines tells of the surviving Filipinas demanding justice in the form of a formal apology from the Japanese government. The world now knows the bitter story of wartime rape by the Japanese army that forced Asian women, some as young as 12 years old, into sexual slavery in brothels (institutionalized 'comfort stations') run and authorized by the Japanese government. Most of the Comfort Women have died while the survivors, nearing the age of 90, wait for an apology if not monetary reparations to compensate for all the abuses and violence committed against young Filipinas along with their sisters from Korea, Indonesia and China. The intensely dramatic monologue 'Say It' represents decades of these women's plea for justice that resonates again this day as women in war-ravaged countries have become systematic weapon of war and genocide.

6. The FWN continues to build partnerships with feminist organizations as well as Asian Pacific organizations working to advocate for women in the workplace who are exploited and underpaid. Efforts include participation in gender dialogues and take on media for its continuing portrayal of women as sex objects. FWM promoted the 2011 documentary *Miss Representation*, a documentary that explores women's under-representation in positions of power and influence in America and challenges the limited portrayal of women in mainstream media.

7. FWN promoted Filipina image by giving recognition to the 100 Most Influential Filipinas since 2007. That influence that spreads worldwide is the celebration in this publication.

8. In 2013 FWN proudly stood as a partner to the One Billion Rising, a global call which saw more than a billion people in 207 countries rise and dance to demand an end to violence against women and girls. The campaign, launched on Valentime's Day 2012, began as a call to action based on the staggering statistic that 1 in 3 women on the planet will be beaten or raped during her lifetime. With the world population at 7 billion, this adds up to more that one billion women and girls. In 2014 the effort was expanded to a call on women and men everywhere to rise, release, dance, and demand justice. In San Francisco FWN joined hundreds of organizations including law enforcement on the front steps of City Hall to celebrate its women force and demand an end to rape, battery, slavery and other gender-based crimes that seek community-based solutions.

9. PINAY POWER 2012 has arrived! The year 2006 became the banner year that launched a decisive campaign to double the number of Filipina leaders by 2012. The idea, as envisioned by Filipinas whose outstanding work in their community is worth emulating, was tooled with succession planning. To implement the campaign the search for the 100 Most Most Influential Filipina Women in the United States began in 2007. The selected awardees are tasked with giving back to the future of the Global Filipina community by mentoring another Filipina who becomes a part of the talent pipeline of Filipina leaders.

10. FEMTORING has arrived! What could be a more sustainable step that will support the Filipina leadership locally and globally than to establish an innovative partnership using accessible technology? FEMtorMatch consists of the 100 Most Influential Filipina awardees (from 2007 thru 2013) making good of their pledge that came with their working award that they will share their competencies and skills set with a Filipina Femtee (or multiple Femtees) within their family, community or the Filipinas in the broader global community.

The ten years I spent with *Vagina Monologues* is about building a movement among Filipinas and supporting its growth. However it was the mutually beneficial art of empowering women that hooked me to cruising the freeways to San Francisco. I also count ten years of 200-mile commute from the central valley for each meeting, rehearsal, special event and even for the one-on-one coaching with cast who have become my good friends. The inter-generational production group, the sense of community and involvement of their family and friends and an always appreciative audience inspired me to no end.

I was also once part of a movement for alternative theater in the Philippines that made me realize the power of the performers to speak the truth and how it intensely impacts people's hearts and mind. I experienced first hand that theater is really for the masses, hence a strong vehicle for social action and movements.

LEADERSHIP TIPS

1. ***Know history, know self.*** Knowing and appreciating the depths of my being an Ilongga, my provincial origin, was a necessary step to my growing up. I felt the sense of pride in my family that had nothing to do with class or social status. On the contrary it was humble and perennially humbling. Being Ilongga brought me self-confidence. It also made me interested in aspects of history that formed my Filipino-ness. In her book *Sinaunang Habi – Philippine Ancestral Weave*, Nikki Coseteng affirmed my own belief: "We are a culture that did not build Parthenon or Borobodor. A non-monumentally inclined people, our ancestors devoted themselves to the fine representation of spiritually complex worlds – in such exquisite media as textiles that show love for the smallest detail, the most elusive of motifs, the most nuanced aesthetics. This is our heritage. We must value it for its intrinsic qualities, instead of pining for the measures of excellence of other societies. In this world, only those who have a strong sense of who they are, can insist on their own terms. Only those that can value their real nature can exercise power over global forces." She was talking about textiles but I thought she was talking to me!

2. ***Be authentic.*** This seems easily understood and learned but only if one goes through a process of understanding one's priorities and values. It is a sound approach to being yourself and being part of others. It is the opposite of pretense that invites inner conflict and turmoil. I remember putting on an act called Pretty-In-Pink (dressed like the movie) in the first FWN gathering of professional Filipinas and intentionally disrupting their notions of aggressive leadership and climbing the career ladder. The message was that million dollar business suit means nothing if you lack authenticity.

3. ***Be a motivator; spend time with optimists.*** This is somewhat similar to surrounding yourself with positive people. But there is an obvious trade-off. One must also be a motivator of positivity. This is a much needed requirement in the workplace. In my years as a supervisor, I would tell my staff to bring a solution if you want to tell me about a problem. This results in healthy exchange that is free from guilt, blame, finger-pointing, or distrust of each other's judgment.

4. ***Study excellence.*** People, co-workers, or friends are living books of leadership. Instead of simply trying to understand "what makes them tick..." take the matter a notch higher. Take lessons and take notes from people who make a difference or from people who are different. If one believes in the human capacity to excel, then everyone in the room is a study in excellence.

5. ***Empower women.*** This is the most expansive of all leadership traits. It's a game changer. And it doesn't get old.

Stepping Up

Gloria T. Caoile

National Political Director
Asian Pacific American Labor Alliance
Chair, FWN Advisory Board

Abstract

I did not design my career path, nor did I initially foresee what issues I would be passionate enough about to devote my professional life to. All I knew from the beginning was that I had to make something of myself and not let my parents down, especially after their efforts and sacrifices to give my siblings and I a better future. This chapter starts with my involvement with the Filipina Woman's Network (FWN) and my constant message to women, especially Filipinas, Filipina Americans, Filipinas in the diaspora: "Step up and power up." I then outline my life's journey, starting with the story behind my family's immigration and the series of jobs and employers I had, which led me to dedicating over three decades of my life to the labor movement and making people realize that their voices mattered. My story illustrates how passion, people skills, courage, and competence helped me overcome serious challenges in life and accomplish far beyond what I would have imagined. I learned the difficult way that while there are people who take advantage of the innocent, there are also those who go over and beyond to create avenues for others to excel. Even though I did not initially have a lot of experience and connections; my hard work, integrity, and ability to build relationships eventually opened doors for me. To enable others and create similar pathways for them is what I have tried to do throughout my career. I want to keep sharing the message that if a once naïve, inexperienced young Filipina-American such as myself somehow managed to navigate the physical and political terrains of Washington, D.C., then anybody else can too. I end this chapter with a summary of leadership tips focused on how Filipinas can step up.

Stepping Up

"Step up!" is my lifelong mantra. Whenever and wherever I am asked to talk to women about leadership and political empowerment, my one constant message is that I tell women they must "step up" and participate equally with men in decision-making. Women's voices need to be heard in all governance institutions at all levels. I remind my listeners, "Influence the decisions that impact your future and that of your families, communities, and nations." But how?

Participate in civic life. Be involved in parent-teacher associations, business and professional organizations, church groups, community clubs, sports leagues, and more. Realize that the bounty you enjoy is not free. Public safety, roads, utility and transportation systems, libraries, schools, parks, and the many amenities that all of us enjoy in our communities, cities, counties, and states are the result of the labor of other citizens who volunteer on boards and commissions. The amenities are the result of the labor of good people that run for public office, and the thousands of dedicated public servants that run public institutions.

Working with Filipina Women's Network has allowed me to emphasize female participation in the civic life of the U.S. I firmly believe that Filipina American women can be leaders and outstanding contributors to the civic and political life of the U.S. For Filipinas in the diaspora, you too can step up in the political and civic processes of your adopted countries.

Filipina leadership is not uncommon. Although barriers to resources and political clout still exist, according to a United Nations Human Development report, the Philippines has one of the highest levels of gender empowerment in East Asia. More than thirty-five percent of administrators and managers in the Philippines are women, one of the highest in the world. Additionally, close to twenty percent of legislative seats is held by women, and two-thirds of technical and professional workers are women. Furthermore, the Philippines has had two women presidents.

Our participation in the electoral and political processes of the U.S. is necessary because we can bring our Filipino American values to the table and influence the direction and future of the U.S. Sisters, step up! You too Filipina sisters in the diaspora, power up!

My Leadership Journey

Let me share with you how I have this conviction and commitment
-- based on my own journey right from the day I arrived in the US at
the tender age of 17 to my career in the labor movement, culminating
in being complimented by the President of the United States for a lifetime of work and service!

Early Career

I worked in Washington, D.C. for more than 40 years. Driving from
my home in Virginia, I would cross the Potomac River and glimpse
the monuments; the marble and granite obelisk dedicated to George
Washington, the Greek Doric temple memorializing Abraham Lin-
coln, and the pantheon-like and neoclassical building honoring Thomas Jefferson. As the years went by, traffic congestion grew and I avoided the gridlock by rerouting, passing the White House and sometimes
on to the avenue leading to the U.S. Capitol building. From my first
day to the day I left, I remained awestruck by the grandeur of the city.

I arrived in Washington, D.C. in 1962. I was seventeen. My mother and I traveled across the Pacific on an ocean liner because it was
cheaper than flying. My father and four siblings remained in the Philippines. My mother arranged my stay with a relative in Virginia. What
little savings she and my father had she spent, enrolling me in a highly regarded secretarial school. She then returned home to the Philippines and trusted I would acquire some skills, find a job, and become
an independent woman. My mother had so much faith in me that I was
committed to not letting her down.

Even though power and politics are the primary business in Washington, D.C., I did not get involved with either power or politics until later. My first job was personal secretary to an Asian woman. She
lived in the Watergate complex, and, at my job interview at her residence, I sat on a rosewood armchair, nervously waiting, completely mesmerized with my surroundings. My eyes fixated on a standing
Chinese print screen with flowers and birds framed by *huanghuali*

[Chinese term for a beautiful rosewood] wood.

Supple and graceful, Anna Chennault walked towards me to introduce herself. I knew very little about her other than what the employment agency told me; she was widow of the late Lieutenant General Claire Lee Chennault. He was commander of the 'Flying Tigers,' the first group of American pilots to fight the Japanese in World War II. It was only after I got hired that I learned that prior to her marriage to General Chennault, she worked as a war correspondent in Shanghai. When he died, she stayed in Washington, D.C. to manage the aviation-related business he built in China. She was also in-charge of the Chinese Refugee Relief Organization. My job was to organize her schedule, prepare correspondence, and transcribe notes for her memoir. It did not take me long to discover how well connected she was to power brokers in Washington, D.C., especially among elite Republicans.

Mrs. Chennault, as I addressed her, gave me very little feedback on my job performance. Nevertheless, I enthusiastically reported to work and admired her. Here was a woman who commanded attention the moment she walked into a room. I was young, impressionable, and thought the way she carried herself was a standard I should emulate. I worked hard, showed initiative at my job, and longed to get a compliment. But it never came.

Then one day, Mrs. Chennault approached me and told me to go to the Embassy of Ethiopia. Emperor Haile Selassie, supreme ruler of Ethiopia, was coming to the United States for an official state visit. Mrs. Chennault was friends with the Ambassador of Ethiopia and she told him her top-notch assistant could show the embassy how to organize for the Emperor's state visit. I was totally flabbergasted! I never imagined that my boss held my organizational skills in high regard. Her only encouragement for me was "You can do this."

And she was right. Even though it was my first foray into organizing events, I performed so well the Ambassador offered me a permanent job, which I took. The experience taught me something that I tell young people today when they ask what it takes to succeed in the workplace: Don't wait for the compliments; work hard, show initiative, and good things happen.

The job at the embassy allowed me to navigate into new realms. My social milieu expanded, my office skills improved, and I met exciting people. The problem was compensation. Embassies in Washington, D.C. were notorious for keeping female workers in low-paying clerical positions. There were no health benefits, no paid vacation and sick leave, no paid maternity leave, and no retirement plans. Noncitizens took the jobs because the embassies offered diplomatic visas.

I, on the other hand, had no visa problems. When the Americans liberated Manila in the closing days of World War II, the first evacuees out of the Philippines were American prisoners of war and their families. My grandfather and pregnant mother were on the first military transport to the United States. Months later, my father followed. I was born in Lawton, Oklahoma, a natural-born citizen of the United States. Still, there were many obstacles blocking my path to better employment. My barriers were my lack of connections, sparse information on what was possible, and no one to give me career advice. Having my family thousands of miles away made navigating the world of employment very challenging.

I had outgrown the embassy job so I ventured out of my comfort zone and explored other opportunities in the private sector. Barely 20 years old, I was hired to provide secretarial support to the general manager of an American Express branch office located on K Street in Washington, D.C. Today, K Street is synonymous with the political industrial complex: lobbyists, pollsters, consultants, media buyers, fundraisers and campaign workers have their offices along this street. In the 1970s, insurance companies, travel agencies, and law firms populated the area.

Less than a year at my job at American Express, I accepted an offer of employment from one of the agents starting his own travel agency. I was ambitious and thought it was an opportunity to advance. This was one of my worst decisions, which I discovered one Sunday morning when two policemen came to my apartment to question me! I found out the agent who hired me had expropriated monies from the office, but he informed his partner and investor group that I was responsible. I was overwhelmed, devastated, and frightened. But most of all, I was determined. I could not let anyone denigrate me and my family and I vowed no one would take away my integrity. Ready to fight the false accusations, I searched the yellow pages of the telephone directory and randomly found a brilliant and kind lawyer to defend me. Thankfully, the justice system worked. I was exonerated.

Nonetheless, that sense of vulnerability continued to live in the recess of my mind. It has motivated me in advocacy, workers' rights, and issues of social justice, because I do not want anyone to ever have to experience what happened to me. Young women have the right to be protected from predators of all kinds.

My next job was at an insurance company. I was executive assistant to three top-selling insurance agents. In addition to providing them with administrative support, I was tasked with training college students to become insurance salespersons. I was quite good at it and enjoyed the work. I was getting positive feedback, along with periodic pay increases so I felt that my life was going well, both professionally and personally. I had just gotten married and was expecting a child.

When my baby came, I took some time off. Shortly after I returned to work, my office manager began to behave differently. He regularly found fault in my work and opined that motherhood was affecting my job performance. He denied me my pay increase. He told me I would never be able to find a job anywhere else. He denounced anyone that would hire a woman with a three-month-old baby. I was astonished, angry, and in disbelief. How can anyone have such views?

I was so insulted and disgusted with him that I called the employment agency I previously used and inquired if they knew of any job openings. My contact said there was a job at a labor union, but the pay was less than what I was making. I told her I did not care and asked her to schedule me for an interview during my lunch hour.

I did not know anything about labor unions. I walked into the office of the American Federation of State, County, and Municipal Employees (AFSCME), headed to the education department and interviewed for a secretarial position. At the end of my interview, I was asked when I could start and I said "Today." I walked back to the insurance office and my office manager haughtily said, "Oh, we're now taking two-hour lunches." I replied, "I would have been back sooner if the guy in-charge of approving my hire was not on the golf course. I quit!" I gathered my personal belongings and walked out of the door to start a most rewarding career.

Labor, Power, and Politics

AFSCME opened my eyes to a whole new world. I found myself in an organization that valued the worker and public service. The heart of the union was the pursuit of collective bargaining rights for public employees. Collective bargaining allows working people to negotiate with their employers issues such as pay, benefits, leave, health and safety policies, working hours, and ways to balance work and family. What a revelation it was for me to learn that workers, through their unions, could actually negotiate contracts with their employers that determine the terms of employment.

I thrived at my new job. My productivity exceeded expectations. One day, at a meeting with the president of the union, my boss bragged about my performance. The president said that if I was so outstanding, why then was I not working directly with him? I was transferred to the executive floor.

By the end of my 33-year career at AFSCME, I had served two presidents, taken charge of convention and travel, and organized bi-annual conventions for 8,000 delegates and their families. I was responsible for the office facilities of 600 employees and I directed human resources personnel. The union grew to 1.3 million members; men and women who earned livable wages, who were fairly compensated, and enjoyed health care and retirement benefits. For me, to know that in some ways I was part of improving the quality of life of so many people made it all worthwhile.

Working in the AFSCME president's office allowed me to get involved in the business of power and politics. I was privy to negotiations among local and state governments. I was witness to agreements and decisions made by domestic and international officials, members of Congress, and the White House. I became very respectful of the democratic process and grew to appreciate the greatness of this country. Thus, began my involvement with political and civic engagement. Seeing how decisions were made, I felt strongly that a truly representative democracy should include Asian Pacific Americans. I became involved in encouraging members of the immigrant community to vote, to volunteer in civic organizations, and to do their part in helping America maintain a healthy democracy.

After I retired, AFSCME continued to call on me for special assignments. I led disaster relief teams to assist union members devastated by wildfires in Southern California, flooding in Iowa, Hurricane Katrina in New Orleans, and the 9/11 tragedy in New York.

Participation in the Political Process

Outside of work, I became active in the Filipino American community. My being Filipino is very much a part of who I am. I may have lived in the United States for most of my life, but my formative years were in the Philippines. I am proud to be a Filipino American.

I briefly took the helm of the Asian Pacific American Labor Alliance, a labor-affiliated organization I helped found. This allowed me to continue my work in voter participation and to serve as a bridge connecting labor to the broader Asian Pacific American community. I was able to get resources to conduct voter registration, voter education, and get-out-the vote programs in cities where there were large populations of Asian Pacific Americans, and in particular, Filipino Americans. Las Vegas, Nevada was one of our program sites. Fortuitously, I ended up retiring in Las Vegas.

My own personal experience and journey has helped me sort out my political priorities: immigration, gender equality, civil rights, health care, and economic security. I frequently remark that my siblings and I won the ovarian lottery because we were entitled to come to the United States from the day of our birth, with citizenship for my siblings derived from our mother and mine from my place of birth. But there are many who are not so lucky. There are families in crisis, threatened daily by their immigration status. There is still plenty of work left before immigration reform can become a reality.

Gender equality issues need to be resolved. When women are denied equality of opportunity and are not paid for equal work, such disempowerment cripples societal prosperity. I hope that when my lovely granddaughter enters the workforce, gender inequality will be a thing of the past.

Crimes of hatred and prejudice have no place in America. We need to remain vigilant to insure hard won rights are not taken away.

I am a breast cancer survivor. I am healthy today because I was fortunate to have access to one of the world's best health care systems. However, millions of young children, women, and families in this country still lack access to health care. I cannot comprehend why anyone would deny them this right.

Issues related to the economy concern me. I came to the U.S. decades ago because my parents believed I would have a better future here. Unequivocally, they made the right choice. My family including my husband, daughter, sisters, nieces, nephews, in-laws have been able to compete in the workforce. Many others are not so fortunate. We need to improve access to education so that the next generation can be employable. They need to have the tools to compete in the global economy.

Political participation is all about making sure our government responds to these values and priorities. It is about influencing the direction and future of this country and I believe it is our duty to engage.

A Passion to Succeed

Over the years, I have received numerous honors and accolades for my achievements including a presidential appointment to the President's Advisory Commission on Asian Americans and Pacific Islanders; the distinguished service award from the Asian American Justice Center for my involvement in advancing equality and service on various boards that promote social and economic justice; the *Filipinas Magazine* achievement award for community service; and the Philippines' highest civic award, the Presidential Merit of Honor, for my involvement in fighting poverty in the Philippines. My most surprising (and cherished) award is from my high school, the St. Scholastica's College Pax Award, given to an outstanding alumna. I never imagined I would ever get an award from my school as I was a mischief-maker when I was young.

While I am highly appreciative of the public recognition, it is my private life and family that provides me with the greatest satisfaction. My husband, Ben, and daughter, Melanie, are my source of strength. Our granddaughter, Ciara, is our fountain of joy.

As I reflect back on my experiences, I want to share four salient qualities that have helped me: passion, people skills, courage, and competence.

First, nothing substitutes for passion. You need to love what you do. Passion makes you believe in yourself. It is motivating. It is infectious. It is the key to long-term success.

Second, having people skills: being approachable, friendly, pleasant and respectful of others require that you actually interact with humans. This sounds laughable, but in our highly technological world, we have become dependent on our computers to communicate with each other. I cannot emphasize enough that face time is essential to establishing relationships and that pleasantries are not antiquated. Today's work environment is so highly integrated that it requires cooperation, collaboration, and sharing of information. When you are able to make others feel at ease, they are more likely to cooperate. Everyone becomes vested in the outcome and shares in the success.

At AFSCME, as special assistant to the president of our labor union, I was able to control the flow of information and access to the president. That made me an important cog in the organization. Even though I was in a position of authority and power, I made it a point to be approachable, friendly, and pleasant. I put people at ease. So when I had ideas on what our organization needed to do, I sold my ideas by going to the people who I thought needed to buy into my ideas. I could have just as easily gone to the president. Instead, I took the time to go to key people who I thought would be affected by the decision, and I would work with them in fashioning proposals that were workable for them but aligned with my concepts. I learned that it did not matter where you are in the hierarchy; if you know how to approach people, if you take the extra steps to nurture your relationships, then most likely you will experience success.

Third, have courage. Resolve to go forward even when risk is involved. Courage in the workplace takes many forms. The existence of gender and racial disparities cannot be denied. To be successful, one must have the courage to fight the stereotypes. I advise young people to assert themselves and be confident.

Finally, to be influential and have power, you need to be competent. How often have you heard expressions like 'value-added' or 'value proposition,' 'bringing something to the table,' 'enhancements'? These are basically terms that ask, "What is your contribution?" I have learned that you cannot bluff your way to success. When you lack competence and substance, you doom yourself. As a woman and a minority, I learned being good was not enough. I had to be excellent. To achieve excellence, one must put in the extra time, the extra effort, and go the extra mile.

Don't Wait for Compliments

At AFSCME, I was involved in an event called Solidarity Day. A million union members were marching to Washington, D.C. My task was to make sure our members got to Washington D.C. from all over the country. We needed to secure transportation. We needed buses. Over 100 unions had the same task, so competition was fierce. When the bus companies stopped taking orders over the phone, I decided to go to New York, camp at their offices, and negotiate with them directly. I did not leave anything to chance. Needless to say, we were the largest group represented that day. I credit my success with going the extra mile.

When I was at AFSCME, a young governor from Arkansas named Bill Clinton met with my boss and sold him on the idea that he would become President of the United States. My boss liked him a lot. They became good friends.

As I reached my 30 years of service at the union, I was so busy preparing for another convention that I did not even have time to think about my upcoming milestone. I was too busy finding hotel accommodations for delegates and their families, organizing the program, ensuring booths were in place, printing materials, ordering the audio visuals, arranging the banquets, and so on.

Our keynote speaker was President Clinton. President Clinton walked on stage while I remained backstage with the secret service agents, headsets on, giving orders to the program director. The president made his way to the microphone and then announced he wanted to congratulate someone who had worked 30 years at the union. He said my name and then started a litany of compliments. I got so excited I hurdled over decorative plants, leaped from the back of the stage to the podium, and gave him a hug. I completely lost my mind and forgot about presidential decorum. My boss thought for sure the Secret Service would immobilize me. I ended up on the front page of the *Chicago Sun-Times* and on CNN with the headline "Even the President Needs a Hug." I was lucky that they didn't say "Crazy Woman Hugs the President"!

This was one of my more humorous moments in life. But it was also meaningful. I had a flashback to the young woman who arrived in Washington, D.C. many decades ago. This is where her journey took her, standing in front of 8,000 people, being complimented by the President of the United States for a lifetime of work and service. At that moment, I knew I had kept my promise to my mother. I did not let her down.

Though I am retired, my passion for service has not diminished. In all my endeavors, I try to do the best that I can. Tomorrow is promised to no one, but for each day that I have, I try to make the world a little bit better.

LEADERSHIP TIPS

1. ***Love what you do.*** Nothing substitutes for passion. Passion makes you believe in yourself. It is motivating. It is infectious. It is the key to long-term success.

2. ***Develop your people skills.*** Having people skills; being approachable, friendly, pleasant and respectful of others; requires that you actually interact with humans. Even in a technology-centric world, face time is essential to establishing relationships. When you are able to make others feel at ease, they are more likely to cooperate.

3. *Have courage.* Resolve to go forward even when risk is involved. Have the courage to fight racial and gender stereotypes. Assert yourself and be confident.

4. *Build competence.* To be influential and have power, you need to be competent and bring value through your contributions. As a woman and a minority, being good is not enough; you have to be excellent by putting in extra time and effort.

5. *Step up and get involved.* Work hard and work for others. Use your network to enable others and create the same pathways for them. Participate in civic life, whether it is community clubs or sports leagues. Realize that the bounty you enjoy is not free.

6. *Don't wait for the compliments.* Work hard, show initiative, and good things will happen. But also guard against those who may sabotage you or demean your work.

Transforming Self: Personal Narratives

For the Love of Racing

Michele Bumgarner
Michele Bumgarner Racing, LLC

Abstract

While growing up I spent countless hours at the kart track driving hundreds of laps with my brother. Back at a time when girls did not race, I was undeterred in driving. Driving was fun. This chapter explains how my love for driving evolved into a passion for racing. Although my first win was at Kartzone race in Cebu, my first true victory was convincing my father, after repeated tries, to get me my own kart. What had been a hobby turned into a personal quest of blazing a trail for women and representing the Philippines in unchartered territory. I detail my racing journey, from local tracks to competing nationally, then in Asia, Europe, and America. I continue to marvel at how open-wheel racing was merely a dream of mine that has now become my reality. I describe the growth of my passion, skills and ambitions, as well as the challenges I have faced and how I have responded to them over the years. I underscore the importance of hard work and never leaving room for complacence. I end my chapter by emphasizing the value of being yourself and how there is no contradiction between being competitive in a male-dominated sport and being feminine; if anything, I have made sure that being a woman is an advantage.

Introduction and Early Years

My love for racing started when my dad first opened the Subic Le'Mans fun kart track around 1995. For as long as I can remember, my brother, Mark and I would spend hours at the kart track and drive hundreds of laps a day. We would never get sick of it and you just could not keep us off the track.

My dad started racing karts all over the Philippines the following year and would bring along the entire family, my mum and us four kids.

Back then there were not that many permanent kart tracks to race on, so they improvised with temporary layouts in parking lots. It was not fancy at all, but we had a big group of people, like Mike Potenciano, Carlos and Mike Anton, George Apacible, to name a few, who just travelled all over together and raced and had fun. We were one big dysfunctional family and I have lots of good memories.

That same year, when my brother was about five years old, my dad got him his very first mini go-kart and he would drive around the track on his own during lunch break (there was no class available at the time). Mike Anton shortly followed by getting his two kids, Mica and Pocholo, karts of their own. My dad eventually decided to start a class for kids, which was Cadet 60cc and they started racing in 1997.

In 1997, young girls did not race. As of that year, only two women drivers had ever competed in the Indy 500, the greatest race in the world since its beginning in 1911. Women were not even allowed in the garage area, not even to get the passenger car keys from their husbands, until the late 70s. So to say that racing is a male dominated sport is almost an understatement.

So when I first asked my Dad to get me a kart, the answer was "No." According to him, girls did not race. However, after lots of begging and persuasion, my Dad finally gave me the 'go' signal to race and I had my very first year kart racing in 1998. While my Dad may have said "no" at first, I think he wanted to see how much I wanted it. But once he did say "yes," he and my mum have never wavered on their support. For that I am very grateful.

The Taste of Victory

That first year, I would have to be completely honest and say I was rubbish and just not good. I was not fast; everyone would lap me two or three times during an average race. But I did not care. That did not stop me at all because all I wanted to do was drive and have fun. During my first year and a half of racing I looked at it more as a hobby than anything. That quickly changed when I won my very first race at Kartzone, Cebu in 1999 in the Cadet 85cc Class. That's when I thought, "Oh, well maybe I can do this as a career." That was the end of Michele Bumgarner, *the driver* and the beginning of Michele Bumgarner, *the racer*.

From there I went up the ladder from Cadet 85cc to JR KT, then to JR ICA representing the Philippines in the very first race of the Asian Karting Open Championship in Malaysia in 2002. By 2003 I was Asian Intercontinental Junior Karting Overall Champion as well the Philippines Karter of the Year and recipient of the Philippines Golden Wheel Award for overall Motorsports Driver of the Year.

The following year, I was the Overall Champion in the Asian Karting Open Championships in the Open Class as well as recipient of the Philippines' Sports Citation for Karting, Recipient of Automobile Association of the Philippine Motorsports Award, and again the Golden Wheel Award for overall Motorsports Driver of the Year. The year 2004 was also the first year I got into formula cars, open-wheeled single-seater race cars. By this time, I had extensive experience racing karts, but my karts only had two pedals, the accelerator and the brakes, so I had no clue how to drive a car with manual transmission. Nonetheless, I was offered a great ride in the Formula Toyota Class that I just could not refuse and came in First Runner Up, and also won several races throughout the year.

On to Europe

A big year for me was 2005 because that was my debut into the Professional World of Karting in Europe. Karting in Europe is the 'Lion's Den.' The competition is ruthless. You have to really be willing to deal with other driver's tagging you and then tagging them right back! I remember when I first arrived, my team showed me my kart and I started to work on putting the seat and the pedals in the proper place for me. They seemed really surprised that I was working on my kart. But that was part of my training, so I just got after it and made it happen. The day that I qualified in the top tier of the field was a big day. It is always fun to surpass people's expectations.

As well as racing a full season in Europe, I was the Overall Champion for the AKOC in the Open Class for the second year in a row, Overall Champion in the Shell Super Karting Series, and Karter of

the Year in the ICA Class at the Carmona Kart Track. At Carmona
I was the Track Record Holder with a time of 42.36 seconds. In addition, I was selected for the Red Bull Young Drivers Search semi-finals round for karting in Sonoma, California and finished fourth after qualifying for pole position out of 90 drivers. I was the heat race winner in the Asia Pacific Championships in Suzuka, Japan, setting the fastest lap times twice in the event to become the first female and the first Filipina driver to win an outside international kart race. To top it off, I also won the Formula BMW Scholarship by Formula BMW Racing School in Bahrain at the F1 track. It was quite a year and would be my last year racing in the Asian Karting Open Championships.

The following year marked my second year in European karting as well as my first year in the Asian Formula 3 Series. I was first Runner Up in a heat race in the World Cup ICA Class Karting Championships in Suzuka, Japan. I also raced in the ICA Class in the World Karting Championships in Angerville, France and the Macau World Karting Gran Prix in the Formula A Class, becoming the first Filipina to compete in both events. I also became the first ever-female winner in the AF3 Series after winning the season opener at Batangas Racing Circuit, eventually clinching third overall after winning a couple more races and missing a few races at the end of the year due to my karting schedule. The European karting experience was one that I still benefit from today. It was just so intense, but I really loved it and felt like I thrived on the competition.

On to America

Between 2007 and 2009, I moved to America to continue racing. In 2008, I raced a few Star Mazda races as well as being a Factory Driver for American Kart Manufacturer, MARGAY. I became the first ever female to win a race at the Rock Island Grand Prix in Rock Island, Illinois. Just to prove the point, I successfully defended that race becoming back to back champion the following year. EKarting News named me Driver of the Month for September in America. After all the success on track, I had a forced hiatus from racing between

2010 and 2014. Motorsports racing is not cheap, to say the least and with the world economic problems, a racing budget was very difficult. In the minor leagues of racing, drivers have to fund their careers, even when you are a champion driver with records and awards. That is the way the business of motorsports works. So it was important for me to stay positive and keep in shape by continuing my workouts and a few test sessions.

My goal was to enter the newly created Mazda Road to Indy. This is the development ladder system for drivers who want to compete at the top level of Indy Car racing, which of course includes the Indianapolis 500. The Indy 500 is the most famous and most prestigious race in the world. What a dream, what a goal! But how to get there?

Speed Bumps and Potholes

I am asked a lot about what challenges I have faced competing in a male dominated sport. The short answer is that certainly there have been some. There were guys that did not think a girl should be on a track and would tease me. I remember that my first driver suit was purple, because I wanted to make sure they knew I was a girl. My helmet had a big butterfly on it. I have always loved butterflies, but again, I just wanted them to know I was a girl. When I made a pass, all they would see is that butterfly flying by them—well that was great fun! So it did not seem challenging at the time. It is just what I wanted to do, and I was not going to take no for an answer.

However, as I have moved up the ladder and into bigger cars with more horsepower and more speed, the challenges have changed. I have earned the right to compete, but every day, every race, all drivers have to prove themselves again and again. The competition gets tougher, the budgets get bigger, the attention gets larger, and there is a lot of pressure on what becomes a full time job with serious responsibilities.

As the cars get bigger, one of my challenges is staying physically fit. Driving a race car takes a lot of endurance. If you get tired, you can lose focus. Loss of focus even for a tenth of second can mean a crash. It is also an issue of strength. As drivers, we have to tolerate serious G-forces. For example, in going through a corner we might carry speeds that will create 2-G's of pressure. That is two-times my body weight pressing down on me. Staying in physical shape to take that pressure for the required length of the race requires serious fitness. So I work out every day at a specialized center for driver training that includes upper body fitness, endurance training, reactionary skills, and so on. As a woman, this could be a big hurdle. But I feel fortunate that I have been an athlete all my life. I love tennis and almost chose a career on the courts instead of the track. At 5'9", I also have the stature to be physically competitive in the car.

Advantage: Women!

The big budgets are also tough. The competition for dollars is steep, but I think being a woman and especially a Filipina, gives me an advantage. Let's face it, women look better standing next to cars than men do. And as the only driver, much less a woman, from the Philippines to be racing, I can do a lot to represent companies that have Philippines interest, both at home and internationally.

So as I move up the ranks, I am aware of the exposure and the attention that I can bring to help grow the Philippine economy. Handling all of this responsibility is a lot of hard work. You spend more hours working on the business and promotion side than you do actually driving the car.

To succeed as a race car driver, you have to build a team around yourself that you can depend on and trust. But ultimately it is my reputation, my face, my life that is at stake. So I am learning that as a driver, I am also the boss of me, Michele Bumgarner Racing, LLC. It is important that all the things I do outside the car, reflect who I am. And I am a girlie-girl. I think a lot of people believe that girls that drive race cars are maybe rough around the edges or a bit boyish. But I love 4" heels! When I have time, a manicure is fabulous! And when you see a feature on my hobbies, it will be shopping with girl friends! Yet, when I put the helmet on, I am told that my face changes. The helmet goes on and my inner fierce comes out! I love racing!

Backtrack to 1998

In my first year of racing, if anyone would have told me that in ten years or so, I would have accomplished all I have done, I would probably say that you are full of it. Was it love at first sight? Of course, I was hooked! But did I think that I would ever take it this far? Never, Formula racing was merely a dream of mine and now it is my life. It is not an easy goal by any means. I know I have a long ways to go, but I am ready and prepared to go the distance and become a top world class racer representing the Philippines.

I hope that my story can inspire others to really listen to their own heart and follow what it tells them. It is that inner passion that gives you the strength to really pursue a dream. I did not start down this path just to prove that a girl could race. I wanted to race. Following a dream should never be gender specific. If it is your passion, that will give you the strength to go for it!

LEADERSHIP TIPS

1. *Follow Your Heart.* It may sound simple enough, but sometimes people who are not as brave or as passionate will try and talk you out of dreams that to them seems crazy. But when your heart says "go," do not let anybody stop you. No matter how many "no's," how many hurdles, how much time it may take, do not stop. Just do not stop. You will never be who you were meant to be, if you do not follow your heart!

2. *Be Ready to Work Hard.* Dreams that are worth pursuing will take hard work. They will take dedication. But again, if you are following you heart, if it is your passion, it will not be a problem. Yes, you will get tired. You will get frustrated. You might, like me, get delayed and have to sit on the side lines for a few years. But having the passion in your heart will make the journey possible.

3. ***As for working in a man's world, allow femininity to be an asset!*** The natural tendency when you are surrounded by all guys is that you need to act like one of the guys to get along. But it is not about fitting in. I have seen some other women drivers think that if they did not get angry about an incident on track, that the guys would not take them seriously. Instead, it negatively impacted their public persona. It is more important to be true to who you are as a woman. Women build consensus. We pull together to solve problems and on a race team, that is a helpful skill. Racing is a team sport, but the driver is the team leader. So it is important to be firm, but by doing so with a smile, it makes it hard for people to tell you, "No."

CHEF TO THE CHIEFS

Cris Comerford
White House Executive Chef

Abstract

*I*n this chapter, I recount the road that led me from being a reluctant chef to feeding the chiefs of countries worldwide. I look back at the steps leading to my appointment as executive chef of the White House, including the meal that won me the position, and reflect on the significance of becoming the first female and ethnic minority to earn this role. I take the reader back to my home in Manila where I helped my mom in the kitchen cook for a large brood when I was a young third grader. Through my mom, I developed a love for cooking and the ability to cater to a diverse palate, characteristics I would carry with me throughout my jobs in the U.S. and Austria, from managing a salad bar to running the kitchen of the most famous house in the world. In this reflection on almost three decades of journey in the culinary world, I emphasize the importance of keeping an open mind, continuing to evolve, and having a community and family which anchored me to what matters most, including being true to my Filipino heritage. I share various stories throughout my career that fit together as puzzle pieces forming the picture of who I am now as a professional, family person, and humanitarian, and provide a glimpse of what could possibly be next.

Introduction: Waiting in the Wings

It was the night before the announcement of my appointment as President George W. Bush's executive chef. I had a long, somewhat chaotic road leading up to this point and the details are a bit blurry. It started when I discovered that First Lady Bush had expressed her desire for a new head since Executive Chef Walter Scheib III would be stepping down. I did not pay much attention to the conversations about a new executive chef, but I did hear that the Association of Women Chefs and Restaurateurs had reached out to Mrs. Laura Bush urging her to appoint a woman as Head Chef in the White House who could serve as a role model for women. They argued that the time was right for a woman to be in charge of feeding America's first family as women have been feeding American families throughout its history. They also highlighted the gender disparity in the food and service industry where women hold less than four percent of the leadership jobs but make up over fifty percent of the workers. I will never know for certain the influence of the Association of Women Chefs and Restaurateurs on my appointment.

What I do know is that around 450 chefs from all over the U.S. applied for the executive chef position. The pool was eventually narrowed down to ten candidates and then to three. All the finalists had to prepare a tasting menu and it was my responsibility to help them succeed in their presentations. During this time, the head position was already vacant and as executive sous chef, I had to step in. On top of that, a state dinner for the Prime Minister of India was looming over me and I was trying to figure out when I would get around to preparing for my own tasting menu. I found it somewhat ironic and amusing that I was an applicant for the role of executive chef, while helping others get the role and performing the duties of the actual executive chef. If there was one thing I learned well from the trenches of the kitchen over the years, it was to go with the flow and that is what I did.

Unbeknownst to me, the state dinner for the Prime Minister of India turned out to be my final test. I tried to trace back to my thought process in preparing that meal to understand what worked for me. I was definitely challenged when I discovered that I would be catering to dignitaries from India, given their rich culinary tradition. I wanted to honor that but at the same time give them a taste of American flavors so I decided to marry ingredients from both traditions. I came up with: chilled asparagus soup, pan-roasted halibut, basmati rice with pistachios and currants, herbed summer vegetables, trio of celery hearts, leaves and roots, and mango, chocolate-cardamom and cashew ice creams. I did not hear any complaints from the 136 guests in attendance and I was satisfied with the outcome.

There was so much excitement and even controversy around my possible appointment that at times a part of me just wanted to get it over with. Then I would catch myself thinking about this and pause. I had to remind myself that this was important and if anything, it was the public that helped me the most in realizing the magnitude of the accomplishment—First ever female Executive Chef in the White House history! First ever ethnic minority! My mind wandered back to when I was working in Austria and one of the apprentices there came up to me excited and almost in disbelief to meet the first female sous chef she had ever seen. She said she wanted to be a sous chef someday, too.

Two days after my official announcement as executive chef, *The Washington Post* published an article about me with the headline, 'Toque of the Town.' When I saw that I immediately remembered the apprentice in Austria and wished she would see it so that she would know that someday, she can be more than just a sous chef too.

A Reluctant Chef

When my father, Honesto Pasia, suggested I go to culinary school, I almost laughed at this because becoming a chef was the last thing I wanted to do. I grew up around food and loved it but never really envisioned myself doing that as a profession. But the more I thought about it, the more it made sense. My mom, Erlinda, instilled in me a love for cooking and as early as third grade, I started helping her in the kitchen and got my hands on whatever I could. She prepared a wide variety of authentic Filipino food without ever using a recipe or measuring the ingredients. She made what she was doing look like second nature but she was a perfectionist when it came to me, always telling me my food was either too salty or overcooked. I grew up in Sampaloc in Manila and came from a big clan: a blended family with a total of 11 children so we almost never ate out and there were a lot of opportunities to practice cooking. That is also a lot of people to please, so I was grateful that I picked up my mom's ability to blend flavors and satisfy everyone in the family.

I eventually deferred to my father and decided to give culinary school a try. Who would have thought that years later I would end up not just cooking for my family, friends, and clients, but for heads of state from all over the world? I would never have imagined ending up in the White House after having starting off as a 'salad girl' as my brother teased me. My first job in the U.S. was being in charge of the salad bar at a Sheraton Hotel. I had to be picked up and dropped off since I did not have a car at the time. I did not see this job as anything special and it was not the type of glamorous role that one envisions oneself doing someday, but it was a start. Looking back now, I realize it was one of my most important experiences as it taught me how to be organized, how to work well with other people, and most of all, to really love what I do. Every job we have is important in shaping us and now I rely on my other team members to manage the work I used to do.

I got my foundation in cooking at the University of the Philippines where I took courses in Food Technology. When my visa for the U.S. was approved, I had to move immediately and discontinue my studies. However, my love for food remained so I continued developing my skills. Since then, I have worked as a chef in hotels and restaurants in Chicago and Washington, D.C. and spent six months as Chef Tournant in Vienna, Austria.

Cooking by Instinct, Not by Formula

One of the greatest turning points in my career and life would have to be when I was recruited by the White House Executive Chef Walter Scheib III in 1995 to be his assistant. It took me a while to seriously consider the role but once I joined the White House, it became a place for tremendous growth as a professional, a leader, and a Filipina. I will always be grateful that Walter treated me as a co-chef and allowed me creative license in the kitchen. He was a great supporter of my creations and every year I spent with him contributed to my growth.

Expressing my identity through my cooking has always been important to me. Growing up in a Filipino household that loves food and flavors distinct to our cuisine means that food just runs in my veins. While I do not feel the need to always have a Filipino theme in my dishes when I cook for work, the flavors, ingredients, and philosophy always manage to make their way to the dishes I create. I keep getting asked if I serve Filipino food at the White House. My response is that usually instead of serving *adobo* or another well-known Philippine specific dish as they are, I incorporate them into meals, as a stuffing for example. I love embracing my heritage and sharing it with others even in different forms or one element at a time. One of the biggest compliments I get is when people are able to identify every ingredient in what I plate. My meals are distinctly known for the Asian spice, colors, and the extra garlic.

The diversity of the food I prepare is a priority for me and is based on knowing who I am serving. I believe I picked up the ability to concoct an eclectic range of food from my mom, just like her gift for cooking with instinct and not with a formula. Once for a state dinner, I was asked to prepare a "quintessentially American" dinner and for someone who was born in the Philippines, French-trained, and married to a man of Irish descent, I simply took that to mean to prepare something that reminds one of home.

I approach starting any meal by surveying the best locally available ingredients and from there I combine ingredients until the dishes begin to take shape. A lot of the creative process also happens in my 2004 Volvo during my drive to work. The drive is where a lot of ideas come to me or where details for meals are finalized including the ingredients and the plating, so that when I arrive at work, I only have to instruct the staff to execute what I have envisioned.

Ultimately, I believe that great cooking comes from people who have an inherent capacity to taste, see, and smell. I do not usually measure the seasoning and just taste the food as I go, always relying on my palate, experience, and at times my assistants to figure out when I have hit the right notes. My former boss at Le Ciel reinforced this when he said that I have that certain feeling that is difficult to describe, a way of putting food together, not just cooking it but presenting it.

Evolution as a Chef and Leader

When I was appointed by First Lady Laura Bush in 2005 to take over the reins of the White House kitchen, I knew that my life would never be the same. The state dinner for the Prime Minister of India clinched the position for me. I learned later that it was not only my food that was evaluated by the First Lady, but also how I executed my job, how I interacted with people, and how gracefully I managed pressure.

While taking the head position in the White House kitchen was initially a shock, I also knew that I had earned the position. My career is made up of a series of steps involving hard work and determination that led to an incredible destination. What makes this accomplishment extra special and has caught the attention of the food industry and beyond is that I am the first ever female and minority to ever assume the top spot in the White House kitchen. People and the press were so fascinated by this that my story made national news, with one editorial even commenting that my résumé reads like a classic American success story.

I have to admit that all the attention that followed the public announcement of my appointment was rather surreal and overwhelming. One day, I even looked myself up on Google out of curiosity to see the extent of the coverage I was getting. I almost had to pinch myself to see if I will wake up from a dream and I was extremely humbled by the support I received and positive reactions to the appointment. It was reassuring to hear that my colleagues had faith in my ability to assume a very demanding position and thought that I would be consistent in my level of performance and focus.

How does one get to this level in a career? Unlike recipes that have secret ingredients, I do not think there is a secret or trick to achieving the seemingly unattainable. The combination of exceptional competence, interpersonal abilities, and hard work can produce results beyond one's imagination. As I progressed in my career, I had to be more than just a great cook, but had to learn to become even a greater manager and listener. I had to stay focused at all times, especially on the biggest needs of the moment.

On a regular day at the White House, I manage a small team but when there are big, high-profile events such as the state dinner for China, I had to put together a team of 41 chefs. This is when a lot of preparation and rehearsals well in advance can make or break the success of a dinner. The hand signals I have developed for my staff so that chaos could be avoided in the kitchen and serving area have also made a big difference in executing a flawless dinner, in near silence. This could almost be likened to a ballet with a well-rehearsed staff performing a choreography. However, despite impeccable planning, the unexpected always happens so it is crucial to know how to react and adapt to a situation when a dish or ingredient does not turn out right.

Given the unpredictable nature of my work, my flexibility in new or tough situations has served me well, along with my ability to have good relationships with people. Great talent is important but no one will want to work with you unless you know how to adapt to different situations and personalities. People know I am quite friendly and even-tempered but underneath that surface I am very tough. I am fortunate to have earned the respect of my team and peers in the industry and they know to take me seriously even if I relate to them in a very relaxed and cheerful manner.

When Chef Scheib referred to me as an "all-around great chef," I think that what he meant is one who is more than just able to envision and execute a delicious and eclectic spread, but also has excellent leadership and interpersonal skills and is always looking to grow. That is why it is essential for me to refine my skills by keeping up with trends in the industry and having a robust network. I travel regularly and belong to the Club des Chefs des Chefs, a network of chefs of heads of state worldwide dedicated to promoting and preserving culinary traditions. Participation in this club exposes me to new ideas, ingredients, and practices and allows me to exchange tips and information with the best in the field. I truly believe that sharing tricks is a mark of a good chef.

Another quality that has worked for me in my career is that I have simply been myself. I always maintain a professional demeanor but I am also the same person to the kitchen staff and the highest ranking officials. In 2009, I was honored to find out that the Obamas wanted to retain me as their head chef. I discovered that part of the deciding factor was the First Lady Michelle Obama's being able to relate to me, especially being a mother to a young daughter myself and valuing healthy eating and a healthy lifestyle as much as she does.

I have also been a rather private person and taking on the public persona of this job has been a challenge. When I was first appointed as the head chef in 2005, I heard that I had over 500 requests from the press for interviews. Thankfully, I already had a family trip planned at the time and I managed to slip away quietly and let the White House handle the press release and public relations. But as I mentioned, flexibility is important and even though I have kept my public appearances to a minimum, I am open to them especially when there is a greater purpose such as Mrs. Obama's 'Let's Move' initiative. I even did an appearance on *Food Network's* Iron Chef and The White House's video series, both of which promote healthy eating and showcase the White House's vegetable garden. It is so much easier for me to relate with the public when the attention is not on me, but on something I find important.

What Really Matters

My most valuable lesson from all the attention that my appointment as Executive Chef generated, is that I need to channel all of the blessings I am receiving for the greater good. From that moment I knew that I will have to be more purposeful about giving back to the community, especially through mentorship. I think mentorship is a key factor in the success of the White House kitchen. I personally believe that the things I do and my accomplishments are not just for myself, but it is my responsibility to bring others along. I have since then done my best to take more initiative to inspire other chefs and those in leadership to do the same; to remind them that that the younger generation of chefs are looking up to them.

Another way I have taken advantage of my position is by putting a spotlight on issues that are important to me and this focus on issues has in turn increased my motivation. My involvement with Mrs. Obama's 'Let's Move' initiative allowed me to partner healthy eating and learning to grow my own vegetables. I was inspired to have my own garden at home and my whole family has gotten into this as well, so much so that my daughter now loves to grow herbs and even reminds me when I have too little broccoli on my plate. I even lost fifteen pounds as a result of being more mindful about what I cook and eat. When I do work in public, it is important for me to demonstrate making dishes that can be prepared with ingredients that everyday Americans find in their refrigerators. The Obamas are pretty simple eaters and are easily satisfied with food that most families find in their refrigerators.

I have also been able to take healthy eating one step further by collaborating with Chef Ming Tsai, the White House Initiative on Asian Americans and Pacific Islanders (AAPI), and the U.S. Department of Agriculture (USDA) to help promote healthy and traditional Asian American and Pacific Islander cuisine. We are demonstrating different ways to prepare traditional meals in a healthier way with different techniques under the guidance of the USDA's MyPlate food icon. I am a firm believer that it is unnecessary to completely sacrifice the food that you love and grew up with, when moderation is the key to maintaining a healthy and nutritious diet. Chef Ming Tsai and I created videos where we prepare various AAPI recipes in the White House kitchen which we hope will encourage viewers to try the healthier version of the ethnic foods their families are accustomed to eating (https://www.youtube.com/watch?v=BKKF-HryVsg). For me, Filipino food is much more than just the actual dish, but it is a big part of my identity and culture and like with other Filipinos, food is what brings and connects families together. I love that my daughter Danielle, who is half-Filipino, adores Filipino food, especially for breakfast. I do not see us ever giving up our traditional *tocino* [bacon] and *longanisa* [sausage], but we consume them in moderation and increase our vegetable intake and do regular exercise.

Above all, through the course of my work at the White House, I have come to appreciate my family and church community more than I thought possible. I am humbled by the selflessness of my husband John, who said to me when I first got appointed in 2005 that he is aware of how much that job will demand of me and decided he will fill the void created by spending more time with our daughter. To have him, a fellow chef, be so understanding and supportive of every step of my career has been a true blessing. The more success I gained in my career, the more I realized that even though work is a big part of my life, I should never miss out on my family and that anything I accomplish through my work will ultimately be shared with them.

Also, my involvement with my church community and role there as a deacon has helped keep me stay grounded over the years. The regular Bible study with my group has helped me keep my priorities straight and has been a source of guidance and wisdom in the various stages of my life.

I am not sure if the evolution of my career was completely by design, but I do know that where I am now all began because I kept an open mind. If I had not let my father convince me to go to culinary school, I do not know where I would be now. Even though I had thought that I was not chef material at the time, perhaps my dad knew me better, so I think it is important to pay attention to the feedback of those who know us well as they have the ability to plant seeds in us and nurture them.

It is also important to love what you do; for me, in a way it just happened organically where my love for helping my mom and for food transferred over to sharing with others the love of food and being creative through my dishes. It is also no secret how food has the power to create bonds between those who share them and the ability to evoke strong emotional reactions, whether it is the nostalgia for home and childhood or the sheer pleasure from experiencing a delightful meal.

At this point in my career, I have gotten questions around where I will be next as I am already at the pinnacle with my White House role. I see it differently because when we think of pinnacles, there is really nowhere to go but down and it does not feel that way for me. I have no immediate plans, but let us say I end up doing more volunteer work, I do not think that will be a step down at all. I believe in constantly growing and transforming, without necessarily having a defined end goal, other than having a satisfying and meaningful outcome for all I do and making sure that those around me share in and also benefit from the blessings I have received.

LEADERSHIP TIPS

1. *Play the part you want, even before you have it.* Treating every-day like an audition for our dream role and never being complacent prepares us better to get there and excel. When we develop the habit of constantly raising our level of performance, we only get better and possibly become the best at what we do. This entails always aiming high and being willing to be the first to accomplish something.

2. *Listen.* It is important to be attuned both to what people tell us and to our circumstances. While we cannot take in everyone and every-thing, developing an ear for important lessons and the most pressing needs to address allow us to be the most effective in our actions. This includes knowing our priorities and being able to balance the demands of our professional and personal lives.

3. *Embrace who you are and share it.* Honoring what makes us unique and expressing that in all we do makes them all the more fulfilling and also allow us to stand out. Our authenticity has the power to draw others and share the satisfaction of celebrating a blend of our heritage, personality, style and talent reflected in our identities.

4. *Keep learning, keep growing.* It is the combination of extraordinary talent, managing relationships and pressure gracefully and working harder than others that opens doors to great opportunities. We need to be constantly developing these different facets and be proactive in finding the best resources and space for practice to allow us to cultivate our best.

5. *Bring others along.* Developing others is the true mark of a lead-er. We must pass on the lessons we gained along the way and cre-ate pathways for others to work for their own successes. Accom-plishments are most meaningful and satisfying when we are able to share them with others and become a source of inspiration and motivation.

CHRONICLES OF A MEETING QUEEN: ON LEADERSHIP

Kristine M. Custodio, ACP

Senior Paralegal and Business Development Director
Butterfield Schecter and Van Clief, LLP

Abstract

*T*his chapter presents a second-generation Filipina's journey to discovering the path to leadership in the U.S., and
is a poignant, honest personal accounting of life's lessons
and insight about community, faith, family, and self. This chapter
chronicles my life experiences as a Filipina leader in the paralegal
field. Major topics include individual leadership style, leadership
skills and traits, group dynamics, succeeding when faced with failure, and leader behavior. This chapter also examines the immigrant
values and cultural influences as a second-generation Filipina coming of age in the U.S.

Introduction

Sometimes I feel as if my life is one long meeting. Meetings consume
most of my evenings. Yes, I am a meeting queen but always with purpose and the spirit of collaboration at hand. With the constant hustle and juggling of people, places and things, I am always asked how I
accomplish so many things in a day, week, and month. The truth is I
do not know. I do know that I was born with a lot of energy, at least
enough to accomplish all the things that any busy modern-day woman
needs to check off of her to-do list. I am sure many women can relate.
In fact, I know my first and most influential role model, my mother, Zenaida Pinpin Custodio, passed her extraordinary energy on to me. She
can move mountains. She is in every sense of the word, a true Filipina.

On Role Models, Mentors, and Career Advocates

Zenaida Pinpin Custodio, or Zena for short, was born on March 31, 1940, in Pampanga, Philippines. Zena is one of six children born to Eusebio Garcia Pinpin and Guadalupe Dizon Pinpin. Zena grew up with modest means. Her father was a tailor and her mother a house-wife with a fifth-grade education. My grandparents beamed with pride as they boasted to family and friends at every opportunity that all of their children and grandchildren were college graduates. Education, hard work, family, perseverance, and God were the cornerstones of my mother's upbringing. These values built me in every sense of the word.

My mother, with her college degree and $200 in her pocket, im-migrated to the U.S. in 1974, blazing a path that most of her siblings would follow. My mother met my father, Roland Mojica Custodio, in 1975 in the U.S. It was a whirlwind romance resulting in marriage and the birth of my sister, Ria, that same year. I joined the family on Octo-ber 11, 1976. We lived in Northern California at the time but moved to Kauai, Hawaii soon thereafter. Our journey next took us to San Diego, California where our family currently resides.

My mother is my hero. She is everything I am and hope to be: cou-rageous, talented, intelligent, and fearless. When I think about all of the things that my mother has accomplished in spite of the many chal-lenges that she faced as a woman, as a 'foreigner' with an accent, I am left awestruck.

I am often told stories of the difficulties that my parents endured, particularly my mother, when they first immigrated to this country during the civil rights and women's liberation movements, from op-portunities denied to misguided assumptions. But my mother refused to allow other people's perception of who she was and where she was going to stop her from achieving her goals and dreams. I was always taught the virtues of hard work: rewards will be reaped with a strong mind, a good work ethic, and keeping faith.

For a single woman of modest means to immigrate, get married, start a small business, and build a successful life is a testament to liv-ing the ubiquitous 'American dream' that so many Filipinos immigrat-ing to the United States chase. It also speaks volumes of her relentless fortitude and desire for success. But her dream was indeed a journey that spanned the course of over 40 years.

My mother was a teacher by training. In fact, she was my pre-school teacher in Kauai, Hawaii. She sparked my lifelong love of learning and teaching. It is not surprising that my favorite job thus far has been as an adult educator.

My mother once told me that she approaches life like a puzzle. She is a gifted problem-solver and fact gatherer. She is on a constant quest for knowledge and learning and paying it forward. She enjoys a challenge. That is how she approaches all of the challenges in her life both great and small.

My mother shared stories with me of when we lived in Hawaii, reminiscing about our little island paradise. My memories of Hawaii have come alive in my mind with the lilting cadence of her storytelling and how the businesswoman emerged.

"Do you know how I made extra income when we lived in Hawaii? I learned a new hobby and made a business out of it. I learned how to make ceramics and sold my pieces at the flea market on the weekends. I was the only one who did not have to bring home any unsold pieces every weekend." She laughs. I hear the competitiveness in her voice. Then she continues.

"You know I was a Super Mom. I worked, took care of our home, and took you to your music lessons. Even when I was not working full-time, I thought of ways to bring in income. I became a salesperson. Remember, that is how you got your encyclopedias?" Yes, I remember those wonderful red leather books with gold trim whose pages fueled my desire to learn and research.

When I think of all the experiences that shaped who I am as a leader today, I have to credit my parents for giving me the gifts of curiosity and exploration. My parents possess an indomitable spirit to travel, explore, and seek adventures. We moved from Kauai, Hawaii to San Diego, California in the early 1980s. Hardly a weekend or school break would pass without a road trip or destination vacation planned. My parents, especially my mother, sacrificed time and money to provide my sister and me with every opportunity to explore the world around us, even if that meant shuttling us to the many private lessons and extracurricular activities until our high school years. But one thing stands out in my mind from childhood. With the privileges I enjoyed in my youth, my parents always emphasized the importance of paying it forward and giving back. We were also taught to be mindful of the environment. I think my mother was a hippie, but she will never admit it.

During my high school years, I joined the orchestra playing the violin, which taught me a great deal about discipline, dedication, teamwork, and the beauty of music. I was also active in the Key Club (Rotarians) and the environment club. The focal point of service to others above self remains with me until today. I am a servant leader. I learned from the best servant leaders, my grandparents.

My grandparents helped raise me. They lived with us or near us until they both passed away. The beauty of Filipino culture includes the extended family. My grandparents were known in their community for their hospitality and generosity. I am still reduced to tears when I think of the incredible fortune of being raised and shaped by my grandparents, the grandest teachers of all time.

My parents' journey was not an easy one. It took tremendous discipline and perseverance to enjoy the fruits of their labor daily. It is the peaks and valleys of life, the failures and adversity that built character. This was a life lesson that I would learn as a second generation Filipina.

On Faith, Failure and Other Life Lessons

Life lessons have a way of smacking you in the face, remaining in the depths of your mind, and finding little means for escape. I will not forget my honors speech and debate teacher who informed me that I simply did not have what it took to be in his class. It sounds so clichéd, but when one door closes another truly opens. The universe has a way of taking care of itself.

We were in mid-term. I was in ninth grade, an insecure freshman and filled with doubt. I felt uneasy in Mr. P's class even though I had been in advanced classes since fourth grade. It helps when your mother is a teacher and your own personal tutor and advocate. So here I was with the same kids that I had always been in class with since childhood.

As a somewhat shy, hormonal, angst-ridden teen, I lacked the poise and confidence to excel in my Advanced Placement speech and debate class, and Mr. P let me know it. In the face of defeat, I transferred into Ms. Glenda Mechling's English class. To my surprise and great fortune, Ms. Mechling nurtured and molded this aspiring motivational speaker and lover of words. She was preparing me for what was to come. I survived failure. Just as every successful leader will tell you, failure, perhaps not at the very moment it is happening, can be awesome. Failure provides opportunities for creativity, growth, and resilience.

As I embarked on my next journey, leaving home for college, my tenacity and perseverance would be put to the test. I was 17 years old and on my own. I moved to Long Beach, California to pursue my future career as a physical therapist. Or so I thought. I quickly learned that with freedom comes great responsibility.

I had always prided myself in my academic prowess. I love school. I love learning new things. Not surprising, as my mother was a teacher. Well, my first semester in college resulted in my being placed on academic probation. Still, that first semester was certainly fun-filled and full of learning as I adapted to a different and diverse environment. That experience could have shattered me, but it did not. Instead, the drive for success burned inside me.

College, for me, was more than just training for my career. It is where I discovered who I was, who I am, who I am becoming, and the stuff of what I am made. I learned to stand on my own two feet amidst adversity and challenge. The shyness and insecurity of that young girl melted away. I transformed. I found my voice. I became stronger both mentally and physically. Running became my outlet. I adopted a vegetarian diet. I faced more failures, but dealt with them head on. I empowered myself and surrounded myself with good people and good books. I worked hard and had faith.

On the other side of failure is faith. Faith in a higher power, in self, in the belief that everything will always be okay; it is the key to success. I have always known my truth, deep down inside where every fiber of my being and DNA exists. Even when I doubted myself, with faith I knew that I would be a purveyor of justice and my gifts of spoken and written word would be put to great use.

During my last semester of college, my mother had a stroke. My faith was shaken to its core as my world turned upside down. I took the summer off and moved back home to San Diego. By this time, my mother had already started another business, a board and care facility for developmentally disabled adults. Not only was I responsible for helping my mother in her rehabilitation, but suddenly I also found myself, at the age of 21, stepping into my mother's shoes and running her business.

Eventually, I assumed the role as Administrator of our family's business, a role that I hold until today. After all, I am my mother's daughter. I am as much a savvy businesswoman as my mother. Although I enjoy our family's business and the people that we serve, I had a personal goal from childhood that I wanted to pursue. I have a passion for justice and the law.

I always thought that I would be in the medical field because I love people and helping people, especially those in need. My role as Administrator for our board and care facility aligned with that belief. But my interest in the law drew me to study to become a paralegal, and I enrolled in the paralegal program at the University of California at San Diego Extension's paralegal program. Fast-forward fifteen years. I had the honor and privilege of serving as the commencement speaker at the UCSD Extension's paralegal program commencement ceremony just six years after I, too, completed my paralegal training and embarked upon the path to my new career.

Beginning a new career without any legal experience challenged me in ways that shaped my future success in the field. In 2008, after five years as a paralegal, I would have never imagined that I would be a contender for a national award, Paralegal of the Year; it was even more of a shock to me that I was selected a runner up for the award. I learned the importance of the following leadership qualities and skills in my path to becoming the President of the San Diego Paralegal Association.

Some Lessons I Have Learned

Network, network, network! Your network really is your net worth. Find a career veteran to ask questions to about your career or to vent to, you will need a strong network.

Suit up and show up. This is half the battle. Show up to all the classes, events, and mixers that you can possibly attend and meet everyone you can.

Find a mentor. I have also maintained a close network of friends and colleagues who I feel comfortable to call upon during my times of need. My mentors have truly been an important part of my life and have helped me to achieve all of the success I have enjoyed. And it is always great to be able to share resources with one another.

Attitude is everything. Learn to be a team player and lead when needed. Be positive. Your resume may boast a 4.0 GPA, but if you are hard to get along with, the whole dynamics of your team may be affected. Heard of the saying, "One bad apple spoils the whole bunch?" We spend eight hours a day and often more with our co-workers.

Work hard. Earn your team's respect with your work ethic and work product. Things will not be handed to you on a silver platter. Your education is the foundation of your knowledge base, but it is up to you to take your career to the next level.

Do not compromise your ethics! You are the one who ultimately has to wake up every morning and face yourself. Make wise choices and decisions not only in your career but in your life. Pay it forward. When you are fortunate enough to reap the fruits of your labor, share your success, be it by mentoring someone, volunteering, or lending a hand. Whatever it is that you are most passionate about. go after it with great gusto and be generous with your blessings. Live life and mean it. Success will be sure to follow.

On the Future: Pearls of Wisdom for NextGen Leaders

Great leaders come in all forms. But what makes a great leader? From a global perspective, one may argue a great leader impacts world awareness of injustice and affects the change in societal mores. Leadership characteristics include charisma, poise, articulate communication skills, and courage. But what ultimately makes a great leader? It is the recognition that the complacency about the status quo is far worse than the possible consequences of taking a stand and acting for the betterment of humanity.

Not all of us will be the next great world leader, but we all can decide to be a great leader to our children and families, to our friends, and to our colleagues. We can decide to inspire not only with our words but with our actions. Great leaders share similar skillsets. Under immense pressure, we get the job done. We find ways. We use our resources, networks, power of persuasion, experience, and our commitment to our responsibilities as fuel to get things done.

In summary, my words of final advice on leadership and success: work hard, remain true to yourself, follow your passion, and everything else will fall into place. In the end, it is not the fame and fortune that are important to me. I am reminded by the American essayist and poet Ralph Waldo Emerson that the definition of success is: "To laugh much; to win respect of intelligent persons and the affections of children; to earn the approbation of honest critics and endure the betrayal of false friends; to appreciate beauty; to find the best in others; to give one's self; to leave the world a little better, whether by a healthy child, a garden patch, or a redeemed social condition; to have played and laughed with enthusiasm, and sung with exultation; to know even one life has breathed easier because you have lived—this is to have succeeded."

Leadership Tips

For the next generation of leaders, here are the pearls of wisdom that have been imparted to me by way of experience, mentors, role models, and influencers of both friend and foe:

1. *Keep alive your spirit of curiosity and exploration.* As my parents modeled to my sister and to me, life is to be lived. Get out and explore, especially in nature.

2. *Learn from failures.* Failures can be a source of creativity, growth, and resilience. Adversity builds strength of character.

3. *Keep your faith alive.* Max Ehrmann's prose poem entitled "Desiderata" so eloquently stated: "With all its sham, drudgery and broken dreams, it is still a beautiful world."

4. *Network with the wider community.* My approach to life is that I can learn something from every person I meet. In other words, every person I meet is my teacher.

5. *Know thyself and thy boundaries.* Saying 'No' is permitted. I still struggle with this one every day because I feel like I can do it all. A sign of a great leader is to have the foresight and courage to know your limits.

6. *Stay true to yourself despite the opinion of others.* No one knows you better than you do. I have to remind myself daily that other people's opinion of me is none of my business.

7. *You do not have to be disagreeable to disagree.* Keep calm, be poised and articulate. You can get your point across without destroying others. Happy and content people do not seek to destroy others.

8. *Practice, practice, practice.* Whatever your chosen profession, strive for excellence and hone your craft. Live with great passion each day. Life is a gift, and we are not guaranteed tomorrow.

9. *Ask questions until you understand why.* Do not just go along to get along.

10. *Be flexible.* Life will not always go as you plan but even in the most challenging moments, life lessons abound and the rewards are great.

11. *Take risks.* Throw caution to the wind. In the words of Harvard professor, Laurel Thatcher Ulrich: "Well-behaved women seldom make history."

12. *Health is wealth.* Guard and protect your health and physical fitness. Moving mountains takes a lot of energy.

13. *Don't give up. Persevere.* Success is usually just around the corner.

14. *You are here for a reason.* Live with purpose and passion every day.

15. *Be positive.* Be confident in who you are. Surround yourself with positive people who will help you become the best version of yourself.

16. *Do something that scares you every day.* Today, I am frequently asked to speak about my experience as a paralegal and about professional development, leadership, and ethics. Had I accepted the belief that I was not equipped to excel at public speaking, I would not be where I am today.

FROM THE BOONDOCKS TO THE BOARDROOM

Sonia T. Delen-Fitzsimmons
Senior Vice President, Bank of America Merrill Lynch

Abstract

I believe in changing the world one small step at a time. In this chapter, I share how I have made my mark in the Filipino-American community in the San Francisco Bay Area and the Philippines as a business executive, philanthropist, board member and mentor. Growing up in a rural town in the Philippines, I remember always trying to excel in all of my endeavors in school and the community, a quality that I have carried with me to the corporate world in the U.S. I highlight the series of steps I took not only to develop my career but also to give the attention and commitment that having a family entailed. From a nine-year old assistant to my father, who helped farmers with land deeds, to being the highest-ranking Filipina in Global Leasing at Bank of America, where I am responsible for the negotiation of multi-million asset financings for Fortune 500 clients, I share how I have consistently embodied my commitment to the community through my work. The common thread in my life has been an innate desire to go as far as I can while serving communities and facing the challenges of life head on and turning challenges into successes. My humble beginnings fueled my ambition for a better life in order to eventually give back to society. My son's disability made me more empathetic and compassionate with families who share a similar plight and has motivated my efforts to create a community with them. I end the chapter with the qualities that created for me a life filled with both accomplishments and meaning. I hope that sharing my story will benefit aspiring leaders.

Introduction

Recently, I was chatting with a good friend about life, loves, relationships and current events when our discussion turned to our childhood years. We shared about our early experiences, even though we grew up in different cities and circumstances. As we were talking, it was with some surprise and gratitude that I realized how far I have come in my personal and professional life.

Humble Beginnings

My journey began in Batangas, in a simple home located in an underdeveloped barrio called Conde Labak, not far from Batangas City. The community had no modern infrastructure. Homes had no running water and electricity. I remember my sisters Ester, Delza and I used to trek down the hill to the community well. With two full pails hanging at the end of a long pole, which we carried across our shoulders, we carefully walked back to the house so we would have water for drinking, washing, cooking and bathing. It was physically difficult to make that trek back home, but I would spend the time thinking about what I could do to help make life a bit easier for us.

My mother and father were educators, and they worked hard to provide us with a good life and education. As part of a handful of people who could read and write, they were often pressed upon by the farmers in the area, most of them uneducated, to help them understand legal documents, file claims and deeds, and communicate with the outside world.

There were nights when our house would be brimming with farmers and their families, clutching land deeds, seeking my father's help in filling out forms and records with the appropriate city government agencies. Long into the night (of course using hurricane lamps), my father would gently talk to the farmers and help them out. I would watch in awe as my father extended his support. The farmers were stressed when they came to seek assistance, but left with a lighter load once my father explained what was needed, and how he would help. Seeing the relief in their eyes made me proud of my father and ignited my desire to assist in the process.

I remember asking my dad to send me to typing school so I could help him with the documentation. So, on the weekends, I took the bus and attended typing school in the city. At the age of nine, I became my dad's assistant, typing all those documents. It was a tedious task. One mistake on the form and I would have to start all over. Auto-correct and computers did not exist at that time. Erasers would smudge the paper and white-out did not exist. While helping my dad with the forms, I somehow assimilated the ability to read and understand contracts. That experience was my first foray in community service, and it felt good.

More Than An Education

A few years later, while in high school, I continued to support the community by leading the Young Christian Life Community (YCLC), a group organized by the nuns who ran the all-girls exclusive catholic school I attended. We organized retreats, led the student body and helped out in our community. We also became involved in national concerns. I remember on one occasion, when the neighboring province of Quezon was flooded by strong typhoons, riding on *bancas* [canoes] to deliver food and clothing we had collected, and sleeping on the cold, hard floors of the governor's mansion to weather the storms.

I went to the University of the Philippines where I pursued a degree in Foreign Service. It was a chaotic era for the Philippines: Marcos was in power; martial law was in effect; the opposition was restless; free speech was curtailed; journalists and critics of the government were harassed or even disappeared. The university's student government was suspended and in its place, the Consultative Committee on Student Affairs (Concomsa) was formed. Then student and civil rights leader, Arno Sanidad approached me to lead the group. Concomsa's goal was to champion the rights of the students and the underprivileged. I had a strong sense of justice and wanted to help, so I accepted the challenge and led the organization. The experience strengthened my organizational skills and my tenacity.

The chaos did not limit itself to the streets or the media. Concomsa was closely monitored by the government and because of the prevailing activism, members of the organization were watched closely and threatened, including myself. It was a thrilling, yet dangerous time, but I thrived in it.

A Major Shift

In 1982, I decided to migrate to the United States, where I felt that I could seek better opportunities to help my family. During my first year here, I gave birth to my first-born, David, who was born blind and hearing impaired. As a single mother (by choice, for the first seven years), I knew that I wanted to give David a good life, and he inspired me to strive and find opportunities so I could provide for him.

Having no experience working in the U.S., I applied for entry-level positions. My first job was an administrative assistant. My communication skills were hampered by language and fluency issues. Recognizing that I needed to strengthen those skills, I enrolled in a night class at the UC Berkeley Extension.

As I worked to better myself, I had to find the right support for David. I scoured the yellow pages to find community agencies which could help me with David. I met dedicated case workers who specialized in disability cases. They assisted me in finding the best doctors, education and support programs. I met with other families and got involved with parent groups and my local school district. In the quest to find assistance for my son, I developed another passion: helping other children impacted with disability. I served on the boards of two organizations: Support for Families of Children with Disabilities, and the Blind Babies Foundation. To this day, I remain a strong advocate for children and adults with special needs.

My Quest to Do Better

With David by my side, it became imperative to better our lot in life. As an administrative assistant, a woman and a member of a minority group, my career track was very limited. I looked at the structure of the company where I was employed at the time and identified where I wanted to be in the company. Once I had set a goal, I made a plan and approached the head of contracts administration. I outlined my skills, and we discussed how I could be an asset to her group. There was no job opening at that time, but I continued to check in with her. A few months later, she called me. The opportunity came when there was a large fleet acquisition. Although I was not part of her current department, she remembered me and that I had the determination, dedication and skills needed for a newly created position. She offered me the job, which I happily accepted. This was my stepping stone. I successfully rose through the company by a series of promotions and was recognized in the financial arena for my expertise and hard work.

After a few years, I joined Bank of America Merrill Lynch where I am currently a Senior Vice President and the highest ranking Filipina in the Leasing subsidiary. As global financial services companies merged and evolved, I had to be nimble, learn and adapt to the changing financial environment, and be firm and steadfast in my knowledge and skills. More often than not, I find myself to be the only woman at the bargaining table. I love what I do, and because I love and thrive in it, I continue to find success in my efforts. It is daunting but it can be done. I have come to share the viewpoint of Barbara Annis and John Gray who recommend in their book *Work with Me: The 8 Blind Spots Between Men and Women in Business*, that the key to success is being mindful of gender-intelligence, knowing that men and women are equal and embracing being a woman. It is important to maintain harmony, working towards achieving high levels of performance and becoming successful in the workplace and at home.

Passion Comes with Action

I have been asked regularly how I continue to work with community organizations in addition to job and family. It is my passion and I choose to act on it. I am proud of my involvement with the Filipina Women's Network, aimed at 'femtoring' and empowering women and girls globally; and the Philippine International Aid, providing educational benefits to the disadvantaged youth in the Philippines and the San Francisco Bay Area. I am honored to chair the health initiative of the Apl.de.ap Foundation International's "Campaign for Filipino Children," which will provide special medical equipment and training to targeted regional hospitals in the Philippines, with the goal of eradicating blindness in premature babies caused by retinopathy of prematurity.

Elevating our culture to the world stage is a high priority for me. I am proud of coining the phrase "Let's Go Filipino" and co-founding "Kulinarya" with the Philippine Department of Tourism and the Consulate General in San Francisco. The goal of Kulinarya is to raise awareness about Filipino cuisine and celebrate the culinary talents of Fil-Am chefs in the U.S. Now in its fifth year, the annual live cooking competition has attracted contestants from San Francisco, Los Angeles, Honolulu, New York and Chicago. Kulinarya's success has boosted the popularity of Fil-Am chefs, restaurants, and Philippine food suppliers in the San Francisco Bay Area and across the U.S.

The Long and Winding Road

Yes, the Beatles said it well. It is a long and winding road to success and personal fulfillment. Many times, young women who I mentor ask me what they can do to succeed. Here are some tenets that I firmly believe in.

Determine Your Measure of Success

Staying at home, raising a family and being available to your children is a measure of success for some. Reaching the top of Mt. Kilimanjaro, or retiring at the age of 40, or becoming an acclaimed violinist are other measures of success. For me, success has been a combination of ensuring the right support for David, my first born who has a disability, nurturing my three sons to be the best they can be, earning Senior Vice President title at the Bank of America Merrill Lynch, taking time to enjoy the concerts with my husband, and putting passion into action. What is important is to determine what success means to you. Once you have set your goal, the next step is to formulate a plan on how to get there.

You Are Never Too Young or Too Old to Learn

The astounding proliferation of very young chief executive officers, successful entrepreneurs and innovators affirms my belief that leadership skills start at a young age, much younger than what many are accustomed to. At age nine, I learned about contracts by osmosis.

We are fortunate to have role models and mentors as well as seasoned and veteran leaders to whom we can relate and look up to. Finding mentors, coaches and sponsors has been important in my own leadership development. These supporters have believed in my talents, advocated for my promotion, and helped with navigating pitfalls and challenges.

In order to navigate and position yourself as a leader in the industry you choose, you will need to increase your experience so that you can project the confidence that you know how to lead. Find out and discover your passion. Live your dreams. Rebecca Shambaugh, in *It's Not a Glass Ceiling, It's a Sticky Floor: Free Yourself From the Hidden Behaviors Sabotaging Your Career Success*, indicates that you should be clear on what you want, what career development means to you, and what your strengths, weaknesses, values and motivations are. Then develop your career, create a diverse network of contacts, and manage your time to achieve work/life balance. And this strategy also applies to the more experienced or veteran workers or leaders to achieve success in their endeavors. Focus on the road map to get you there, so you can achieve your ultimate goal.

Credibility, Dignity and Integrity

These are universal values. In any activity, assignment or task, strive towards credibility. Demonstrate that you are able to deliver what is expected of you in a timely manner, with a high standard of quality of work. Always research, ask questions, listen carefully, and then when you are clear on the subject, speak with authority. Never try to wing it; be fair and you will be worthy of respect. Such is dignity, that you will be taken seriously and have pride in yourself.

With credibility and dignity, doing the right thing and being fair, comes integrity. If there is anything that I value the most, it is integrity. It cannot be bought and it cannot be handed over to you. I subscribe to the Merriam-Webster dictionary definition of integrity as "the quality of being honest and fair; the state of being complete or whole" (www.merriam-webster.com/dictionary/integrity).

Believe in Yourself

Sheryl Sandberg, in *Lean In: Women, Work, and the Will to Lead*, encourages women to "sit at the table," seek challenges, take risks, and pursue their goals with gusto. That is what I have done to rise through the ranks, gain recognition, and be promoted in my company.

Speak up and participate during meetings and team events. In other words, be engaged. Assert yourself without being aggressive and off-putting. Familiarize yourself with the subject and the people you will be meeting. When the opportunity to show your knowledge or leadership qualities presents itself, grab it, even though it may be outside of your comfort zone.

Do not let your fear of making mistakes hold you back. Be bold, and when (not if) you make a mistake, dig into what went wrong, absorb it, learn from it, then move forward. Try your best not to make the same mistake again.

Open your eyes, learn and be well informed by reading about topics that expand your thinking. Learn to appreciate the circumstances that you are in, be they hard or easy.

Picture what success looks like to you or emulate a person who you feel is successful. Project an aura of strength and dependability by being comfortable with your abilities and competencies, carrying yourself with dignity, and dressing for success.

Honor your commitments and be respectful of each other's time. Many successful people are pulled in different directions, and their time is valuable. Be punctual at all times.

When interacting with someone, show interest by keeping eye contact with them. Put the technology away for that period of time, and give them your full attention.

Withhold any judgments you may have. Be open-minded, a good team player and be supportive of others – that makes a good leader.

Adapt to New Challenges

Keep excelling in every domain. By choice, I immigrated to the U.S. as a single mother-to-be. By circumstance, my son David was born totally blind and hearing-impaired. I faced the challenge with courage. I was driven by my personal mantra to learn, explore, excel and be credible.

Never stop the thirst to learn, to develop, to absorb, and to innovate. Adapt to situations physically, emotionally, and mentally. Stay out of company politics, but be mindful of the power plays in your environment. Do not get entangled with games. However, it is important that you know your superiors and their interests, so you can engage them in conversations appropriately.

The key to standing out is to be relevant. Any changes in your environment mean you need to identify how you add value and clearly show that you are a collaborator and a leader.

Be insatiable in making yourself better by challenging yourself to excel in your role or assignment, whatever that may be. Go out of your comfort zone, think out of the box and implement your plans with precision and thoughtfulness.

Set Aside Time for Reflection and Growth

We are led to believe that we must work harder and harder. Working hard is good, as long as you find time every day for reflection. Take a step back and look at what is going on with your life, and ask yourself if it makes you happy. For me, the perfect combination to a fulfilled life is a healthy body and a healthy mind. After so much 'extroverted' activity and action, I take some 'introverted' time to let things seep in and to allow new ideas to come to the surface. I enjoy golf and classical music with my husband, among other things.

Take time to meditate. Be grateful for all the graces, no matter how small or how large. Be thankful for those who keep you secure, calm and happy. Reflection is important as it enables us to regenerate, reinvigorate, and find direction, peace, and understanding in our lives and workplace. You need to make a conscious effort and look introspectively and with determination. A good technique is to keep a journal to record your feelings, your disappointments, your accomplishments, and tasks ahead. You will be amazed to see how you have grown when you read your entries and see where you were, where you are now—and how you got there.

Discipline yourself to generate ideas, find the rationale and champion them. Pursue them with vigor and be results-oriented. Soon, it will be part of your lifestyle to see where you are in the present, and where you want to be.

Give Back to Society

Always be grateful for your life, whatever your station in life or wherever you are. Travelling the road to get where you want to be can be a beautiful experience. Along the way, you will meet others who may not be as blessed as you. Reach out to them with compassion. We are blessed with good fortune, happiness and love. We did not reach our station in life without the help of others, and it is incumbent upon us to do the right thing by sharing our blessings with the community.

You do not have to be rich to make a difference in making the world a better place. If you do not have the funds, donate your time or your expertise. Be understanding of those who are suffering. In volunteering, my involvement with the Filipino community and foundations has given me new perspective, and working with others has increased my self-esteem and built relationships and connections.

Giving back to the community is a fulfilling job, because you now have the ability to share yourself and reach out to other people.

Leadership Tips

1. *Determine your measure of success.* Success comes in many forms and situations, and is different for everyone. What is important is that you determine what success means to you. Once you have set your bar, you now have a goal to aspire to. The next step is to plan how to get there.

2. *You are never too young or too old to dream.* Discover your passion. Live your dreams. Focus on the road map to get you there, so you can achieve your ultimate goal. Work hard and know your stuff! Knowledge is power. How do you gain knowledge? Ask questions. Explore. Listen. Absorb. Study.

3. *Have credibility, dignity and integrity.* Always strive for credibility and deliver what is expected of you and on time, with a high standard of quality of work. With credibility, doing the right thing and being fair, comes integrity. It cannot be bought and it cannot be handed to you.

4. *Believe in yourself.* If you do not believe in yourself, how will others have faith in you? Do not just sit in meetings or team events, speak up and be engaged. Be bold and do not let your fear of making mistakes hinder you: if they happen, learn from them, then move forward. Project an aura of strength and dependability; the key to that is being comfortable: picture what success looks like to you and carry yourself with dignity like the person you aspire to be.

5. *Adapt to new challenges and keep excelling in every domain.* There will be times when you will be uprooted, either by choice or by circumstance, so be courageous in facing the challenge. Understand your surroundings, and never lose the thirst to learn, to develop, to absorb, and to innovate. Go out of your comfort zone, think out of the box and implement your plans with precision and thoughtfulness.

6. *Set aside time for reflection and growth.* Working hard is good, as long as you find time every day for reflection. Take a step back and look at what is going with your life, and ask yourself if it makes you happy. Reflection is important as it enables us to regenerate, reinvigorate, and find direction, peace and understanding in our lives and workplace.

7. *Give back to society.* Civic engagement happens in the present, not when you retire. To make a difference in the world is not dependent on being rich. If you do not have the funds to donate, volunteer your time or your expertise. By volunteering, you gain a new perspective and a sense of fulfillment from sharing yourself.

LEADERSHIP BY INSPIRATION

Ernestina de los Santos-Mac, M.D.

President, PACCM

Abstract

My professional and management skills and close attention to details made me successful in my career as a pediatrician. In my career, I give importance and priority to being an advocate for the best interests of my patients. My leadership style is anchored on my passion, commitment, and dedication to the goals of the organization I lead. In my civic undertakings, organizational advocacy comes first. As a leader, my style calls for me to work behind the scenes, delegate responsibilities to others, and generously give credit to where credit is due. Knowing the respective strengths and expertise of my fellow officers is important in the efforts to achieve the mission and vision of the organization. This is actually teamwork which is crucial in any endeavor of the organization. Without teamwork, not much can be done. My values as a Filipina are my indispensable tools in my efforts to attain success. I learned these values while I was growing up in a poor family. My parents gave me a good sense of self and ambition to rise from poverty. My late mother told me: "Nothing is impossible if you are patient, hardworking, and focused on what you are trying to achieve." My late father instilled in us the importance of integrity, kindness, and goodwill. In this chapter, I share how obstacles such as poverty, lack of support, and personal loss can be transformed into opportunity. I recount my humble beginnings in Ligao, Albay, Philippines where I faced a slew of opposition and doubters in my ability, including an initially unsupportive father and school administrators who disapproved of women with ambitions for higher education. Often taking matters into my own hands while also soliciting the help of others, I remained steadfast in my resolve to finish my education and fulfill my dreams of becoming a doctor in the United States. I urge the new generation of female leaders to foster a culture of reciprocity, have faith, work hard, get involved, and to lead with credibility through action, inspiration, and kindness.

Introduction

The world was in turmoil on the day I was born. It was two days after the Japanese bombed Pearl Harbor in a massive aerial attack that triggered World War II. My parents, Braulio de los Santos and Corazon Hernandez, remembered well that on the day of my birth a male *partera* [midwife] named Tiong Lucio, delivered me while the public market in our town, Ligao, Albay, Philippine, was blasted with bombs by Japanese kamikaze pilots.

Extremely Difficult Life

Life was extremely difficult during the war. We stayed at our *retirada* [retreat house] in Tula-tula, Ligao where we hid from the Japanese. But even at an early age, I felt that the Japanese imperial soldiers were to be feared no more than the guerrillas who were supposed to protect us.

As soon as the guerrillas learned about our abundant food supply, they raided and pillaged our home, acting entitled to take whatever we had. The raids happened several times. I observed these abuses committed by fellow Filipinos with indignation and vowed to myself that from then on, I would work for the common good.

My father worked for an American company, ALAMEN Transport Co. As a young girl, I remember that we hosted a few Americans, a certain 'Mr. Stoddard' and 'Mr. and Mrs. Ayton.' (I never knew the correct spellings) in our home.

I was six years old during the Philippine liberation. I still vividly remember wearing clothes made of American parachutes. My experience with the Americans during the war introduced me to the positive values of the United States of America, and since then I nurtured my dream of coming to America. We looked forward to receiving our share of relief goods distributed by American soldiers. I felt then that the Americans were our saviors. With this in mind as a young child, I made it a goal to get out of poverty and fulfill my ambition to come to America.

Sole Breadwinner

My father was the sole breadwinner of our family. He was responsible for feeding 13 mouths including one grandmother, two grand aunts, four adopted cousins, two uncles, my mama and three biological children, including myself, the eldest and only daughter.

Primary or elementary school was nice and easy. Mrs. Rosal, my first grade teacher, was great. I was one of the first few pupils who was able to read "Bantay, Bow-wow-wow." My *katon* [spelling book for beginners] teacher, Tiang Sila, taught me the ABAKADA.

Intermediate school was a different story. Somehow, my fifth grade teacher did not like me and gave me low grades. But this did not weaken my determination to study hard. In sixth grade, Mrs. Cam (may God bless her soul) was one of my beloved teachers. She laid the foundations of my budding values such as honesty and integrity. But I found out later that my advocate was Mr. Ramon Sanchez. He fought for me behind the scenes. I eventually graduated salutatorian. Nelia, our valedictorian, deserved it.

When we were in college, my mama engaged in a small-scale buy-and-sell business to help my papa earn money for our household expenses. School was easy for me but my greatest obstacles were the doubters. They included teachers who told my parents that it was not wise to send me to school because I was a girl. I would retort, "So what if I am a girl?" I never considered being a girl an impediment.

Happiest Times of My Life

I attended secondary or high school in the 1950s at Mayon High School in Tabacalera There were two factions at school, the 'haves' and the 'have-nots.' It was obvious to which group I belonged. I was the ringleader for both the poor boys and girls. The two groups fought in almost gangland style but without the violence. These were some of my happiest times as I had no serious concern about life outside the confines of the schoolyard. With nothing to lose, we used to raid the fruit orchards of the stingy rich people for our *merienda* [snack].

In high school, I developed an interest in writing that led to my involvement with the school newspaper. I was also a captain of the

Philippine Military Training (PMT). Sabers and guns were my forte and I had a penchant for declamation.

Some Sort of *Déjà Vu*

In my senior year, I experienced some sort of *déjà vu*. I found out that I was going to graduate with fourth honorable mention. I was upset and scared to show my less than ideal grades to my parents. I had hopes of applying for scholarships but graduating with fourth honorable mention compromised my chance for a full-ride scholarship. I knew I had to take matters into my own hands.

I started my own investigation. I went to the principal who could not understand why I had such a low grade average. It turned out that my home economics teacher gave me a very bad grade, but when confronted she made it look like she had made a mistake and the correction was promptly made. As a result, I graduated salutatorian. On stage, it was announced that the point difference between the salutatorian and the valedictorian was .0007 percent.

After high school, I attended Legazpi College (Don Erquiaga School) where I took up liberal arts. There I excelled. Sciences were my forte. I remember Mr. Delgado who was my professor in botany and zoology, and Mr. Soliman, my chemistry professor. It was in college where I started to sharpen my leadership skills. To me at the time, the meaning of leadership was working hard: *you have to work hard so you can lead the pack*. In hindsight, I can say, "When you want something enough and you think it is right for you and for the common good, you fight for it."

ROTC Commander

It was at Legazpi College where I became the commander of the only female Reserve Officer Training Corps (ROTC) company in the country. During the ROTC days, we competed against our male counterparts and we always worked as a team to keep improving our skills. As a result, we always won the contests in the dismantling and assembling of MI rifles. "Never be intimidated by the opposite sex" was our battle cry.

I eventually graduated with honors from Legazpi College. I passed the entrance examination at the University of Santo Tomas (UST) where I was granted a partial scholarship. Going to UST in Manila, was my first trip to the big city. We lived in the slums of San Andres Bukid, Manila in a small, attached dwelling. I became very familiar with the Nagtahan bus. I saved 25 centavos every day by riding the bus that stopped in front of the old Far Eastern University campus. I then would walk the length of Morayta St. to reach UST on Espana St. everyday.

Medical school at UST was four years of hard work full of blood, sweat, and tears; but with faith, I was able to persevere. My medical internship came and with it, more struggles. Working at the San Lazaro Hospital on Rizal Avenue, Sta. Cruz, Manila, the other interns and I were exposed to the risk of contracting cholera, as an epidemic of the deadly disease was raging. The emergency room at San Lazaro was crowded with many sick children on tables, busy with new doctors like myself sticking *sueros* [IV] into their scalps. To encourage my co-interns, I volunteered to complete the daunting task. "This is what we are here for," I exhorted them. We also encouraged the parents to be hopeful for the survival of their children.

Fight against Cholera

In the fight against cholera, we won some and lost some. We suffered deep heartaches as we witnessed little ones convulse and die. At the same time, we were grateful that we were able to save many of them from death.

The risk of contracting tuberculosis was a looming danger during my internship at the Quezon Institute. In the back of our minds, we were fearful of the possibility of infection. But somehow we were unfazed, and again I led my co-interns by demonstrating how to insert a chest tube under the guidance of the attending physician. I told my fellow interns confidently, "This is not going to kill you as long as you protect yourself." They believed my guidance and followed the procedure accordingly. All of us emerged alive without contracting TB (thank you, Lord).

Upon passing the rotation, we were assigned to the Maternity and

Children's Hospital. This assignment was an eye opener for me. As in the past, many of my classmates and buddies came from well-to-do families who had a hard time getting their hands dirty and were not used to toiling away. Some of them found it difficult to deliver 13 babies each per night. They asked me how I made it that far. I answered simply, "It is a matter of survival."

Light Moments

Although it was hard work most of the time, there were also light moments at the Maternity and Children's Hospital. I remember one particular incident when I read "Ill" on a seemingly healthy patient's chart. Confused, I asked my friend Remy, "*Wala naman sakit bakit 'ill'?* ["He's not sick, why does it say "ill"?] She laughed uproariously then answered, "*Tanga* [Stupid], 'ill' as in illegitimate." I was floored when I realized that 80 percent of the newborn babies were illegitimate children. Because there is no divorce in the Philippines, many couples whose marriage have ended just separate and take on a common-law living relationship. Thus several of the "illegitimate" births are due mainly to a structural societal policy.

At that time, there was a severe lack of family planning education for Filipino women. Today, this lack of family planning education continues to bedevil Philippine demographics. It breaks my heart to see wayward kids on the streets, slums, barrios, and mountains seemingly happy, not knowing that they are facing a very dim future. Poverty incidence is about 20 percent (National Statistics Office 2014, 60).

Recognizing their sad plight, I want to help them. Increasingly, mission work has become a platform in which I can apply my leadership skills. I try to inspire unfortunate children through leading by example. I share my story. I tell them that once upon a time I was like them, but with hard work and education, I was able to extricate myself from the quagmire of poverty. I call this method 'leadership by inspiration.'

The Next Hurdle

I graduated from the UST Medical School on May 18, 1965. My parents, may God bless their souls, were very proud of me. Deep within me, a little voice kept saying, "You have earned it." None of my professors personally knew me because I was not like my other classmates who had drivers and flashy cars with license plates with single-digit or double-digit numbers that signified high status.

My next hurdle as a young medical intern was the board exam. All of us interns studied very hard, burning the midnight oil during our review, and fortunately most of us passed the test. Some six months before graduation, we applied to take the examination for Educational Council for Foreign Medical Graduates (ECFMG).

My father was very much against my plan to take the ECFMG. Though my father refused because he could not afford to pay the fee, I was undeterred. I took matters into my own hands again. Against his wishes, I went to Tito Bito, my father's youngest brother, and asked him to loan me the money I needed to take the exam. Tito Bio was a willing conspirator and our arrangement was kept a tightly guarded secret. I was able to take the exam in confidence.

I waited patiently for the results of the exam that was to determine my fate. The fateful day was May 18, 1965, the same day as my graduation. I jumped in jubilation, I finally had my ticket to 'freedom' and the key to the fulfillment of my dream.

When my father learned that I had passed the exam, he cried unashamedly. It was the first time I saw my father cry. I felt then that it was a cry of joy and pride. During the summer after graduation while waiting for the results of the board exam, I worked for a doctor who was running for office. To say the least, he was not a good boss. Nevertheless, I was grateful to him for the opportunity to work with people who needed medical care. Whatever money I earned from my job, I saved for my trip to America.

Travel to the U.S.

I was set to come to America, and though I anticipated some barriers to come in the way of my plans, I was determined to overcome them.

Nothing was going to stop me from starting my new life in the U.S. I applied to a hospital in Meriden, Connecticut which hired me and sponsored my plane fare. The date of my departure was January 3rd, 1966.

My father finally came to terms with my departure and he was ultimately happy to let me go. He later died at a comparatively young age due to a bleeding ulcer possibly caused by work stress. My mother, on the other hand, had always been supportive of me as she had high hopes and ambitions for all of her children. She was ecstatic that her daughter, not just anyone from Barrio Guilid, Ligao, Albay had not only become a doctor but was also embarking on a new journey to America.

First Taste of Steak

On the way to the U.S., my flight had a long layover in Hawaii. The long wait made me anxious and I feared that the Philippine Airlines plane had mechanical problems. My anxiety subsided when we were fed American steak and crunchy celery, fanciful food that at that point, I had only seen in the movies.

Afterwards, I boarded an American Airlines plane and arrived in New York City in the dead of winter. The situation was aggravated by a Port Authority bus strike, but the hospital that employed me had a contingency plan. There was a taxicab waiting to transport me to Meriden, along with other passengers who were going to different hospitals. I was the last one to be dropped off.

The hospital staff helped me to settle in the interns' quarters. When I arrived, one of my classmates, Dr. Remy Raquiza, who later became my daughter's godmother, was there waiting for her newest roommate. There was another Filipina doctor in the hospital, who I came to know very well, Dr. Lourdes Andaya, a respected neurologist in Michigan.

Adjustment Not Difficult

Although we were on call every other night, the adjustment to our new environment was fairly smooth. Some of my classmates from UST came to join us in July 1966. The new recruits included Dr. Teresita Sinaguinan, who later became Dr. Teresita S. Platon; Dr. Ted Quintos; Dr. Edilberto David; Dr. Dick Ruiz; Dr. Olive Gonzales who later became Dr. Olive G. Quintos; and Dr. Linda San Antonio. Together with Remy and Lourdes, we formed a tight 'family.' I was their *Ate* [big sister] in Meriden and their cook, too. I showed them the ropes. I always reminded them not to take 'BS' from anyone, and I advised them to work hard and always give it their best shot.

I felt like a little puppy when I first saw snow. I picked up a handful and tasted it.

I never went to driving school. I did not have a car, but I got around because Remy had a Corbet, not Corvette. Theresa, my Italian friend, taught me how to drive. It took a lot of guts to start the ignition of a Dodge Plymouth 1958 in mint condition. But she was not a bit scared, and I drove her confidently around downtown Meriden. Up to now, I can still hear Theresa's voice instructing me, "When in doubt, hit the brakes." I eventually got my driver's license but still did not have a car. Ted Quintos bought his first car and we all took turns driving it.

While I was still in Connecticut, I met a Columban nun who was the sister of one of the obstetricians at the hospital. At the time, I wanted to become a missionary. She took me to the monastery in Hyde Park, Massachusetts where I met the mother superior and a Filipina novice. The mother superior advised me to finish my residency before embarking on a mission. The mother superior indicated that it was possible that my first assignment would be Lima, Peru.

Time to Leave Meriden

Then it was time for me to leave. I followed Dr. Lourdes Andaya to Detroit. Later, all my classmates in Meriden followed me to the Detroit area where we all worked in different hospitals. I ended up working at Harper Hospital and the Children's Hospital of Michigan where I finished my residency and had a stint in pediatric cardiology.

A Fateful Year

Looking back, 1967 was a fateful year for me. Some of us were moonlighting at Herman Keiffer Hospital during July of 1967 when the in famous riots hit Detroit. I remember being transported in a military tank from there to Harper.

At Harper, I was one of three new, immature and naïve female doctors; none of whom had a boyfriend at the time. Whenever a new batch of resident doctors was introduced, we all used to say, "*May maliwanag na mukha.*" [There are bright faces.]

We used to take the same elevator with a *pogi* [handsome] Filipino resident physician who seldom reciprocated our curious gaze. After he got out of the elevator, we would giggle in unison. I used to tell my doctor friends, "*Matira ang matibay.*"[May the best person win.] Little did I know that this elusive resident doctor, Frankie Mac, had something up his sleeve: I was his unknowing target. Later, years into our marriage, Frankie disclosed that he first saw me in April of 1967 when he came in for his interview at Harper. He saw me and said to himself, "She is the girl I am going to marry." I replied, "*Yabang, suerte mo lang.*" [Show off, you just got lucky.]

In our most tender moments, he would say that he fell in love with me because I looked so innocent but very self-assured. He would reminisce, "When you walked in the hall of the wards, you always looked like you were the one in charge." Indeed, I was.

First Boyfriend in Person

Frankie was my first real boyfriend and he was the reason I did not become a Columban sister.

Before Frankie came into my life, I had a friendship developed through letters with a graduate of fine arts who was studying medicine at the University of the Philippines. He had plans to follow me in the U.S. To me, he was a leader in his own right, practicing leadership by inspiration. He taught me how to be honest with myself and how it felt to be truly loved and adored by somebody.

Though he was a good influence, I was honest with myself when I discovered that I was truly in love with Dr. Mac. I promptly wrote a letter to my pen pal, breaking up our relationship.

I was married to Frank Mac for over 27 years. We had three

children; one girl and two boys, all of whom we raised to become beautiful human beings.

Unfathomable Reason

I believe that all things happen for a reason. And so for some unfathomable reason, my blissful married life suddenly came to an end. September 16, 1995 was one of the most painful and saddest days of my life. I came home to my son, Ernest, choking back his tears as he struggled to tell me what had happened to his father

When I finally understood what Ernest was saying, I realized that my Frankie was gone, *gone forever*. What came next felt like the longest car ride of my life. It felt like an eternity to reach the hospital.

Most Painful Moment

When I arrived at the hospital, I was met by a Catholic sister and all of Frankie's friends quietly sitting, looking very sad and somber.

It was painful to see my children wailing as they stroked the lifeless body of their father. It was the most painful moment in my life.

I realized I had a responsibility so heavy that I could not even cry. I had to keep my faith. I had to keep a handle of what was going on. I was seized with the urge to lead my family through this crisis. Through this family tragedy, I realized that leadership is not just a matter of leading a big company to make millions. To me, leadership also means extricating oneself from a seemingly hopeless situation, getting up and continuing to put your best foot forward. The pain of losing my beloved is always and will be always in my heart but the antidote to my suffering is to look at all the positive things that have happened in my life.

I look at my life as a life exclusively designed for me by the Almighty. Despite the lingering heartache, I found perspective and independence. It dawned on me that the loss of Frankie gave me the opportunity to step up my community and charity work.

My Biggest Supporters

My children have inherited the generous and caring heart of their father who had big dreams for the Philippine American Community Center of Michigan (PACCM). They are the biggest supporters of my passion for working with the PACCM. Building upon Frankie's legacy, I held the position of President of the PACCM for six years. I entrusted responsibilities to good-hearted and dedicated fellow PACCM officers and board members. I led by delegating a lot of responsibilities, while I worked behind the scenes.

Through my work at the PACCM, I learned the importance of gaining support from those who have similar values and commitments. A good leader makes others feel truly valued. A good leader knows that an organization is destined to succeed if everyone works together, with each individual knowing that they are an integral part of the group's shared mission and vision.

My many community activities include the following: Commissioner of the Michigan Asian Pacific American Affairs Commission for six years; Board Director of the Asian Pacific American Chamber of Commerce; Board Director of the World Medical Relief; President of the Filamcco Foundation; and past Chairperson of PACCM. I have the same level of commitment for the mission and vision of all these organizations.

International Family

I am blessed with what I call my international family. My Princeton graduate-daughter Nathalie married a wonderful lawyer, Glenn. When they got married, the wedding planner was – who else? – yours truly. I feel so blessed that my daughter married into a humble and beautiful family. Glenn and Nathalie have given me the greatest gift of all, my grandson Dash. To see them interact with each other gives me pure joy.

Our second son, Anthony, married Irina, a girl from Estonia. She is a wonderful person, and I could not ask for a better daughter-in-law. My son is blessed and fortunate to have her as his life's partner. An only child, Irina has many talents and is very smart. She is now a CPA. Her parents are very lovely people.

Our youngest son, Ernest, is a graduate of medicine from Wayne University. He is married to a lovely Indian doctor, Ami, whose equally lovely family lives nearby.

With all these blessings, I cannot ask for more.

Medical and Charity Missions

Since my husband passed away, I have continued to inspire leadership by completing medical charity missions. I try my best to give back, and hope to inspire other Filipinos living in the U.S. to give back to our homeland.

In addition to my volunteer work in the U.S., I have conducted medical charity missions in the Philippines for 18 years. I try to harness both my medical and leadership skills to save children from imminent death. Though I am not particularly wealthy, God has given me the blessings and tools to help those in need.

Missionary work keeps me grounded because it always reminds me of where I came from. Poor children deserve a better life and a chance to succeed. To inspire them to improve their lot, I share my own story. I tell them where I came from and how I overcame obstacle after obstacle. If I inspire one child to improve his or her life and that of his or her family, I feel that I have done my job. The act of giving can be very rewarding.

Leadership by Giving Back

Last year, my nephew, Kagawad JJ de los Santos took me to the poorest *barangay* [village] in Mandaluyong, Metro Manila. It broke my heart to see kids living in unbelievably miserable conditions. Last Christmas, I sent toys and clothing to the kids living in this *barangay*. I made a promise to my nephew that I would conduct a solo pediatric-medical mission next year for these unfortunate children.

On another occasion, I donated badly-needed desks to a classroom orphanage in Bicol, one of the beneficiaries of my missionary work. This is an example of leadership by giving back. At the Iliyan school in Bicol where indigenous children study, I provided the school with a new white board and P.E. T-shirts. This is leadership by sharing and inspiration.

It takes leadership to overcome daunting tasks. And sometimes, doing good requires commitment as it entails more work and extra sacrifice. To enable me to provide medical care, medication, and other essential needs to the most vulnerable children in the Philippines, I have to work hard to earn the needed money and other resources to complete my mission.

Most Outstanding Physician

In recognition of my charitable activities, Beaumont Health System cited me last year as one of the Most Outstanding Physicians in Humanitarian Endeavors.

Perhaps my most coveted award is the Woman of Substance Award given on International Women's Day on March 8, 2001. In part the award states:

> To Ernestina de los Santos Mac, the professional, affable woman who remains the ever faithful, unassuming, benevolent citizen of Ligao with excellent academic record and successful family life to her name, distinctly passing an admirable, fundamental nature best demonstrated in her continuing community service here and abroad epitomizes the breed of women of today the world needs more of.

When people look up to you as a leader and believe in you so much so that they name you one of 100 Most Influential Filipina Women of the World, I was both gratified that my initiatives based on my commitments had been recognized and encouraged to become an even more effective leader.

Leadership Tips

1. ***Be credible to the public.*** Next-generation leaders would do well if they are credible not only to their followers but also to the public. It is impossible for leaders to lead effectively if they are not credible. Leaders are credible only if they do whatever they are advocating. In this way, they lead by example. You should not just 'talk the talk' but 'walk the walk.' Actions speak louder than words, so back up your promises with actual delivery. This way you will improve your track record and credibility, especially to outside audiences who may not know you as well as your teammates, colleagues and employers.

2. ***Be good listeners.*** They should have the patience to listen in earnest to the opinions or arguments of their followers. This would show that the leaders are open-minded and willing to accept change in their positions on issues. Empathy is a big part of leadership, and being a good listener helps. Good connection comes from your followers knowing that you understand them, that you have been an effective sounding board for them. This takes time and genuine understanding, and leaders need to show that they are not just thrusting their own viewpoint on others. Listening helps build consensus and alignment.

3. ***Inspire your teams.*** If the leaders are employers, they would also do well if they keep on saying or doing things that could inspire their employees. To be able to inspire their subordinates, the leaders should be good at explaining issues and concerns. Giving incentives would likewise go a long way in inspiring employees. These can be of various types, ranging from awards to rewards, from regular encouragement to rousing oratory. One part of leadership comes from building deep relationships, another important part comes from inspiring the broader organization and society with whom you may not have the time or opportunity to build close intimate relationships. Communication and inspiration are key here to help others rise to and beyond their true potential.

4. ***Give back to society.*** Quality leaders should develop in themselves the 'culture of giving back.' Leaders blessed with this virtue are looked up to not only by the beneficiaries of their generous heart but also by the entire public. This is so because it is a manifestation of one's pure intention—which is to help those in need of help. This culture of giving back is not a one-way street: Both the beneficiary and benefactor experience a profound sense of high spirit. This is particularly true with the benefactor whose heart is full of joy upon seeing the beneficiaries smile as they receive, say, relief goods or seeing poor children's eyes flicker with hope upon receiving, say, slippers or notebooks.

Nevada's First Filipina District Court Judge

The Honorable Cheryl Nora Moss

Abstract

*J*udge Cheryl Moss is the first Filipina-American lawyer elected as a District Court Judge in the State of Nevada's history. Judge Moss's journey begins with her graduation from law school in Washington, D.C. and relocating to Las Vegas, Nevada shortly thereafter. In a span of six years, she became licensed to practice law in Nevada, opened her solo law firm, and was elected to the judicial bench at a young age. Judge Moss won three contested elections successively, and she recounts her fourteen-year career as a family court judge.

Introduction

The year 2014 marks the Sesquicentennial Birthday of the State of Nevada. In 150 years since Nevada was admitted to the Union on October 31, 1864, no Filipina lawyer had ever run for political office to District Court until the year 2000. I, Cheryl Nora Moss, daughter of Dr. Demetrio Torres Nora and Dr. Rena Oquendo Magno Nora, decided to take the challenge to run in a contested primary election for a newly-created department in Clark County's Family Court established in 1993 as a specialized court handling domestic relations and juvenile cases.

After graduating in 1994 from The Catholic University of America Columbus School of Law in Washington D.C., I was excited and motivated to assist people who needed legal help and representation. After several years of working full-time at a successful law firm as a law clerk and at the same time attending law school in the evening,

I was fortunate to attain a prestigious judicial law clerk position with the Honorable John H. Bayly, Jr. at the Superior Court of the District of Columbia. I was barely five months into my year-long judicial clerkship when I received a call from my parents. They informed me they had decided to relocate from New Jersey to Nevada, and they would continue working as physicians with the Veterans Administration Medical Center in Las Vegas.

I Knew what that Call Meant

Growing up as a Filipino-American, I learned that family always came first. I wished to be close to my parents and to spend time with them as they approached their retirement age. I discussed with Judge Bayly my decision to follow my parents to Las Vegas. He was very supportive of my decision to move out west. I had already passed the bar exam and received my licenses to practice law in the State of Maryland and the District of Columbia.

I had to give up a budding and lucrative career in Washington, D.C. I had to start all over again in Nevada, take the bar exam in Las Vegas, and hoped to get a job in a city where I had no connections. In Washington D.C., I received several job offers over the telephone without even having to submit a letter of application and resume. Working for a judge virtually guaranteed me a job with any law firm of my choice.

I arrived in Las Vegas in January 1995 after driving for five days across the United States. I initially lived with my parents until I could secure a job with a law firm and save money to take the Nevada bar exam. I sent a hundred cover letters and my resumes to nearly every law firm in Las Vegas. Job offers were very scarce despite my graduating in the top 25% of my law school class and having worked for a distinguished judge in Washington, D.C. After several months passed, I still was without a job offer, but I did not give up. I took part-time jobs in the legal field until I was admitted to practice law in the State of Nevada in October 1997. From the time I took the oath to become a licensed Nevada attorney, I knew I wanted to open a solo law firm, The Law Office of Cheryl B. Moss, Chartered.

For approximately three years, I enjoyed building up my law

practice, litigating in the courtroom daily, and helping poor clients. During that time, there were very few Filipino-Americans living in Las Vegas and even fewer Filipino lawyers.

Running for Public Office

When I considered running for an elected office, I knew I was a double minority, a Filipina in a male-dominated profession and a solo-practicing attorney in Las Vegas with no prior campaign experience.

In Nevada, voters elect judges by popular vote unless the governor appoints one in special circumstances such as the demise or retirement of a sitting judge. I recall how I was truly an underdog with limited financial resources to run a contested campaign. But my circumstance woke a sleeping giant. When the Filipino-American community in Las Vegas learned that one of their own was seeking to run for a prominent political office, they rallied behind me. In the year 2000, there were approximately 30,000 Filipino-Americans residing in Clark County. A good number of them were eligible to register and vote.

On my own, I started attending local community events and meeting the leaders of various Asian-American organizations and political groups. My mother, Dr. Rena Nora, was of great help. She had the altruism and professional abilities to easily make friends and make contacts in the Filipino community. Her rise to prominent leadership in the community paved the way for me to gain public exposure and build a network of friends. She introduced to me to the organizations within a short span of time.

Networking and meeting people in social and civic settings were the best and least expensive form of advertising. Whenever I met a new person, I was able to establish a connection. So the next time I would meet that person, I knew that we would have something in common to talk about. It was important to find the right contacts to help spread the word about my campaign to become the first Filipina and first Asian-American elected to District Court in the history of the State of Nevada.

The mutual friendships with community leaders, especially Filipinos and other Asian-American leaders, remained for over a decade. They were vital to my successful re-election bids for two more terms. For each of my campaigns, I considered how many campaign signs were needed to cover a county with over one million residents, how much television and radio spots were affordable based on a small budget, and how many volunteers were willing to help.

Seeking endorsements from unions and other community organizations were also vital to getting votes. I had to build my self-confidence. I had to learn how to dress for the occasion, and hone my public speaking skills. My past successes in winning three consecutive elections made me unique. I still remain the only Filipina to ever be elected to public office in Nevada's history. Other Filipinos have run for office, but I am the only one to break through ethnic barriers to public office at the state level. I am proud to be the face and representative of all Filipinos in the Las Vegas metropolitan area. One thing I learned was that Filipinos are 'affectionately clannish' and their votes have always given me the extra push to succeed on Election Day and garner two-thirds of the votes.

Serving the People of Las Vegas and a Special Relationship with the Filipino Community

The Filipino-Americans in Las Vegas are proud to have me as their only Pinay judge in Nevada. Being Nevada's only Filipina judge, I am a living example to our future generations that running for a political office can unite a community, increase their pride and their morale, increase political participation, and be living proof that the 'American Dream' can be achieved.

Winning an election to political office as a District Court Judge came from sweat and tears as well. From manual labor such as putting up campaign signs in 112-degree heat in Las Vegas, to preparing for endorsement interviews and submitting candidate questionnaire responses, to attending hundreds of events in a span of six to ten months, meant involving myself with voters; greeting them, shaking their hands, and speaking with them about my campaign platform and experience.

After being re-elected, my duties as a public servant and representative of the Filipino community required me to give back to the people who voted me into office. Community service is at the core of my values as a Filipino-American. When the Filipino organizations and civic groups invite me to induct their officers or deliver a keynote speech, I made it a priority to attend despite my busy schedule since I am the only Filipina judge available to officiate and speak at Filipino gatherings.

I have spoken to the Filipino youth at leadership symposia to stress the importance of education, hard work, and respect for elders. During my childhood years, my mother would organize and host youth leadership conferences, and she always required me and my siblings to attend. I came to realize over the years what an impression the Filipino leaders had made on me and how appreciative I am for having had the opportunity to be exposed to such community events.

I firmly believe that the Filipino communities in the U.S. should regularly devote time and resources to Filipino youth organizations to promote our proud heritage and diverse culture. The Las Vegas Filipino organizations have raised money for educational scholarships for Filipino students. Although I was born and raised in the U.S., I have always been and will always remain proud to be Filipino.

Being a Filipino-American leader means being the Filipinos' representative in a high level political office. I have always endeavored to promote my Filipino heritage and to raise community awareness so that Filipinos will be unified and be a powerful voting group in Las Vegas. In recent years, political candidates for various offices in government have regularly attended Filipino gala dinners, picnics, and fundraisers in the hope of winning the Filipino voters' support on Election Day. Filipino organizations have grown in number and have increased visibly in the political arena. The fact that Filipinos went to the voting booths to support me sparked their growing interest to be more participative in Las Vegas politics. I am inspired by their dedication to helping one of their own through three victorious elections.

My 14-year career as a Filipino-American judge speaks of my dedication to be 'The Face of the Filipino Community' in Clark County, Nevada. Having such a long tenure on the judicial bench means long days and numerous hours devoted to work, campaigning, community service, and balancing work with family life. Being the only Filipina judge means receiving frequent invitations, attending Filipino events, and always saying "Yes" when invited.

I think of my career as two full-time jobs: being a judge and being a political candidate. When I am out of the courtroom, I devote many hours to reading court cases, preparing for the up-coming week, writing trial decisions, and handling administrative matters relative to my position. The rest of my out-of-court time is spent attending events and making myself available to the Filipino community.

Nevada judges run for re-election every six years. I ran in 2000 and again in 2002 to synchronize with the election cycle for District Court Judges as required by the Nevada Constitution. My third election was in 2008, and I am running for reelection during Nevada's Sesquicentennial Birthday in 2014.

For me, campaigning means being visible within the Filipino community and doing community service whether it is an election year or not. I describe this as 'political maintenance.' This means remaining in touch with all constituents and voters in Nevada and maintaining a special relationship with the Filipino community. My main motivation, however, is not so much about political maintenance, but rather unselfishly giving back to the community that voted for me.

Being a Judge for All

On my first day on the bench as a judge, I was like a 'deer in head-lights.' The idea of wearing a black robe for the very first time and see-ing a courtroom full of people stand up and rise out of respect for the court and the newly-elected judge was quite an extraordinary experi-ence. It was nerve-wracking, but my first day at work went smoothly, and soon I began to settle in.

As I look back on the 14 years I have served as a judge, I recall how I matured and learned the ropes. I spent a lot of time in the court-room, the back hallways, and in my judicial chambers. I would run into other judges who are my colleagues, some senior judges, and other court personnel. The discussions ranged from simple hellos as we passed each other by or discussions about court administrative matters. In the courtroom, I have heard cases involving custody matters, some extremely contentious, child support issues, alimony issues, and many other issues ranging from disputes over the sale of a marital residence to accusations of serious domestic violence and abuse, including sexual abuse.

As I gained more and more experience handling domestic relations cases, I sharpened my sensitivity to people's credibility and continuously focused on understanding why people end up in the courtroom, what should be done in the interim, what could be done to resolve the matter expeditiously, and to bring closure with the goal of hopefully not having the parties return to court.

There were times when I have had really trying days in court and I would arrive home late in the evening and take several hours to unwind. The stress of listening to contentious and acrimonious matters on a daily basis took its toll on my health at times. However, I have always enjoyed my job despite the trials and tribulations. I ran for political office to help families and children, not for the prestige of the office.

Truth be told, it is somewhat difficult to describe what it was like being a rookie judge compared to being a judge now with 14 years of experience under my belt. I can say though that there is a marked difference in my sensibility, and I am less quick to react. I have also learned that diplomacy and neutrality are extremely important. A good leader does not 'burn bridges.'

First impressions may never be accurate. One should not be too quick to dismiss a potentially valuable networking contact merely on first impressions alone. I was told once that it is always best to be 'Switzerland' as it is the most neutral country in the world. A good judge strives to be fair and impartial even outside the courtroom and in their personal lives. By being neutral and independent in my beliefs, I have found it easier to navigate through life.

Investing in Filipino and American Youth

I have always believed in investing in Filipino and American youth, our nation's future leaders. As part of my community service throughout my 14 years as a family court judge, I strived to regularly attend and support youth leadership events. The Filipino community should continue to endeavor to teach our Filipino youth the significance of growing up Filipino-American and our desires to always be achievers and leaders.

The community should also continue to instill in the Filipino youth the deep pride we have for our Filipino culture and heritage. With these basic principles and foundations, our Filipino youth will be able to pass on to their future generations the importance of family, education, and what it means to be a Filipino-American leader and role model.

LEADERSHIP TIPS

"Aspire rather to be a hero than merely appear one."

Balthasar Gracian

1. ***Take on risks and challenges.*** I am fortunate to have succeeded in taking the plunge into politics. I grew up as a Filipino-American in the U.S. in a culture and environment where I personally never thought or dreamed of running for political office. Indeed, as a teenager or as a young adult professional, it never crossed my mind until a colleague casually mentioned to me that the Nevada Legislature passed a bill to expand the Clark County Family Court by adding three new departments. Three new judges were to be elected to preside over the departments.

2. ***Think strategy.*** There were five people in my 2000 Election race. I was the only female in the race. I faced four male attorneys in the primary election. If I could count on the female voters, Filipino voters, other Asian voters, and people who knew me and my mother, Dr. Rena Nora, I believed I would have an advantage despite having a tiny campaign budget. One of the male candidates had already announced he had a large budget for his campaign. That fact did not deter me.

3. ***Understand media, technology, and social media.*** In my 2000 election, I did not have Facebook, Twitter or other social media. My campaign communicated with the voters and contributors by fax and emails. I allocated my small budget for production of a campaign TV commercial and purchasing TV spots on local cable stations. Even if my TV commercial aired at 3:00 A.M., I knew that Las Vegas is a 24-hour city that never sleeps. Casino workers who worked swing and graveyard shifts saw my TV commercial.

4. ***Keep promises and maintain a good reputation.*** Upon being elected and re-elected for two subsequent terms, I have maintained professionalism on the bench and stayed connected with the community by volunteering to do inductions of officers, judging high school mock trial competitions, and doing speaking engagements to educate the public about family court and the law.

5. ***As a leader, stay humble.*** A leader wants to help guide people in the right direction, protect the interests of families and children, educate the public, and provide access to justice. A leader does not seek power for personal gain or arrogance.

WRITING FOR SAINTHOOD

Janet Susan R. Nepales

Hollywood Journalist
Member, Hollywood Foreign Press Association

Abstract

I remember as a child I always dreamt of *sainthood*. It is a crazy thought but it was my goal when I was a child. I wanted to be like St. Therese of the Child Jesus whose childlike attitude made her closer to God, closer to *perfection*. But then, reality hit me and I know I am but human with many imperfections. So knowing I cannot be a saint, I decided to become the next best thing for me—to be a *journalist*. I love to write. I have been *writing* since I was in first grade. It was in high school, though, when my *journalism* teacher, Mrs. Lourdes N. Tacorda, picked me during my junior year to be the editor-in-chief of our school paper, *The Capitol*. Her confidence in me inspired me. I loved being a journalist! I decided to take up Journalism in college despite my father's protests. "You will never get rich in Journalism," he told me. He may be right but I became rich not materially but in life experiences—meeting all these interesting people I would have never met or being in places in this world I would only read about. Journalism has opened many doors for me and being the first and only Filipina journalist in the 70 plus-history of the *Hollywood Foreign Press Association* that does the *Golden Globes* annually is beyond my dreams. But it is not really the glamour and the glitz that make me proud of being a member of the HFPA but the *philanthropic* activities it does—helping brilliant but needy students who want to take up journalism or filmmaking, helping preserve our history by donating to organizations and schools that preserve our old movies or TV shows, or assisting countries like our very own *Philippines* during Typhoon Sendong or Typhoon Haiyan when the organization donated $25,000 and $100,000, respectively. I hope, by sharing my own short story, one young girl will pursue her own perfect dreams in an imperfect world because that to me is the beginning of sainthood.

Introduction

I have always believed that you are what you make of yourself.

I have never thought of myself as outstanding but I work hard to be one. I have never thought of myself as excellent but I always aim to be one.

Perfection is not really my goal but being close to perfect is. Yes, you may say I may be hard on myself but I am also my worst critic.

I remember as a child that I always dreamt of sainthood. It is a crazy thought but it was my goal when I was a child. I wanted to be like St. Therese of the Child Jesus whose childlike attitude made her closer to God, closer to perfection.

I always thought, if these 'ordinary' people can do it, I can do it too.

My paternal grandfather, Narciso Rodriguez, who was half-Spanish, half-Filipino, may not have been the most religious man on earth but he was the one who kept buying me prayer books, novenas, books with prayers for everyday needs, stories of saints, and other religious stories.

So while other kids were reading comic books, I was reading novenas and books about saints.

I did not know why my *Lolo* [grandfather] bought me those books but I read everything that he gave me. I devoured them as if my life depended on them; that my goal of sainthood would be fulfilled if I found out what the saints' 'secrets' were.

I was curious. I wanted to discover the shortcut to sainthood. I am sure there must be an easy way, I naively thought.

I spent days reading all of the books from cover to cover, fascinated by the fact that the saints were able to turn their 'ordinary' lives into meaningful, significant, blessed lives.

When I was in high school, reality hit me. I realized that I was but human with many imperfections. And that sainthood was such a tall order for me to aim for. I realized I was not perfect.

So knowing that I could not be a saint, I decided to become the next best thing for me — I became a journalist.

My Inspirations

My paternal grandmother, Cecilia Castillo Rodriguez, who was then the District Superintendent of Schools of Quezon City, taught me how to read every time I spent weekends at her house.

My *Lola* [grandmother] Celing, as I called her, was more patient and less strict than my parents when it came to mentoring. I think that was because my father and mother seemed to be always stressed out making both ends meet while raising six kids on their limited income. He was a business consultant; she was a grade school teacher.

My *Lola* also taught me to love socializing. Even though I was just a kid, she brought me to most of her events. She also showed me off to her teachers. Some grandmothers show off their grandchildren's singing or dancing prowess; my grandmother showed off my writing skills.

I was only six or seven years old when she would give me a topic out of the blue and tell me to write a poem or a short story about it. I would diligently and easily whip out one in English to the amazement of the teachers that she was supervising.

It was not a boring task for me. It was like a game.

Unknowingly on my part, it was the beginning of my love for writing.

It was in Quezon City High School in Kamuning when my Journalism teacher, Mrs. Lourdes N. Tacorda, picked me during my junior year to be the editor-in-chief of our school paper, *The Capitol*. Her confidence in me inspired me.

She challenged me. She nurtured me. She mentored me.

And I loved it!

I loved being a journalist-in-training. I enjoyed being an Editor-in-Chief. I loved interviewing people, writing their stories, finding out how they became who they were, the challenges they went through, how they overcame them, and sharing their stories.

It was just like getting to know my saints. It was fun. It was inspiring.

I decided to take up Journalism in college at the University of Santo Tomas despite my father's protests. "You will never get rich in Journalism," he told me as if that was the most important thing in life. If you are good, money will follow, I told him.

It was a lame answer, I thought, but it was something to keep him quiet for a while. Money was not my goal, anyway. I just wanted to pursue my passion. I wanted to write.

This Girl is on Fire

In college, I blossomed as a writer and as an editor.

In my freshman year, I made it to *The Varsitarian*, the official school paper of the University of Santo Tomas (UST). I started as a reporter. I became the Managing Editor in my senior year.

As a freshman, I also made it to *The Flame*, the official magazine of the Faculty of Arts and Letters. From a reporter, I became the Editor-in-Chief in my junior year.

I became the President of the Journalism Club at UST. I invited well-known journalists, writers, and people in the entertainment field to preside in forums and speaking engagements. I invited the late *Philippine Daily Inquirer* publisher Isagani Yambot who was then an editor at *The Times Journal*. I invited the late director-writer-activist Behn Cervantes to speak. He was also living in Kamuning. We learned a lot from them. They inspired a lot of students. Later in life, these two great men also became my close friends.

We had interesting forums. They inspired me to do more.

I joined press workshops and events as a representative of the school paper and college magazine. Aside from our annual Batangas writing retreats with *The Varsitarian* staff, I attended professional media workshops and forums where they allow student journalists to participate. My college mentors, the late Felix Bautista (who was then also the Publications Director of *The Varsitarian*) and Ramon 'Kiko' Francisco (who was also the Faculty Advisor of our Journalism class), encouraged me to do more, to spread my wings and to get out of the confines of the school premises.

I did and it ignited the fire in me some more.

I networked with the professional journalists.

Soon, I found myself contributing articles to magazines, including *Mr. & Ms.*, *Mod*, *Woman's Home Companion*, *Women's* and *Panorama*, even while I was still in college.

I got published so often that my classmates thought I was already a professional who was simply taking night classes.

Before I knew it, the late Fred Marquez, who jumped from editing *Mod* magazine to *Times Journal's Parade* magazine, took me under his wing as his editorial assistant and feature writer.

Parade magazine, which came out every Sunday with the *Times Journal*, was the entertainment, sports and feature magazine of the paper.

Soon, I was interviewing Hollywood celebrities who were visiting the country or had shows in the Philippines. Fred also assigned me to interview local actors, actresses, writers and directors.

It was the start of my foray in the entertainment field. Soon, I was the magazine's go-to journalist every time there was a foreign act in town. I did a lot of cover stories for the magazine.

While at *Parade* magazine, I was the youngest journalist to be invited to join the inaugural flight of British Airways from Manila to London. It was my first trip out of the country. I was 21 then.

I found myself traveling for a week in London with veteran journalists and editors like Luisa Linsangan, Domini Torrevillas-Suarez, Ernie Evora-Sioco, Joe Quirino and Corazon Fiel, among others. Traveling outside the Philippines for the first time opened my eyes. There is a big wide world out there waiting to be discovered. My love for travel began.

The *Times Journal* soon came out with an edition for Saudi Arabia that reprinted my Parade articles. *The Architectural Digest Philippines* magazine of the *Times Journal* asked me to write about celebrity homes as well.

Chinatown East magazine that was headed by Veronica Velosoyap, soon got me involved too. I wrote about the country's Filipino-Chinese business leaders, from Lucio Tan to Henry Sy, as well as top fashion models like Alta Tan.

After *Chinatown East*, I moved to the *Times Journal's Lifestyle* section where I did features on fashion, art, and other fields. The experience made me appreciate the fashion world and designers.

From there, I moved to *People's Journal* where I wrote front page stories, including one on Lynda Carter, the former 'Wonder Woman,' who visited the Philippines. I helped her find a little girl from the province that she was helping send to school. They had an emotional first-time meeting at Manila Hotel where Lynda was staying. I was happy I helped arrange the very moving meeting.

It was New Year's Eve. I found myself at my newspaper desk, writing about that story, typing away on my sturdy old typewriter (no computers back then!), trying to meet the deadline.

My editor, Tony 'Father' Friginal, hovered over me. "You have five more minutes!" he reminded me. I did not feel sorry for myself that I was working on a big holiday eve. I was excited. Deadlines give me an adrenaline rush. I was on fire.

I met my deadline.

The following day, New Year's Day, was the best day. I started the year with a front page story and a scoop.

I felt so fulfilled seeing my story in print and on the front page. I felt happier too knowing that I was instrumental in helping somebody. It was a good day.

Challenges: Taking it a Day at a Time

If the road to sainthood is thorny, the road to journalism is scary.

If I had not been passionate about and dedicated to my craft, I would have given up. But to me, success is reached by making those baby steps, one day at a time; and standing up every time you fall.

There was the challenge of proving myself.

As early as in college, I had to prove myself. In my senior year, my Public Relations professor, Bettina Olmedo, told our entire Journalism class, "Nobody in this room will end up as a journalist. I will throw my hat to whoever in this room becomes one."

Instead of inspiring us, she put us all down. However, while my classmates felt downhearted and disappointed, I took it as a challenge.

In that class of 25, four of us ended up as professional journalists working for the top newspapers of the country. Somebody had to throw her hat at us.

There was the challenge of staying true to your craft.

Being truthful and helping others to tell the truth is hard. As a journalist, it is my duty to write the truth. The challenge comes when I have to squeeze out the truth from my subject. You have to make your subject comfortable so he will relax and open up to you.

Teaching others to be truthful and honest was a challenge.

When I moved to the U.S., I saw my articles being copied in various Filipino-American newspapers. I was not given proper credit for my work or my quotes. It was frustrating to call editors or reporters of newspapers and tell them that if they were to use my work, they better give me proper credit. We have to stop 'cut and paste journalism' and give credit where credit is due. We have to stop plagiarism.

Journalism involves a lot of hard work and patience. If you do not want to work hard, you do not have any patience and you just want to 'copy and paste,' do not be a journalist.

The work of a journalist is her intellectual property and stealing it without giving proper credit is unlawful and unethical.

Being an honest journalist is indeed like trying to be a saint.

There is the challenge of temptation.

As my father warned me, "There are a lot of dirty old men (also known as DOMs) in journalism." Indeed, in the journalism field, or at least during my time, many senior male editors will try to make a pass at single young female reporters. But as I told my dad, "There are a lot of DOMs in any field. Everything really depends on how you handle yourself."

A good childhood foundation helps one make the right choices in any field in life.

Getting Close to Sainthood

But true enough, as my dad said, "You will never be rich as a journalist."

Indeed, I did not become rich materially. However, I was rich in life experiences. I traveled around the world to attend film festivals, press junkets, set visits, and do exclusive interviews. I met many interesting people, from Oprah Winfrey to Barbra Streisand, from Michelle

Obama to White House Executive Chef, Fil-Am Cris Pasia Comerford. These are my heroes, my idols.

Journalism has opened many doors for me. Being the first and only Filipina member in the 70 plus-history of the Hollywood Foreign Press Association (HFPA) that presents the Golden Globes annually was beyond my dreams.

It is not really the glamour and the glitz that make me proud of being a member of the HFPA but the philanthropic activities that we do including helping brilliant but needy students who want to take up journalism or filmmaking, helping preserve history by donating to organizations and schools that preserve classic movies or TV shows, or assisting countries like our very own Philippines after it was severely affected by Typhoon Sendong or Typhoon Haiyan. HFPA donated $25,000 and $100,000 respectively to UNICEF Philippines to aid the victims and to help in the relief operations in those calamities.

I am also proud to write about Filipinos who do well in Hollywood including to name a few: Oscar-nominated cinematographer Matthew Libatique and actress Hailee Steinfeld, international singer-actress Lea Salonga, talented singer-actress Vanessa Hudgens, "Glee's" triple-threat Darren Criss, award-winning singer Bruno Mars, "Grimm's" and "Pirates of the Caribbean's" Reggie Lee, outstanding fashion designers Monique Lhuillier, Michael Cinco, Furne One, Alan Del Rosario, Oliver Tolentino, David Tupaz, Francis Libiran and Carlyn Nuyda Calloway.

Giving back and helping others fulfill their dreams is also important to me. Since 2007, I have been giving scholarships to deserving and outstanding high school journalists at my alma mater, Quezon City High School.

The students, who display excellence in writing as staff writers of the school's papers, *The Capitol* (English) and *Ang Parola* (Tagalog), are recommended by their journalism advisor and teachers to receive the Janet Susan Rodriguez Nepales Journalism Scholarship.

Hopefully, with these scholarships, these young writers will be inspired to continue to pursue journalism in college and then, ultimately, as a career.

I pray that by sharing my own short story, there will be at least one young girl, maybe someone going to a public school in Kamuning, Quezon City, who will be inspired to dream big and proclaim, "I want to be a journalist!"

She may want to change the world. She may want to influence people. She may want to inspire, to educate, to tell the truth at all cost, to help others tell the truth, to be true to herself and to the world.

Because if she does, if she pursues her dream in this imperfect world, that is already close to attaining sainthood.

Leadership Tips

1. ***Dream big and achieve.*** Start in your neighborhood. Dreams are free. So instead of dreaming small, dream big. You have nothing to lose. Aim high. So even if you fall, you will still be among the stars. Start in your own neighborhood. Organize a Journalism Club. Begin a community newsletter. Be active. Be the voice of the community. Find out what's happening in your neighborhood and see how you can help and serve. Make your voice be heard. Propose ways to improve the community. Find where change needs to be done. Do not just be a critic. Be an activist.

2. ***You are what you make of yourself.*** The world is one big educational playground. Learn. Do not be afraid to make mistakes. Learn from those mistakes. Be a sponge. Make every experience an educational one. Everybody is given tools (your talents) by God. Do not waste those tools by doing nothing or worse, ignoring them.

3. ***Honesty and integrity are important; do not plagiarize: Give credit where credit is due.*** You have only one name. Take care of it. A bluff can only carry you so far. In due time, the truth will come out. Do not be a copycat. Be original. Be yourself. Always aim for the truth. Learn to acknowledge the people who helped you. Be grateful. Be thankful. As they say, be good to people on your way up because you might meet them again on your way down.

4. ***Give back to the next generation.*** For example, donate to a student scholarship. Share your talents, your God-given resources with the next generation. Do whatever you can to help our future leaders. Give back in any way you can. Teach. Reach out. Be accessible, helpful and accommodating. Do not be stingy when sharing knowledge and wisdom.

5. ***Be proud to be a Filipina.*** You are a Filipina. Stand tall. You come from a stock of women who are versatile, strong and fierce.

Beating the Odds *

Colonel Shirley S. Raguindin

Chief of Diversity, National Guard Bureau
Chief Diversity Officer, Air National Guard

Abstract

*I*n this chapter I identify how cultural barriers can either help or hurt in the development of leadership competencies of minority women, specifically focused on the experience of a Filipina woman in the military who was able to beat the odds, even at birth. As the demographic workforce is rapidly changing, Filipinas provide a unique leadership competency to the workforce. To enhance the image of Filipina women globally, I share my experiences and hope to inspire emerging leaders to use our culture as a strength rather than a weakness to overcome what may seem as insurmountable barriers. What is most profound for today's youth and emerging leaders of diverse backgrounds is to understand that the only barriers to goals in life are not the ones created by others; but the ones we create in ourselves.

Can your destiny ever be pre-determined?

Today as Chief Diversity Officer I am responsible for the strategic direction, implementation, and alignment of the National Guard's integrated global diversity and inclusion initiatives. These initiatives are considered critical for achieving the highest state of military readiness for over 458,000 soldiers, airmen, and civilians. Prior to my current assignment, I served as Senior Military Liaison, Department of Defense Transformation Agency Enterprise Planning and

---

* The views presented are those of the author and do not necessarily represent the views of DoD or its components.

Investment, Office of the Secretary of Defense. Throughout my career, I have served in numerous readiness programs, leading change through policy, strategic planning, and attention to quality of life issues that impact mission readiness.

What does a typical day look like for me? Our morning starts at 5:00 a.m. After I am dressed in my military uniform, I prepare my son's breakfast and drop him off at elementary school. Every morning I start with a prayer to count my blessings being married to my best friend and re-dedicate my life to being a servant leader. The workday starts with a checklist of priorities and meetings. I start with the director's meeting where I cover the top three functional areas issues. I monitor the organization's strategic plan for global diversity and ensure there is follow up and that new programs are on track. Before lunch, I make time to mentor a member of the organization or to recruit a new member into the organization. During the afternoon, I meet with the Director of the Air National Guard, a three-star general. We review the nationwide implementation of diversity initiatives and may check with the 30 committee members with responsibility for diversity. We assess the organizational culture by comparing it with our diversity strategies and identify new initiatives to ensure that every member is able to reach their maximum potential. After school, my husband takes our son to Taekwondo which allows me the time to work out at the gym and run a few miles. After dinner, our son completes his homework, and goes to sleep. This allows me time to spend a few hours working on the completion of my Advanced Joint Professional Military Education studies at U.S. Joint Forces College, located in Norfolk, VA.

Among the many challenges I face are insufficient manpower and resources to get the job done. It is the responsibility of my leadership team to find new approaches based on collaboration that will allow us to tap into the talents of others, develop and harness their talent, and leverage technology. One of the many joys of this job is seeing how positive cultural transformation based on effective and dedicated leadership impacts mission readiness, one leader at a time.

My destiny was determined prior to my birth, even before I could begin to think about what I wanted to do with my life. My story begins when my mother, Maria, a "picture bride" [a term used for matchmaking of brides from the Philippines and laborers in Hawaii where the matchmaker paired bride and groom using photographs and family recommendations] from San Nicolas, Ilocos Norte, Philippines, married my father, Isabelo, a truck driver in Waipahu, Hawaii on the picturesque island of Oahu. My family started their humble life on the Oahu Sugar Cane plantation, amidst the endless fields of towering waving tassels where sugar cane fields dominated the western region of the islands. I am the oldest daughter and number three of the six siblings, with three boys and three girls. My Hawaii roots provided the experience of growing up in a place where many ethnicities worked together. As the family grew, we moved from the plantation fields into the suburbs. I will never forget the excitement when my oldest brother graduated from high school and received a car from my parents as a graduation gift. I assumed, I would follow in my brother's footsteps. I graduated with honors; was awarded several scholarships, and received a letter endorsed by Hawaii Senator Daniel K. Inouye to attend the U.S. Air Force Academy. I believed a car had already been picked out for me. However when graduation day arrived, my parents delivered the news that a 24 year old engineer, was scheduled to arrive from the Philippines and would be my new husband. My parents explained the agreement for the arranged marriage was made with their friends on the day I was born. At this point, I realized the car I had anticipated for years was never going to materialize. I was even more concerned that I would not have the opportunity to drive my own future. It seemed that I was trapped in my own environment and that my future was in the hands of my parents' traditional Filipino culture. In most Asian cultures women are generally expected to take a subservient role rather than work for a living. My parents believed this pre-arranged marriage would complete my life and allow me to move forward. As they proudly continued to describe my to-be husband and the date he was scheduled to arrive for the wedding, I realized my vision of attending the military academy was quickly disappearing. Panic-stricken, I firmly said to my parents, without hesitation, that I wanted to attend the Air Force Academy and then serve in the military. I asked if the arranged marriage could be postponed until after I graduated. To even sweeten the deal, I mentioned tuition would be covered by a full four year scholarship. However, my father objected and said that the Air Force Academy was for men as he pointed to a pamphlet that showed a large welcome sign, 'Bring Me Your Men' on the campus. In no time, I was kicked out of the home since I had not only disappointed my family; I had also disappointed their lifetime friends. This was a difficult time in my life. Without the permission of my parents I could not attend the Air Force Academy, but I could still attend the University of Hawaii Air Force Reserve Officer Training Corps (AFROTC) program. I was selected for a four year AFROTC scholarship and accepted for a Junior Fellowship Program to work as a meteorological aid at National Oceanic and Atmospheric Administration (NOAA) at the Honolulu International Airport. The years of diligent studying and achieving above average grades allowed me to be ready for opportunities. I learned it is better to be prepared for an opportunity, than not be prepared for an opportunity at all.

Many of my family members, friends, co-workers, and professors at the university tried to discourage me from attending the university and my goal then of serving in the military with comments like, "You'll fail calculus," "There will never be any jobs available after you graduate," "You're only going to college for an MRS degree" (intended as a joke to just go to school to get married). I conditioned my mind so that all of these disparaging remarks from my friends and associates were compartmentalized as 'background noise' and kept my focus on education. Frankly, I did not have the luxury to worry about what other people thought. During this time, I remained close to my faith and prayed for patience. So I kept my focus on my studies. My mother encouraged me and reminded me to "Do unto others as others do unto you." A quote from Mother Teresa helped me get through this time:

> People are often unreasonable and self-centered, forgive them anyway. If you are kind, people may accuse you of selfish, ulterior motives, be kind anyway. If you are successful, you will win some false friends and true enemies, succeed anyway. If you are honest and frank, people may cheat you, be honest and frank anyway. If you find serenity and happiness, they may be jealous, be happy anyway. The good you do today, people will often forget tomorrow, do good anyway. Give the world the best you have and it may

never be enough, give your best anyway. For you see, in the end, it is between you and God, It was never between you and them anyway.

After four years of attending the university, I was recognized as a distinguished graduate, the first female minority Corps Commander, and honored by Hawaii Governor George Ariyoshi. This was a day I could not forget. My parent's greatest gift to me was their presence at my graduation and commissioning ceremony. They never again brought up the topic of marriage.

As a lieutenant in the Air Force, my first assignment was to Yokota Air Base in Japan with the 475th Air Base Wing. During my first assignment, I worked on my Master's degree and played on the Pacific Air Force Tennis Team. As a member of the Air Force Tennis team, I competed in the Asian-Pacific region and earned the recognition of number one in doubles and number two in singles competition. This was also the year my father passed away and I returned to Hawaii to deliver the eulogy on behalf of my family. I recognized that my father's influence molded me into who I am today, despite his reluctance about my joining the military. As my belief in God and spirituality grew, I reflected on my father's overprotectiveness and realized it prepared me to survive an uncertain future. My father taught me a very special thing: as I looked forward to the future, I should never forget where I came from.

Although my father was no longer with us, my mother mentored me with the right advice at the right time. I learned how our lives had been similar when her father insisted she work with the family pottery business even though her goal was to become a nurse. Despite her feelings of regret, my mother showed me that it was out of love that she gave up a career to allow her children to be successful. Through the years, I remembered her sacrifice as I was promoted through the ranks and developed the ability to succeed in a variety of environments. It was common for me to be the only Asian female officer in the organization and every once in a while, I would think to myself, maybe my father was right, and I should have married the young man from the Philippines. But the thought lingered for only a few seconds. Because of the rigors of travel and military training, and moving three times in seven years from Japan to Arizona and to Washington, there was no time to plan for a family or marriage. I called my family, especially my mother, weekly to keep up with the family events including the birthdays, graduations, and anniversaries I could not attend. During these calls, my mother would share her wisdom and ask me about my financial planning and the purchase of my first home. She would remind me to think about starting a family and having children while also reminding me to continually strive to do well at work.

While the military was in the midst of ending Desert Storm, I received an offer to join corporate America to work for Procter and Gamble as a project engineer and manager in a pharmaceutical plant. I would also be able to maintain my military career part-time with the Air National Guard. Again I kept my focus on goal alignment. Through my mother's coaching, I learned how to become immune to derogatory female comments. It was about this time that I knew something was missing. I learned more about myself by serving others in the community. I began serving as a mentor at high risk schools with a message to do well in school in order to be able to take advantages of possible opportunities in corporate industry, the military, or the federal government. When I visited my family in Hawaii I also made it a point to visit my alma mater, Waipahu High School, to mentor students about the need to prepare themselves for college or other opportunities. In order to find myself, I needed to lose myself in the service of others. This created a domino effect in influencing others to do the same for others.

As described by Sheryl Sandberg, Chief Operating Officer of Facebook and author of *Lean In*, my career path is best described as a "jungle gym, moving in and out of the non-traditional path" that have allowed me to strategically sharpen the skills needed. After working as a Pharmaceutical Engineer and Team Manager for 40 technicians at Procter and Gamble, I rejoined the military, this time the Air National Guard where I work full time in Human Capital Resources at the State-level Headquarters level. I then gained command level experience as a Military Personnel Director during the Global War on Terror. This opened doors for me to serve later on as the Director of Property and Fiscal Office of a Joint Task Force; and finally I was selected to serve as senior advisor to the Adjutant General at State-level Headquarters for ten years. Although there were many opportunities for promotion if I compromised my position and self-worth, I opted not to compromise and chose the professional path. No promotion is worth losing my character, self-respect, and core values. Making a difference, personal fulfillment, and serving a cause greater than me was the path I chose as a servant leader.

The tipping point for my development as a leader was enrolling in several leadership courses and learning about leadership and management and enrolling in a diversity leadership course. Sir Winston Churchill once said, "To every man there comes in his lifetime that special moment when he is figuratively tapped on the shoulder and offered a choice to do a very special thing; unique to him and fitted to his talents; what a tragedy if that moment finds him unprepared or unqualified for the work that would be his finest hour." Looking back, there is a reason for all that happens in our lives. It is not just what we learn along the way that makes us who we are, but equally important are the choices we make. Failure can be a blessing in disguise and I have learned enough from my failures in a short span of time to not repeat them again. Despite the barriers I faced, one could argue I was able to beat the odds. This book contains similar stories of success that exemplify the courage and heart of Filipina women to, in the words of Sir Winston Churchill, "Never, ever, ever give up."

Becoming the leader I am today has been helped by having many mentors and organizations like Filipina Women's Network (FWN). They have provided access to successful Filipina women who could share their experiences with breaking through cultural barriers. One of the most difficult decisions in my career and as a mother and wife to a husband, who retired from the military, was to choose between a promotion if I stayed in my job at that time, or move to a new city, apply for a new job and start from scratch to build a new network. Because family is one of my top priorities, I moved and learned after a year, I was back on track. Dealing with the uncertainty and stress that comes from moving, finding affordable child care, and dealing with a new job was tumultuous. What kept me on course was my faith and belief in a higher power and never forgetting how my parents were able to take risks, make the right choices. and their many sacrifices necessary to keep us together as a family. Having a global network of successful Filipinas in almost every state was also very helpful as well as knowing Filipina professionals who are doctors, lawyers, artists, CEOs, mayors, judges, scientists, government officials, university professors and high military ranking officials in all military services. It was comforting to know that I was not alone. As a result, I make time to mentor youth whenever I can and wherever I go. Dr. Stephen Covey, author of *The Seven Habits of Highly Effective People*, said it best: "Leadership is communicating to people their value and potential so clearly they begin to see it in themselves."

Can your destiny be pre-determined? The answer lies within you; and not with anyone else.

LEADERSHIP TIPS

1. *Be prepared for any new opportunities.* Make a choice to find your purpose, to fulfill your destiny and establish goals larger than yourself. Be prepared to benefit the greater good. When you do this, you will be ready for any challenge.

2. *To find yourself, lose yourself in the service of others.* Mother Teresa once said, "When you have nothing, you have everything". You don't need a big title, nor do you need to be rich to serve others; all you need is a big heart. You can start by being kind to one person every day.

3. *Look toward the future but never forget where you came from.* Based on their love for me, my parents, like many parents only wanted what was best for their children. Recognize the challenges in our Filipino culture and traditions, and turn these challenges into strengths while giving back to society and mentoring the next generation of leaders.

4. *No promotion is worth the loss of your character, self-respect, and core values.* My mother always emphasized education as key to success. Don't take short cuts. Always be prepared and ready for the next big opportunity.

5. *There is a reason for everything, trust and walk in faith.* Do what you can in the time that you have in the place where you are. Unfortunately my family lost our beloved mother, Maria, this year. She is remembered as a role model who taught us it is important to live simply, so that others may simply live. A life not lived for others, is not a life.

I will end with two of my favorite inspiring quotes:

"Leadership is communicating to people their worth and potential so clearly they begin to see it in themselves." — Dr. Stephen Covey

"Never ever, ever, give up." — Sir Winston Churchill

BLACKAPINA

Janet Stickmon

Professor of Humanities, Napa Valley College

Abstract

lackapina is an essay that reveals my experience of being a biracial woman of African-American and Filipino-American descent. It is divided into three "movements": (a) The Intersection, (b) Multiple Contexts, and (c) The Blend. Through these "movements," I explore my progression from identifying as "half African-American" and "half Filipino-American" to embracing hybridity as a Blackapina. From the death of my parents to the birth of my child, I describe pivotal moments in my life that have shaped my understanding of myself as a multidimensional human being, specifically drawing upon the concept of psychosynthesis and its application to multiracial people. This essay becomes an opportunity to explore and recognize the fruits of existing in that in-between space of Filipino-American identity and African-American identity.

First Movement: The Intersection
(adapted from Stickmon 2014)

People of multiethnic backgrounds are accustomed to existing at the intersections of multiple worlds and multiple identities, holding and juggling those spaces in tension. We become adept at navigating in and out and through numerous ethnoracial and ethnocultural contexts. The more one enters and exits these contexts, and the more one critically examines racial hierarchy and essentialism and their impact on the dynamics between racial groups, the more pronounced one's experience of multiraciality and multiethnicity becomes. An understanding of critical race theory coupled with the experience of existing within the interstices of life, surviving and thriving in a world dominated by binary thought and then being inspired to rise above the surface "unfragmented are vital for multiethnic people who seek to live out the fullness of their humanity." It requires a creativity that is prompted by the mere existence of the intersection in the road, as well as the time taken to reflect upon the ramifications of that intersection.

As a Blackapina, a woman of African-American and FilipinoAmerican descent, I regularly reflect upon how truly I am embracing both sides of my heritage and how well I am serving the populations on both sides of my bloodline. Existing in this in-between space of ethnicities and critically examining this intersectionality informs and strengthens my ability to recognize the complexities and nuances that characterize life's mosaic. We, as multiethnic people, have the potential to navigate this world of complexity and nuance. We have the potential to create unconventional solutions for the intersections of life and inspire deep, reflective transformation. Living in the intersection forces us to deal with the multiple paths that come together; if those paths never meet, if the crossroads don't exist, there is almost no reason, no opportunity for creative outcomes to arise.

So what does it mean to be at the crossroads? It means to stand at any intersection, any meeting of multiple paths, and ask the question: So what do I do now? It is to welcome transition.

Binary thinking would suggest selecting one of two paths. Perhaps a more nuanced way of thinking that informs the experience of many multiethnic people would suggest entertaining or exploring the possibility of taking multiple paths simultaneously. It means daring ourselves to believe that it is possible to walk multiple paths at the same time, embracing the transition, defying the conventional, the orthodox, the hegemonic and actively walking all of those paths; becoming a living, breathing mosaic. And as one bravely walks the multiple paths, one can clear the way, knocking down all obstacles that obstruct the flow of understanding, of compassion, of cooperation. This strengthens the ability of humanity to co-create a world predicated on our capacity to remain in dialogue and allow our ideas to build upon each other as opposed to being combative in nature. Consequently, any collaboration amongst human beings should reflect this spirit of interdependence, manifesting in a force that brings healing wherever there is brokenness

Second Movement: Multiple Contexts

Having a Filipino-American mother and an African-American father, I juggled both of my ethnic backgrounds throughout my childhood and adolescence. Momma was from the *barangay* [village] of Labangon in Cebu and left a clerical job to come to the U.S., the country she considered the 'land of milk and honey.' Da'y (short for Daddy) was from Shreveport, Louisiana and hopped freight trains to California. He was one of approximately six million African-Americans who fled the oppression of the South during what came to be known as the Great Migration (Wilkerson 2010, 9). My biracial experience began with the very basic influences of food and language, eating Momma's *biko* [a rice cake] and *bijon* [rice noodle] and Da'y's hoe cakes and hot cakes, hearing Da'y sound 'country' and Momma speak Cebuano.

It was 1989 when Momma died and Da'y was put in a convalescent hospital; I was 15 years old. Three years later, Da'y died, and I officially became an orphan, continuing to juggle my dual heritage along with the meaning of life in the absence of parental love. I was tossed around from one social worker to the next, telling my story over and over again, becoming attached to no one. Though the most immediate lifelines to my history were gone, my sense of self was informed by the memories my parents left behind, the Filipino relatives I moved in with, the holidays spent with my African-American relatives, and close high school and college friends. In the public sphere, school, church, work, commerce, etc., I learned what was acceptable and unacceptable according to Eurocentric standards. Though my family was from a poor, working class background, I quickly learned how to operate effectively within a social environment that was predominantly white, middle-class, and Christian-centered. While I received messages about how certain ways of speaking and behaving commanded respect from those who lay at the intersection of these social categories, I had to also remain socially fluent within predominantly Filipino and African-American environments, as well.

Death. New family. New school. More death. These were my adolescent years. And out of all of this, I was trying to figure out who I was and what purpose I had. I was a fairly quiet and private person to begin with, but losing Momma and Da'y drove me into a deeper silence where lethargy coiled around my spirit, making hope seem hilarious. I always planned for the worst so I could be prepared for disappointment. I cried and cried until I had no tears left; it wasn't as though the pain stopped; a raw ache always lingered, but tears only brought me partial relief, and I was sick of crying. I developed a callousness toward life, promising myself I'd never get hurt again. Little did I know that when you shut off one emotion, you end up shutting off others; so as I became numb to pain, I became numb to joy, and all my laughs were hollow.

When I was around people I could trust, people who knew how to be gentle with me, but also recognized my strengths and knew how much I hated pity, I was vibrant, playful, and vocal. Some of these angels were relatives like my cousin Alison Rodriguez on my Filipino side, her husband Martin, and their two children, JoAnna and Chris. Alison became a lifeline to my Filipino family and implicitly reminded me that indeed there was a time when Momma did exist. Martin became a symbol of what it meant to let go of the past as he embraced members of our family who initially didn't accept him because he was Mexican. Eventually, his family in Cuernavaca became my family and introduced a third culture into my upbringing. I felt a special connection to JoAnna and Chris partly because they were biracial like me. I assumed the responsibility of being the best *tia* [aunt] I could be, which included nurturing their Mexipina(o) identity.

Most of the angels in my life were friends, teachers, and mentors, or a combination. In my adulthood, a period in life when I thought I wouldn't need parents, I found a new mother and father amidst this group of angels. It took me over 20 years before I was able to embrace new parents and not feel as though I was betraying my birth parents. Many adults struggle to express their new "grown-up" needs to parents who had always known them, but perhaps never completely understood or accepted them. I have somehow been spared this experience;

instead, I am able to choose the new parents of my adulthood not only according to how well they suit my emotional and spiritual needs, but also based on how well we relate to one another. Today, I am blessed with their love and blessed with opportunities to share my love with them.

My new father, Tom Shepardson, is my former high school history teacher. He is white of Italian, English, Scottish, German, Austrian, Dutch, and Native-American ancestry. His gentleness and patience have been priceless. Observing his comfort with being an introvert allowed me to accept my own introvert side. His ability to listen to me and affirm me throughout my adolescent and adult life is the reason why I believe I am a sane and loving person today. I consider Tom, his wife Diana, and their three children Katie, Anna, and Louis to be blood.

Vangie Canonizado Buell, a Filipino-African-American woman and mother to many (including three loving daughters of her own) has become my mom, auntie, confidant, mentor, and the *lola* [grandmother] to my daughter. We share a common ethnic mix and complex family history. This woman is an activist and what Gladwell (2000, 38-48) called a "connector," taking great pleasure in introducing good people to good people. She is a patient, good listener, with a keen awareness about the various systems of oppression and privilege that exist in the United States. I can rest in her spirit and find inspiration there; a feeling I thought I'd never experience again.

Mama Vangie and Dad have never met, yet they have me in common. My new parents have been a constant source of support and guidance. Their warmth and wisdom have sustained and strengthened me. They have always believed in my integrity, generosity, intellect, and strength of character, and never doubted that my African-American and Filipino-American heritages were integral to my beauty as a human being.

Third Movement: The Blend

Being both African-American and Filipino-American means having the benefit of drawing from the richness of both ethnicities and bearing the responsibility of sharing both ethnicities with all I come in contact with. It means understanding and living out the complex interplay between culture, race, and ethnicity on a daily basis. Throughout my life, I was constantly searching for a word or label that would communicate my pride in both sides. Identifying as only African-American or Filipino-American never felt right because it just wasn't true. College and scholarship applications told me, "Please choose one," but categories like African-American and Asian/Pacific Islander felt too constraining. Friends, family, and strangers frequently asked me, "Are you more Filipino than Black or more Black than Filipino," questions that reflect a dangerous polarization and discomfort with nuance. Such binary thinking dictates how many of us operating in a Western context tend to approach people and ideas; we are conditioned to choose between or identify with one of two extremes; black and white, rich and poor, good and evil. Having to choose suggests that one couldn't possibly: (1) identify with more than one thing at the same time, (2) embrace a perspective or state of being somewhere in between, or (3) have multiple options to choose from other than the two presented.

Though such things were limiting, I never felt so frustrated by racial categories or questions reflecting binary thought that I longed to identify as 'just human.' This didn't fully capture what I was about either, especially since being both Black and Filipina shaped my human experience. My humanity was not something that could be extracted from its ethnic milieu. I was one who valued the unique histories of both sides and wanted to celebrate how being African-American and Filipina-American have shaped my human experience.

For many years I identified as half Black and half Filipino, figuring this was a way I could declare to the world that I was both. However, identifying in terms of fractions reinforced a fragmented self-perception; it signified my silent insecurity about believing I was a diluted or counterfeit version of each ethnicity. Since my Filipino features were not immediately noticeable to most people in Lancaster, California, I became aware that phenotypically I looked Black and therefore regularly reminded others that I was also Filipino, being sure to use the few Cebuano words I knew. This was done partly to show pride in my Filipino side, but also to show myself off as not-your-average-Black-person; someone with an 'interesting' twist. I discovered that I received more attention when people learned I was mixed but not necessarily always good attention. So as early as elementary school, long before I had the language for it, I had done what many had done to me: I exoticized myself. I continued to do so until I became aware of some direct consequences of exoticization; not always feeling special and unique in a positive sense, but instead feeling freakish and less human.

During my late teens and early twenties, I noticed that I felt pressured to believe I had to turn on and off each side of my ethnic identity depending on who was around. I thought that in order to be accepted as Black within an all Black social environment, I had to 'turn on' my Black side (whatever that meant) and leave behind or downplay my Filipino side; when I was in an all Filipino environment I felt that I had to 'turn on' my Filipino-ness (whatever that meant) and downplay my Black side. I felt like I was contextualizing; however, this was not satisfying and I continued to search for a way to contextualize without denying my other half. I wanted to bring all of me wherever I went, and I wanted all of me to be accepted regardless of whose company I was in.

Making attempts to be in touch with both sides, learning about the history of both and remaining socially connected to each community, I eventually became comfortable saying I was 100% African-American and 100% Filipino-American and devised various combinations of these terms. I was and am fully both. Identifying as such seemed to be a defiant response to the questions, "Are you more Filipino than Black? More Black than Filipino?" Not only was I proud to be both, but I was also proud to be a woman. So, beginning in my late twenties, I found ways to embrace my womanhood as I bounced between several ways of identifying: Filipino-African-American woman. African-Filipino-American woman. Filipina-African-American. African-Filipina-American. These names communicated the ideas of 'together' and 'distinct' at the same time.

Around this time, while working on my Master's thesis on pre-colonial West African and Filipino tricksters at San Francisco State

University, I came across *Heirs of Prophecy*, a fantasy novel by Lisa Smedman (2012), whose main character, Larajin, was half elf and half human. I was fascinated with how she invoked the deities from both her human and elven sides. This caused me to stop thinking of being biracial as a deficit or an impurity. I began to wonder if instead I had the potential to be emotionally and spiritually stronger and more capable of facing life's challenges because I could call upon the assistance and guidance of deities on both sides of my ethnic heritage. From that point on, I've expanded the circle of deities that I address and thank during prayer, calling out to God, Eshu, Oshun, Yemaya, Bathala, Apolaki, Lakapati, and Diyan Masalanta. Consequently, I have learned more about the multidimensionality of the Divine, gaining greater clarity about the multiple ways the Divine manifests itself on Earth.

In early 2007, the possibility of identifying as 'Blackapino' or 'Blackapina' crossed my mind. The term floated around in my head for a bit, but did not seem to get concretized for quite some time. I did not have the courage to use it, but I could not completely articulate why. In retrospect, I know some of this had to do with my discomfort with blending terms, as if the process of blending would corrupt the ethnic essence of each side. This was an indication that I was still afraid of being viewed as a diluted version of a Filipina or African-American. I was also hesitant to use the term because to untutored ears it evoked only laughter and was never taken seriously; hidden in the laughter, I could almost hear people say, "Aw, that's cute and catchy. But is that real? Is that a real, lived experience?"

Folded into this transition were memories of a number of scholars who researched and published articles on multiracial identity. Such scholars either used blended terms or used concepts that involved blending. I remember the early writing of Rudy Guevarra, Jr. in which he explored the experiences of multiethnic people of Mexican and Filipino descent, becoming the first to use the term 'Mexipinos' in a published work (Guevarra 2003). From his clothing line, Multiracial Apparel, I bought some shirts for my niece and nephew that read, 'Mexipino' and 'Mexipina' (Guevarra 2012). Shortly following the release of my memoir in 2005, I met Matthew

M. Andrews, the first to conduct research focusing on multiracial identity specifically amongst those of both African-American and Filipino-American descent (Andrews 2005, 27-38).

A few years later, during the summer of 2007, I delivered a presentation at the Loving Decision Conference on precolonial West African and Filipino tricksters being empowering, decolonizing role models for biracial people of African-American and Filipino-American descent. There, I had the pleasure of listening to Rebecca Romo (2008) present her research about biracial people of African-American and Mexican-American descent and remember how freeing it was to hear her use the label 'Blaxican.' Susan Leksander presented research on applying the concept of psychosynthesis to multiracial clients. Leksander described psychosynthesis as a process within Western psychology that drew from various traditions including an African worldview describing how each human being is "seen as a community in and of itself, including a plurality of selves" (Ogbonnaya 1994 as cited in Leksander 2007, 2). Leksander pointed out the normalcy of each person having many subpersonalities and stated the following:

> Subpersonalities are thought to form in response to a "unifying center," a center of meaning that evokes a deep response in us. Different subpersonalities might arise in relationship to many different unifying centers—"parents, siblings, school, profession, philosophical systems, religious environments and the natural world." I would add to this cultural and ethnic communities. A unifying center can be contacted at any age, from our earliest relationships to experiences late in life. What one experiences as outside of oneself, with enough exposure and meaning, eventually becomes internalized as a subpersonality. This new identity internalizes and consolidates the skills, gifts, drives, qualities, beliefs and values activated and gained in response to the unifying center. (Leksander 2007, 12)

Leksander's research put my complex relationship with my African-American and Filipino-American backgrounds into perspective. At various times throughout my life, different aspects of each ethnicity seemed to be 'outside' of myself since I had fashioned my life after the white dominant paradigm. In order to fully understand what it meant to live out my African-American and Filipino-American identity with depth and integrity, I consciously exposed myself to the people, language, arts, and history of each side to the point where each ethnicity gradually became internalized as one of my subpersonalities. My nucleus of subpersonalities was and will continue to be strengthened by my continuous immersion in social circles consisting of African-Americans, Filipino-Americans, women, introverts, extroverts, artists, athletes, theologians, healers, the various subgroups lying within each circle, and the intersection of all these and more. This nucleus is a tight, yet fluid, ever-expansive, ever-evolving blend housed within my spirit. I possess an authenticity that laughs in the face of essentialism. I am 'Blackapina.' Black. Filipino-American. Woman. I am an African-American unafraid of identifying as Black because it hearkens back to the Black Power Movement when Black, the color and the culture, were embraced with pride.

I also use Blackapina because *bibi*, the word for "black" amongst the Sonay of Mali, referred only to "the essential goodness of things," a definition predating the distortion and demonization of the color (Nobles 2006, 329). I am a second-generation Filipina-American, holding my mother's immigrant dreams and sacrifices; as my *utang na loob* [debt from within], I offer Momma the fruits of my work as professor of Filipina(o)-American Heritage and Africana Studies. I am a woman who menstruates and gives birth and nurses and nurtures and fights. I am each of these and more. I am all these at the same time. I live at the crossroads, straddling multiple worlds. Hybridity is my home where transition and nuance are always welcome. At the interstices, you'll hear my breath. When I walk, listen for the sound of ancestral spirits and deities hailing from the African continent and the Philippine Islands; hear them pulse and drift, cry and whisper, laugh and pray as they clear the way for their children to walk the world protected, guided, and strengthened. *Ashe.*

Leadership Tips

1. *Cultivate the knowledge and skills that will allow you to be an expert in your field.* This expertise can be one vital source of confidence. People trust you when you are competent and are more likely to continue seeking your expertise.

2. *Remember that there is a dialectical relationship between a leader and her followers.* Followers respect and learn from a leader who has the ability to respect and learn from her followers. A good strong leader is not domineering or condescending toward her followers or her peers/colleagues. An abusive leader will never last long; such a person will either be usurped by the victims of their abuse or their own hatred and anger will cause them to self-destruct. A good, strong leader earnestly shares her wealth of knowledge with her followers, but also recognizes and affirms the knowledge/input that her followers bring to the table and does not attempt to take credit for their input.

3. *Be friendly, approachable, and honest.* A good leader recognizes that these qualities bring out the best in people. However, be aware that some may unfortunately, (a) misconstrue these qualities as a sign of weakness or naiveté, or (b) use these qualities as tools for personal gain. Don't let such people distract or disturb you; when you genuinely practice friendliness, approachability, and honesty, you are modeling respectable behavior that can quickly become contagious as long as you believe in its power.

4. *Maintain a continuous connection to your ancestors and the Divine.* They will be your source of strength, hope, and love. They will be a constant reminder to remain proud of your ethnic heritage(s) and continue to use your skills and knowledge to serve your community in the spirit of collectivity.

Leading Organizations

A Filipina Leans In

Nina D. Aguas

CEO, Philippine Bank of Communications

Abstract

*B*eing a woman is an asset, not a liability. Nina D. Aguas illustrates how being a woman and a Filipina has helped her achieve many firsts in her career: shattering the proverbial glass ceiling several times during her 30 years working for global financial institutions and leading her to her current position as President and CEO of the Philippine Bank of Communications. While banking is known as one of the most dynamic, competitive, and male-dominated industries, Aguas shares how she has leveraged her unique Filipina qualities to go head to head with a diverse set of colleagues while maintaining her values, grace, and dignity. A daughter, sister, wife, and mother; she recognizes that each aspect of her life has influenced her as a business leader. Her story is a testament to how we can take advantage of our circumstances. With the right attitude, perseverance, and faith, there is much that can be achieved.

Early in my career with Citigroup, I had the opportunity to sit at a table with the Worldwide Chairman of Citigroup, who, at the time was in town for his one and only visit to the Philippines. Over dinner he asked me what I hoped to become within the company. Being one of over 250,000 employees worldwide, I found it amusing that he would ask such a question. My reply was one that anyone in a high-powered organization might consider inappropriate or even audacious, particularly for someone aiming to achieve a significant position within the company as I was. I replied with certainty: "Someday I will be the president of a Filipino bank."

Though my answer was unexpected, he quickly responded: "Why not at Citi?" I simply said: "Look at the room. The women do not even comprise 10 percent." I got his attention, and move up within Citi I did. At that time, I had already become the first female Regional Audit Director across our global footprint and, in the years that followed, I became the first female Country Business Manager in the Asia-Pacific region (Dumlao 2001). My climb to the top was seemingly a series of fortunate events, some might say almost accidental. Looking back, however, I think I also did things right. Living is about circumstances, events, access to opportunities, and being in the right place at the right time. More importantly, it is about taking advantage of opportunities you do find or that find you.

Today, I am President and CEO of the Philippine Bank of Communications. This is, in many ways, a dream come true. Eleanor Roosevelt once said: "The future belongs to those who believe in the beauty of their dreams." My journey has not been without its share of challenges and unexpected turns, but by believing in myself and taking charge of each situation I am faced with, I put myself in a positive frame of mind that impacts every decision I make and, ultimately, my life. When you view yourself as being at an advantage, then you are at an advantage.

Even though I came from humble beginnings in Tarlac City, Philippines and was not from a prominent family, I never felt discouraged from pursuing my dreams. We are all able to influence our circumstances. With the right attitude, perseverance, and faith, there is much that can be achieved. My growing up years with my sisters, brothers, and cousins were glorious and joyful. We were of very modest means but definitely not wanting. We climbed trees, ran in the rain, gazed at the stars, and swam by the river banks under the watchful eye of our grandmother, who made sure we did not swim too far out. We did not have a television or toys. I did not even have a doll. Instead we used our imagination and improvised. We played dress up with our pillow cases and made tents out of our blankets. We strategized to master traditional Filipino games such as *patintero* [a team tag game], *piko* [hopskotch], and *taguan* [hide and seek]. We played with simple everyday objects: marbles, jackstones, plastic balloons, rubber bands, and clay pots. I also had my share of chores which included helping to clean our house and to carry my mother's shopping basket. From her I learned the art of haggling. Mother asked all of us girls to help out in the kitchen and so we all became reasonable cooks. When I was six, I saw the house that our father helped build burn down. I had the consciousness to gather up my things, wake up my sister, and lead her down the stairs to safety. As young as I was, I felt I had to step up; she was depending on me to help find our way out.

As a little girl, I only spoke our dialect, *Kapampangan*, so when I was old enough to attend our town's private Catholic school for girls, I had to spend the entire summer learning to read and write in English from our mother. School was demanding and rigorous. We were taught by the nuns what it meant to be a good Catholic. Yet it was all the activities outside of the classroom that I believe really brought out the best in all of us. I was very good at reading poetry and leading prayer. I was often asked to stay after class to help those who were weak in math and reading which, as an eight or nine year old, I did not appreciate, as it took me away from my time to play. Looking back, these little tasks were actually the roots for my mentoring skills.

There are a few unhappy memories though, for who is ever spared such? Much as I wanted to be, I was never picked to be an angel for the First Communicants as I was brown-skinned. I wanted to do this so badly, but at the time, only the fair were chosen. Hopefully it is no longer so these days. There were years in high school that were quite uncomfortable. Why, you might ask? I was such a certified wall flower that I made lame excuses not to attend dance parties. I just told myself I was being saved from the teenage boys for a greater purpose. Seeing them again decades later, indeed I was saved!

From grade school to university, I was at the forefront of student politics as President of the class and involved in student organizations. My professors agreed I was a natural leader. I spoke convincingly, passionately, and emotionally during campaigns. I used my energy to influence changes for the greater good. These were years leading to the declaration of Martial Law. I was not militant by disposition and preferred to take the middle ground. I did not take my politics to the streets but stayed within the campus and university corridors. Doing so took courage, given the fervor and political tensions of the times but if I am to speak candidly, my fear of my father was stronger than my political will. As you can see, even in my teens, I was already picking my battles.

My mother asked me to take up commerce and accounting. I became a Certified Public Accountant (CPA) because I was an obedient daughter. As a fresh graduate, I joined the prestigious accounting firm SGV as a junior auditor. It was a field job I found uninspiring. I increasingly became drawn to the client's side of the business. Despite my lack of enthusiasm, I persevered and gave this opportunity my best. Eventually clients did take notice and offered me jobs.

I was always attracted to banking, propelled more by the seeming glamour and the opportunity to travel than by the excitement of the trade. My transformational entry into banking was by God's grace. I had done some work for another foreign bank but I had to give it up in order to join my husband who was overseas for study and a temporary posting. I came back from living in the U.S. to an open position with the largest foreign bank in the country, Citibank, which in later years would be known as Citigroup or Citi. I was very drawn to the institution. I told myself I was going to work for Citi one day. I liked everything about the bank including its reach, its global presence, and the seemingly boundless opportunities for learning and growth. I believed then that anyone who wanted a fulfilling banking career must go through Citi. As the song goes, "if you can make it there, you'll make it anywhere."

Banking is one of the most dynamic, competitive and, admittedly, male-dominated industries in the world. An American Banker article published in May 2014 indicated that while women represent 54% of the finance and banking workforce, only 23% of senior officer positions are actually held by women (Detjen 2014). Despite this, I personally never felt that I was any different or less capable than anyone else while working in the industry both in the Philippines and overseas. These thoughts crossed my mind occasionally but I was neither daunted nor very awed by my male colleagues who held positions of power. Perhaps I have been fortunate as the Philippines is an exception to the rule and one of the Top Ten countries where women occupy roles in senior management (Grant Thornton IBR 2013). As my career progressed I moved into roles that involved foreign assignments, I did not feel that my gender was an issue.

Having "grown up" in a global bank, I gained the confidence of interacting with colleagues of different nationalities and cultural backgrounds. Working in the U.S., however, made me realize the extent towhich diversity is an issue. Having come from an environment in the Philippines that was more tolerant and inclusive, diversity was not high in my consciousness. I may have not even recognized that I was being discriminated against as a Filipina. It seemed to me that the talk about the uniqueness of each group magnified the differences rather than leveraging the differences and finding common ground to build upon. Sensitivity and mutual respect are key. My journey certainly has its share of setbacks as things have not always gone my way. Twice in my career I was passed over for critical appointments. In both cases, I believed I was the best person for the job. I also believed that in a system of meritocracy, where hard work and performance would eventually be rewarded, a promotion would naturally be handed to me without asking. I was really naïve in that sense. That I had the full support of my peers in both instances made the rejection no less upsetting. In both incidents, a male expatriate colleague was appointed but did not last. In the first instance, I did eventually get the job. In the other, I received an even more senior post. My lesson from these experiences was key: NO ONE IS AS INVESTED IN YOU AS **YOU** ARE. As one reaches the tip of the pyramid and attains more senior level positions in a huge organization, there will naturally be less of the prized assignments and an oversupply of talent. There can only be one CEO. You must lean in, state your case, and be ready to fight for it. This does not come naturally to us Filipinas, as we are socialized to believe in the virtue of humility, albeit sometimes false. We hesitate and hold back no matter how badly we want something. One self-discovery on my part is how de-motivating it was to be forced to work for some one incompetent. I would rather be "it." Yet failures are part of the path to success and, if handled properly, allow one to gain courage. I learned to face disappointments with grace, leveraging adversity as a way to stay focused and strengthen myself and my team.

I have always believed that being a woman is a unique quality that makes people sit up and take notice. And while we are raised to be respectful and ensure that we do not offend anyone, in a highly competitive work environment, Filipinas have the extra advantage of being able to go head-to-head with a diverse set of colleagues. Being a Filipina carries with it a precious set of skills including tenacity, quiet strength, generosity of spirit, and courage; the very bricks of success. The Filipina is quintessentially a paradox, quiet, shy, and *mahinhin* [demure] on the exterior, but sharp, secure, and decisive at heart; a unique combination that drives achievement and ultimately, success. She is intuitive and quick-witted, adaptive, and resilient. She instinctively knows when to lean in and when to lean out!

While I was always driven to arrive at a better place, I was not consumed by the desire to succeed. My detachment to the idea and measures of success gave me the space for critical thinking. I believe it is important for the journey to be joyful and exhilarating. I also believe the journey needs to be shared with like-minded people with similar passions, values, and desire to work with women and men who are equally purposeful, competent, and willing to share. I draw strength from their collective genius and from what each individual brings to the table.

Living is a team sport and I believe one cannot live and journey through life alone.

My journey has not simply been about standing out amongst peers in board rooms, for one must effectively lead in order to succeed. I believe leadership requires compassion, an ability to listen, learn from others, and inspire them to excel. To be a leader is not just an act of giving and forgiving, but also an act of harnessing, not just your own skills but also recognizing and harnessing the skills of those you lead. Both competence and incompetence trigger in me a strong desire to lean in and step up. I cannot let unfulfilled matters go by. I am restless until I extend myself and take charge. I am awed by excellence and learn from the talent that I am surrounded with. As such, creating a culture of mentorship has been a personal passion throughout my career.

Often people ask—is leadership more influenced by nature or nurture? I believe that we are the sum of many parts. We are influenced by great women in our lives including the saints, grandmothers, mothers, sisters, teachers and women leaders—and, yes, also by the men. We are inspired by those we hold dear, as well as those with whom we work each day. Our society and culture equip us with the values, skills, and determination necessary to seize opportunities and shape our destiny. As a woman, I wear multiple hats. I am not just a business leader but I am also a daughter, wife, sister, and mother. While there is a common notion that this balancing act can be a deterrent to a woman's advancement, to me, this has been an advantage. Each hat I wear has equipped me with a unique set of insights, which together, has shaped the leader I have become. I believe I am diversely skilled and emotionally stronger as a result, so I can better deal with multi-faceted and complex issues.

Being raised by a headstrong mother and growing up with four equally strong-willed sisters taught me grace and humility. Among us there is no jealousy as we all pursued our passions and took different paths. From them, I learned to respect differences and celebrate each other's personal triumphs.

Early in our marriage, my husband was awarded a scholarship, and then offered a post in the U.S. I put my career on hold, packed my bags and joined him. Years later, following his retirement, it would be his turn to take a back seat, supporting my foreign assignments with Citi and ANZ. My marriage has taught me about compromise and remains a constant reminder of what is truly important. Indeed, the Filipina has the potential for greatness, and our experiences both in the workplace and beyond allow us opportunities to harness and develop the leader within. However as the old adage goes, *noblesse oblige*, or in recent times, "With great power comes great responsibility."

At some point, we may find ourselves to be on top and the best at what we do. We should always remember, however, that all these may come to pass and that someone stronger or younger may come along. Instead of focusing solely on being the best we need to focus also on doing the best. As former *National Geographic* photographer Dewitt Jones once asked, "Do you want to be the best in the world or the best for the world?"

I have given many years of my life working for large multinational financial institutions where I interacted with high net worth individuals and big corporations. It was compelling, high octane, a constant battle of wits, and I must admit, quite glamorous and heady. We hardly noticed who or what we lost along the way. The strong, the best, and the brightest ruled. Running successful businesses energized me, and I believe I delivered far more times than I failed. Along the way, however, I hit a crossroad.

Three years ago, I chose to go down a path that is less travelled by those who share my professional background. I gave up a high-paying job in the private banking world overseas and chose to come home to the Philippines and work locally. This was propelled by a strong desire to serve our country's poor, under-served, and under-banked. A report on financial inclusion published by the Bangko Sentral ng Pilipinas (Central Bank of the Philippines) in 2012 indicates that 37% of municipalities in the Philippines does not have a banking institution. Additionally, in over 60% of these unbanked municipalities, not only is there an absence of a bank, but a lack of alternative access points to financial services such as ATMs or payment centers (Bangko Sentral ng Pilipinas 2012). During my time with Citi, I had the opportunity to see first-hand how microfinance institutions empower people and allow them to escape from poverty (Aguas 2004). While my career took me elsewhere, both geographically and functionally, parts of my mind and heart remained focused on this vulnerable sector of Philippine society.

Yes, I reached the point where I made a conscious choice between money and meaning. I came home with a hope and a prayer that I could achieve both success and significance by leaning in courageously and providing banking access and financial solutions for the poorest Filipinos.

As I continue on my journey, I thank God for having given me a grateful heart. Big and small people, simple and complex matters, and magnificent and plain creations give me reasons to smile and for my heart to beat a little faster. A sincere smile begets other smiles and brings out joyfulness in the workplace, within family, and among friends. And this is what this journey is all about: bringing joy to those we love, those we work with, and those we serve. It is for this that I wake up to each new day, and, again and again, choose to *lean in*.

LEADERSHIP TIPS

1. *Think positive, dream big.* Eleanor Roosevelt once said: "The future belongs to those who believe in the beauty of their dreams." We are all able to influence the circumstances we find ourselves in. With the right attitude, perseverance and faith, there is much and more that can be achieved. When you view yourself as being at an advantage, then you are at an advantage.

2. *Keep true to your core but remain open to other viewpoints and possibilities.* Having core principles and beliefs provide us with a backbone that guides our decisions and actions, however, we must remain open to other philosophies and possibilities. In today's fast-changing and increasingly diverse world, we need to be adaptable and learn to adjust how we do things without compromising what we stand for.

3. *Invest in your people.* As leaders, we must recognize that our success also depends on the success of those around us. We must have the generosity of spirit to inspire them to excel and to think of others as extensions of ourselves - be as invested in their careers as we are in our own.

4. *Failure is part of success.* Things will not always go well, nor will things always go your way. At one point or another, we all experience failure. You have to be able to rise from that failure, for what is important is not the failure itself, but rather how you rise from it and what you learn in the process. While the end goal is to succeed, what truly matters is the quality of the journey that gets us there.

5. *Keep your sense of humor.* Sometimes life throws curve balls and we encounter challenges and face unexpected turns. We must be resilient and find ways to bounce back. Apart from faith and being with those whom we hold dear, nothing is more healing than laughter. Humor can narrow differences, build bridges and lighten grief. The ability to laugh at ourselves keeps us human and grounded. We must remember to keep things light, let go and share a laugh every once in a while.

6. ***Be a good listener.*** Living is a team sport. One cannot live and journey through life alone. And with any team endeavour, communication is important. As leaders, daughters, sisters, wives, mothers and friends, we must learn not just to speak, but also to listen.

7. ***Walk with confidence.*** It was not very long ago that a female would be dismissed as being "just a woman," but that is no longer the case. We must stand proud and hold our heads high. If we present ourselves with confidence, we will command attention, recognition, and respect.

8. ***Prioritize.*** Circumstance will push you to wear multiple hats. The key is how you handle it. The need to juggle and multi-task should not be seen as a burden, but as an opportunity to learn balance and recognize what is important. You cannot be everything to everyone at the same time. The key is to prioritize.

Barefoot in the Barrio to American Madame Mayor

Mayor Ruth Uy Asmundson, Ph.D.

Ambassador, Davis Sister Cities
Special Assistant to University of California Davis Vice Provost on
University Outreach and International Programs
Former Mayor of Davis

Abstract

"*T*o dream the impossible dream...
To reach the unreachable star."

As a young girl, I was a dreamer and no dream was too big. In first grade, being the smallest with the shortest name and seated at the back of the class, one of my dreams was to become a doctor and marry a tall, good looking man with a long name that begins with 'A.' This is my story in search of that dream, how I as young girl went from a remote barrio of Mabini, Gamu, Isabela, Philippines to the center of an American city's political life; an amazing journey that led me to become the first Asian mayor of Davis, California, and first Filipina immigrant mayor in the continental U.S. My journey took me to Manila for my undergraduate degree and with Fulbright scholarships obtained an M.S. and Ph.D. degrees in the U.S. While in graduate school, I met the young, dashing Davis Mayor, Vigfus Asmundson, and my life's course changed. We have four daughters and also raised two nephews. While raising my children, I was active in many school and community organizations and awarded many honors, including 1989 Davis' Citizen of the Year, Philippine Presidential *Pamana ng Pilipino* award in 2006, and one of Filipina Women's Network '100 Most Influential Filipina Women in the U.S.' in 2007. I served on the Davis Board of Education, two terms as mayor of Davis, and currently as Ambassador to Davis Sister Cities and Special Assistant to UC Davis Vice Provost on University Outreach and International Programs.

In the Beginning:
Dreaming for the Unreachable Star!

It was the tail end of the 1940s, as a five-year-old, I quietly watched the remains of my 32-year-old father, Uy Chusing, laid to rest in the remote hinterlands of Isabela. My father was born in Xiamen, China and moved to the Philippines with his uncle when he was eight. Ten years later, he met and married a 14-year-old girl named Virginia Lacaste, who bore him four daughters and two sons. I am the fourth. Our family settled in Mabini, a barrio of Gamu, Isabela. All eight of us lived together in a two-bedroom house without running water, without an indoor toilet, without electricity; typical in the barrio at the time. I had to study my lessons at night using a small kerosene lamp until my stepfather eventually installed a small generator to light our home for two hours every night.

My mother had quit school after the sixth grade, but always had an appetite for books. During World War II, my parents hid American soldiers from the invading Japanese forces in our house inside hollowed-out stacks of bales of tobacco. After the war, the grateful soldiers sent her books, American magazines, and newspapers. She always kept learning and passed on her passion for new knowledge to her children.

While growing up in the barrio, there were three obstacles for me that I had to overcome. First, my mother had eventually married my father's cousin, Uy Tie, and he wanted the children to attend Chinese language schools after we finished elementary school. Second, my surname, Uy, placed me at the end of an alphabetically-arranged classroom. Third, the Ibanag majority of Gamu look down on the barrio folks of Mabini.

Determined to follow my dreams, I set personal goals and worked to find opportunities to pursue them. The first goal was that I would go to English-language schools and continue my education to become a doctor which did not endear me to my stepfather. My second was to marry a tall, good-looking man with a long surname that started with 'A.' My third was to be an active contributing citizen to make my community the best place to live.

I had learned from my mother that success comes hand-in-hand with a good education, and I worked hard to be the top of my class.

Starting in second grade, I represented Mabini Elementary School every year in competitions that pitted me against a peer from Gamu Elementary School. However, the girl from the barrio, always bested the girl from the town, and I suffered the insults heaped on me by my rival's Ibanag mother.

Because Mabini did not have a high school, I had to transfer to Gamu after elementary school. But as the valedictorian of Mabini Elementary, I continued to work hard and received higher grades than my rival, the valedictorian from Gamu Elementary. I was a friend to everyone including my rival. I attained the highest positions in student government. I played softball and volleyball and attended regional Girl Scout conferences. My teachers relied on me to organize all kinds of student activities.

Even more than my school activities, I enjoyed talking to all sorts of people. On my way to my elementary school in the morning, I would greet everyone I saw along the way, mothers sweeping their front yards, fathers getting ready to go to the field, and other people starting their days. I knew everyone and everyone knew me, they waited for me and they knew when I was sick.

This scene would ultimately replay over and over in the different places I would find myself. In high school, my ability to connect and lead made me president in all my classes and the student body president in my senior year. At Adamson University in Manila, my list of friends would range from the neighborhood housemaids who threw out the weekly trash, the *zapatero* [shoemaker] on my way to get my *jeepney* ride to school, to University luminaries, such as the Adamsons themselves.

I was the first in the family to finish high school, but I was not content to stop there. After graduating, I enrolled in a B.S. Chemistry program at Adamson University. I received a scholarship that I was determined to put to good use. It also helped that one of my older sisters had settled in Manila a few years earlier. However, the significance of all that I had accomplished thus far was lost on my stepfather who refused to support me to go to college. Therefore I supplemented my scholarship by selling nuts, candies, and underwear to my classmates. Seeing my determination for further education, my older sisters realized that they could also further their education. They worked during the day and went to night school. All of my sisters eventually finished high school and trade school. One older sister went on to college to become a certified public accountant.

After my first year at Adamson, my stepfather expected me to know how to make soap. That was what was important to him, *SOAP!* Of course I did not know how to make soap.

My ignorance of the finer details of soap-making, however, was masked by my ability to build relationships. In my first year at Adamson, I was often asked during special occasions to entertain Mr. and Mrs. Adamson. The couple liked me, and took me under their wing. My newfound confidence drove me not only to join many organizations inside and outside of Adamson University but also to form, with my circle of friends, a sorority in the school.

And still I did not think twice about eating at the bus drivers' table on my trips back to Isabela. I would often ask my sister's maid, whom she sent as a chaperone during these eight-hour trips home, to change roles with me when we joined the all-male drivers for meals. The little girl who used to greet everyone on her way to school had never really changed. I could joke and laugh with the bus drivers with ease. They would ask what I did for a living and told them that I was a maid but they did not believe me. They told me that I had 'class' and that I had a refreshing genuineness that came to the surface and audacity that made me stand out.

Immediately after graduation, I put one of my mother's favorite sayings to good use, from Matthew 7:7-12: "Ask and You Shall Receive," by striding into President Adamson's office and telling him, "Mr. President! I'm done! Do you have a job for me?" My forthright attitude landed me work as a laboratory researcher that summer and as a chemistry instructor the following school year at Adamson University. My first day of teaching was memorable. I was 19 years old and as I walked to class, it dawned on me that I would be teaching students many years older than I. I could barely walk to my classroom due to nervousness and panic. I was scared, so I leaned on a wall by the door and said a little prayer. And then I had an epiphany, that I knew more than anyone in the class, and that none of them would know whether what I was telling them was correct! I have never been nervous again. I was a popular teacher with students lining-up outside my classroom to listen to my lectures. I used real life examples and analogies that resonated with them to explain and clarify the mysteries in chemistry, such as discussions of ionic bonding and covalent bonding of elements in the periodic table. I would compare ionic bonding to the intense attraction that happens when a beautiful young lady and a handsome young man meet and covalent bonding happening when two young ladies or two young men meet, like each other and become friends but the attraction is not as intense. That was in the 1960s when gay and lesbian issues were not a hot topic.

The Journey Begins:
To Reach For The Unreachable Star!

It was my professor of Physical Chemistry who encouraged me to apply for a Fulbright Scholarship. I was reluctant to apply since no Adamson University graduate had ever received one. However, my professor insisted that I try, telling me: "Nothing ventured, nothing gained. If you get it, it is wonderful, if not, take it as a good learning experience." I then encouraged several former classmates to apply as well. The director of admissions at Adamson snickered at us, saying that we were just wasting our time. His son had graduated the year before as a magna cum laude, applied, but did not get a Fulbright. I told him that it would be a good experience and repeated my now favorite saying "Nothing ventured, nothing gained." In my interview at the U.S. Embassy, I applied my experience of talking to all sorts of people and charmed the international professors. When the panel chair introduced himself, he said that he was from Australia. I asked "Are you from the outback?" They roared with laughter because it was like I was asking him if he was from the boondocks. But that was all I knew about Australia from my reading of romance novels, my favorite escape from reality during my college days. And so he gave me a geography lesson on Australia. When the other panel members from New Zealand, Canada, and the U.S. introduced themselves, I also asked a little of what I knew about their countries and we had a lively conversation. They could tell that with my inquisitive nature and work ethic, I would make the most of any opportunity. Halfway through the interview, the chair finally said that they needed to ask their interview questions. The first was a question on velocity, one that I was not sure of the correct answer, but I thought it made no sense for him to ask a question requiring complicated calculations. So I answered confidently, "Of course it is zero." I surprised them. I was told that I was the first to answer it correctly. They asked several more questions, of which I only knew answers to a few, but they still thought I was brilliant for having answered the first question correctly.

I got the scholarship and soon found myself at the orientation for Fulbright students in Hawaii. Although I was anxious about leaving the Philippines and familiar places, I was determined to learn to fit in. I befriended our orientation adviser, and peppered him with questions. He told me: "Americans love to talk about themselves, and if you want to start a conversation, just ask them about themselves, then again ask another question and they'll think you are a great conversationalist." It worked. Now, I am that American who loves to talk when asked a question.

I became a student at Wilkes University in Wilkes-Barre, Pennsylvania in 1966. While there, on November 18, 1966 at four o'clock in the afternoon, I was walking by a dormitory and wondered why people were having such a big pillow fight. It was my first sight of snow. After I received my master's degree in chemistry in 1968, I proceeded to UC Davis for my Ph.D.

One of my mottos is the three "bodies" in every group: *Somebody*, *Anybody*, and *Nobody*. "When the chairman asked for volunteers, he said, "*Anybody* can do it." *Everybody* thought *Somebody* would but *Nobody* did. *Somebody* decided since *Anybody* could but *Nobody* did, *Somebody* should and he volunteered. When *Everybody* saw *Somebody* doing what *Anybody* could, *Everybody* gladly lent a hand and soon the job was done!!!"

True to my motto, I immediately got involved in Davis and threw myself into the busy job of volunteering for UC Davis' international students' organization. Because of my friendly ways and natural ability to instantly make everyone feel welcome, I was charged with setting up dinners for newcomers in the Fall. During my third year, I was given the extra task of providing entertainment for the new foreign students and distinguished guests. Since I could not get anyone to perform, I ended-up dancing the *Binasuan*, a dance involving balancing three full wine glasses on my head and palms.

As fate would have it, the newly elected, mayor of Davis, Vigfus Asmundson, was on hand for the event. He told me later that he could not take his eyes off me, and was enchanted with my charm.

I had befriended Vigfus's mother, my next-door neighbor, a year before I met him. A bachelor, and often featured in the local paper, my roommates and I would tease each other that it was the mayor calling when the phone rang. The older Mrs. Asmundson had often attempted to introduce me to her son and even arranged dinners for the two of us to meet. Vigfus, however, weary of his mother's constant attempts as a matchmaker, had previously fended off his mother's invitations. When he finally called, I thought my roommates were joking again.

On our first date, he asked me if I liked children and I said, "Of course!" The second time we met, he took me on a tour around 'his' city to show me the landfill, the dumpsite, the waste water treatment facility, places which I did not feel were romantic at all! However, it fit with his frugal nature as a child who grew up during the Great Depression. On the third date, he asked me to marry him and I said yes because, he was the man I have been waiting for since I was in first grade, the tall good-looking man with a long name that begins with 'A.' We continued dating until I finished my Ph.D.

However, my contract with the Fulbright scholarship program interrupted the two-year romance. I returned to the Philippines where I became chairperson of Adamson's graduate program in chemistry at age 28. Although eligible Filipinos presented themselves to me, I could not quite shake off from my head or my heart the image of the tall, handsome American named 'Asmundson.' We continued corresponding, and when Vigfus visited his brother in New Zealand some six months later, he said he was "in the neighborhood" and could he visit the Philippines. Again he proposed marriage and for the second time I said, "Yes." Vigfus put his Harvard law training to good use and succeeded in getting my visa to return to America.

A Fork In The Road: From Science To Politics!

Ours was a marriage of opposites. He was raised in the city, I in the countryside. He had a long name at the beginning of the alphabet, mine was merely two letters and lay at the opposite end. He was 6'2" and I was 5'1". He was a Republican, I am a Democrat. Somehow all these 'opposites' seemed moot because we shared the same core values. Our love for each other was the only thing that really mattered.

Vigfus wanted ten children, I wanted two, so we compromised on four and eventually had four daughters, and later raised my two nephews after my sister and brother-in-law passed away. The circumstances surrounding Vigfus' ascent as mayor were mirrored in my political career some 30 years later. He won a seat in the Davis City Council with the highest number of votes in 1968 and was later elected mayor. I won a seat in the Davis City Council in 2002, also with the highest number of votes. Because of a new ordinance, automatically became mayor two years later. We are the only husband and wife to both serve as mayors of Davis.

My public service in Davis started with volunteer work at Valley Oak Elementary School where our children attended. I also became the International House's first office manager (later serving as vice president of the Board of Directors), member of the Davis School Arts Foundation Board of Directors, and many other organizations. At one time, I held simultaneously several key leadership positions in the schools and city, including PTA presidents at Valley Oak Elementary School and Emerson Junior High School, hospitality committee chair at Davis Senior High School, president of Davis School Arts Foundation, vice president of International House, Davis, and scholarship committee chair for University Farm Circle. As an active parent volunteer in the school district I advocated for new programs and educational options such as offering a Spanish Immersion program which eventually became a K-6 school, and extending the gifted and talented education program to several more grades. In addition, for 26 years, after my marriage in 1973, I served as my husband's law office manager. I believe the keys to my success were my passion for all my causes, hard work, my ability to multitask, and a bedtime of 2:30 a.m. In recognition of my accomplishments, I was later awarded the 'Davis Citizen of the Year' award in 1989.

"To run where the brave dare not go... and the world will be better for this"

I started my career in politics in 1990 when I was appointed to a vacant position on the Davis Board of Education. The other finalist was a Hispanic administrative law judge whose supporters filled the board meeting. When I was appointed, the head of the other finalist's supporters angrily complained that the School Board "missed their chance of appointing a person of color" and everybody looked at me. After the meeting, I asked him to lunch the next day requested he explain to me why he thought that I, as a Filipina, was not a person of color. He told me that the board should have appointed his friend since there were more Hispanics in Davis than Filipinos. I countered that if that was the case then the board should have appointed a white person since there are more white residents in Davis than Hispanics! We have been good friends ever since. This was typical of my approach of confronting conflicts, to communicate, and to solve the problem directly with the people involved or being affected right away and gain new friends. Two years after my appointment, I was overwhelmingly elected and was again re-elected four years later. During my ten years on the Board of Education, I served as Board President twice.

I strongly believe in investing in future generations. As a board member I founded the Davis Educational Foundation, advocated for more and better school facilities, pushed for more funding from the state, and pushed for more challenging and rigorous curriculum. During my term, an Independent Study School, an alternative high school was opened, three additional elementary schools were built, older schools facilities were renovated, and we worked with the Davis City Council to acquire school sites at minimal cost to the school district. I remained a constant voice for sensible budgets, even when it was unpopular. The then mayor Lois Wolk and I also started a 'Youth In Government' program at Davis Senior High School. This program continues to make Davis high school students aware of their civic duties and expose them to real life political processes and issues in the school district and the city.

While on the Davis School Board, I was also active on the California School Boards Association (CSBA) as director-at-large for Asian Pacific Islanders for several years, and on the National School Boards Association policy committee. Whenever a school board member was needed for a state-wide mathematics and science task forces or committees, CSBA recommended me. In these capacities, I advocated for more parental involvement in schools, removing calculators from elementary school, and more rigorous curricula in mathematics and science. I developed a reputation for thoroughly reading reports, consistently attending meetings, and answering correspondence late into the night. Even as mayor, I personally read and answered all my emails, which averaged over 80 a day.

Although I intended to retire from politics after serving on the Board of Education, the citizens of Davis had other ideas. The community was well aware of my core values and many accomplishments and was unwilling to let me retire. I had earned the respect and trust of the community. As a school board member I served and represented the school children and parents well. Talking and listening to students, parents, teachers, administrators and community members was an integral part in my decision making process. I made decisions based on my guiding principle of what is best for the school children rather than what was expedient. I made sure that I remained available and accessible to all. Everybody, even little children, knew my personal phone number, 753-RUTH. "Exacting, energetic, and engaging" were the words of Dr. Orville Thompson, Professor Emeritus of UC Davis. "I have known Ruth for possibly 30 years. Her husband was our paperboy when we first came to Davis." He added: "One of Ruth's greatest strengths is her passion for people. I know of no one in Davis better known than Ruth. She wants to know what people need." After taking two years off and following repeated pleas from members of the community including my husband, who himself had desired to run again but could not because of his Parkinson's disease, I ran and was elected to the Davis City Council in 2002. I was re-elected in 2006, receiving the highest number of votes in each election. I served as Mayor of Davis during both terms, and I am one of only three mayors to do so since the late 1940s. I led the council in sensible budgeting, and voters knew they could trust me to be fair about competing priorities.

During my years of public service, I received many awards. The ones I am most proud of are: Davis Citizen of the Year in 1989, 'Distinguished Service Award' and 'Outstanding School Board Member' from the Yolo County School Board Members Association; 'Women of Distinction Award' from the Soroptimist International of Davis; 'Woman of the Year' awards by the Philippine and other Asian Headlines; one of 200 outstanding Filipinos in '*Mga Bagong Bayani:* Inspiring Filipinos Overseas,' and recipient of the 2010 Award of Distinction at UC Davis 22nd College Celebration. I was featured in 2014 in the One UC Davis banner series on campus honoring the people who had made UC Davis the unparalleled institution that it is. In 2006, I went to Malacañang Palace to accept the *Pamana ng Pilipino* award from President Gloria Macapagal Arroyo. In 2007, I was recognized by the Filipina Women's Network as one of the '100 Most Influential Filipina Women in the U.S.'

I have always wanted to make my community a better place. Besides the service I have contributed to Davis and surrounding cities, I returned many times with my husband to Mabini, where we helped rebuild and restock the community library destroyed by a typhoon, gave scholarships to motivate students to aspire for higher education, and inspired students to attend university. As a result, Mabini finally has its own high school. As a child in Mabini, it was my dream to have a good education in order to attain a brighter future and a better life. Having achieved this dream, I want others to have that same opportunity and I helped Mabini become a model for the surrounding barrios.

In addition to providing a library in Mabini, I also pushed the community to address health-related issues, including better living conditions and having a more green community. I acquired funding from the Philippine government to buy a thousand tree saplings and we had a tree-planting day, in the late 1970's, along all the streets in Mabini. Those trees are now grown and provide beautiful canopies, shade, and fresher air.

After a seven-year battle with Parkinson's disease, Vigfus died in 2003. Prior to his passing, he saw me elected to the Davis City Council. While his public service was finished, mine would continue. He achieved a lot as mayor and before he died, he challenged me to surpass his four major accomplishments: one of them was the 1972 city general plan that became a model for other cities in California. It was a tall order but I am proud to say that my legacy is as good as his, perhaps a little bit more but different. As mayor, I was confronted with many major issues such as growth, city infrastructure, dwindling revenues, employee negotiations, water and waste water treatment, climate change and many more. My job involved working with the community to find solutions in a systematic way. We prioritized our needs and set goals. California State Senator Lois Wolk said in one of her testimonials: "Ruth is a smart, dedicated public servant who cares a great deal for our community and the people who live here.... She has always been a leader, never shying away from the controversial issues of the day, whatever they may be." In my eight years of service on the City Council, I spearheaded initiatives that brought more affordable housing to the city of Davis, generated more tax revenue through economic development, brought in a Target store for more affordable shopping options in Davis and our favorite grocery store, Trader Joe's, and created better working relationships between the city, Yolo County, the Davis Joint Unified School District, and the University of California, Davis.

For me, two projects stand out as particular points of pride. The first was a push for alternative transportation, continuing efforts to make Davis the Bicycle City in the U.S. I formed a bicycle advisory commission and funded a city bicycle coordinator. Davis now enjoys 100 miles of bicycle lanes, paths, and tunnels. Davis has more bicycles than cars. Streets are better and safer for bikers because of clearer delineation between bike lanes and car lanes. A bike overpass over the freeway was built for easier access from north to south Davis. Davis competed and won against 23 other major cities in the U.S., to relocate the Bicycle Hall of Fame from New Jersey. In addition, the National Bicycle Museum is now located in Davis. As a result, Davis, since 2004, has consistently received a platinum 'Bicycle Friendly

Community' rating, the highest level, from the League of American Bicyclists.

The second point of pride for me is adding four more sister cities to Davis: Los Baños and Muñoz in the Philippines, Wuxi in China, and Sangju in South Korea; bringing the total to eight. I remain a part of Davis' sister cities program, as they have grown to rely on my hospitality and friendship and always request that I be a part of any delegation.

I was appointed by the Davis City Council in 2010 as the Ambassador to Davis Sister Cities. In the same year, I also became Special Assistant to UC Davis Vice Provost on University Outreach and International Programs. I continue to serve in both positions.

This Is My Quest...My Reachable Star!

Even after retiring in 2010, I continued my involvement in the community, and my civic work continues. I was actively involved in the formation of a new Korean Cultural School in Davis, which graduated its first class in 2014. I am a strong supporter of the new *Eskwela Natin* [Our School] in Sacramento, the first Filipino American Cultural School in Northern California. This also graduated its first class in 2014. I try to help whenever and wherever I can. Immediately after the Philippines was hit with typhoon Haiyan/Yolanda in 2013, I mobilized the Davis community to raise thousands of dollars to support victims in Tacloban, Iloilo, and Samar, similar to my efforts for the Asian tsunami victims in Sri Lanka in 2006.

Life has been good to me. I was blessed with a good husband and a happy married life for 30 years, raised children to become good contributing citizens of the world, and I am able to continue to be involved in their lives. I love to babysit and enjoy my growing number of grandchildren, my 'little Zs,' Zypher, Zach, Zhayne, Zoe and Zander and care for my 93-year-old mother.

"And I know if I'll only be true
to this glorious quest" — Lessons Learned

It was indeed an amazing journey paved with many exciting,

challenging opportunities, and obstacles overcome but a journey that provided wonderful experiences, and valuable lessons. Being a dreamer, I learned early in life that having goals, big and small, will lead me to where I want to go. It is like sailing, if you do not have a port destination in mind, you will just drift and never get there, but, if you know where you're going, it is easier to overcome all the obstacles along the way because you are focused on getting to your port of destination, your goal.

Look for mentors that can help you along the way to make your life better. "Ask and you shall receive." Listen to their advice. I have had many wonderful mentors who helped shaped my life and I cannot thank them enough: my mom, my teachers, my physical chemistry professor, the Adamsons, and more, too many to mention. I especially cannot forget to thank my late husband who taught me to be a good and caring politician. Bob Dunning, Davis political columnist wrote: "Vigfus, a giant in the civic life of Davis, was from a generation of citizens who saw service on the City Council as a duty, not some sort of exercise of ego...a solid citizen who approached each issue, not part of some grand scheme that had to fit into a specific political agenda...In his mind we were all equals, all deserving of having our voices heard." I strove to embody that sentiment in my political life. Vigfus told me that as a public servant I was there to serve, not just those who voted for me, but the entire community. People will be critical and insulting but to remember that I am a good person and that they are only critical of my position on issues. I need to listen to all sides of the issue before making a decision and to vote for what I believe is right and best for the city. I must remain courteous and respectful at all times, agree to disagree, be friendly, be nice, be kind, and treat others the way I want to be treated.

Have fun!

Leadership Tips

1. ***Help others the way you have been helped.*** We have all had lucky breaks, e.g. my professor recommending me for a Fulbright scholarship. Pass on the good luck many-fold, invest in the next generation. At the same time, acknowledge and thank the people who have helped you along the way to make your life better.

2. ***Learn how to talk to and relate to everyone equally.*** We are all human beings, whether laborer or professor, driver or diplomat. Treat people the way you want to be treated. Walk in someone else's shoes.

3. ***Institutionalize good will.*** To make sure good energy and initiatives become sustainable, formalize them and write them into clear processes, procedures and foundations.

4. ***Do not avoid conflict—face it head on, and stick to your principles.*** One day, even those who consider you as opponent may eventually concede if you are right.

5. ***Be involved, get involved.*** When you say "somebody will do it" be that somebody to get things done. Give back to deserving and needy people especially in the aftermath of disasters. Be a mentor to young people.

6. ***Go global.*** Take your ideas, vision, best practices and models of governance to other countries also, e.g. Twin/Sister City programs.

7. ***Politics is a tool to do good things but it is also seductive.*** In addition to being seductive, politics is addictive, and teeming with temptations. As a good and caring politician, keep yourself grounded at all times and be aware of what is important to serve your constituents. As a public servant, you are there to serve, not yourself, but your people and community. Make decisions based on what is best for them rather than what is expedient. Do what is right especially when nobody is looking. Be a role model as an upstanding citizen for your people in words, deeds and action.

Crossing Borders In Pursuit of Excellence

Mary Jane Alvero Al-Mahdi
Chief Executive Officer
Geoscience Testing Laboratory, UAE

Abstract

As Chief Executive Officer (CEO) of Geoscience Testing Laboratory (GTL), a multi-disciplinary testing company, I head a multimillion-dollar company based in the United Arab Emirates (UAE) with four branches and 20 site laboratories. GTL is a diversified independent testing laboratory providing specialized testing services in the fields of Construction Material Testing, Geotechnical Investigations, Environmental Analysis, and Microbiological Testing. GTL counts the prestigious Burj Khalifa, Downtown Dubai, and the Dubai Metro as but a few of our impressive projects. I have been instrumental in growing my team from eight to a staff of over 450. Becoming a CEO is the greatest leap that I have made in my career. In this chapter I discuss the management and leadership capabilities that are required to maintain our competitive edge and ensure customer satisfaction. Since our technical expertise is mainly the source of income, I am also the Chief Learning Officer (CLO) focusing on training and development for the employees. I also stress the need to pursue excellence through membership in professional associations. Despite my busy corporate role, I also find time to give back to the community through charitable causes. To help Filipinos in the UAE upgrade their skills with free education, I co-founded the Filipino Digerati Association, which was a recipient of the Philippines Presidential *Banaag* Award in 2012 accorded by His Excellency President Benigno Aquino Jr.

Introduction

I have been working at GTL for the last 15 years. In 2003, I rose to the position of CEO. With the leadership, management skills, and experiences I gained through 22 years in quality control and analytical laboratory services, I am able and confident about my ability to run every aspect of the business. Having the right attitude, making emotional connections, solid management practices, and employing logical thinking make me an effective female leader breaking through the glass ceiling.

My role as the CEO requires two important capabilities: management and leadership. I create core processes, plan strategies, develop a performance management system, organize, and plan. I consider this 'management.' As a leader, I create a compelling purpose, tell a story about aspirations and vision for the company, and articulate clear values and behaviors for the organization. An essential part of my role is to motivate and engage employees, give direction, and manage change. At the same time, I am adept at the human, relational aspects of leading the top team and interacting with all stakeholders; and that is 'leadership.'

I am a creative and visionary leader who understands what is working and what is missing in the organization. I strongly believe that achievement and value creation in the organization will not be sustained if one is without the other. It is my duty to build a culture. Work gets done through people, and people are profoundly affected by culture. A lousy place to work can drive away high performers. After all, they have their pick of places to work. And a great place to work can attract and retain the very best. Culture is built in dozens of ways and I set the tone. My every action sets cultural messages. The clothes I wear, whom I talk to, whom I fire, and whom I put up with and reward, all powerfully shape the culture of our organization.

Gender is not a hindrance in climbing the corporate ladder. My strongest traits as female CEO are assertiveness and persuasiveness. I have a strong need to get things done and I am willing to take risks. I am emphatic and flexible, as well as strong in interpersonal skills which enable me to read situations accurately and take information in from all sides. Being a female leader, I am able to bring my team around to my point of view because I genuinely understand and care about where they are coming from, and want them to feel understood, supported, and valued. Compared to some male executives, my level of engagement and support is higher. The women's leadership and communication styles are compatible with gender-diversity objectives in the corporate culture of an organization. The feminine way of leading helps me to achieve my duties and responsibilities, and helps the entire organization understand and implement the values that really matter.

What My Job Role Means to Me

My leadership strategy links to the organization's business strategy. We have established a leadership development program that trains, supports, and selects people who drive our business strategy. We build execution into the culture. Promoting a leadership culture of customer service, growth and development, entrepreneurship, and market offerings have made our business successful. We believe in our company philosophy that 'everyone is a leader' and each individual is given the responsibility to understand the business and make decisions which support the mission of the entire organization. Our leaders grow as the company grows.

The continuity of training and development among the employees and its results have a major impact on the return on investment of our organization. The experiences and the skills I have acquired in the laboratory testing business over 22 years have helped me establish a systemic corporate governance that demonstrates and provides the structure through which our organization pursues its objectives, while reflecting the context of the social, regulatory, and market environment. Governance involves monitoring the actions, policies and procedures of the company, and the alignment of interests among the stakeholders. My role requires ensuring that GTL management system is accredited to ISO 17025 and ISO 9001. ISO is the International Organization for Standardization which has responsibility for defining, establishing, and maintaining a quality assurance system for manufacturing and service industries.

As a leader, I integrate and develop strategic initiatives by matching portfolios to levels of leadership in the organization. I lead the growth strategy by weighing our organization's strategic options against its ability to launch new businesses, new approaches, and other forms of breakthrough performance. Planning the path towards a predetermined strategic goal while taking into account the quantity, timing, and mix of human resources, managers and leaders requires leadership. I lead the organization by creating a principle-centered environment with a culture of learning.

My focus on vision is one of my strong leadership qualities. The experiences and the skills I have acquired in the laboratory testing business have helped me understand how the organization operates currently and the future demands. I am a builder and a renovator.

Customer service has contributed to our growth as one of the biggest laboratories in the Middle East. I have trained my people to handle and surpass customers' expectations. The culture of understanding and integrity inside the organization is reflected in how we deal with our customers.

I am committed to leading through learning, and am also the CLO for the organization. Since our technical expertise is largely the source of our income; training and development for the employees are given emphasis. As a leader, part of my job is to inspire the people around me to push themselves—and, in turn push, the company to greatness. I model this by pushing myself.

The financial performance of our company made us strong in the market. The salaries of my employees have never been delayed. The scheduled payments for suppliers are strictly monitored. I set budgets within the firm, fund projects which support the strategy, and ramp-down projects which lose money or do not support the strategy. I consider carefully the organization's major expenditures, and manage the firm's capital.

How Did I Get in this Field

I earned a Bachelor of Science degree in Chemical Engineering in Manila, Philippines. Leaving my country for a greener pasture was a necessity for me in order to help my family back home. When I arrived in Dubai in 1992, my first job was Quality Control Inspector in a textile factory with a salary of AED 1000. With my competency, I realized that I was over-qualified for the job and I could do better. So I explored other work opportunities closely related to my profession.

After eight months of working at the textile factory, I was appointed as a Chemist in one of the most reputable construction quality control laboratories in the Middle East at that time. I was able to grow based on the day-to-day learning and working experiences in the laboratory. It was an interesting job for me. Technical know-how, information and knowledge had to be developed. My colleagues in the laboratory were all male but it was never a hindrance for me to grow and develop myself. It was a rare opportunity for a female to be working in a man's world 22 years ago.

I worked as a chemist for six years and then moved to GTL in 1998 as a Quality Assurance Officer. When I joined GTL, we were only eight employees. I was promoted to General Manager within six months and to CEO in 2003. The Chairman noticed my management and leadership skills when I started growing the organization. The number of accredited tests increased from nine to over a hundred today, manpower from eight to 450, one branch to four all over the UAE, and from a congested laboratory of 1200 square feet in Rashidiya to a sprawling 140,000 square feet lab in Dubai Industrial City.

Just like passing through a labyrinth, I have successfully faced challenges climbing the corporate ladder. Advancing my career through learning and investing in my education have helped me create opportunities for my employees as well as given me the ability to lead the business confidently. Every person who knows my success story is amazed at how I handled it and got through it. It is my passion, and with that passion comes the power to reach the stage where I am now. My triumphs prove that making dreams a reality is not bound by gender, in fact, at the end of the day, gender has nothing to do with my achievements and accomplishments. Hard work, dedication, and commitment to the dream are the true qualities for making and leaving a mark in any industry.

Professional Networks

In addition to professional qualifications, I have also extended my learning circle and professional community network through member-ship in industry and alumni associations. I have an MBA and a BS in Chemical Engineering. I am also a certified Six Sigma Black Belt, and an evaluator for Emirates Women Awards (2010-2014) for the Dubai Quality Group as well as the European Foundation for Quality Man-agement Excellence Model (EFQM 2010 Excellence). For ISO, I am a Quality Management System (QMS) Lead Auditor for ISO 9001:2008 and for ISO 14000 Environmental Management Systems. Other qual-ifications include ISO 18001 OHSAS and HACCP (Food Hygiene).

I am a member of numerous local and international professional or-ganizations including: European Foundation for Quality Management Excellence Model, Dubai Quality Group (member at large), Dubai Accreditation Center (representative), American Management Asso-ciation, USA (member), Society for Human Resources Management, USA (member), UAE Society of Engineers (member), Filipino Dige-rati Association (founder/board of director), and Adamson University Alumni Association (UAE and Manila chapter). Memberships in these professional networks ensure that not only I but also the rest of my technical team keep abreast with the latest quality standards.

Maintaining the Passion

I have the passion to lead and I believe in the growth of the people I work with. Seeing people grow to the next level of leadership is ful-filling. Sustaining the passion to lead wholeheartedly takes not only skill, it takes courage, inner strength, and spirit. Meanwhile, I moti-vate and engage people to discover themselves, their blind spots, and their behavior patterns in a safe, trusting, and professional environ-ment. At the core of my leadership is the core of my persona. I devel-op my leadership skills as I develop other emerging leaders. It involves motivation, introspection, reflection, integrity, and courage paired with self-awareness and the ongoing desire to learn. Purpose plays a critical role in maintaining my passion. Understanding the purpose of my passion will ultimately lead to success.

My passion to lead is extended to the community and results in empowerment of the community. I am one of the Filipino community leaders in the UAE. With my passion to lead is my desire to help. We organized a non-profit social club which promotes educational and professional advancement among Filipinos. I am one of the founders of this club and one of the volunteer trainers as well. It aims to help Filipinos working overseas enhance their skills by providing training without requiring the payment of tuition. The organization also prepares the Filipino migrant workers for their future by giving them workshops on entrepreneurship and livelihood programs which will help them during their reintegration into the Philippines.

Biggest Achievement

Of the many awards I have received (see list below), I treasure the Emirates Businesswoman Award, Runner-up in the professional category. The award was given in 2008 by Dubai Quality Group, under the patronage of Sheikh Ahmed Al Maktoum. The award aims to recognize the role of women in the economy of UAE and their contribution to its growth and development. It honors the contribution of those who have excelled in their field and inspires women to achieve their potential. I never even dreamt of this award but one of my employees nominated me. Completion of the required documents for this award helped me realize how far I have come. The Emirates Businesswoman Award has opened numerous opportunities for me to help, to lead, and to create new leaders. I was the first and, to date, the only Filipina executive who has received this award. This award has given me more confidence to represent our business in the market and gain trust from customers. There is no happiness more satisfying than when your contributions are recognized. Many women, especially Filipinas, have been inspired with my success story. I believe that I brought honor and pride to my country. With this achievement, I hope to inspire women to go outside the box and explore opportunities in their career.

Biggest Hurdle

I faced the biggest hurdle in my life when my father fell sick. All the savings of my family were spent on his illness. When he died, we were left with nothing and it was painful to watch my mom work hard just for us to survive. Because of this, I promised myself to study hard and at the same time to work part-time to cover my other expenses.

Today, my biggest hurdle in life is balancing my personal and career life. With loads of work responsibilities on my shoulder, I find it hard to enjoy quality time with my children. However, my family is my priority. In some situations, I sacrifice my work to meet the needs of my family.

Biggest Inspiration

My biggest inspiration in life is my mother. For me, she is a role model. I saw how she took the responsibilities of both a mother and a father when my father was bed-ridden till he died. She did her best to to provide a comfortbale upbringing for my siblings and myself. My mother worked hard and sacrificed a lot for the family. Her everlasting love for my dad is an inspiration for me to be the best wife for my husband and the best mother for my children. She made us proud of her by the values and ethics she instilled in us.

Ultimate Goal

One of my ultimate goals is to build a foundation for street children. This foundation will protect the rights of homeless children; provide food and shelter, and proper education to help them in building their future. I am in the planning stage at this moment. Funds will be generated from my own earnings and the networks and sponsors who believe in and buy into, my vision. Within the next seven years, the foundation is expected to be operational.

Awards and Recognitions

- **Gr8t Women Awards 2014, Middle East: Special Mention in the field of Geoscience.** Celebrates women who are pushing the boundaries of personal and professional excellence; acknowledged across the subcontinent as the ultimate accolade.

- **100 Most Influential Filipina Women in the World for 2013: Innovators and Thought Leaders Category.** Recognizes women who have broken new ground in the marketplace, have delivered new and unique applications of emerging technology transforming the way people think, or have improved the lives of others.

- **Emirates Woman, Woman of the Year Award 2013, Visionary Category.** Honors and celebrates the achievements of women in the business, arts and culture, philanthropic, and visionary fields in the UAE.

- *Pamana ng Pilipino* **Award 2012: Presidential Award for Filipino Individuals and Organizations Overseas.** Conferred on Filipinos overseas who have exemplified the talent and industry of the Filipino and have brought the country honor and recognition through excellence and distinction in the pursuit of their work or profession.

- **Emirates Businesswoman Award 2008: Runner-up, Professional Category.** Recognizes the role of women to the economy of UAE and its growth and development. It honors the contribution of those who have excelled in their field and inspire women to achieve their potential.

- **Blas Ople Award** *para sa Natatanging Bagong Bayani* **[Excellent New Heroes] 2009, Philippines.** Recognizes the most outstanding overseas Filipino worker who has been nominated, qualified, and excelled in the field of his/her profession as well as having the commitment for community and social service.

- *Bagong Bayani* [New Hero] Award for Outstanding Employee 2009, Philippines. Honors an employee who has earned the respect, trust, and confidence of his or her employer, superiors, and co-workers; has proven his or her competence by being promoted in status or in rank, or awarded citation for distinguished and outstanding performance.

- **Young Asian Achiever Award in UAE, 2011.** Highlights those in the age group of 25-45 who have made a mark for themselves in various fields: business, fashion designing, journalism, social work, and architecture.

- **International Achiever's Award 2012 (Global Adamsonian), California.** Recognizes the winner's distinguished and outstanding performance and accomplishments through unwavering and relentless efforts dignifying the profession, continually aiming to improve quality of life for fellow citizens in UAE. It recognizes achievements, brilliance, personal integrity, and dedication to work.

- **Most Distinguished Chemical Engineer 2009: Professional Regulation Commission, Chemical Engineering Board, Philippines.** Recognizes the winner's inspiring and outstanding works in field of strategic planning, quality system, and effective successful management of an enterprise in a foreign country. Moreover, the award recognizes the continuous quest for higher education to raise the level and expand the practice of the chemical engineering profession in UAE.

- **Woman of Substance 2009 Honoree,** *Illustrado* **Magazine, Dubai, UAE.** Recognizes the true measure of a woman, not only with her beauty, possessions, stature, or popularity; but the capacity of her heart, the strength of her character, the sharpness of her intellect, the charity of her dream and the largesse of her spirit. Her very substance.

Leadership Tips

1. *We can all be leaders.* I used to think that leaders were just born. The life struggles and the difficulties I have been through have made me a better leader and also enabled me to help others appreciate their potential. After winning the prestigious Emirates Businesswoman Award in 2008 and receiving a succession of recognitions, I realized that leaders are developed and shaped by life experiences. As we grow, we have the opportunity to influence others by our values and need to seize every opportunity to lead others to greatness.

2. *Leadership is the ability to get results.* Leaders emerge when people need other people to get results and leaders take action with no guarantee of success. Leaders can get off-track when they try to be everything to everyone. They should focus on their areas of strength and identify their weaknesses. They should bring people who will compliment their strengths and fill in the gaps. The power of good leadership forms not only a well-rounded individual but an accomplished team. True leadership comes not from position but from participation and effectiveness.

3. *Focus on purpose.* Effective leaders focus on purpose and take up activities that are critical to their success, such as networking. They need to be proactive in developing links. Links can serve as a means to a larger purpose, such as developing new business.

4. *Adopt a leader identity.* We become leaders by adopting a leadership identity and developing a sense of purpose. A person affirms leadership by taking purposeful action, taking responsibility for their choices. When a person's leadership competencies develop, opportunities reveal themselves and challenging assignments become more probable. Affirmation by others gives the person the determination to step outside a comfort zone and explore unaccustomed behaviors and new ways of exercising leadership. An absence of affirmation, however, lessens self-confidence and discourages people from seeking growing opportunities.

CREATING INITIATIVES FOR CHANGE

Suzie Moya Benitez

Trustee and Executive Director
Bayanihan Folk Arts Foundation

Abstract

Creating Initiatives for Change is a study of the impact of Bayanihan's initiatives to change selected aspects of how it does music and dance. As the Executive Director of the Bayanihan Folk Arts Foundation, it has been my honor to play a leadership role in these changes. Bayanihan has meant joy and pride for the Filipinos worldwide. Bayanihan has helped forged a united national identity for the variety of ethnic groups who live in the different corners of the Philippines' 7,100 islands. It has helped preserve and promote Philippine culture through the development of dance theaters. It attempts to bring folklore to theater by raising ethnic and regional dances to the level of stage art. Its idea of choreography and staging has included the adaptation of indigenous dance to the modern theater. I recognized that in order to ensure the sustainability of efforts at preserving cultural heritage, changes were needed to make Bayanihan performances compatible with sophisticated contemporary theatrical expectations. We initiated a study among a sample of high school students in Metro Manila for feedback on needed innovations and changes. The youth have indicated they are inspired by the beauty and richness of their culture, delivered to them in the language they know best. Increasing appreciation of our rich cultural heritage and cultivating positive values through dance and music among the young could bring unity, as it builds their ability to contribute to their own enrichment and participate in the growth and development of our communities and our country.

Introduction

In the 1950s, although independent of America, the Philippine land-scape was still very much a reflection of the American way of life, and daily life for the Filipinos was still dominated by American culture. Ball-room dancing, American jazz, and loud blaring music were the craze. The preservation of Philippine heritage became the primary goal of cultural educator Helena Z. Benitez. She was strongly influenced by her father Dean Conrado C. Benitez, an ardent nationalist, the first Filipi-no Dean of the University of the Philippines (UP) College of Liberal Arts, founding dean of the UP College of business administration, his-torian, lawyer and constitutionalist.

> Helen wanted every Filipino to share her passion and commitment for preserving indigenous culture. Her cultural endeavors ranged from encouraging cultural experiments at the Philippine Women's University (PWU) to influencing national policy as lobbyist or leg-islator. In time, she was to lay the foundations for establishing the dance legend that was to become known as the Bayanihan (Santos 1994).

Helena Z. Benitez would go on to be on the board of trustees of PWU, a senator and the first Filipina chairperson of the UN Commis-sion on the Status of Women.

The Dance Company

"*Bayanihan*" is an ancient Filipino tradition that means "working to-gether as a community for a common good." Central to the Filipino's social ethic, the PWU community headed by Helena encouraged stu-dents in the Physical Education club to perform Philippine dances. They performed for the first time a choreographed version of the rice cycle from planting to harvesting, threshing, winnowing, and pounding. Their performance showcased the beauty of Filipino life and work in the Philippine countryside.

A summer tour to Japan in 1956 headed by Dean Conrado was en-thusiastically received and gave birth to the idea of forming a folk dance group that would tour the world. Thus the Bayanihan dance group was formed <http://www.bayanihannationaldanceco.ph/>. Its first formal performance was during the World Confederation of Teaching Profession on August 1, 1956.

The Bayanihan Folk Arts Center

In 1957, the Bayanihan Folk Arts Center was organized with the following goals:

1. To conduct and coordinate research on Filipino culture.
2. To collect and preserve indigenous art forms and encourage their use in present day living.
3. To provide instruction for those interested in Filipino dance and music.
4. To give presentations or performances at home and abroad which would stimulate and enhance the appreciation and understanding of Philippine Art and Culture.

In order to achieve these goals, a more formal corporate body was formed, the Bayanihan Folk Arts Association, Inc. For more than 40 years, the association saw the dance company through 14 world tours and more than a hundred short tours. Tours were met with great world acclaim and earned various distinctions for their world class standards. It was my privilege as a young dancer to participate in several of these tours and to learn first-hand about the response of audiences and the efforts necessary to make presentations successful.

The Bayanihan Folk Arts Foundation

On October 7, 1997, the Bayanihan Folk Arts Foundation was established. The Foundation superseded the Association and a second generation of directors were appointed to lead and bring new methods and approaches to the "new" Bayanihan.

Realizing that the greatest challenge leaders face today is staying competitive and relevant to the rapidly changing taste of the new generation of audience, I opted to make a strategic move to increase the agility, creativity, and efficiency of the organization. The goal was to complement rather than completely replace the traditional organizational structure.

Restructuring the organization required veering away from leadership by individual specialists and moving towards a team concept. The first step was the creation of the artistic team. The artistic team was charged with constantly seeking new ways to remain on top in the highly competitive entertainment environment. I was able to apply concepts from my lecture series on "Corporate Image, Social Graces, Business Etiquette & Leadership Skills" to the evolution of the Bayanihan.

Despite the protests and personal attacks from a noisy minority of the Bayanihan alumni, I led its artistic team to focus on re-building and re-inventing the dance company. I was prodded by my late husband, Noel Benitez to stop seeking popularity and just listen to my inner voice. He would say: "If you believe in it, just do it!"

Reinventing Bayanihan through Various Development Programs

1. *The Culture Exchange Program*

The greatest challenge to us in this century is to give meaning to life and learn to grow with each other in this highly technologically developed world. Today, there is no denying that the world has become closely wired through modern communications and technology. Translating this to Bayanihan's mission, vision and goals, the company must strive to keep up with global developments through culture exchanges.

I am committed to investing human and material resources to access quickly cultural information needed by the Bayanihan. A primary way of accessing this information is through festival exchanges around the world. I have used cyberspace tools to participate in discussions with folk society leaders around the globe and to update global partners through its websites and e-news. Bayanihan welcomes foreign dance companies to perform back to back with them and arranges for these companies to teach and share their dances and music in workshops that are open and free to the public.

2. *Teaching and Touching Lives*

In order to use art, music, and dance as a catalyst for values education and for uplifting the nation's spirit through art and culture at the community level, I designed a social mobilization program called "Teaching and Touching Lives." I proposed the project in 2002 so that the Foundation could embark on an educational program that would bring the Bayanihan's programs to towns and cities all over the Philippines. In so doing, the project opened the doors for cultural exchanges involving top dance companies from other countries.

It also aimed to:

1. Develop the youth and take pride in one's own cultural heritage.

2. Build self-esteem and confidence in one's potentials.

3. Develop the young people's native talents particularly their love for dance, singing, and acting.

4. Develop a strong sense of identity and pride in being a Filipino.

5. Eradicate problems such as gambling, drinking, petty crimes, and drug use among idle youth in their communities.

6. Hone the skills of the young people and eventually help them organize their own theater groups focused on their provincial life and region.

3. *Sayaw Workshop*

The aim of the Sayaw workshop was to encourage the young and the young at heart to learn, love, and successfully achieve great things onstage while appreciating our rich cultural heritage, especially our music and dances. This annual summer workshop has drawn over 100 students each year.

4. *Innovation through New Creative Works*

In our effort to create a new image for Bayanihan that builds on more than 50 years of artistic life, the artistic team, under my direction, has pursued research and created new works each year. For its regular season production at the Cultural Center of the Philippines, Bayanihan created works that infused new technology.

5. Participation in World Dance Competitions

I took the initiative in bringing the company to compete in prestigious world dance competitions. The objective was to expose the dance company to the highest level of performance standards found in the world as well as to toughen the already high spirit of competitiveness among the core performers.

When Tita Helen Benitez asked me why I had to join world competitions when Bayanihan was already acclaimed internationally, I replied: "I want to test the mettle and competitiveness of our directors, performers, dancers, and musicians vis a vis the world's best." Immediately she gave her blessings.

6. Reduction of the Size of the Cast for Each Show

While earlier the dance company used a cast of 30 to 50 performers for a show, today Bayanihan can present a one-hour show with a select core of 10-12 members, and even with an uneven number of girls and boys. I encourage every member to be a tough and able performer who can handle fast changes and stand the punishing schedule as well as the demands of the new strenuous dance movements.

By limiting the number of the cast, the Bayanihan is able to accommodate two bookings at a time, locally or internationally and not be faced with a lack of cast members.

7. Infusion of Mix Media and Electronic Sound

Today, Bayanihan benefits from stage effects using mix media and innovating with new interpretations of electronic sounds. This is to achieve a NOW image, which we have found appeals to the young generation. To widen the audience base, Bayanihan innovated without losing the essence of folk. This strategy has aimed to expand the market and to widen the audience to reach its quotas. This has complimented the company's efforts to achieve sustainability.

8. Registration of All the Works of the Bayanihan

In the past there was free access to all the works and choreography of Bayanihan, but today all the works of Bayanihan are registered. The foundation owns the intellectual property rights to all the works, including choreography, music, concepts, titles, costume design and colors. We now have a marketing plan and the Bayanihan brand is strictly followed in logos, brochures, program formats, program notes, and uniforms. We have also established a separate office for business transactions that handles performance requests. This limits the individuals involved in booking to the booking officer and myself.

Survey Results

I initiated a survey early in the innovation process focused on a sample of high school students in Metro Manila. Questionnaires were completed after watching the Bayanihan's two-hour presentation "On Golden Wings of Dance" at the Cultural Center of the Philippines. The survey provided almost immediate feedback on some of the innovations.

I recognized that innovations increased the vulnerability of the Bayanihan and that the team needed assurance from its target market that indeed the innovations in dance and music helped the audience appreciate their Filipino heritage better. The study showed that 93% of the respondents enjoyed the innovative show and would be interested in attending future shows.

The study generated the following insights:

1. Bayanihan must work to keep Filipino folk dances and music relevant and alive for the next generation.

2. It must continue its research to come up with new exciting works.

3. It must expand into modern themes that relate to younger audiences.

4. It must increase visual impact by employing theatricalized folk forms acceptable to a wider audience base.

5. It must produce videos and sound recordings of international quality of its theater productions on the new DVD format.

6. Given the popularity of MTV, Bayanihan needs to create its own MTV as part of its marketing plans.

7. Bayanihan should continue to evolve, preserving Philippine music and dances through continuous research, creating from these materials new interpretations of the dances, adding theater, and elevating performances to an art form.

8. Bayanihan must continue its "Teaching and Touching Lives" program, sharing its modules on folk dance and music with elementary and high school students. Folk dance should not be merely a physical education requirement but can be a strong character building and formation educational vehicle.

9. Increasing the appreciation of our rich cultural heritage and cultivating positive values through dance and music among the young can bring unity among Filipinos and contribute to the growth and development of our nation.

10. Last but not the least, the results of the research can be used to build Bayanihan's future audience.

The insights from the research affirmed the need to invest in continued research on what appeals to young audiences.

Conclusion

The Bayanihan was declared the national folk dance company of the Philippines in 1998 by virtue of Republic Act 8626. To date, it is an eight-time World Dance Grand Prize Winner. The Bayanihan has been a consistent winner in world competitions since 2002. The Bayanihan is now ready to respond to a new generation with different perceptions and inclinations. It is able to communicate in the language of the 21st century. In the future, the Bayanihan can be expected to evolve into a fundamentally new form of organization, peopled by leaders who will grab every opportunity to act now and transform to meet the challenges of the future. Helena Benitez (2009) noted: "People and their culture evolve in tune and in time with generational succession. Those who remain frozen in time and cultural dimension are soon left behind. They become irrelevant and uninteresting and uninspiring. They cannot excite new audiences." Thankfully, Bayanihan has avoided getting into this rut.

Bayanihan and its new leadership under my direction have chosen to be agile in meeting the demands of a continually changing theater landscape. The Artistic Team, with Isabel Santos, Ferdinand Jose, Melito Vale Cruz and myself, continue to be proactive, on our toes, to be steps ahead in learning, re-learning, injecting, deleting, changing and constantly improving the Bayanihan. We are convinced the Bayanihan represents the best of what Filipinos can achieve.

Former President Fidel V. Ramos, who signed the law declaring Bayanihan as the national folk dance company, said: "Today, the word Bayanihan is practically synonymous with not only excellence in dance or cultural promotion but also excellence of the Filipino. It has given us cause to be proud of our heritage and proud of ourselves as a people."

The most enduring legacy of an institution such as the Bayanihan Folk Arts Foundation and its performing arm, the National Folk Dance Company of the Philippines, is a continuing development process that results in change by empowering people to seek the best for themselves, while searching for ways to grow and looking for ways to perform what is best for their communities and their country. I do not have to be told that I have a big responsibility.

Today, that inner voice continues to push me onward. My late husband Noel Benitez would remind me time and time again: "If in your principled center you truly believe it to be right, then don't fear, **Just Do It !!!**"

Leadership Tips

1. *Make a choice to dream big.* When Bayanihan Founder, Dr. Helena Z. Benitez invited me to help the dance company become sustainable, she prodded me not to be afraid to dream big. "Soar," she said. Indeed, achieving one's dreams and goals starts with making the choice to dream BIG, taking the risk, and moving out of one's comfort zone. Every endeavor requires an effort to always do better than the ordinary. Do not just set goals that are easily achieved!

2. *Overcome your detractors.* Only when one dares to take risks can one achieve significance. Oftentimes we worry about criticism that can be hurtful to us, thereby limiting our creative initiatives. Do not allow criticisms or detractors to suppress your moves or to turn success into impossible dreams. Of course, it is easier said than done. In my own personal experience, even those whom I thought would support me, made up untrue tales to block the strategies of the "new" Bayanihan. But in the end, making a choice to achieve what one thinks unachievable and being persistent and honest in the purpose one has set is worth the hurt and pain.

3. *Try infusing new technology and stay up to date.* There is no limit to one's creative imagination. Infusing new technologies to your existing works will keep you at par with the rest and the best in the world. There is room for innovation, for new research, and for new interpretations of masterpieces. In Bayanihan's case a group of alumni often protested the "new look" in our productions. Only when the shows got rave reviews and Bayanihan started winning top prizes internationally did protest stop. Innovations can always widen your audience base.

A Guided Path: My Career in Medicine, Research and Public Service

Carmencita M. David-Padilla, M.D.

Professor of Pediatrics, College of Medicine,
University of the Philippines (UP) Manila

Abstract

As a young and soft-spoken girl, I had strict parents and a disciplined education at the College of the Holy Spirit, a convent school. If not for Martial Law that was declared in 1972, my parents would not have allowed me to pursue college at the University of the Philippines Diliman, the bastion of student activism. I was sure of what I wanted in life: to be a doctor, pursue Pediatrics, get married, start a family and be a neonatologist practicing in Manila. Everything was on schedule except for the last one. Embedded in three short vignettes in this chapter are 10 important life lessons: 1) Dream; 2) Life is made up of choices; 3) Have a high tolerance for frustration; 4) No man is an island; 5) Leadership is a critical element of a successful program; 6) Believe in other people; 7) Service to humanity is noble; 8) Time management; 9) Enjoy life; and 10) Prayer is a companion. In God's plan, there is a purpose for every person in this world. So interpret life in this spirit.

Life is a journey.

Life is an adventure.

Life is good to live.

I was a quiet, soft-spoken student in elementary and high school. I spent my formative years with very strict parents and was educated in a convent school run by German nuns, the College of the Holy Spirit located in Mendiola, next to Malacañang Palace where the President resides and holds office. The world outside my immediate home, however, was in turmoil the last two years of my high school. Student protests happened daily throughout the city, and the center of it all was the University of the Philippines (UP). The newspapers were flooded with stories of the 'First Quarter Storm,' a series of protests in January 1970 where students launched protests in several areas of Metro Manila to protest against the policies and programs implemented by the administration of President Ferdinand Marcos (Solis 2010). Since my high school was next to Malacañang, we witnessed all the rallies, the shouting marches, the bonfires and the protest slogans painted on the walls of our school as well as the nearby schools: San Beda College, La Consolacion College and Centro Escolar University.

I was set to go to the University of Santo Tomas for my college degree because the University of the Philippines (UP) was not an option. My parents were concerned about the protest rallies since UP was the bastion of student activism. The historic uprising of UP Diliman students, known as the Diliman Commune, was the height of the protests when professors and staff stood in solidarity with transport workers in February 1971 (Tagiwalo 2011). Then in September 1972, Ferdinand Marcos declared Martial Law when I was a senior in high school. The social unrest ceased almost immediately. If not for martial law, my parents would not have allowed me to pursue college at UP upon graduation from high school in 1973. At that time, the only thing that was clear in my mind was that I wanted to become a doctor. Entering UP was the beginning of a new journey in my life.

Life Lessons

I would like to share three short stories with life lessons. The first is on how I landed in the field of genetics. The second story is on newborn screening and the last story is on birth defects surveillance.

On becoming a geneticist

Early on, I wanted to become a doctor and so I did—a pediatrician. I wanted to become a neonatologist—a specialist who takes care of very sick newborns and premature babies. Everything was set for my training in London after my residency. But I guess God had other plans for me. In the early 1980s, the lone geneticist at the Philippine General Hospital (PGH) unexpectedly died of cancer, leaving a vacancy in our department. There was only one other doctor who could have stepped into genetics but she got married and this changed her plans. On a bright sunny day in May 1987, I was summoned to the office of the Chair of the Department of Pediatrics where the four senior professors, Amelia Fernandez, Luis Mabilangan, Carmelita Domingo and the late Perla Santos Ocampo were waiting for me. Being the youngest faculty member, I was convinced, maybe the correct word is coerced, by my mentors to change my course from neonatology to genetics. Although it was a very difficult decision for me to agree to pursue a scientific field that was less traveled at that time, 28 years ago, I said "Yes." Why? Because I am of that generation when the young MUST follow the recommendations of the old. Regrets? I have none. I am happy I made that difficult decision in 1987. It was a major turning point in my life.

I was offered a fellowship in Clinical Genetics at the Royal Alexandra Hospital for Children, Sydney, Australia. Upon my return from Australia, I had the sole responsibility of setting up genetic clinical services at the PGH and various genetic laboratories that were eventually moved to the National Institutes of Health (NIH). First I set up the Cytogenetics Laboratory in 1990 at PGH and this was transferred to NIH in 1997. Then I set up the first Newborn Screening laboratory in 1997, a Biochemical Genetics laboratory in 1999, and a Molecular Genetics laboratory in 2000, all at NIH. Then I set up a series of newborn screening laboratories throughout the country because of the expansion of the newborn screening program: in Iloilo (2005) to service the Visayas, in Davao (2010) to service Mindanao, in Angeles City (2011) to service Northern Luzon, and recently in Batangas (2013) to service Southern Luzon.

Had I pursued the path of a neonatologist, I would be working in the nursery of two or three Metro Manila hospitals taking care of patients only from these hospitals. Because I made the difficult decision of becoming a geneticist, I have been able to set up all of these laboratories to serve patients all over the country.

Here are my first two lessons.

LESSON NO 1. *You must dream.* It is free. Not all of our dreams will come true but it is wise to aim for something. Life cannot be free-wheeling. Just like with any relationship, you have to invest time with yourself and think of what you want to do in life.

LESSON NO. 2. *Life is made up of choices.* In every turning point in one's life, we have a choice. The best choice is not always the easiest. The right choice is not necessarily what we want. Sometimes the choice is not what we want but somehow, there is a voice in our heart that tells us that this is the right one.

The Newborn Screening Story

Because of my special training in genetics, I became instrumental in setting up the newborn screening pilot project in 24 hospitals in the Philippines in 1996. Of the many accomplishments in my career, this was the most significant since data generated from my research was the basis for Republic Act No. 9288 or the Newborn Screening Act of 2004. It is now being offered in over 5,000 hospitals throughout the country and has saved more than 90,000 babies from mental retardation and death. Newborn screening is a test done on newborns after 24 hours of life. A few drops of blood are drawn from the baby's heel and examined to test if a baby will have a condition that will cause mental retardation or death.

Newborn bloodspot screening was introduced by U.S.-based researcher Dr. Robert Guthrie in the early 1960s. Newborn screening subsequently spread throughout the world especially in the developed countries. In Asia-Pacific, the newborn screening started in New Zealand, Japan and Australia in the mid '60s. There is a universal recommendation now that newborns be screened for a set of diseases that can be treated at birth, thus preventing mental retardation and death.

Starting a new program in a country beset with other equally important health problems was a challenge. Upon the advice of Dr. Alfredo Ramirez, Dean of College of Medicine, I visited the Department of Health (DOH) in 1992, soon after I arrived from my training in Genetics. I talked to the DOH Assistant Secretary Alejandro de Leon, who was also a professor at UP College of Medicine. I introduced the concept of newborn screening. He was very accommodating but at the end, he said, "No data, no policy." He said newborn screening would compete with existing health programs of the country. I went home disappointed. Of course it was clear that I needed another entry point.

In 1996, together with my mentor Dr. Carmelita Domingo, we started a pilot research project to generate data for the country. We invited all the hospitals in Metro Manila -- 75 hospitals -- to a meeting to explain the project and its merits to the future generations in the country. Only 28 responded to our letter and eventually only 24 hospitals joined the pilot project. The group named itself the Newborn Screening Study Group and the project was called the Philippine Newborn Screening Project (Padilla and Domingo 2002; Padilla, Basilio and Oliveros 2009).

The group was excited because we were able to gather good data after only two years. We gave the data to DOH. Unfortunately although declared as good data, the DOH was not ready to take on the project. The DOH had other priorities that were equally important. So the leaders of the 24 hospitals decided to expand the program to other hospitals on their own. A program with a slogan "Save your baby from mental retardation and death" was definitely attractive to the public (Padilla, Krotoski and Therell 2010). By 1999, there were 69 hospitals; by 2003, there were 323 hospitals offering newborn screening. But there were over 5,000 hospitals that needed to be reached. At this rate, it would mean my whole career life and beyond.

Without a public policy on newborn screening, some private hospitals took advantage of the situation and overpriced the cost of the test. Soon, fly-by-night laboratories were being set up. Although DOH repeatedly took the position that a law was needed to implement this program, it was not ready to take it on as a national program nor integrate it into the public health delivery system. It was at this time I decided to make a bold move of enrolling in a Master of Arts in Health Policy Studies at the College of Public Health, UP Manila. I considered this a step towards gaining the skills to write policies on newborn screening. The World Health Organization had already adopted the principles of universal screening set by Wilson and Junger in 1968. A law in place in the Philippines would be able to mandate the offering of newborn screening throughout the country.

I wrote the draft bill on the nights of February 13 and 14, 2003 during an official trip in Singapore. I circulated the draft bill to as many stakeholders I could reach, including DOH officials, lawyers, policy staff of senators and congressmen, physicians, midwives and nurses. When I finalized the draft bill on newborn screening, I gave it to a former DOH Secretary and now Senator Juan Flavier, whom I chose as the best person to lobby the bill. I had to deal with legislators and their staff who were predominantly male. I personally lobbied at both the Senate and Congress and never in my whole lobbying stint did I have to bribe anybody. It is possible! I patiently waited in their offices or outside the plenary halls that are seen on television. Lobbying for a bill was an experience. Being a woman probably became my strength at the end. Considered as one of the fastest bills to be legislated at that time, it was God after all who said, "It is time!" It is history now that the implementation of the newborn screening is guided by Republic Act No. 9288 or the Newborn Screening Law signed on April 6, 2004. Now, every newborn in the Philippines has the opportunity to be screened and be saved. The lead agency is DOH and testing is covered by insurance for members of the Philippine Health Insurance Corporation. To this day I am still very much part of the national program as a technical partner. There are many caveats in this 18 year history of newborn screening. I do want to share some lessons.

Lesson No 3. *One must have a high tolerance for frustration.* Do not let frustrations get you down. For the past 18 years of the newborn screening program, I have a litany of disappointments that I can discuss in another paper. The important thing is that one must learn how to get up and move on. If I had given up in 1992 after that first meeting with the Assistant DOH Secretary, we would not have the national program today. In 2003, just before I gave the bill to Senator Flavier, DOH Secretary Manuel Dayrit asked me why I needed a law. My response was that a law would ensure the mandate remains immune to changes of political administrations.

LESSON NO 4. *Although written by John Donne in the 19ᵗʰ century in his Meditation XVII, the cliché "No man is an island" is true for all generations.* I may have been the face for newborn screening but how to get 5,000 hospitals to follow was a challenge. Legislation was one strategy. But getting the program to where it is right now, needed a lot of good will. The people implementing the program must believe it is a good program. It cannot be offered merely as lip service. I had to rely on a lot of people to set up the newborn screening service in the best and most professional manner possible in their hospital or community.

LESSON NO 5. *Leadership is a critical element of a successful program.* The newborn screening program has a team of leaders. Each one of the 5,000 hospitals implementing the program has a coordinator. He or she must implement the program in his or her hospital. Doctors, nurses and midwives must follow them. I cannot implement a national program without a team of leaders.

Can you be a leader? The answer is "Yes." You can also be a leader. I was not a leader in elementary or high school. It was in college when I started holding key positions in student organizations. I was always a class officer through medical school and eventually became a treasurer of the Medicine Student Council. By residency training in pediatrics, I emerged as a promising leader. I eventually became a chief resident, the assistant of the Chair of the department in implementing training, service and research.

At present, I hold three key positions. I am the Executive Director of the Philippine Genome Center, a new office that cuts across all campuses of the University of the Philippines <www.pgc.up.edu.ph>. I am the Director of the Newborn Screening Reference Center at the National Institutes of Health <www.newbornscreening.ph>. This office is the technical partner of the Department of Health in the implementation of the national newborn screening program. Lastly, I am Interim Director of the Institute of Health Innovation and Translational Medicine of the Philippine California Research Institutes at the Commission on Higher Education <www.ched.gov.ph>. All these three positions I did not apply for. I was chosen to lead.

Some jobs are applied for and you have to prove that you have done exceptionally well in your other positions. Some positions are by invitation because you are nominated or selected to lead. Regardless of whether you applied for a leadership position or nominated to the position, the expectations are the same.

So what makes a good leader? A leader is creative. A leader thinks outside the box, a thinker of new solutions for old problems. Everybody starts at the bottom of the ladder. Consistency in excellence is critical. You cannot be a performer today and be a lazy employee next month. It does not matter if your task is minor; do it well all the time. You have to project the image that you are responsible and can assume a bigger role in the hierarchy of the company. In your job do not be afraid to speak up. Participate actively in discussions. Always put your best foot forward. Nothing really comes on a silver platter.

Birth Defects Surveillance Project

The Birth Defects Surveillance Project is another favorite of mine. Birth defects are physical defects that are obvious to the eye. The cleft lip and palate are the ones that most people are familiar with but there are hundreds of other conditions that can be identified. The important thing is that they are identified and remedied by the public health system. Data shows that birth defects or congenital anomalies (medical term), have remained to be in the top 10 causes of infant mortality for the past 50 years. However, there is insufficient data to develop public policies resulting in legislation. After several attempts to launch a birth defects surveillance project,I managed to do a pilot project similar to the newborn screening program but not enough to write and lobby for policy.

LESSON NO 6. *Believe in other people.* In March 2014, I was in Negros

Occidental to deliver a message at the launch of the province-wide pilot on the Birth Defects Surveillance Project. The governor, mayors, municipal health officers, chiefs of hospitals and representatives from both private and government hospitals were in attendance. Their task was to conduct the pilot project, generate the data and hopefully, their data will be the basis of future policies on the care of patients with birth defects.

Governor Alfredo Maranon asked, "Why Negros Occidental?" My answer was very simple. I said, "I believe in your people; they are passionate, dedicated, committed, outside the box thinkers, responsible. I just know that Negros Occidental is the right place." Negros Occidental is home to 11 exemplary awardees and 13 outstanding awardees in newborn screening. The leadership created new ordinances to ensure newborns in Negro Occidental are given the opportunity to live a normal life. They had to come up with creative strategies to enroll in the program as many babies in their province.

At the presidential table, Governor Maranon then asked me, "What else can I do?" I said "Write ordinances that will institutionalize all the activities in your province; and provide scholarships for students who will help your province push forward this project." The next comment was very interesting. He said, "I do not necessarily want the brightest. I want the average students who have a heart, the heart to help Negros." Governor Maranon knew that to be an effective leader, he had to think beyond the project, come up with sustainable measures beyond his term of office, and provide enabling tools that will guarantee the success of their model project.

Passion is important. The people around you will know if you are passionate about your cause.

Allow me to conclude by sharing a few more lessons learned from my professional career.

LESSON NO 7. *Service to humanity is noble.* When I was interviewed for admission at the UP College of Medicine, I was asked: "Why be a doctor?" I said, "I want to serve humanity." It was just an answer to an interview question. It was hard to explain how I would put this into action. But my career has more than proven to me the nobility I have felt and continue to feel through my work as a doctor and a geneticist. In the end, I have merged my passion for caring for at-risk newborns—not as a neonatologist, but as a geneticist and working with birth screening and surveillance.

LESSSON NO 8. *Time management.* Life cannot be all work. Life must have a balance.

LESSON NO. 9. *Enjoy life.* Find the time to enjoy your family. A balance in life is crucial. In a 2005 magazine interview, I was asked "What do you do to unwind given your very busy schedule?" I spend the very little free time that I have with my family. We go to the mall, or the gym, watch a movie or simply stay at home. During business trips, I take my son along so we can be together. We both love seeing new places and experiencing new things together. It is our way of bonding despite our very busy schedules. One of the most unique experiences was probably in Cagayan De Oro. My son and my staff organized a rafting activity. My concept of rafting was simply to sit in this big raft and float on the river. What they did not tell me was that you have to jump off a bridge, suspended 35 feet in the air to get to the raft, after which you had to navigate through the rapids. At first, I could not do it, but my staff and my son convinced me to do it. The next activity was 'caving.' But to get inside the cave, you first had to rappel down to reach the Cueva de Oro, which was only 100 feet below. And we did not just walk through the cave, we had to crawl through small holes, jump into pools of water, and swim through tunnels to be able to get to the other end of the cave. All of this we did in complete darkness, aided only by the flashlights connected in our safety hats. It is like *Fear Factor*, but I told myself, "I've dealt with other forms of stressors, I will survive this one!" It was a different experience. Everyone should try adventures like these to reduce stress but do not do these things on your own! We had the guidance of local tour guides.

LESSON NO 10. *Prayer is a companion.* In the many trials in my life, prayer has been my companion. I believe that God always answers our prayers. Sometimes, *He* readily says "Yes" because it is our destiny. Sometimes, *He* gives something slightly different. And sometimes, *He* says "No" because *He* has something better for us. I believe that in God's plan, there is a purpose for every person in this world.

God has a plan for you!

LEADERSHIP TIPS

1. ***You must dream. It is free.*** Not all of our dreams will come true but it is wise to aim for something. Life cannot be freewheeling. Just like with any relationship, you have to invest time with yourself and think of what you want to do in life.

2. ***Life is made up of choices.*** In every turning point in one's life, we have a choice. The best choice is not always the easiest. The right choice is not necessarily what we want. Sometimes the choice is not what we want but somehow, there is a voice in our heart that tells us that it is the right one.

3. ***One must have a high tolerance for frustration.*** Do not let frustrations get you down. The important thing is that one must learn how to get up and move on.

4. *Although written by John Donne in the 19th century in his Meditation XVII, the cliché "No man is an island" is true for all generations.*

5. *Leadership is a critical element of a successful program.*

6. ***Believe in other people.*** They are passionate, dedicated, committed, outside the box thinkers, responsible.

7. ***Service to humanity is noble.*** A true leadership career will prove to you the nobility of work and dedication to the human race.

8. ***Time management.*** Life cannot be all work. Life must have a balance.

9. ***Enjoy life.*** Find the time to enjoy your family, they are critical as well—beyond just bonding and solace.

10. ***Prayer is a companion.*** In the many trials of life, God always answers prayers—sometimes readily, sometimes in a different manner.

Pakikisama: Building Relationships, Building an Industry

Adela Sering-Fojas
CEO and Co-Founder of SevenSeven Corporate Group
with
Miguel Fojas

Abstract

My beloved father often emphasized the adage 'lead by example.' He has inspired me to assume full responsibility for whatever I do and to lead with passionate initiative, resilient perseverance, and relentless fortitude.

Although my father can no longer witness my corporate achievements and individual successes in life, he served as an authentic role model and a genuine inspiration for my leadership. The predominantly male, and often cutthroat, information technology (IT) industry presented challenges to me as a Filipina minority pioneer, but having a positive attitude, an authoritative presence, and a fair disposition has contributed to my success in this environment.

My father taught me to have an open mind and a healthy curiosity, and to learn various networking qualities centered around the Filipino ethos of *pakikisama*. These qualities helped me make the transformation from being a successful textile buyer in the garment industry to becoming a prominent Filipina-American leader in the IT service sector of global banking, financial services, and insurance.

I am the CEO and co-founder of the Seven Seven Corporate Group, an exclusive IT developer platform provider of a sophisticated offshore business operation that caters to top financial services institutions around the world. Founded in 1996, the Seven Seven Corporate Group offers Information Technology Enterprise Solutions (ITES). I founded the firm with the belief that our fellow

Filipinos and Filipinas with IT talent can compete with the very best in the U.S. market. The firm has since crated thousands of jobs and established offices in the U.S., Philippines, and Singapore.

My emphasis on ethical business practices, dedication to exceptional customer service, and attention to the importance of interpersonal relationships has produced profitable results and made Seven Seven Corporate Group a leading corporate pioneer in next IT generation of Knowledge Process Outsourcing (KPO) services.

I have led by example and modeled an ethical style of management, key to the Seven Seven Corporate Group's being a consistent recipient of DiversityBusiness.com's Top Business Award. I have been recognized in the Top 50 Asian-American Business Awards in 2011 in New York City. I have also been named as one of the 100 Most Influential Filipina Women in the United States in 2009 and as one of the Global FWN100 in 2013 by the Filipina Women's Network.

This chapter touches on my entrepreneurial career as a Filipina pioneer and an intercultural leader within the IT and Business Process Outsourcing (BPO) industries. As the CEO, I have had predominant responsibility for meaningful interpersonal interactions with our Fortune 500 clientele, a major factor in Seven Seven's exponential growth during the past seventeen years. The principle of *pakikisama* has been very important in being able to adjust to the dynamics of different countries. This invaluable principle of networking truly helped me expand the of our firm and grow this industry that employs a total of one-million Filipinos and Filipinas, and is expected to contribute US$18 billion in service revenues to the Philippines at the end of 2014.

I shared the stories that shaped my leadership with my son Miguel, who is studying for his MBA in International Business at the Antwerp Business School in Belgium. He tells my story in his own words.

Introduction

My mother is always a ball of energy the moment she gets up from bed to start each day anew, but this morning as she switched off the ringing alarm on one of her two mobile phones, she is also contemplative and nostalgic. She knows she must remain alert for any customer service issues from any one of Seven Seven's clients and check for email updates on her mobile phones. But occasionally, she finds time to pause and wonder at the beautiful summer day and reflect on the blessings in her family and professional life, and think of what has led her here, including a particular incident that occurred during her school days at Siena College in Manila.

The Unforgettable Flag Ceremony

One of her fondest memories was about a congratulatory flag ceremony that provided some good luck and somehow turned a corner in her life. She felt rather nervous because she sensed (rightly or wrongly) that her name might have been on the superintendent's list of students to be expelled. In the Philippines, expulsion from any esteemed academy, like Siena College, would mean that a student is ostracized by other academic institutions.

She genuinely enjoyed being a student at Siena College; she clearly did not desire to send any a damaging impression that would upset her school administrators. She did not want to be considered a reckless rebel, which could result in expulsion by Sister Felicia, the superintendent. Since she genuinely craved to maintain her *amor propio* [self-image] at Siena College intact, she looked for a strategy to evade expulsion and avoid bringing *hiya* [disgrace] on her Filipino family's surname.

Unexpectedly, she saw some schoolmates trampling on a plastic bag while Sister Felicia monitored the flag ceremony activities. Sister Felicia was distracted by the plastic bag and she obviously expected someone to pick up the plastic trash, which was starting to whistle in the wind. Since no one took action, my mother decided to pick up this piece of plastic trash from the ground and to place it in the nearest trash bin. Sister Felicia recognized her by name for what she called a leadership action. My mother had discovered the importance of taking action, and she endeavored to build a solid rapport with the school administrators.

She had realized that her survival was contingent on creating meaningful relationships. Building, maintaining, and sustaining relationships became a central element in formulating a distinct leadership strategy revolving around my grandfather's (her father) proverbial saying, "Lead by example." This principle of networking helped facilitate the prosperous growth and strategic success of the company, which she was to establish years later, the Seven Seven Corporate Group.

My Beginnings as a Filipina Pioneer

Her narrative as a Filipina pioneer began with the story of her first job doing clerical work. At the young age of twenty, my mother emigrated from the Philippines and travelled to the United States under direct orders from my grandfather. Often characterized as a military man, he has truly motivated her to formulate a regimented routine in fulfilling her responsibilities. However, she failed to carry out my grandfather's disciplined outlook on life in the beginning.

My grandmother arranged my mother's first job in America: working for an infant clothing manufacturer in the Garment District of New York City. She worked as a clerk from 8 AM to 5 PM. The night was spent enjoying time with friends and barely sleeping. As a result, she usually arrived at work feeling exhausted. Fortunately, her Filipina colleagues covered for her by completing her clerical duties while she slept in the storage space of the company. She felt gratitude to her Filipina colleagues for helping her make the adjustment to the American work environment, and to my grandmother for placing her in the company of Filipinas. In hindsight, she now recognizes that her Filipina colleagues were practicing the relational dynamics of *pakikisama*, cooperating for the greater good of significant others. Without the Filipina *pakikisama*, her adjustment would have been more traumatic.

As one of her duties, she was asked to perform the exceptionally tedious task of numbering pages from a logbook of corporate purchase orders for this infant clothing company. Unfortunately, one day when she reached order 999, she did not realize that she skipped to the number 2000. As a result of her error, she was terminated from this job. She learned the importance of attention to details.

She felt determined to learn from her mistake by being more ambitious and by aspiring to become a successful textile buyer for a fashion design manufacturer in the infant clothing industry.

A Filipina Businesswoman in the Making

She remembered my grandfather's advice to assume responsibility for everything that she did. She learned that she must become more detail-oriented and more organized in her approach toward achieving desirable behaviors such as having a regimented work ethic, a disciplined mindset, and a positive mentality. More importantly, she realized that her negligence could lead to a serious loss of corporate profits regardless of the selected industry.

Although my grandfather can no longer share in the joy of my mother's corporate achievements and individual successes in life, he has always served as an authentic role model and a genuine inspiration for her leadership actions. In retrospect, she said, she learned that strategic business relationships have a truly pivotal connection between the strategic effectiveness of an influential leader and the desirable result of creating sustainable value for the organization.

Since she had been raised in a traditional household with an ancestral family history of Filipino politicians who campaigned for positive change in the Philippines, she fully understood the extraordinary significance of maintaining smooth interpersonal relationships with both adversaries and supporters. She learned the value of relational leadership and how meaningful interaction leads to sustainable personal and business relationships. Once she had grown a genuine appreciation for influential people with strong political personalities, she valued the importance of cultivating invaluable interpersonal skills. She sincerely believed that strong interpersonal skills helped establish the needed authoritative presence of an effective organizational leader who can also serve as an authentic role model for others to emulate. She learned that positive relationships among colleagues and clients and among administrative employees and strategic resource individuals create value for everyone involved. She learned that strong interpersonal skills could help create the authoritative presence needed by an effective organizational leader.

Rising through the ranks of an infant clothing company helped my mother realize that clerical work or any organization's back office business operations did not provide her with the passion she needed. What she genuinely desired was to be part of the hustle and bustle of being with people with more knowledge and experience than she had.

Through the years, she came to realize that strong interpersonal skills could offer an influential presence in the course of any business-related discussions with executives who were able to assist her in providing sustainable value. She also believes that the ethical principle of trust is required for meaningful interaction with business relationships if one intends to generate profitable results for the company. Using her ethical style of salesmanship, she relies upon an expansive network to ensure profitable customer service results where trust is the most important ingredient.

In thinking about growing the industry she chose, my mother recognized that she could add more value by persistently interacting with service clientele and delivering superb customer service results for any organization's front office needs. She became proactive by "floating" around the work floors to search for and build more connections. She continues to operate under good faith principles commonly associated with ethical salesmanship and remain convinced that she must conduct all business affairs with a great moral sense of integrity. This reputation of being ethical and operating with integrity has contributed to the growth of the company she established.

The Metamorphosis of a Filipina Entrepreneur

My mother became a successful textile buyer for an infant fashion company by being energetic and sustaining interactive business relationships and interpersonal connections in New York City. Then her long time mentor, a senior executive in a global company in the Financial District of Manhattan who had known her since before she was married, presented her with a bewildering but irresistible proposition that would capitalize on the IT knowledge and talents of Filipinos and place them with promising job opportunities that would allow them to progressively excel in the highly competitive Wall Street environment.

At the time, her mentor referred her to a firm that had a job vacancy for a computer programmer. Fortunately my mother knew of a programmer who was competent and had experience in developing computer mainframe application programs. Her mentor was required to identify a representative agent for the applicant and he listed my mother using her maiden name and the rest, as they say, is history. Listing her as the representative agent for the job candidate was an excellent move that influenced the course of my mother's life and led to the creation of the Seven Seven Corporate Group. The investment banking firm decided to hire the applicant and the hiring executive of the firm asked her mentor about Adela Sering, the representative agent for this particular job candidate. She received a phone call from the global investment banking office asking if she represented the afore-mentioned job applicant. She said "Yes." Evidently, she impressed the firm's hiring executive. As a result, she received a fair commission for placing the right job candidate to fill the vacancy. Her mentor believed that if she repeated this recruitment procedure for other job-seeking applicants, she could make a profitable markup from several global investment banking businesses within the New York metropolitan area and build a business out of it. Based on the strong sales skills she had acquired and lessons she had learned in the Garment District of New York City, she decided to roam around the back offices of firms to pro-actively search for IT program managers who might be interested in hiring talented Filipino application developers. After finding staff positions for four Filipino programmers, she resigned from her position as a textile buyer and initiated a new professional career as a Filipina entrepreneur in the IT service industry. With the encouragement of her mentor and the euphoric experience of placing four successive job requirements, she established the Seven Seven Corporate Group.

The Ingenuity of the Filipino and Filipina

Whenever she has been faced with a controversial challenge in any business negotiation, being a Filipina leader has repeatedly served as a unique intercultural differentiator that has given her a competitive advantage over business rivals. Being a Filipina has given her a positive attitude, an authoritative presence, and a commitment to fairness that have proved invaluable in the corporate environment.

Although she is not proficient in the IT language of Java, she knows enough to assist Filipinos and Filipinas who are proficient in computer coding to find positions and place them into appropriate firms. While she may have very little knowledge of developing IT application programs, she can help anyone who needs assistance to enhance his or her IT programming skills.

Seven Seven's vision is to harness the true Filipino potential, provide a showcase for hardworking IT professional programmers and match them with premier Fortune 500 companies. As her partner in visioning towards a long term growth for Seven Seven, my father, Macario "Mac" Fojas has helped lead our firm to be one of the largest Filipino-owned IT service providers in the Philippines.

Our value proposition is one-stop ITO and business process outsourcing (BPO) services. We have a unique onshore-offshore engagement model, and we follow stringent data connectivity and security standards. Maintaining our firm's credibility to deliver these services requires a talented workforce. Our firm is composed of the best computer science and engineering graduates. All our Java engineers are 100% Java certified. Our mainframe group is made up of experienced and seasoned programmers.

Fortunately, my parents were able to employ thousands of Filipinos in high level jobs in information technology and back office services, not only contributing much-needed jobs in the Philippines but also making significant strides in developing key competencies that enhanced the country's portfolio of capabilities. As one of the first Filipino-owned companies in this industry, Seven Seven Corporate Group has become known to truly represent nation building in the information technology sector. During the nascent years of the information technology services industry when an obscure economics and statistics Connecticut research firm published a report with the Philippines ranking Number 1 globally in terms of knowledge jobs (Source: Global New e-Economy Index 1999 and http://www.computerworld.com.au/article/85917/meta_launches_global_new_e-economy_index_/), my parents were among those consulted by the Philippine government to help develop the country's value proposition. By then, Seven Seven had been in business more than three years and had grown tenfold its job creation record.

Among our key initiatives is the creation of the company's program for professional development centralized on technology training to showcase the best talents of the Philippine IT experts in the globalized economy. Through the years, this program has guided the skills training and career advancement of hundreds of talented graduates from the top colleges and universities of the Philippines. Today, the Seven Seven Corporate Group is advancing the professional careers of thousands of Filipinos and Filipinas who are able to competently stand shoulder-to-shoulder with their counterparts in the U.S., Singapore, India, and other knowledge worker cultures around the world, proud to be delighting their customers with excellent service and seamless problem resolution, and intent in their primary purpose of making a difference in society.

Handling the Volatility of the IT Business

Once the Seven Seven Corporate Group has invested the time, effort, and resources to sustain a strategic business relationship with a particular managerial executive who may ultimately have complete control over the staffing procedures and recruitment practices of an IT department, my mother normally expects that the Seven Seven Corporate Group will maintain the strategic business relationship as an ongoing concern. However, the strategic business relationship is unfortunately contingent on the organizational tenure of the invested individuals. Since strategic business relationships have always served as the focal point for creating sustainable value for the IT services firm, she honestly admits that the firm's client accounts have rapidly evolved over the past seventeen years as a majority of our clients have undergone radical changes in executive management. As a result of mergers and acquisitions, executive turnover has been high, often adversely affecting influential positions and, hence, our business relationships.

Fortunately, my grandfather had taught her the significance of being well prepared for any situational experience, especially in the advent of an emergency. Based on his personal experiences in the military, he taught her that building moral character involves having courage whenever it is necessary to perform any leadership action, regardless of the circumstances or the consequences. While she has personally endeavored to embody specific leadership characteristics of my grandfather, she believes that she may not have demonstrated every behavioral practice that showed his best relational leadership qualities. Nonetheless, these qualities have inspired her to follow the knowing-being-doing model in regard to relational leadership. For example, she has been confronted with a hypothetical scenario that involves being in a position where the location site is under siege. Even if the location site is in serious danger, she should try not to be in a frenzied, panicked state of mind as long as she has acknowledged the hazardous condition of her present situation.

Moreover, she should not lose focus on being in the current moment by concentrating on figuring a practical way out of the potentially harmful situation. Instead, keeping all pressures at bay, she should keep a clear mind and line up all possible options. Finally, she must take action to strategically detect the nearest possible exit strategy at the quickest possible time and with minimum damage.

Although neither our office building nor our household was ever under threat of war, we have figuratively experienced the metaphorical siege, namely the financial crisis of 2008.

A Real-Life Example

When BNP Paribas refused to accept withdrawals from three hedge funds by reporting a complete evaporation in liquidity, an incalculable number of corporate investment banking businesses suffered from the financial crisis of 2008 during a period known as the Great Recession. Business analysts estimate that the global economic decline cost the United States approximately fourteen trillion dollars in unrecoverable revenue. Since the Great Recession had resulted in the loss of nearly an entire year's worth of financial activity, the United States experienced one of the steepest economic downturns in American history. While the Federal Reserve assessed the reported damage to the American economy, the Great Recession subsequently caused several investment banking institutions to descend into a relative abyss of corporate oblivion. The crisis affected our strategic business alliances. The Seven Seven Corporate Group endeavored to mitigate the relational damage and focused on stabilizing relationships with our valued clients in the Financial District of Manhattan, providing strong support so these associates can be successful in their roles and trailing after them when they move on to other arenas.

Whenever a client filed for corporate dissolution, my mother became more determined to strengthen her resolve not to get upset over the loss of business and personal relationships. My mother sustains a high level of enthusiasm, remain optimistic, and look for a new corporate entity that might emerge from a corporate dissolution agreement. She continues to rely on relational leadership for strategic success. The Seven Seven Corporate Group's relational leadership model has provided exceptional service results by consistently creating compelling IT solutions for nearly two decades. Since 1996, she has wholeheartedly invested an immeasurable amount of strategic effort, valuable time, and financial resources toward proactively sustaining the strategic business alliances with many multinational institutions—previous corporate client accounts that underwent major managerial changes before becoming either a corporate defunct entity or a legendary corporate behemoth within their respective industry verticals. However, she recognizes that every single one of these corporate business entities has undergone key executive transitional changes as part of divesting away from prior structural failures that adversely affected their bottom lines. Consequently, dissociation is used as a tactic by most senior executive managers in order to restore the reputation and integrity of the firm's newly formed corporate entity.

While patiently awaiting an organizational decision that could affect the future of the firm, she regularly has client conversations with pertinent managerial members in order to earn the cooperative trust of the new corporate entity. Leading with passionate initiative, resilient perseverance and relentless fortitude, along with the deeply ingrained value of *pakikisama*, she has been able to preserve strategic relations with Seven Seven's resource individuals who are operating under new corporate entities. However, relational leadership must be accompanied by the ability to do a thorough examination of pertinent corporate financial documents. The professional guidance of my father has been helpful in this regard.

As a result of her optimistic efforts, several newly established corporate entities favorably increased the size of the Seven Seven Corporate Group by providing more job opportunities to the hardworking people of the Philippines. Since the new corporate entity has tripled the organizational size of our company, the Seven Seven Corporate Group assists its Filipino and Filipina employees who are striving to achieve and experience the "American Dream" and who are contributing to the Philippine brand of excellent customer service that is now recognized around the world.

Conclusion

A vision without a task is but a dream,
A task without a vision is drudgery,
A vision and a task is the hope of the world.
— G.F Simons C. Vazquez and P. R. Harris, Transcultural Leadership, 1993

Although my mother's story as a professional may have begun as a Filipina entrepreneur with very little knowledge in her chosen field of expertise, she was genetically blessed with quick intelligence, an enthusiastic curiosity, and a high level of energy to absorb and process information at a fast rate. With the insightful guidance of my father, she progressively learned more about the information technology industry. Based on his recommendations, she read countless informative articles and written publications on successful entrepreneurs from *Forbes* magazine and other business publications. She tried to model the networking strategies discussed in these articles. Eventually, she formed several strategic corporate alliances with Wall Street firms that morphed from business acquaintances that proved very beneficial to the Seven Seven Corporate Group. After more than seventeen years in the IT business, the Seven Seven Corporate

Group has evolved from a few individuals working from a home office into one of the most prestigious women-run and minority-owned IT service providers serving the greater New York area, as well as the largest Filipino-American ITES company in operation today.

As my mother snaps out of her reflective state of mind, she proceeds with the usual tasks necessary to successfully execute her business strategy. I am gratified that my parents, hand in hand, started the Seven Seven Corporate Group in order to make a difference in society. My father's vision coupled with my mother's networking strategies and her value system that is deeply ingrained in *pakikisama* make for a perfect recipe for success. As a result, the Seven Seven Corporate Group is a reliable and trustworthy IT service vendor for its Fortune 500 clientele in the U.S. and the blue chip companies in Asia Pacific because we are committed to client loyalty, employee integrity, and organizational excellence.

An authentic vision inspires enthusiastic energy and meaningful purpose. Her father—my grandfather—taught my mother that every inspirational leader must have a clearly articulated vision. This transparent vision can guide one into proactive action in order to serve a specific cause that makes a difference in society. Once colleagues and clients rally behind this identified cause, passionate initiative will drive the organization to create positive change in resolving conflicts and finding common ground among employees.

From my mother, I learned that a meaningful purpose involves sharing this 'can do' attitude with others. By having a 'can do' attitude, one can get others actively involved and truly committed to the authentic vision-building process. Pulling people together with resilience and perseverance allows these individuals to collectively work for positive change within the organization. Individuals will have an opportunity to use this leverage to connect with other like-minded individuals or corporate entities in order to sustainably stimulate productive lead generation.

She always emphasized that an established ethical standard helps guide a person's decisions and actions. Relational leadership is driven by core values, which positively impact thousands of lives from around the world. Relational leadership involves having a meaningful purpose aligned with core values that are reflected in one's behavior. Ethical standards affect an organization's actions and its ability to achieve its goal-oriented vision. Having relentless fortitude develops an individual's ethical voice and is necessary for attaining sustainable value for the company.

LEADERSHIP TIPS

1. *An authentic vision inspires enthusiastic energy and meaningful purpose.* Every inspirational leader must have a clearly articulated vision. This transparent vision can guide one into proactive action in order to serve a specific cause that makes a difference in society. Once colleagues and clients rally behind this identified cause, passionate initiative will drive the organization to create positive change in resolving conflicts and finding common ground among employees.

2. *A meaningful purpose involves sharing this 'can do' attitude with others.* By having a 'can do' attitude, one can get others actively involved and truly committed to the authentic vision-building process. Pulling people together with resilience and perseverance allows these individuals to collectively work for positive change within the organization. Individuals will have an opportunity to use this leverage to connect with other like-minded individuals or corporate entities in order to sustainably stimulate productive lead generation.

3. *An established ethical standard helps guide a person's decisions and actions.* Relational leadership is driven by core values, which positively impact thousands of lives from around the world. Relational leadership involves having a meaningful purpose aligned with core values that are reflected in one's behavior. Ethical standards affect an organization's actions and its ability to achieve its goal-oriented vision. Having relentless fortitude develops an individual's ethical voice and is necessary for attaining sustainable value for the company.

THE POWER OF DREAMS

Soledad Muesco Manaay, PhD
President, Xicepta Sciences

Abstract

Global mobility and e-commerce have provided the frame-work for the successful pursuit of my dreams. I write about what global leadership means and what global leaders must do in order to successfully reduce conflict among their diverse employees. My recommendations include emphatic attitude, non-violent communication, and compassionate leadership. I stress the importance of sensitivity to cultural differences, perspectives, and context when dealing with diversity. Based on my experience I encourage leaders to apply critical thinking and a wider worldview when addressing challenges. Since a person or group's cultural values and beliefs are often extended to their business culture; there is a need for cultural intelligence (CQ) when doing business across the globe. Global leaders with CQ not only understand but are able to successfully solve problems and effectively adapt in various cultural settings. Business leaders can contribute to social changes through corporate social responsibility or through advocacy of programs and causes that can make a difference in people's lives. Meaning-making is an important aspect in a leader's life. I use part of my personal story to illustrate that poverty should not be a hindrance to success and that education, hard work, and perseverance can change one's social status. I briefly describe my journey to co-founding and being President of Xicepta Sciences, a company in Silicon Valley that manufactures molecular wellness supplements.

Introduction

Dream Big and Dream in Color

As a child, I often gazed at the expansive blue sky and imagined the many other places it covered. This was how I began to entertain the idea of traveling and living abroad. Psychologists and child development specialists maintain that a child's culture is influenced by the people around the child and this cultural experience expands as the child grows up and acquire new culture. I guess I expanded my culture beyond the four corners of our small abode at an early age through my imagination. My mother did brag to her friends that as a child I always knew what I wanted to be when I grew up.

My yearning to see foreign lands at an early age was intensified by the Irish priests who taught at my school, San Ramon Catholic School at Suay, Himamaylan, Negros Occidental. Most memorable was the handsome and kind Father John Doohan, who forced us to speak English without the Ilonggo sing-song accent. Though his strong Irish accent was difficult to understand, his ocean-blue eyes communicated what he could not say in our native dialect and so all was well. I was fascinated by the color of his skin and I remember wondering how he kept it so white but what's even more fascinating in my young mind was what he represented; the other people in the world whom I wanted to meet, learn from, and even marry someday.

I also decided that someday I would earn my own money, lots of it, so I could improve our way of life; "our" included my parents and my brothers (I was the only girl). Although I had no concept of 'rich' or what was 'quality' life at such a young age, I knew that there was a better way of life, one where I don't have to walk under the pouring rain or the hot sun just to use a toilet, or sleep on a torturously hard bamboo bed in between two of my siblings who either kick in their sleep, snore loudly, or worse, wet the blanket that we all shared. There are worst images I could describe to represent the poverty I have experienced as a child but doing so would just dramatize things and that is not really the intention of this chapter. Besides, they are now just memories, ones that I laughingly treasure and would lovingly share with my future grandchildren and great grandchildren when the time comes, provided of course that I retain my mental clarity. This vision makes me smile. I could almost hear my yet-to-be-born grandchildren whispering to each other in between giggles, "Granny sure tells great fairy tales."

Fairy Tales Do Come True with Hardwork

I do feel that my life is a fairy tale, one complete with demons, brutes, a pot of gold, and of course, a handsome prince. The pot of gold is an exaggeration, for all I have is a collection of a few gold coins. The handsome prince is my charming and genius husband, a medical scientist with an MD degree and a PhD in Molecular Biology, whose scientific verbose drives me insane. As far as demons and brutes, I know many women can easily empathize with me having their fair share of demons and brutes. The demons are of course imaginary, often the result of what the brutes do; but that is a totally different topic which will be included in my memoir as soon as I gather the courage to write it!

Many people who knew me say that I am such a plucky girl and that I have all the luck in the world for having escaped poverty and achieved success. Success, I believe, is subjective but given my humble beginnings, I guess where I am now can be considered 'success.' About luck, it may have helped in the sense that I happened to be at the right place at the right time though I firmly believe that hard work, perseverance, and determination were the real forces behind everything I have accomplished. One thing is sure, I never forget to thank the Divine Providence for being around to listen to my prayers and wishes.

At 16 and during my senior year at Madeleine Academy, a Catholic High School at Hinigaran, Negros Occidental, my parents who have always treated me with tenderness and love, punished me with scathing words because of a *tsismis* [gossip] they had heard. The year was 1973 and in a barrio where gossip was the order of the day, a boy winking at a girl could end up sounding like a boy humping a girl by the time it reached the ears of the girl's parents. And that was exactly what happened in my case which prompted me to run away from the simpler life of the province to the complex life of a big city that was Manila. I was disappointed and hurt that my parents mistrusted me.

If truth be told, the boy had not even stolen a kiss from me though I wished he did just for the experience. As for my parents and all six brothers, I am sure they would have preferred me to remain a virgin even after four marriages.

As a young girl I had dreamt big dreams and these dreams were my vision of the future. Alas, every vision requires action. No matter what challenges you face, you must focus on your vision and choose the right path that would take you where you want to go. Be strong and unyielding. I learned from an early age that nothing was easy, except giving up, which I am glad has never been in my vocabulary.

When I left Negros Occidental in haste, I gave up an academic scholarship, my only hope to get into college. Although I am not a big believer of fate, as I believe that we can will our destiny, I do think that the event was meant to happen. How else would I have found my way to America had I stayed under the watchful eyes of my over-bearing brothers and overly strict parents? I will be honest in saying that my mother loved me very much and she only wanted what was best for me. And for her, the best certainly were not the homeboys with tattered pants most of whom worked at the sugar mill when not attending school.

My mother was my idol, even now. She was ahead of her time, that I am certain. She sang and performed in her family's traveling *Zarzuela* [folk opera], her melodious voice was comparable to Judy Garland's and I was told she could dance like Ginger Rogers. She was also a talented dressmaker. I remember how she made a dress for a woman in less than an hour without measuring her for size. I was very young when that happened but I remember how thrilled the woman was and in fact she came back the following day to report that many men had paid her compliments and that many women had gazed at her with envy. She was sure it was because of the dress that my mother sewed for her. I must admit that in my young eyes she did look absolutely smashing in that dress. On the way to Manila aboard a ship, I parked my under-fed figure on a cot that was to be my bed for two days while at sea and began planning my course of action: get a job, attend college, and find my way to America, my chosen destination. I had heard it being referred to as the land of the free, the land of milk and honey, and many other awe-inducing descriptions. I would get there one day, I told myself.

Lying on my cot, I tried to divert my focus away from my seasickness. I visualized Manila based upon what I have heard from my rich classmates who frequented the big city with their parents: big buildings, busy traffic, sidewalks full of vendors, and people from all walks of life whirling their way to their respective destinations. I began to see myself among the people walking along the busy sidewalk. I was wearing a well-pressed white and blue college uniform, my back hunched from carrying my big bag full of schoolbooks. I saw myself wiping my sweating brow with the hand-embroidered hanky that my mother made for me. I felt myself missing my mother and wishing she was beside me.

Alas, my visual image of life in Manila while in that ship was inaccurate. You see, I had an uncle, my mother's brother, who worked at the Office of the Chief of Staff of the Philippine Armed Forces at Camp Aguinaldo (GHQ or general headquarters). For some reason, I had the impression that he was rich and powerful, lived in a big beautiful house, and would help finance my education. I remembered him visiting us in Negros with his lovely wife, remembered him offering to send me to school in Manila. "It is the place to be if you want to achieve success in life," my uncle declared. I remembered declining his offer saying "No thank you. I have a full academic scholarship." I was always a class valedictorian, and my parents were already informed by my school that if I maintained academic honors, I would be awarded full college scholarship. I was confident no one could upset my standing.

My childhood memory of my uncle's visit centered on his wife being dressed so elegantly, of him speaking so eloquently, and of both of them displaying a certain air that gave me the impression they were 'somebody.' I was partly right. Fact 1: my uncle was very close to the most powerful at GHQ, the Chief of Staff himself, being his driver and trusted clerk. To many, this was a coveted position, after all, he was with him almost every day, he knew all his secrets and he can speak to him anytime he wanted—and this was a privilege in itself. Fact 2: my uncle could not afford to send me to college as he could barely afford to support his wife and five young children, all girls. Apparently, he wanted a son and so they kept making babies hoping the next one would be a boy. Fact 3: Manila was not the colorful city I had visualized but rather grayish even under the bright sun. Picture gray garbage. Picture gray being the color of the homeless children's tattered clothes. Picture the dark moldy cardboards which they built their homes with. Picture gray being the color of the big guns that the guards toted so they could shoot anyone they want. It was Martial Law and lawlessness was the law.

When Life Hands You a Lemon, Bake a Lemon Meringue

There I was with shattered dreams. For almost a year, I worked as a nanny and all-around helper at my uncle's house. My only joy was my interaction with my sometimes naughty but overall loveable five young cousins. It was a big leap from having six brothers. With them, I was a leader. Every chance I got, when the kids were having their nap, I would sneak out with a neighborhood girl whom I befriended, another teenager who traveled to Manila with big dreams but ended up with the same fate as mine, though she was lucky her uncle only had one child. One day, she dragged me to a t-shirt factory swearing that she knew the owner and that we would sure get jobs as seamstresses. *"Pag tinanong ka kung may experience ka, sabihin mo opo."* [When she asks you if you have experience as a seamstress just say yes!] *"Di ba ang nanay mo mananahi?"* [You said your mom is a dressmaker, right?] I nodded my head while thinking "where is she going with this?" Ester (I just remembered her name) would have been a great motivational speaker provided she drops her horse manure tactics. To cut the story short, I got the job but got fired within an hour. I guess the owner did not like a t-shirt with sleeves attached to the neck opening. Instead of going home with my head bowed, I decided to visit my uncle's office to help him with paperwork. I had the afternoon off with my auntie watching the children and I decided I would not let the t-shirt fiasco ruin my day. Along the way, I saw young women flocking to an office building. I followed them and eavesdropped a little. I found out they there to apply for the Women's Auxiliary Corps (WAC) recruitment.

Being a WAC wasn't exactly my ambition but I needed a job and so I decided to try my luck. When I encouraged my friend, Ester, to apply with me, she laughed at the idea. Her uncle had already mentioned this to her but he made it clear that the criteria was a college degree. I only heard what I wanted to hear and so I ignored whatever information she had that was not useful to my purpose. There were hundreds of applicants with only 30 positions. I was among the very few with no college degree and one of the youngest, My uncle was very supportive. In fact, he was able to secure an educational waiver from his boss on the condition that I pass all other requirements which included academic and physical exams. Armed with a waiver (every applicant was backed by some high-powered individual), I found myself being scrutinized by about a dozen high-ranking officers whose intention was more to discourage you rather than motivate you. I responded to their questions with every ounce of intelligence and confidence I could muster. The series of exams included an IQ test, a general comprehensive test, and a physical exam that I considered intrusive. I had a valid question: why would the government be interested in whether I was a virgin or not?

I guess the selection board scored me high since a few months later I was among the 30 "special recruit" for medical service who immediately began a series of training. Almost every one of these 30 were to be medical technologists and midwives. Despite the fact that I was the only one with only a high school diploma, I was constantly among the top 10. Consequently, I earned the respect of my batch mates. I was no longer ostracized as though I had a malignant disease; though I continued to receive the most punishment, which consisted of duck walks and trips around the training center under the rain for the simplest of reason: I walk like a girl. "You must walk like a man, ready to fight battles!" I remember my drill sergeant screaming at me. For anyone with principles, self-esteem, and dignity, be ready to mask those when you join the military.

The rigorous basic training exceeded anything that I had ever imagined and I would have given if not for my educational goals. The year that followed witnessed the girl in me turned into a woman. I was an instant Operating Room assistant to a military surgeon with a long line of patients to cut and sew. At the time, truckloads of wounded military personnel from the war-torn Mindanao were being airlifted to V-Luna Military Hospital. Soon after, I was rotated to different departments. The following year, I worked at Radiology, Pediatrics, Cancer Ward, Orthopedics, and what was then referred to as the Mental Ward. It would be difficult to work in these departments if you have no compassion. It is doubly difficult when you have compassion as you, too, would bleed with the wounded, would die a little with the terminally ill, and would ache at the sight of children suffering from debilitating illnesses. After about a year I decided that I was not meant for hospital work.

I enrolled at night school all the while planning to get reassigned somewhere that could get me closer to where I wanted to go. I was not sure where but I knew the place existed. In the meantime, I made good with my promise to help my parents. Every pay day I mailed them an envelope containing half of my pay. The other half was for my tuition and subsistence.

Sometimes Opportunity Doesn't Exactly Knock.
One Must Seek It and Once Found, Grab It Tight.

Well, just maybe, the wind did whisper in my ears that there was an opening for a junior writer at some 'secret' Executive Assistant's office at Malacañang. Yes, you guessed right, I applied and to my surprise, I got the job! Soon I found myself with a desk overflowing with stacks of documents and my job was to read the volumes of words into a few sentences. My boss would either edit or sign my drafts, usually a "Memorandum for His Eyes Only." Who would ever have thought that the girl from nowhere would end up working at Malacañang!

At this job, I would rush to finish my work by 4:30 and at five o'clock sharp I would be out of the door and off to the nearby University of Manila where I studied Foreign Service. Rain or shine, I never missed school. There were other challenges that seemed insurmountable during that period in my life but distance and time helped heal the wound although the scar remained. I am talking about the first brute I met: an officer seven years my senior who stole something valuable from me in the guise of love. When I said stole I meant without permission, and forcibly. This was during a time when women's rights in the Philippines were unheard of. One would think that remembering this episode that happened over three decades ago would be easy but it never gets easy. What bothers me the most is that this person never apologized and I suspect his sense of entitlement allowed him to think that what he did was normal.

Being a woman could be both detrimental and empowering depending on how you respond to certain situations. Where I worked before I came to the US, powerful men preyed at young women, which was probably common in many workplaces at the time. Bosses felt they had the right to slap or squeeze their secretary's bottoms just because they are the boss. Many dirty old men who felt their status symbol was not complete without a mistress or two got the shock of their lives when I said no to their proposals. Saying no is empowering. When you are faced with this situation, it is important not to be swayed by the glitter of diamonds being offered to you. It is a short-term thrill and the long-term effect is destructive. Focus on your dream and follow your path even if you have to crawl to get there. The rewards are sweeter and far more satisfying.

Being a woman also means we are the child-bearers, housekeepers, disciplinarians, caregivers, and in many cases we also carry the burden of being wage earners in addition to being dutiful wives. We play many roles and in the process, we give up our dreams and our personal identity. Sometimes we even feel inadequate especially when our abusive spouse tells us so. Whatever your role, it is important to make the right choices, to stand your ground, to hold on to your dreams, and to not lose your identity.

When Success Happens, Celebrate!

My trip to Manila aboard an overcrowded and rasping ship was very memorable because of its significance in my life; it brought me closer to my dream. My first airplane ride was even more memorable. I remember that early evening on July 21, 1980, of how worried I was when my plane took off despite the merciless rain. I watched through the window as the old Manila International Airport and the nearby city got smaller and smaller until there was nothing to see but the murky clouds dancing around the wings of the Philippine Airlines plane. I knew I was coming back but at that moment, it felt like I was forever leaving my homeland and everything and everyone that I loved. My destination was Hawaii, USA, where I would serve as Media Analyst at the Philippine Consulate General. I distinctly remember my seat- mate, a French gentleman whose bodily odor made me wonder if all Frenchmen smelled the way he did. His smell bothered me so much that finding a way to transfer to another seat was all I could think of thus forgetting my already full-blown homesickness. I managed to reprogram my mind by envisioning the beautiful and colorful sights that awaited me. Soon I found yet another source of comfort: the knowledge that finally, finally, my dreams have come true.

It was not by happenstance or pure luck that I achieved my goal. I had a dream and I was relentless in pursuing that dream. I did not rest on my laurels. Let me clarify by saying that there is nothing wrong in being contented and happy with whatever you have, in fact, it is a blissful ideal. In my case, I just happened to be passionate about exploring my potential and expanding my world.

How I landed my foreign assignment was unbelievable even to me. Still in my early 20s and working in a job that others would have killed for, I should have felt jubilant. Somehow, some aspects of the job made me realize I had to move on. And so, I turned my radar up again and learned of the foreign service assignment that the Ministry of Information offered. Right then, I knew I had found my dream job. I applied to take the Foreign Information Officers' course attended mostly by high-ranking officers and future Foreign Military Attaches. Again, sheer determination, smarts, and my competitive spirit gave me the edge over others. And this I could not have achieved had I been lackadaisical and unfocused in my self-development strategies. I happened to develop a penchant for reading at an early age. I read everything from fish wrapper to comic books and anything else I could lay my hands on. Books were rare to find at the time in my corner of the globe. This activity helped enhance my communication skill and my command of the English language. Oh yeah, Father Doohan, God rest his soul, should also be given credit.

I was lucky to have had an excellent foundation at San Ramon Catholic School, and with my mother inspiring me to be more than what society had expected of me during those times. Poverty may have been our social status but my parents instilled in us integrity and self-respect and these have been the bases of my confidence. My mother was a very refined woman and she successfully stimulated in me grace and self-esteem. My father on the other hand inspired in me adventure and nobility in spirit. He was a Judo and Arnis instructor, and a self-professed philosopher, who shared his skills without asking for monetary reward, which was why we were penniless. He was not a tall person but very high in ideals. He hammered us with values such as respect for others and honesty. "Don't lie or cheat, and be humble!" I could still hear his voice in my head.

Building your confidence is not difficult especially if your childhood culture established this at an early age. If not, you have a need to reinvent yourself. As you grow and expand your knowledge and experiences, you should also expand your worldview and adapt to what is current, appropriate, and applicable. We all have this capacity.

Acculturate and Be Open to Changes

Life in Hawaii was delightful. Today, I think of Hawaii as a perfect example of a place where culturally diverse individuals live together in harmony. How they embrace each other and form an *Ohana* [extended family] is just admirable. And yes, almost every day in Hawaii was beach day!

I lived in Waikiki where it was normal to see scantily clad people walking the streets. I was both shocked and amazed to see women of every size, shape, and age parading in 'barely there' swim wear. I remember the credo that the Catholic nuns, and my parents, implanted in me. Hide your body—flaunting it is sinful! Remembering this, initially I would go to the beach and lie on the sand in my muumuu.

Watching an 80-year-old woman with sun-damaged skin hanging all over her body proudly walk the street dressed in a thong-like bikini bottom made me say to myself: "that is real confidence; that is real freedom." The message that the older adult woman put out, of being confident and free, must have been contagious because not even a week later, I was among the bathing suit-clad crowd answering to the summons of Waikiki Beach. That evening back in my apartment, I reflected upon my action of donning a bikini and parading my body for everyone to see. I asked myself the question: "Was that un-Filipina of me? Am I becoming what my parents feared I would become: shamefully Americanized?" I mentally debated on the issue and the new Sol (my nickname) won over the old Sol. I know that my parents would have preferred me to be fully wrapped by either a *patadyong* [wrap skirt which is usually worn with a loose blouse] or a *kulambo* [mosquito net material] and the wider and longer the wrap is, the better it was for my virtue, in their book. Understandably so for they were operating under their old values and beliefs, the same values and beliefs I held until I realized that values and beliefs can be expanded and that one can balance old values with newly acquired ones.

The statement "when in Rome do what the Romans do" is really quite insightful. It tells us that life is easier when one assimilates into the dominant culture. The beauty about the whole issue of acculturation is that you could assimilate as intensely or extensively without losing your core values or belief system. As you acculturate, you gain new values that will allow you to navigate more successfully in your new environment. For example, learning the language of your host country allows you to communicate better and in addition helps you form social connections and even get a better job. Also, enjoying the local food and practicing the local tradition help add new meaning and dimension to your life especially when in return you share with your hosts a taste of your food or tradition. Acculturation breeds sharing and in sharing we find that our culture and worldview expand (Sam and Berry 2010). In their article, Sam and Berry (2010) conclude that those who acculturate or assimilate into a bigger society adjusts better than those who segregate themselves or remain partial to just one culture.

I said earlier that life in Hawaii was delightful and it was; nevertheless, challenges were ever present. When I got married, I was forced to resign my position with the Philippines Consulate General but fortunately, a job at the mayor's office awaited me. Life with my musician ex-husband was not the life I envisioned and for many reasons our marriage did not survive the seven-year itch. Lonely, broke, and feeling alone because I refused to run to friends for comfort, I clung to my daughter as if she were my lifeline. I guess she was my lifeline. This was when I realized that life in America was not everything that people say it was. It was not the land of milk and honey and I had to take on three jobs; part time radio announcer, freelance writer, and real estate broker. They were the best options I had as a single mom. They enabled me to have the best of both worlds: take care of my baby and pay my bills. It was exhausting and frustrating but I found the joys of motherhood invigorating, which balanced the ride. I learned the trade, and soon, I became a constant top producer as a realtor; unfortunately, before I could even begin to build my wealth, the market crashed in early 1990s. And this happened while I was enrolled in a graduate program at the Hawaii Pacific University. With much difficulty, I decided to begin the process of moving forward to new challenge and adventure.

In 1997, I moved to California where I believed greener pasture awaited me. I left dearest friends, who served as my surrogate family, and uprooted my daughter who was 12 years old at the time. She vehemently (and tearfully) opposed our move. I was afraid that her resentment would last forever and the thought worried me. She resented me for taking her out of her circle of friends and family, the only ones she had besides me. Luckily for both her and me, not even a month later the twinkle in her eyes returned and she eagerly assumed her new life with her new-found friends. She acculturated really well for which I was thankful. Yes, children have high resiliency level and they do adapt to their surroundings much faster than adults in many cases.

Execute Your Vision

Prior to my current position as President of Xicepta Sciences, an innovative and socially-conscious company that manufactures natural, safe, and cutting-edge molecular supplements and skin care products, I owned and managed a senior home care agency, Care On Call, Inc. which I sold in November 2013. Over the course of six years, I must have employed well over 300 caregivers and at the same time I had acquired quite a number of older adult clients. Years before, I was Executive Director of a prestigious 150-capacity assisted living facility in Menlo Park, CA with almost 100 staff members including Department Directors. I learned from these two jobs that the complexity of leadership is made simple by following a few rules: (1) Understanding the perspective of others; (2) Applying critical thinking; (3) Leadership through empathy; (4) Framing your presentation in a way that connects to your audience's belief system and lets them know that what you're proposing is a "win-win" deal; and (5) Knowing that different groups require different approaches (see Gundling, Hogan, & Cvitkovich 2011).

As a leader of my small firm, Care On Call, Inc., I learned tremendously from the different situations I faced every moment of that chapter of my life. I definitely made mistakes, but I also learned from those mistakes. Having come from a country where power and gender distance was high, I found myself wanting and needing to study people's behavior, their motivation, and their mental programming. This was partly what drove me to go back to school to pursue my Doctorate in International Psychology: to increase my knowledge of multiculturalism that would benefit my interaction with people around me. I did not want to be a clinician and so I chose Industrial and Organizational psychology as my concentration. Prior to my Ph.D. program, I completed a Master's program in Psychology and Gerontology (health care for the aging) while working full time. I also had a year and a half stint at law school. Despite the times I stumbled and fell, got wounded, and felt unsure and afraid; I felt proud knowing that I was paving the road to my future.

Even though over 70 percent of our employees at Care On Call, Inc. were from the Philippines diversity was still an issue. Everyone represents diversity in many ways. The rest of the employees were from other countries including India, Samoa, Mexico, Fiji, and even Korea. The diversity of nationalities made my task more challenging.

Successful mobility requires proper acculturation and looking back, I realized that while many of our workers had acculturated to the macro culture, there were those who struggled and they were the ones who did not make the cut. Helpful as I am, I faced the dilemma of whether to hire and be helpful of *kababayans* [fellow citizens] or follow our strict hiring procedure to protect clients' welfare. There was no doubt about it: the welfare and needs of our older adult clients came first. Come to think of it, hiring unqualified persons just to be helpful to them is really a double-edge sword; you are setting them up for failure and you are setting yourself up for possible liabilities.

I found that the key to enriching your life is not by acquiring more money but by how you can affect others. And so as my business grew, my philanthropic activity also grew, not to mention my support to my *barangay* [village]-size family back home. I still remember the joy I felt when I visited my hometown in Negros to inaugurate the library that I donated with the help of Books from the Barrio which had shipped thousands of books on my behalf. I believed that education empowered me and broke my family's cycle of poverty and this was my reason for donating the library with books. With our business, Xicepta Sciences, philanthropy is vital to our existence and it is incorporated in our mission and purpose. Scholarships would be part of our giving back program. Luckily, my husband shares my passion to advocate for children with special needs, to empower through education, and to help install social justice in the world in all possible ways. These are monumental organizational values, which, if many companies emulate, could have tremendous effect in the world we live in.

When the Going Gets Tough, Get Tougher

Many of Care On Call's older adult clients came from Europe and they were rooted in a culture with which the caregivers were unfamiliar. In addition, many of them had illnesses co-morbid with aging and this required special people with special caregiving skills and a compassionate attitude. I addressed this challenge by providing hands-on training and intervention whenever there was a conflict. I scheduled cultural sensitivity training and care-related training as often as possible. For the most part, my job was enjoyable and rewarding though there were times when I felt like the weight of the world was on my shoulder and all I wanted to do was to unload the burden as quickly as possible. Several events in my life contributed to this; in fact, they drove me to almost a state of despondency and seclusion. (1) Two of my brothers died of cancer within a month of each other. Before they died, I was traveling back and forth to the Philippines to help oversee their care. (2) My third brother had a stroke and almost died and this happened during the wake at our family residence for my deceased youngest brother. (3) The following year my house almost burned to the ground because of a malfunctioning water heater.

I tried to solve the mystery of life's complexity but I found no answer except that there are events that need to happen because they serve a purpose. And these events in my life taught me that God gave us the capacity to withstand trials and that there is nothing that can break us except our weak resolve. It also taught me that materials things are just that, material things; they are inconsequential. Life and health, including mental health, are far more important. Family, loyal friends, and relationship with self and others are also vital to our meaningful existence. And, for as long as we live, we have hope. Having said this, I considered all the negative events in my life as instruments of learning, tools for character building, and opportunities to reflect and reach down at the very core of my humanity. In reflecting, I understood the meaning of my life, my purpose on this earth, and what I want to do before I move on to the next world.

Advocate for Yourself and Empower Others

In many of the positions I held, it helped that the buck stopped with me, making it easy for me to make management decisions. Empowering and providing support was foremost in my agenda as the firm's head. While many caregivers considered me as their friend and an advocate, I was thankful that they also managed to maintain a respectful boundary. My office was open for anyone who had an issue to discuss or just wanted to stop by to say hello. My employees appreciated this policy. To show appreciation to our family of caregivers, we held parties and fun events.

Many Filipinos who worked with us as caregivers were highly educated. Some of them were nurses back home and I knew of a couple with doctoral degrees. Some who had come straight from the provinces required additional technical training and sometimes were unfamiliar with the household amenities of our economically-advantaged clients. Many of them proved to be the most caring and compassionate caregivers one could ask for.

With almost every one of the caregivers coming from a collectivist society, one would think that working harmoniously would be the normal course of events. Interestingly, diversity in many areas ignited misunderstanding and it took some digging into individuals' perspectives to truly understand the root of the conflict. In most cases, stereotyping played a part but once addressed and clarified, the situation improved.

The Ph.D. program that I embarked on helped me realize that understanding culture is an important aspect of managing employees, and that global leadership is about being adaptive and having a worldview that goes beyond one's national boundary. Some leaders act as though leadership is a crown to wear or a belt of authority that can be used to whip people into obedience. Leadership, rather, is an activity that should bring people to understand issues and resolve them in a win-win manner. Leadership is also about effecting good and using your power to empower others.

Explore the World and Expand Your Knowledge

I have been fortunate to travel to many countries including Australia, Indonesia, China, Japan, and at least seven countries in Europe. My trip to Indonesia and China were part of my doctoral curriculum and the rest were more for fun and recreation; however, I treated them all the same, a great learning experience. Every country has its own beauty and grandeur, and each proved to be a cultural marvel.

True, nowadays one doesn't have to leave one's office chair or kitchen table to view the world. Our advance technology can virtually bring us anywhere we want to go and even allow us to hold a face to face chat with people from distant places. But, nothing can duplicate the act of being present—to inhale the local air whether stale or fresh, to brush shoulders with the residents and in so doing, connecting with them, warm flesh to warm flesh, tasting the foods that keep them alive, hearing their music, dancing their dance, and most importantly, sharing stories with them. I imagine this is how cultures are spread, how friendships across the shores are formed, and how cross-cultural knowledge is gained.

The not-so-great thing about virtual travel or cross-cultural learning through the media is the technology's influence and ability to twist facts or slant the message to the extent that it is difficult to ascertain whether what it puts out is fact, fiction, or a sensationalist's view. And this is a caveat for would be global leaders; when doing research for professional or academic use, do not rely on news articles alone; nothing is better than cited scholarly article and actual study in your area of interest.

Earlier, I spoke about the importance of knowing cultural similarities and differences. Only in knowing our differences can we begin to appreciate each other and only by being aware of our similarities can we begin to forge better understanding of other people's perspective.

When my daughter and I were in Germany two years ago, we rode the buses aimlessly and at one point we decided to disembark and explore the area. To my amazement, the modest town reminded me of the town I grew up except for the architecture and the food. The surroundings was unsophisticated with small stores and eateries that reminded me of the *sari sari* stores [small convenience/variety stores, often at the front of a house] and *carenderias* [public eating-place, where pre-cooked foods are served] back home. That morning we had a chance to walk around Frankfurt's cobble stone streets. We gushed at the sights of gigantic half-timbered houses and we marveled at the modernity of the shopping district. What a contrasting sight in one day and an exhilarating experience which will be forever etched in my memory.

The Relevance of Global Leadership

Global leaders can positively impact world situation in many ways:

(1) By understanding the mechanics of mobility and addressing its effects on the workforce; (2) By using global mobility as an opportunity to study and learn multiculturalism and diversity; (3) By bringing back knowledge and technology learned to enhance globalization since this seems to be where we are going; (4) By promoting a company culture that is supportive, sensitive, and respectful of the differences that exist between people of diverse backgrounds; and (5) By incorporating CSR in their mission and philanthropic programs that contribute to social changes and effect social justice.

Sometimes we forget that we are culturally diverse in many levels, including ethnicity, gender, religion, culture, educational level, socio-economic status, skin color, among others. It is important to embrace the differences and avoid biases. It is also beneficial to acquire and maintain a worldview that is beyond what you have developed or acquired during childhood. We need to be open to possibilities!

The secret is to know that underneath a person's behavior is a set of beliefs and values they have learned from their own environment. If we want to avoid conflict, we must filter our own prejudices and view the situation from the other person's perspective. If everyone takes the time to exercise this, I am willing to wager that harmony will prevail over violence.

There are many cultural variables both in interpersonal level and institutional level that a leader must be sensitive about. For those of us who are professionals in the west, it is important to remember that an ethnocentric attitude is not helpful (Munroe & Munroe 1997). Hofstede, Hofstede and Minkov (2011) said that conflict is common among people who think, feel, and act differently. Despite these differences, we must work together to find a solution to our common problem. In order to solve the problem, we must not ignore the differences that divide us. My interpretation of this is that understanding why and how we differ in our thoughts, feelings, and action will help us communicate and negotiate better.

Finally, we live in a world that is fragile; people often get lost in the wars of religion, political affiliation, and other unfathomable reasons. There are also those, including women and children, who experience marginalization and abuse. Poverty is everywhere. As global leaders, we can endeavor to make a difference in the lives of others through a variety of ways. We can empower employees by listening, by being patient, and by being fair and supportive. More importantly, we can contribute to social changes through philanthropic programs. Every company should exercise corporate social responsibility (CSR) activities not just to promote their business but also to contribute to the good of mankind. We can advocate for the marginalized as part of our CSR. We can speak to oppose human rights violation, discrimination, racism, and violence against women and children. As global leaders we have a voice and influence. We must use it for a greater good!

It can be told now that the day I ran away from home marked the beginning of an exciting albeit bittersweet and life-changing journey that catapulted me to what I am today; a mother of a feisty, intelligent, and outspoken educator and novice film editor; Co-founder and President of Xicepta Sciences, a company that manufactures molecular wellness supplements (I did not intend for this to sound like an advertisement); consultant in the areas of multiculturalism, parenting and industrial and organizational psychology; author of two young adult books and a few more waiting to be published; and among other roles, wife and business partner of a former federal medical scientist, an MD and molecular biologist, who was diagnosed as autistic savant (the disclosure is with his permission), a role that is quite a journey in and of itself.

LEADERSHIP TIPS

1. ***Remember your roots but expand your worldview.*** Don't forget where you came from and where you were when you started your long journey. Let your starting point be a reference point to chart your progress and growth. Expand your world view, learn to appreciate and understand other cultures. Look at things from their perspective and understand the basis of your own perspectives. Frame your views and decisions in a way that connects to your audience's belief system.

2. ***Apply critical thinking.*** Critically evaluate your approaches, your decisions, your context and your priorities. Question why things are the way they are. Ask 'what if' things could be different—and how.' This is called "critical thinking," a highly valued leadership asset. Learn from your mistakes and the mistakes of others—treat them as learning opportunities for a thinking leader. Globalization is not homogeneity, understand and master its nuances. Nurture interactions and open communication within your organization.

3. ***Lead through empathy.*** Effective leadership is not about giving orders. Leadership comes by understanding where people are and what got them there, and most importantly, what motivates them. Leadership is about being flexible and knowing your own purpose in life. Leaders should empower as empowerment builds trust and strengthens teamwork. Know that underneath a person's behavior is a set of beliefs and values they have absorbed from their own growth paths and ecosystems.

4. ***Use your power wisely: for a greater good.*** There seems to be no end to problems in our world. You can help make things better through every single pro-active gesture and contribution you can give. Advocate for change, support those who are empowering others, and oppose injustice. Use your voice, influence, and experience for a greater good. Remember that the survival of our world and the future of our generation will largely depend on the actions of today's leaders.

5. **_Set aside time to enjoy life._** Find meaning and satisfaction in your daily life. Surround yourself with good company and anchor yourself in organizations outside of your workplace. This includes your family, spiritual organization, sports club and volunteer groups, all of which could bring more meaning in your life. Enjoy friendships with people you trust and can grow with. An enjoyable personal life makes a better executive

Mommyla, Popsy and Me: Leading by Example through the Generations

Susie Quesada
President, Ramar Foods International

Abstract

*I*n this chapter, you will understand how a husband and wife team in the Philippines was able to set up multiple successful businesses in the Philippines and then do the same in the U.S. while passing on the entrepreneurial spirit to the next two generations. There is no substitute for hard work, a good education, and a positive outlook. The Quesada family was able to overcome the many challenges of starting businesses in a new country as well as the unique dynamics of working in a family business. Led by a strong Pinay with vision and energy, Maria Quesada started most of her businesses based on what her family's needs were at the time. Her husband, Ramon was the practical partner who was supportive and helped execute the ideas. Just as she raised her children to be hardworking and intelligent, she knew the key to her success was enlisting smart and hardworking employees and the ability to develop their potential and talents. She knew the importance of being able to lead by providing examples of collaboration and teamwork needed to elevate the business to the next level and to embody the company's larger mission of giving back to the community.

Introduction

In the Philippines, as in many cultures, a name can mean so much. Whether it is your given name or a nickname or a term of endearment, the names we use to call our loved ones evoke a special feeling: *Mommyla, Daddylo, Popsy, Ramar*. As I say each one in my head the memories come flooding in and their words of wisdom follow. All families are unique and sometimes our choices in professions tend to follow from generation to generation. In the case of my family, the entrepreneurial spirit has been going strong for three generations. It all began with Mommyla.

Mommyla

Mommlya was my *lola* [grandmother] who asked her grandchildren to call her Mommyla. She passed away when I was eight years old and I remember that she was very warm and welcoming as well as religious. When we went to Mommyla's house in Atherton, California, the house would be loud and bustling with at least 50 family members. All the grandkids would play upstairs in this gigantic playroom that had three sofa sets in it. We would build forts and play hide and seek in the dark with no adult supervision. The older cousins would just watch the younger cousins. When the adults had finished preparing the food, they would call us and we would rush down the stairs trying to be the first in line as we were surrounded by the smell of *pancit bihon* [thin rice noodles], *adobo* [meat braised in vinegar or soy sauce or coconut or a combination], *bistek* [beef steak], crab, and the myriad of dishes to choose from.

It was only as an adult that I learned about my grandmother's business side. People tell me that I am like her because I am also a teacher turned businesswoman. How did a Filipina mother of 11 find the time to start over 10 businesses? Is that even possible? It was her perseverance and vision that began Ramar Foods International in 1969 and why it is thriving today as a third generation family business. I was too young to learn first-hand about her leadership style and thoughts on business. Luckily, she passed on the gift of entrepreneurship to her 11 children and this has made a huge impact on my own personal leadership style.

I am currently the President of Ramar Foods International, the largest Specialty Filipino and Asian Frozen Food Manufacturer in the US. It is difficult to tell the story of how I got here without telling the story behind my family's entrepreneurial spirit.

Mommyla started doing business based on personal experiences that she knew would give back to the community. In the Philippines, children, formulated a cough medicine after one of their children passed away from a common cold. Pushed by the hope that no one else would have to suffer such a terrible loss, they began manufacturing and selling it, and Doctor's Pharmaceuticals, Inc was born. It was this first business that opened the gateway for her interest in business. Daddylo and Mommyla had the energy and gumption to start businesses that she saw would be beneficial for her community. Mommyla had the vision and the ideas while Daddylo would be the more practical and methodical of the team, instrumental in the execution of her ideas. Together they balanced each other well. Once she learned of a new opportunity, she would jump into it and both would work very hard to make sure it succeeded. Later on, when the older children finished college, many of her 11 children were drafted to manage the businesses; and then Mommyla and Daddylo would start something new. Daddylo passed away in 1973, but he was the other half of the entrepreneurial spirit that elevated the Quesada family into many businesses.

This led to more businesses including a restaurant (Bonanza), the first automatic pin setting bowling center in the Philippines, a movie theatre, piggeries and poultry farms, ham production, and the building of housing subdivisions including the pioneer low-cost GSIS housing. Each business idea came out of a need she saw for her family and surrounding community. Her connections and networking in these industries led to her owning and operating one of the biggest franchises in the Philippines: Kentucky Fried Chicken. She continued in the U.S. by investing in residential apartments, motel operations, drive-in restaurants, pizza and popcorn distribution routes and day care for preschoolers—all after Mommyla and Daddylo started Ramar Foods (formerly Orientex Foods) to keep the family busy while the younger children finished their schooling.

She was a hard worker and great at delegating and getting results. She made sure she had the right people in place to deliver the results she was looking for. As her kids grew up, they would work in the different businesses, whether it was folding boxes for the medications or working the cash register at a restaurant or teaching at the day care. She instilled in her children the importance of education and hard work. She was also quite organized as you can imagine having 11 children running around at so many different ages. The custom of having help in the house to cook, drive, and care for her family helped. There was a board in the living room keeping track of which kid had which car with which driver. Mommyla was also very philanthropic and active in the civic and religious community. She and Daddylo were always helping other families and giving back. Not all of her businesses succeeded, but she continued to push out new ideas and was never deterred by failures.

The U.S. Journey

When she saw the opportunities that were available in America, she took her family there on vacation with the intention of finding a way to stay. Some of her children had been married at this point and started their own businesses and families. She took the remaining children with her to Palo Alto, California. In the U.S,. Mommyla continued to try new business ventures. It was the beginnings of Ramar Foods International that granted the family the trader's visa to stay in the U.S. First, she brought handicrafts from the Philippines and started selling them at the local flea market. There were enough Filipino immigrants looking for her wares that she opened a brick-and-mortar store in Mountain View called Orientex and started carrying imported foods from the Philippines. As the Filipino population grew, more customers were looking for foodstuffs that would provide a taste of home. And more stores were popping up in the Bay Area just like hers owned by fellow *kababayan* [fellow citizens] from home. They started buying goods from her and pretty soon Mommlya was supplying imported food to all the Filipino stores in the area. Daddylo was there every step of the way making sure that each investment made sense. Of course as the business grew, Mommyla put her children to work. It was my father Primo Quesada and his brother Delfin who took care of the day-to-day operations. They would unload the containers, take the orders, fulfill the orders, and drive the trucks for delivery. At this point, Mommyla started to focus on new business ventures. She bought and operated apartments, hotels, and restaurants as well as started a day care center. As she embarked on a new business idea she would share her ideas with her children and get their perspectives on how to proceed. This type of collaborative effort gave her children practical business knowledge and led to their future successful businesses.

My father Primo was working at Orientex while he finished college, and as a new graduate he decided to open a travel agency. This was hard work. My mom recalls that they would attend every single party in the Filipino community and spread the word that he could take care of everyone's travel needs. This form of networking paid off and soon Orientex Travel, named after the already well known Orientex Distribution company, was thriving. My mother Evangeline joined my father at the travel agency doing the bookkeeping and accounting. She left a career in the hotel industry to have more flexible hours at the agency. Another husband and wife business team was born. In the early 70s, Orientex Distribution was on the verge of bankruptcy so Mommyla asked my dad to take over and see if he could salvage the business before they had to close the doors. The cost to import products and maintain the delivery trucks was not generating enough profit to sustain the distributorship.

From Distribution to Manufacturing

Having attended the University of the Philippines (UP) College of Business and finishing his studies at Menlo College in Accounting in Menlo Park, my dad started by listening to his customers and friends in the growing Filipino community. Filipinos were looking for products from home that he was not able to import due to U.S. government regulations, such as ice cream, *longanisa* [sausage] and *lumpia* [spring rolls]. He saw the potential in the market and decided to develop these products. First, he tried to see if he could work with San Miguel Corporation in the Philippines to import Magnolia Ice Cream. They were not interested in the small Filipino community in California and sent a letter denying his request. That is when he decided to start a new Magnolia Ice Cream in the U.S.: one that would use the delicious fruits from the Philippines but the high quality milk of California. It was this decision to move into manufacturing that saved the company.

Getting into manufacturing required a major investment and Primo relied on his strong accounting background and took a page from his mom. He always noticed that she wasn't afraid to ask questions so he surrounded himself with people who could share the knowledge he needed to get started. Using his own capital and with approval from the board of directors which consisted of his brothers and sisters, he invested in an ice cream making machine and began manufacturing Magnolia Ice Cream in the US. At last, the Filipino American community could taste the flavors of mango, *ube* [purple yam] and *macapuno* [coconut sport] in a high quality ice cream. The investment started to pay off and Primo started to search for other lines that he could sell during the cold months when ice cream sales slowed down.

One Quesada super ability that I have to stress is the ability to know what great food tastes like. It was in our little kitchen in Walnut Creek, CA that my mom would prepare the multiple recipes of *longanisa* [sausage] and my parents' friends would come through our doors voting on their favorite recipe until my dad was convinced that we had the right flavor profile to take to market. This was my first taste of working for the family business. Our first meat products included the introduction of Orientex brand *longanisa*, *tocino* [bacon], and *lumpia*. A whole new set of challenges started because producing meat required the U.S. Department of Agriculture to be involved from start to finish. The meat plant had to be built to code and who was better to build it then my father himself.

Primo was interested in building and selling property, so he studied for his General Contractor's license and Real Estate license. Just like my grandmother, he continued to challenge himself by embarking on new business ventures. At the same time, his siblings were starting their own businesses. *Tito* [uncle] Tim came to work with him at Orientex. *Tito* Papin owned Betsy's Bakeries in the San Diego area. *Tita* [aunt] Liza continued running Orientex Travel. Tita Lena ran Barbizon Modeling School with her husband. It was only Tito Jack, the eldest, who followed Daddylo's footsteps and became a doctor. One thing I remember while growing up is that both my parents worked hard. They took every opportunity to learn something new and they talked to my two brothers and myself constantly about how they saw new information through a business lens. Yet, they never told us that we would be working for them some day. They encouraged us to follow our own paths. Perhaps it is this secret that helped us find our way back to the family business.

As Orientex Foods grew, my dad built our factories and also started many business including construction and real estate. Of course, my mom would help on the accounting side in each business. She graduated from UP Diliman with a degree in hotel and restaurant management so her back-of-the-house skills were an asset to each venture he started. And her front-of-the-house customer service skills proved to be helpful as well. He built and sold apartment complexes and homes. He developed eight brands including Turo Turo Gourmet, Bestaste, and Manila Gold. Each brand filled a unique space in the Asian grocery stores and soon our market grew to include the growing Asian population in the U.S. and Canada. In 1999, he and the stockholders decided to rename the company 'Ramar Foods' in honor of his parents Ramon and Maria. The name of the company was built on the names of its founders.

My dad is always eager to learn and is not afraid to do something he has never done before. He makes a point to always surround himself with smart hard working people and that is how he gets results.

He tried not to get in the way of any employee who had a better idea to accomplish the tasks at hand. His leadership style was motivating yet at the same time practical. His great judgement of character helped him find out what really drives people and bring out the best in them. My dad led by example and showed us that hard work and the commitment to try new things can lead to success.

A COO — and More

Being the third generation leader in a company is tricky. People have preconceived notions of a COO, child of an owner, and question whether or not they earned the position or were just given the position. I am happy to say that in the Quesada family you have to earn your place in the family business. Daddylo and Mommyla started this tradition and we continue it today.

I began working for the company at the age of eight. My dad paid one cent per label that I affixed to the lid of containers of Magnolia Ice Cream. Throughout my childhood I worked summers scooping ice cream at Filipino festivals, filing in at the head office, or doing food demonstrations in Asian Supermarkets. Was I forced to do these jobs? Not at all. My dad offered them as an opportunity for us to learn the value of hard work and the satisfaction you get from spending the money you earned. He did not steer us into the family business but instead encouraged us to follow our own path.

Growing up, my passions included reading, cooking, team sports, and outdoor sports. While I was attending college at the University of California at Berkeley, I had some inspiring teachers in my Asian American Literature and Latino American Literature classes. I enjoyed learning the history of cultures through reading. Having coached and tutored youth in my community in high school, I pursued additional paths for connecting with youth and my passion for education blossomed. This led me to a career in education. After graduating from college, I pursued a Multiple Subject Teaching Credential at St. Mary's College and taught sixth through eighth grades in San Lorenzo, CA. One of the reasons I chose this school was the large population of Filipino American and Asian American students.

My goal was to be a mentor and convince them that they could be leaders in their community. I was blessed to be surrounded by motivating staff who encouraged me to get involved. The vision was clear at Washington Manor Middle School under then Principal Diane Carris. The staff was motivated to do what was best for the students and the culture was that of volunteering for the greater good. We made decisions by consensus, which is no easy task with over 45 educators, but everyone felt heard and supported. Within four years I was coach of the soccer team, founded the Diversity Club, helped start the Safe School Ambassadors program, and served on district committees for Diversity and Reading.

In 2004, my uncle passed away and my father saw an opportunity for an important discussion with me. He took me to a fancy restaurant with white table cloths, not the usual hole-in-the wall taqueria we normally frequent and asked me this question: "What if something happened to me and no one knew the family business?" By the end of dinner, I had agreed to take a two-year leave of absence from my tenured public school teaching position to learn the family business. "It will take you two years to like it," he said.

He rotated me through the accounting, logistics, and marketing departments. I can not say that I liked it at first. My passion for teaching is strong and the creativity and autonomy that you have as a teacher in the classroom is hard to find in other careers. In the marketing department, which at that time consisted of one person, I started to see how the pieces to the company puzzle came together. Now I was working *with* all of the departments and not just *in* the individual departments. I made mistakes in the beginning and learned how they affected the bottom line. Sometimes, you learn the most from mistakes and mistakes helped me think about all aspects of a decision. Luckily, my father was there every step of the way to guide and nurture even when it felt like I was drowning in an unknown land. "Business is just common sense," he says. "If you think about all the scenarios, how it will affect everyone involved, it is easy." I was very aware of the fact that I was the boss's daughter. Without having to be told, I made sure I was the first one in the office and last one to leave. I had to earn the trust and respect of our long time employees and prove that even with my education background I could bring something to Ramar that would lead us to growth and success.

My passion for education told me to take some business classes but my dad insisted that I was learning more working in the business. Eventually I realized that teachers surrounded me. My father was very good at hiring and motivating people, and the turnover at the company was very small. The same people I had known growing up as a kid at the Ramar Christmas parties were now nurturing my business and leadership skills.

Evolution of Family Businesses

I was surprised when both of my brothers asked my dad if they could join his company. First PJ, the youngest of the three, left his own production and marketing firm MOSS productions to become our first in-house graphic designer. His company was already making our TV commercials, so it was a natural fit. Next, Ron Quesada worked out a deal with my dad where he could manage the properties that he built and that my mother was managing, and still continue to be an integral part of the Filipino American arts community where he could showcase his musical talents playing multiple instruments including *rondalla* [an ensemble of stringed instruments including *bandurria*, *laud*, *octavina*, guitar, and bass guitar] and *kulintang* [gongs from the Southern Philippines].

In the meantime, the Quesada cousins, Mommyla's grandchildren, have embarked on their own business as well. Tricia Quesada-Sakai started BabyJellyBeans.com with her husband. Jon Quesada helped found CupsCo. Nikki Quesada has a designer bag and shoe company called Shiq. Broddie Quesada is chef and co-owner of two restaurant concepts—Bonanza Roaster Calf and Chuckwagon Roast Beef. Lorie May Quesada-Abrahams is co-owner of Glamour Rouge Makeup and Hair Artistry. Mico Quesada, is developer and co-owner of a Persian Rug company with sister Nikki and cousin Frenjick. Frenjick Quesada is a successful interior designer and co-owner of Design HQ, a design firm in Metro Manila. Eros Resmini is an investor in tech startups. Winnie Santos is in the sugar-flour bakery business. Lena Marie Quesada is now running Barbizon Modeling Schools.

Slowly, my parents started to travel more and spend more time away from the office. I think my dad knew that I had earned the trust of the department heads and people at the office before he decided to let go of the reigns. PJ is now VP of marketing and Ron is on the Board of Directors for Ramar and manages the real estate side of the business. My brothers and I work together and consult each other on all major decisions. Although our titles are different and we bring unique perspectives to the table, we collaborate when it comes to strategic directions of Ramar and consult our employees and network to come to conclusions on how to proceed. We have been watching our father do this for years and with his guidance we have opened up new growth markets for Ramar.

Ramar Foods International did not have a mission statement or core value statement. My brothers and I recognized this and decided we needed to write one. We did not have too much trouble because the way my father had built the business made it very easy to identify the mission after spending some time in any of our businesses.

Ramar Foods Mission Statement

1. Treat everyone like family. Whether it is our employees,
   customers, suppliers or vendors, it is in our company
   culture to treat everyone with respect and trust.

2. Make it the best. Whether it is the quality of our products,
   the processes and procedures to manufacture and sell them
   or the customer service we provide, we make it the best.

3. Be Ramarkable. To be Ramarkable is to attract notice for
   being exceptional or amazing.

Giving Back

Now as my parents have retired, it has been my pleasure to oversee
the day-to-day operations and take care of our loyal employees who
we treat like family. Before retiring in 2013, my dad started the Ramar
Scholarship Foundations in the Philippines and the U.S. The combined
Foundations have supported over 45 students to date who might not
otherwise have attended college. This is my parents' way of giving back
to the community. They continue to be active in these Foundations, interviewing students, and raising funds as well as acting as mentors for
the scholars. They are also very active in supporting their alma mater,
the UP High School.

    Besides my father, I had the support of many different mentors .
The principal and staff at Washington Manor Middle school helped
me gain confidence in trying new things and how to motivate people.
As I started to learn about the corporate landscape, the Filipina Wom-
en's Network has been an integral part of my personal growth. I have
been a member since 2007 when Elena Mangahas and Marily Monde-
har invited me to my first Power Lunch, and I had the opportunity to
rub elbows with so many successful Filipinas who were making strides
in their own industries. Having access to so many resources from different perspectives helps me feel good about the decisions I make for
Ramar. I accepted the role of President of FWN in 2013 so I could give
back to the community that has supported and inspired me, and so
that I can ensure that the next generation of Filipina Leaders will have

an organization that can cultivate their successes across all industries.

My leadership style is always evolving because I am eager for knowledge, but it will always be grounded by the entrepreneurial spirit I hold in my heart. Hard work does pay off. Treat everyone like family. Lead by example. Take risks and learn from every experience. Find a mentor and be a mentor. Live your life with a sense of purpose and always give back to your community.

At Ramar Foods International we strive to be extraordinary in everything that we do just like Ramon and Maria and Primo and Evangeline before us. My father Primo has the same vision and work ethic that his parents, Daddylo and Mommyla instilled in all of their kids. You can not tell anyone to work hard, you have to show them. In fact, almost all ten of my dad's siblings are successful business owners. And the third generation of 35 grandchildren is carrying on Mommyla's entrepreneurial spirit with their own businesses. I am very proud to carry on my grandparents' legacy of leading by example and giving back to the community. For 42 years Ramar Foods has been the leading manufacturer of Filipino and Asian foods in the U.S. We have achieved this through the quality of our products and the quality of our people. It continues to grow as Americans learn how to enjoy Filipino flavors and learn about Filipino culture. And everything we do is grounded in our mission: to make Ramar Foods synonymous with Filipino Food in the U.S. Today, I hear the name of our company and I can not help but think about my grandparents and how their entrepreneurial spirit fueled two more generations of leaders in a variety of fields. *Ramar*, *Mommyla*, *Daddylo*, and *Popsy*. That is right, I forgot to mention that Popsy is my father Primo and every day we work hard for him and our grandparents' legacy.

LEADERSHIP TIPS

1. ***Learn to build a core foundation in business from which you can diversify.*** When you start a business, master the foundations of the corporate world including process, finance, innovation, culture, and communication. This will become a valuable foundation from which you can launch a series of complementary businesses and a whole conglomerate of companies. From starting and leading a single organization, Doctor's Pharmaceuticals in the Philippines, Mommyla diversified into restaurants, motels, Ramar Foods, and other business in the U.S.

2. ***See opportunity in adversity.*** From a terrible loss, Daddylo and Mommyla came up with an idea so that others will not suffer the same loss. Learn to see problems as blessing in disguise. Adversity is a way of reminding you of other ways to do things, of new ways to prioritize your life, and of novel ways of framing perspectives.

3. ***Align business interests with social contributions.*** There is more to life than money, and there is more to business success than profits. If you can overlap your business opportunity with social contribution, you get a win-win situation. Choose a business which also has a positive social impact, and you can be doubly happy. Leadership is in the boardroom as well as in the homes and souls of your employees and consumers.

4. ***Learn every aspect of your business, do not just live off owners' privileges.*** Even if you come from a privileged background, learn the basics of business from the ground up, as I did. Put in your sweat equity. Leverage the connections you have, but earn your status from a position of merit as well. That will bring you much more buy-in from your organization and give you the respect you deserve.

5. ***Build a culture of community, quality, and excellence.*** Leaders are known not just for the milestones they reach but the way they create a lasting culture in their organizations. Long after you have departed, people should remember you for the community spirit you created in the organization, your passion for quality, and your drive

for internal and external excellence. To be Ramarkable is to attract notice for being exceptional or amazing.

6. ***Give back to society and build the next generation of leaders.*** Pass on the baton, create positive energy in society by mentoring the next generation of leaders. Give back to society generously, to the underprivileged. Give more than money, put in your effort and energy. Become a mentor, a coach, a sounding board for the next generation of leaders.

Leading an Industry: My Journey with 55,000 Heroes

Marife Zamora

Senior Vice President and Chairperson
Convergys Philippines

Abstract

My life journey in leadership began with my parents inculcating in me during my childhood a passion for excellence, and has continued to my professional and personal experiences as a corporate leader. My advocacy for integrity and women leadership has contributed to my developing into who I am today. In this chapter, I speak mainly of my ongoing 11 year career journey in Convergys, from the time I joined in 2003 as employee No. 2 in the Philippines, as Country Manager setting up the global customer management company's operations in the country, to my current role as Chairperson of Convergys Philippines. I am joined in this extraordinary journey by the 55,000 men and women of the company and by the parallel journeys of our colleagues in other geographical locations. As a leader in a people business, this story is not really just about me, but about all of us as a collective team. I talk about what is important for us, who we are, and what we stand for. I am proud to share that beyond the fast pace of the Convergys story especially in the Philippines, our story is about sharing a passion that makes extraordinary things possible. It is about proving that with exceptional performance, adaptability and resilience, the Filipino talent can really be the best in the world. It is a story of a collaborative spirit that can steer the nation to greatness.

Introduction

Setting the Standard, Steering the Nation

What does it take to be an incredible business leader, and what is the journey of a 'pioneer' like, especially one that sets the standard for the industry? These are the questions I often get asked as an individual, and about the organization I am in, Convergys. There are many things to consider, but I believe it starts with a vision that helps build the nation and shape the world.

Building the Philippines' economic and social capability depends significantly on employment— providing meaningful jobs and career opportunities for talented Filipinos, who in turn make a difference in improving their families' lives, of the clients and customers they serve, and the communities where they live and work.

As the first Philippines Country Manager for Convergys Corporation, a people business and global leader in customer management, I was tasked to build the company's footprint in the Philippines— from its first contact center with a handful of employees when operations began in 2003, to its current 34 sites nationwide and over 55,000 employees. With the help of my excellent leadership team, discussed below, the company achieved extraordinary growth, and now holds status as Convergys' largest geographical location in the world, and the Philippines' largest private employer since 2010. The global company supports Fortune 500 (including half of the Fortune 50) companies in industries such as communications, technology, financial services, retail, entertainment, automotive, and healthcare. We have 125,000 employees globally, spread across more than 150 centers. The Philippine operations span the globe and serves clients and their customers in North America, Europe, Australia, Latin America, and Asia.

Currently, I am Chairperson of Convergys Philippines, continuing to support the country's leadership team as well as representing the company in various industry associations and speaking forums. As I often share: a large part of our success is our clarity of vision, and the resilience and passion to realize that vision. When we started building the company, it was not about building a business. It was to do one simple thing: to help the Philippines. It was not growth for its own sake, nor was it solely about commerce. It was to accomplish something useful and significant that could have a real impact on the Filipino people: employment, keeping families together, and improving quality of life. And when you successfully get your team to articulate and embrace that vision, great things follow. I am fortunate to have seen the Convergys Philippines journey unfold from the very beginning.

The Convergys Journey:
Passion that Makes the Extraordinary Possible

My journey with Convergys and the company's remarkable growth in size runs parallel with the rise of the Philippine Business Process Outsourcing (BPO) industry. Convergys' success certainly contributed to helping the Philippines become the No. 1 voice-based outsourcing destination in the world, and No. 2 for overall outsourcing, second only to India. According to the IT-Business Process Outsourcing Association of the Philippines (IBPAP), the Philippine BPO industry has been the fastest growing industry for the last 10 years, with 2013 revenue at USD 16 billion. The entire workforce is expected to exceed one million headcount within the year 2014, and in 2016, revenue is expected to be between USD 20 to 25 billion.

With Convergys' position as the country's largest private employer, I consider this to be a story about sharing a passion that makes extraordinary things possible. It is about proving that the Filipino talent can take on the world with exceptional performance, adaptability and resilience. It is a testament that, with a collaborative spirit, we can all steer our nation to greatness and be modern day heroes.

It is important to go back to the beginning of this extraordinary journey. In 2003, Convergys established its presence in the Philippines. I was employee No. 2, hired then as Country Manager with the objective of setting up two operating centers with 800 employees. We were a small to medium enterprise (SME) when we started 11 years ago, but we had big dreams that resulted in 34 operating centers today and 55,000 employees nationwide; from Baguio in North Luzon, all the way to Davao in Mindanao.

From my perspective, the starting point of that journey was setting up a winning strategy. The underlying strategy has always been focus on excellence, being the best in everything we do, be it the search for talent, work location and environment, best practice tweaked to account for local nuances, and state-of-the-art tools needed by the business. The strategy of excellence in everything we do was commonplace.

I remember the time when we were brainstorming about the first print advertisement that we would run. A manager showed me a contract for a quarter page ad. And we said, "No. We're one of the biggest contact center companies in the world. We want to attract the best and the brightest. Let's go for front page, full page ad in all the major dailies." And that is what we did. It was our first ad campaign, and it was about celebrating our size and scale as among the world's biggest and best, and telling everyone that "we will not set limits to our growth." It was a coup; we set the bar high. No BPO company was ever in the front page of the Sunday recruitment pages of the nation's top three newspapers, and no single BPO ad had covered the whole front page before. We had the luxury of having the best talent walk through our doors! With 800 people and our big dreams, we were acting already as what we wanted to be: the biggest and the best.

And that big dream indeed happened and continues to happen to this day.

Starting Right with an Exceptional Philippines Leadership Team

This story is not just about me. I consider the journey as being one with the rest of Convergys Philippines' 55,000 employees, who take pride in their work and entrust their careers and growth to Convergys. They are the ones who help us set the standard as the nation's largest private employer and strongest BPO company. They are the ones who, by their daily work, have changed their lives and the lives of others in the process. They are our heroes!

In this light, I see myself as the temporary steward of this great enterprise. I come to work every day not as head of an organization or captain of industry. I come to work every day to work hand in hand with colleagues in trying to make it better, stronger, and more influential.

It has always been the company's philosophy to harness a local

leadership team in the locations where we operate. When we set up in
the Philippines, the quality of leadership was something on which we
did not compromise. A year and four months after starting operations,
we found and attracted the best contact center operations management executive in the country, Ivic Mueco. Ivic started in Convergys
as Head of Operations and succeeded me in 2011 as Country Manager.
Ivic is the major contributor to the growth of the business, ably assisted by her entire leadership team. Our mantra was to go for the best in
talent, process, and tools. And Ivic and the rest of the team made the
strategy work in the Philippines and share the responsibility for the
success we enjoy today.

I take special pride in saying that the members of the executive
management team complement one another; each plays to his or her
individual strengths. Everyone shares ownership and accountability.
For instance, recruiting goals and challenges are not just the responsibility of the Head of Recruiting. Human Resources (HR), Training,
Operations, Facilities, and IT issues are not just each department's
problems to address. For me, this collaborative spirit is important, especially when you have a company that has grown at double-digit percentage rates each year. Every leader has to come together and move as
one. This is the only way a team can move with such speed and agility
amidst changes. In fact, it is a norm in our BPO industry to experience
changes all the time because this industry is very dynamic. We need to
adjust and help address both the challenges and opportunities that our
clients experience in their respective industries, across the globe.

It is also common for many companies that experience growth to
consider it as a turbulent or chaotic experience, like riding through
choppy waters. I can attest to this, given Convergys' double-digit
percentage headcount growth every single year, over 11 years from
800 to 55,000 people. I believe it is important that everyone works
together to overcome the constant waves of change that accompany
a growth experience. In my experience with my team, no problem
is beneath anyone. There was a time when we were growing rapidly
and at the same time hiring for an HR leadership position. The head
of our Finance department volunteered to temporarily lead the HR
organization as well, to ensure no disruption to the business while

we were in the process of seeking the new HR talent. I could not be prouder of this leadership team. Not only do we continue to achieve stellar financial and operational success for our global company, we also continue to achieve significant retention, including of our topmost leaders, despite the intense grapple over leadership talent in the marketplace for our industry. For an 11-year old company in such a competitive environment, the average tenure of our executive leadership team is seven years! Now that's commitment!

Shared Values, Unshakeable Integrity and Social Commitment

Convergys prides itself in having a shared set of corporate values that enable a values-centric high performing environment. These corporate values guide the decisions around how we operate and care for our clients, shareholders and employees. But the real influence occurs when each member of the Convergys team applies these values to their daily work and interactions with one another and the wider world.

For instance, Convergys' value for integrity goes beyond the company walls. For me specifically, I am a member of the board of the Philippine Integrity Initiative, a nationwide movement to institutionalize ethical standards in the country. Convergys is a pioneering BPO partner committed to the Integrity Initiative from the time it began in 2010, and was first to sign the Integrity Pledge. The impact of Convergys' participation? Role modeling by our employees, as well as processes, and standards that extended even to our vendor partners. More than a hundred of our vendor partners have signed the Integrity pledge, and Convergys employees are also participating in the initiative's public events such as its annual integrity run. Overall, these contributions have earned Convergys the position of being one of, if not the number one, partner of the movement.

I believe that integrity is the cornerstone of our success. Integrity is who we are, what we stand for. It is the value we seek in the people we invite to join our team, and is the value we uphold in everything that we do. Our identity as a company and as individuals impels Team Convergys to support the Philippine Integrity Initiative. At 55,000-strong in the Philippines and 125,000-strong across the world, we would like to share this light with the rest of the world, starting in the countries in which we operate.

As the company is in the field of providing customer service, employees regularly deal with confidential customer information, making integrity of paramount importance in every interaction. Employees are also the first line of defense against the threat of fraud. In this industry, which is people-centric and global in nature, it helps to straightforwardly and consistently set the tone of integrity, transparency, and meritocracy in all transactions. We also use integrity, transparency, and meritocracy as well as objectivity in measuring performance and developing the careers of our people. Our company's solidarity with the Integrity Initiative demonstrates how we stand for integrity, inside and outside the workplace. For Convergys as an organization, this is one of the ways that we show the nation and the world that in the fight against corruption, each person counts.

In fact, Convergys is the only BPO and one of five companies in the Philippines that earned an 'Advanced' rating from the Integrity Initiative's Validation System (IVS). The IVS begins with a voluntary self-assessment taken by companies who are signatories to the Integrity Pledge, a commitment to conduct all business transactions and processes with integrity and transparency. The self-assessment is followed by an independent validation by the Integrity Initiative. Companies that have 'Advanced' rating from this process are considered to have maintained extensive and effective practices in their organizations and are demonstrating best practices in six focus areas: Top Management, Dealing with Employees, Dealing with Clients, Dealing with Business Partners, Dealing with Finances and Dealing with Government, Communities, Environment and other Key Stakeholders. To share best practices in line with integrity, Convergys is also a regular participant or speaker at the annual Philippine Integrity Summit.

Giving Back to the Communities
Where We Live and Work

Any industry leader, be it an individual or an organization, needs to be a role model in contributing to the improvement of lives in the community. Convergys' unique approach is to drive philanthropy where our employees live and work, and enable them to give back and help build a strong foundation that enables the success of tomorrow's workforce. This is another way we demonstrate that by making a positive difference, we can be heroes for our countrymen.

Called Convergys Community Action Network (CAN), employees at each site are empowered to choose the beneficiaries they will support, whether it is to help access or remove barriers to education that include poverty and illness, or support healthy communities in which wellness and/or educational opportunities thrive.

I am both humbled and proud of this aspect of our work and people. Corporate Citizenship is also one of Convergys' eight values. Thousands of generous Convergys employees in all of our sites collectively volunteer their time, talent, and treasure, making this value very real in our organization. We are grateful to them for keeping alive the spirit of giving. They are an inspiration to me and the Convergys global leadership team, and to our other thousands of colleagues across the globe who are part of Convergys CAN and who are aware of the positive impact that we are making for our countrymen. We are also thankful to our partner organizations, for working hand in hand with us in our shared vision of improving education for children, who are the workforce of tomorrow. Indeed, what everyone does encompasses much more than the word 'work' can describe. What we do together is a mission that is bigger than our organizations combined. The mission that we are accomplishing today will outlive us all.

Convergys has also been recognized for this unique philanthropic approach, the Convergys CAN. The CAN was the winner of the 2013 American Chamber of Commerce CSR Awardee for Access to Quality Education, and was one of the companies selected as 2014 Best in CSR, at the Fourth Asian Excellence Awards.

Nurturing Others to Reach
their Highest Potential

Another Convergys value, of which I am a firm believer and supporter since day one, is 'Developing People.' I also personally refer to it as our 'Build-from-Within' philosophy. At least 80% of our leaders are grown from within our employee base and promoted within their careers.

This is a testament to the efforts of the company and the executive management in establishing a robust leadership development processes and programs precisely to provide career opportunities for our people to grow. 'Build-from-Within' is critical in sustaining the company's extraordinary growth. To lead the industry, we must build strong leaders in our organization.

With a view on the growth in my own role, I often share my insights and learnings, such as my experience taking an Executive Sponsor role in the Convergys Global Women's Network (GWN). The GWN is open to employees beginning at supervisor level, all the way to our top leaders, and it spans the globe. GWN aims to provide additional expertise and support opportunities for career development among women leaders. In one of those sessions I shared with the GWN the story of building our footprint in the Philippines and the way we leveraged our strengths and talents to become the employer and destination of choice for business process outsourcing.

Leadership that Conquers the Uncharted

I am fortunate to have received honor and recognition during my entire career, especially in Convergys. I am regarded as the only Filipino BPO executive with a global C-suite role, with C-suite understood as a corporation's most important senior executives since top senior executives' titles tend to start with the letter C, chief executive officer, chief operating officer, and chief information officer for example. I certainly hope that I won't be the only Filipina in a global C-suite role and for this number to grow as soon as possible!

I am also thankful to have been awarded the Global Filipino Executive of the Year at the 2011 Asia CEO Awards, the 'Go Negosyo' Woman STARpreneuer Awardee in the 2012 Women Entrepreneurship Summit, and last but of course not least, the 2013 Global 100 Most Influential Filipinas awarded by the Filipina Women's Network.

I always give back recognition to our team. I am especially proud of the industry recognition Convergys has earned, that speaks to our financial growth, employer and operational excellence, managerial and leadership competencies, and social commitment. This includes the company being inducted into the Philippine Economic Zone Authority (PEZA) Hall of Fame based on being recognized as Top Employer and Top Exporter for three consecutive years in both categories. Convergys Philippines was also hailed as the first Information Communication Technology (ICT) Hall of Fame awardee, for Best BPO Employer, after having won the award three times. Additionally, Convergys was also a two-time recipient of ICT BPO Company of the Year.

My own growth in my role in the company is also a wonderful aspect of my journey. After being Philippines Country Manager, I was given the role of Senior Vice President and Managing Director for Asia Pacific, Europe, Middle East, and Africa in 2011. In this role, I managed Convergys' largest region (Philippines, India and UK) which accounted for approximately 44,500 of the global company's headcount at the time and through 2012.

As a testament to the caliber of excellence of our teams beyond the Philippines, the geographic locations of India, and UK continue to gain significant recognition as well. Convergys India was recognized in the 2011 Dataquest Top 20 BPO companies list, the 2012 Golden Peacock Award for Most Innovative Service for its free, comprehensive employee transport system, and being in the Global InfoWeek 500 Innovation list for the same service. Convergys United Kingdom also won Contact Centre Team of the Year (2012) and Outsourced Contact Centre of the Year (2013) in the Northeast Contact Centre Awards, UK.

To further help our country gain international prominence, I believe that we should also support our industry as a whole, such as the Information and Communications Technology (ICT) industry, and associations such as the Contact Center Association of the Philippines (a member of the IT-Business Process Outsourcing Association of the Philippines or IT-BPAP), and the American Chamber of Commerce, and many more. I have been privileged to have taken roles in these organizations as well.

Prior to joining Convergys, I served as Managing Director for Headstrong Incorporated, a global provider of integrated solutions and digital technologies. Previous to that, I was with IBM Philippines where I held a number of sales, marketing, and management positions during my 18 year tenure with the company.

Greatness that Comes from Within:
Being Marife Zamora

I consider my passion for excellence as something I developed early on in life. I feel fortunate to have parents who have a deep commitment to making a difference in the world, and to doing things excellently. When I was a child, every time I would complain that I was bored, my mother would urge me to go help someone—anyone—in need.

My parents also truly believed that things work out well if one keeps on learning and studies harder. And while I was not always in first place in school during my childhood (in fact when my grandfather would visit and have pictures with the grandkids who were top of the class, I was not in those pictures!), the discipline to keep on learning and studying hard was ingrained in me. I pushed myself to always strive to be better. Discipline and persistence leads to so-called 'greatness,' or what I would simply call success. I still remember my mother saying: "We are systematically creating a race out of something that ought to be a journey." We know that success is not about simply running faster than everyone else in some predetermined direction. Yet the message we are sending from birth is that if you do not become the Spelling Bee champ or get into an Ivy League school, then you will somehow finish life with fewer points than everyone else. That is not right. You will eventually succeed, with the lifelong habits of discipline and persistence.

I also believe that positive reinforcement is worth developing throughout one's life. My mother will surely be bursting with pride now seeing me where I am but she was also bursting with pride when I had a bad piano recital when I was in Grade 2. My mother's positive reinforcement definitely gave me the winning attitude that helped me, and in turn, those whom I lead, get to where we are today. It is also important to recognize that one must be purposive in giving positive reinforcement. You have to know what desired behaviors to reinforce, and make sure that those behaviors are the ones you truly recognize and reward.

Effective positive reinforcement goes beyond words of praise and reassurance, and goes deeper than material rewards or incentives. It has to be sincere. And sincerity, as well as kindness, takes time and commitment. You can never err with treating everyone in the organization with respect, thoughtfulness, and a kind word. Every one of our employees is an essential employee. Every one of them wants to be viewed that way. And if you treat them that way, they will view you that way. They will not let you down or let you fail. They will accomplish whatever you have put in front of them. The person who comes to clean my office every night is no less a person than the Chairperson of Convergys. They deserve and get a 'thank you' from me, a token every Christmas, and an inquiry on how they are doing. These actions let them know they are valued. Being kind does not mean being soft or a wimp. Kindness is not a sign of weakness. It is a sign of confidence.

Let me share a personal experience: I have a Facebook (FB) account and my FB friends include our call center agents. I once saw an FB posting from a Team Leader about her joy in being ranked No. 1 in her program for three consecutive months. That level of a performance is a mean feat. So I posted a congratulatory note on her page. I was pleasantly surprised with her response, which went, "When the boss of all bosses likes your pic, I go chicken dancing." So I believe, as the old saying puts it, "To the world, you may be one person but to one person, you may be the world." Positive reinforcement, having faith in the greatness that is within the person, and expressing this, changes lives.

I take special pride in the fact that Convergys has positively changed 55,000 lives in the Philippines alone, and is still growing rapidly. For me, this success is achieved first and foremost by delivering excellent performance for our clients and their customers around the world. And because we are a people business, that excellence is delivered by the dedicated men and women who are our employees, to whom the company is equally committed to support in their growth and development.

Women Leaders — Taking the Top Spot

Speaking further of excellence, I believe that being No. 1 by a mile, setting the standard as a leader, requires one to push boundaries and challenge individuals to go for the top spot. The topic of women leadership is especially close to my heart, and is a personal advocacy.

I recently started speaking up about the challenges women face in the workforce, something I was given the opportunity to do at the Asia CEO Forum last year and once again this year. I was actually inspired by Sheryl Sandberg, COO of Facebook and her book, *Lean In*. As a result, a group of us launched an advocacy for women in the workplace and the will to lead. With the help of Sharon Dayaon of KPMG and funding from Noel Bonoan, COO of KPMG, we did a count of women CEOs in the Philippines who are not 'COOs — Children of Owners.' Lo and behold, out of the top 1,000 corporations in the country, we only got 20 names. These 20 will be the backbone of the 'Lean In Circle' that we formed.

To further cite my learnings from Sheryl Sandberg's *Lean In* book and global movement, I believe and agree that we need to acknowledge openly that gender remains an issue at the highest levels of leadership. We need to start talking about this. We need to start talking about how women underestimate their abilities compared to men; and for women, but not men, success and likeability are negatively correlated. That means that as a woman is more successful in the workplace, she will be less liked. This then means that women probably need a different form of management and mentorship, a different form of sponsorship and encouragement, and some protection, in some ways perhaps more than men.

Doing my own share of speaking at various leadership forums, I implore everyone, men and women alike, to 'raise their hands' for tough jobs and risky assignments, and to take advantage of rigorous performance reviews which are the best time to get coaching, or to even seek it proactively whenever necessary, not limited to performance review schedules. I encourage everyone to seek opportunities to stand out in the crowd, ask for what we want, and to speak up and "toot our horns" when we hit a goal.

Therefore, do not wait to get noticed. The most important factor to determine whether you will succeed is not your gender, it is YOU. Be open to opportunity and take risks. In fact, take the most difficult, the so called messiest, the most challenging assignment you can find, and then take control. It is wise for aspiring leaders to cultivate risk-taking. Pursue new skills relentlessly along the career path. Change job or role after you have mastered the current one. Also remember that career growth is not just about vertical progression. Be willing to go sideways on the career track or even backward, to pick up key expertise or command a business unit.

This advocacy I have committed to women, the workplace, and the will to lead, is not easy. As the objective of this pursuit is to have more women leaders at the top, I believe that if we make a collective effort to positively reinforce the behaviors that will take us to this result, it will become a reality; and as such will take soul searching, brutal honesty, and making hard choices.

To illustrate my own experience during the early years of my career, I remember the time people would ask me how I brought my children up, and I would always reply that they brought themselves up. I was always out during their childhood years traveling to Hongkong for three weeks of entry level sales class, another three weeks for advanced class, another two weeks of marketing school, a week of media training, weeks of trips to the U.S. or Asia to attend a roadshow with a client, going home late to crank out a proposal or being in a social engagement. I considered myself a delinquent mother. I still feel guilty having done this.

However to my delight, when I asked my daughter Tina who was then in kindergarten what she wanted to be when she grows up, she replied that she wanted to be like me; traveling around the world. That reply made my heart sing. By the way, if I were one of the stars of IBM during my time, Tina is much better than I am in selling a value proposition and making it successful. So, I must have done something right!

A New Chapter in the Journey

These days, whenever not at work, I am very much enjoying the company of my family, my daughter Tina, son Ian and his wife Jhoana, and their two-year old son Ayrton Raphael. My grandson Ayrton is the "love of my life." And these days, in my household, I am called "Mamita!" My Facebook page is strewn with family photos, featuring Ayrton prominently of course! I gladly wake up very early in the morning on most days, as I love bringing him to his pre-school. During my most recent vacation in May, I visited San Francisco and Las Vegas in the U.S., together with Ayrton, Jhoana and Tina. It makes me chuckle recalling how that trip went, because two-year old Ayrton pretty much dictated how much time we spent at each place. So if we are shopping and he already wants to leave, we follow him! With Ayrton, I am so excited for so many new experiences to come. And to close this chapter, I leave you with this quote: "A life is about its events; it's about challenges met and overcome— or not. It is about successes and failures. But more than all of these put together, it's about how we touch and are touched by the people we meet. The people in my life made me who I am." This little man Ayrton is already a great influence on who I will be.

LEADERSHIP TIPS

I believe there are four key qualities of an effective leader.

1. *A skillful and intuitive portfolio strategist.* Think long-term and have a differentiating edge over competition.

2. *Focused and analytical thinking.* Leverage facts and market trends, make sense of those and make decisions accordingly. But after the homework is done, trust your instincts.

3. *Competitiveness.* From the start of my career until now, I have injected my competitive nature into every fiber of my work. Our industry sets very high standards for growth margins, market leadership, and near-flawless quality, standards we call "stretch goals" which require our employees to reach as high as possible—but we also expect standards to be met and maintained. Also, if you do not have a competitive advantage, get out of the game. Control your own destiny or someone else will. Be No.1 by a mile!

4. *Flexibility and communication.* My leadership style is flexible and constantly adapting. Beyond being a CEO, one should be seen as a management role model, an oracle, as well as an icon for those who hope to ascend to the top. Also be a good communicator and motivator. Addressing large groups was something I had to learn. Good communication is simply everyone having the same set of facts.

What I also consider true is that the most successful individuals populating the top rung of the corporate ladder are those who attract top talent and inspire them to exceptional levels of performance. They are concerned about the careers of their subordinate, as much, or more than, their own. Benevolent leadership is also good, because in that environment, information and authority flow freely. Honesty abounds. People can question authority without retribution. Creativity reigns. Each team member feels accountable to other team members as well as to their leader.

My final advice to next-generation leaders concerns the always present topic of work-life balance. In my view, there is no such thing as work-life balance. There is work, and there is life. You need to decide on your priorities, every day. No matter your gender, what is important is getting the right amount and type of support to help you grow, not just professionally, but also personally. If you get that support, you can make it to the very top.

Transcending Boundaries

HARMONIZING GLOBAL TEAMS IN AFGHANISTAN

Maria Africa Beebe, Ph.D.

Director, Global Networks

Abstract

I was actively involved in networking various African and U.S. universities around telecommunications policy and regulation in 2005, when Afghanistan came 'calling.' Afghanistan is a microcosm of the world. This case study is a reflection of my experiences from 2005 to 2008, as Chief of Party of the Afghan eQuality Alliances, funded by the United States Agency for International Development (USAID) as a Global Development Alliance (GDA). I have identified leadership concepts that led to the success of this activity within the socio-economic context of a single but complex country, Afghanistan. I have examined the multiple sources of leadership in the Afghan eQuality Alliances, the shared purpose, the alliance dynamics of collaboration and competition, and the challenges for global teams posed by functions of leadership, culture, and Islam. The case study concludes with lessons learned from harmonizing global teams in Afghanistan from the perspective of a Filipina, naturalized as an American, and representing U.S. interests. As part of my conclusion, I identify implications for leadership development.

Qatra qatra daryaa mesha . . .
Drop by drop, it becomes an ocean . . .
(Dari Proverb)

Introduction and the Path to Afghanistan

In this chapter, I reflect on my experience as Chief of Party for the Afghan eQuality Alliances between 2005-2008. When asked "Why Afghanistan," my answer has been "Afghanistan called me." In 2005, I was successfully engaged in networking various African and U.S. universities to develop telecommunications policy and regulation. Networking African and U.S. universities was consistent with my life-long sense of purpose, of being able to make a difference and contribute to society. I have a proven commitment to the implementation of international development assistance by the joint definition of goals and strategies and the sharing of resources and risks. Moreover, the timing was right. I felt I was ready because of my higher education qualifications, technical background, international development experience with Peace Corps, USAID, Oregon State University and Washington State University embedded in *pakikipagkapwa*. (See synthesis chapter for a more detailed explanation of the term.) Moreover, I had the courage to say "yes" and then to say "no" when I knew that I had trained and mentored enough Afghans to carry on.

"She will travel around the world," declared the midwife when I was born in Zamboanga del Sur where my parents were living in 1948. And travel the world I did as life happened. My sense of home is very much related to the global community. First, there was working as a Peace Corps Volunteer with the Igorot mountain peoples, and then being an international development contractor while accompanying my husband, James, for his Department of State USAID postings in the Sudan, Philippines, Liberia, and South Africa. I also did consulting work in Poland, Kenya, Laos, Nepal, Switzerland, Nigeria, Botswana, Zimbabwe, Mozambique, Ethiopia, and then Afghanistan through academic appointments with Oregon State University, and Washington State University. My sense of purpose is inextricably tied to seeking local and global connections. This global experience is the reason for establishing Global Networks. My personal challenge has been to ask people around me: "What is the opportunity for local and global connections that will contribute to the common good?"

Becoming a Peace Corps Volunteer was an unintended consequence of falling in love with and getting married to a U.S. Peace Corps volunteer in 1970, visiting Peace Corps headquarters in Washington, D.C., and being told: "You would be a perfect volunteer since you have language, a knowledge of Philippine culture, and teaching skills, but to be a Peace Corps Volunteer you have to be a U.S. citizen. However, if you see yourself as a U.S. Peace Corps Volunteer, we may be able to make it happen." I said, "Yes." Peace Corps requested and received approval for expeditious citizenship for me and within six weeks, I became a U.S. citizen and a Peace Corps volunteer assigned to Bontoc, Mt Province. The lesson here is that within bureaucracies there are humans who can make things happen.

The Development Context

The choice to be called the 'Government of the Islamic Republic of Afghanistan' is a public affirmation of Islamic values. However, Afghanistan has been variously referred to as a rogue state (Khalilzad and Byman 2000), fragmented state (Rubin 2002), and failed state (Ghani and Lockhart 2008). This is due to a long history of internal strife and external invasions and pressures, resulting in alternating fusion and fission (Dupree 1973). The external invasions have contributed to Afghanistan's heritage including Buddhism followed by Islam. In 1979 a rebellion by the *mujahideen*, Islamic fighters, against the Marxist government led to an invasion by the Soviet Union. The *mujahideens*, with covert aid from the US, fought the Soviets who pulled out in 1989. Power sharing among the *mujahideens* disintegrated in 1994 and they turned their guns on each other. Afghanistan's ethnic diversity resulted in different warlords governing different geographic areas with support by different external interests. Disillusioned *mujahideen* fighters, mostly Pushtuns, then formed the Taliban movement. In 1996, the Taliban seized control of Kabul.

After September 11, 2001, the U.S. invaded Afghanistan as part of its war on terror. President Hamid Karzai became transitional president in December 2001 and was subsequently elected as President. Given the significant role of multilateral agencies in Afghanistan, many observers question whether Afghanistan is a sovereign country or is an instance of what Bothe and Fisher-Lescano (2002) refer to as global governance. The issue of sovereignty brings into question aid effectiveness and sustainability.

In December 2001, Afghanistan began a slow process of recon-struction. The magnitude and complexity of the problems faced by the Afghans are reflected in higher education institutions. These in-stitutions are critical for providing the leadership, managers, and per-sonnel that run and operate the key institutions of society, including the government civil service, private sector, and civil society organi-zations. However, the decades of conflict had a disastrous impact on Afghan higher education institutions that became isolated from their global peers, and lacked opportunities for professional development. These institutions needed to build their capacity to respond to the needs of contemporary students. There was a critical need to enrich their experiences by bringing research and engagement into the cur-riculum and by offering practical opportunities for students to pre-pare for the world. To help address this challenge, USAID provided funding to Washington State University for a Global Development Alliance (GDA). The GDA was tasked with creating and supporting alliances for higher education through the Afghan eQuality Alliances project. All GDAs represent USAID's commitment to change their way of implementing international development assistance through the joint definition of the development goal and the means to achieve it, shared resources and risks, joint effort, innovative approaches, and leveraging resources (USAID 2009). GDA activities are designed to be transformational. The objective is to work with U.S. partners around the world, "to build and sustain democratic, well-governed states that will respond to the needs of their people and conduct themselves re-sponsibly in the international system" (Rice 2006).

Geography, ethnicity and language, power struggles, human devel-opment indicators, the role of women, and the state of higher edu-cation are among the socio-cultural, political, and economic factors that posed complex leadership challenges for the GDA work in Af-ghanistan. Moreover, the role of Islam in development and Islamic leadership principles particularly in the context of Afghanistan were regarded as 'stumbling blocks' by many in the development com-munity and not appreciated as potential building blocks to achieve development goals. This case study includes a brief comparison of

Islamic principles of leadership with the generally accepted principles of leadership espoused in the west. The study concludes with implications for leadership development and intercultural leadership in a globalized world.

The Global Development Alliance

The project name, Afghan eQuality Alliances, was significant as each word emphasized the long-term goal of Afghan ownership, equal access to quality education and e-education resources as a shared vision, and alliances to address jointly the capacity development challenges in higher education. By working together, the hope was that alliance partners could achieve solutions that would not be possible if individuals, bilateral partnerships, or traditional donor projects acted alone in silos.

Afghan Ownership and Leadership

Nurturing local ownership and leadership is consistent with the Paris Declaration (2005) on assistance effectiveness. The Paris Declaration defines ownership as the exercise of effective leadership over a country's own development policies and strategies. To ensure Afghan ownership, in defining higher education development priorities, the potential alliance partners consulted with a broad set of stakeholders including university chancellors, ministry officials, and students. However, consultation early on was not sufficient to sustain Afghan ownership and leadership. Continuing challenges have resulted from changes in leadership during the three year life of the project, including two Ministers of Higher Education, two Deputy Ministers of Academic Affairs, four Kabul University Chancellors, and three Kabul University Vice Chancellors for Academic Affairs. Meanwhile activities had to proceed to meet the donor timetable even as efforts were renewed constantly to ensure Afghan ownership of activities. At the same time, there was as much change in leadership on the donor side.

Equality a Shared Purpose

Equality meant a shared vision of equal access to quality education and e-education resources. This shared vision has required balancing pedagogy, content, technology resources, and other factors. These factors were not always in harmony, given the changes in leadership and differences in basic cultural assumptions concerning equal access, quality education, and the use of e-education.

Nature of the Alliances

The level of collaboration and sharing envisioned for this activity required a unique project structure. A macro-team served as an umbrella for several overlapping micro-teams to achieve a common goal (see Figure 1).

FIGURE 1.
Macro and Micro Teams

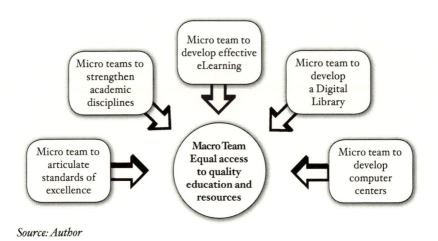

Source: Author

Leadership in Global Teams

Multiple Sources of leadership

Because the project was designed as an alliance, there has been the involvement of numerous leaders from diverse nationality, gender, and functional backgrounds. From the Afghan side, key leaders have included the Minister of Higher Education, the Deputy Minister for Academic Affairs, Chancellors, Vice-Chancellors, Deans, professors, and lecturers, at Kabul University, Kabul Polytechnic University, Kabul Medical University, Heart University, Balkh University, Nangarhar University, Kandahar University, the Afghanistan Civil Service Institute, and the Institute of Diplomacy of the Ministry of Foreign Affairs. From international partners, sources of leadership have included deans and lecturers from the Indian Institute of Public Administration, Aga Khan University in Pakistan, Tokyo University of Foreign Studies in Japan, University of Western Cape in South Africa, Asian Institute of Management in the Philippines, TU Berlin, University of Groningen, and Springerlink in the Netherlands. From the U.S. sources of leadership have included the Chief of Party, professors, and lecturers from University of Arizona, Colorado, Maryland, Ohio, Colgate, Hartford, Washington, Washington State University, and Gonzaga University. From the donor-side, sources of leadership have included NATO, USAID, German Aid, World Bank, Indian government, Japan International Cooperation Agency (JICA), and provincial reconstruction teams.

For the Afghanistan case, the multiple sources of leadership can be viewed using a model suggested by Morgeson, DeRue and Karam (2010) that considers the locus of leadership (internal and external) and formality of leadership (formal and informal). These relationships are shown in Table 1.

Along the formality dimension, WSU had formal responsibility for the team's overall performance. The major sponsor, USAID, formally assigned a leader, called a Cognizant Technical Officer (CTO). The Ministry of Higher Education served as the government representative. These external leaders did not perform any of the team's day-to-day tasks. What became problematic was when external

TABLE I.

Multiple Sources of Leadership and Locus of Leadership for the Afghan eQuality Alliance

FORMALITY OF LEADERSHIP		
Formal	Responsible for team performance	
Informal	No direct responsibility for team performance	
LOCUS OF LEADERSHIP		
Internal	Engaged in day-to-day activities. Shared responsibility.	1. Macro Team Leader– WSU in US 2. Macro Project Manager – WSU Chief of Party in Afghanistan 3. Micro Team Leaders
External	Not engaged in day-to-day activities. Supporters and advocates	1. Sponsor–USAID 2. GoIRA–Ministry of Higher Education (MoHE)

Source: Adapted from Morgeson, DeRue, and Karam (2010)

leaders viewed their role as micro-managing day-to-day activities. Along the informal dimension, shared leadership among team members did occur, with some Afghan team members emerging as leaders, while officials from USAID, MoHE, Kabul University, and other higher education institutions acted as mentors and champions; providing feedback, supporting a positive social climate and engaging in problem solving.

Because the alliances included provision for grants, the sources of leadership tended to shift. When a grant was given, for example, to Hartford University to improve the quality of engineering education, the formal internal leadership for that function moved to Hartford University, and WSU, who had overall responsibility, provided the external leadership within the formal dimension of leadership.

Collaboration and Competition

The overall goal was to build strength in higher education through collaborative. In general, higher education institutions in both Afghanistan and outside Afghanistan were just learning to understand

and appreciate the alliance model and its requirements for good faith agreements ranging from contractual and affiliation arrangements to full mergers. A complicating factor was that key leadership even from the same institutions operated by different principles and used different measures of success and work modes. My role as the Chief of Party was that of a conductor of multiple jazz bands and a juggler of morphing and often ill-defined balls.

WSU provided overall leadership and was responsible for maximizing synergy, locating human and financial resources, and entering into agreements with alliance partners. Partners received support from the project while also contributing their own resources. WSU had to manage a range of transitory, intermittent, and more lasting alliance partners; make timely choices about different partners; and manage transitions as various partners entered and exited the process.

The relationship among the alliance partners unfolded in overlapping phases, similar to those identified by Kanter (1994). The overlapping phases included starting with an initial meeting to discover compatibility, drawing up plans, discovering and bridging differences, and, gaining from the collaborative advantage. As participants changed, situations evolved and priorities shifted. As the alliances developed overtime, different alliance partners were engaged in helping define the project. Several of the alliance partners have, at one time or another, displayed what Schon (1971) called the Rashomon effect, where the telling of the same story by several participants had become several different, oftentimes ambiguous, and sometimes incompatible stories.

When asked about their motivation for working in Afghanistan, the most common answer by the external alliance partners was based on altruism: "They need help the most. We can help make a difference."

Alliance partners had to develop trust while calculating how others were likely to behave. Trust was especially critical when partners were required to act as agents for each other. The complex challenges posed by the socio-political and cultural factors have required a range of capabilities and commitments by the different institutions working on the shared goal of improving higher education. The range of alliances among partners is characterized by a variety of collaborative interactions similar to those identified by Mandell (2003). Mandell noted that these different collaborative interactions require different leadership styles and communication .

1. The most basic alliance used networking for dialogue, exchanging information, and creating common understanding. These intermittent alliances have loosely defined roles with low-key leadership, minimal decision-making, and informal communication. An example would be an informal donor group convened by the World Bank that met sporadically to share information on human resources.

2. The next level of alliances required coordination. In addition to exchanging information, partners worked together on implementing activities. More defined roles, facilitative leadership, and formal communication were necessary. An example of this type of alliance was the provision of different levels of computer education in order to improve the use of information technologies (IT) for teaching and learning. The Ministry of Higher Education IT coordinator chaired a working group, facilitated the work of NATO to provide bandwidth for all higher education institutions, and reviewed the activities and results of the Cisco Networking Academy, TU Berlin, the Afghans Next Generation e-Learning Centers of the Afghan eQuality Alliances, and other activities with IT components.

3. Cooperation was needed when alliances with numerous partners were working with different local partners and resources had to be shared. An example was an engineering alliance where different universities from abroad worked with different local Afghan universities on curriculum. This type of an alliance required cooperation among the donors, cooperation among the local institutions, and cooperation with the local administrative structure. This more complex arrangement required shared leadership among the different teams involved in the activity.

4. The most complex alliances required ongoing collaboration on both design and implementation of activities. Collaboration required exchange of information, joint implementation of activities, sharing of resources, and, enhancing the capacity of another organization. An example was the collaboration required to implement an executive master's degree program, a program at the government funded Kabul University (KU). The executive master's curriculum and many of its instructors were provided by foreign partners but with increasing responsibility transferred to local partners over the life of the project life. In some cases the local counterparts had to be trained and mentored in the use of the new curriculum.

Not all participants recognized the need for the different ways of working together depending on the level of collaborations that activities required. This became a source of tension when, for example, one or more alliance partners demanded approvals of actions when all that was sought was the sharing of information about actions.

My role was that of translator and cultural informant for concepts that were often equally new for Afghans and non-Afghans and that of a referee in a game where the rules were in constant change.

Functions of Leadership

The leadership functions can be conceptualized based on the action phases suggested by Morgeson, deRue, and Karam (2010). At the transition phase, the leadership functions are to: compose team, define mission, establish expectations and goals, structure and plan, train and develop team, make sense, and provide feedback. At the action phase, the team leadership functions are to: monitor team, manage team boundaries, challenge team, perform team task, solve problems, provide resources, encourage team-self management, and support social climate (9-27).

Hill's team leadership model (2010) provides a more nuanced tool for understanding the complexities of team leadership in a multicultural environment, as in the case of the GDA in Afghanistan. As shown in Figure 2, the leadership decisions to improve team effectiveness were (a) to continue monitoring or intervene; (b) to intervene at the internal or external level—in the team's environment; and (c) to intervene at the task or relational level. These layers of leadership decisions were complicated by the interactions between leadership actions, different cultural clusters, and Islam (see discussion below).

FIGURE 2. Leadership Decisions.

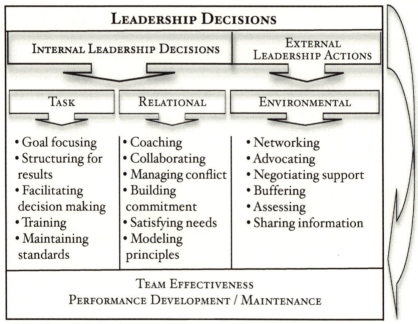

Adopted from Hill (2010)

Leadership and Culture Clusters

The GLOBE study (House et al. 2004) is useful in understanding the challenges posed by culture for leadership in Afghanistan. GLOBE researchers used data on cultural dimensions from 62 countries to form 10 regional clusters. Three of these clusters that were represented in the Afghan project are Anglo, Germanic Europe, and Southern Asia (that includes Philippines, India, and Iran and would likely include Afghanistan). The researchers for the GLOBE study also identified six global leadership behaviors, based on how different cultural clusters viewed the leadership behavior of others: charismatic/value based, team-oriented, participative, humane oriented, autonomous, and self-protective. GLOBE researchers then related the regional clusters to the global leadership behaviors. The Southern Asia cluster viewed self-protective leadership as very important whereas self-protective leadership was least important for both the Anglo and Germanic Europe clusters. While the GLOBE study is useful for making generalizations about culture and leadership, it is not sufficient to explain the dynamics of leadership in the multicultural teams in the Afghanistan GDA. For example, in the GLOBE study, participative leadership is viewed as least important by the Southern Asia cluster. This desire for autocratic leadership seems to contradict one of the basic principles of Islamic leadership; the need for *shura* [consultation].

Islam and Leadership

In "Islamic Leadership Principles," Adalat Khan (2007) identified the sources of Islamic leadership principles as the Holy Quran; the life, way of life (*seerah*), and the sayings (*hadiths*) of the Prophet (*pbuh*), the wise caliphs, and pious followers. Some of the studies of Islamic leadership available in English are based on a Western framework that then find relevant concepts from Islamic sources to explain the principle. For example, Beekun (2006, 117-129) takes Kouzes and Posner's (1995) *The Leadership Challenge* and links it to Islamic values:

1. **Challenging the Process.** Following Islam's *shura* mandate, to consult with people, regardless of whether or not they belong to your organization or whether or not you agree with them, listen to your most demanding critics to improve the status quo.

2. *Inspiring a Shared Vision.* Engaging in *shura* by praying or asking Allah to validate the vision, content and direction of the organization's future.
3. *Enabling Others to Act.* Using power to foster collaboration, empower and delegate to strengthen others, and considering other people's interests above your own.
4. *Modeling the Way.* Following the timeless and virtuous example of the prophet (pbuh). "*And you stand an exalted standard of character.*" (Qur'an, 68:4 quoted by Beekun, 2006, 103)
5. *Encouraging the Heart.* Preparing for continuous challenges.

An alternative to beginning with a Western framework for examining Islamic leadership is to take a story from the Quran and derive leadership principles from it. For example, Unus and Beekun (2007) takes the story of Dhuk-Qarnayn told in Surah Kahf [Surah 18] in the Holy Quran. Unus and Beekun (2007) indicated that although no one really knows whether Dhuk-Qarnayn was Alexander the Greek or Cyrus, King of Persia, what is important are the leadership lessons derived from his story. These lessons are consistent with some of the recent statements of western leadership theory and are as follows:

1. Leaders expect the best from those to whom tasks are delegated and are responsible for providing them, to the extent possible, with the material resources and the training needed to get the job done.
2. Leaders distinguish between the righteous and those who are not and are expected to be fair in providing rewards and honors for good people and punishment for wrong-doers.
3. Leaders are generous while remaining humble since it is Allah who has given everything what a leader has.
4. Leaders need followers and of course Allah's help. Good leaders accomplish their mission by making followers partners in solving the problem and giving help according to their means.

5. Leaders are also good followers by modeling the most challenging and difficult behaviors.

, 6. Leaders need to remember and remind the people that the true source of all is Allah (SWT).

To summarize, "What should be" in Islamic leadership is generally attuned to the western concepts of leadership, especially servant leadership. However, "what is" is not always in harmony with "what should be" as was the case of the GDA in Afghanistan. Why this was could be partially explained by Beekun and Badawi's (1999, 6) observation that "a typical Islamic organization rarely transitions to implementation" due to "endless fine-tuning" or "analysis-paralysis."

Although these negative forces presented continuing challenges to the GDA leadership, the positive aspects of Islamic leadership were also evident. The multicultural team, including the Afghans, would have benefitted from an explicit reminder that leadership in Islam is rooted in belief and willing submission and service to Allah (Beekun and Badawi 1999, 17-34). According to Beekun and Badawi (1999) the Islamic model requires the leader to:

- Inspire the vision (to serve Islam)
- Strengthen the heart (with *Iman* [faith in God] and *Taqwa* [inner consciousness toward Allah])
- Lead the way (with the Quran and the Sunnah)
- Assess actions (accountability of actions)
- Mobilize the community (to develop an Islamic civilization).

My role was that of a humble student trying to understand and share with the different participants in the project some of the implications of Islam.

Accomplishments of the Afghan eQuality Alliance

I am very proud of my role in contributing to the success of the Afghan eQuality Alliance. In partnership with the Ministry of Higher

Education, the Afghan eQuality Alliances program contributed to capacity building in Afghanistan's higher education institutions. The program piloted new curricula, degree and certificate programs, and faculty development activities in Kabul based universities that can be replicated in regional and provincial universities. The Afghan eQuality Alliances established elearning centers in nine regional Afghan universities that have increased faculty and student research capacity, improved the quality of classroom instruction, and improved English language computer literacy for thousands of students and hundreds of instructors.

The Afghan eQuality Alliances also improved the qualifications of Afghan civil servants and professors through development of a Masters Degree in Public Policy and Administration (MPPA) for Kabul University. The project established a digital library, which has enabled access to educational resource materials in the country and elsewhere. It improved the quality of instruction in priority academic disciplines, namely education, engineering, computer science, and geo science by supporting professors in those disciplines to attain advanced qualifications. Partnerships were established between eight Afghan, eight U.S., and five third country universities to facilitate improving the quality of teaching and learning in Afghanistan.

Conclusions and Implications for Leadership Development

Afghanistan is a microcosm of a globalized world where leadership and cultural contact occurs within a context of interdependent but unequal political and economic power. As part of USAID's commitment to improving international development assistance, USAID advocated for joint definition of issues. However this was complicated by the lack of consensus among Afghans mirrored by a similar lack of consensus among outsider partners. The time needed to build consensus got in the way of western timeframes for implementation and the push for quick results. Moreover, externally funded development programs seem to favor and reinforce Anglo and Germanic cultural values and work styles that appear to conflict with some

Afghan culture and Islamic principles of leadership. Leadership principles derived from Islam are mostly consistent with western models of leadership and instead of being considered a stumbling blocks could be viewed as building blocks for leadership development. Acknowledging this requires active engagement to discover our common humanity despite differences in expressions of cultural norms and religion or spirituality. What is needed is the development of cultural empathy, patience, non-reactivity, compassion, and wisdom. As a Filipina, I was in a unique position to help bridge some of the cultural divide. I shared many of the cultural values of my Afghan colleagues including a focus on relationships (the Filipino value of *pakikipagkapwa*) and sensitivity about the imposition of values on others.

As a Filipina, representing American interests in higher education, the lessons I learned about harmonizing global teams in Afghanistan are the need to:

1. Recognize that the globalized world has porous boundaries that make it impossible to escape the role of culture. Thus we need not just to tolerate each other but also to learn new ways to benefit each other.
2. Consider cultural clusters as complementarities and consider cultural norms as heterogeneous. We need to emphasize our shared humanity while accommodating differences. As we build our individual intercultural sensitivity there is a need to also help partners undertake multicultural approaches.
3. Develop competence in generic management and leadership tasks, such as goal focusing, structuring for results, facilitating decision-making, training and maintaining standards. Equally important are leadership relational actions that include coaching, collaborating, managing conflict, building commitment, satisfying needs, and modeling principles. Moreover, there is a need to develop cross-cultural skills for networking, advocating, negotiating support, buffering, assessing, and sharing information.

Because of their potential to make significant contributions to development, it is incumbent for Filipinas to be willing to answer the call to provide leadership in unanticipated fields and settings.

Leadership Tips

1. ***Embrace the positive aspects of our Philippine culture.*** My early socialization in the Philippines provided the building blocks for my ability to negotiate different levels of relationships with many different nationalities from *makitungo* [dealing with] to *makisama* [being with] to *makiisa* [being one with] that proved helpful in reaching into and maintaining social capital, in sometimes unconscious ways.

2. ***Draw on positive memories.*** My *Lola* [grandmother] used to say, "In addition to being intelligent, you have the blood of a *katipunero* [19th century Philippine revolutionary], your *Apong* Juan was a runner for the *Katipunan* [secret 19th century Philippine revolutionary association] when he was still a young boy" and she would add with suppressed delight, "And I was known as *Kumander Dayang-dayang* during the Hukbalahap days." This memory has served as a touchstone for perseverance and fortitude; challenging myself as I challenge others; speaking up for what is right even if there is opposition; acting on convictions even if unpopular, and taking actions that require courage.

3. ***Connect the dots and reflect on how your experiences helped shape your character.*** Playing *patintero* and other childhood games taught me to be collaborative with my team and competitive with other teams. Spinning records as a disc jockey, another college job, taught me how to make seconds count. Dancing the Tinikling and other folkdances during college taught me discipline.

4. ***Decide on priorities when you can.*** I put the Ph.D. dissertation on hold for a long time, in part to nurture my children David and Ligaya during their formative years. When I decided it was time to finish my dissertation, I concentrated on it. I am glad I did, as the Ph.D. gave me the intellectual capital, thought leadership, and clout to work in international development.

5. ***Make meaning where you can.*** I can think of several moments that reminded me of the fundamental unity and interrelatedness of the universe. Walking on the Nubian desert made me think of "I am but a small grain of sand in this whole universe." Being buffeted by a storm while in a small canoe in the Philippine sea made me think of "nearer my God to thee." And an Afghan mother who said, "I wish for my daughter to be able to read her own love letters" made me think of how we all wish the best for our children and our children's children.

AD ASTRA, PER ASPIRA:
TO THE STARS
THROUGH DIFFICULTIES

Penélope V. Flores, Ph.D.
Professor Emerita, SFSU

Abstract

*I*n this chapter I will emphasize three things. I will explain the Academic University ranking ladder, I will clarify how I earned University tenure, and I will show that through difficulties, I tried to reach for the stars as in *Ad Astra per Aspira* (To the stars, through difficulties). I will attempt to share two *t*hings that shaped my academic life. The first is how my Philippine heritage background shaped my general outlook under a fierce competitive promotion atmosphere. The second is how I earned my tenure, struggling to be accepted into the community of scholars. I will also highlight my global academic experience. Out of my experience in the Philippines, in the U.S. and in international development, I will share my leadership tips by quoting some of my favorite authors.

Introduction

I am enjoying my well-earned and blessed retirement from San Francisco State University (SFSU), where I retired as a Distinguished Professor Emerita. Since retiring I have found myself extremely busy. In Spanish, the word for retirement is *jubilada*, an apt word. In "jubilation" I can undertake projects without pressure. I taught higher education courses for the last 35 years. My academic university level appointment was at the University of the Philippines, Diliman, Quezon City, at the Assistant Professor level. My last academic post was at SFSU, as Full Professor.

Organization and Structure

In this chapter, instead of using a chronological structure, I will start right in the middle of things. In creative writing this approach is called in medias res, (Bernays and Painter 2004). First, I will share how I obtained tenure within the California State University system. Constraints about the teaching credential program will be presented. Second, I will give background information on my family, my educational qualifications, professional growth, and achievement using a "story-telling" format. For this reason, my already published life story will be cited liberally, perhaps showing how I am also a victim of my own success. Finally, I will share my leadership tips by quoting from some of my favorite authors.

THE DEFINITION OF PROFESSOR. There are two definitions of the word professor. The first is the nominalized verb. It is the action of professing something. Any teacher, usually an instructor in a college setting, is called a professor, an occupation. The second definition is a noun classifier. It is an academic rank characterized by a hierarchical system of office defined by special skills and experiences and bestowed by peers. For this chapter, I am using this second definition.

The California University System's Tenure Process

Entering a tenure-track academic post

A career in academe is fraught with dangers. In the academic world, there is a high degree of non-acceptance of women. For women of color, it is a particularly dangerous undertaking: a double whammy.

The pressure points reside within the deep recesses of the hierarchical California University System. It is no fun entering the tenure-track academic pool but my advice is, "Have fun having no fun."

How I got a tenure track post.

In 1989, the Chronicle of Higher Education announced a tenure-track hiring spurt at SFSU, College of Ethnic Studies. I was in the market for a University tenure track position not at the lecturer level. I sent in my application just so people in the academe could read my CV. Of course my qualifications and experience did not fit the job description. No matter. I never expected an invitation for an interview anyway. However, the Hiring Committee reviewed my resumé and was impressed. My documents remained in their active file.

Hiring committees always have some faculty from other divisions. Somebody from the College of Education was on that hiring committee. The following year, a tenure-track position in mathematics education opened in the Secondary Department, College of Education. Luckily, somebody remembered my previous application and I was invited to reapply. My strategy worked. I was favorably noticed. This time the job description mirrored my experience.

My achievement and qualifications stood out. I was offered the position. The rank published in the hiring advertisement was at the Assistant Professor level. The administration carried out a thorough review and found that my qualifications and experience went beyond the entry-level post of Assistant Professor. To their credit they immediately redefined the position to Associate Professor. The Hiring Committee recognized that my research coordinator's job at a prestigious research university was equivalent to an Associate Professor's rank. To be sure, it was understood that the first year is probationary. The second year is either a termination year or advancement to the next level year.

The Bait

For SFSU, 1990 was the beginning of an overall push for faculty diversification. To many, the College of Education seemed reserved for only white old men, so as an incentive to diversity, the dean was promised two additional faculty positions for each qualified minority hired. The department went all out encouraging the applications of young qualified women candidates. Three women were hired: a Mathematics major from Oregon, a Middle School specialist from Alaska, and a Mathematics educator from Chicago, originally from Manila.

It was dismaying to know that I was the BAIT! In order to get their catch of two young white women, the department had to hire me first. My running thought went: "Great! Officially two of them are equal to one of me! What a subversive yet exhilarating thought! "

However, I knew then that to be successful I needed mentoring and support from the department. I asked for and was assigned a caring and professionally competent mentor.

Categories for Professoriate Promotion and Advancement

The three criteria for professoriate promotion and advancement were excellent and outstanding evaluations in the areas below (Academic Senate Bill #S07-241).

1. Teaching effectiveness.
2. Professional achievement and growth
3. Contributions to campus and community.

First Criteria for Earning Tenure: Teaching Effectiveness

All California State Universities (CSU) are teaching universities. That year, the Mathematics major from the University of Oregon received bad teaching evaluations. She had no publications. She was given her exit papers. The middle school expert had many shortcomings. Her wasted mind was focused elsewhere.

In contrast, I earned glowing teaching evaluations. Once, I invited a small group of freshmen members of the Pilipino American College Endeavor (PACE) to my teacher training class. Then, with the whole class watching, I modeled a mini lesson. Finally the class critiqued and discussed how they could improve on what I had just demonstrated. This mini-teaching technique was a hit with both the young and the old. One wrote, "Amazing! A Filipina Ph.D. and a Professor! I never had a Filipino professor before."

Teaching in the credential program was challenging. Many of the teacher candidates were already teaching as 'temporaries.' They had an attitude with me! I remember one teacher candidate who asked, "What does she know about teaching in our schools?"

Shedding the natural Filipino modesty I strongly became aggressive. All of a sudden, I grew *cojones* [balls] and quickly began to brag about my qualifications and accomplishments.

In other words, my response was overkill. I projected on Power point my lifetime teaching certificate obtained from Philadelphia in Bilingual Education (Spanish, English and Pilipino). I said, "Look here. I offer a State University approved multicultural course. If you are successful here, you will earn your Multicultural teaching certificate. Believe me, you need my signature for a permanent teaching job."

Then, I showed my Mathematics teaching credentials from Chicago. For some unexplained reason and with the concomitant snobbish-appeal, a Mathematics teaching credential always elicits a WOW response! People forget race, and gender as they predictably admit, "I was never good at math."

On Classroom Management

I love to tell that I taught high school in the ghetto like South Chicago school district. My sophomore students towered over my five-foot frame. I had a pain-in-the-ass tall basketball hero, Keith. One trying day, I approached him.

"You know what, Keith," I said. "I want to give you a scholarship to the downtown YMCA."

"What for?" he wanted to know.

I replied smugly, "I teach Judo and Karate at the Y Gym."

"Oh?" he laughed nervously as I continued;

"If you don't mind, why don't you at least visit?"

"Why should I?"

I whispered so that everybody would strain to listen.

"Because before you know it, I'll put your spindly legs into a tight knot as a class remembrance for you."

Of course, that was the most brazen of all white lies; as white and toxic as zinc oxide! But the credential class understood my point. When using one's authoritarian teacher-voice effectively, declarations become seeds of truth. Ultimately, I told them, my entire class-room was composed of South Chicago gangster-type teen-agers who were transformed into a choir of angels singing the Pythagorean theorem.

The Second Criteria for Tenure: Professional Achievement and Growth

I am always on stage, performing, either as a lecturer, presenter, or professor. Teaching is a passion with me, learned young at my mother's knees. But for obtaining a promotion to full professor, a love for teaching is not enough. I had to publish or perish.

One day, as I was carrying a stack of index cards: a bibliography of my publications, I dropped it accidentally in class. It cascaded dramatically like the Pagsanjan waterfalls in the Philippines onto the floor in the center of the room. I said, "Sorry, but these are my publications." A respectful silence descended. "Writing research articles enhances my university teaching," I explained. I ignored the humming murmurs. My students thought I did it purposely and never forgot that episode. During my evaluation for professorship, many submitted letters about my exceptional publication record. My credential graduate students loved my dramatic flair. In Tagalog, I was a *pasikat* [show-off].

How did I get all these publications that reveal professional achievement? I submitted my articles to mainstream periodicals. After receiving many rejections, I cried, "Enough!" I went to the Vice President for Faculty Development for help. He got me a small faculty grant. Soon a Filipino-themed journal, the first of its kind in the U.S., was born.

I became the editor of *The Journal of the American Association for Philippine Psychology* (JAAPP), a peer-reviewed journal. The JAAPP became the venue for tenure-track Filipino Americans to be published. The first volume's theme was *Pilipino Kahit Saan, Kahit Kailan* [Filipino Wherever, Whenever]. It included the following articles:

Indigenous Psychology, V. Enriquez;
Cultural Identity of Third-Wave Filipino Americans,
  L. M. Strobel;
Victim's Discourses, M.C. Kirk;

Philippine American Youth Between Two Expectations,
P. V. Flores;
Liminal Identity, B.C. Hill;
Mental Health Services: The Case for Filipino Americans,
A.B. Canlas and L. Mesa.

The next issue had as its theme: Taking Roots, Breaking Ground with the following articles.

Cognitive Styles of Selected Filipino Immigrant Children at the Filipino Education Center, San Francisco, P. Fermin;
Understanding Language Maintenance and Language Shift, R. Galang;
Effects of Family Environment on the Academic Performance of Filipino American College Students in San Diego, R. Monzon;
Madness and Deviance in Filipino Folk Medicine in Hawaii, D. Aquino.

In the midst of its remarkable success, a ubiquitous mentality reared up its ugly head. It is of the genus Crab, species Filipino. The Filipino crab mentality, for those who are not familiar with the metaphor goes thus:

A hot cauldron full of crabs is left on the stove. Whenever one crab succeeds in climbing to the rim of the pot, the other crabs below pull him down.

It happens many times among all kinds of organizations. So as the journal was getting off ground, an editorial board member suggested, "The editorship should be rotated." With dampened enthusiasm, I stopped my efforts to solicit articles.

In the meantime, I courted the multicultural and interdisciplinary professional crowd. The World Council for Curriculum and instruction, North American Chapter responded. I co-founded and served as co-editor for 15 years (1997 to 2011) of *The Journal of Interdisciplinary Education* (JIE).

Yes, I am a repeat offender when it comes to founding academic juried journals. But the JIE survives to this day, a well-respected periodical. In contrast JAAPP appeared as a passing ship in the night disappearing in the Narrows of Babuyan Bay (Pig Pen's Bay) and plunging into the Philippine Deep.

The Manila Bulletin USA is a weekly newspaper published in San Francisco. It carries regular news articles by various journalists and opinion columns. I proposed writing a half page column on Philippine history, society, and culture for young readers who have little or no knowledge of the antecedents of why we do things the way we do. I promised a scholarly sociological and historical contribution every week. The editor loved the idea.

A year has 52 weeks. Therefore for my tenure promotion, I could count on 104 published articles in every two-year review period. That was an astounding and spectacular feat! If my academic competitors were lucky they might have one or two articles published in a year.

My Filipino heritage and background knowledge had pushed me up and over the ceiling. But I also authored a scholarly tome, based on my dissertation, *The Progress of Philippine Education* (2004).

I had arrived at the time of my initial hire armed with co-authorship of *Algebra for 7th Grade*, *Advanced Algebra for 8th Grade*, *Geometry for High School Freshmen* and *Pre-Calculus for Juniors*, published by the University of Chicago School Math Project. McGraw Hill picked up these titles as a textbook series. In the series we introduced Geometry a year earlier than it was in the standard curriculum. Offering Geometry provided for the abstract thinking development in a gradual manner. Even in the early renaissance period, Da Vinci proved that the study of Geometry was the portal to nimble thinking and creativity. Geometry was the Middle Ages' SAT exam. My article "How Dick and Jane Achieve Differently in Geometry" was the most cited in the index of citations in two fields: Gender Studies, and Mathematics education.

Thus, at the Associate Professor rank, the next step towards Full Professor, I sped forth with a giant whoosh like an express train. I gained my full professorship rank in record time. The normal time to go from Assistant to Associate is seven year, and another seven years to go to Full Professor. I shortened the period to four years. I had assured myself fame for my originality based on my academic rank advancement. It took grit, hard work, and most importantly, a narcissistic self-involvement. One needed these to do the job of getting tenure.

Third Criteria for Tenure:
Contributions to Campus and Community

I wrote proposals and earned grants. I sat as a member of the California Humanities Council for six years, two three-year terms, and ensured that my SFSU contributions were on par with the rest of the community of scholars. I directed the Math and Science Teacher Education Program.

I established a teacher education partnership with the Philippine Normal University and the University of the Philippines and sent my student teachers to teach in Manila and Diliman, Quezon City schools. My student teachers were all Caucasians teaching in San Francisco's Filipino-impacted schools. In the Philippines they taught English and in their major subject areas. Consequently, they were thrilled to have these experiences. One remarked, "My students address me 'Sir,' and unlike my students in the US, they do as they are told."

The Filipino Americans considered my community involvement extraordinary. I regularly convened and organized conferences on issues regarding Filipino identity. I graced every function and celebration. I fattened up with *lumpia* [spring roll] and *pancit* [noodles]. At every gathering I listened carefully to their problems and struggles and produced articles published in the *Journal of Interdisciplinary Education* about their concerns (Flores and Resus 1997; Resus and Flores 1998; Flores and Resus 1999; Flores 2004;).

The Filipino American community recognized my leadership role and gave me Outstanding and Most Influential achievement awards. The Daly City public school district rejoiced "Finally, we have a Filipino American professor at SFSU who can help us deal with the issues of the ever growing Filipino immigrant school population." In one school, 40 percent of the students were Filipinos. I used this school as a clinical venue where I assigned student teachers and where I also conducted my own research. This resulted in the book *The Philippine Jeepney: A Metaphor for Understanding the Filipino American Family* (Flores and Resus, 2010.)

Portfolios were prepared for my tenure and promotion with extensive documentation and edited with the assistance of my very supportive spouse Manuel. I could not have made it without his tender loving care, organizational acumen, editorial skill. and continued inspiration and encouragement. Behind every successful Filipina is an understanding Filipino husband.

Being the first Filipina tenured professor at SFSU gave me the stature. When I had reached the Full Professorship level, I became less fettered by the rules of academia. How did I meet all these challenges? I attribute it to my family background, educational achievement, and international experience.

My Family Background, Schooling, and International Experience

I was born in Gapan, Nueva Ecija, in 1931 to a physician father and a teacher mother. They provided a privileged lifestyle for myself and three siblings. My father, Dr. José Viola Villarica belonged to the *ilustrado* [elite] social class. On one hand, I am sort of embarrassed to admit it, but on the other hand, it makes me proud. His maternal uncle, Máximo Viola, studied medicine in Barcelona, Spain. It was Dr. Máximo Viola who in 1886 provided his friend, Dr. José Rizal, the Philippine national hero, with a subsidy of 300 pesetas to publish Rizal's book, *Noli me Tángere*. In today's parlance, Viola was the first Filipino 'venture capitalist.' Rizal's novel inspired the Philippine revolutionaries to rise against Spain (Guerrero 1961).

My father, although born in Bulacan, established his successful medical practice in Calapan, Oriental Mindoro. He was also a literati, [a poet]. He published the English parallel translation of Balagtas' Tagalog epic poem *Florante at Laura* (Villarica, 1957). My mother turned it into a study guide for Tagalog courses. My parents' joint contribution to Philippine studies can be found in "Far Above Cayuga's Waters" (Lozada 2008, 386-397).

Beginning in grade school, all my subjects were taught using English as the language of instruction while Tagalog was my mother tongue. The effect was interesting. I spelled out my frustration in *Reflections: Readings for the Young and Old* (2002,13-18).

Unfortunately, my father died during the war. All of a sudden, at age eleven, being the eldest daughter, I grew up quickly. The war was a great equalizer. The rich and poor suffered equally. The social order was shaken vigorously, and we found ourselves cash poor. Sure we had large land-holdings, but they were in areas controlled by guerillas and the New People's Army (NPA). The land was unproductive, and later included in land-reform programs that distributed the land to the actual farmers.

The war years saw my family always running from the brutality of the Japanese Army's occupying forces. What it felt like to be always on the run, hunted by the enemy is reflected in my article "Run Ebony, Run" (Lozada 2008, 380-385).

With a strong resolute single mother, we were raised with high expectations and lofty aspirations. She said, "Riches are lost. Beauty fades, but intellectual achievement endures."

She wanted her girls to be socially and academically educated. So she sent us to a private secondary school, the College of the Holy Spirit branch in Calapan, Oriental Mindoro where we were taught by German nuns from Bavaria. I describe my life as a convent girl in the volume *Behind the Walls, Life of Convent Girls* (Brainard and Orosa, 2005).

When we remember life within the convent walls, we speak of contradictions; the errors and the innocence, of mistaken views but of good intentions, of ignorance but of devotion, of torment short of redemption. We have 'yes' and 'no' simultaneously upon our lips. Life within the convent walls is supreme egotism resulting in supreme denial. Within the convent, we were told we suffer that we may enjoy (Flores 2005, 52).

I graduated in 1956 with a Bachelor of Science degree in Education, Cum Laude, from the Philippine Normal University (PNU), Manila. It was at PNU where I blossomed as a natural leader, to wit: editor of the university paper *The Torch*, delegate representative at nation-wide college conferences, and club president of a couple of campus organizations. I even starred as a folk-dancer specializing in the popular dances: *Fandango sa (Nabagsak) na Ilaw* [Dance of the Dropped Lights] and *(Napilay sa pag Ti)-Tinikling* [Crushed ankles from dancing the Tinikling].

After college, I married my long-time sweetheart Manuel G. Flores, a UP grad who worked as a paleontologist at the Bureau of Mines and moonlighted as a lecturer at Far Eastern University in the evenings. We have two sons, Norman and Ivan.

Even in childbearing, I went for 'tenure.' My firstborn were twins! Norman had a twin, Raymond, who sadly passed away during childbirth. Ivan was born a year later. My friends, who knew I had twins, but did not know I lost one of the pair, assumed Norman and Ivan are my twins. They grew up alike in almost all aspects.

My Teaching Experience

While a teacher at the UP Elementary School, I was awarded a Faculty scholarship in 1965 to the University of Pennsylvania, Philadelphia. My master's degree specialization was Educational Leadership. That emphasis was instrumental in climbing the ladder of appointments and positions within a short time. I stepped up from UP Elementary school teacher to Vice Principal, to Assistant Professor teaching foundation courses at the UP College of Education, and then to the Professor Executive Officer of UNESCO's Asian Institute for Teacher Education (AITE). This last post opened up my international commitment.

Facing the Brand New World

My nuclear family immigrated to the U.S. after Marcos declared martial law in 1972. My husband and I had dreams of our sons studying in the U.S. We were afraid that martial law's oppressive policies might prevent any travel abroad. So, on January 3rd 1974, with $200 in my pocket, the four of us (Manuel, Norman age 8, and Ivan age 7 and I) left our little cottage home within the UP Diliman compound bound for Philadelphia carrying our green cards. Manuel's first job was at Colonial Penn Insurance. I found work as a substitute teacher in the public schools. Then Manuel was offered a Research Biology appointment in

Chicago's Industrial Bio–Tech complex. His career advanced quickly in the 'Windy City.' While enrolled in the Ph.D. program at University of Chicago (U of C), I also taught in a private K-12 school in the Hyde Park-Woodlawn neighborhood. This neighborhood is where the Obamas lived before moving over to the White House.

I taught at Harvard. My school's name was Harvard School for Boys. It offered a Latin preparatory curriculum that honed the academic skills of the sons of the elite for admission to Harvard University. Heads of corporate businesses, and African American CEOs, needed this special school for their sons. Unlike today's euphemistic labels such as 'special schools for the disadvantaged,' the Harvard School for Boys was known as 'The Special School.'

In my letters home, I impressed everybody about teaching at Harvard. Well, I conveniently forgot to add 'School for Boys.' My mother replied tersely, "Harvard is in Boston, not Chicago."

I earned a Ph.D. degree in Comparative and International Education, Division of Social Science, University of Chicago. The University holds graduation commencement exercises every quarter and thus we did not have to wait for the traditional Spring graduation. I joined the commencement in December 1984.

A week later, I was hired as the Evaluation Research Coordinator for the University of Chicago School Math Project (UCSMP). My job was to establish experimental and control classes in high schools that used our U of C's Algebra and Geometry textbooks. I analyzed and wrote reports. That meant that I had to travel to U.S. states using the UCSM material. When it was deadly hot in Chicago I visited the coolness of Vermont schools and I scheduled visits in balmy Tejeras, Texas during Chicago winter months.

Sisyphusean Program of Studies

Working at UCSMP also meant I was still mulling around the department, greeting my professors, friends, and graduate students. Those who had not seen me graduate, jokingly said, "Penélope's Ph.D. must be the longest ever in the department's history." The average length of time for a working student to obtain a Ph.D. in the Social Science at the U of C is seven years. I completed mine within six. Not bad.

Adding six more years as Evaluation Research Coordinator meant that for 12 years I was seen around the department.

There is a standing unwritten rule that no one asks about the progress of someone's dissertation. So no one asked me. It was assumed I was still laboriously and painfully edging my way towards completion of my dissertation. Considered a virtual Sisyphus, I apparently was one eternally doomed in a cycle of despair, to push a stone up hill only to see it fall down as it neared the top.

After obtaining my Ph.D. I could easily have gotten a lecturer's job in the smaller colleges around the Chicago area, a big frog in a small pond. But my professor advised, "Stay here. You'll accumulate scholarly advantage with the U of C's experience." It proved so true.

My global academic experience

Operation Brotherhood (OB), the Junior Chamber of Commerce (JC) International, and the Lao Government formed a consortium to provide medical and socio-economic development. As the OB team social worker and teacher, I opened village schools where our medical teams were based. I mostly did ethnographic studies based on collected personal stories. Years later, I wrote *Good-bye Vientiane: The Untold Stories of the Filipinos in Laos, 1957-1973* (Flores 2008). The appetite to know about this untold story resulted in the book being sold out. I donated the book proceeds to a Tiruray tribal school in Davao, Mindanao. The second edition came out in 2010.

A UNESCO professional appointment in Nepal was extraordinary. My formal consultancy title was 'Expert.' I was full of myself and intrigued with my official title. My calling card shouted: 'UNESCO Expert in Primary Education, Nepal.' Cool! My sons in grade school, Norman and Ivan, attended the International School in Kathmandu. Embedded in their curriculum was a teacher-led month-long trek to the Solo-Khumbo base camp region on the way to Mt. Everest.

In Dhankuta, a village perched up in the Himalayan mountain ranges, I was known as the Teacher in the Basket. I opened a girl's primary teacher-training school there. The only way to reach it is by trekking. I was, and still am, a terrible mountain trekker and a grumpy complainer. My Sherpa porter once plucked me up and sat me deep into his backpack basket. With my torso in and my legs hanging out of the basket, he carried me on his back. I was in a terrible fright, but the children were amused. "Here comes the teacher in the basket," they cried.

I worked briefly for UNESCO with assignments in Afghanistan, before the Taliban, and in Iran, before the Ayatollahs. What a treat!

For the United States Agency for International Development (USAID), I worked in Indonesia (twice; 1987 and 2005) where I first served as a Research and Development Consultant, and the second time, as the Primary Education Adviser for Indonesia. In Ethiopia I was the Research and Development Consultant in Primary Education for American Education Development (AED).

Ethiopia is a unique country. It has a long and ancient Christian Orthodox tradition. Ethiopia is mentioned in the Bible where it is written that in Paradise there are four rivers. One is the Gihon, flowing in the land of Cush, Ethiopia (Genesis 2:10). I visited Gihon. It feeds into Lake Tana, in the Tigray region. Legend claims Mary raised the baby Jesus in one of the islands there. I published this story as The Maryam Monastery, Lake Tana, Tigray, Ethiopia (Brainard 2012, 18-25).

Lake Tana river tributaries flow out of the Ethiopian plateau in a spectacular waterfall to become the beginning of the 'Blue' Nile that in turn joins the 'White' Nile in the Sudan and. together the river meanders through the Valley of the Kings in Egypt to become 'The Gift of the Nile.'

My Curriculum and Development Global Network System

The World Council for Curriculum and Instruction (WCCI) provided me the international networking opportunities in various countries of the world. Its conferences were first held triennially in England, Turkey, Philippines, Canada, Japan, Netherlands, Egypt, India, Thailand, Spain, Australia, and then biennially in Philippines, Antalya, Turkey, Hungary, and Taiwan. I presented papers at every international conference starting with the conference in the Netherlands. These papers served as points in the tenure race. I founded and edited their Journal of Interdisciplinary Education. I coordinated the different Special Interest Groups. I was in a leadership position in several international conferences. It was a promise and a challenge.

In most instances, my university bases were at the U of C and SFSU.

The Rizal Scholar

Beginning 2001, before starting my early retirement, I launched a new area of research and re-invented myself. By studying Rizal's correspondences to his family, friends, and especially his political and literary articles, I began to re-trace his travels in Europe. In Heidelberg, Germany, I was a *Rizal Forscherin* [Rizal Scholar] as reported in a news article (Rhine-Neckar Zeitung April, 2014). Based on my studies of Rizal's travels in Europe, I realized that for six months he had a traveling companion. And guess who this person was? None other than my grand uncle, Dr. Máximo Viola! I immediately dug back into our family archives and re-read Viola's (1913) memoirs *Mis Viajes con el Doctor José Rizal*. What a revelation! Viola described details about Rizal only someone who had shared a one-to-one relationship knew or could ever tell.

I depleted my dwindling resources, visiting the various Rizal and Viola sites. With great precision I can now put historical images in my blog <http:// penelopevflores.blogspot.com> about the many European cities in the life of Dr. José Rizal through the eyes of his best friend, Dr. Máximo Viola. There is no mention of these travels in any of Rizal books. I made it my objective to have this wonderful tale of friendship published. My Viola-Rizal manuscript soon will be in the hands of my editor. I have already invited my friends to the book launch.

My Left and Right Brain Activities

I am a fulfilled, happy Professor Emerita. I continue to travel widely and write voluminously.

Luckily, my left and right brain hemispheres manage to talk to each other. The left-brain does the verbal, logical, sequential and analytical tasks. The right brain is in charge of the visual, perceptive, simultaneous and out-of-the-box thinking. When I get bogged down with writing articles, research reports, and statistical data analysis, I let my right-brain surface by playing classical guitar, (Caruli, Carcassi, Fortea) and piano. (Beethoven, Chopin, Shubert, Schumann). I do not sing.

Having converted my San Francisco apartment into an art gallery and the headquarters of San Francisco's Pigment, Easel and Brush Society (PEBS), it should be aevident that I love to paint. My formal training consisted of summer courses at the Galleria Italiana di Bellas Artis, Florence, Italy. Copying the Masters at the Uffizi Museum helped develop my compositional and color schemas. There we were taught that the perfect artistic form is the nude. I must have been the most celebrated senior citizen painter drawing the gloriously constructed male nude models posing at Michelangelo's art school: the Galleria. I continue to be involved in Museums as a docent or storyteller volunteer at San Francisco Asian Art Museum. I remain an artiste at heart. My selected paintings have been exhibited at the Oakland Asian Cultural Center (2011), San Francisco's Philippine Consulate (on-going), and San Bruno Art Gallery (2014).

Ad Astra per Aspira: To the Stars through Difficulties

The road to the stars has not always been rosy. Subtle prejudice and discrimination lurk in the shadows of every ivory tower. It is carefully crafted. One needs to have a sensitive antenna to catch it. But it is there.

Through difficulties and challenges, I am proud to be one of the original founders, past president, and currently board member of the Philippine American Writers and Artists (PAWA), Inc. My contribution was in making PAWA, Inc. a non-profit organization. Authors and artists remember the Calatagan Literary awards I gave out to deserving writers and artists. The trophy is a stylized replica of the 15th century earthenware pot excavated in Calatagan, Batangas Philippines. The artifact was inscribed around the shoulder rim with the native ancient syllabary *Baybayin* script (see cover page. Flores and Gaborro 2004). It is proof that when the Spaniards colonized the Philippines, this native script was already in use. It was replaced with the Roman alphabet. I continue to contribute occasional articles to *Filipinas Magazine*, and currently to the e-magazine *Positively Filipino*.

PAWA has gained a wide national reach and has provided services to many aspiring creative artists in the Bay Area. PAWA's Manuel G. Flores Prize Fund, established after my spouse's death in 2008 following 47 years of marriage, continues to benefit many young local writers of Filipino heritage. To quote: from a 2014 letter by Chris Santiago of Pasadena, CA:

> I write with the warmest regards to thank you and PAWA for the Manuel G. Flores Scholarship, which made it possible for me to attend the 2013 Kundiman Retreat in New York. It is no exaggeration to say that it was a life-changing experience that not only helped me regain my bearings in terms of my creativity and the ground from which I speak, but introduced me to true friends and mentors with whom I will share a life-long bond.

From emigrating to the U.S., I have learned that the true value of freedom is to be what I want to be, and to do what I love to do. As a Filipino *kahit saan, kahit kailan* [wherever, whenever] my aspirations and expectations have strengthened me into a showcase of which my family and friends can be proud.

In ending this chapter, let me share with you my leadership tips by quoting my favorite authors.

Leadership Tips

1. *Remember, we didn't learn to walk following rules. We learned by taking small steps and falling over (Richard Branson).* If we all started to walk without falling over and subsequently picking ourselves up bravely, we would not have developed a sharp initiative thrust to learn from our failures.

2. *Courage is the ladder on which all our virtues mount (Clare Booth Luce).* In the ladder metaphor, first we choose the kind of ladder to carry. Then we pull ourselves up at every rung. Overcoming the first rung is the best training for success.

3. *Whenever one aims for perfection one may find it is a moving target (George Fisher).* In this year and age of multi-tasking, immensely important in attaining our goals are flexibility, checking, and re-checking our coordinates.

4. *Keep your integrity.* Do not exaggerate so that you'll always be credible (Dr. José Rizal). When Rizal was writing for *La Solidaridad*, (1890) a fortnightly magazine of the Philippine Propaganda Movement in Spain, he noted many of his contemporaries were submitting exaggerated news and articles against the friars. He reminded them to be honest and truthful, declared, "Everything I wrote in my novel *Noli me tángere* can be truthfully supported and documented."

5. *A good head and a good heart are always a formidable combination (Nelson Mandela).* Mandela had a good head when he constructed South Africa's Constitution. He added his heart by not exacting revenge but promoting peace. He was a great example of a good leader worthy of emulation.

6. *Be faithful in small things, because it is in them where your strength lies (Mother Teresa).* There was this boy who carried a pail of water and dropped it into the sea. When asked why he was doing it, he replied in all innocence, "My small drop of water will create an ocean." Such compelling faith is where one's strength lies.

7. *About the only thing that comes to us without effort is old age (Gloria Pitzer).* I love this leadership tip. Now that I'm sitting prettily in my youthful old-days as an 84-going 85 year-old lady, I can say with all sincerity and with an elderly and professorial tone, "Have fun and enjoy every moment of it!" And that's an order.

Grit: Leadership
Through Social Media

Mira Gillet

Founder and Chief Director
Peace Game Online, USA

Abstract

Grit: Leadership through Social Media aims to demonstrate how free online courses have the potential to develop the leadership skills of individuals to contribute towards significant global impact. I discuss the evolution of Peace Game Online, a digital game I co-developed that was voted Best Learning Game out of 285 projects. Stanford University offers special Massive Open Online Courses (MOOC) through Venture Lab. One of these MOOCs is the Designing a New Learning Environment (DNLE) course which allowed me to contemplate the intersection of technology, design, and empathy. What resulted was a platform that surpassed the barriers of culture, religion, and time zones among others, to create a forum for global understanding and promoting peace. This chapter traces the hurdles and successes from the development of the initial game as a MOOC project into an actual course that harnessed the interest, energy, and determination of participants worldwide to promote peace through a new learning model. The experiences of the game developers who came from diverse backgrounds and locations worldwide illustrate a transformation in their critical thinking. Through the development of the Peace Game, team members also gained technology skills, evolved their critical thinking skills, and developed a commitment to scaling the game and building bridges online well after the course was completed. Through interaction while testing the game, the team members learned the actual possibility of peace despite their initial skepticism about whether true friendships could form organically online. The chapter concludes with beneficial outcomes of developing and playing Peace Game Online and my leadership tips.

Introduction

Having grown up in the Bay Area, I was exposed to the high tech world of Silicon Valley innovation as well as the cultural challenges of the immigrant experience. This chapter shows how my work was influenced both by traditional foundations from the Philippines as well as cutting edge design concepts from digital work. I describe some of my lessons learned from the hurdles, successes and surprises I experienced during the evolution of Peace Game Online.

Peace Game Online is my brainchild. Inspired by the idea of John Hunter's World Peace Game, I led a team that turned this board game into an online game. The World Peace Game is a hands-on political simulation in the form of a board game that gives players the opportunity to explore the connectedness of the global community despite crises like war. Major global problems are represented in the board, and the game's goal is to extricate each country from dangerous circumstances with the least amount of military intervention.

The Peace Game Online is a microcosm of the struggles of the varied cast of characters in the real world. The hope was to use this virtual game to empower the global community to combine their effort to resolve real-life problems. Instead of waiting for politicians to fix problems, game players solve challenges together for the benefit of all. By making friends, game players can pause, if not stop fighting, and instead concentrate on problem solving to help the underprivileged. The game allows top game players to earn points they can use to give or receive interest-free micro-loans, micro-funds, or micro-credits for social entrepreneurship activities that can improve the quality of life. Thus, any donations or grants generated by Peace Game Online go to these activities.

Empathy and understanding is the core of everything I teach. I teach technology, design, and innovation to students. On the surface, this might seem counterintuitive. What does innovation and leadership have to do with peace? My design philosophy is that in order to create something needed by the end user, you must first understand the user as a person. You must empathize with the user's situation. Only by understanding the end user can you truly create something that will be of use to them. With this pedagogy in mind, it was natural to reverse the process: if technology functions best when its design is based on empathy, why not use technology as a platform to *teach* empathy?

The purpose of this chapter is to demonstrate how significant global impact can be made through online platforms. The next generation of youth is wired and plugged into digital media like no other, and leadership opportunities of the 21ˢᵗ century will undeniably call for harnessing the online world. I also hope to inspire young women to develop themselves and their communities by taking advantage of available resources, including free online classes, such as those from universities like Stanford.

I took the DNLE course, a MOOC offered by Stanford through Venture Lab (now called Novoed) that is available for free to anyone. The goal of the course is to promote systematic design thinking and through the use of technology, make learning more interactive, collaborative, and constructive. The course assignments led to the formation of a team to design Peace Game Online, voted Top Learning Game out of 285 projects <https://dnle.stanford.edu/>.

The DNLE course attracted diverse participants. They included educators, students, researchers, designers, technologists, and entrepreneurs from countries all over the world. Participants in DNLE learned to use communication technologies efficiently, intelligently and globally, and they also demonstrated the use of such technologies while submitting their individual and team project assignments. Learning to work as a team and to collaborate with each other in a competitive but supportive environment is another key feature of any MOOC, including DNLE that motivated me to form the Peace Game team. As a disruptive technology, a MOOC needed the involvement of people from around the world to be effective.

The Peace Game Team

As team leader, I decided to gather a team that would create an online game dedicated to peace. Peace Game Online uses a MOOC platform to provide players of the game with a safe space to discuss religious, cultural, or national issues that divided them. The team included students from Pakistan, Kenya, Bulgaria, South Korea, and the United States. By creating and playing the game together, the team, some of whom had never traveled internationally, developed friendships across national, cultural, and religious borders and identities. My Peace Game partner, Talal, co-founder and manager of Peace Game, learned about MOOCs and DNLE from a Turkish friend. Talal remarked:

> MOOCs immediately captured my attention and I began to explore courses offered by different universities, and then I saw DNLE offered by Stanford University Venture Labs. I immediately enrolled despite the fact that I am a Chartered Accountancy student and I have no experience of pedagogy and the educational studies field at all. At that point in time, I didn't know how DNLE would empower us with the vision and tools to change the world!

Part One: Play for Peace

The Peace Game <https://www.openlearning.com/courses/> brought together a diverse range of individuals with a shared passion for exploring the potential applications of new technologies to learning environments.

The vision of changing education resulted in an experiment that would eventually become a lifelong adventure for some. It is definitely a life-changing experience for those who took advantage of the opportunity provided by the game and reached out to the rest of the world. The learning portal makes it possible for individuals to use the game to practice global collaboration. Collaboration is crucial to the game's success and equally crucial to the world.

Talal noted that the Peace Game team was identified as the developer of the most successful game. Talal recognized that he developed leadership skills when he was given a chance to lead the diverse global game team. Talal worked with me on the final team project every day for many hours via Skype and emails. By doing this, Talal learned to use different digital technologies. He also learned to maintain working connections with other teams as well. According to Talal:

This is an unparalleled and unforgettable experience that helped me later on when we decided to start our own MOOC. DNLE was so engaging that the skills I gained are now a part of my thinking process. I would say that DNLE has produced leaders with the vision. In my example, I am a student of accountancy and earned distinction in DNLE. It indicates that DNLE provides a level playing field to its students from diversified backgrounds.

As the first experience of a 21st Century Higher Global Education, the DNLE course empowered Peace Game team members to make real world improvements for the underprivileged (see our discussion of sample micro projects below). Our team applied almost every concept learned from DNLE assignments and lectures. An example is the role of online communication, collaboration, and visualization technology in the behavioral, cognitive, constructivist, and social dimensions of learning. "Peace Game MOOC is the best example of DNLE in action!" according to Talal. In order for our Peace Game project to go to scale, the team understood they were the role models. With each team member representing his/her home country, each country impacted another through team members' conversation and engagement. Because of DNLE community support, the team was able to achieve success in demonstrating meaningful learning interaction around the issue of peace.

Alison Burek chose to join Peace Game Online because it was designed around the idea of ordinary citizens of the world coming together in conversation to discuss global issues. Alison studied international economic development as an undergraduate. According to her, the greatest lesson she learned was not from textbooks or from lectures, but from other students from other countries. "In African Politics class, there were several students from Africa. One day the professor, to his credit, turned the floor over to them because they wanted to discuss a critique they had of our class. We only studied material written by Westerners, from a Western point of view, which however well intentioned, tended to be quite paternalistic," says Alison. Peace Game is designed to facilitate an equal playing field and a safe space in which to discuss issues with people from a wide range of backgrounds.

Part Two: Collaboration not Always Peaceful

The team's collaboration had not been as peaceful as one would think. Below are some of the hurdles that Peace Game Team faced while collaborating, followed by the successes that have motivated us to keep moving forward with the project.

Hurdle One: Connectivity and Time Zones

In Pakistan, Talal worked through power outages that occurred at the worst time for our project. Despite working through different time zones, Talal's youthful tenacity contributed to the success of the Peace Game and exclaimed that, "It is good to be young!" The older people on the team had trouble working through the night to work synchronously at different time zones. In general, our team was able to Skype across time zones from Pakistan and India through South Korea and America. In Alison's words:

> We chose to expand our course format to include the medium of Skype. Old-fashioned human conversation is the best medium for cultivating empathy and understanding. New technology enables us to have these conversations over the Internet in the form of free video chat. This allows us to combine the benefits of an asynchronous course structure—in which students may participate at a time and place of their choice—with the benefits of synchronous person-to-person exchange of ideas.

Hurdle Two: Deep-seated Differences

Although I delegated team leadership to Talal in Pakistan, one team member in India chose to continue communication with me for his own reasons. One reason could have been concerns about Talal and his age, as he was only 23 years old at the time. Another reason could have been contextual; the ongoing conflict between Pakistan and

India concerning Kashmir and the potential animosity between Hindus and Muslims.

Hurdle Three: Conflicts and Sensitive Issues

A team member from France who was critical of our work asked us a thought provoking question: "How can we measure learning?" This team member, who self-identified as an atheist, said we would just be arguing on the basis of dogma and ideology if religion were discussed. However, the success of Peace Game proved him wrong, as it is one of the few places in the world where anyone can have a frank discussion on religion. Talal remarked:

> Through this amazing Peace Game, I am now able to think differently, reaching out to people outside my culture and religion is the most exciting experience for me. I heard people saying that we should not discuss religion, and I always argue, when beliefs and religions exist, we must recognize their existence instead of hiding it. Peace Team recognized that more than half of the population of the world shares some form of religious belief or spiritual faith.

Talal continued: "When you open this door of recognition, there opens a pathway to a strong and trustworthy communication channel that helps in exchanging ideas and imparting education in one's mind. I think this is the critical success we had in this project, and I consider it a breakthrough in the era where conflicts are taking a religious face." By their open and honest discussion, Peace Team members started to appreciate each other's points of view.

Hurdle Four: Seven Miles from Stanford for Some, Thousands of Miles for Others

When I started a job as an innovation instructor with Workshop Education, I learned about John Hunter's board game on peace. At the time, Stanford University was also initiating its MOOC programs. I was only seven miles from Stanford, while others contributing to the

Peace Game were many more miles away. Talal, was 7,600 miles away. Most of the original team of writers, artists, teachers, engineers, accountants, musicians, designers, and programmers lived on opposite sides of the planet.

Hurdle Five:
Publicity and Moving Peace Game beyond DNLE

In addition to being awarded Best Learning Game, Peace Game also received recognition from the Open Learning Innovation at MIT. Peace Game met their criteria of using open-access and open-license technologies along with innovative learning.

The feedback we received from Peace Game MOOC students suggested the need for publicity and exposure. I emailed key agents who are influential in the promotion of world peace such as the Vatican, Dali Lama, Oprah Winfrey, Bill Gates, Randi Zuckerberg, the World Bank, Nobel Peace Prize.org, and others to invite them to play the Peace Game and to pass it on. We will continue to reach out to individuals who are influential in promoting peace.

With support from DNLE, our Peace Game class project turned into a new learning environment after the end of class. Peace Game was voted the top learning game in the class. In order for the game to become a full MOOC, it needed architecture similar to Stanford's MOOCs. The team selected a free platform, together with other technologies that combine the best features of asynchronous and synchronous learning. Talal explains:

> We learned educational design concepts, and we have designed our own MOOC, we learned how to form successful teams, we made our team, we learned how to get along with people from different backgrounds, and we are dealing with our Peace Game MOOC participants from all around the world. Most importantly, we have combined our vision with Dr. Paul Kim's vision about reaching out to everyone and to empower everyone with education!

According to Alison:

> The MOOC format, together with some other technologies that the
> the team employed combines the best features of asynchronous and
> synchronous learning. Old-fashioned human conversation is still the
> best medium for cultivating empathy and understanding. New tech-
> nology enables us to have these conversations over the Internet in
> the form of free video chat. The time zone issues can be a bit of a
> challenge, but it's worth it to learn from others all over the world.

In addition, the team had to evaluate whether the technology encouraged higher-level thinking, and whether it promoted learning.
Instead of design-based assignments, we focused on finding solutions
for the 15 Global Challenges of the Millennium Project <http://millen-
nium-project.org/challenges.html>. These challenges are: sustainable
development and climate change, clean water, population, democra-
tization, global foresight, IT, rich-poor gap, health, education, peace
and conflict, status of women, transnational crime, energy, science and
technology, and global ethics.

Success One: Empathy in the Digital Realm

Peace Game found two of its most passionate members near the end
of the game development process. Originally, Yibin and Ionna were on
different teams. Yibin, the leader of SMILE@Tibet, had a team with
the vision of using micro-funding to increase accessibility to financial
services for entrepreneurs and small businesses that lacked access to
traditional banking institutions. Micro-funding was seen as a tool for
reducing the gap between rich and poor in the Global South. Ioanna
from Greece saw that the Peace Game team needed help and she made
a video for us. Like a traditional face-to-face classroom, the DNLE
class got to know one another and learned to care about each other
even though we never physically met.

Success Two: Building Trust and a Safe Space

Team collaboration improved as Peace Team realized the potential
that the team had for empowering others. Students in DNLE and the
players of the Peace Game do not fear people. The team built mutual

trust which was essential for collaboration and for innovation to germinate. The Peace Game allowed us to make friends without social pressures. Traditional socio-political and religious barriers were mitigated through the implementation and use of the digital space. In Peace Game, no one could reprimand another for making friends with the so-called enemy. People are safe to talk about challenging social and political issues that are often avoided. By learning from each other, people become friends, albeit virtually.

Success Three: The Learning Continues

Classmates from our DNLE class enrolled in our Peace Game MOOC. Little did I know that transitioning from a MOOC student to a MOOC teacher could lead to so many opportunities. I was just thinking of it as another learning experience and an opportunity to show others how to play for Peace.

Success Four: Motivation from the Wise

Here is the feedback from our instructors:

> It is unfortunate that the cultural divide sometimes undermines pure intentions. But this is exactly why YOUR TEAM was chosen to be highlighted. You have the potential of being a role model if your team is able to portray a well-balanced persona, which does NOT trigger any unwanted unnecessary controversy. MORE IMPORTANTLY, it would open the doors for intercultural and interfaith TRUST. As you know, many misunderstandings in the world are fed by ignorance and prejudice. Learning how to play a neutral public lead role is not easy, especially when we also try to stay true to our individual beliefs. But for the greater good, it is important that we do.

Part Three

The Peace Game Online yielded some unanticipated beneficial outcomes with implications for global leadership development based on social media.

Surprise One: Friendship and Forgiveness as Tension-Relievers

Peace Game encourages participants to make friends with people they would never have talked to. The type of initial encounter enabled by Peace Game is necessary to reduce tension among nations. One of Talal's friends in Karachi, after trying the game, remarked, "So the Peace Game is starting a conversation." Players take risks because of their recognition of the value of more peace. For players, Peace Game can be an amazing adventure that fosters the empathy and collaboration needed to solve Global Challenges. The game also allows for forgiveness to occur online. I noticed that Palestinians and Israelis often kept their friendships secret for fear of being criticized by others in their respective groups. It was obvious that people who were unable to forgive each other at the beginning of the game, were not able to communicate meaningfully with other players and blocked the possibility of peace. Forgiveness, even online, has allowed for friendships to get started.

Surprise Two: Overcoming Media Control

The biggest surprise for the team was discovering the unreliability of mainstream media outlets. By collecting firsthand accounts of what was going on in each other's country, game players could make better informed decisions about conflicts or news stories. For example, the story of Malala Yousafzai, the courageous young girl that was shot for advocating for education for girls was on the cover of *Time* magazine in April 2013. She was huge news in America. But when I skyped Rija, a Peace Game MOOC student, who is connected to women's rights in Pakistan, she told me that Malala was in the news for a few days and then disappeared. No one in Pakistan knows what happened to her, with some suggesting that Malala's incident had been staged. Meanwhile, the American public was getting details about Malala's condition in a British hospital as she recovered. The insight from Rija helped to contextualize the ways in which the mainstream media in one's home country can skew the presentation of an event taking place in another country based on the values or ideologies the home country wishes to promote. Through the Peace Game, the player had the ability to bypass media control by directly sending and receiving information.

Surprise Three: Jews for Palestine

While playing the Peace Game, one of the peace team members interacted with someone of Jewish ancestry for the first time. "Jews for Palestine? Impossible!" he said. This person showed him that there are Jews who support Palestine's right to statehood. Under the 'Peace' umbrella, it is possible to learn from each other by conversing about sensitive issues. Interfaith dialogue is encouraged and can diminish conflicts between people based on preconceived notions.

Surprise Four: Letting Africans Lead Africa

According to Alison, nobody knows better than Africans how to identify and solve the problems faced by their own countries. More importantly, nobody else has the right to dictate to these countries what their development priorities should be, or how they should participate in the world economy. And yet, many Western "aid" organizations often do not consult the people in the countries they are trying to support.

With the leadership of Jonathan Leibenberg, a student in Peace Game MOOC and now leader of 'Peace Game: Africa,' the Peace Game team has started to gather representatives from each of the 50 countries in Africa. These individuals will be expected to interact and to share their knowledge, expertise, and resources in a joint effort to discuss solutions for reducing the gap between rich and poor in Africa, and maybe, to implement those solutions that are feasible.

Surprise Five: Helping the underprivileged

The End of Poverty by American economist Jeffrey Sachs (2006) helped me to better understand the relationship between economics, climate, and geography. He contextualized issues of poverty wherein richer countries have a better climate to produce while countries on the equator, such as Malawi, are particularly vulnerable to diseases like malaria that require costly public health interventions. After a

Peace Game play, donations were given to the Malaria Fund of World Vision for mosquito bed nets for families where the need is greatest. Other projects for disadvantaged people are detailed below:

> $25 micro-loan to Ghana for livestock.
> $18 for bed net for malaria protection to Zomba, Malawi.
> $15 Pakistan flood relief.
> $20 education support for Tibet immigrant children
> through World Vision.
> $15 to Lifewater in Northern Uganda.
> $20 for bed nets to Honor World Malaria Day 2013,
> to New Delhi, India.
> $20 to a HIV AIDS fund and health education activity in Fiji.
> $40 to find and rehabilitate trafficked girls in the Philippines
> through www.visayanforum.org

While these micro-funded projects are very micro they were life-lines for those who benefitted. Despite facing challenges related to limited resources, our team intends to develop more micro-fund projects.

Surprise Six: Immediate Application of Learning

David, another player, used his new skill to create a rapid wireframe for the Peace Game interface so that the team could have its own architecture outside of Peace Game MOOC.

Talal explains:

> We are moving in the right direction. We consider Peace Game MOOC as the testing phase of our innovation. We have plans to move beyond the boundaries, cultures and religions. If we succeed to build a proper platform for Peace Game, then it can be the most disruptive learning technology that will combine human centered learning approach with higher education. We imagine our innovation as a social media platform where people will engage with each other to solve their problems by playing scenarios.

Alison explains:

> I expect that as we progress in the Peace Game, we will be constantly using these rubrics to learn and evaluate our own technology, thus making it more effective as a learning tool.

The team believes that the Peace Game MOOC has become a disruptive game-based interactive course where students learn critical thinking skills that prepare them to make decisions that can lead to world peace. Students also learn to address their own challenges as well. Taking advantage of MOOC's disruptive power enables students to discuss sensitive issues while also promoting the active engagement of individuals from different sides of the globe. Our learning environment is highly dynamic because it incorporates all dimensions of every field of life. It is sustainable because of its structure's flexibility.

Surprise Seven: Movement Beyond and Post-Peace Game MOOC

The Peace Game has resulted in several other initiatives and joint activities. Vonivate from Fiji and I have become friends and are learning from each other. Jonathan in South Africa gave me the name of his Tanzania contact and I shared the information about a water initiative contest that will award a laptop in Tanzania. Meanwhile, Jonathan has connected with Noel in Malawi.

Since the inception of the Peace Game, Ali and I received further training at the Stanford Mobile Inquiry Learning Environment (SMILE). I have been developing Peace Game questions for inquiry learning with Talal's assistance.

Adam Brimo, co-founder of OpenLearning.com in Australia gave us data on the various players and countries that participated in the Peace Game MOOC. Adams data indicates the website had 6913 page views from 100 countries.

Talal proposed bringing Peace Game into the redesign efforts for The Design Thinking Action Lab of Leticia Britos Cavagnaro at Stanford University. The lab started on July 22, 2013 with only six people on each team. Five teams were formed with participants from Iran, China, England, the Philippines, Egypt, Buenos Aires, Spain, Pakistan, United States, Brazil, France, Morocco, Mexico, Uruguay, Germany, and Venezuela. Each team will try to redesign the Peace Game using design-thinking skills starting with empathy.. Talal, Sara, and I are team leaders. My team was composed of children from ages 9 to 13. Online Peace Game continues to evolve based on collaborative efforts.

Lastly, Peace Game has also been able to shift perspectives. Alison's sentiment about peace prior to the Peace Game was nothing short of skeptical. According to Alison:

> I'm sad to admit it but I don't believe world peace is attainable. I'm kind of a crusty old cynic. The issues facing the world are incredibly complex—poverty, inequality, environmental degradation, and religious and cultural differences just to name a few. I also know that there will always be plenty of greedy, violent people in the world. I don't know that true peace is attainable.

Although Alison remains cynical about the attainment of world peace, she believes that the ideal is worth pursuing. Talal maintains that:

> We are working close to idealism, and we are contributing our part to make this world better, education is the most effective tool to empower minds of people, and we have made education, especially MOOC education as a carrier to enter into people's minds and to develop their capabilities that will help them to create and live in a peaceful environment.

Our professor called for the design of a new learning environment that is engaging, educationally sound, accessible, and sustainable. The Peace Game team considered the professor's call as empowering the team to create a new design concept to establish meaningful connection between people all over the world. Like the quest to achieve world peace, the development of the game itself is ongoing and requires the teamwork of many. Ultimately, the Peace Team discovered that conflicts are not so much related to religion as they are to issues such as water, culture, politics, and money. But by enabling a space for courageous conversations, Peace Game helps to bridge the disconnect between people.

Global Reach

The MOOC course resulted in a Peace Game Online which became a MOOC course itself. The MOOC Peace Game has been tested with me collaboratively leading teams with diverse skills. The experience with testing the new course has significantly increased my global friends and collaborators. My global circle now includes Roz Hussin, Dr. Kim, Saed Awwad, Alexa Frisbie, John Hunter, Joyce in Kenya, Deepak in India, Joseph in South Korea, Nicky in Hong Kong, James with Seeds of Empowerment in Tanzania, Dariana from Bulgaria, Yibin in mainland China but working in Tibet, Ioanna from Greece, Noel in Malawi, Mark Roest, Ankie from Canada, Jonathon in South Africa, and Sara in Spain. Among us, we are able to speak Mandarin, Cantonese, Spanish, Swahili, Punjabi, Urdu, Hindi, Sindi, French, Italian, Bulgarian, Greek, and English.

I continue to interact with players of the Peace Game from diverse backgrounds, races, ethnicities, and religions.

LEADERSHIP TIPS

1. *Draw on your virtues and values.* Resilience gives me the confidence to not give up, grit gives me insight to get through pain, determination gives me focus to do good with the talent God has given me, patience gives me the advantage to look at the long term goals, humility gives me the insight to skip taking it easy and drive gives me motivation to go for my dreams and what is expected of me.

2. *Utilize leadership skills that are already at your disposal.* Being an immigrant means I have to work twice as hard to prove I am as good as anyone else; humility, empathy at the beginning stage of human centered design, and peace making, that is, seeing both sides to solve conflict comes naturally to me.

3. *Celebrate being a Filipina.* As typical of Filipino culture, my father taught me how to smile even while others are trying to discourage me, knowing that person would regret their impulsiveness. My mother taught me to work hard and had high expectations of me. Jesus showed me to love my enemies and use my gifts for others. Coming from an immigrant background made me comfortable in taking appropriate risks on what gives a better return on investment.

4. *Be true to your core identity. Working with you should be both productive and pleasurable.* My core identity is my relationship with Christ as a child of God. I often advise people to do what you need to do and not care what other people think, only care what God thinks. He does not change His mind or make careless opinions.

5. *Recognize how your Philippine heritage has informed your values, sense of purpose, leadership style and outlook on the world.* I was born in America because of the sacrifices my parents went through leaving everything to start a new life in a new country.

Because I am aware of this sacrifice on my parent's part, I know that I could not waste opportunity. I needed to make opportunity by being proactive.

6. ***Don't be over ambitious.*** Don't step on other people's shoes. Give credit where credit is due for a successful undertaking.

7. ***Learn from your experiences.*** My experiences beyond home challenged or reinforced my notions of leadership, and since Filipinos have experienced racism and prejudice, I have empathy for all people who are not treated with respect and know that I have been blessed to bless others.

8. ***Tradition is not necessarily at odds with success in the global workplace.*** I do not believe Philippine traditional beliefs are at odds with the requirements of success in the global workplace. Since the Philippines has had their first female president and America has not, I consider the Philippines to be advanced in important areas.

9. ***Harness technology to benefit you and others.*** Please remember that behind every technology is a smart user. You too can lead a diverse global team through social media.

FULL CIRCLE

Lenore RS Lim

President and Founder
Lenore RS Lim Foundation for the Arts

Abstract

My family migrated to Vancouver, Canada in 1975 and we later moved to New York in 1988. Since the 1960s, my passion for art has driven my life. Juggling my teaching, parenting, and creating artwork was not an easy balancing task. Nevertheless, with my Filipino ingenuity, I managed successfully to hold numerous solo art exhibits in all four corners of the world. By showcasing the Philippines' cultural tradition and heritage in my art, I represent the world-class talent of Filipinos in the visual arts as well as promoting international goodwill and better understanding of our country worldwide. Altogether, my artworks constitute my visual serenade to my country. In 2000, I made history by being the only Filipino artist to be included in the international art exhibition titled, 'Progress of the World's Women' held at the United Nations in New York. I continued to hoist the banner for Filipino artists at the Venice Open 2002 with my installation entitled, 'Comfort House' as a tribute and a memorial to the thousands of comfort women in Asia who were subjected to unimaginable indignities during the World War II. I share my talents and cutting edge techniques by giving free workshops to promising art students, particularly in developing countries. Though I am not living in my homeland, I am a part of the Filipino diaspora and that allows me to give back to our motherland, revitalize printmaking in the Philippines and contribute to the global artists community.

Introduction and Inspiration

Any success I am blessed to have is shared with all the people and places that have inspired and continue to inspire me.

When I was a child, my father, Arsenio Raquel-Santos bought me my first art book when he noticed my growing interest in drawing. In high school, Sister Araceli, my art teacher at the College of the Holy Spirit, gave me free art lessons outside the classroom every Saturday morning. Without their support and encouragement, I might not have developed into the artist that I am today.

The memories of early childhood growing up in the Philippines come naturally to me and these continue to inspire me every day: the tranquil and idyllic countryside, the lush green fields, the mountains and rivers, the clear blue skies, the sunsets, the people, and everything in the Philippines.

The Robert Blackburn Printmaking Workshop in New York City offered me a sanctum and environment where I explored, experimented and collaborated with my visions in prints. Robert Blackburn was a very special person who left a mark on many contemporary artists who have had the good fortune to meet and work with him. Even in his later years, he continued to reinforce the belief that all artists, black, white, young and old, native and foreign born matter. For Blackburn, their expressions affirmed the most important elements of humanity. He believed that the light cast by artists illuminates us all. I had the pleasure to know him personally and visited him before he passed away. He touched my life so deeply that I feel I have a responsibility to continue what he passed about art on to me and others. I have to maintain a high level of creative and artistic quality, support and encourage innovation, and pioneer opportunities for artists from minority communities and developing countries.

Background

I graduated from the University of the Philippines, College of Architecture and Fine Arts in 1967. In my senior year, I was elected Student Council President. After graduation, I taught art at the International

School from 1968 to 1974, rising to Art and Special Subjects leader from 1972 to 1973 in the elementary department. I also taught art at the high school department of Assumption Convent in Manila from 1968 to 1970. My concerns for the pedagogy of art lead me to become Secretary of the Philippine Art Educators Association (PAEA) from 1973 to 1974.

My teaching career brought me to Mobile, Alabama USA in 1975 as an Art Resource Teacher in the Mobile County Public School System. I then moved to Vancouver, British Columbia (B.C.) to start a family. I gave art lessons at Place des Arts from 1984 to 1985.

To understand and learn more about bringing up my two young children, I finished a Certificate in Early Childhood Education at the Douglas College in New Westminster, B.C. in 1985. I then started a multi-cultural pre-school for Our Lady of Lourdes School in Coquitlam,B.C. in 1985. I served as the pre-school's supervisor until 1988 when I accepted a position teaching at the Early Childhood level at the United Nations International School in New York. In Vancouver, my husband and I were regularly involved in various projects that promoted and contributed to showcasing and promoting Philippine culture. We sponsored and hosted Philippine Nights at different parishes, as well as presented concerts and shows featuring Filipino performing artists from the Philippines.

Our family's move from a Canadian suburb to New York in the late 1980s was the biggest change in my life. There were museums, galleries, art stores with extensive choices of art materials, art schools, and of course people. I was constantly around exceptional artists from all over the globe. Living in New York opened new perspectives and insights from which I derived new ideas and inspirations. Over the years, I have continued to learn and grow as an artist in New York and the influence is undeniably reflected in my work.

An accident in the late eighties in New York caused such serious injuries that I was bedridden for some time. To occupy my time, I began to turn the pages of a beautiful book titled *Impressionism and Post Impressionism* given by a dear friend Victor Huang. All of a sudden there was a strong reawakening of feeling and a renewed sense of commitment and dedication to pursue my art when I recovered. It was a pledge I made to myself and was to be an important turning point in the way I would relate to art. I began to take courses in printmaking and computer art at the School of Visual Arts (SVA) from 1990 to 1995. I interacted with artists and teachers who were the pioneers of computer art, among them Larry Wright, Gunars Prande, Elaine Breiger and David Sandlin. Since then, I have explored new techniques that combine traditional modes with the use of computers.

In 1991, the Museum of Modern Art (MoMA) in New York had a show of seven printmakers. One of the artists that left a tremendous impression on me was Robert Rauschenberg. He had big, beautiful art pieces. I thought that perhaps I should concentrate on printmaking and one day I could come up with equally wonderful work. On my first trip to Boston in the early 1980s, my friend Emy Masigan Mercado took me to a gallery and got me interested in some etchings by Salvador Dali. I liked his prints so much that I decided to take lessons in printmaking. I took many art classes at the School of Visual Arts in New York.

Philippines Ambassador Philip and Mrs. Mabilagan, were instrumental in encouraging me to apply for a grant. Ada Mabilangan was the first to refer to me as an "established artist." A subsequent grant from the Pollock Krasner Foundation cemented the self-confidence I needed to continue my career upward.

As a Global Filipina, my three worlds greatly influence my work. In New York where I taught and was exposed to the United Nations international community, I learned a significant amount from the diversity of cultures. There are different points of view on divergent subjects and even simple discussions on current issues can be a very interesting and enriching experience. I had the opportunity to meet many important people like Kofi Annan, the then UN Secretary General; Agnes Gund, President Emeritus of the Museum of Modern Art; Thomas Krens, Director of the Guggenheim Museum, and many foreign ambassadors and dignitaries. New York City by itself is always a living and vibrant influence on any artist who lives and works there. I may conceive an idea while taking a quiet walk by the water in Vancouver but eventually continue to work on it in New York. Or, when I go on holiday to the Philippines, I may pick up some inspiration and material and bring them back to New York to work further on them. Eventually I would come out with a number of artworks based on what I had experienced in Manila, but flavored, crafted, and blended in a North American setting. I guess I can say I do my art wherever I am and with whoever I am at any given time but the influence of New York manifests itself clearly in the finished product.

Balance

One definition of success for me is living a balanced life. A successful life is where I can balance family, career, community, and spirituality.

Being a teacher complemented my being an artist. Both fields require discipline, dedication, organization, setting timetables, and focusing on one's goals. Both involve hard work and a supportive family.

Since I was a full time teacher, I did my art after school hours and on the weekends. I set aside spring breaks and the summer vacation to do my exhibitions. I also had to think ahead. When I moved to New York, I wrote down my goals and made plans to achieve them. I wrote down the year when a specific goal had to be worked on. This has been my guide. I had to be flexible, too. I had to do some adjustments like when I was ill. I used those years for study and to further develop concepts.

Art and music were family activities; both my children were studying violin. So while I was at the studio, they would do their music lessons. We would make trips together collecting and buying my art materials. As a family, we coordinate our schedule to meet everyone's needs. My husband who is in real estate often would have property showings and once in a while the family would assist him in presentation and staging property.

Besides being an artist, I was also a full time teacher, mother, wife, and an active member of numerous organizations in the community. I have had to manage my time efficiently. Computer technology, which I embraced at its infancy in the eighties, has helped me fulfill the different demanding roles I have played. Through the computer I am able to do my work for school, research my design studies, and organize my schedule. The computer has given me more time to do my art after school hours. Before the computer, I used the fax machine to contact galleries to prepare for an art show. I use technology not only to do computer-generated designs but also to reach my colleagues at school and in the art community. I may use the computer to ask questions or to invite people to see my exhibit.

Computer art was a relatively new field in the 1980s. I ventured into it thinking it was a challenge. Back then, I was not sure how people would respond to my art. My first show at the Philippines Center in New York in 1991 with a number of computer oriented art pieces was very well received. Over the years, I have improved my printmaking techniques. I have experimented with bigger pieces like my installation, Comfort House for the show OPEN 2002 in Venice. For the installation my prints were digitally printed on acetate and laminated onto plexiglas.

My husband Jose and children Claire and Justin learned how to use PageMaker and Photoshop with me. Together we worked on newsletters and catalogues. With their help we would put my guest list in a database. The family supports me whenever I have an art show. They help me with press releases, brochure, price lists, and title cards. Email has been an important tool in connecting with the other artists. My art exhibits are often planned, coordinated, and arranged through email. Sharing my websites has also been helpful and saves a lot of time.

I have embraced the Christian Life Community (CLC) way of life. Rooted in Ignatian spirituality, it has helped me realize that all that I am is from God and that I should develop all my talents and abilities to glorify Him. One way of glorifying God is by helping others in the best way I know. I am also constantly reminded of God's presence in all things. I am thankful for all of God's gifts, including the beauty in nature. That is why when I do my art I always begin with a prayer; it helps bring the peace of knowing God to my art.

Transcending Challenge: Illness

My spirituality has always helped me maintain perspective and manage anything that comes my way.

I was quite ill for a while and had my intimations of immortality. During this period of my life, I found I had a lot of time on my hands and yet, ironically because of my illness, I was not sure of how much time there was really left for me. During that period I did a lot of introspection. What kind of legacy would I leave? This was when I noticed my art begin to mature. I slowly veered away from just pretty pieces that were acceptable. My latter work reflects a new attitude. The pieces reveal greater depth, soul, and passion.

The Pollock-Krasner grant was a prestigious honor that I received in 1999. I had to live up to the expectations of being a grantee, so I strove to work even harder. The grant also freed me from financial constraints and allowed me to hire an assistant, and I was able to create bigger and more challenging pieces, despite being sick at that time.

Through my art consultant Clint White, I was introduced to Tally Beck. Tally offered to host a solo exhibit of my work at the Tally Beck Gallery on the Lower Eastside of New York. The Gallery brings my work to the Art Fairs in San Francisco, Texas and the Hamptons. At the last Market Art Fair, my artwork was a Critic's Pick.

Giving Back

I hope to be able to give back even a fraction of the blessings I have received.

In 2000, prior to retiring from teaching at the United Nations International School, I founded the Lenore RS Lim Foundation for the Arts. Its mission is to inspire and to help develop the artistic potential of deserving individuals regardless of their economic and social background. The Foundation promotes the greater appreciation and understanding of Fine Arts in the community at large, and in so doing enhances the public exposure to the artists the Foundation supports.

The Foundation co-sponsored the exhibits of Manuel Rodriguez, Sr. at the Philippine Center in New York in 2007. At the same venue, the Foundation also co-sponsored the UP Landmarks Exhibit in 2008. Also in 2008, the Foundation published Nik Ricio's photo-etchings Kalibo and Ati-Atihan and sponsored the solo exhibit of Myrna Reyes at the GSIS Museum in Manila.

In 2009, the Foundation sponsored the solo exhibit of Francisco V. Coching, the Filipino Master Komiks Artist, and the concert of Sharon Tan at the Philippine Center.

The Foundation conducts workshops at the University of the Philippines and the Philippine Association of Printmakers. In 2010, the Foundation sponsored several master printmakers from the Robert Blackburn Printmaking Workshop including Devraj Dacoji and Elizabeth Harington. They conducted workshops in lithography and intaglio. Students and professional artists participated in this successful project. In 2012, the Foundation again sponsored master printmaker Devraj Dacoji to conduct an advanced lithograph workshop. In addition, the Foundation invited Justin Sanz, New York printmaker, to demonstrate watercolor monotype and advanced woodcut techniques.

To celebrate the Centennial Anniversary of the College of the Holy Spirit, in 2013, the Foundation organized and sponsored the High Spirit Exhibition and Artists talk at the Cultural Center of the Philippines. In 2014, the Foundation sponsored Print Expressions, a printmaking exhibit and conducted a three-day printmaking workshop at the College of the Holy Spirit College of Fine Arts in Mendiola, Manila.

The Foundation published the books: *Manuel Rodriguez, Sr. Into the Threshold*, a book on the life, art and teachings of the Father of Philippine Modern Printmaking, and *Imelda Cajipe Endaya: Stitching Paint into Collage*, six essays about the artist's work and the culture that nurtured her art.

Other Community Service

When we moved to Vancouver in 1975, we started our family and we were active members of the All Saints Parish in Coquitlam. As a member of the parish, I helped with fundraising events for the parish and with my husband, we coordinated the Philippine Night where we got the other Filipinos involved in preparing the dinner, program, and dance for the parish. Later, two other Catholic church parishes in the area asked for our help to organize their Philippine Nights.

I founded the Filipino Music and Art Foundation in 1980 to be able to support Filipino artists from New York and the Philippines to present a concert to enhance the Filipino image. Among the artists we sponsored were Raul Sunico, Gil Lopez Kabayao, Fides Cuyugan, Jimmy Melendrez and Rene Dalandan.

Between 1981 and 1984, I was the president of the University of the Philippine Alumnae Association in B.C. The organization sponsored various cultural presentations such as The Bayanihan Dance Company, The University of the Philippines Concert Chorus and the Madrigal Singers.

I was president of the Society of Philippine American Artist (SPAA) from 2006 to 2008 and a second time from 2010 to 2011. The SPAA is a non-profit organization based in New York City that promotes and highlights Filipino talent overseas. The society promotes the appreciation of the arts, unites artists, assists aspiring artists, and assists its members to advance their skills, derive economic benefits from their work, and develop rapport with the public through workshops and activities that bring art to the people. We have sponsored the annual SPAA Art exhibit for the past 20 years and have published three SPAA books.

As Trustee of the Philippine Pastoral Center, Chapel of San Lorenzo Ruiz, New York City from 2002 to 2008, I organized a number of Day of Prayers for the community and fund raising activities for the Chapel. In 2009, I was the co-chair of the San Lorenzo Endowment Fundraising Project with the wife of then Philippines Ambassador to the UN, Hilario Davide.

I was President of the College of the Holy Spirit Alumnae Association USA / Canada from 2000 to 2003. During my term, the association became a registered not-for-profit organization. The association serves as the link to the alma mater in the Philippines and organizes reunions for the alumnae in U.S. and Canada. Since 2003, I have been a volunteer member of the Art Committee of the Philippine Center New York. The Philippine Center exhibits works of Filipino artists regularly and the Art Committee reviews the portfolios of the artists applying to exhibit at the Philippine Center. I coordinated the artists applying to exhibit at the Philippine Center. I coordinated the event Tribute to Manuel Rodriguez Sr. and coordinated publishing the book for the Philippine Consulate, Art at the Philippine Center

New York in 2010.

As an active member of the Philippine Association of Printmakers (PAP) and a member of the Board of Director since 2010, I have conducted workshops for printmakers and have sponsored the two PAP exhibits at the Philippine Center New York.

Since 1988, together with the CLC, I have been involved in coordinating the Days of Prayer during Lent for the Filipino community in New York. This is an opportunity for all of us to grow spiritually.

Encouragement and Support for Emerging Filipino Artists

Since I left the Philippines in 1974 to go to the U.S., I have been involved in assisting Filipino artists in any way I can. In Vancouver, I co-founded a non-profit music foundation that regularly sponsored performances of world-class Filipino performers. When I relocated to New York, I focused more on assisting Filipino visual artists both from within the Philippines and the diaspora by encouraging them, giving them ideas based on my personal experiences, and helping them organize art shows.

When I visit the Philippines, I am always impressed by the beautiful art works I see from Filipino printmakers. Considering the high cost of materials in the Philippines, the limited space and equipment they have to work with, and the minimal government financial assistance available, they are still able to produce high quality artwork.

One area where I can assist Filipino printmakers is to help educate the public about the value of printmaking. Compared to other media, such as painting, printmaking is a painstaking medium that is still not widely appreciated in the Philippines as it is in Europe and the Western world. By helping create a larger market for prints, young and deserving Filipino printmakers will be encouraged and motivated to attain a level of self-sufficiency and to advance their art to the next level. Towards this objective, I regularly hold free workshops and artists talks for both students and artists at various schools in the Philippines and even as far away as Peru. I share not only cutting edge techniques but create a forum for an exchange of ideas and experimentation in printmaking that is designed to contribute long lasting benefit to popularizing the medium to a larger audience.

As I fly in and out of my established homes in the Philippines, Canada, and the U.S., the global Pinay diaspora, is no longer separate from my homeland. Instead, it has become a coming together, a full circle; a state of opportunity to dialogue and to exchange thoughts and ideas in order to give back to our motherland and the global community.

Leadership Tips

To the next group of aspiring leaders:

1. ***Believe that you are a born leader.*** Believe that you have been individually gifted by God with unique talents and abilities that you alone possess and may bring to the community. Remember that Christ chose twelve uneducated fishermen and laborers to build His church. Today, the church has a billion believers spread across very corner of the globe making positive contribution to mankind.

2. ***Look within and examine why you want to lead.*** After self-examination and understanding your motivation, accept and pursue your role as a leader with deep passion and consistency. Always remain focused on your mission, never wavering even in times of difficulty and after setbacks. The fruits of your work over time will surprise you. I was driven early in life to be of service to others by my upbringing and convent education. This would eventually lead me to volunteer in campus activities and to get involved in student government. Later when I immigrated to Canada with my ehusband, my pride in being a Filipina and my desire to let others know about our culture was the driving force that got me engaged in various community activities. To this day, I remain steadfast in projecting the best of the Philippines in words and deeds. In the process, I also continue to advance my career as an artist and as an effective community leader.

3. ***Be people-oriented.*** It is through social interaction that you will be able to gain the social skills to build a team for whatever undertaking you pursue. There is nothing I have accomplished without the help of others.

4. ***Do not be afraid to delegate work to others.*** Delegate even if you know you can do the job better and more efficiently. By getting more people involved, you will be getting more people to take ownership of the work at hand. That can only be beneficial in team-building, training of new leaders, and the accomplishment of objectives.

5. ***Be the last to accept credit or honors.*** Credit or honors for work accomplished or goals achieved should be given to the members of the team who were involved in the work. The achievement of what you sought to achieve is more than enough reward for your heart and soul.

Japan: A Love–Hate Relationship

Isabelita Tiopianco Manalastas-Watanabe

President and Representative Director
SPEED Money Transfer Japan

Abstract

*I*t has been a love-hate relationship for more than 30 years with my adopted country, Japan, and it still is. The beautiful memories of my first visit to Japan in 1975 stayed with me long after I had left the country, pulling me like a magnet to return to the Land of the Rising Sun. Return I did, leaving behind my first love, and being led to an exciting life, first as a student, an international civil servant, then as a bank executive, and finally the President of a company I established. I have overcome many challenges along the way, and have been successful thus far. Even though challenges may still come my way, I know that with the continued trust, support and understanding of my family, I will overcome. I will not stop nurturing bigger dreams. I also firmly believe in the power of prayer, and that if it will be for the greater good, it will be answered.

The Start of A Life's Journey

Autumn of 1975. Thirty youth ambassadors of goodwill from each of the five ASEAN member countries (Indonesia, Malaysia, the Philippines, Singapore and Thailand), and thirty from Japan converged in Singapore, to participate in the Ship for Southeast Asian Youth program sponsored by the Japanese Prime Minister's Office. I was one of them, an economic researcher from the Philippines' National Economic and Development Authority (NEDA), representing the category of 'young professionals.' We boarded the Nippon Maru, which became our home for more than a month, and sailed to six countries, with Japan as our last port of call, before flying back to our home countries.

It was a journey of a lifetime, changing the lives of many, including mine. Many friendships were forged, some lasting even to this day. Love relationships developed, some resulting in marriages.

Although I did not realize it right away, I had changed after that first voyage to foreign lands. Suddenly, my horizons widened. I wanted to learn more about other people, about their culture, about everything that was new to me.

All the places we visited were beautiful, but it was love at first sight with me for Japan. The beautiful memories of that first visit to Japan; the blazing red and gold autumn leaves, the dizzying speed of their bullet trains, the very clean and comparatively safe streets, the brightly lit nights of Tokyo, and yes, the delicate food that is also a feast for the eyes; all these stayed with me long after I flew home. Japan was like a magnet, pulling me back to the Land of the Rising Sun.

When the chance came for me to receive a Japanese government scholarship, I did not think twice, even if this meant convincing my high school sweetheart to postpone our church wedding until after I had completed my research and then my graduate studies in Japan.

Was I Stupid?

Many of my friends thought it was a stupid idea, when they learned that I had chosen to do my graduate studies in Japan, instead of in a country like the U.S. In Japan I would have to learn my '3 Rs' again. I had to learn to read in Japanese, write in Japanese, and do aRithmetic; my math skills were shockingly bad compared to those of my Japanese classmates. Six months of Japanese language training as part of my scholarship grant were completely inadequate. I only had one econometrics subject during my four years of undergraduate course in business economics at the University of the Philippines and we did not have the chance to work with computers during my time. But at my Japanese university, lengthy and complicated mathematical equations were the usual fare. The knowledge and mastery of computers seemed to be the norm, and were required even to pass my political science subjects.

There were some other surprising things, like being invited for a beer by my professor, and inside the university! But it was absolutely normal, I found out later, and something I appreciated. It was during those drinking sessions between professors and students, and between company employees and their bosses, that everyone feels equal to everyone else. Everyone becomes more relaxed, able to speak more freely, and able to release the stress of the vertical hierarchy in Japan.

I learned all these and many other things along the way. I also learned that three years were probably too long for someone to wait.

I lost my first love.

I got my degree.

Was I stupid?

The Early Professional Years

When the Philippine government, through the Department of Foreign Affairs, sought nominations from Philippine governmental agencies for the post of Deputy Director for Investments at the ASEAN-Japan Centre in Tokyo, I had just returned from my studies in Japan. The Deputy Director for Investment would represent not only the Philippines but all of the ASEAN countries. NEDA, where I returned soon after I completed my MA studies in Japan, nominated me. I did not have any investment experience, but I had a significant advantage over the other candidates; I had knowledge of Japan, its people and its language. I got the job.

Young, Pretty, Filipina: An Asset?

Youth, they say is not an asset in Japan, where corporate seniority is almost always equated with chronological age. A pretty face? Yes, definitely! But generally appreciated only in the entertainment and related industries. A Filipina? Depends on what industry you are employed in or what kind of business you are engaged in.

I was 27 when I held the post of Deputy Director at the ASEAN-Japan Centre in Tokyo. The Japanese colleagues seconded to the Centre by the Japanese government, with equal rank, were about twice my age. I also had the disadvantage of being female in a country where men dominated the corporate boardrooms, and women CEOs and top executives were still a rarity.

I tried to make myself look older by wearing suits in conservative colors and tying my waist-long hair into a bun. I hid behind my rank. I instructed my staff to introduce me as Manalastas, *Jichou* [Deputy Director] whenever anyone invited someone from the Centre to speak regarding investing in the ASEAN countries. In Japan, it is normal to address a business person using one's family name, followed by the rank or position. So I was Manalastas, Deputy Director.

I became somewhat of a curiosity in Japan. I was invited to appear in TV programs. Many articles about me, my work and my experiences in Japan, appeared in various Japanese publications. I even graced the covers of some.

Let me share with you some of my early experiences.

"Mr." Manalastas

My office got an invitation to send a speaker to a Japanese investment seminar in Nagoya. I was the one who went. I arrived at the seminar room early, greeted the Japanese officer from the seminar organizer, *"Konnichiwa,"* but I did not introduce myself. He just ignored me. Young, Japanese looking female; maybe he thought I was one of the tea servers. Or maybe one of the simultaneous interpreters for the seminar? Definitely not the main speaker! I would soon find out why. When I glanced at the presidential table, my name was written as "MR. MANALASTAS." Imagine the shock of this Japanese officer when I sat down at the presidential table behind this name plate.

Lesson learned: Immediately offer your *meishi* [calling card] when meeting someone for business. The calling card will set the tone for discussions, as the other party can gauge how high you are on the corporate ladder, and whether or not you are the decision maker. Then the doors will open, a little or widely, depending on your rank and on the other party's interest in doing business with you.

Filipina? Prostitute!

Question: *Why is it that there are no longer many young and pretty Filipinas in the Philippines?*
Answer: *They are all working in Japan!*

Only a joke, of course. But the truth was that there were indeed many young and pretty Filipinas in Japan working as entertainers when I first started working there in the 1980s. I lost my cool once when I was told by a Japanese that Filipina entertainers were really nothing but prostitutes. I asked that person, so what if we were entertainers? Being an entertainer is a profession and there is nothing wrong with being one. So what if what he claimed were really true? Who was more noble, and more decent: the Japanese entertainer who worked because she wanted to buy expensive material things, or the Filipina who sacrificed herself to earn money to send back home to support her family?

Judge not, lest ye be judged. Well, I did judge! From that time on, I lost my respect for Japanese men and I vowed that I would never, ever marry one!

Watashiwa Hawaii Karadesu!

The stereotyped images that the Japanese have of the Philippines (Smokey Mountain; slums) and Filipinas in Japan (prostitutes) have hurt me so much. I even allowed myself to deny my identity as a Filipina at one point in my early days in Japan. This, despite the fact that I was one of the few Filipinas blessed with a career and job. I can speak Japanese, maybe for two minutes or so, and get away with not being detected as a non-Japanese. But after some time, the Japanese listener will immediately be able to determine I am not Japanese and the inevitable question "*O kuniwa...?*"[from which country are you?] Once, I answered spontaneously, "*Watashiwa Hawaii karadesu*".

I felt shame afterwards. I wrote an article in *Ugnayan*, a Filipino newsletter in Japan, maybe as a way of purging myself of the guilt I felt. I also wanted to share my thoughts with my *kababayans* [fellow citizens from the Philippines] in Japan that we should never, ever and Filipinas in Japan all the time! Whatever career we may have, do this. We should raise our heads high and be proud to be Filipinos whatever job we may do, when we do it out of love and caring for our families back home, the job becomes noble.

Whoever is clean and pure, cast the first stone.

Harassment of a Kept (?) Woman

"Your footsteps are so noisy!" (I was seated, watching TV, when the woman living directly below me called to complain.)

"Your garbage is not properly sorted out." (How did they know it was my garbage?)

"Sorry, I had to open your mansion while you were away," said my building caretaker, "as one of the laundry baskets was missing. I found it inside your place and returned it to the common laundry room." (I stole that laundry basket?!!! A pink, plastic laundry basket anyone can buy in a nearby store, the price of which will not even buy a decent lunch. Of course, I went down to the common laundry room and 'stole' back my laundry basket.)

This was the last straw of the many harassing incidents while I was living at that high-end mansion provided by the ASEAN-Japan Centre. The *hanagatakai* [literally 'high nose'] residents could not believe that a young Filipina could afford to live there on her own.

I finally decided to move out and find another mansion. By the way, 'mansion' is what the Japanese call a condo, even a small one. But one of my colleagues at the office suggested, "Why not fight back?"

Fight back, I did, but not physically. I intentionally dropped my *Gaimusho* (Japan's Ministry of Foreign Affairs) issued I.D. in front of the office of the building caretaker, and then went up to my mansion. At that time foreigners in Japan used an alien registration card as their I.D. Since I was working for an inter-governmental, regional organization my I.D. was different. As I expected, after a few minutes came a knock, I opened the door, and there was my building caretaker saying, "Did you drop something very important?" I feigned surprise and bewilderment, an Oscar award-winning performance, shook my head, and asked him why. "Oh, you must be very careful not to lose this important I.D."

End of harassment. No more complaints. No more *tsismis* [gossip] that I was the mistress of a rich Japanese. I had won! I stayed in my mansion.

Fast forward to 2014, more than two decades after my first employment in Japan. Nothing much had changed. Even in government, only a few women occupied top positions. As of June 2014 there were only two women in the 19-person cabinet of Prime Minister Shinzo Abe. Sexism is common in the nation's work place, as illustrated by CNN coverage in June 2014 of sexist comments hurled at Ayaka Shiomura, a young Assembly woman during her speech at a Tokyo Assembly meeting about the need for more services for women. Japanese male colleagues heckled her and interrupted her with comments urging her to get married and questioning whether she was too old to bear children (she was 35). The last coverage I saw on this incident was in a Japanese TV program where one of the lawmaker-hecklers apologized to the Assembly woman. Other hecklers have yet to come out in the open.

Other foreign media like BBC also carried the news. Mariko Oi, a Japanese newscaster at BBC, was interviewed regarding her views and opinion of the incident. She was obviously pregnant, and she told the BBC interviewer that she was at first wary about how her supervisor would respond to her pregnancy. She need not have worried as she worked outside a Japanese setting. In Japan, there is the so called 'M' curve for the female labor force; join the labor force when one graduates, leave when one gets pregnant or to raise a child, go back to the labor force (normally on a part-time basis) when the children are grown up or are independent, and then retire; up, down, up, down.

Good that the heckling incident received international coverage. It may have influenced the Japanese Prime Minister to announce plans to encourage Japanese companies to increase the number of women managers, from the current 7% share, to around 30% by 2020.

Juggling Career And Motherhood

I had an exciting, happy, but also stressful first nine years as a professional in Japan.

Reviewing old newspaper and magazine clippings of various write-ups on myself, I found one where I was the cover story. "*Shigoto Ni*

Ikigai Demo Hitori De Utsukushiku Toshi Wa Toritakunai" [Working With Purpose, But I Do Not Want to Grow Old Beautiful and Alone] was the title of my story. I probably gave myself away during the interview, as the title reflected my deepest emotions at the time.

It was time to take stock of what I had accomplished so far. I had to decide on what I would still like to do with my life. I needed to just let things flow and lead me to the next phase. My former boss at the NEDA had told me that to have a fulfilled and complete life, one had to plant a tree, write a book, and have a child. I had already planted a tree and written a chapter in a Japanese book. I needed to accomplish just one more task: have a child.

I moved to the U.S. and had just given birth to my son, JC, when the phone rang. It was my former boss at the NEDA, now a top-ranking official of the Philippine National Bank (PNB). Would I consider going back to Japan to help PNB open its Tokyo Representative Office? With my six-week old baby in my arms, I flew back to Tokyo. I was to take a job in a field where, again, I had no prior experience. In a short span of time, I was able to upgrade the Representative Office license to that of a full banking license. I was even able to open a branch in southwestern Japan. The bank, with a minimum capital of only US$1.5 million, was in the black in less than a year. I was promoted one rank after the other, until I became First Senior Vice President. At the time, I headed not only the Japan operations of the bank, but was Area Head for Asia and the Pacific.

My being Filipina was now an asset; my clients were our own *kababayans* [fellow citizens]. These were the thousands of Overseas Filipino Workers (OFWs) who were more comfortable talking and dealing with another Filipino/Filipina, than with a Japanese at another bank. Being a ranking senior bank officer and now also more senior in years, I was able to open most doors, just by being myself. My working hours were spent with my Filipino staff and my Filipino clients. I also had a Japanese Deputy Managing Director, senior in years, having retired already from a Japanese bank, doing all the tasks that involved dealing with matters Japanese. I was in the best of both worlds: working in a Philippine environment, in a Philippine company, but based in Japan.

I faced other challenges like how to juggle motherhood with my career. I had my mother and my baby's nanny to support me, but still, it was not easy. I remember rushing back home during lunch hours, to breastfeed JC, and then rushing back to the office. There were many sleepless nights when my baby was awake and I, tired from long hours of work, needed to catch up on sleep myself. I tried to bond with my son as much as possible, taking him with me during frequent marketing trips all over Japan, and even to overseas business trips. But there was always guilt, with my son spending more time with his nanny than his own mother. Tears flowed when I went home to the Philippines to pick-up my son and his nanny, after a month-long medical procedure there for my son's bowed legs. He refused to come to me, not recognizing me at first. My heart broke.

I read books about parenting. I learned that it was not the number of hours spent with your children, but the quality time spent with them that mattered.

The Agony of Making the Decision: Quit Working and Become a Full Time Wife And Mother

The last post I held at PNB was First Senior Vice President and Area Head for Europe, Israel and Africa, based in Italy. My son was in the U.S., my husband and two daughters in Tokyo, and I was in Rome. Four long years of separation and of living alone, thousands of miles away from my loved ones. The bank was very considerate of my family situation and moved me back to Asia in February 2010, first on a special assignment at the PNB Tokyo Branch, and then to Hong Kong where I would head the bank's operations there and for Asia.

But lingering memories of going home to a dark house, cooking my own meals and eating them alone, the guilt of not having spent time with family, and news of high school classmates' untimely deaths, made me debate whether I should continue to be in the rat race. What was the use of earning all that money and then just dying suddenly, and God forbid, dying alone, in a foreign land?

But can I really stop working? Will I not get bored and become a nagging wife?

The thought of taking off for a full month vacation, for the first time ever in my professional life, and spending time with son JC, became irresistible.

I prayed for the right decision. On the day I was to send my resignation letter to the President of PNB, I left the PNB Tokyo Branch to go to church. I prayed and asked for final guidance from God. It was still the same decision after my prayers, resign and spend time with family. I pushed the send button of my computer to email a copy of my resignation letter, and suddenly my computer screen went black. I called a close Filipino businessman-friend and told him "Ayaw siguro ng Diyos na mag-resign ako" [God probably did not want me to resign, after all]. He laughed, and said "Bulok lang siguro ang computer mo" [Perhaps your computer is down].

So I went out of the office again, went to another church and prayed again. Returning to the office, with the final decision still the same, but with tears falling, I pushed the send button again. This time, my email went though. I felt a certain calm, a release, a relief.

It Was Not Meant To Be

After sending my resignation letter, the very first thing I planned to do was to take a long vacation and spend it with my son and with my brother and his family in the U.S. This was in July, 2010.

I could not drive in America. I ended up just sitting in the house, day in and day out. I was just waiting for everyone to come back from work or from school, and then seeing them off again the next morning. It was the same routine of leaving home and coming back early evening. I could of course walk to the shopping mall, or to the church, the distance to which were close by Tokyo standards, and I felt reluctant to take a taxi. But I felt very self-conscious being the only one walking home from the mall, carrying bags filled with what I had purchased. I thought everyone was staring at me. I also realized that my son was at that age where he would be happier being with his friends and more so, with his girlfriend, rather than with his ageing mother.

Too much idle time on my hands. I missed my daily grind. To be a full time wife and mother was not meant for me. By August, I was already flying back to Tokyo, ready to take up another challenge.

The Final Challenge — Setting Up a Company and Making it Succeed

'Shacho'

"Say hello to *Shacho*," our *ninong* [godfather] tells my husband. I still can not get used to being addressed as Shacho, even in a playful manner. But I confess to loving the sound of it. I am not only the *Shacho*, the President of a company in Japan, I am also *Daihyo Torishimariyaku Shacho*, the term normally used for the President and Chairman of the Board of a Japanese company.

To become *Shacho* of a company is not that difficult. Just get yourself a lawyer, pay him for setting up and registering a company that you would like to set up, and register yourself as the *Shacho*. But setting up a company was probably the easier part. Coming up with the large amount of capital needed to run the business in high-cost Japan; getting the building owner to agree to lease office space; convincing office furniture and equipment leasing companies to return your calls, much less to meet with you; opening your corporate bank account; these can discourage the faint of heart.

The First US$600,000

While I was still in the U.S., I sent a flurry of emails. I tried to locate my lawyer-contact who helped me in the past with the application for a full banking license for PNB Tokyo. I asked a former colleague at the bank if he remembered the offer given to me in the past of free use of the front end remittance system of a Dutch Central Bank-licensed money transfer company, should I decide to set up my own remittance business. I read about the newly enacted Japan Payments Act of April 2010, which would make it possible to have not only fully licensed banks, but non-banks as well, engage in the money transfer business. My confidence in myself grew every minute. I could do this!!! And the wheels turned very fast. Within a couple of days, I re-connected with my lawyer. I requested him to start the process of setting up and registering the company, even though I was not yet back in Tokyo. The other good news was the confirmation from my Dutch company contact that they were serious about their offer for a remittance system. Could I present a business plan to them?

I booked a flight for Amsterdam, and made my presentation to the Managing Director of the Dutch company, his brother the Chief Financial Officer, and their father the Chairman of the Board of their family-owned bank. The father was the final decision maker.

Maybe I did a good presentation. Or, maybe the business prospects really looked good. Even before my last power point slide was shown when I hesitantly asked whether they would be interested in investing maybe a US$100,000, the patriarch of the family said "Make that US$300,000!!!" I had a committed first investor. I flew back to the U.S. the very next day. I kept thinking of how I could raise around US$1.5 million. This was the minimum amount needed to operate my money transfer business smoothly, in very high-cost Japan.

I contacted my closest Filipino businessman-friend. I asked him if he would also be interested in investing. He asked me how much the Dutch businessman's commitment was and then told me, "I will match his."

I was in business!

The Dutch businessman's actual investment was less than the original commitment. The Filipino businessman's actual investment was more than his original commitment. I later acquired the 23% shareholdings of the Filipino businessman and now own 74% of the company.

Japanese Kone

With the proper kone [connection], it was much easier to open doors in Japan. But there were doors that seemed to remain locked if the one knocking was not Japanese. My Japanese legal counsel helped open the door to the leasing company where we leased much of our furniture, fixtures, and equipment, saving us much needed liquidity. My husband, Fumio, was connected to the same university as the real estate manager's sister and that kone made it easier for the office building owner to approve me as a tenant. But before the leases for the office could commence, I still needed a Japanese guarantor to guarantee the lease payments. My husband Fumio became the guarantor!

No regrets in having married a Japanese!

None other than Discrimination

Discrimination was what I felt when my request to open a corporate account with one of the biggest Japanese banks was all but refused. I could not operate the money transfer business without opening bank accounts. This was necessary not only for the company's daily operating needs of depositing and withdrawing funds, but also more importantly, for funds settlement with my remittance tie-up partners overseas. To open remittance catching accounts in Japanese banks where OFWs can transfer their funds was an absolute necessity if we were to service not only walk-in clients, but clients living all over Japan, especially in places where we did not have a physical presence.

You be the judge.

Excerpts from my letter to the bank on my company letterhead:

21 April 2011

Mr. President:

Please allow me to relay to you my experience with your Ginza Branch. I do hope the treatment I got was not because I was a foreigner, and a victim of discrimination by your bank.

I went to your Ginza Branch in the afternoon today, to open a corporate account. (list of document I presented...

Your officer at your Ginza Branch wanted more documents from us in Japanese. I explained that we do not have the company profile in Japanese as our clients are mainly non-Japanese. I also said our homepage is in English...

Before I left, I asked for his name, so that I can look for him the next day, but he did not even have the courtesy of telling me, nor to offer his name card. But now, I decided I will not go and bring those thick documents and demean myself further, and appear like begging...

I felt so bad that I am almost tempted to sue for possible harm to my business if I am unable to open an account and thus, delay unnecessarily my target start of business on May 1st. But I will not do that.

I still have some respect for this country which has been my home for almost 30 years.

Sincerely yours,
Isabelita Manalastas
President and Representative Director

Next time we visited this bank, we got the attention we wanted, and the desired results.

It Must Have Been Fate

May 1, 2014 is the fourth year anniversary of our business, Speed Money Transfer Japan K.K. In Autumn 2014, we will open our Osaka Branch, the fifth branch. We were already earning enough that my dream of sharing profits with all Speed's staff has become a reality. Speed's shareholders who have given their trust to a David amongst the Goliaths in Japan, will not be disappointed. My lifetime's savings, which I have invested in Speed, will be safe, and can continue to provide for my children and their children's needs.

I continue to dream bigger dreams, like setting up an OFW Bank, also migrant-owned, and migrant-managed like Speed, and offering cradle-to-grave financial services to Filipino migrants and their families.

I am still in Japan, sharing my decades-long experiences living and working in Japan, through speaking engagements and writing a regular advice column in a widely circulated Philippine newspaper in Japan— *The Jeepney Press*.

I will probably leave Japan again in the very near future, to retire in the Philippines. But as it has always happened in the past, I am sure I will keep coming back. The love-hate relationship continues, but as fate will have it, love will always prevail.

A Good Mother, a Good Career—
Can They go Hand in Hand?

Mother's Day, 2014. I received the following email from my son, JC. Now grown, and still living and working in the U.S.

Hi, Ma!

Happy Mother's Day to the greatest mother that a son could ask for. Although today is a day to celebrate everything that a mother does for her children, do not think that it is the only day that I appreciate everything you have ever done for me. Not a day goes by that I am not thankful for everything you have done and sacrificed for me. From carrying a fat younger version of myself on the train during rush hour to take me to school, to having to put up with my 'tampo' [sulk] and hot-headedness during my teenage years, to supporting my indecisiveness in university. The bottom line is, you are the definition of unconditional love. You have never and will never give up on me. You have taught me the value of that, and I can only hope and strive to love my future children (your future grandchildren!) as much as you have loved me. I know that sometimes you feel guilty that you could not be there all the time for me when I was younger, some missed basketball games, choir concerts, school plays, whatever it may have been; but please know that I understand, and have understood for a long time that you were doing the job of two parents, finding a balance was understandably hard, and even sometimes impossible simply because you wanted to provide ME the best. Now the time has come for it to be all about YOU. Not only on this day dedicated to mothers like you, but everyday should be all about you now. I will always be here, but I'll be the one taking care of you this time. I'll be the one to carry you on the train during rush hour (or any place that you'll need me). I'll be the one to provide you the best that you deserve. I love you very much, and thank you for being, simply, you.

Love,
Your *anak*! [child]

It *is* possible to be a good mother and have a good career, after all.

LEADERSHIP TIPS

1. *Follow your passion.* Success is powered by passion. Even if there are obstacles on the way which others may think are insurmountable, let your passion show them and yourself that you can get what you aim for. The passion will drive you to get the skills, contacts and knowledge you will need to succeed. It all begins with passion.

2. *In Rome do as the Romans do.* In a globalized economy, you will get to work with people from around the world, travel far and wide, and even choose another country as your home base. Be perceptive and pick up the business and social norms of your host home. Learn the language, know the culture. Don't forget your roots but morph them into your new reality.

3. *Overcome stereotypes of gender and nationality.* Wherever you go, it is but natural that people will have pre-conceived notions of gender and nationality which will affect you. Understand where these biases are coming from, and learn how to challenge and overcome the stereotypes. Show them that you can be as good as or better than anyone else as a Filipina.

4. *Don't be afraid to break barriers.* Though tolerance and progress on the gender front seem to be picking up in many areas, there are still new frontiers and domains where barriers to women and Filipinos exist. Don't be afraid to be the first to venture out into new territory. There may be no peers and mentors where you venture, but don't hold back from carving out your turf.

5. *Don't ignore the family.* Professionally qualified and skilled though you may be, don't ignore the powerful foundation that family gives you. Be grateful to those who shaped you, and also live up to your responsibilities to your own children. Find out in your own way how you can have it all—at work and at home.

6. *Power of prayer.* Life is a long, tough journey full of upheaval and changes. But the only constant through thick and thin is the Divine Force, and the power of prayer. Spiritual energy is always there for you, see the power of prayer as a source of guiding light, calming peace and uplifting drive.

LEARNINGS FROM SEVERAL LIFETIMES

Imelda M. Nicolas

Chairperson, Commission on Filipinos Overseas (CFO)
Cabinet-level Secretary
Office of the President of the Philippines

Abstract

*T*here have been several essays about my life written by others and by me. With the exciting offer of the Filipina Women's Network to be one of the contributors to its unprecedented book about Filipinas who have demonstrated leadership around the world, I decided that this would be an opportunity to recap some of the lessons I have learned about leadership as a Filipina and to consider the personal growth and self-awareness that have influenced my understanding of leadership.

I have traversed the world as a student. I have been an entrepreneur in New York, an executive of a multinational company with offices in France, Spain, and Ireland, and a part-owner of a business in China. Yet, I unfailingly find my way back home to the Philippines again and again.

I have gone through several lifetimes and personas from an idyllic, bucolic childhood in Sorsogon and life in a highly disciplined all-girls board school in Legaspi City run by the Benedictine sisters, to the intellectual and cosmopolitan environment of St. Theresa's College in Manila where I majored in the humanities and graduated *magna cum laude*, and to Columbia University in New York for further studies in Art History.

My activist years started before and continued during and after the Marcos regime. I was a staff member to then Senator Benigno 'Ninoy' Aquino, Jr., a political prisoner during the early years of martial law, a parliamentarian of the street, a campaigner for presidential candidate Corazon C. Aquino and later her Assistant Appointments Secretary with an office next door to her, and an advocate for women's cause as chair of the National Commission on the Role of Filipino Women during the Ramos administration.

Now as Chairperson/Cabinet-rank Secretary of the Commission of Filipinos Overseas, I look after the interests of 10.5 million overseas Filipinos in more than 200 countries. In between my years of government service, I took on a corporate persona: first, as assistant to my sister, Loida Nicolas Lewis the chair and executive officer of the New York-based multinational TLC Beatrice International Holdings; and then, as CEO and part-owner of TLC Beatrice/China, a chain of food stores in mainland China.

Introduction and Getting Involved:
The Early Years

I was born in Manila on December 27, 1945. I was the fourth of five children of Magdalena and Francisco Nicolas. To say that both my parents were involved in business is an understatement. Our family owned an entertainment center that had a movie house, a drugstore, and a bowling alley in the heart of Sorsogon, a town in the southernmost tip of Luzon, one of the country's major islands and part of the Bicol region. We lived on the second floor of the Center where, even during meals, business was the main topic of conversation.

Aside from business, my parents also talked about community concerns. My parents were actively involved in civic, religious, and social work. They never lectured us about being involved in the community or the need to be involved beyond the home, family, school, and work. Neither did they lecture us about the needs of those who are less privileged, marginalized, or discriminated upon. Instead, they demonstrated what they stood for. Their example taught all of us how to become socially responsible. The unspoken but accepted principle in our family was 'for whom much has been given, much is also expected.'

My older sister Loida, also raised my social consciousness. In the late 1950s, we were in high school and in our early teens, when we heard that the local government officials had issued a permit to allow prostitution in Sorsogon. My sister started a petition for the townspeople to sign asking the local government to revoke the permit. With a significant number of signatures secured, my sister, some of our fellow teenagers, and I went to the municipal hall where we presented the manifesto to the mayor. Surprisingly, the mayor acceded to the demand of the manifesto and the place never opened. This kind of protest was unheard of even in Manila, much more in a province like Sorsogon. Actually I just went along with my sister. This was 100 percent her initiative.

What follows are lessons I shared in the book *Crossover Leadership in Asia: Staying Whole in Two Halves, from Civil Society to Government* (International Center for Innovation, Transformation and Excellence in Governance 2008). The book featured Florencio 'Butch' Abad, Teresita 'Ging' Quintos-Deles, Corazon 'Dinky' Juliano-Soliman and myself. We were the founding members of the International Center for Innovation, Transformation and Excellence in Governance (INCITEGov). We were also four of the 10 high government officials/cabinet-level Secretaries who resigned in 2005 from the Gloria Macapagal-Arroyo administration due to the presidential election anomaly and allegations of massive corruption on the part of the Macapagal-Arroyo administration. The media dubbed us the 'Hyatt 10' as we declared our resignation and read our statement in a press conference in that hotel.

Looking back, another very good lesson learned from my parents without their 'lecturing' us was their lack of bias towards people on the basis of the color of their skin or their lack of education, or whether one is rich or poor, or whether their children are boys or girls.

I recalled that by late afternoon, after our classes in the town's public elementary school, I would be playing usually barefoot *patintero* [team tag game] or some other children's games with the daughters of the neighborhood's barber and farmers from the barrio, the so-called *kanto boys* [street corner boys], and the children of my father's employees. My parents would call me for dinner and there was not one word of reproach from them regarding my playmates. No big deal.

They also did not treat us their children, whether boys or girls, differently. They did not have gender stereotypes. I never heard them say that I should behave in a certain way because I am a girl or that only my brothers are allowed to do some things because they are boys. Later on in my life, they never mentioned or pressured me about my marital status or lack thereof. Whether single or married, they accepted us as we are and our respective significant others.

My parents taught us by example what Martin Luther King, Jr. heralded in his magnificent "I Have a Dream" speech delivered in 1963: "I have a dream that my four little children will one day live in a nation where they will not be judged by the color of their skin but by the content of their character."

Through the years, as I got more and more exposed to different kinds of people in various work and social environments, inside and outside the Philippines, I have recognized the stereotypes that exist in society. But because bias of any kind was never part of our family's DNA, I did not exhibit stereotypical behavior. Thus, my lifetime commitment is to create a truly egalitarian society, working towards the dream of Martin Luther King, Jr.

My Life as an *Interna*

In June 1955, I was entering the fourth grade, and without knowing why, I found myself, together with my older sister Loida who was in sixth grade, being enrolled by my mother in St. Agnes' Academy, a convent school run by German Benedictine sisters in Legaspi. Since the school was 50 kilometers away from Sorsogon, it was taken for granted that both Loida and I would be *internas* [resident students] or boarders in St. Agnes. We lived with the nuns, sharing a dormitory with eighty-odd girls from places in the Bicol region, many of which I heard for the first time: Masbate, Guinobatan, Pilar, Daet, Iriga; the list seemed endless.

I am not surprised that my first days in St. Agnes were a haze. I am sure I suffered from sensory overload with the majestic Mayon Volcano in the background, the elegant façade of the school, and the nuns in their traditional black and white habits, clucking like mother hens. I remember feeling relief in the early morning with the coming of the light and the singing of the sisters in the chapel. Sometimes, in between sleep and waking up, I easily imagined that I had died and gone to heaven. But the inevitable bells would rudely bring me back to reality. As boarders, we were obligated to attend the early morning mass with the nuns, followed by an unexciting breakfast and then off to our respective classrooms. You can learn more about my experience and those of other 'convent girls' in *Behind the Walls, Life of Convent Girls* (Brainard and Ysip-Orosa 2005).

Lessons learned

Again, not by words but by immersion, I internalized, without my knowing it, the 'personal relationship' with God, that is beyond the rituals and the "thou shalt" and "thou shall not" of the Ten Commandments. As an *interna*, we were living practically like nuns. There was childish resentment and reluctance to go to daily masses, weekly confessions and the Sunday Adoration of the Blessed Sacrament, wearing white long-sleeved dresses and veils, sweating in the chapel without air-conditioning.

But eventually and unknowingly, the spirituality, not the religiosity, became part of my soul. It took another thirty years before I acknowledged this fact and appreciated Ephesians 2:8: "For by grace you have been saved through faith. And this is not your own doing; it is the gift of God." Whether in times of difficulties or in my day-to-day existence, I have learned to tap deep into my spiritual roots, going beyond the words of scripture to their true essence.

Another sometimes difficult lesson I learned in St. Agnes is how to live (literally) with all kinds of people, fellow students and nuns alike. In my mind's eye, I can see the dormitory as one large hall full of uniform beds and drawers, overflowing with my soon-to-be fellow boarders, who came in all sizes and shapes—from the youngest, teeny-weeny first grader to the most senior graduating high school students who towered over me like giants. As I got to know the girls I would be living with for the next 300 school days, I found out soon enough that their characters, quirks, and upbringing were even more varied than their sizes and shapes.

Looking back to those days and my "miserable" (I was homesick all the time) and "inexplicable" (at least to my child's mind) days away from home, I have learned to connect the dots in my life. Unforeseen and even forced changes can yield clues to the paths I would later take and the roles I would later play, bring out new heretofore unexercised 'muscles,' and lead to an unexplored 'inner world.'

Unforeseen events have led to finding lifelong friends whom I would have never met if I stayed where I was and to discovering strength of spirit that I never suspected I had. And no matter how I hated it then, the Benedictine discipline of the German nuns of St. Agnes gave me the backbone and the work attitude that would mark me throughout my life.

Nurturing Community Involvement the Theresian Way

My early orientation to community service guided me during my college years from 1961 to 1965 at St. Theresa's College (STC) in Manila. The STC brand of education integrated involvement in the extracurricular activities with organizations such as the National Union of Students of the Philippines (NUSP) and the Student Catholic Action (SCA). At the time, Catholicism in the Philippines was very dynamic, a product of the revolutionary Ecumenical Council called by Pope John XXXIII. There was a black-and-white struggle between communism and anti-communism, which made SCA the Church's 'Army of Youth.' It employed the same tools used by communists like organizing by cell, discussion groups, and so on.

I joined the SCA as a freshman because I had no choice but to be a member of SCA, unthinkable in this age of personal choices. Upon reflection, I am grateful to have been forced to be an SCA member where through SCA committees I taught catechism in public schools and brought weekly relief goods to families who were living under the Del Pan Bridge.

In other words, I was "forced" to go outside my "comfort zone," to see beyond the convent walls of St. Theresa's and the gated Belair Village, where our family lived, to realize that most of us in the "exclusive girls' schools" led sheltered lives, did not know the realities of abject poverty and the miserable living conditions of the majority of our people. The realization led to social action.

Through the annual SCA Leadership Conference in Baguio, I had the heady experience of meeting with all the other student leaders of other schools in the Archdiocese of Maila. Without my knowing it,

I was *volunteered* by my sister Loida's friends, also known as the Girls Friday, to be one of the officers of the SCA Council of the Archdiocese of Manila, first as Press Relations Officer in 1963-1964, then as President of the Council for Women for 1964-1965.

As President, I led this 'Army of Youth' composed of SCA Councils from almost all the major universities and colleges in the Archdiocese of Manila. Again, this position "forced" upon me one of the best things that happened to me; it gave me the opportunity to discover and develop my leadership ability and provided me my first taste of public service.

In short, the core of my values in terms of serving our people was first manifested because of SCA! For this I will always be grateful. See (Manlapaz, Villacorta and Nicolas 2011) for a collection of personal memories about SCA.

Lessons learned

Many of us are not aware of our potential. Most of the time, it would take some other people, usually other women, to discover our potential and *force* us to recognize the *brave, new world* in us and out there. While exploring this world, we need mentors and role models that would help us navigate the *treacherous* rivers and circuitous roads we face in the careers, professions, work, or type of public service we choose. I was lucky to have mentors and role models, usually women, throughout my life, starting back in SCA.

A word to our next generation of leaders

Lucky as I was to have mentors, I recognized a debt to the unlucky, the marginalized, and the vulnerable. I urge you to get out of your comfort zone and reach out to people who may not be in your customary circle of friends and acquaintances. Help them to become empowered. Stop talking about "social responsibility," just do it. Walk the walk and don't just talk the talk.

Political Awakening through a War and a Storm: The Vietnam War

In 1967, I left to study Art History, first, in George Washington

University in Washington, D.C., and then in Columbia University in New York. This was a time of upheaval with massive protests against the Vietnam War. The U.S. was quite literally "an explosive cauldron of movements, from the anti-Vietnam War militants, to feminist activists, from the Black Panthers to the flower children with their underground counter-culture." While at Columbia, I found myself in the thick of things. Our building was the first to be occupied by the Students for a Democratic Society (SDS)/Weathermen. I did not go to my classes for almost a week until the police finally came and took the SDS occupiers out. This environment awakened my political consciousness as a leader and as a woman, which proved necessary as I confronted the next challenges that lay ahead of me in the Philippines. (See *Crossover Leadership in Asia: Staying Whole in Two Halves, from Civil Society to Government*, Mislang 2008).

First Quarter Storm

I left the U.S. at the height of protests, only to find myself in the middle of the First Quarter Storm back in the Philippines. I joined the marches and demonstrations, without becoming a member of any of the militant organizations—such as *Makibaka, Samahan ng Demokratikong Kabataan* (SDK), *Kabataang Makabayan* (KM), and others. Despite my non-affiliation with any of these organizations, the military arrested me from my home on December 8, 1972, just three months after the declaration of Martial Law. I thought of several reasons for my arrest. First reason was my apprenticeship under Senator Ninoy Aquino. I was assigned by Senator Ninoy Aquino to be the research assistant of Nick Joaquin who was doing the senator's biography as he was preparing to run for president. The second reason could have been my task, as Senator Ninoy Aquino's liaison officer, to give money to members of the *KM, Makibaka* and other organizations. I knew most of the leaders of these organizations who were eventually detained. The third reason could have been my involvement as publisher of a lampoon underground paper called *Imelda's Monthly*. I got it from very reliable sources that Imelda was quite incensed with the publication, which was brought to her by her palace sycophants.

To this day, the exact reason for my arrest remains unclear. What remains very clear in my memory, however, are the details of arrest. I am usually very poor with dates but I remember the date of my arrest, December 8, because the day before, there was an assassination attempt against the First Lady Imelda Marcos in *Nayong Pilipino*. The military declared that there would be a second wave of arrests, this time of those identified as anti-Imelda Marcos.

Several truckloads of soldiers surrounded our Bel-Air house in the early morning of December 8, 1972 and since there was curfew at that time, I knew immediately that those ringing our doorbell in order to get in were not 'friendly forces.' I was brought to Camp Aguinaldo, where I was never informed of the charges leveled against me. Luckily enough, I had two uncles who were colonels and I was eventually released.

However, a month later, I was arrested again, this time I was confined first in Camp Crame and then later on transferred to Fort Bonifacio where I was detained for six months. I was one of the graduates of *ABC University*, that is Aguinaldo, Bonifacio and Crame, the three military camps in Metro Manila. Ironically, I could not be given amnesty because I was not a member of any of the identified communist groups. My father negotiated with the Judge Advocate General Office (JAGO) for my release. It was so many years later that my sister Loida told me that our father was able to arrange for my release in exchange for furniture! (Our family business, more popularly known as NIC-FUR, was in furniture.)

My detention was not the traumatic experience that it could have been. When you are young, you are very naïve and resilient. I was arrested when I was 23. I reasoned to myself that even if they kept me there for 10 years, I would still be young when I left.

What I did not expect was the long duration of Martial Law and the loss of freedom, the affront of civil liberties, and the complete disregard for human rights. I think people who did not go through Martial Law could never really appreciate their freedom as much as those who were there. When you think about it, all those who were against President Arroyo like Dinky (Juliano-Soliman),

Ging (Quintos-Deles) and Butch (Abad), *lahat kami* [all of us] had been through Martial Law and we knew that the conditions in 2005 were nearing Martial Law proportions. (See *Crossover Leadership in Asia: Staying Whole in Two Halves, from Civil Society to Government*, Mislang 2008.)

Lessons learned

Ronald Reagan during his inaugural address in 1967 as Governor of California for his first term said: "Freedom is a fragile thing and is never more than one generation away from extinction. It is not ours by inheritance; it must be fought for and defended constantly by each generation, for it comes only once to a people."

Our country and our people should take heed of these words. Freedom is a fragile thing. Why must we lose it before we appreciate it? Cherish what so many people have died for including Senator Ninoy Aquino, the father of our President Benigno "Noynoy" S. Aquino. Defend it constantly—everyday, if we must. It took almost two decades before our people removed from their neck the yoke of dictatorship. That is a price too heavy to pay, too long to be without freedom. Never again!

To the generations we now call Gen X, Gen Y and Millennials: the fight for freedom is never over. To have been a political prisoner during the Martial Law years is now a badge of honor. But in your time and age, that badge of honor could take a different form. It is up to you to carry on the fight, no matter what.

Crossing Over to Government

In 1983, Senator Ninoy Aquino, perceived to be the strongest contender for president against Marcos, was assassinated on the tarmac of the Manila International Airport (now known as the Ninoy Aquino International Airport). Following Aquino's death, I completely submerged myself in the fight against the Marcos dictatorship.

Assistant Appointments Secretary, Aquino Administration, 1986 to 1988

Aquino's widow Cory and youngest brother Paul knew who I was from my early ties with Senator Aquino as his research assistant and liaison officer. So when Cory Aquino decided to run for president, Paul asked me to prepare a 'black book' of issues of national interest and their corresponding responses that Cory could use as a reference tool. I consulted some friends and experts to find answers to some of the most common questions that the media might ask Cory. I consolidated these questions and answers in this 'black book' that I personally delivered to Cory at her home. When I met with her, she and Paul asked me to be part of a four-person team going with her to campaign in Mindanao and the Visayas. So together with Aquilino 'Nene' Pimentel, Cory's son-in-law Eldon Cruz, and Fritzi Aragon, I joined her presidential campaign.

It was an exciting time for me accompanying Cory wherever she went, as assistant, bodyguard, PR/media person and her all-around factotum! I vividly remember the overwhelming support we received in the places we visited. I think the response of the public at that time was something that I will never see again in my lifetime. They wore yellow and adorned their houses with anything yellow. It was not difficult at all to bring people together.

I was not thinking about any role in the new administration beyond the campaign. But after the People Power revolution of 1986, President Corazon Aquino invited me to work with her in Malacañang Palace, the official residence and principal workplace of the President of the Philippines. In one of the first few meetings of the newly elected president, held at the Cojuangco Building, her campaign headquarters, Aquino would invite me to assist Ching Escaler, the appointments secretary. I readily agreed and was already at work in Malacañang the day President Aquino transferred from the Cojuangco Building to the Palace.

Those were exhilarating days! Schedules included international celebrities and leaders who wanted to pay homage to the new president and arrangements for the president's triumphal appearance in a joint session of the U.S. Congress (see Aquino's 1986 speech). It was an honor to accompany her on her courtesy call to the Pope at the Vatican. The President would even be voted *Time Magazine*'s "Man of the Year" for the year 1986.

One of the things I am most proud of during my stint with the Office of the Appointments Secretary was the restoration of integrity in the office. We were told that during the time of President Marcos the appointments secretary or whoever arranged for a meeting with Marcos received significant monetary gifts. As a team, we made sure that the during the entire term of President Aquino, there would be not even be a single hint of impropriety in the Office of the Appointment Secretary. (See *Crossover Leadership in Asia: Staying Whole in Two Halves, from Civil Society to Government*, Mislang 2008.)

Dragon Lady of the Aquino Administration

None of us who had worked for the election of President Cory Aquino, prepared for victory. We were a motley group of people who were, for the most part very good in fighting the Marcos dictatorship. We had not yet learned to meet the challenges of governance. We were oppositionists, we had not really been trained for governance. When I joined the Aquino administration as assistant appointments secretary for President Aquino, I felt that I was very good at organizing people and setting up events, strengths that I had carried over from my experience in business. I was systems and tasks-oriented but I had very little political and people skills. So very early on, I was branded the "dragon lady" in Malacañang. That was quite traumatic for me.

That moniker amplified not only the negative impression the Palace staff had about me but also the power that my boss, Ching Escaler, and I had as the persons responsible for scheduling presidential engagements. This perception of the power of the appointments office made it vulnerable to intrigues, and at the height of these intrigues, I decided to accept my 'reappointment' as presidential assistant. (See *Crossover Leadership in Asia: Staying Whole in Two Halves, from Civil Society to Government*, Mislang 2008).

Lessons learned

Poets and public speakers alike say: "Revolution is poetry while governance is prose." Those of us who jumped from the so-called "parliament of the streets" during the Marcos dictatorship to the seats of power in Malacanang and Congress during President Cory Aquino years found this adage bitterly true but that did not deter us from doing the right thing.

Chairperson of the National Commission on the Role of Filipino Women (NCRFW)–Ramos administration, 1993 to 1998

As Chairperson of the NCRFW under President Aquino, I also pushed the women's agenda. The NCRFW was tasked with gender and development (GAD) training and I felt that NCRFW was in a unique position to institutionalize GAD in government.

Thus, upon request of several women's organizations I asked the newly-elected President Fidel Ramos, for whom I had campaigned in the 1992 Presidential Elections, to appoint me as Chairperson of the NCRFW. President Ramos was quite willing to attend to women's concerns and suggested that the NCRFW board meet with him on a quarterly basis, instead of annually.

While at the helm of the NCRFW, I led the institutionalization of the GAD. I advocated for the 'Women's Budget,' a five percent allocation across the board in the total budget for all agencies at the national and local levels. The women's budget is used by GAD advocates to monitor the progress of GAD's institutionalization in government. (See *Crossover Leadership in Asia: Staying Whole in Two Halves, from Civil Society to Government*, Mislang 2008.)

Lessons learned

Government is the best way for institutionalizing one's advocacy. Governance is both a science and an art that one must learn if we are to translate speeches into reality that makes a difference and is sustainable over time. To institutionalize anything in government, one must be strategic in one's thinking and action.

Change is constant as people change roles, organizations transform, and Philippine elections change national leaderships every six years. But keep your core values the same. You may adjust their applications to different contexts but you must remain true to yourself and to your conscience. This is so easy to say but very difficult to do. So take heed!

You must constantly examine your conscience and critique yourself. Although criticisms are hard to swallow, they may have kernels of truth in them. It is up to you to discover and discern them for what they are and act accordingly.

TLC Beatrice Foods: a Detour to Private Sector

In 1994, my sister Loida assumed the leadership of the TLC Beatrice International Holdings, Inc. after her husband and business tycoon Reginald F. Lewis passed away. Beatrice International that Lewis, had acquired through a US$984 million leveraged buyout in December of 1987, was then the largest African-American company in the U.S.

Loida would seek out my help as her younger sister, upon taking up the reins of the company. Basically, I started as Loida's assistant, and then eventually became Vice-President for development and training of the company. My team would go on to develop TLC Beatrice China, which operated more than 200 Western-style community stores. The community stores are similar in concept to 7-Elevens, an American chain of convenience stores but slightly bigger. Community stores were revolutionary for China because Beatrice was the first Western company to be given a license to operate in China in the small store format. Loida sold the TLC Beatrice Foods International companies in 1998 and paid off all the shareholders. TLC Beatrice China was eventually closed in 2008.

Returning Back to Government: Secretary General, National Anti-Poverty Commission (NAPC) –Arroyo Administration, 2004 to 2005

After the 2004 Presidential Elections, President Arroyo told her friend, my sister Loida, that she was appointing me as secretary general of the National Anti-Poverty Commission (NAPC). Loida immediately shared the good news with me. All I knew then was the position was a cabinet-level position. I said "Yes" immediately.

Community-based Monitoring System

After studying thoroughly what NAPC is all about, I focused on several items that were strategic in nature. I strongly advocated for the more effective implementation and nation-wide use of the community-based monitoring system (CBMS). I considered the CBMS to be an innovative and cutting-edge tool and process that empowers the community and the local government units. By using local poverty indicators, both the community and local government units were able to establish their baseline poverty data, identify and target the poorest households in their areas, and design and implement poverty-reduction plans, programs, and projects using the data that they themselves had collected and analyzed.

Microfinance and Rural Micro-enterprise Program

I also pushed for microfinance as a poverty alleviation measure based on studies conducted by the United Nations Development Program (UNDP), the Japan International Cooperation Agency (JICA), the Asian Development Bank (ADB), and the International Fund for Agricultural Development (IFAD). These studies reveal that the impact of microfinance on poor households has been positive with reports of higher incomes and assets, as well as the movement of poor households out of poverty after several loan cycles. I believe that microfinance institutions have the ability to adapt and to enhance traditional microfinance technologies that could help accelerate inclusive growth. In view of this, I focused my attention on the implementation of the People's Development Trust Fund (PDTF) established under RA 8424 (Social Reform and Poverty Alleviation Act), the same law that created the National Anti-Poverty Commission. I also tried to re-channel the activities of the National Livelihood Support Fund (NLDF), which had approximately three billion pesos, to capacity building rather than to lending. It seemed there were enough resources to fund the lending but not capacity development. (See *Crossover Leadership in Asia: Staying Whole in Two Halves, from Civil Society to Government*, Mislang 2008.)

Resigning From the Government:
The Garci Tapes and Hyatt 10

In June 2005, tapes of the conversations between President Gloria Macapagal-Arroyo and former COMELEC Commissioner Virgilio Garcillano surfaced suggesting the possible manipulations of the 2004 elections. The tapes caused widespread public fury and outrage. It was the worst crisis faced by the Arroyo administration and inevitably drove ten Cabinet members, including myself, to the edge and eventually, out the door.

Initially, the revelation by Press Secretary Ignacio Bunye on June 6, 2005 of the two tapes that would implicate the president did not seriously worry most of the cabinet members. To restore the positive image of the president, the entire Cabinet agreed to make at least two recommendations to be shared with the President. The first recommendation was that Mike Arroyo, the First Gentleman should exit from Philippine politics. The second recommendation was to ensure that the people associated with the First Gentleman, who were appointed in revenue generating institutions in government, would also leave. While the President seemed to agree to the first recommendation, she balked at the second recommendation. But eventually, President Arroyo did not do as she promised. Even her 'public apology' related to her call to Garcillano was not done according to the discussions during various Cabinet meetings.

Dinky Soliman detailed the points and counterpoints made at these meetings in *Crossover Leadership in Asia: Staying Whole in Two Halves, from Civil Society to Government*. The tipping point for some of the Cabinet members came when President Arroyo declared "the framework for governance is national security. We should bring out the fear factor."

Thus, 10 cabinet secretaries and top government officials decided to resign en masse on July 8, 2005. These included: Butch Abad (Department of Education Secretary), Johnny Santos (Department of Trade and Industry Secretary), Cesar Purisima (Department of Finance Secretary), Emilia Boncodin (Department of Budget and Management Secretary), Ging Quintos-Deles (Presidential Adviser on the Peace Process), Rene Villa (Department of Agrarian Reform Secretary), Bert Lina (Bureau of Customs Commissioner), Willy Parayno (Bureau of Internal Revenue Commissioner), Dinky Juliano-Soliman (Department of Social Welfare and Development Secretary) and myself (National Anti-Poverty Commission Secretary-General).

Lessons learned

I have described my experiences of moving from activism to being in government in the book, *Crossover Leadership in Asia: Staying Whole in Two Halves, from Civil Society to Government.* One of the most ridiculous accusations hurled at the Hyatt 10 was that we were power-grabbers. Given the entire range of Cabinet portfolio represented by us, we held the most important and influential positions in government, from finance to trade, from budget to education, from social welfare and development to the peace process, from poverty reduction to revenue generation to agrarian reform! So what additional power did we need to grab?

And the perks of power could be addictive which is why some people will do anything to stay in power. And here we were, all ten of us, giving up these perks willingly for what we felt was in the best interest of the country, not for our own self-interest or other vested interest.

But of course, we are human too. After our resignation, we would joke among ourselves about how we missed some of the things we took for granted or enjoyed while we were in the Cabinet. We reminisced about how people would hang on to our every word during meetings as if we were talking from a burning bush in Mt. Sinai, how we would get the best VIP seats in meetings and conferences, how our meetings and schedules were efficiently arranged by our executive assistants to the point that they practically managed and ran our lives, how our drivers would know where to go and how to get there in the fastest possible time, how we could cut short conversations and discussions without apparently offending people in order to get down to business. It was incredibly easy for our offices to get people, whoever they may be, to talk and meet with us. These were some of the thousand and one seemingly insignificant things that went with the position.

Having done this cross-over more than once, I was psychologically and emotionally prepared for the loss of these accoutrements of power because even while in power, I kept reminding myself that all these were temporary; that I should not start thinking that I am entitled to them and that I should definitely not allow these perks of power to define me.

On a macro level, as a Cabinet Secretary, I had a better appreciation for how government is such a gigantic force in the shaping of and making a difference in ordinary people's lives. So after leaving government, one of the things that I really regretted was that there was still so much to be done that could be accomplished under the purview of government.

Lessons Learned

To our next generation of leaders: Be wary of the perks of power and power itself. Both can be very addictive. That is why people will do anything to stay in power. They lose their moral compass and lose their way. The Bible says it best: "What does it profit a man, if he gains the whole world but lose his soul?"

The Next Chapter: Chairperson/Cabinet-rank Secretary of the Commission on Filipinos Overseas

Another opportunity to serve came in 2010. This chapter is still being written as I was appointed by President Benigno S. Aquino III as Chairperson/Cabinet-rank Secretary of the Commission on Filipinos Overseas (CFO).

Early on, when asked about the job, I said, "This is the best job in the world." And I quoted one of my favorite affirmations:

> Where I am at this moment is perfect. My past is my friend today as I take the lessons that I can from it and say thank you. Everything that has brought me to this present moment is a gift and I am a stronger and wiser person because of it.

Leadership Tips

1. *Make spirituality, not religiosity, become part of your soul.*
   Whether in times of difficulties or in your day-to-day existence, learn to tap deep into your spiritual roots, going beyond the words of your religion to their true essence. Harness the wisdom of your religion, but do not denigrate other religions. Each religion has common religious cores, which you have to respect.

2. *Learn how to live with the full spectrum of people.* As your leadership takes you around the world and up and down organizations, you must learn how to live and work with all kinds of people. You will need to accept or negotiate their differences in character, quirks, values, agendas and motivation.

3. *Discover and recognize the force within you to face the brave, new world.* By being self-aware, you can seek out mentors and role models who can help you navigate your career and life pathway. Learn how to accept criticisms, discover and discern the "kernel" of truth in them and act accordingly.

4. *Serve the people. Lucky as you are, you owe a debt to the unlucky, the disenfranchised, the disillusioned, the marginalized and the vulnerable.* Get out of your comfort zone and reach out to people who may not be in your usual circle of friends and family. Give them the opportunities to develop their full potential, in every which way.

5. *Keep alive the fight for freedom.* Each new wave of political, social and technological change opens up new challenges to society. Freedom is redefined and reinterpreted in multiple ways – and therefore freedom must be defended constantly by each generation. Remember freedom is a fragile thing, once lost, it is very difficult to recover.

6. ***Learn the art and science of governance.*** The path of law and government is a good way for institutionalizing one's advocacy. But it is not easy to jump from the parliament of the street or the private sector to the seat of political power. Learn to be a strategic thinker and doer. Hone your people skills without sacrificing your principles.

7. ***Beware of the perks of power.*** As you rise in leadership ranks, so do the privileges accorded to you. But remember that these perks are temporary. Abuse of these perks and arrogance can cause your downfall when you least expect it. Perks and power can be addictive. So do not allow them to alter your moral compass. Do not let them define you! In government, you must always remind yourself – that you are there to serve and not to be served!

ORA ET LABORA:
A GIRL NAMED LOIDA OF SORSOGON

Loida Nicolas-Lewis
with
Rocio Casimiro Nuyda

Abstract

*T*his chapter captures the life story and leadership lessons of Loida Nicolas, who grew up in an entrepreneurial family and imbibed leadership values at an early age. She carried on her spirit of faith in humanity and God right through her career at the top of a billion dollar company. Despite extensive media coverage and a high-profile corporate status, she retained core principles of simplicity and sensitivity. *Vanity Fair* named her one of the 200 Most Influential Women in America, thanks to her achievements as an industrialist, philanthropist, civic leader, motivational speaker, author, and lawyer. Years later, once she realized that she had lost the stamina and enthusiasm to run a business, she exited the commercial world and devoted herself to community and civic organizations in the U.S. and the Philippines, such as U.S. Pinoys for Good Governance, Global Diaspora of Overseas Filipinos, National Federation of Filipino American Associations (NAFFAA), and People's Alternative Livelihood Foundation of Sorsogon. "Global Filipinos cannot ignore the abject poverty, lack of adequate housing and education of 30 million Filipinos in the native land. We must do more towards its development. Writing a check is not enough," she eloquently says. The chapter also brings out her progressive philosophy as a mother.

* Author's Note. I have requested my close friend and classmate at our high school days in St Agnes Academy, Rocio Casimiro Nuyda, to expand her original nomination of me for the Centennial of our school in 2012. This chapter then is her own words but I take full responsibility for its contents.

Introduction

Loida Nicolas was a Sodality member and graduated Valedictorian of her High School Class 1959. It is easy to understand how 55 years later, she has lived the life of a true Benedictine child, guided by the spirit and dogma of *ora et labora* [pray and work].

She was raised in the small town of Sorsogon, by entrepreneurial parents who grew their business through hard work and sheer determination. Loida proudly declares that "my parents were hard workers, their value system was intact, their faith in God was strong, and they had ambition."

Growing up, Loida was surrounded by a business environment that made leadership her natural way of life. When asked how she differs from others whose parents were not as entrepreneurial as hers, she remarked, "It is how you make of yourself. My father was orphaned at 11, and lived with a rich business man uncle." She suggested that being an orphan had not been an obstacle to her father reaching the highest level of his business career. She continued to share that "my father was class valedictorian but when he kissed a girl, he was told by the principal that it disqualified him from being the valedictorian and he would be the salutatorian." To the question of whether she is luckier than most, she demurely responded, "You have to be prepared when luck comes. You have to be connected to your inner self."

Assuming Responsibility for a $1.7 Billion Company

In February 1994, Loida Nicolas Lewis took over the helm of TLC Beatrice International Holdings after the sudden death of her entrepreneur-husband Atty. Reginald Lewis. During his life, Reginald Lewis was listed by *Forbes Magazine* as one of the 400 wealthiest Americans in 1992. She had a billion dollar problem to solve and a husband's reputation to preserve. If you inherited a $1.7 billion company from your husband, and you were a pretty, petite thing with a charming Filipino accent pitted against the global Masters of the Universe, you might want to begin your first board meeting with some kind of table-banging display.

The story goes that Loida Nicolas Lewis started with a prayer. "Because the Lord God helps me," she said, "I shall not be dismayed." Eyes rolled, brows rose, and there were snickers, Loida recalls.

This was, after all, TLC Beatrice International Holdings, the global food operation battled over by, among others, business giants such as Henry Kravis, Michael Milken, and the Franprix Supermarket Chain. It was the $985 million leveraged buyout, the biggest of an overseas company in 1987 with holdings of 63 companies in 31 countries that made Reginald Lewis the richest African American in America. Loida intimates that her husband's brilliance was in creating wealth. He won the bid because he dared to win it. The brilliance was in the foresight to start liquidating as soon as he had the contract to sell. In three years, he reduced the debt to $350 million.

But if anything speaks to the essence of Loida Nicolas Lewis, it is her unassuming and strong-in-faith unplanned arrival into global business and the favorite prayer she chose, Isaiah 50:7: "Therefore, I have set my face like flint to do His will. And I know that I will triumph."

Number One of the Top 50 Women Business Owners of America

In 1995, Loida landed on the front cover of the Working Woman magazine and was voted as the Number One of the Top 50 Women Business Owners of America. Martha Ingram of Ingram Industries was second to her in the list of 50.

In their testimonial, the magazine wrote, "Loida is a devoutly spiritual Catholic who clearly believes she is on a mission. And if the inspiration comes from God, the very earthly goals were set by her husband. In one year, Loida proved she's got what it takes to play in the corporate big leagues, bringing focus, faith, and discipline to TLC's disparate operations." As cliché as it may sound, Loida set her eyes on taking Beatrice public, and plunged in to finish what Reginald Lewis had left undone.

As the ones who had snickered quickly learned, the prayer was only the beginning. Loida infused TLC with a gentle air that would be remarkable. A hug from her became a key corporate incentive, and she handed out copies of *The Little Book of Hugs*. The corporate Christmas card was signed Peace and Love. And, she packed off the entire

New York staff, from Executive Vice President to secretary, to an over-night annual retreat led by Jesuit priests.

At one of her high level meetings, Loida listened for a few min-utes as her top lieutenants complained about a European manager's style. Loida broke in and chastised them. She suggested that they did not know what was going on in his life. Beatrice executives noted that Loida's ability to ask probing but considerate and sensitive questions and then listen to the answers, created a disciplined but collegial at-mosphere.

Changing Directions

Her leadership was tough and yet tender. The following years Loida modified the course of the company and started by reducing the op-ulence that her late husband had relished. Her simplicity was evident when she sold the company jet and limousines, moved the company to more modest office space, sold the marginal companies, and persuad-ed Goldman Sachs and BT Securities to back a high-yield offering of $175 million during the company's first return to U.S. capital markets since a couple of aborted attempts during her husband's tenure. She also tamed the balance sheet by refinancing some costly debt, readying the company to go public.

When a potato processing plant in Ireland was sold, Loida delayed the closing of escrow; in order to negotiate a $1 million pool to be shared by the workers, proportionate to their years of service. She ne-gotiated for the buyer to also retain the services of the loyal and effec-tive manager. When the profits were shared, the highest amount was given to a worker who had been peeling potatoes for three decades. Loida strongly felt that the profits should be shared with those who created value for the shareholders. In 1997, she liquidated TLC Be-atrice and sold the last business in 2000, resulting in a 35% internal rate of return on investment for the shareholders of the company.

She shared that the growth years of TLC Beatrice were a contrast to the failures of business ventures in China and the Philippines. Emerg-ing and basking on the successes of TLC Beatrice, she became over confident. Even after conditions changed, she continued to apply the same principles that had worked during the peak of the European and global business boom. She failed to either recognize or fully understand the difference between European and Asian businesses. In Europe, all that was needed was to make monthly visits and oversee the highly experienced managers who were themselves often the former owners of the business unit and could be relied upon for their business acumen and ethics. Her full presence was not required. She failed to recognize that the difference is that the European businesses were entrenched in long standing practices, whereas running the Asian businesses needed full time attention because in Loida's term, "they were startup businesses."

Selling the China Business

She was committed to creating wealth on her own apart from the wealth that she inherited. It took her seven years, from 2000 to 2007, to realize that she had lost the stamina and enthusiasm to run a business 24/7. She realized that she had failed in running the China business. "It was a humbling and desolate experience," Loida recalls.

In 2007 she sold the China business at a loss. "The fault, dear Brutus, is not in the stars but in ourselves that we are underlings," she says. It was a high price to pay but she no longer had the passion to be in business. She agonized over this, until her daughter Leslie one day told her, "Mom, you have to forgive yourself." It was only then that she was able to release herself from self-recrimination.

Loida's *ora et labora* [prayer and work] philosophy is: "Wealth has to come from profits with honor." She quickly admits that this is not original, that such a belief is rooted in her spiritual belief, "love everyone as Jesus has loved you." As part of her *ora* [pray] she keeps and maintains a prayer journal. In it are pages of her reflections. "I journal what happened the day before, what made me happy, what made me sad. Normally as an optimist, I reflect on happy thoughts. I do 15 minutes of quiet time in the principles of Zen practice. I sit, I breathe, I count, and am aware of the present moment. When you do, God touches you as much as you touch God." She professes that this helps in keeping her grounded. It is in the same principle of examination of conscience that St. Ignatius Loyola described as consolation and desolation.

Contributions to Church, Home, and Society

Loida's community and civic advocate based activities in the U.S. and the Philippines are incalculable. She co-founded or founded a wide range of notable organizations.

- Founded in 2009 and is current Chair of U.S. Pinoys for Good Governance. Financed and raised funds to monitor the National Capital Region of 17 cities and 7 municipalities during the 2010 Philippine Presidential election.

- Mobilized and headed the US delegation to participate in the Global Summit of Filipino Diaspora held at the Philippine International Convention Center (PICC) Manila. The thrust of participation was to respond to the call of the Commission of Filipinos Overseas and the present administration to alleviate the poverty in the Philippines. Similarly, the organization acts as a watchdog in the oversight of anti-corruption in the national government.

- Co-founded the Global Diaspora of Overseas Filipinos.

- Concurrent Chair of the Reginald F. Lewis Foundation, which has donated to Harvard Law School, Museum of Maryland African American History and Culture and Virginia State University, all of which named buildings after Mr. Reginald Lewis.

- Challenged in 2004 the COMELEC in the Philippine Supreme Court on it's decision to deny dual citizens (Filipinos living abroad who reacquired their Filipino citizenship), the right to vote in the Philippine National Election. Won a landmark Constitutional case, Nicolas-Lewis Vs. COMELEC giving the right to vote to dual citizens.

- Co-founded with Alex Esclamado as its Visionary Founder the Federation of Filipino American Associations (NAFFAA), a national, non-profit, non-partisan organization based in Washington D.C. with affiliates in 12 U.S. regions. Promotes national affairs and monitors legislations and public policies that affect Filipino Americans' interests, such as legislations in the U.S. Congress to recognize the FilAm Veterans of World War II and the Portability of Medicare for Filipino Americans who retire in the Philippines. This organization continues to be at the forefront of advocacy and action to secure political, legal, economical, and cultural development for Asians and Filipino Americans.

• Founded in 1999 The Lewis College (TLC) in Sorsogon City, offering education at the Pre-K, grade school, and college levels and offering a six months TESDA-approved, U.S. curriculum-based nursing assistant course. TLC is now recognized throughout the Bicol Region as a leader in information technology having won the regional competition in 2010. Several graduates are now working abroad as nursing assistants and English teachers through placement programs operated by TLC. Recently, TLC admitted Asian students, mostly Japanese, for intensive English language courses. TLC also offers instruction in Japanese to locals.

• Funded $25,000 to start the church-based microfinance People's Alternative Livelihood Foundation of Sorsogon Inc. (PALFSI) under Bishop Jesus Varela in 1998. The donated fund was the basis of initiating the program to lift Sorsoganons from poverty. The foundation started with four families and has since helped 20,000 families who have been lifted from poverty to middle class status through micro-lending.

• From 1988 to 1999, organized prayer groups at St. Joseph Catholic Church in Paris, France and at St. Vincent Ferrer Catholic Church, Manhattan, New York.

• One of the founders of the Asian American Legal Defense Fund in New York (AALDEF) in 1974, a legal service center that protects and promotes the civil rights of Asian Americans, works with Asian Americans across the country to secure human rights for all, provides legal service to those affected by racial and economic injustice, works with the poor and Asian Americans who are not proficient in English, and participates in the coalition against anti-Asian violence. Campaigned against the deportation of Filipino doctors who were recruited to fill shortage of medical personnel in the U.S., testified in Washington, D.C., House Committee on Census and Population, about the impact of immigration law on census count of Asian Americans.

- Worked as paralegal with Manhattan Legal Services in East Harlem from 1969 to 1973.

- Former Board Member of the National Catholic Reporter.

- Member, Board of Directors of the Apollo Theater Foundation.

- Former Board member, National Foundation for Teaching Entrepreneurship, motivational speaker, and lecturer on wealth generation and career planning.

- Author, *How to Get a Green Card*, now in its 10th edition, a best seller in its genre, sought after by immigrants and helpful for their quest of permanent residency.

- Former Chair, Sorsogon Provincial Tourism Council (SPTC).

- Founder and Part Owner, Fernando Hotel & Fernando Mall.

- Former Member of the Board of Trustees, Philippine Development Foundation (formerly Ayala Foundation USA).

- Chair, the RFL Foundation, which funded the Reginald F. Lewis Museum, Baltimore, Maryland and the Francisco Nicolas, Sr. Scholarship Foundation, University of the Philippines (UP) Diliman, Quezon City.

- Completed the pledge of her husband to the Reginald F Lewis International Law Center, Harvard, the biggest by an individual in 1992.

Awards and Citations

- 2011 – Eleanor Roosevelt Award, NY State Women's Council. For being a good role model for women who aspire for success in the home, career, business, and society.

- 2009 – NaFFAA *Pamana* Award.
- 2009 – The Forum's Eminent Person Award, Manila, Philippines.
- 2008 – Global Entrepreneur Award, Centennial Celebration UP, Diliman.
- 2007 – Asian Hall of Fame, Seattle, Washington, U.S. (first Asian Woman awarded for community, business and political activism).
- 2005 – Honorary Doctorate Degree, Morgan State University, Maryland for exemplary management of TLC Beatrice International Holdings Inc.
- 2002 – Leadership Award, National Federation of Filipino American Associations.
- 1999 – Corporate Leadership Award by the *Filipinas* Magazine.
- 1998 – *Vanity Fair* Magazine saluted the achievements of American women. This ranking of 200 Influential women included Loida Nicolas Lewis along with former First Lady and former U.S. Secretary of State Hillary Clinton, former U.S. Secretary of State Madeleine Albright, former U.S. Secretary of Justice Janet Reno, U.S. Supreme Court Justices Sandra O'Connor and Ruth Ginsburg, U.S. Senators Elizabeth Dole, Barbara Boxer, Dianne Feinstein, Mary Landrieu, Kay Hutchinson, and Susan Collins.
- 1997 – *Pamana* Award by the President of the Philippines (during President Joseph Estrada's term).
- 2013 – Recognized by the Filipina Womens Network as one of 100 Most Influential Filipinas in America and as one of 100 Most Influential Filipinas in the World.
- 1998 – Outstanding Mother Award.
- Won a discrimination case against the U.S. Immigration and Naturalization Service.
- 1995 – Leadership in Community Award, Asian American Legal Defense and Education Fund.
- 1963 – Student Catholic Action Award upon graduation, St Theresa's College, for spearheading and organizing the social services component of SCA that started student visits to the slums and the sick of Tondo, Manila.

The Early Years and her Benedictine Education

Throughout the years following her graduation from St. Agnes' Academy, she embodied her Christian and Benedictine education. The combination and balance of prayer and work never wavered in her actions and spoken words.

As a young girl, I remember her diligence as a student, her competitiveness about being at the top of her class academically. Her blue and white jumper uniform always being pressed neatly compared to the rest of us who were often caught with ripped hemlines. She wore a scholarly looking pair of eyeglasses, combed her hair away from her face, and stood taller than most. She and her younger sister Imelda were *internas* [resident students] in the school's dormitory during the school week and would be picked up on weekends for the drive home in Sorsogon so they could spend time with their parents. It came naturally to her to lead the class, her dorm-mates, and the entire school in activities that needed to be led. Academically, she was at the top of competitions between all the Catholic schools in the region. And yet, her demeanor was always mild mannered, pleasant, and humble. Early on, traces of what she would become as a global and international leader were evident. Loida was born to lead and to have positive impacts on the lives of people in her community and the world.

She spoke about *ora* [pray] before the Global Summit of Filipinos in the Diaspora: "Global Filipinos cannot ignore the abject poverty, lack of adequate housing and education of 30 million Filipinos in the native land. We must do more towards its development. Writing a check is not enough."

She continued, "Whether we sit in an executive office as a CEO or a baby sitter in a private home, our being Filipinos enables us to anticipate how the other person is feeling and we respond positively or react humanely." She believes that this Filipino character trait springs from the Filipinos' deep-seated spirituality and faith in God's grace: "nothing can separate us from the love of God, and this also explains why we take up leadership in our community. Our contemplation and intimacy with God brings us to action."

She has also been quoted as having said to the media during

numerous interviews: "During my darkest nights, I never lost faith in a Loving God." She was speaking of widowhood and trying moments of her Chairmanship of one of the largest food conglomerate in the world.

When asked about The Lewis College: "It is paying back to get Bicolanos out of poverty through education. We must never forget that there is a time to pay back for all of life's blessings." The Lewis College has successively won championship in Computer Programming from 2010 to 2013 for the Bicol region, a championship that speaks of high academic standards of The Lewis College.

Her *labora* [work] is best described on the pages of *Vanity Fair* when along with Hillary Clinton and other distinguished American women, Loida was named one of 200 Most Influential Women in America. *Vanity Fair* wrote: "Is it patronizing in a so-called post feminist era to salute the achievements of American women? The fact that this question occurs suggests that even now, after decades of transformation and upheaval, the subject of women, their lives and all the possible roles those lives encompass, remains dynamic. Their stories have one thing in common: no dull moments. Faced with choices, they have usually wanted everything. And that is what they have often gotten. They are remarkable people whose contributions go beyond gender. *Vanity Fair* salutes them."

Her *labora* [work] also lies in her diligence in writing down the demands of the day. This is her to-do list of work, whether the day is devoted to fundraising, speaking engagements, or any of her favorite advocacies. She begins each year by going over the past year's resolutions with her daughters. Together they create the new resolutions and set goals for the coming year.

Upon the death of her husband, Loida carried on the roles of both father and mother to her two daughters, Leslie and Christina. Both graduated Cum Laude from Harvard University and Christina garnered honors grade in French Literature and History. Leslie is a certified yoga instructor and a fitness competitor in the Arnold competitions for this sport. Christina is founder and president of All Star Code, an organization that trains young high school men of color to become innovators and entrepreneurs in the technological industry. Loida is the grandmother of Christian and Savilla Sword and Calvin Halpern. She speaks four languages, Filipino, French, Spanish and English.

Progressive Philosophy as a Mother

Her progressive philosophy as a mother is a contrast to her traditional personal ways. She believes in letting her children make mistakes, even if she sees the mistakes coming. She hopes that she raised them well enough to learn from their mistakes. She believes in saying it once and that something said is something heard. To the question of how she talks to them, she responded: "Do not sound like a mother superior and treat them as a daughter inferior. You must talk to them without sounding like an advisor. You either say, may I suggest or you keep your mouth shut and your wallet open."

As a young mother with aspirations to pass the bar examination in the U.S. she did so with a characteristic resolve. Supported by her late husband, she arranged to leave the care of her first born to her mother-in-law for the whole duration of her law review studies. Her perseverance paid off when she received the coveted honor of being the first Asian woman to pass the bar exam without having taken the law courses in the U.S. Loida was once again victorious.

When her first born child, Leslie told her mother that she was separating from her husband, Loida hoped that it was a passing rush of emotions. But, she realized that children are responsible for their own happiness. "You have to let them live their lives and choose their destinies. Unless they ask, I try not offer advice."

These days, she finds absolute relaxation and joy in walking her grandchildren in the park. She relives the days of motherhood through her two-and-a-half year old grandson Calvin, child of daughter Christina and Dan. She talks to him constantly and delights in the child's new words, especially if he learned them from her.

Strongly rooted in her Catholic faith, she facilitated the baptism and first communion rites of her grandchildren. It brought her immeasurable happiness when Christina, who had earlier indicated she could not break away from work, called Loida to say that she would be attending the baptism of her son, Calvin. On the same day, her grand-children, Christian and Savilla by daughter Leslie and Gavin Sword re-ceived their first communion.

Select Causes

These days, she is active in meaningful, selfless advocacy activities that she leads with grit and daring. She is visibly outspoken in her cen-sure of the Chinese intrusion into Philippine territory and water. She forcefully emphasizes that this intrusion endangers the Philippines' rights to billions of dollars of oil reserve and trillions of cubic feet of natural gas. China has the capability to rob the Philippines of its right of ownership granted by the United Nations Convention on the Law of the Sea (UNCLOS). Her unrelenting resolve to bring this to the forefront of international attention landed her on a China television newscast where she was identified as China's "public enemy number 1." She laughs about this.

She is emphatic that she chooses areas for advocacy based on what-ever comes her way. When she learned about Dondon Lanuza, a Fil-ipino who was sentenced to death by beheading in Saudi Arabia, she studied the case, spoke to his mother, was impressed by his mother's strong faith, and went about raising 'blood money' for his release. Don-don was given $100,000 or PHP4 million from the Philippine govern-ment. She raised $122,000 or PHP5 million from the Filipinos in the Philippines and the global diaspora, still short of the PHP35 million demanded for his release. Dondon Lanuza was set free after the Prince of Saudi Arabia offered to make up the difference. Loida was once again victorious in the global arena of power negotiations.

On July 4, 2014 she gathered a group of friends in her home to champion the cause of granting Temporary Protective Status to un-documented Filipinos in the U.S. in view of the damage caused by ty-phoon Haiyan.

"I am a Filipina through and through," she affirms. Recently, she produced the *Noli Me Tangere* opera and took it on the road, from New York to Washington, and then to Manila. During a press conference in Manila, she was quoted as having said, "In the 19th century during the lifetime of José Rizal, the Filipino people were subjected to persecution, prejudice, utter disrespect by the ruling class. It is my hope that this opera will enlighten the minds of the young and they will have a better understanding of how we got here, why we are who we are."

On June 1, 2014, Loida spent four days in Los Angeles to support me as I chaired a high profile benefit dinner to rebuild the St. Scholastica's College in Tacloban, Philippines in a fundraiser called 'Hope After Haiyan.' With her as the driving force, this too proved to be remarkably successful.

Reflections on the Future

I asked her if she will ever marry again, or if she had even considered marrying again. She confided that she was once married to a king and she asked if there can be another king? As schoolmates in high school, we have maintained a special bond of friendship. For all that she has become, she remains unaffected. Her staff here and abroad professes that they will never leave 'Mrs. Lewis.' Global leadership in all shapes and forms defines her. During one of her trips to Los Angeles, I met her at the airport, on her late night arrival. She would not hear of dining out because she says she has dinner in her purse. Sure enough, out comes a packaged cup of noodles from her Birkin purse. She sits with me in a kitchen work table for two without the trappings of fine linen, rather paper napkins on the side, chatting the night away over the hot noodle soup that came out of her purse. The lady sleeps in my guest room and compliments me on how warm and comfortable she is.

She opens her East Hampton vacation home to me, and schoolmates, in celebration of my birthdays and spoils us with large servings of lobsters. We prance around in our PJs like schoolgirls and we know she genuinely relishes it all. She sends me text messages to ask whether I am available for a phone call, I mean the lady can just call. She eats crabs with her hands and pounds on them with fervor, because she loves eating in the company of friends. She doses off quickly in seconds, catnaps that she says energize her for the next task at hand. On a night when we are caught in her Fifth Avenue apartment by an electrical interruption in the neighborhood, she pulls out candles and sticks them without hesitation on drinking glasses instead of her Tiffany candleholders. She squeezes herself into a bed with four other schoolmates, just as others would do. She is generous with her compliments, but she is quick to point out what does not look right. She and I share the same outlook about every woman's right of choice if faced with the dilemma of pro-life or pro-choice. She quotes Pope Francis: "Who are we to judge." Indeed, she is as human as one can get but the lady has her own brand and style. A woman steeped in the precept of "Ora Et Labora."

The day that Reginald Lewis agreed to a blind date was the day that Loida's destiny was written. She was desolate when he died, but she says that looking at it now, God had a purpose. She would become an instrument for that purpose. She ends our interview with this parting quote: "All things work together unto good to those who love God, to those who are called according to His purpose."

The woman is an industrialist, philanthropist, civic leader, motivational speaker, author, lawyer, mother, and friend. She is the girl named Loida of Sorsogon.

Leadership Tips

1. ***Strengthen your sense of family.*** In a world where competitiveness, career ambition, social identity and economic competence seem to dominate the daily grind, it is important to stay connected and rooted to family as the central source of values and inspiration. Parents must continue to cultivate the possibilities for children to whom the baton can be passed over.

2. ***Success begins by putting people first.*** Do not get obsessed with business numbers and process alone, focus on the human aspects of your colleagues and employees also. There is more to their story than meets the eye, find out what is happening in their lives before you judge them. Encourage them with simple things like appreciation and hugs.

3. ***Connect to your inner self.*** Have a regular inner dialogue with yourself, and have regular resolutions and plans about your life and where it is going. Listen to your inner voice and develop your sense of instinct. This inner self will surface during your toughest moments and show you the way.

4. ***Value simplicity.*** Wealth does not have to become flashy opulence. Especially when you are a public figure, your spending habits come under scrutiny and send out all kinds of messages. Be simple and frugal, don't chase what does not seem natural or appropriate.

5. ***Respect cultural differences.*** In a globalized economy and culture, it is all the more important to understand, recognize, and value cultural differences. The U.S. and Europe differ as Western nations, and even among Asian countries there are lots of differences. Learn how this affects communication, power and governance.

6. ***Leadership begins even in school.*** Even in your student years, there are opportunities and lessons for leadership. Starting off with your class-mates and continuing right up to school; there are chances for you to learn about and exercise leadership. Grab it with both hands.

7. ***Parents should be advisors not rulers.*** Treat your children with respect, not as 'mother superior child inferior.' Be advisors to your children, not rulers or supervisors. The confidence that will last them throughout their lives begins its journey at home. Set a good foundation for them.

8. ***Give back to society.*** Just because you are better off or live elsewhere does not mean you can cut yourself off from the problems of your fellow citizens and your roots. Give back to the unfortunate and the deprived, and give them more than a check; spend time and energy on their issues and causes.

9. ***Have a sense of history and faith.*** Have a sense of history and know where you are coming from, and see the connection between yourself and the divine power. Everything has a purpose in life, give gratitude to your people and to God for His blessings. Let this influence your professional and personal life, and be proud of your faith.

BEING A WOMAN AMBASSADOR*

Patricia Ann V. Paez

*Ambassador of the Republic of the Philippines to Poland
and Non-resident Ambassador to Lithuania, Estonia, and Latvia*

Abstract

*T*his chapter presents the experiences of a woman ambassador who is a career diplomat and rose through the ranks of the Philippines' Department of Foreign Affairs (DFA). It dispels common notions that the rarified field of diplomacy is a world of glitz and glamor, dizzying whirl of cocktail receptions, rubbing elbows with the 'movers and shakers' in government and society, and constant globe-trotting. It provides insight into how a Philippine envoy prepares and is honed for 'prime time,' gives a glimpse into the upsides and downsides of being an ambassador, and the challenges of juggling multiple roles as the envoy from a country which, in recent years, has regained pride in its place among Asian countries. This chapter gives an insider's view of the tough, demanding, and exacting work of an ambassador and the special problems faced by a woman ambassador. Love of country is the only fuel that sustains one to forge ahead as an ambassador with tenacity, focus, and resolve. Foreign Secretary Albert F. del Rosario has exhorted us that it is imperative "to reach beyond one's grasp." But precisely because it is a tough job, the joys that come with success are immense and immeasurable. For a woman ambassador, grit and guts are her shield and armor.

Introduction

Many people think an ambassador 's life is glamorous, jetsetting and full of cocktail parties and high profile ntworking. Enhancing this image is the fact that protocol dictates that an ambassador, whose full

---

*The views presented are those of the author and do not necessarily represent the views of the Philippine Government.

official title is Ambassador Extraordinary and Plenipotentiary (AEP), be always majestically addressed as His or Her Excellency even by his or her peers in the diplomatic circle.

Tough Core of an Ambassador's Job

But this is only the outer layer. At its core, an ambassador's job is very tough, exacting, and demanding; and being a woman makes it even tougher. It becomes triple tough when one represents a country, which has been weighed down by an image problem.

Today's crop of Philippine envoys are expected to meet stringent standards of performance and produce tangible results, both qualitative and quantitative. Coming as he does from the private sector, Secretary Albert F. del Rosario's first initiative was to retool all ambassadors with essential skills. This is to ensure that they can carry on their mandates effectively within the framework of the three pillars of Philippine foreign policy.

Three Pillars of Philippine Foreign Policy

These three pillars are: first, promoting national security; second, enhancing economic diplomacy; and third, protecting the rights and welfare of Filipinos overseas.

A new global environment requires that ambassadors are invested with a new set of skills. Secretary del Rosario enlisted the support of the Asian Institute of Management (AIM) to train Philippine diplomats on management and economic diplomacy. Passing the AIM courses is now a prerequisite before a diplomat can be assigned abroad as an ambassador. This pro-active measure is extremely vital not only for acquiring new skills but also for imbuing ambassadors with a 'corporate culture' aligned with the Aquino administration's goals of poverty alleviation, job creation, and good governance. It is worth noting that in his inaugural speech, President Benigno S. Aquino III said that "our foremost duty is to lift the nation from poverty through honest and effective governance," adding that "our goal is to create jobs at home so that there will be no need to look for employment abroad."

It also bears recalling that on his first day in office at the DFA, Secretary del Rosario gave brief remarks before the entire foreign service corps and his key messages were: first, "if you do not love your country, you should not be in the foreign service;" and second, "always reach beyond your grasp."

These messages deserve to be heeded. This is because love of country is the only fuel that will keep you forging ahead as you undertake your primary task of representing the Philippines while pursuing the Philippines' national interests in credible and effective ways. An ambassador who is committed to making a positive difference and who is determined to deliver results is invariably overworked, underpaid, and under-appreciated. Sometimes, ambassadors will have to draw from their own goodwill and dare to do things which might not always seem to follow all the rules to be true to the mandate. In other words, as an ambassador you have to do whatever it takes to get the job done and you do it with passion. You answer the call to duty motivated by an abiding love of country.

Multiple Roles of an Ambassador

An ambassador plays multiple roles as a leader and a role model for the embassy team and to the Filipino community. An ambassador is a change-agent and innovator who must be ready to improve or experiment to get things done; a manager who oversees the day-to-day operations of the embassy; a communicator who delivers speeches and remarks before different audiences and accepts media interviews; a negotiator who engages in talks on possible bilateral agreements in different fields; a quasi-lawyer who carefully reviews the drafts of such agreements; an advocate who is involved in the cases of Filipino nationals who find themselves in trouble; a public relations (PR) person who networks with those who 'push the levers and press the buttons' within and outside of government; an organizer and events planner; a techie; a field marketing and sales representative who promotes Philippine tourism, encourages investors to invest in the Philippines, and traders to trade with the Philippines; a 'culturati' who promotes our country's culture and heritage; a cheerleader for and unifier of the Filipino community; even a quasi-therapist to Filipino nationals in distress; a perpetual student or lifelong learner whose thirst for new knowledge, information, and expertise must be unquenchable; and an efficient multitasker.

Preparing for Prime Time

To be able to understand these roles and be ready for "prime time" in the realm of international diplomacy requires painstaking preparations.

An aspiring ambassador who wants to make the grade on the basis of merit and not on the basis of political connections must first pass the rigorous Foreign Service Officers (FSO) exam. Once she passes the test, she automatically joins the ranks of the career corps with an entry level rank of FSO IV. From this rank, it will take her an average of at least 15 years before she becomes a full-fledged ambassador. Prior to becoming an ambassador, she must again pass another exam to qualify as a Career Minister, the rank immediately below the rank of Chief of Mission Class II and a rank which already qualifies one to be designated as an ambassador. The highest rank is Chief of Mission Class I.

This slow ascent to the top rung of the career ladder is a process of continuous on-the-job training for higher responsibilities as one serves at an embassy or consulate overseas and at the Home Office in Manila. This entails taking turns doing the work of a consular officer, an administrative officer, a cultural officer, a press and information officer, an economic officer, and a political officer.

At the Home Office in Manila, an officer can be assigned to any of the DFA's geographical offices, to the consular, public information, communication, personnel and administration, fiscal, or legal offices, or to any of the offices of the three undersecretaries or to the office of the Foreign Secretary.

The molding and honing process takes more than a decade and involves doing diverse functions, as well as adjusting to the working or management styles, and personalities of different bosses as one is shifted from one office or overseas post to another. Every semester or every six months, the work performance of an officer, regardless of rank, is rated. It is only when an officer gets a performance rating of "very satisfactory" in the most recent four semesters during the cycle of promotion, will she be considered for promotion to the next higher rank. Each promotion is also subjected to the confirmation process of the Commission on Appointments.

Even before one travels to her country of assignment, an ambassador must also know various things ranging from the most significant to the mundane.

Ideally, she must have at least a conversational or a basic proficiency in the language of her country of assignment. In addition, she must be steeped in Philippine history and culture as well as in current events. She must also know the host country's history, its profile which includes its system of government and the nature of its economy, its culture, and other relevant information including the bilateral relations between the Philippines and the host country and the living conditions there.

It also helps to know what furniture or items the Embassy has or does not have, as well as its physical layout, so that they can be supplemented with items which can only be sourced from the Philippines. These may include works of art by Filipinos, native decor and handicraft, coffee table books on the Philippines and other literature; and Philippine produce which are non-perishable such as wines and liquor for giveaways. The Philippine Embassy has to be a showcase of Filipino creativity and talents.

A Typical Work Day at the Embassy

A typical work day of an ambassador involves reviewing all the incoming communications from the Manila Office and routing them to the relevant staff with specific instructions and deadlines. She also reads the outgoing communications all of which go out over her signature prior to their transmittal to the Home Office and signs vouchers for bills to be paid. Her day is mostly consumed by meetings. These include making representations before the host government on various matters; for instance, informing counterparts about the Philippine position on the West Philippine Sea/South China Sea issue; lobbying the host government to support the candidatures of Philippine government nominees to international bodies; or taking up a vital issue which impinges on the Philippines' national interests. An ambassador also has to have a lot of 'face time' with other sectors outside of government since 'public diplomacy' is the handmaiden of 'official diplomacy.' People-to-people contacts form the solid bedrock that will sustain and nourish relations between governments and countries.

Usually, an ambassador's schedule is filled at least two months ahead of the actual dates. Since she must actively engage in diplomatic representation services and in economic diplomacy, she must constantly meet with all key stakeholders. She is also invited to various speaking engagements and to conferences on an array of issues, attends the National Day celebrations hosted by other ambassadors, receives visitors at the embassy, hosts meetings or diplomatic receptions, launches projects such as information campaigns to increase awareness about the Philippines, and projects a positive image of the country. She also participates in tourism and trade fairs, conducts 'roadshows' in the host country's major cities to inform the private sector of the business opportunities in the Philippines, arranges exchanges of high-level visits, conducts media interviews, arranges business missions and tourism-related familiarization tours to the Philippines, and stages cultural shows. Her responsibilities include initiating *pulong-bayan* or town hall type of meetings to inform the Filipino community about pressing issues relevant to them and assisting Filipino nationals in distress for whatever reason, and the list goes on.

Working as an ambassador is a non-stop routine of networking and pro-active initiation of new projects. As one's network expands, so do the opportunities to strengthen bilateral relations which must be seized because they may never come again.

One must also be thoroughly prepared, especially on the substantive issues, when meeting with foreign officials because their most important resource, like that of a hard-working ambassador, is their time. An ambassador cannot run the risk of leaving an impression that she just wasted a foreign counterpart's time because she will likely not be received again by that official or important figure.

An ambassador must also have a clear objective in mind before requesting a meeting. On the meeting day itself, she must be able to convey her key messages in a clear and concise manner. She must be articulate, well-groomed, mindful of protocol, and must always leave a positive impression. An ambassador must also always dress appropriately for any occasion; thus, in one day, she may have to change from her business attire to a cocktail dress for an evening diplomatic reception.

Credibility is the most essential capital of an ambassador. In the era of the Internet, everyone has access to information and could readily vet any information for its validity or authenticity.

Humility is also an important trait for an ambassador as well as the ability to develop positive rapport since people will help you, if they like you. An envoy must always cultivate their contacts to sustain good working relations.

Joys and Challenges
of Being a Woman Ambassador

Joy for an ambassador comes in many shapes and forms. I am filled with joy when I know that the embassy team has taken to heart my injunction that 'this will do attitude' will not work for me since I expect everyone to give their all and do their best.

It was such a great joy for all of us when the Philippine embassy booth won the prize as 'the most creative and most professional booth' in the first-ever tourism trade fair that we participated in, here in Poland.

We were very pleased when volunteers from the Filipino community in Poland agreed to our request to form the Mabuhay Folk Dance Group and when they gave their debut performance during the 2013 Philippine National Day diplomatic reception. It is a source of immense joy when key people in the host country offer their help or take active partnership with an ambassador so that she can achieve her goals, especially if they are not asking or expecting anything in return.

This was the case when the editors of Poland's two biggest national dailies, published a full page open letter of appeal to the people of Poland for donations to the Philippine National Red Cross for the victims of typhoon Haiyan. It was followed by the lighting ceremony of the Philippine *parol* [Christmas lantern] which was installed in a window of the Presidential Palace or residence. Earlier, we gave the *parol* to President Bronislaw Komorowski and First Lady Anna Komoroswka of Poland as a way of thanking them for making direct media appeals and meeting with Polish NGOs so that they would support the Philippines in the aftermath of that typhoon. The government of the City of Warsaw led by Mayor Hanna Gronkiewicz-Waltz also installed another Philippine *parol* in its biggest outdoor Christmas tree in Warsaw's New Town Square.

Success in attaining one's diplomatic objectives is the major source of an ambassador's pleasure. An example of attaining a major objective was the first-ever familiarization tour to the Philippines of the Polish Chamber of Tourism led by no less than its President Mr. Pawel Niewiadomski. I was elated when the Country Manager of Qatar Airways (QA) in Poland sponsored the round-trip airfare for eight participants. Offers of help from several sectors of Polish society and government continue to come our way but we can not avail of all of the offers at once due to lack of personnel on our part. But we are committed to responding to offers of help one at a time. Right now, we are giving priority to organizing a business and economic mission to the Philippines of the Polish private sector, in partnership with the Polish Chamber of Commerce.

Challenges exist but for as long as one is imbued with a 'can do' mindset, nothing is insurmountable.

From the time I started working after my graduation from college, I have often found myself as the only female, or one of the few females, in most work situations. This experience helped prepare me to be the first woman ambassador to Poland and to the Baltic States.

As a new envoy 'on the block,' you always arouse curiosity and interest and create impressions about yourself with whoever you meet. Mindful of this fact, I always make it a point to do my homework before any meeting so I can convey to the people across the table that I fully know what I am talking about. This includes having ready answers to whatever questions they may throw based on anticipating a whole range of possible questions.

My 'talking points' or the content of all the presentations that I make, whether in PowerPoint or whatever form, must be well-researched, must be factual and accurate, and packaged in digestible amounts since the attention span of the audience, whether of one or a hundred or more, is limited. Presentations must also appeal to the senses, requiring appropriate visuals or background sound. All events that the embassy stages must be tackled like a stage production to ensure positive and lasting impact. In other words, we cannot afford to be mediocre or to be rated simply as average. All engagements must approximate excellence, if not, be actually excellent and must have a 'wow' factor.

In sum, a woman ambassador can only prevail over the challenges by demonstrating intelligence and excellence which, in turn, entails a lot of hard work, perseverance, focus, concentration, and dogged determination. Not only must you do this one time, you must do this ALL OF THE TIME since you are only as good as your last performance. This is where love of country serves as the compelling motivating force to be a cut above the rest and to strive for excellence in all endeavors, in keeping with Foreign Secretary Albert del Rosario's exhortation to each and every ambassador, "to reach beyond your grasp."

Leadership Tips

To the next-generation of leaders who aspire to join the DFA in the Philippines and become a successful ambassador—not just an ambassador in title alone—you must ask yourself whether this is really what you want to do, and be fully cognizant of the fact that your journey will be an amazingly difficult one since you have to keep raising the bar in terms of performance.

1. *Choose the career which brings out your passion.* In diplomacy or any field of endeavor, a prerequisite to success is passion and definitely not mere obsession. You may obsess about becoming an ambassador but if you are not truly passionate about it, you might still become an ambassador and yet not make any indelible mark. As in romance, passion in the pursuit of diplomacy drives one to heights of selflessness, particularly to selfless service to country. This passion invests one with the capacity to fully embrace all the challenges that may come along the way and not in any way be daunted by them. It also invests one with the corresponding resolve to hurdle all obstacles, and at the end of the day, still be fully gratified by the experience.

2. *Put your ego aside and be a people person.* Personality-wise, you must also ascertain whether you are a 'people person.' Diplomacy is not a profession for solo players. You have to network, network, and network because all the goals that you have to attain require harnessing the active participation of many people. Diplomacy is also not for the egotistical. If you do not mind to whom the credit goes, you will be able to accomplish most of your goals. In my personal experience, if you allow others to take center stage and relegate yourself to the backstage while still 'keeping your eye on the ball,' many helping hands will be on the deck.

3. *Shine in academics.* A young aspiring ambassador must first complete the necessary academic credentials, and as much as possible, with flying colors because these lend you with gravitas, especially when combined with a sterling professional experience later on. The following academic disciplines are important: history, economics,

international relations, and diplomacy. But this is not a cut-and-dried prerequisite. Many good ambassadors have earned their Bachelor of Arts degree, Master's degree, or Doctoral degree in other fields, aside from the ones that I just cited.

4. ***Pick up language skills and fluent communications.*** In diplomacy, it is important to have language proficiency, both written and oral, in at least one language, aside from English and whatever your native tongue is. Spanish and French are especially useful in multilateral diplomacy. It helps to take the qualifying exam for Philippines FSO (for information on this, please access <http://www.dfa.gov.ph/index.php/fsoexams>) as soon as you graduate so that what you have learned is still fresh in your mind. Develop your writing skills because you will have to a lot of writing to do ranging from 'bread and butter letters' to Notes Verbale, Aide Memoire, other types of diplomatic correspondence, speeches, and diplomatic communications to the Home Office, 'talking points,' briefing papers, and so on. For diplomatic reports, train yourself to write in a concise and direct-to-the-point manner because a one-pager memo is what is usually desired by an extremely busy Foreign Secretary or Minister.

5. ***Stay on top of the news and dig beneath it.*** Keep reading continuously and extensively in order to stay abreast of current developments, and sharpen your memory and your ability to store them in your mental back file so that you can be conversant about them at any given time. You have to be well-rounded and should be able to carry on conversations about world history, culture, philosophy, the arts, music, cinema, sports, and other topics.

6. ***Develop speaking skills ranging from small talk to public speeches.*** If you are shy by nature, you can overcome shyness by enrolling in special courses that will train you in public speaking. Being a diplomat entails accepting invitations to many speaking engagements. A pleasant sense of humor and the ability to engage in 'small talk' are equally important because attending diplomatic cocktails and receptions is actually an extension of your work past regular office hours. They provide good avenues to network and establish rapport with people you will have to work with. At times it can feel like you are 'speed dating.'

7. ***Always be self-aware and confident but not arrogant.*** Self-confidence, not arrogance, will see you through. You must also not fear rejection because it is a must for you to reach out to people who do not know you but whom you must know. If you are able to cite a compelling reason for that V.I.P. to meet with you at a mutually convenient time, the possibility of rejection is remote. But you have to come very well prepared for that meeting, or it may be your last, or you can just as quickly be shown the door even before you have warmed your seat. It should not come as a surprise to you if you get talked about in the country where you serve as an ambassador. It is really a small village and the people you meet and come across will invariably compare notes about you.

Over and above these crucial traits, it is very important for you to bear in mind that you should always comport yourself in a manner worthy of respect, whether you are performing an official function as an ambassador or just shopping in a mall because your title as an ambassador never leaves you, even if you retire or, heaven forbid, even when you die.

UPHILL ROAD TO SUCCESS IN SCIENCE AND ACADEME

Delia B. Rodriguez-Amaya, Ph.D.

President, International Academy
of Food Science and Technology
Senior Visiting Professor
Universidade Federal da Fronteira Sul

Abstract

*T*his chapter tells the story of my journey, from a small town in the Philippines to becoming the president of the International Academy of Food Science and Technology. My professional path took me first to Manila for my undergraduate degree, then to Honolulu for my M.S. degree, and Davis, California for my Ph.D. It continued on to Kingston, Rhode Island for a postdoctoral stint and to Campinas, Brazil where I have spent most of my professional years. The road was often uphill, winding, and thorny; but being a Filipina, dedication, determination, persistence, and adaptability carried me through. The solid education I got from the Philippines, guiding principles from parents and teachers, research expertise from the U.S., and above all, God's blessings, were fundamental to my professional success. That success can be gauged from: scientific publications, invited seminars and lectures, research paper presentations, international courses for researchers, advising Master and Ph.D. theses, coordination of financed research projects, editorship or membership of editorial boards of international and Brazilian scientific journals, administrative positions, organization of international conferences, consultancy or serving as scientific adviser of international agencies or projects, participation in Brazilian and international technical and policy making committees, and numerous awards.

Introduction

In August 2014, at the 17th World Congress of Food Science and Technology in Montreal, Canada, I was inducted as the first woman President of the International Academy of Food Science and Technology (IAFoST), and the second president from a developing country. I was elected a fellow in 2003 in recognition of "outstanding service to the field internationally." I have been elected a member of the Academy's Executive Council three times since 2008.

Growing up in a small town in the Philippines, I did not foresee that one day I would hold one of the most prestigious international positions in my field of study. Looking back, the road to this success was tough and thorny, but typical Filipina traits have sustained me all the way. These traits include dedication, determination, persistence, and integrity. A bio-sketch in the Asian Journal (Pimentel 2013) added humility and grace as fundamental in my journey to the top.

My Hometown

Where do I come from? The answer is in my following verse:

Where is home?

Must I roam the world to find where is my home?
Is it in a sleepy town nestled at the foot of majestic Mt. Mayon where
stories of a happy childhood are forever recalled?
Is it in bustling Manila where I sought and got my university diploma
and taught Chemistry for the first time?
Is it in a place many call "Paradise," where Diamond Head guards
over vivid blue waters, and East meets West at a Center?
Is it in the city of Davis where day and night I did bench work in a
darkened lab, to earn a PhD that is recognized far and wide?
Is it in scenic Kingston where I finally saw the four seasons unfold,
each with its own charm to behold?
Is it in Griffin, near Atlanta, where I took care of Katherine Grace,
my firstborn?

Or is it in Campinas, Brazil, where I spent most of my professional years?
If "home is where the heart is," then mine is where it all began, in a
tiny town called Santo Domingo, in the Province of Albay.

June 17, 2001

Educational Background

At a conference in Rome in 1995, sponsored by the United Nations
Food and Agriculture Organization (FAO), I gave two talks and coordinated one of the sessions. At the conference I was approached by
Latin Americans, Asians, participants from other developing countries, and women; all claiming me as their representative. It was then
that I realized that my unofficial mandate was far greater than I ever
imagined.

In retrospect, I think I was prepared for that role. My writing,
speaking, and organizational skills were acquired from the Philippines,
including my basic education. My research expertise was mostly developed in the U.S. My degrees are: B.S. in Food Technology, Araneta University, Magna Cum Laude; M.S. in Food Science, University of
Hawaii, East West Center grantee and recipient of the East West Center Professional Award for high scholastic achievement; and Ph.D. in
Agricultural Chemistry, University of California, Davis, Board of Re-
gents' Graduate Intern Fellow.

I was a full scholar from high school at Legazpi College, now Aqui-
nas University, Albay, through undergraduate and graduate studies.
In the Philippines, it is not enough to excel academically; scholars
are expected to be student leaders as well. In high school, I was editor-in-chief of our official publication and monitor of my class. We
did folk and modern dancing, singing, public speaking, acting, gym-
nastics at programs and special events. I even won a gold medal for
placing first in a Spanish Declamation Contest with José Rizal's *Me
Piden Versos*, trained by my Filipino-Spanish maternal grandfather,
Diego Balin. My undergraduate extracurricular activities included:
being president of the Rizal Club, president of the Science Club,
vice-president and president of the Student Catholic Action, treasurer of the Honor Society, and secretary of the Senior Organization.

I received four gold and one bronze medals for high scholastic achievement and a gold medal for leadership. I learned to multitask, organize, lead, speak, and write.

Professional Achievements

As a professor from 1978 to 2010 in the Faculty of Food Engineering, University of Campinas, Brazil, my teaching responsibilities consisted mainly of the undergraduate subjects, Food Analysis and Food Chemistry, and the graduate subjects, Food Analysis by Chromatographic Methods, Chemistry of Food Color and Flavor, and Chemical Changes during Processing and Storage of Foods. Highly rated by professors and students, these classes had large numbers of students. Added to these regular classes were numerous short courses for students and professors of other universities, researchers of institutes, and technical staff of food industries.

I also advised 24 students for their Masters theses and 24 students for their Doctoral theses, as well as 15 undergraduate students for Research Initiation projects. It is customary in Brazil for graduating classes to honor the professors who they think contributed most to their academic development. Four graduating classes of Food Engineering honored me at their Commencement Ceremonies. This was considered rather unusual because Engineering students generally dislike Chemistry.

My administrative positions included: Chairman of the Department of Food Science; General Coordinator, equivalent to Dean, for two terms of the Graduate Programs, Master and Doctoral, in Food Science, Food Technology, Food Engineering, and Nutritional Sciences, programs with total enrollment of about 500 doctoral and master students and a faculty of more than 60 Ph.D. professors; Coordinator for four terms of the Academic Council of the Faculty of Food Engineering; and Coordinator of 25 financed research including two interuniversity projects funded under the Brazilian projects, Ministry of Science and Technology's Program for Research Centers of Excellence.

My research expertise is reflected in more than 240 scientific publications in books, book chapters, reviews, and research articles in indexed journals, mostly in international publications; more than 210 invited lectures in more than 30 countries; and more than 240 research papers presented at international conferences in more than 25 countries and Brazilian conferences. I was research fellow in the highest category of the Brazilian National Council for Science and Technology for twenty years (1990-2010) and the first woman to reach the highest category in the area of Food Science and Technology (FST). Advocating for quality research in developing countries, I gave 15-day hands-on intensive courses for researchers and professors in the Philippines, Mexico, Argentina, Chile, Brazil, South Africa, Tanzania, and China, mostly sponsored by FAO and by the international project Harvest-Plus. I also conducted research training in my laboratory in Campinas for young scientists from Argentina, Chile, Colombia, Ecuador, Guatemala, Mexico, Peru, South Africa, Sri Lanka, Philippines, Canada, and Portugal.

I was invited to participate in several FAO-WHO Expert Consultation Meetings, in India, Brazil, UK, and Serbia; and served as a scientific adviser of Vitamin A Partnership for Africa, a joint project of seven African countries. I also served as a collaborator and scientific adviser of HarvestPlus' Breeding Crops for Better Nutrition- International Biofortification Program. I have also been recognized internationally for organizing high level scientific programs, such as those of the Latin American Symposium on Food Science, held every two years since 1995, and the 16th World Congress of Food Science and Technology in 2012.

The Ministries of the Brazilian government make good use of university professors as consultants and collaborators in various activities. I was a member and subsequently coordinator of the Brazilian Ministry of Education's Commission for Graduate Studies in FST, with the principal mandate of evaluating and promoting high standards for Master and Doctoral programs in the field. I also was a member of the Advisory Committee on FST of the Brazilian National Council for Science and Technology for two terms; a member of *ad hoc* technical advisory committees of the Brazilian Ministry of Health and the Brazilian Ministry of the Environment, and a Councilor of the Brazilian Society of Food Science and Technology for four terms. Even after retiring from the University of Campinas, my professional activities continued. Since retiring I have served as visiting senior professor at Universidade Federal da Fronteira Sul, a new federal university in Southern Brazil, helping them to set up their Graduate Program in FST; a scientific adviser of the International Foundation for Science (based in Sweden); the editor of *Current Opinion in Food Chemistry and Biochemistry*; a review editor of *Frontiers in Nutrition*; and a member of the Editorial Boards of *Trends in Food Science and Technology*, *Plant Foods for Human Nutrition*, *Archivos Latinoamericanos de Nutrición*, *Alimentos e Nutrição*, and *Revista do Instituto Adolfo Lutz*. I served as a member of the editorial boards of six other journals, including 10 years on the editorial board of the *Journal of Food Composition and Analysis*.

In the Philippines, my professional positions included: Instructor, Department of Chemistry, Araneta University (1962-1964); Researcher (1966-1968) and Assistant Professor (1972-1973) of the Department of Food Science and Nutrition, University of the Philippines, Diliman. Also at the same time I was a Professorial Lecturer at the Graduate Schools of the University of Santo Tomas and the Centro Escolar University (1972-1973). In 1994 I was a Transfer of Knowledge through Expatriates (TOKTEN) fellow at the Philippine Food and Nutrition Research Institute and University of the Philippines Diliman, under the auspices of the UN Development Program and the Philippine Secretary of Foreign Affairs.

The Story Behind the Achievements

While a listing of professional achievements can be impressive, the back-story is even more indicative of professional endeavors.

I could have stayed in the U.S., where modern research facilities and ample funding make research less difficult, and international recognition comes more easily, but I wanted to contribute to science in the developing countries, where I belong.

As my husband and I were preparing to go to Brazil, friends, colleagues, and even former professors were advising us to carefully examine our options. Some of them argued that going to a developing country may mean professional suicide as researchers. In my first years in

Brazil, I thought I did just that. It took me one year before I got hired. I learned later that people did not believe my Curriculum Vitae: If she were that good, why is she here? Why did she not stay in the US? Others thought that I would be a threat to their own professional careers.

Summing up in this verse, my professional journey involved huge hurdles:

An uphill walk to recognition

Experimental science is harsh on those
who are not in the mainstream.
Months or years to acquire funds
to get the laboratory into working.
To once again be deterred by equipment
starting to need costly repair.
Reagents, solvents and other materials
that are imported at prohibitive prices.
And an infrastructure that is not there
or is simply precarious.
To top it all, the misconception that researchers
in the third world are but third-rate scientists.
Ratified by a colonial mentality that accepts
that third-world
science is inferior.
And if a woman, in the eyes of many,
naturally weak in engineering, math and physics.
All these barriers while science elsewhere
advances at an exponential pace.
But a thinking mind is not exclusive
of the rich and privileged.
And though utterly tempting to join
the brain drain statistics,
scientists in developing countries
can still tread the long uphill road to success.

January 21, 2005, on JAL flight 047 from New York to Tokyo

One of my older thesis advisees said that my problem was "doing first-world research under third-world conditions." Indeed, the obstacles seemed insurmountable. Financially, a scientist in a developing country has to cope with limited funds and lack of infrastructure on one hand, and very high costs of instruments, materials, and technical assistance on the other hand. Bureaucracy works very slowly, as in importing equipment and reagents. The greatest barrier, however, is invisible: prejudice against third-world scientists. I had gotten tired of hearing first-world scientists (fortunately, only a few) affirming: "They do bad science there" with 'there' meaning developing countries. At a closed (invited participants only) meeting in the 1990s in Washington DC, I was questioning, as diplomatically as I could, the experimental design of one of the speakers from a developed country. Obviously furious, she said, "Who are you to question my research?" I counted up to ten and simply replied, "I asked a technical question, I would like a technical answer." My response conquered the other participants. That was in the morning; in the afternoon, I was coordinating the session.

Even people from developing countries are biased against third-world scientists. On a weekend while I was giving a short course on carotenoid analysis at the Cape Town Medical Research Center, where the famous first heart transplant was done by Dr. Barnard, I was being given a tour of lovely Cape Town by a young and articulate guide. He treated me very well, but I could perceive that there was something about me that bothered him. At the end of the day, he asked: "What does a Latin American woman know that our best scientists don't already know?" I laughed and replied: "So that was what was bothering you about me all day. Don't worry, I also lecture in the US, Canada, and European countries."

What carried me through those difficult years? A good disposition would be on top of my list:

A bright day

In the morning I wake up eager to discover what the day
has in store for me.
Through the wide-open
window, I first let the sunshine through.

Out in the garden the dewdrops glisten against the green grass,
a perfect backdrop for the flowers in splendid colors so pleasing
to the eyes.
The birds are chirping as they merrily hop from tree to tree,
replacing last night's barking of the neighbor's dog with pedigree.
Without delay I must now hurry to go to the university,
where I must use professional prowess earnestly.
Trying to give classes with the stamina of many years ago,
but with the knowledge and experience that time
has allowed me to accrue.
Advising graduate students in their research projects to insure
that science is well served as future scientists are being prepared.
As I put the finishing touches in the latest paper we want to publish,
it occurs to me, how exacting but fascinating science can be!
Out of my office window, I notice the purple ipê trees fully in bloom,
so I pause for a moment to admire Mother Nature's generosity.
Amidst all these, I must not forget to send emails
to colleagues and friends.
Luckily, there's lunchtime or suppertime to get a glimpse
of my daughters' day.
I have already done so with my husband's in the car
as we drive to and fro.
As nightfall approaches, I find myself back home comfortably.
I must do the exercise modern Health Science and my family
have convinced me to do,
while the national and international news tell me
what the world has been through.
As scenes of wars, anguish and conflicts blast the TV screen,
I search for stories of human compassion which, fortunately, come on.
Before the news ends I even get to chuckle
at the politicians' latest gaffes.
But now the day is ending, I must say a prayer or two,
to thank the good Lord for this bright day and tomorrow, too.

June 19, 2001

I used my God-given talents to the fullest, but I knew my limits. At the times I could not soar as a condor or an eagle, I flew low, as the butterflies, but I flew:

Fly away, butterflies

From the unattractive caterpillars you emerged,
mosaics of varied designs and colors, of the same shape.
Singly or in flocks of impressive numbers,
noteworthy additions to nature's charming creations.
Your freedom, as your life span, is not unlimited.
You cannot soar as high as the birds,
and your life time is ever so short.
But you can fly from flower to flower,
from plant to plant, from garden to garden.
Fly away, butterflies, make the most of your freedom,
while it lasts.

March 7, 2003

The Support of Family, Mentors, and Friends

My parents and teachers gave me priceless guiding principles:

Lessons learned

Many a lesson I have learned which I wish to pass on.
As a child I was taught that time was precious,
never recovered when lost.
From Dad, an emphatic advice: honesty must be upheld,
no matter what,
having this virtue, the other admirable traits naturally follow.
And from Mom, a gentle reminder: the golden rule must prevail,
success is gratifying only when won by hard work and competence,
never by stepping on other people's toes.
From a favorite elementary school teacher, my dad's best friend,
came the warning that opportunity would come but once,
like a bald man,

bald from behind, when not grabbed when approaching,
would not be held back.
A university professor reiterated that God-given
talents should not be wasted,
but used not only for oneself but for everybody's advantage.
And my Master's adviser's refrain that my greatest professional property
is my name,
never to use it in vain, putting it in papers, not worthy of the name.

June 18, 2001

It is often said that behind a successful man is a woman. I would say that behind a successful woman is a supportive, understanding man. I have had not one, but at least four.

First, there was my father, Serafin Rodriguez, who believed in women's capacity and competence. Of course, he had no choice. He had six daughters and only two sons. He was generous with his compliments. After reading my book Guide to Carotenoid Analysis in Foods, which I suspected he, not being a scientist, did not understand, he praised: "It is science written in beautiful prose."

My M.S. adviser, Dr. Hilmer Frank, said that the best thing he ever did for me was to get out of my way. He was referring to the fact that he allowed me to do my thesis independently, although I knew he was watching from a distance. Long after I left Hawaii until he passed on, he would send me a nice note each time he found a paper of mine in a journal.

I talked with my Ph. D. adviser, Dr. C. O. Chichester, about my thesis twice: when we decided what the topic would be and when I gave him the final thesis a month ahead of the promised date. I finished my Ph.D. in three years. My thesis was approved without any correction from him or from the other members of the Thesis Committee. A year before Dr. Chichester's death, his wife asked him why he never helped me, not as a student and not as a professional, when he always said that I was his favorite student and he gave a big helping hand to the others, who were mostly men. His answer: "One, she did not need help. Two, because she is a woman working in a developing country, had I helped her, people would think that she became successful because of me. Because I did not, now that she is so successful, all the credit goes rightfully to her."

Many of my successful female colleagues are either single or divorced. Those who are divorced invariably say that their profession has gotten in the way of their marriage. My older sister Emma has often told me that I have been lucky that my husband Jaime has been very supportive of my career. A couple of years after we joined University of Campinas, one of the older professors, a dictatorial Brazilian-Italian, confronted Jaime, telling him that he was setting a bad example for the other husbands in the Faculty because he was letting me travel to conferences on my own. He said that his wife only went to conferences with him, but was now also wanting to go on her own. Jaime simply replied: "What's the matter? Don't you trust your wife?"

Of course, there were women, too, especially my mother Beatriz, my daughters Katherine Grace and Melisa Ann, and my sisters Emma, Ophel, Malou, Evelyn, and Judith. My two brothers, Bobby and Boyette, aunts and uncles could be counted on too.

A female co-professor has always said that to her, family comes first because a professional career, no matter how successful, is temporary and will soon be forgotten, at which time, what remains is the family. I agree, adding friends, too:

Family and friends

God gave me so many treasures,
but family and friends I cherish the most.
People I can turn to, whenever I wish to.
To tell stories or share concerns.
To crack jokes or soothe fears.
To burst into laughter or dry tears.
To relish good food or take a pleasant walk.
To discuss the news or listen to a poem or song.
To lighten chores or delight in leisure.
To celebrate conquests or soften falls.
Or just spend time together, with no purpose or aim.

> Never forgetting that family and friends
> are lifelong
> riches for me to claim.
>
> *June 18, 2001*

For the party my former thesis advisees gave me when I retired, they prepared a video of my professional life, while my daughters did one on my personal life. Both were heartwarming.

My daughters' video ended with two messages:

> You have been an inspiration for many. Mom, thank you for being also our inspiration in so many ways.
> *Karen and Melisa*

> It has been something admirable to see you along the years make more out of a career anyone could and set an example for many Brazilians, other Latin American, and even people from the First-World countries to follow.
> *Jaime*

Recognition at Last

I have often been asked how I got to be internationally renowned. My answer: "through my papers." As of February 28, 2014, my journal papers had 2,229 citations according to Scopus and 2,542 according to the ISI Web of Knowledge. These numbers are substantial, considering that FST is a specialized field and citation numbers are much lower than in Chemistry or Biology. Several of my papers were in the top ten most cited and/or most read lists of international journals. Not included in the above citations of articles are my three monographs, all published in Washington DC, which are even more widely cited in articles published in international journals: *A Guide to Carotenoid Analysis in Foods* published in 1999 (cited 641 times as of 2/28/2014); *Carotenoids and Food Preparation: Retention of Provitamin A Carotenoids in Prepared, Processed, and Stored Foods* published in 1997 (cited 225 times);

and *HavestPlus Handbook for Carotenoid Analysis* published in 2004 (cited 248 times). Notably, the first monograph is still widely cited about two decades after its publication. In his book review in *Carotenoid News*, Gary R. Beecher, prominent scientist of the USDA Agricultural Research Center, wrote:

> Every technician, student, post-doc and scientist involved in carotenoid research should have a copy of this monograph on their desk and lab bench... Even though it focuses on food analysis, most of the monograph is applicable to carotenoid in general.

Of the second book, well-known vitamin A scientist Donald S. McLaren wrote in Xerophthalmia Club Bulletin (1997):

> This is an attractively produced, very well written and most informative document which I shall prize as a valuable source on this important subject for some time to come. Dr. Rodriguez-Amaya has been a leader in this field for a number of years . . . This monograph should be in the hands of all who are concerned in any way with programmes aimed at promoting better vitamin A nutrition.

However, my first publication that gained international recognition and took me firmly into the international arena was "Critical Review of Provitamin A Determination in Plant Foods," accepted as submitted for immediate publication in the *Journal of Micronutrient Analysis* (Rodriguez-Amaya 1989). From then on, one of my great pleasures has been to see that a paper or a book I have written in my little corner of the world is read and used as a reference worldwide.

I have now received many awards, including the 2012 Philippine Presidential Award *"Pamana ng Pilipino,"* the 2010 East West Center Distinguished Alumni Award, the University of Campinas Zeferino Vaz Recognition Award for excellence in teaching and research three times (1994, 1997, 2003), the Brazilian Society of Food Science and Technology's Andre Tosello Award (2005), and the Philippine Association of Food Technologists' 50th Anniversary Recognition Award (2010). My husband has jokingly told me to stop receiving awards, otherwise he would have to make an extension to our house just to accommodate more plaques and trophies. Even before I received the 2012

Presidential Award, I already considered myself a winner. Philippine Ambassador to Brazil, Eva G. Betita, kindly sent me copies of the letters of support from my colleagues, and they were all highly complimentary. Below are excerpts from these letters:

> She is internationally recognized as a research investigator who has established a record of exceptional productivity, valuable contributions, and leadership... One of the very important important attributes is her ability to view a subject in scientific depth but also with a much broader international and societal perspective. This is clearly demonstrated by her being actively involved beyond the realm of just scientific knowledge to participation in many professional and societal activities directed to serving the common good... She is proud of her Filipino heritage and brings tremendous honor and recognition to the Philippines as I have witnessed many times...

David R. Lineback, Former Director, Joint Institute for Food Safety and Applied Nutrition, University of Maryland; Past President, International Union of Food Science and Technology IUFoST), Council of Agricultural Science and Technology, Institute of Food Technologists (IFT), and AACC International

> Her stellar record of achievement is laid out: peer-reviewed papers published, books published, students mentored, honors held, and positions held. These are clear indications that Dr. Rodriguez-Amaya is a wonderful and talented scientist, a collaborator with her colleagues to improve processing of foods to deliver more nutrition to the consumers...

Daryl Lund, Emeritus Professor of Food Science, University of Wisconsin Madison; Past President, IAFoST, IFT; Emeritus Editor-in-Chief, IFT Peer-Reviewed Journals (2003-2012)

I have known Dr. Rodriguez-Amaya since the mid-1990's firstly when I was the nutrition advisor for the USAID micronutrient programme and later as the manager of the micronutrient research portfolio. I also worked closely with her when I worked for the International Food Policy Research Institute as the Nutrition Coordinator for the global biofortification project. Dr. Rodriguez-Amaya was an exceptional colleague from the outset... She showed both excellence and leadership... She pioneered work on the development of analytical methods that can be used in laboratories that range from basic to highly sophisticated, and which can be adapted to diverse food crops. Dr. Rodriguez Amaya's work has been instrumental in helping to solve vitamin A malnutrition in developing countries... She rarely takes on work for her own benefit. Instead, she uses her natural talents as a leader and identifies and pursues to the end the nurturing and development of young professionals... Dr. Rodriguez-Amaya has a long and distinguished career as an analytical food scientist and her impressive publication ecord is testimony to this. Likewise the many invitations she has had to organize and lead high level conferences and meetings and the numerous awards she has received... Dr. Rodriguez-Amaya is immensely generous with her time and never hesitates to help untangle complex multi-disciplinary challenges.

Penelope Nestel, Institute of Human Nutrition,
Faculty of Medicine, University of Southampton, UK

In IUFoST, her involvement in, and presentations at, a succession of its biennial World Congresses of Food Science and Technology and especially her role as Programme Committee Chairman for the forthcoming World Congress in Brazil have made her well-known and greatly esteemed worldwide. It is that esteem which first resulted in her being elected in 2003 a Fellow of the International Academy, then being elected to the five- person Academy Executive Council for 2008-2010 and again for 2010-2012 and finally her just having been elected as the Academy President Elect for 2012-2014 and therefore as its President for 2014-2016...

J. Ralph Blanchfield, Past President, IAFoST

Presently, I am assisting Professor Rodriguez-Amaya in her role as Chair of the Scientific Committee of the IUFoST 16th World Congress of Food Science and Technology... She has done a superb job of putting together an exciting and comprehensive program populated with researchers ranging from up and coming young researchers to world-renowned experts. This is a congress/program which will be spoken about for years to come and is a testament to her vast knowledge and experience. It is also a reflection of her reputation, standing and stature in the global food science and technology community...

Rickey Y. Yada, Canada Research Chair in Food Protein Structure; Professor, Department of Food Science, University of Guelph, Canada

The Thorns Among the Roses

The journey was not all 'wine and roses.' Along with the beautiful roses, there have been formidable thorns. Two First-world professors tried to block my professional advancement in every possible way because I was too independent and I did not want to work for them. More painful was when a former Ph.D. advisee, someone I had trained and promoted professionally and even sent for postdoctoral studies with one of my colleagues in Europe, turned against me because she wanted to be the leading authority in Brazil in our research field. As coordinator of the evaluating committee for research grants in one funding agency, she made sure that all my proposals were rejected. Colleagues in two other agencies have also blocked me from receiving grants. Unfortunately for them, two typical Filipina traits guaranteed my professional survival: adaptability and persistence.

There is a Filipino folklore titled 'Pliant like the Bamboo' that impressed me when I was in high school. Its essence says that Filipinos are like the bamboo, it does not break, even in a storm, because it sways with the wind. So when my research and student fellowship proposals were being rejected, I changed course. These rejections were evidently not technical; our research papers continued to be well received and widely cited internationally. Besides, the scientific productions of those whose proposals had been approved were inferior to mine. To be fair, I will always be grateful to these funding agencies that for 25 years from the time I started my professional career in Brazil, approved 100% of my proposals.

Now the time has come to say goodbye to experimental research, retire from the University of Campinas, and dedicate my time mainly to writing books, book chapters, and review articles, which will not require research grants and student fellowships. This decision turned out to be one of my wisest Already a review article titled 'Quantitative Analysis, *In Vitro* Assessment of Bioavailability and Antioxidant Activity of Food Carotenoids: A Review' has made it to the Top Ten Hottest Articles of the *Journal of Food Composition and Analysis* (Rodriguez-Amaya 2010). I am writing as sole author a comprehensive book, about 500 printed pages, tentatively titled *Food Carotenoids: Chemistry, Biology and Technology* to be published for international distribution by John Wiley-IFT. International invitations to serve as scientific adviser, consultant, speaker, editor or author continue. God has been tremendously generous with me. Every time a door is slammed close for me, He opens another; wider and better. All along my professional career, I stood firm even when things were not going my way:

Persistence

So many times I feel like rowing against the tide,
trying with all my might to take a step forward
only to find that I have taken two backwards.
Valiantly, against all odds, I try again to move on,
but the tide keeps holding me back.
Then, with no obvious reason, except for my persistence,
I miraculously find myself three steps in front.
So step by step I am able to push ahead.
And when I balance it off,
I come face to face with something akin to success.

August 11, 2001, written with migraine headache

My father had often told us that every experience is valuable. The happy ones can be simply added to our mental file of happy moments to be revisited every now and then for pleasure. The sad ones are those from which we can draw precious lessons.

Concluding Remarks

I took the long, winding, and uphill road to success in science and academe, but I got there. I did it with courage along with humility, determination along with respect for others, persistence along with grace, always with integrity, pride in being a Filipina, and above all, with God's blessings and generosity. In closing, some final thoughts in two verses:

The roads not taken

It is now the afternoon of my life
or is it early evening?
No matter, it is time to look back and ponder
the roads taken and not taken.
In some I found myself without thinking,
but the outcomes were fulfilling.
With others I took time to make a decision,
but in the end were not so satisfying.
Still others were uphill, rugged or winding
that led to nowhere in spite of my trying.
But now 'tis the roads untaken that are puzzling.
What if . . . I can only wonder.
A friend once described a situation so common then,
"I am at the crossroads and I like all the roads."
Though a blessing to have options to choose from,
a doubt lingers—were the right choices taken?
But on the whole, am I not content with the roads
I wittingly or unwittingly followed?

So why must I bother with those not pursued,
unless it is merely to test a dimming imagination?

January 21, 2005, on JAL flight 047
from New York to Tokyo

Professional fulfillment

Which do I treasure more – success or fulfillment?
But don't they mean the same thing?
Success is generally measured in numbers,
though quality sometimes comes to the fore –
books written, theses defended, articles published,
awards received, classes and lectures given,
projects executed, conferences organized
or attended, administration, consultancy.
Immeasurable, fulfillment goes far beyond,
a feeling of satisfaction that one's work has implications.
Using one's knowledge and findings in chemistry,
to help save children from preventable blindness,
and from morbidity and premature mortality,
and to promote general health, especially of the elderly.
Training young scientists, especially in developing countries,
so that they can do their research competently,
and science is passed on efficiently.
Helping to provide sufficient, safe, nutritious,
good quality food for the entire population,
including sustainable use of biodiversity.
One is good for the ego, the other for the heart.
One will be forgotten in due course,
the other has more lasting consequences.

March 6, 2005

Leadership Tips

1. *Be an accomplished professional in your field of study first.* In science and academe, there are no shortcuts to lasting leadership. It is the consequence of professional achievement, not an end by itself.

2. *Maintain your integrity.* Once credibility is lost, it is hardly recovered.

3. *Work, work, work, but work efficiently.* Be a doer rather than a dreamer.

4. *Working with you should be both productive and pleasurable.* Cultivate a good sense of humor—it is good for you and for people around you.

5. *Have the humility to go for lower positions first.* You may be denying yourself the opportunity to become an outstanding president by going directly to it, instead of taking a lower position first to gain experience.

6. *Don't be over-ambitious.* Don't step on other people's shoes. Give credit where credit is due for a successful undertaking.

7. *Be courageous and assume responsibility for mistakes or failures.* But get up and try again with greater zeal and competence.

8. *Decide wisely and act promptly.* Delayed action is typical of weak leadership and can have detrimental consequences.

9. *Be perceptive.* Perceive and take advantage of opportunities to move forward, but also perceive impending problems so that they can be solved before they become gigantic.

10. ***Polish your speaking and writing ability as well as your organizational skills.***

11. ***Do not sacrifice your personal life.*** Your family and friends are your greatest treasures, your constant supporters, at happy or at trying moments.

12. ***Remember your greatest Ally for all times.*** Pray always not only to ask for but also to thank God for His blessings.

A Filipina in a Word,
a Filipina in the World

Astrid S. Tuminez, Ph.D.

Regional Director
Microsoft Legal and Corporate Affairs, Southeast Asia

Abstract

*H*ave you heard of the Christian Children's Fund or CCF? This is a program where, for $18 a month, a sponsor, usually from a developed country, can support a young child in the Third World. I was a CCF child. My sponsor was Margaret Brighton, an 18-year old young woman from Iowa. By the time Margaret sponsored me, I had already left my village and moved with my family to the slums of Iloilo City. Some nuns from the Daughters of Charity found my sisters and me when they were visiting the slums and invited us to attend their expensive school for free. Margaret's $18 helped me buy pens and notebooks at the start of the school year and get a new dress and new sandals at Christmas time. I never had breakfast as a child. I had one pair of socks that I could wash only once a week. I did not have money to buy leather shoes like the rich kids who attended my school. When it rained, I plugged the holes in the sole of one shoe with lollipop wrappers. Yet I never let my circumstances kill my ability to dream. Dreams are FREE! I dreamt that I would leave the Philippines. I dreamt that I would see the world and meet with global leaders. I dreamt of seeing the world and speaking many languages. When I was about 11 years old, I got a copy of *Time* magazine from the school library. I read about New York City and the United Nations (UN). Later, two young American Mormon missionaries came to my home and asked me what I wanted to be when I grew up. I confidently declared, "I am going to New York City and will be Secretary General of the United Nations." I did not become Secretary General, but I actually worked in the UN one summer and, even better, lived in New York City for 13 glorious years. My life is a story of unbelievables. I have ended up studying in some of the best universities in the world (Harvard and MIT), working with global leaders, and living in five different countries. After 22 years abroad, in 2003 I got a call from a former U.S. ambassador to the Philippines to ask if I would work on a project commissioned by the White House to help expedite a peace process in the Philippines. That was the start of my journey 'home.' My chapter will elucidate my leadership journey from the slums of Iloilo to Harvard to 'forgetting' being a Filipino and then returning 'home' to contribute to the land of my birth.

Introduction

It was 1992 and I had recently returned to New York City from Moscow, where I had been living and working. My husband of nearly four years was then a young associate at a big Manhattan law firm. One weekend, we were invited to a party hosted by one of his firm's partners at a beautiful cottage on Fire Island. The partner's wife, a chic middle-aged woman who curated a museum, struck up a conversation with me. She asked about my education and work. She queried if I was from the Philippines, then quipped, "Are you related to the Marcoses?" I thought she was joking, but her face was utterly serious. "Not even remotely," I replied. "Oh!" she said, "I had assumed that, with your elite education, you were probably related to that family!" I laughed and walked away, saying nothing more about who I was. My acquaintance's question amused me, but also elicited a feeling that I had felt many times, of being an impostor. I had been invited to a party where I did not belong. I was showing up in places alien to my upbringing. I was feeling equal to people whose birth and life circumstances should have kept them away from the likes of me.

Childhood

I was born in a small village in Iloilo province on Panay Island, an hour's plane ride south of Manila. The village was accessible only by foot. The pathways were muddy when it rained, dusty when the sun shone. The villagers did not know electricity or other comforts of modernity. I would have grown up in that village and become a farm girl or a farmer's wife had my mother, herself bordering on being destitute most of her life, not decided to act on dreams that she had. She knew that ignorance and hardship awaited her six children if we stayed in the village, so she moved the whole family to find luck and fortune in the big city.

That big city was Iloilo City, circa 1966. I do not recall much of the first home we had, which I understood from my siblings was a rented room somewhere in the city. But, proving her resourcefulness, my mother helped in the political campaign of a local politician. As a reward, she was granted the privilege of building a home on a tiny square plot of black sand on Gomez Beach, where a small multitude of slum dwellings had already been erected. Everyone in the family was thrilled. My earliest memory was at the age of two, when my whole family gathered in the living room of our new hut. My father took a stool and a piece of chalk, and wrote "1966" on the beam above the doorway that separated our living and dining quarters. My father had brief stints at various jobs, but the one he held longest was that of tax collector at the local wet market. As children of 11 and 10 years, my older sister and I had the task of filling out tax receipts ahead of time for our father, using pre-printed government forms and carbon paper for copies, and signing our father's name over and over on the forms. The amount for the tax was always the same. My father would hand out these forms to small merchants selling fish or vegetables. I assumed the receipts my father handed out were discounted because the sellers always gave him discounts on their products in return, or gave him free pieces of fish or vegetables outright.

Our poverty was quite ordinary in a Catholic country that stigmatized birth control while regarding children as a form of wealth. My family was not unusual: large and poor. There were seven children, with me being second-to-the-youngest. Some years we seemed to have enough food; other times, less so. The worst times were when my father did not work at all. We had to depend then on the kindness of relatives and neighbors, who shared with us sweet potatoes, or corn and rice mixtures that they got from farms they and their families tilled outside the city. Our hut had no electricity, running water, books, or luxuries of any kind. We cooked on a dirt stove, using cooking coal or firewood. We fetched our water from a well a block or so away from the beach, up the street where richer people lived. My older siblings had attended the local village school, and then the public school in the city, but our educational fortunes changed drastically just a few years into our city lives. Nuns from the Daughters of Charity, a Catholic order, happened to be doing their 'slumming' in our neighborhood one day. That is when these nuns visited families, often bringing donated canned goods or used clothes, and teaching catechism and morals and values to children and adults. The nuns spoke to my mother and older siblings, and asked if there were more children. The other younger ones and I were rounded up. We were very talkative and the nuns thought we were smart. So they basically let us win an undeclared 'lottery.' That lottery was the opportunity to go to their exclusive school for free. They had just started a 'free' department for underprivileged children, and we were only too overjoyed to say "Yes." On enrollment day, a few months' shy of my sixth birthday, an aunt accompanied me to the school. She did not know my official information, I had no birth certificate, and was not even sure how my real name was spelled since she called me only by my nickname. So, on the form, I was enrolled as 'Astred Tuminez.' Fortunately, one of my older siblings later told me how my name was actually spelled, so we were able to edit it properly. I was a typical squatter child, ignorant, malnourished, and insecure. I did not know my letters and numbers. I did not know I carried a name borrowed from the queen of Belgium. I was unsure about this thing called school.

Education

The thing I was unsure about turned out to be my salvation. The nuns and teachers of my school, Colegio del Sagrado Corazon de Jesus, opened up a universe I did not even know existed. The first few months were tough. I thought 'o' was '100,' for example, and was flying high on my first quizzes that had a 'o' on them. I did not get discouraged. In fact, I took it as a challenge when the teacher, on the first day of school, said that the smartest girl would be seated in the first seat, first row, and the dumbest in the last seat, last row. After a few days of observation, she put me in the last seat, last row. No matter. I loved learning to read, I loved writing on the blackboard, I loved adding numbers. Before the school year had ended, I was in the first seat, first row. And, sometimes, my martinet of a teacher even put me completely in charge of class when she had to go out for a period of time. Even though I was only a 'visitor' at the start of the year, I was too young and unskilled to be considered a full-fledged first grader, they decided nonetheless to promote me to second grade the following year.

In third grade, the 'Free Department' for indigent kids was abolished, and those of us who were selected to remain at the school were added to the regular mix of rich, tuition-paying kids in the main building. A new arena of competition unfolded, where girls looked at my shabby clothes and plasticky shoes and non-existent school supplies, and occasionally snickered. That bothered me a little, but not so much that it dampened my love of learning. I discovered Nancy Drew, the Hardy Boys, Dr. Seuss, and Shakespeare in abridged version. I remember starting books on one end of the bookcase and not stopping till I had finished all the books in a row. I was learning to love the English language and its colors and nuances and variety. I loved grammar. In fifth and sixth grades, my favorite teacher thought me smart enough that she had me grade all the essay exams. I discovered self-esteem, generated from the fact that I was good at something. I discovered that I was a natural leader and that I loved leading. I discovered God because the nuns and teachers taught me daily about Christian living. In fact, they basically instilled the fear of God in me, effectively done with pictures of people being tortured with fire and constantly stabbed with a pitchfork in hell! I discovered speech and drama and cheerleading and biology and earth science and *Time* magazine and dissection and T. S. Eliot and, oh, what a magical world that all was!

One day, the nuns asked if I would be interested in going to the U.S. They were actually teasing me in a nice way because they wanted to enroll me in a program called the Christian Children's Fund (CCF). CCF enlisted donors from the U.S. who, for $18 a month, would sponsor a child in the Third World. I gladly accepted. My donor was Margaret

Brighton, an 18-year old from Iowa. We exchanged letters, but I never knew her exact address because it was expurgated from her letters. I understood the CCF organization's fear that donors might be inundated with requests for money if the children actually had their personal addresses. Margaret's $18 a month helped to buy me notebooks at the beginning of school, a new dress and sandals at Christmas time, and a few painting lessons with an instructor who taught orphans at an orphanage called Asilo de Molo. I felt privileged and blessed. My universe kept expanding and I understood then that I could dream bigger dreams. I began before the age of ten to think seriously about the big world outside my birth and life circumstances. I dreamt of living in New York City. I wanted to work for the U.N. I wanted to fly a lot of airplanes and see the world. I wanted to live big. It was possible, just like in all the books and magazines I had read!

During my last year of high school I had to move to Manila because my family and the nuns who sponsored us were in conflict. My siblings and I had joined the Church of Jesus Christ of Latter-day Saints and, understandably, deeply hurt the feelings of the nuns who had been so helpful to us. We never openly discussed the tension and situation, but my family was asked to pay tuition, which we could not afford. At the same time, my *nipa* [leaves of the nipa palm are used as roof material for thatched houses] hut got broken into by thieves who drugged my aunt and siblings and stole money from their purses. We no longer felt safe and decided to move to Manila to be with my mother.

I moved to Manila with no transcripts or funds, but my mother and I got a meeting with the guidance counselor at Union High School of Manila. On sheer faith and a promissory note, he let me enroll in the school. I thus managed to finish high school, getting voted 'Most Likely to Succeed' by my class. Then I received a government scholarship to the University of the Philippines, where I attended for three semesters. Subsequently, I got accepted to Brigham Young University in Utah, where I studied Russian language and literature, and international relations, on a full scholarship except for the first semester. From there, I went to Harvard University for a master's degree in Soviet Studies, and then to the Massachusetts Institute of Technology for a Ph.D. in political science. I did not spend a cent for my education,

an education that has made all the difference in my leadership journey.
Indeed, I have been one of the lucky ones, perhaps the luckiest.

A Filipina in the World

My education and work since I left the Philippines in November 1982
have transformed me from a girl from a squatter settlement to a Filipino out and about in the world. In the last three decades, I have studied, lived, and worked in five countries: the Philippines, the U.S., the
Soviet Union, Hong Kong, and Singapore. I lived in Moscow and had
the chance then and later to meet four times with Mikhail Gorbachev.
He and I even exchanged autographed copies of each other's books
after he was no longer President of the Soviet Union. I also worked
with Gorbachev's Foreign Minister at the time, Eduard Shevardnadze.
I also worked closely with the first Chief Judge of the first post-So-
viet Russian Constitutional Court. My professional affiliations have
included Harvard University, Carnegie Corporation of New York, the
World Bank, Brunswick Warburg (now UBS), AIG Global Investment
Corp., the Salzburg Global Seminar, the U.S. Institute of Peace, the
City University of Hong Kong, the Lee Kuan Yew School of Public
Policy (National University of Singapore), and Microsoft, Inc. I have
worked with many illustrious policy-makers and scholars from around
the world, and been involved in many interesting projects in academia,
philanthropy, foreign affairs, venture capital, the arts, political activism, and peace-making.

What has allowed me to pursue such a varied and global career, and
enabled me to contribute as a leader in the last two and a half decades?
Two foundational variables are faith and education. Faith preceded
my education, but my education strengthened my faith and expanded
my curiosity about the world. As worlds of learning opened to me, I
also simultaneously felt and sought a calling to do good, make a difference, keep an open mind, and continue exploring. This approach has
informed my job choices, my combination of family commitment with
professional ambitions, and my motivations for doing what I do; and
leading others. There is a distinct 'Filipina' element to the ethos that
has informed my international career: that element is the sum total of

my upbringing in a culture that generally does not stigmatize strong girls and women, and my foundational education and training by women (nuns) adhering to strict religious codes and a firm commitment to service. This ethos gelled further when I became a Latter-day Saint (Mormon) at the age of 11. Two American Mormon missionaries came to my nipa hut and taught my siblings and me. Even more than Catholics, Latter-day Saints subscribe to demanding commitments to serve family, community, church, country, and the world. We also subscribe to a strong ethos of individual perfectibility tempered by compassion and humility.

Although my graduate education was more secular than anything that came before, the fact of the matter was that I had already been largely formed as a person with solid values and ethics by the time I left the Philippines at the age of eighteen. I would also underline toughness, forged in the squatter life of my childhood and early teen years, as a critical factor in my success as a Filipina out and about in the world. I am not easily intimidated. And even if I felt intimidated or nervous or unsure, I would never let it show. I always felt like I had a core that was steel-hard yet flexible. Perhaps that came from having few illusions in the squatter settlements, where I saw my first murder victim when I was only ten years old. In my neighborhood, children routinely broke bones, or drowned, or died with worms coming out their noses. I learned early on that the world was a tough place. Self-help, coupled with faith and the friendship and kindness of others, were critical to my ability to survive and thrive. I learned at an early age that I had literally nothing to lose, and everything to gain. Making the necessary effort while also being humble to ask for and accept others' help were crucial to any meaningful success.

A Filipina in Hong Kong

Having lived in the U.S. for 22 years, 13 of those in New York City, I had practically forgotten that I was a Filipina. My world consisted mainly of American, European, and Russian institutions and colleagues. I behaved like an American, I thought like an American. I was proud to be an American! After all, I was quite certain when still a little girl that the Philippines was not the right place for me, given my lack of social and familial connections that seemed so critical for success in the country. As an adult, I was far distant from the Philippines, going back only very occasionally as a tourist since all of my immediate family had migrated to the U.S. Nothing in my work and specialization touched upon the Philippines or Asia. But, in 2005, that would all change. My husband, who was a banker for HSBC, was asked if he would like to move to Hong Kong to head structuring for HSBC's Structured Credit Products group. We discussed it and said, "Why not?" I went to Hong Kong for a day in early 2005 for a "look see." I arrived on a Saturday and checked into the old Ritz Carlton on Exchange Square, in the very heart of Central, Hong Kong. Waking up the next morning, I asked the concierge where I might take a walk. He pointed me to places on the map, and out I stepped into the Hong Kong sunshine. What a shock! I was greeted by thousands of Filipinas sitting on benches and sidewalks, chatting, doing manicures and pedicures, cutting hair, and even dancing. I was astounded! "Why were all these Filipinos here?" I asked. I did not know that hundreds of thousands of Filipina women worked in Hong Kong as domestic helpers. It was all a curious thing for me, but I did not make much of it because I thought myself an American and, therefore, all these women on the pavement were not so relevant to who I was.

Hong Kong was a rude awakening, a jolting prelude to what I might call the rediscovery of 'My Skin and I.' Soon after we moved to Hong Kong, I noticed that people, especially the Chinese, treated me funny. I took a salsa class at the Hong Kong Country Club, and the instructor asked if I was a member. She asked no one else in class that question! I met up with my husband and kids for an American Thanksgiving dinner at the Marriott, and their security guy with the special earpiece quietly but menacingly came up to me to ask what I was doing in the lobby. Later, I figured out that he thought I was a sex worker. One day, after a massage, and dressed in old jeans and a t-shirt, my own doorman stopped me and asked what I was doing in the building. And, when my apartment needed repairs, the building concierge came up with some workmen and asked me, "Where is Mrs. Tolk?" To top it all, I was going out to a party one evening, bedecked in party finery, and a Filipina helper in the elevator commented, "Wow, you look so nice. Is it your day off?" AAARGH!

I could forgive the Filipina helper who mistook me as a fellow maid because her comment was borne out of sincere ignorance. But I was furious about the insulting, oppressive, offensive, and haughty treatment from other people in Hong Kong. How dare these people think they were so superior to the women who were raising their children? A Korean-American friend gave me pointers on how to cope: behave like an imperialist snob, carry an outrageously expensive designer purse all the time, and refuse to greet anyone lower than me in status. I considered her suggestions briefly, and then decided I would do better.

Through my church, I started to give talks on self-esteem and communication to hundreds of Filipina women working in Hong Kong. Sometimes these women came to me with sad stories, asking for my help and intercession. But I told them that, sad as their stories were, mine was even sadder. I did not want them to think that I was their savior. I did not want them to believe that the solution to their problems lay in the hands of someone other than themselves. I did not want them to think that they were intrinsically inferior to anyone, including their employers. I urged them to learn to speak in front of their employers, to thank them for their jobs, and to say that they would work very hard and do their best in everything. But I also urged them to tell their bosses explicitly that locking them in an apartment without a key, or not allowing them to call their families, or not giving them a day off, or giving them a ration of only a cup of rice and a fish head a day were WRONG!

It was during my time in Hong Kong that I painfully and unequivocally re-discovered myself as a Filipina. It did not matter that I had an Ivy League education or spoke six languages or had a track record of leadership. The shallow category of skin color and ethnicity mattered more. This was, I must say, a difficult thing to accept. In Manhattan, I got used to the fact that I was just one of everybody else in my gentrified neighborhood. In Hong Kong, I was definitely pinned down as a member of the underclass. The experience awakened in me a new pride in being a Filipina, a new empathy for the hard-working Filipina domestic workers in Hong Kong, and a new commitment to carry my identity with pride and assertiveness in all my circles of interaction on the island.

I also came to the disappointing conclusion that, despite the decades since I left the Philippines, not much had changed in terms of public policy in my country of origin. Corruption and incompetence remained as central obstacles to progress. Hence, ten percent of the population lived outside the country, many in tough, demeaning or dangerous circumstances, in order to be able to send the remittances that funded education, consumption, and some investment at home. Policymakers in my home country still had not awakened to compassionate nationalism. I mean a nationalism that did not vaunt Filipino identity versus foreigners per se, but one that sought through effective and systematic policies to remove the shame of poverty and human degradation that blighted the lives of millions of common Filipinos.

"At Home," At Last

During my time in Hong Kong, I worked for a project funded by the U.S. State Department and based at the U.S. Institute of Peace in Washington, D.C. to help expedite a peace process in the southern Philippines between the Moro Islamic Liberation Front and the Philippine government. The job actually started in 2003, while I was still living in New York City. I made long trips to Manila and Mindanao while living in New York, and was thrilled to cut my 24-hour commute to less than two hours once I had moved to Hong Kong.

When I first started going to Mindanao, I knew very little about the Moros or Muslim minority of the Philippines. I had to do much homework to learn about Moro ethnic groups, Moro history, Islam, and the many failed efforts to find a lasting peace in the south. It was a profoundly humbling experience for me to listen to people on the ground in places like Cotabato, Marawi City, Sulu, Basilan, Tawi-tawi, and other remote areas. I worked closely with young Moro leaders, who struggled with their own identities as Filipinos and/or Moros, and who wondered whether they would ever live in a country that accepted them as equals and allowed them space to flourish like others. I uncovered a history that was silent in standard Philippine textbooks. I felt a great empathy with the Moros because of their legitimate historical grievances. I worked with some exemplary and truly courageous leaders on both sides of the negotiations. By getting to know the Moros, I also got to know the even deeper heritage I had as a Filipina. Colonialism had bastardized Philippine "culture" as such, but the fierce people of the south seemed to me to have preserved more of what was original and indigenous in the multi-ethnic and Malay culture of the islands that made up what became the Philippines. It seemed to me a pity that we had considered our Moro brothers and sisters as somehow inferior or hostile, rather than regarding them as part of the national fabric and an asset to the country. The Moros have a proud history, a history that is absent in the national narrative. I was fascinated to discover a whole new part of the Philippine national story in the south. Through a series of research and analytical publications, I have tried to highlight the story of the Moros, the legacy of Spanish and American colonialism, the hopes of younger generations of Filipino Muslims, and the need for Moro history to be integrated into the Philippine narrative and national identity.

I lived in Hong Kong for only three years, and moved to Singapore in 2008. Singapore, too, I discovered, had its share of oppressed Filipina domestic helpers. But Singapore also had a sizeable population of professional Filipinos in the services, academic, technological, medical, artistic, and other fields. In Singapore, I did not encounter the palpable and ubiquitous racism of Hong Kong. But my awakening as a Filipina further intensified. Because of how I looked, everyone assumed I was Filipina and knew everything about the Philippines. Channel News Asia invited me to comment on Philippine politics. I was asked to speak on panels about the Philippines. In my four years as an Assistant Dean and then Vice-Dean of the Lee Kuan Yew School of Public Policy, I had the chance to connect with Filipino students, professors, mayors, journalists, and others. Today, as a regional director of Legal and Corporate Affairs at Microsoft, still based in Singapore, and, as a member of the Board of the Bank of the Philippine Islands, I go to the Philippines on a regular basis. I work with regular people as well as members of the elite. I have reconnected with friend and classmates from three decades ago. I am more knowledgeable on the socio-political developments in the country. My children, niece, and I have launched a small foundation to help schoolchildren in the village schools of Guimaras Island, where my mother was born and raised. In many ways, I feel that I have finally come home as a Filipina.

What does coming home as a Filipina and a leader mean to me? It means, first, a change in my mindset. I think a lot more like a Filipina now, armed with a greater sensitivity to issues, behaviors, and people linked to the Philippines. In many ways, I feel less like a New Yorker or an American. I am more inclined to view the Philippines and Filipinos with patience because the country and its people, like me, are 'a work in progress.' I still wish corruption and incompetence could be eradicated more quickly in the Philippines, but I am inspired by the talent, energy, and honesty that I also see among so many Filipinos. Second, I have become more vocal about my humble origins because I realize that tens of millions of Filipinos remain in the situation that I was in as a child.

Back to the incident on Fire Island in New York, when I was asked if I was related to the Marcoses, I did not dare then elaborate where I was actually from and how I started out in life. I felt ashamed and self-conscious. But, having 'come home,' I see now what a rich and uniquely blessed journey mine has been. By sharing my story, I want to say to those Filipinos living on $2 or less a day: Believe in yourself! Dare to dream because dreams are free! Work very hard! Desire that which is good, work for that which is good, and the universe will find ways to help your own individual potential unfold and bloom. Finally, having 'come home' makes me wonder if I will ever choose to come home literally—to live and work again in the country that I left in 1982.... I do not know the answer to that, but the ellipses at the end of the previous sentence tells me that another story might yet be written in my leadership journey. And though I can only see that "through a glass, darkly," I know that, whatever unfolds and however it unfolds, my re-forged identity as a Filipina will inform what I will contribute and how I live the next chapter of my story.

LEADERSHIP TIPS

1. *Be proud of your identity.* No matter where in the world you go and no matter how high up you rise in the business and political world, do not lose touch with who you are and where you come from. Do not be ashamed of your beginnings, no matter how humble they may be.

2. *Be aware that people may first stereotype you due to their ignorance and bias.* Confront and challenge these stereotypes and show people the breadth and depth of your culture. Do not give in to the prevailing notions of the Philippines being always stuck in corruption and poverty. Be proud of the talent and honesty that also exists there.

3. *Learning about yourself and your people is a life-long occupation.* There is so much to be discovered and reconciled about the Philippines' troubled history, as conflicts in the south reveal. Get to the heart of the matter, because from understanding comes peace.

4. *Be proud of your secular and religious roots.* Many of us have a strong religious upbringing but have also worked in secular settings. Balance the two, think critically, and apply the best of what both worlds can bring to your personal development and service to others.

5. *Dream big dreams and believe that hard work, friendships, and the grace of God will attend you.* No matter how humble your beginnings, remember that your own mind is free to imagine what you can become. Work harder than everybody else. Have fun while you are at it!

6. *Education will set you free.* The way out of the mire of poverty and hardship is learning, knowledge and hard work. Take advantage of any and all opportunities to learn. In the old days, you had to have serious money to get a decent education. Today, so much knowledge is accessible through technology. Take advantage of this.

Developing
Next Generation Leaders

STANDING ON THE SHOULDERS OF FILIPINA GIANTS*

Major Amelia M. Duran-Stanton, U.S. Army, Ph.D.

Inspector General and Physician Assistant
U.S. Army Medical Command

Abstract

I have been in the United States Army since 1992. I attribute my success to being Filipina and to my experiences during my formative years when I lived in the Philippines. Many of the customs and courtesies that I learned growing up, along with a strong work ethic that was ingrained in me by my family of educators and disciplinarians, have enabled me to succeed even in adverse conditions such as deployments and frequent moves. I have been standing on the shoulders of giants, many of whom are women mentors who provided me the right skills to accept challenging roles. They also ensured that I understood I had a responsibility to let the next generation stand on my shoulders. This is why I share my experiences and teach those that I mentor what I have learned over the years. I appreciate the value of mentorship and its influence not only on the mentee but also on the mentor.

Family Tree

The story of my success begins with *pamilya* [family]. Many of the stories about my family are based on me eavesdropping when I was younger, listening to the older folks reminiscing about themselves 'in the olden days.' Many of these stories are those I heard when I lived in the Philippines especially when family members came to visit or when we visited them. My memories are also filled with looking

---

* The views presented are those of the author and do not necessarily represent the views of the Department of Defense, the United States Army, or the United States Army Medical Command.

at old black and white photographs with handwritten descriptions either on the front or the back. I come from a family of educators and professionals who have held a variety of positions in academia. This environment is what I credit for my keen interest in learning, teaching and pursuing challenges. I am fortunate to have had such a background because it left me grounded and motivated to know that I could do anything if I set my mind to it.

In looking back at my family tree, there are some things that I know have made me who I am. I will start with my parents. My father was born in Lubao, Pampanga during World War II. He was an only child. His father was from Ilocos and a second lieutenant in the Philippine Army stationed in Fort Stotsenburg (later known as Clark Air Base) in Pampanga when the war broke out. I learned more of this during my last visit to the Philippines in November 2013 when I saw more old pictures and found his small pocketbook with his address on the front. It seems that I find 'new' history that I did not know and have the opportunity to revisit 'old' history during every visit home. I know that my grandfather died during the Bataan Death March and this left my grandmother a young widow. My grandfather's death also left her with a pension that enabled her to afford my father's schooling. I was told that my grandmother was prompt in paying for needed school uniform and tuition. My father attended Far East Military Academy for high school and the University of the Philippines for his undergraduate studies. He later went to Bloomsburg University in Pennsylvania where he completed a Masters in History.

My mother was also born in Lubao, Pampanga during World War II. She was the fifth of six children and the youngest daughter. Her father was a lawyer and her mother was a school teacher. My mother said her father was the late President Diosdado Macapagal's contemporary and friend; they were from the same hometown of Lubao. She attended St. Scholastica's College in Manila for her undergraduate studies. She applied and was accepted for an internship in Saint Louis University in Missouri where she was awarded a Masters in Dietetics. I unfortunately did not spend much time with my maternal grandparents. I wish I had and most of what I know about them is through my mother, her siblings, and their children.

I am the youngest of four children, the only one born in the Philippines. Coincidence? I think not. I attribute my affinity and fondness for being Filipina to having been born in the Philippines. My older siblings were born in Pennsylvania. My family went home to the Philippines for the Christmas and New Year holidays. My family then lived in the Philippines for a couple of years. When they went back to the U.S., my parents brought my older brothers with them and left my older sister with our paternal grandmother in Manila and left me with our paternal grandaunts in Pampanga. My early memories in Pampanga were also when my sister and paternal grandmother would come home for a visit.

One visit in particular I remember vividly. I was out playing and someone came to get me to tell me that my sister was home. I ran so fast to get home that I tripped, fell, and skinned my knees only to get right back up and run some more. I was so excited. I knew that my sister traveled with our grandmother and their visit meant *pasalubong* [presents] and this visit was no different. They brought *lanzones, rambutan*, and fresh apples. Fresh apples? Wow! It was such a treat to get to eat those back then. Looking back now, it is now more exotic to eat *lanzones* and *rambutan* than apples.

My life in Pampanga was filled with family visits since my grandaunts and I lived in our family's ancestral home. We would have relatives come home from far and wide and I think it was a pilgrimage for them to come and visit their '*Inang* Celang' and '*Inang* Molly.' Sometimes we would also have visitors go to the back of the house and go fishing in our fishpond. I remember climbing trees, running around the neighborhood with friends, and visiting relatives nearby.

But a day after our graduation from the first grade, I was told I was moving to Manila to live with my grandmother, my father, and my sister. This was also around the time that I first remember meeting my father. He had been living with my mother and two older brothers in the U.S. I remember crying, kicking and screaming as they tried to put me in the vehicle to leave. I obviously did not want to go. The only way they were able to convince me to go with them was by telling me I would have the opportunity to come visit often and see my 'Mommy Molly' as I called her back then. I asked many years later why I called her 'Mommy Molly.' I was told it was because I heard my cousin, Net Net (Antoinette), call her mother 'Mommy' and that was when I started calling *Inang* Molly 'Mommy Molly.' I have called her that ever since.

My reflection of women leaders starts here and the first that comes to mind and perhaps the most significant is 'Inang Celang' (Marcela).

Inang Celang

I went home in November 2013 and saw her again. She was already over 80 years old. She is the only living sibling of my paternal grandmother. She was a teacher in Lubao when I was growing up and later became a principal at another school prior to her retirement. Her hair is now mostly gray; and she told me she does not like to travel too far away from home anymore. She mostly sits outside the house reading Danielle Steele books to keep her company. Her eyesight is getting worse, she said. It was nice seeing her. I remember the times when I used to go with her to the school where she taught third grade. My earliest memories are with her and her sister 'Inang Molly' (Angeles). As noted above, I was left under their care while my sister was with our maternal grandmother in Manila.

My first memories of going to church were when she would take me to a beautiful church in San Fernando. I remember the sweet smell of *sampaguita* flowers and kissing the hand of the statue of Jesus. I would sit on her lap as we rode the tricycle and *jeepney* with my right hand on her right leg and my left hand on another passenger's leg, and now realize how small I was then. I remember getting dressed up for Christmas holidays and visiting friends and relatives. We were obliged to *mano po* [sign of respect to bring the back of the hand of an elder to one's forehead] and they always made sure our little shoulder purses were filled with paper pesos before we left. I have fond memories of our walks to and from Graciano Paule Elementary School. I remember sleeping under her desk after lunch and it seemed every time I came back for a visit to the province all her former students remembered me for this. I remember her glass covered desk where she placed pictures of several family members including my brothers and sister. From Inang Celang I learned the love of learning, and the importance of educating the next generation. She taught me by her example that a life is well fulfilled not by what other people do for you but what you do for others. "*Bisa na kang mageskwela*, Amy?" ["Do you want to go to school, Amy?" she asked]. I was about four years old. "*Ali ku pa pu bisa. Manenayan ku pamu kang Ating ku*." ["I do not want to yet," I said to her. "I want to wait for my older sister."]

When I started first grade, I was only five years old, and I did join my sister who was in the same class. I was about two grades ahead of my age group. My sister, who had attended kindergarten in Manila, was about a year ahead. I sat in front of Ms. Malaya Reyes' class with my older sister and our cousin, Net Net. My sister graduated as the class valedictorian. I remember bits and pieces from this year. I especially remember our walks back and forth to school, reading English books at night, and my sister teaching me English rhymes she learned in kindergarten such as "I'm a little teapot." I also remember how simple life was and how much would change after the first grade. I also remember the many visits from my paternal grandmother, Eden, who would travel to Pampanga periodically from Manila.

Eden

Eden was my paternal grandmother. She was stern and strict. She was business minded and was smart with her finances. She owned a fashion school and rental properties. She was well ahead of her times. She instilled in us the value of hard work and doing things right the first time. She had us do chores every morning and on weekends. She was very meticulous. She would not let my sister get a new pen unless she saw that her old one was out of ink. We had to scrub the black soot off the pots and pans and clean every corner of the floors. We had a daily schedule. Many of the skills I learned from her prepared me for the rigors of military life.

There were also things that my grandmother did that I now know were based on life rooted in a colonized Philippines. I remember her telling us that we had to *tilosan* (is that even a word?) our nose. Basically she instructed us to squeeze our nose downward daily so that they would become pointed like Americans and not be flat. She also put a lot of baby powder on our faces for social events and formal pictures to make us look lighter. My grandmother was not the only one who did this. I know that the culture aspired to look American and that being dark had a negative connotation. We even used umbrellas in the sun so that we would not get darker.

She often sent my sister and I out for errands. My sister and I did the grocery shopping and collected rent from the tenants. I remember one time when she sent me by myself to buy hangers from the neighborhood *palengke* [market]. She told me I was not to spend more than *"siete pesos"* for a set. When I went to the market, the vendor lady told me that hers were for sale for *pito pesos*. I told her I was sorry that I could not pay *"pito pesos"* because my grandmother told me not to spend more than *"siete pesos."* Ha! A good lesson learned in translating Tagalog to Spanish is that *pito* is the same as *siete* [seven].

As I got older, I learned to appreciate her more. During my last visit, one of my aunts was telling me that my grandmother was very well respected, beautiful and generous. Another aunt told me she lived with my grandmother for a few years and she would make her dresses. My grandmother owned a fashion school but she had already retired from teaching when I came to live with her. I did not really understand what she could do with that sewing machine aside from helping me and my sister with school projects and the outfits she made for us and for our cousins for special occasions. I do not know her whole story.

I have learned that there are a lot of family secrets, some I learn bits and pieces of, and some it has been safer not to ask about. I think since I was so young when I lived with her, many of the serious discussions were limited. I was told that she spoiled my father who was her only child. My mother, however, came from a family of several children, but I really do not know much about her growing up.

I also do not know how Eden, my grandmother felt about Luz, my mother.

Luz

I do not remember meeting my mother until I was six years old. She came back home to the Philippines because her mother died. After she left, I did not see her again until she came and got me and my sister when I was 11 years old so we could live with her and my brothers in the U.S. Circumstances in our family resulted in my sister and I not living with her for many years. She was a dietitian. She was also hardworking and worked two to three jobs to take care of us as a single parent. My mother also prepared me early for being financially responsible. I remember my sister and I had to work for our grades and my mother made sure that if we wanted something, we contributed to the cost of it. For example, when my sister and I wanted bicycles, my mother paid for half and we had to earn the rest through chores and good grades. My mother had a strict upbringing. In contrast to when we lived in the Philippines, most of the family we saw in the U.S. was from my mother's side. She also set us up for success and her mistakes became lessons for the future. She placed her savings in one 'nest egg' and did not diversify. When that 'nest egg' went out of business, her savings went with it. She told us at the time that we no longer had money to pay for college. She was distraught but eventually did not let this experience dampen her spirits nor ours. However, this made it easy to decide to enlist in the military. And that is exactly what my sister, Angela, and I did through the U.S. Army's delayed entry program (we joined while we were still seniors in high school).

Angela

Angela was my older sister and constant companion growing up. Her full name is Maria Angela Eden; it was a naming custom in the Philippines to add Maria in front of the first name and write it as 'Ma. Angela.' This led to some confusion in the U.S. when they thought she went by 'Maria.' As explained above, she and I were left in the Philippines when we were younger while my parents and older brothers were in the U.S. My sister was very smart and she was a good role model. We had the same struggles growing up and in finding our places in the world. We had similar experiences living in the Philippines. My sister taught me the importance of family and the importance of perseverance. She is one of the family members who has known me the longest and this has taught me that regardless of any misunderstandings or disagreements we will always be family.

We enlisted in the U.S. Army around the same time to earn money for college, to have the chance to serve and travel the world. Once she was done with her enlistment, she put herself through college through the Air Force Reserve Officers' Training Corps (ROTC) program while also holding a part time job. She succeeded and by her actions taught me perseverance, not giving up, and the possibilities of pursuing your dreams. She later became a military intelligence (MI) officer. She was the one who commissioned me as an officer after I had completed the Interservice Physician Assistant Program.

Filipinas in the Military

What is comforting about being in the military is that regardless of where I am stationed or deployed, there is always at least one Filipina there. There is no one particular Filipina I can think of but there were numerous Filipinas who helped me in the military. It seemed that regardless of the harshness and the distance from family of the deployment site, Filipinas were around to make me feel like I was home. This was true in Puerto Rico, Colorado, Texas, Germany, Iraq, Afghanistan, and North Carolina; in every location that the Army has sent me, I always look for Filipinos and for the location of the closest Filipino or Asian market.

The Filipina leaders who serve in the military showed me by their example how I too could succeed. The Filipina military spouses who supported their communities showed me the importance of family. They also reached out to me and ensured that I was part of their family. The military has always been a good place for me to develop as a leader starting as an enlisted Private and now as a Major (officer). There have been many Filipina leaders throughout my military career who by their rank, position, and motivation have served as role models. Based on my experience with these leaders, I reflect back on some of what I want to share with those I mentor.

Standing on My Shoulders: Advise to Femtees

As I reflect upon many mentors in my life and those I have had the opportunity to mentor, I recognize the importance of having grown up in the Philippines. One of our national heroes Dr. Jose Rizal's famous quotes is *"Ang hindi marunong lumingon sa pinangalingan ay hindi makakarating sa paroroonan."* [Persons who do not know how to look-back will never get to their destination.]

First and foremost, embrace and learn about your cultural background, whatever it may be. Who were your *lolo* [grandfather] and *lola* [grandmother]? Have a thorough understanding of what makes you unique and appreciate that it will be different for someone else. Your uniqueness brings a great perspective to any table.

What I also learned growing up is the power of networking. Our first and immediate network is family and each of us, one way or another, is connected. This connection can also be brought to our professional lives. The first habit Stephen Covey mentions in his book *The 7 Habits of Highly Effective People* is "be proactive" (Covey 1989, 65). Being proactive requires self-awareness and taking initiative. Learning about yourself helps you to be self-aware. You must take the initiative to continue the relationships you have and build new ones. My experience with Philippine culture tells me there is always something to celebrate. This can be extended in the work place. Peggy Klaus (2003), the author of *Brag! The Art of Tooting Your Own Horn Without Blowing It* describes the power of "schmoozing" which according to Klaus is nothing more than communication between people by listening, interacting, and responding. Being social and sociable are common Filipino skills. Use them.

The next thing I learned growing up was the importance of resilience. As a Soldier, I had to overcome a lot of adversities including frequent moves, work stressors, and other challenges. When I was younger, I learned that what did not kill me made me stronger. I had frequent moves, lived with different people, was required to perform adult tasks (who collects rent at the age of seven?); but I persevered and my experiences made me stronger. Resilience is important in overcoming obstacles.

What I also learned growing up is the importance of education. It does not matter what your background is but as long as you have a lifelong appreciation for learning, it will take you far. My early days of going with Inang Celang to her school helped me to know the importance of education and that education does not stop in the classroom.

I also learned the importance of taking care of financial matters. Often this is ignored but your current and future successes are dependent upon how you invest in yourself, how you manage financial obligation, and how well you plan for the future by decreasing debt and being fiscally responsible. These are traits others have taught me and what I have learned from reading a variety of books.

Books like Linda Tarr-Whelan's (2013) *Women Lead the Way* describes how vital women are in leadership roles. Tarr-Whelan also provides insights on steps the reader can take to have these roles. Sheryl Sandberg's (2013) book *Lean In* illustrates the power of taking your rightful place at the table. How many times have you told yourself you did not deserve to sit there? Take it or someone else will. A wise leader once told me that if you are not seated AT the table, you will be ON the table.

Dr. Condoleezza Rice's (2010) book *Extraordinary, Ordinary People* described how her parents influenced her by what they stood for. This gave me an appreciation of how extraordinary my life story is and of the "ordinary" mentors who were truly giants and allowed me to stand on their shoulders. Who are the giants in your life? General Colin Powell's (1995) *My American Journey* describes his family's immigrant experience and how it shaped his life. This book gave me a perspective of how unique we all are and how success is not based on where you came from (he came from Harlem, I came from the provinces) but on what you do. These and other autobiographical books by leaders have influenced and taught me how to become a great leader. These are important aspects of anyone's pursuit as a lifelong learner and leader.

Conclusion

Without the foundation of the women who shaped me in my formative years, I would not be where I am today. I am a product of my strong upbringing and I am thankful every day for the experiences I had growing up. The journey and paths I have taken and the emotional rollercoaster I felt writing this chapter have provided me insights on how fortunate I have been and how proud I am to be Filipina. This fortune comes from having experienced life as a Filipina with the rich culture, community and the importance of family. Now, as I mentor other young leaders and subordinates, I emphasize to them the importance of appreciating where they came from and of embracing it. I know and appreciate the value of mentorship and guidance. It is important to share our stories with others. Sharing not only helps them but is also critical for understanding ourselves.

Dacal pung salamat. Maraming salamat po! [Many thanks!]

Note: This chapter received U.S. Army Medical Command (MEDCOM) Operation Security (OPSEC) and Public Affairs Office (PAO) reviews and clearances.

LEADERSHIP TIPS

1. *Leadership opportunities arise in multiple sectors: military, education, business, and at home.* There are willing mentors in every setting and it is just a matter of finding them and being humble to ask for help. Often, the difference in the setting is the climate for accepting the opportunities that are present. Leadership in the military requires set guidelines and requirements that you must have prior to being selected to lead an organization. In education, it will depend on your background and experience in mentoring and educating others. In business, it will depend on your knowledge base in what is required to manage different people. However, the U.S. Army values with the acronym "LDRSHIP"--loyalty, duty, respect, selfless service, honor, integrity and personal courage, are relevant in the education, business, and home settings.

2. *Connect to your roots and cultural background to remain grounded.* You must build upon your family history, and remember those who loved you as a child. You need to reach out proactively to

Leadership Tips

Filipinos wherever you meet them. Being proactive requires self-awareness and taking initiative.

3. ***Persistence, resiliency and passion are key for long term success.*** You may not be the smartest or most qualified person for every job you want. However, by being persistent in identifying your shortcomings and being passionate in taking action to address them, you will succeed. Resiliency is important in overcoming obstacles. There will always be someone who will make negative comments or will not be supportive of the goals that you have for yourself. Being resilient will enable you to ignore the negativity, enable you to pick yourself up quickly when you fall or get pushed down, and to brush yourself off and get back on track.

4. ***Take care of yourself; manage your finances, health, and education.*** You are your best mentor. You are ultimately responsible for your actions. Read inspiring books. Try to manage your finances, your health, and your education because nobody else will do it for you. This applies to anything else in life especially when you want to achieve your goals. You can point a finger at someone else that is 'bringing you down' and not allowing you to succeed, but there are four other fingers pointing back at you. Own it. Your success is up to you.

5. ***Share stories because they are important.*** Stories need to include framing the context, identifying narratives, and noting lessons. Stories help educate the next generation. Storytelling allows leaders to illustrate their intentions so that they can be understood by the next generation. Mentees want to know not only about your success but also when and why you think you have failed. They want to know your personal story about how you got to where you are. They want to experience your trials and tribulations with you. They want to know similarities between your life and theirs. They want to know what you learned along the way so that they too can learn from your mistakes.

WE SPEAK THEIR NAMES

Annalisa Vicente Enrile, Ph.D.

Clinical Associate Professor
University of Southern California (USC)
School of Social Work

Abstract

This chapter explores how the concept and practice of 'sisterhood' has influenced development, behavior and wellbeing. The author traces the importance of sisterhood in personal, political and professional realms, underscoring the intersectionality of all three especially given the multi-faceted roles that Filipina women fulfill. Examining sisterhood from seminal feminist writers like bell hooks, Audre Lorde and Robin Morgan, the author discusses the continued relevance of sisterhood as we move into transnational spaces. The lessons that can be learned from sisterhood are far from objective, but the author provides a first person narrative on the role that sisterhood has played in her own life. As the article states, "The importance of sisterhood to our survival and thriving as Filipina women is essential. I did not always know this. It is perhaps the lesson I have learned that has created the most impact in my life."

Introduction

When I sat down to write this chapter, I thought it would be a good opportunity to share my experiences, reflect, and then write about my continuing journey. Having been blessed with so many diverse life events, I knew I had something to say. And, then something happened. As I began to think about what has made the most difference in my life, I realized it was not about me as an individual, and my real or imagined successes. What have made the most difference in my life are the sisterhoods I have been able to forge. For me, being a sister is being a leader. This chapter is a love letter to all the women who helped make me who I am; all of those who have forged the path ahead, made the journey with me, or continued on.

It is easy, perhaps even trendy for me to define these women as mentors. However, for me, and maybe for most of us, the notion of formal mentorship is not something I grew up with. According to Tintiangco (2009), the connection of global to local practices and the political to personal is based on stories of "struggle, survival, service, sisterhood." Aha! It is here in this intersection that I might locate the notions of mentorship, within the broader and more defined framework of sisterhood. For me, 'sisterhood' is more descriptive of the relationships that have influenced me. Mentors are good examples, role models and coaches, but sisterhood is more than that. Writers from Morgan (1970) to Mohanty (2003) have defined sisterhood as political solidarity, shared struggle, power, global ties, mutual survival and interdependent liberation. It is important to note carefully what hooks (2000,15) wrote:

> We understood that political solidarity between females expressed in sisterhood goes beyond positive recognition of experiences of women and even shared sympathy for common suffering. Feminist sisterhood is rooted in shared commitment to struggle against patriarchal injustice, no matter the form that injustice takes. Political solidarity between women always undermines sexism and sets the stage for the overthrow of patriarchy.

Sisterhood is Personal

My mother was and continues to be one of my greatest (s)heroes. In all of my memories, my mother features greatly. We were a U.S. Navy family, my father marrying my Mapúa Institute of Technology educated mother and taking her to the U.S. where her degree did not mean anything, and then moving every couple of years. I can not imagine what those early days were like for my parents, especially after I was born. But I knew even then how tough my mom was. The navy did not provide that much of a salary, just enough to get by. Maybe it is enough for two people with a baby, but definitely not enough for two people, a baby, and an extended network of brothers, sisters, mothers, fathers, nieces and nephews across the Pacific, who are all depending on remittances. One of my first memories is being in a one-bedroom apartment with very sparse furnishings. In fact, we did not even have a bed, just a mattress. We definitely did not have a television set, but our neighbor did, and the walls were thin. In the morning, my mom would push the mattress up against the wall, feed me breakfast, and get me dressed. Then, we would sit back down on the 'couch' and listen close to the wall because the neighbor's kids would be watching Sesame Street. My mom would act out and pretend to be all the characters we were listening to. She would make funny faces and sing and dance; all to the tunes and script of what we heard behind the wall. It would be another year until I understood what Big Bird actually looked like. From a very early age, I learned that my mother could make a universe out of virtually nothing.

Even as a rebellious teenager, nothing I did would ever make my mom shift from that consistent mixture of "I know best" and unconditional love. She was not one of those mothers that led by sheer example. Sometimes, she practiced the tenet of "because I said so." She was very vocal about her perspectives, which were unconventional compared to other Filipina moms. She also never pressured us to fit a mold. We were never told that we should be doctors, lawyers, or nurses. She just wanted us to learn and love what we did.

My sister, Amy and I were very different personality wise, and my mom dealt with that in stride. Rather than pigeon hole us, my mom learned who we were and treated us accordingly. While I spent a lot of time living in my head intellectually, my sister carried her emotions on her sleeve and her creativity colored every breath. We coexisted and formed alliances in a household that allowed room for difference. It let us emulate the best aspects of each other so that now we are like two sides of the same coin, forged by our mother's example.

Our mother taught us the power of beauty. Writer, Arundahti Roy instructs us to "pursue beauty to its lair" (Zinn 2002). Growing up, there were times, when two new outfits for school was a windfall for us or when we could not go places and do things like our friends did. But, we always had fresh flowers in vases in our rooms and our hair always had bright ribbons. It was a lesson that my sister follows until today. No matter what challenge we face, my sister tackles it with beauty and dignity. When I became an activist, this would be an important lesson to remember; we are not fighting for equity in order to get even. We were fighting to relieve oppression so people can live in a better world. I did not know it, but my mother was teaching me the spirit behind "Bread and Roses" even before I knew the words to the song (Oppenheim 1911).

Auntie Beth. Relative wise, another exemplar for me was my Auntie Beth. She arrived in the U.S. when I was just seven years old. She was very different from the other aunties that immigrated and passed through our home. We always had an extra three or four people crammed in our tiny house. For one thing, she had a job at a bank in Los Angeles and so she only stayed for a while, but we would visit her often. I used to think it was so glamorous to watch her get ready, putting on her makeup which included fake eyelashes, kohl eyeliner, and of course, brown eyebrows. She read novels and quoted Shakespeare and I felt like she was the first relative who lived in the Western World, outside of 'Filipino town.' She took me to plays and museums. And, when I was eight, she drove me all the way down Sunset Blvd. and then went north on Westwood Blvd., stopping at the corner next to a sign that said, 'UCLA.' She leaned across me and pointed out the window. "See," she said, "you are going to be going to school here one day. But, only if you get smart enough." She made me realize you could always improve. I would have to work hard to get there. I did not even know where 'there' was, but I trusted her enough to believe that it should be in my future.

The Vicente Sisters. If we had any doubts that we came from a family of strong women, we only had to look at our aunts. Our aunts are among the millions of Filipina women who exit the Philippines looking for a better life. A few of them, unfortunately, are part of the group that had to leave their family for long years while they worked in the U.S. It is a growing phenomenon that is being replicated by current generations of Filipina migrants. Lindio-McGovern (2013) highlights that despite the overwhelming challenges that immigrants and migrants must face, there are examples of resistance from the macro (policy, organizing, mobilizing) to the micro (self-empowerment). I saw this firsthand in the lives of my aunts, who were about empowering and bettering their lives, but who also helped to build communities and re-create a sense of home for others.

CHARISMA. The first person who taught me what it meant to be a Filipina was a girl who was my own age. This proves that those that guide us are not always older. I first met Charisma when I started going to school at a local Junior High. Having transferred from an elementary school across town, for the first time in my life, I was going to be one of many students that looked like me. But, that was where the similarity ended. I do not know when I first heard the term "white washed" but it would be a whisper that followed me everywhere. It was not even just that I had different interests or that I dressed or acted different. My new classmates frequently complained that I even sounded different. Other than Rosanna, who I knew because my parents were friends with her parents, I did not know anyone else.

I was about to settle into a very lonely year when I met Charisma. She was my opposite in almost every way; a popular girl who had grown up in the 'hood' and who was loved by it. She was confident. Very confident. Although we seemed to be very different, we became fast friends. She understood me in a way that no one else did. And, I honestly wanted to just be like her. In all my glorious awkwardness, she was the epitome of cool. But, instead of encouraging me to follow her like she was some Queen Bee, Charisma pushed me to be myself. She would become my oldest friend, and being myself is still a lesson she constantly reminds me of.

We got into many adventures and took up the banner of countless causes. The first of these was to fight for Tagalog classes. Our school offered language classes that were not relevant to our community, such as German, French, and Portuguese, when the bulk of the student body was Latino and Filipino. There was no reason that the school district could not provide the classes and we decided to demand it.

We made signs, wrote speeches to give in front of the school board, and formed picket lines. I did not even fully understand all the nuances, but I knew that I wanted to be part of this fight, that I had something to contribute. This was my first foray into activism. And, as with most firsts, I never forgot that moment where I sailed from ignorance into action, and then power when the campaign was won.

Tagalog was a language we spoke in my house. My mother insisted. She used the popular Filipino colloquialism that if one understood the language no one could ever 'sell you.' In other words, it was important to always know what was being said in a room; you never wanted to be in the position where someone could lie, steal or cheat you just because you did not know the language. As I got older, I began to learn that language is also about those nonverbal meanings that accompany each word. There is no translation for those words and phrases that have the deepest meanings to us. For example, how could English ever translate all the meanings that my *lola* [grandmother] uses when she leans over to smell my cheek in greeting, smiles, sits back and says, *anak ko?* [my child?] Yes, this was an important lesson, you have to stand up to speak your mind, and you have to have the choice to do so in whatever language is closest to your heart.

MRS. ROGOFF. One of the best things that can happen to you in school is to find a teacher that really cares. In the ninth grade, for us that was Mrs. Rogoff. She was an English teacher who made the written world come alive. She was the kind of teacher that challenged kids who thought they knew it all and made football players carry novels in their back pockets so they could read it between practices. She used to read to us just because she said that some passages were so beautiful they had to be heard. At a time when most adults are writing kids off as "teenagers that don't care," Mrs. Rogoff saw all of us as her personal challenge. She was witty and funny and made real connections to her students. When I became an educator, I would recall her lessons and methods and incorporate them into my own teaching style, but at 15, she was the most important person to me, not because she instilled a love of learning, I already had that from Auntie Beth, but because she taught me to fight for what I deserved.

By the time I was in Mrs. Rogoff's class, I was already looking ahead to high school and an academic program offered there that was referred to as 'I.S.' or 'Independent Seminar.' Not being science minded, I set my goals to joining I.S. The program is basically a school within a school with one cohort selected every year with classes of only about 15-20. Our mostly Latino, African American and Filipino school had a small population of White students and almost all of them were in the I.S. program. It was an important program because it was one of the only ways to get 'out' of the neighborhood and into college.

When I first applied, I was turned down. When I next applied, I was turned down again. I began to panic because I did not think I could get in and in fact, was told to look for other alternatives. I cried to Mrs. Rogoff and she smiled, patted my shoulder, and told me that I would find a way. I looked at her in shocked disbelief. I had expected direction, help, anything but what I thought at the time was trite advice. The next week, she assigned us the book Mila 18 by Leon Uris (1961). The story is about a group of Jewish resistance fighters in a ghetto who take a stand against oppression during World War II. After we read this story, Mrs. Rogoff's parents came to our class and shared their own story of being in the concentration camps and how they survived. As they showed us the faded blue tattoos still inked on their arms, I realized that what Mrs. Rogoff was telling me was not to brush me off. She was telling me there is always a way if you want something badly enough.

The next day, I went to the high school and made an appointment with the Principal. I explained my situation and that I did not understand why I was not allowed into the I.S. program. I was told again about the limitation of space and so on. Instead of accepting it, I said, "I have as much right to be in that program as anyone else. There is no reason that you are giving me that I can not be in the program except for my address." Now, I was not sure if this was true or not, but I had a feeling about it. And, when I used those words, I think that the principal at the time felt that I was making a bigger connection and could cause bigger trouble than I even intended or was conscious of. He said he would consider it and after a week, I received an acceptance letter. In fact, not only did I receive one, but others in my same situation did as well. For the first time, the program doubled in size and our cohort was equal parts students bused in and those of us from the local neighborhood.

MRS. DEPASS. Regardless of getting into the I.S. program, I would spend the next years wondering if I really deserved to be there, or was there because of some quasi-affirmative action because I had raised a fuss too big to ignore. I would like to be able to say that I learned that I was there because my intelligence was too high to be ignored by everyone, but that is not exactly what happened. Regardless of my ability, there were individuals who had a hard time recognizing it. During the second semester of my Junior year, when we were preparing college applications, my counselor pulled me aside when he saw that I was filling out an application to Pepperdine University, a private school in Malibu, California. He looked at me, his sandy hair, thinning across his slightly sweaty forehead and with one finger, he adjusted his wire rimmed glasses, then looked at me with a look of disapproval in his eyes. He said, "Annalisa, don't you have any respect for your parents? Why would you waste their money on a college application to Pepperdine? It is for girls like you, that there are community college transfer programs."

Ethnographer Tatum (2003) posits that every child of color experiences a moment when they know they are not part of the mainstream, middle class, white culture. These experiences, more often than not, are negative. Once experienced, a child cannot go back to pretending her color does not matter. This is what causes children of color to disengage. I was fortunate to have another woman of color, watching out for me, who stepped in when I needed her: Mrs. DePass, a counselor at the school. Mrs. DePass was an African American woman whom I had often worked with on school-wide projects. She noticed something was wrong, talked to me until I told her, and then encouraged me to fill out the applications for the best universities. When I got my acceptance letter into University of California, Los Angeles (UCLA), she was one of the first people I called. It was a call I would make to her for each subsequent academic success, all the way to my Ph.D.

FRIENDSHIPS. Friendships and peer networks in adolescence have been proven as able to mitigate numerous negative outcomes and psychological harm (Adrian et al. 2011). Further, the presence of strong friendships especially during adolescence has been shown to offset negative factors and life events for Filipino adolescents (Espiritu 2003). In my case this translates to: your sisters can save your life. Literally.

By the time I entered my senior year in high school, I knew that I was not going to be in San Diego much longer. I wanted to move out into something bigger and knew without a doubt that San Diego would never be that place. This was why I minimized my romantic relationships, but fate had something else in mind and I fell in love. The relationship was a firestorm of passion and I was swept up in it. It is almost cliché, good girl falls in love with bad boy. Girl gives up herself for boy. Boy takes advantage. Girl ends up heartbroken and disillusioned.

I do not know when it started, but he became more and more controlling, especially after I left for college. Though only two hours away, he would demand to know where I was, who I was with, and I would have to call him at a certain time. Sometimes I stopped on the road, looking for a pay phone so that I would not be 'late' to check in. In retrospect, it sounds stupid that I would willingly do this, but in that moment, there was nothing more compelling.

By the middle of my fall quarter, I was coming home to San Diego every week, sometimes just to spend the day with him, wishing desperately that I could do something that would solve all of our fighting. For the first time, this was something I could not 'smart' or 'think' my way out of. Instead, I pushed and tried to make it work. It was like futilely trying to fit a square puzzle piece into a circular mold. Nothing worked. And, then he hit me. One fist. My face. A push. My back against a wall. His hands. Around my neck. The names he called me. The things he made me feel. Even today, writing this, there is the dull thud of pain.

My childhood was not idyllic, but neither was it fraught with drama. In many ways, it was a typical immigrant household with lots of people in the house. I believed that because no one had ever hurt me in this way, that obviously I was doing something wrong to merit the abuse. For months, I tried to fix it.

One night, after a particularly violent episode, I literally crawled out of his house and I went to Charisma. She made me tell my parents

I do not remember a lot about that night but I do remember the police, who stood in their uniforms, tall and imposing, telling me that if I wanted to press charges that I would be subject to humiliating testimony. The cop said, "You know your parents say you go to UCLA. Don't you just want to forget all this and go back?"

This happened to me before the Violence Against Woman Act, which makes it mandatory for the police to arrest the perpetrator. It was before it was illegal to bully victims so they do not want to testify. It was when the world still thought domestic and dating violence was a nasty little secret that we could keep behind the wall if we all colluded together. I bit the side of my lip that was not busted and I made no effort to stem the tears. I nodded and kept silent and the police made their exit. After that I existed in a strange kind of reality, a limbo where I wandered day and night, wanting to know how to get my life back on track.

How could I have fallen so far? This was not the extraordinary life I had always felt sure I would be living. I had not slept in weeks. I barely weighed a hundred pounds. I had taken an indefinite leave of absence from UCLA and would spend whole days in bed. My parents did not know what to do with me. And, not being equipped for such things thought I would magically come to my senses. That did not happen. What did happen was a lot of sleeping pills, alcohol, and denial. No one talks about this in my family, this period of darkness. Not even my friends talk about it, though they were there and helped me climb out of the place I had found myself in.

Maybe no one talks about it in our whole community. There is so much silence that surrounds depression that there is the ever present caution that whatever statistic is provided is an undercount because of the lack of mental health usage by Filipino American communities. However, studies consistently showed that there was a disproportionate suicide ideation rate for Filipinos, well above other ethnic groups (Wolf 1997; Eaton et al. 2011). But I did not want to be a statistic. Somewhere in the middle of it all, I realized that my life was not over. I had another life to get back to. I just had to choose it, but I also needed support. Unlike other victims who believe that they should be hit because this is the way people show love, or who grew up in households where hits and spanks were more regular than kisses and hugs, I knew different—violence is not a demonstration of love. The silence had to be broken and luckily, I had women around me willing to do that.

They reminded me who I was, what I wanted, and that love should not hurt. I could have gone back to this or another abusive relationship if it was not for these women, but they held a mirror up to me and forced me to look at myself—really look at myself and what I was doing. In the half light of denial, bruised and broken, I knew with certainty, this was not the woman I was supposed to be. I had to fight to get her back. Just as surely as I made that decision and resolved myself to follow it, I knew that these women; Mari, Lea, Rosanna, Dolly, Jenny, and Charisma saved my life.

Sisterhood is Political

I will not minimize the healing process, but I want to say that it happens. Incrementally sometimes, but then one day you get through a whole 24 hours and you realize you are really okay. It is not that you forget, it is just that you find a way to incorporate the pain into your life. It is still there, now a part of you, but it ceases to *be* you.

I did not really understand or even define my relationships as sisterhood until I became an activist and a feminist. The relations of space, feminism and solidarity are particularly sensitive to movement building (Mohanty 2003). I discovered the term *kasama*. Historically, it refers to a system of sharecropping in the Philippines that was so unfair, people needed to work together to survive (Kerkvliet 2002). Literally, *kasama* means 'companion' and during the Anti-Martial Law movement against the Philippine Dictator, Marcos, *kasama* began to have a deeper meaning, that of 'comrade' based on the relationships of those who organized and opposed martial law (Maramba 1997). In college, my relationships took on the stronger tenor of *kasama*. It is described not just in the nature of the relationship, but also embodied political and ideological values.

MILADY. I have always found that one of the best ways to heal yourself is to do something good for somebody else, or for something bigger than we are. Ironically, I would find myself back in a familiar fight, that for relevant education and again, for the right to learn our own language. It seemed that Los Angeles was a beat away from San Diego in this battle, but it raged that much hotter because it was now at the university level. One way to demonstrate the importance of Tagalog language classes was to take them. I enrolled and this was where I met Milady. She was also taking the class and it turned out, she was also from San Diego. At first, we were the two 'ringers' in the class, with much more than basic knowledge of the language. All of these things could have been enough to make us friends, but it was a stronger interest in human rights, justice, and the Philippines that would make us sisters. Milady has this no nonsense way about her that has sometimes gotten her in trouble, but more often, this non-apologetic attitude of hers just earned her admiration. The greater thing that Milady taught me was about loyalty and consistency. She never faltered, in all the years we have known each other. She is always there, steadfast and unwavering. These are good traits for a friend, but they are essential in a *kasama*.

AGNES. With her thick, black hair braided all the way down her back, her huge eyes that tilted at the corners when she laughed, which was often, and her caramel brown skin, the first time I saw Agnes, I thought she was Indian. Agnes was a nurse who had been with the Philippine activist movement from the time she was in her teens to when she immigrated to the U.S. with her family. She has an easy way about her, always taking things in stride and dealing with them in a pragmatic matter. When Milady and I were recruited into the Philippine activist movement, it was Agnes who navigated the way for us. Not only did she translate the dizzying amount of acronyms, but she had an uncanny ability to explain even the most complex things in the simplest of terms. Even when it was a struggle to be part of the struggle, Agnes was the one who always brought us back to the reason why we did this kind of work. Once she told me, "We serve the people. That is the only thing you cannot forget." This reminder was an indication of the deep, abiding love that Agnes feels towards the world. It was not uncommon to see her big eyes well with tears on any number of occasions whether she was happy or sad. Agnes taught me about the humanity in every political issue and the talent of being able to understand the shades of gray within the hard contours of black and white.

LALEE. If there was such a thing as 'Activist Idol,' Lalee would have been it. Her dark lips, espresso brows, tattoos and piercings screamed 'LA chic' but her raised fist and her Marxist analysis made her bad ass. When I met her, Lalee was working in solidarity with peasants in the Philippines. Lalee had such a good grasp of current and historical context that she never had a problem understanding the connections or parallels between what was happening in the Philippines and what was happening in the rest of the world. She was quick to point out the implications of economic trade agreements but could also provide poignant examples from peoples' life stories. There is something about Lalee that draws people to her. It was hard for me to figure out at first since there are so many layers to her that she seemed a sort of enigma. As we became closer, I realized that it was not just one thing with Lalee, it was the sum of who she was: her irreverent humor, her constant search for faith, her belief in a better tomorrow, her attempt to ground herself in the present, and her ability to empathize.

GABRIELA NETWORK. My awakening into feminism and the Philippine movement started almost accidently when I attended a conference. On the surface, the conference was like other conferences I had attended. There were workshop sign-ups, organizers milling about, and a general sense of purpose. The differences became clear soon enough. First, the rooms and hallways were full of Filipinas. And, for the most part, they were only Filipinas. They were from everywhere, and I mean everywhere; from all over the U.S., the Philippines, Europe, and Canada. Just in sheer number, I felt empowered.

I attended additional workshops one after another. It was only then that I started to understand and to listen to the narrative that strung all of these workshops together. Each of the workshops featured speakers who did not lecture or make grandiose pronouncements, but speakers who shared their stories and started discussions. I learned about Mail Order Brides, Overseas Contract Workers, Urban Poor, and Militarism. These were new concepts and phrases that felt foreign but I once again had that distinct feeling of coming home back to myself. In one of the workshops on violence against women, I found myself thinking about my own experiences that by this time I thought I had long buried. I was learning a language that could help me contextualize what happened to me into something that was done to women everywhere. My experience was not unique. And, even if it had stopped happening to me, it was happening to millions of other women. I could not just be a survivor, I had to be a fighter. It was as if my eyes were opening to the realities of being a Filipina woman. It was the cadence of anti-imperialism, justice, human rights, and women's role in society. Women shared stories of their triumphs and also their exploitation. It was the rhythm of revolution. It was the Gabriela Network.

There were countless campaigns to fight against injustice. Flor Contemplacion and her plight as a migrant worker in Singapore who was unjustly killed for a crime she did not commit was one of the largest international campaigns. This issue resonated with many in our communities because there were so many immigrants who could connect with her story of leaving to find work abroad, being away from family, and then being trapped by a system that was difficult to understand. Then, of course, was the case of 'Nicole.' Nicole was a college graduate, celebrating her achievements at the Subic Bay Free Port when she was allegedly grabbed by a group of US Marines, thrown in a van, and then gang raped. All of the officers involved were never tried. Of those who were tried, only one of her rapists was sentenced to jail and he was remanded into U.S. custody. For women like Flor and Nicole justice never comes, but that does not mean that we do not continue to fight. Because of Gabriela Network, some of the mail order bride catalogs were forced to close down and some sex tourism agencies were put out of business. Purple Roses became the symbol of trafficked women and girls. Racism and sexism were questioned, and overall, the U.S. could no longer ignore the plight of Filipina overseas contract workers (Enrile and Levid, 2009).

Throughout the years this type of work not only made me stronger and braver but it gave me a special perspective. I saw first-hand the women's struggle in other countries; different in some ways from ours, but the same in principle and vision. Women who were strangers would clasp hands and call each other comrade and sister. It was not exhilarating just because I was able to speak to thousands of people at an anti-war rally. It was not just exciting when the purple banners heralding the power of women would wave in the breeze. It was breathtaking because again and again, I was privileged to speak with women, hold their stories in my hands, and link arms with them in solidarity.

I do not want to romanticize things, trust me, the women's movement was a struggle. Real sisterhood is messy and full of drama and injustice, competition and pettiness, and even sexism, but it has beauty, too. There was the indestructible, indelible spirit of women which was the beautiful part. With sisterhood, you grew from mistakes and successes alike. With mentors and role models, there would always come that inevitable point of departure where you outgrew each other or your ideas veered in a different direction. With sisterhood, the nature of your relationship could change, but the spirit would remain the same.

When I write about it even now, I am 19 years old again, re-living the experience of being in such a charged, empowered space. I could write pages about the women that I met, women whose strength and courage were awe inspiring, but this is also where I learned the collective spirit of sisterhood. From the indomitable writer and activist Ninotchka Rosca in New York to the tenacious Raquel Sancho in San Francisco, the unwavering Agnes Bartolome, Milady Quito, and Lalee Vicedo in Los Angeles, the militant Liza Maza in the Philippines, and the countless other women I worked with, I learned that the power of sisterhood had moved, and always would be able to move mountains, whole nations, and hold up half the sky.

Where Sisterhood Comes From

There is much speculation and theorizing as to the nature of sisterhood, but also on how we might cultivate sisterhood. The discussion on which spaces are most conducive for the creation and nurturing of sisterhood is hotly debated (Lorde 1995; Morgan 2007). Indeed, even where we are able to find those spaces, we should proceed with caution as Lorde (1986) reminds us, proposing that a homogeneity of experiences and sisterhood does not exist. One must look to the intersections of race, class, gender, sexuality, religion and so on to understand how bonds of solidarity and bridges of understanding have been formed (Brah and Phoenix 2013). These are broad strokes. What I am concerned with has to also do with the basic inquiries: how do we learn to form sisterhood? What is the belief in sisterhood borne out of? As with many things, our beliefs about sisterhood can be traced back to our childhoods and our classrooms.

Sisterhood is Professional

It is unfortunate that the literature about sisterhood in the workplace is rife with cautionary tales about how women tear each other down rather than support each other's climb up the career ladder (Marques 2009). Indeed, this is why the importance of corporate type mentorship is so important; because it has been shown to have a positive impact on women's upward trajectory in the workplace. This is markedly true in my chosen profession of academia and for women of color within institutions of higher education (Varkey et al. 2012). I have witnessed in my lifetime the exponential growth of Filipinos in academia. There were only a few role models for us, and so while we looked to be mentored by these models, we also had to rely on peers. With such small numbers of us, it also meant the creation of instant community and moving beyond the boundaries of mentorship.

DR. PAULINE AGBAYANI. In the late 1990s, Dr. Pauline Agbayani was one of the only Filipina professors in academia who was tenured. She was the only one in the University of California system. She held a joint appointment in both Asian American Studies and Social Welfare. Students fought to get into her class; that is how hungry we were for our history, our stories, and our community. We read her articles and asked if we could be on her research teams. It was with open arms that Pauline was greeted and it was with open arms that she received us.

She had a talent for making you believe in yourself, especially academically. She was challenging but fair. And, through it all she had a great sense of humor. Pauline was exacting in the classroom and rigorous. She would not let you slide just because you were Pinay; on the contrary, it seemed she had even higher standards. She never doubted her students and I think this was because she herself had successfully beat insurmountable odds. Pauline's father was a first generation *manong* [Ilocano term for an older male but often used to refer to exploited Filipino farm laborers]. Her mother was of Irish descent and because of anti-miscegenation laws, they were not allowed to be legally married. They grew up as migrant farmers and at a young age, she was pregnant and unmarried. She did not get to go to college until her own daughters were in college, but once she started college she flew straight through from her undergraduate degree to her Ph.D. Because of her background, she was more than a mentor; she was a heroine.

Pauline was effective because she was about possibilities. That same optimism and commitment carried over into her work with students. Before I even graduated, Pauline encouraged me to get my Ph.D. When I wavered with indecision, instead of giving into my hesitation, Pauline pushed me into another challenge and worked with me to get a Fulbright Fellowship. After a year of doing research in the Philippines, I was ready to continue in academia. Again, Pauline stepped in and helped me secure a place in UCLA's combined MSW/Ph.D. graduate program with a full scholarship. Even when Pauline's career moved her to another school, she still remained my academic mentor until I walked across the stage to get my last diploma.

DR. DAWN MABALON AND DR. ALLYSON TINTIANGCO-CUBALES. Allyson, Dawn, and I went to school together during varying stages of our education at UCLA. Dawn and I started there together as undergraduates and worked together in the community and in academia early on. In fact, she was the one who literally walked my Ph.D. applications to the Social Work Department so that I could make the deadline. There were others of us, too, spread across different campuses in the U.S., but I want to especially mention Allyson and Dawn. It would be remiss of me not to include the two of them in a discussion of Filipina sisterhood, since this is exactly what they embody. They are an example of what positive female relationships in the personal, political, and professional can accomplish. I have never witnessed as uncompromising and unconditional sisterhood as theirs. They have impacted three spheres. It is fitting then that one of their legacies is the Pinay Educational Partnership (PEP), which is a social justice, education leadership pipeline based on the reconfiguration of identity, memory, and action that has been adopted and mainstreamed by urban school districts (Tintiangco-Cubales et al. 2010).

USC SCHOOL OF SOCIAL WORK. I do not know if it was luck or karma or just ordinary hard work that landed me at USC's School of Social Work. I decided to apply after meeting with dynamic faculty members, Dr. Maria Aranda and Dr. Devon Brooks at the Council for Social Work Education's Minority Fellows Program (MFP). At the time, it seemed like a good fit for me as it would give me an opportunity to move beyond research and engage in teaching and creating innovative curriculum while being a part of a resourced institution that I could utilize to help the Filipino American community. Once I started working there, I had to pinch myself for finding my dream job so early in my career. Of course, there are the usual stressors of a complex workplace, but the phenomenal people I have been able to work with have always tipped the balance. The great thing about being in the social work field is that it is a field that is mostly composed of women. We are a school run by strong women whose work ethic, vision and actions go beyond gendered mentorship and are leading efforts to redefine and reshape academia and the field of social work. It is exciting to be at the cutting edge and it is always a reminder of how much more we are capable of doing.

Sisterhood is the Answer

In 2008, my goddaughter and niece, Harley was born. Having this new girl-child in our lives made me re-think the way I wanted the world to be and how to work towards that world. I wish for her, and for all girls and young women a world of justice, free from oppression and exploitation. But most of all, I wish for them real connections to other women, the creation and maintenance of sisterhood. It's the most important thing that we can teach our girls.

I did not always know this. I was not one of those girls who grew up surrounded by other girls. I was like most who were raised to believe that girls should compete against each other and to believe that jealousy and back-stabbing were normal (see Wiseman 2009). This is why I am so mindful about the female relationships I have had in the past and those that are in my life now. I am always in awe of how powerful they are. Whenever my life has been the most tested, when I have been at the end of my rope, I have known that I can reach for the ultimate, never failing, always-to-be-counted on strength of my sisters. There are not enough words to begin to describe the power of women's strength. It is like solid steel melted over a pulsing, beating heart, and it wraps itself around me like a mantle of protection, healing, and providing guidance. People always describe strong women who know their own minds as 'fierce' and I agree with that definition. These are the women that fight fiercely, they think fiercely, and they love fiercely. It is truly the best, most miraculous blessing in my life to be companions with these amazing women. And when I hit rock bottom, it is their fire and their undeniable spirits that hold me up, that make my soul a little more whole, and set my heart a little more free.

Poet Pearl Cleage (2005, 11-12) writes, "sisterhood sometimes seems an abstract idea; and not the living, breathing thing we know and need and want it to be... At these moments, we whisper your names as a talisman and a touchstone; so we will not forget who and what and why we are here...We speak your names, we speak your names."

I am fortunate to know without a doubt that sisterhood is NOT abstract. Real sisterhood changed my life and it changes the world; and so, I speak the names of my sisters and invoke their power: Eliza, Amy, Milagros, Augustina, Tomesita, Carmelita, Dina, Marita, Gemma, Beth, Vicky, Gloria, Lil, MaryAnn, Andrea, Cheryll, Yancy, Ann, Keavy, Colleen, Melanie, Karen, Keara, Charisma, Rosanna, Maribelle, Rhodalene, Lea, Jenny, Lovell, Theresa, Melissa, Anna, Gina, Milady, Lalee, Agnes, Faith, Mel, Meka, Rosie, Maxine, Kat, Haydee, Melanee, Sansu, Yayen, Sally, Tinay, Obet, Liza, Maitet, Mirk, Ninotchka, Doris, Vivien, Caroline, Sockie, Ollie, Wilma, Angel, Jollene, Ivy, Emelyn, Becca, Genice, Marily, Elena, Grace, Alison, Tricia, Meya, Cathy, Glo, Mary, Noemi, Jilly, Ave, Susan, Pauline, Jorja, Diane, Carrie, Elizabeth, Judy, Doni, Martha, Renee, Karra, Kim, Marleen, Saskia, Sierra, Jazlyn, Alana, Rhianne, Mahliya, Genevic,

Mia, Aoife, Talia, Kayla, Maliya, Koa, Tala, Trinity, Nikki, Lorrayne, Mischa, Jewell, Cassie, Ace, Adri, Anielly, Ligaya, Kailyn, Harley...

LEADERSHIP TIPS

1. ***Learn how to Listen.*** Forming any type of relationships, especially sisterhood, is about listening to the needs and the experiences of the other person. For social workers, listening is a skill that we practice. In fact, we call it active listening which requires a number of steps. I will make it a little more simple: listen with your head and your heart, try to put yourself in the other person's shoes, understand their perspective, and ask for clarity to make sure what you think you are hearing is what they are really saying.

2. ***Work for something bigger than yourself.*** We all believe in something. The hard part is standing up for those beliefs and working to create real change. True leadership calls for us to be fighters; to heal and to transform. Life events such as abuse, oppression, exploitation, and other injustices can put us down and make us submissive. And, while, it is important for us to heal ourselves and become stronger, it is not enough. One out of three women are abused during their lifetimes. Every 90 seconds a woman is sexually assaulted. It is not enough to survive, we have to change the world so that women and girls cease to be commodities and targets of violence. Put your own experiences within global contexts. Understand the root causes of what has been done to you. Then take this knowledge to work for change.

3. ***Men can be allies, too.*** Remember, we are a large, Filipino community. It is easy for us to focus only on women, but the reality is we have to work together with our male allies to raise our overall community. Make sure that the men in your life are real allies. Share with them the experiences of women and place on them the high expectation of feminizing themselves. Men can help dismantle

patriarchy, but to do so, we have to teach them; we have to make sure our personal relationships mirror the world we want to see so they must be based on equity and trust.

4. *Never forget where you come from.* The thing about success is that you can lose yourself in it. I call it "buying your own hype." Don't do it. Be humble and realize that there is always room to learn and to grow. One of the best ways to do this is to make sure you are firmly rooted in where you come from, in your culture, your history, and your community. In patriarchal societies, women's histories and experiences are always the first to be erased. In colonial relationships, the native narratives are also destroyed. We live in the margins of both so it is doubly imperative that we treasure, re-tell, and build our knowledge base.

5. *Sisterhood will always catch you, so do not be afraid to take big leaps.* Some things work well with small steps, but others are best achieved via big leaps. Incremental steps may eventually get you where you want, but a quantum leap is quantitatively and qualitatively different. Whether it is a leap of the imagination or a change in career or a move to a new country, taking a big leap puts you in a different dimension altogether. Do not worry about falling—a strong sisterhood will be there to catch you.

ABCs for Global Health

Julieta Gabiola, M.D.

*Clinical Associate Professor of Medicine
and Educator for CARE Faculty at Stanford*

Abstract

I have worked hard in pursuit of my dreams. My story reflects learning at a very young age to be industrious and resourceful, characteristics that have served me well in my journey from humble beginnings to the ivy leagues. With determination, I developed the ability to overcome challenges, whether they were criticisms during my childhood or the early passing of my husband. This combination of determination and ability has allowed me to excel in everything I have set my mind to. My ability to think big has enabled me to have a prosperous career as a physician, academician, and humanitarian. Through my community service and work as an educator, I had the opportunity to demonstrate my leadership abilities and my deep commitment to developing the next-generation of medical professionals and improving the health of all the people I serve whether in the U.S. or the Philippines.

Introduction

Serving the community has always been a big part of my life. I have regularly conducted community health fairs as a professional in the U.S. and have been very active with the American College of Physicians. In fact, one of my most cherished awards came from their recognition of my volunteerism and humanism. I also had a powerful experience at Stanford when I was asked to lead a committee formed in response to the suicide of an intern. The incident was attributed to the rigors and demands in the lives of interns, residents and doctors, and I had the opportunity to promote work and life balance. The death of the intern was a painful way to consider this lesson but I felt honored to have a role in making something positive come out of a tragedy.

Commitment to the ABCs of Health and Giving Back

The accumulation of my experiences in various capacities led me to make a deeper commitment to the cause I care the most about. I have been leading medical missions to the Philippines yearly since 2009. The Philippine Medical Society of Northern California introduced me to the volunteer work of medical mission. In these trips, I organize a team of nurses, doctors, undergraduate, and medical students from the U.S. to provide medical services to anywhere between 5,000 to 8,000 patients. The medical mission is often a life-changing week for the patients. These trips also inspired my research work on preventing hypertension and diabetes in the Philippines and led to the formation of the ABCs for Global Health, a nonprofit organization dedicated to developing community-centered solutions for preventing chronic diseases and the promotion of healthy lifestyles.

Our work stems from the realization that the greatest impact we can have through our medical mission trips is by promoting a sustainable program to help prevent cardiovascular diseases and diabetes. Our two main programs consist of the regular medical mission trips to different parts of the country and the development of the Philippines Chronic Disease Prevention Project, a pilot education program aimed at developing a curriculum for the prevention of hypertension through behavior change. Through the program, we are demonstrating to participants how the interconnection of hypertension, diet, and physical activity affects health outcomes. Our hope is that we can develop culturally sensitive and effective educational programs that can help curb the prevalence of hypertension and diabetes.

My two most recent trips in response to the devastation caused by typhoon Haiyan were particularly moving for two reasons. First, the generosity of the Stanford community was overwhelming. Shortly after the typhoon struck, I was approached by the CEO of Stanford Hospital and Clinics to plan a response and I ultimately ended up joining the Stanford Emergency Medical Program for Emergency Response (SEMPER) team. Together, we ended up serving in areas outside Tacloban City and in the province of Samar that had not been reached by other multinational medical teams. I was struck by my SEMPER colleagues' adaptability to the very resource-scarce conditions and by their selflessness, to the extent that they spent Thanksgiving in the company of Filipino doctors and those affected by the disaster instead of with their own families back in the U.S. They took major risks going into a vulnerable area and for some, this also meant taking unpaid time off from work. This would not have been possible without the full backing of our CEO and leadership at Stanford, along with, the support of staff members who held the fort as their colleagues served on the mission trip. The second striking thing from this experience was being reminded of just how fortunate we are in the U.S. for our abundance compared to other countries. I distinctly remember how much the Filipinos in Tacloban and other areas lost, yet they remained calm and hopeful. They were very appreciative of our mere presence and even the little that we did for and gave them. I admire their resilience, ability to bond in a time of crisis, and determination to rebuild.

This is why the next big project for the ABCs for Global Health is to create free mobile and stationary medical clinics in the Philippines for the less privileged. We want to acknowledge that medical missions are only a temporary fix for chronic diseases and that regular services are needed in the hard to reach areas of the Philippines.

In addition to community service, I have also been very passionate about empowering others, especially medical students. I have been part of Stanford's Educators-4-CARE Program since 2008, a program which is focused on developing medical students into skilled and compassionate physicians. I am dedicated to preparing the next generation of medical practitioners, which is why I have also made time to co-author an interdisciplinary textbook on clinical data gathering written with young health practitioners in mind. This is my way of translating my hard work and determination into something I can leave as part of my legacy.

The Road from Coconuts to Stethoscopes

Getting to where I am now started on a journey when I was five years old. Imagine being that young and selling garlic and onions at a market in San Fernando, Pampanga. Or being seven years old and getting up at 2 or 3 in the morning to count coconuts, by the thousands, as they were delivered to your front yard for your family's business. Imagine learning to crack coconuts with one tiny hand holding a bolo knife or machete and the other hand firmly grasping the coconut as you strike it open with your knife and then shaving it using an industrial machine with sharp blades spinning at high-velocity. Welcome to my life.

Some leaders from Stanford once described me as being "superhuman with boundless energy" and that for me, "a moment of idleness is non-existent." I will have to agree. Looking at my curriculum vitae, I realize there's a large chunk that is missing from it as my official education and training did not begin when I entered nursing school in 1967. It was more like when I was a little over four years old and started first grade in addition to helping my family generate additional income for tuition and living expenses. Beyond selling garlic and counting coconuts, I also had to help distribute *pan de sal* [bread rolls] to different households in our community starting at 5 a.m. and then collected payments after school in the afternoon. I sold popsicles on weekends carrying a makeshift cooler to keep them cold as there was no dry ice back then. On top of that, I eventually also had to learn to collect leftover food or refuse matter from households to feed the pigs we were raising to sell. Talk about having a true piggy bank!

All this hard work prepared me for what would be a lifetime of challenges to overcome and aspirations to realize. When I was 14 years old, the usual age for secondary school graduates in the Philippines, I started a five-year degree at Far Eastern University's College of Nursing. I graduated Cum Laude and Most Outstanding Student. As privileged as I felt to be invited after graduation to be part of the clinical faculty at the College of Nursing, I had to decline as I wanted to pursue my dream of becoming a doctor. This also meant having to leave the Philippines for the U.S. by taking advantage of work visas for nurses.

My nursing education included involvement with the *Kalayaan Makabayan* (KM) [progressive student organization] that staged demonstrations against the Marcos regime. Some of our friends, both men and women, were taken into custody and never seen again. I was fortunate to be able to leave the Philippines right after martial law was declared.

After a year in Temple University trauma unit, I moved to Chicago to start a pre-medical course of studies at Roosevelt University, while continuing to work full-time as an ICU nurse at Rush Presbyterian St. Luke's Medical Center. In 1982, I graduated from Rush University College of Medicine with honors and various recognitions and then proceeded to do my internship and residency at Stanford University Medical School. At Stanford I received the first teaching excellence award as an intern, possibly the only one ever given to an intern.

I then served as a Staff Physician, Assistant Director, Clinical Faculty, Scientific Manager, and private practitioner in Salt Lake City, Utah and Santa Clara and Palo Alto, California. Today, I am a Clinical Associate Professor of Medicine and an Educator for CARE faculty at Stanford University. I am grateful for the journey that led me to where I am and am appreciative of all those who have paved the way for me and supported me. It is my hope that I will be able to do the same for many more young learners.

Mountain Climbing as a Way of Life

Much to the surprise of my children and other people, I am proud that in addition to being an advanced scuba diver, I have also conquered Mount Kilimanjaro, Machu Picchu, and even completed an 11-day Ultimate Hike in New Zealand. It seems like my life has been peppered with mountains to climb, figuratively and literally.

While I have accomplished a tremendous amount over the years, the road was never easy. There was always something, big or small, that tried to get in my way or put me down. For one, while I was growing up I was constantly told that I was not attractive enough, an 'ugly duckling' so to speak. Despite always applying for roles in school performances or wanting to attend parties, I never got invited. So from high school onward, I decided that while I may not be pretty enough for some, I definitely had the talent and intellect to succeed.

And we all know how the ugly duckling story turned out.

I excelled in college earning an academic scholarship and even becoming a leader in student government. Thereafter, I started gaining recognition throughout my career, including membership in honor societies, recipient of distinguished faculty awards, fellowships and most recently, being identified by Filipina Women's Network in 2013 as one of the 100 Most Influential Filipina Women in the World. For as long I can remember, I did not ever just study or work, but juggled both and still managed to maintain honor standing in my classes. I am very fortunate that even my financial difficulties were addressed through the scholarships I received that allowed me to realize my academic potential.

Another major hurdle for me was the unexpected detour my student activism in college took. I was heavily involved with the *Kalayaan Makabayan* (KM) and almost got blacklisted for it. Molotov cocktails and tear gas became common weekly experiences and later, many of my co-activists were either killed or raped in the military camps. These horrific acts forced me to face the reality that I was equally vulnerable as my peers and that my involvement could inevitably jeopardize my future, or worse, cut my life short. Although difficult, I had to make the decision to invest in preparing myself to make long-term and sustainable change. I decided to seek employment in the U.S. as a nurse and then become a physician. This, too, was a struggle because I had to convince my mother to let me go. The case of Richard Speck, the mass murderer who tortured and killed nurses in a Chicago hospital, was still fresh in her mind and she feared I might meet the same fate in the U.S. She ultimately relented when I promised her that I would get a scholarship for medical school.

Of course the challenges did not end there. The first obstacle I faced once I got to the U.S. was that at 19 years old, I was too young to hold a professional license as a nurse, so I first had to accept a nurse position at Temple University Hospital. Additionally, there were other hurdles to overcome, including the language barrier. A lot of things were lost in translation, or even just pronunciation, and then there were simple things such as operating a water fountain. For the life of me, one day I tried to use one but I could not find a knob to turn it on. Imagine my embarrassment when a toddler showed me how it was done, by simply stepping on a pedal! And what about my excitement turning into horror when I bought canned goods for my family in the Philippines thinking I scored a deal because of the discounted price, only to discover the canned goods were *cat food*. Yes, even educated nurses have these moments. After all, no one fed cats with canned food in the Philippines so how was I supposed to know? But if anything, all these moments have done nothing but cultivate a desire to learn and humility to boot!

However, the biggest mountain I have ever had to overcome was coping with the loss of my husband to pancreatic cancer in 1997. I met him when he was a psychiatry resident. Marrying him at Stanford Memorial Church was one of my highlights in my life at Stanford; he was in the prime of his academic career when he passed away at age 46. Beyond being the father of our children, my appreciation for him included the simple things, such as instilling in me a love for the symphony and opera, putting labels on emotions, and enhancing my ability to listen and reflect. Our children were only eight and nine years old when he passed away and I had to quickly learn to play the role of both parents.

Reflecting on the lifetime of challenges I faced and conquered, I realize that what helped me was that I knew my values, my strengths, and how to substitute for my deficiencies. I learned that I did not have to be six feet tall to be a leader or to think big. I also learned to celebrate my successes and never to view failures as such, but rather as challenges to overcome and opportunities from which to learn and grow. I made it a point to look at how I could improve each day and make sure that I had contributed something, even if it is with just one patient or individual whom I have touched. When I became a single parent, I also knew that more than ever, I had to make sure I was well enough to be able to take care of my children. I had to manage my wellness by reflecting more, getting enough rest, and exercise. More importantly, maintaining a positive attitude amidst all adversities has made a difference.

From Academia to Motherhood and Back

When a series of good things start happening in one's life, a time comes when a crossroad is reached and choices have to be made as one cannot have it all; or at least not all at the same time. Such was the case when I was pregnant right about the time I received an offer for a cardiology fellowship at Stanford. This type of situation always poses a dilemma for pregnant women in medicine because the fellowship entailed exposure to radiation from performing cardiac catheterization. Having to make a choice once was tough enough, but two times because I had two consecutive pregnancies and offers, felt almost like fate playing a trick on me. Regardless, I chose motherhood. Twice. I worked at Kaiser Santa Clara Emergency Department for almost five years while my husband pursued a post medical fellowship and we then moved to Utah, where I worked as the Director of the Emergency Department and Admitting Office at the Salt Lake Veteran Affairs Medical Center.

After my husband passed away, I decided to open a private practice. Autonomy was important to me and felt that this would allow me to have a more flexible schedule to raise my children and be more involved in their school and activities. I ended up having one of the most thriving practices in Salt Lake City, something that was not common for women physicians in Utah at the time. Later I decided to move my children back to California so they could continue their studies and be exposed to a different environment. I felt that they were confined in a very sheltered surrounding in Utah and needed to see another world and learn a different way of life.

I accepted a position as the Regional Scientific Director of Novartis Cardiovascular Division but two years later, I was wooed by Stanford to return to academic life and became Co-Chief of the Stanford Medical Group. Clinical practice and education were al-ways my passion and I was joyful to be back in my element of seeing patients and teaching, while also getting to pursue my other interests of doing medical missions and research. I never regretted my choice to care for my children first and things worked out in a way; I ended up having it all.

Slowing Down to Express Gratitude
and to Smell the Roses

I find it humbling that someone who grew up with one of the worst inferiority complexes somehow became someone who now exudes confidence, natural interpersonal abilities, and earns feedback from colleagues such as, "a born leader" and "how she does it all is a model to us." I think I can attribute that to my deep belief that barriers and obstacles are not in my dictionary, only opportunities. Once I have set my mind on something, I just lock in and do all I can until I accomplish what I set out to do.

Two of my parents' words of wisdom that were ingrained in me are "Do not fear voicing your opinion, fight for what you think is right and do not be afraid to question authority" from my father and "Work hard, persevere and do good for people" from my mother. The combination of the two I think created the resolve to go after what I want and back it up with the work needed to be successful. However, thinking about the numerous accolades I have received over the years, I will have to say that my best reward is being blessed with my two children. They are now 25 and 26 years old and doing well, my son is avidly pursuing his career in film and my daughter is starting medical school in the fall.

At this point in my life, as much as I have been known as the Julieta who is always on the go, I would actually like to stop the clock even if for a bit. I want to slow down to experience mindfulness and perhaps, just everything that has led me to this moment. My life is made up of vignettes that have coalesced to form an inspiring human being, one who is full of dreams, boundless energy, and compassion. I am still that person and for now, I think I would like to spend more time getting to know her better and acknowledging all those who have shaped her.

LEADERSHIP TIPS

1. *Get up early and start working before everybody else.* There is wisdom in the adage of 'Some are born with it, others just work harder.' Regardless of one's aptitude, an incredible amount of hard work and consistency can get us farther than most. We must remove from our minds the traditional work hours of 8-5 and dedicate whatever time necessary to get us to where we want.

2. *Delete the words 'obstacle' and 'failure' from your dictionary.* We should see only the opportunities in any given situation and put our resourcefulness to work in order to accomplish what we set out to do. We do not have to be six feet tall to be a leader or to think big. Failures are opportunities to learn and simply another challenge to overcome. We must always celebrate successes big and small.

3. *Take the time to reflect every day.* It is important to ground ourselves in values and priorities and make sure that they are aligned with the effort and time we invest in our actions. This includes knowing when to sacrifice certain things and be confident that while we can not have everything at one time, we can accomplish a lot of things at various points in our life. We must also always look at how we could improve each day and what we have done to make a difference for others.

4. *Focus on your strengths, abilities, and the ultimate goal.* Listening to constructive feedback is crucial to progress, but ignoring sheer negativity and criticisms is even more important. All of us have our differences and it is important that we leverage our strengths and abilities and continue developing them because they will get us to where we want to go.

5. *Serve.* All that we do must matter and there is no better way in doing that than by addressing the needs of society and preparing the next generation of people who will continue the work. Find a cause you are passionate about, can dedicate yourself to and win others to work alongside you.

LETTER TO A YOUNG FILIPINA

So you are looking to the future, to find out how your God-given talents can bring fulfillment to self and to your community? And you are feeling a drive towards science, discovery, and teaching others? May I share with you the lessons I learned having taken that path.

My career goal was to be an independent scientific investigator—in practical terms, the head of my own research laboratory in an academic setting. My assets included the strength of my Filipino cultural background, loyal and generous support of family, habits of discipline, training in logical thinking, and hopeful perseverance inculcated by my mentors, the sisters of St. Theresa's College in Manila. My obstacles were the other side of the coin, including the limitations imposed by a sheltered education at a Catholic college, and my minority status in the U.S. as a Filipina woman.

My goal was to achieve full Professor status at Columbia University in New York. The journey to that end carried the thrills of inquiry and discovery. Nevertheless, it demanded social and interpersonal skills, including effectively connecting with local and global colleagues, and connecting with my own staff. I had to invest time and focused energy to disseminate my work through publications, to speak to large and small groups at conferences and to addressthe special needs of international audiences. Mentoring of students was also a professional requirement. It felt like I was always at work.

Along the way I enjoyed friendships with like-minded and like-spirited colleagues, friendships that transcended nationality, geography, religion, politics, and race. Ultimately, there came joys and satisfactions in the knowledge of having made contributions to a community, and to humanity.

My journey as a Filipino woman in academia required patience and perseverance. Perhaps the largest obstacle was discrimination, mainly based on race. Some of the discrimination was subtle, probably even unrecognized as discrimination by the perpetrator. There were overt instances, too.

It was during my first year as an Assistant Professor at Columbia University. I had finished my post-doctoral fellowship. In a prior job, I had been Project Director of a smoking and lung cancer study and published several research papers on the topic. At Columbia, smoking cessation groups were just beginning to be offered to employees. Because of my background in tobacco and nicotine science, I was asked to give a talk on smoking and health to an employee group. It would be at 1 P.M. in a conference room on the first floor, main building. So at 1 P.M., I knocked on the closed conference room door. It was opened by one of the attendees who looked at me and said, "I am sorry, you are in the wrong room." Well, I informed her, "I am Dr. Covey, I am the guest speaker today." Of course, embarrassed, she let me in, and, the rest is, as they say, history.

To me, the lesson learned was that whether it is higher education or not, and the ivory tower nature of my work- place notwithstanding, my ethnicity, my brown-ness, is an initial assessment factor. It could hold me back, as that lady decided, incorrectly, that I did not belong in the room. But this can happen only if I let it. Color is skin deep. Achievement is rooted beneath the surface of color. Its composition is some talent, a modicum of luck, and, predominantly, hard work. So dream, young friend, then work it. Let it happen. Those university halls are waiting for you.

All the best,

Lirio Sobreviñas-Covey

Lirio Sobreviñas-Covey, PhD
Professor of Clinical Psychology in Psychiatry
Columbia University Medical Center
Research Scientist VI
New York State Psychiatric Institute
New York, NY, USA
Founder and President
Association of Adults with Autism Philippines, Inc.
http://adultautismphil.wordpress.com

Synthesis

Maria Africa Beebe, Ph.D.

*T*he leadership of global Filipina women comes in many forms that share important characteristics. The reflections of Filipina women who have successfully exercised leadership throughout the world provide insight into their diversity and shared values. This chapter is designed to highlight and celebrate their successes while summarizing and analyzing themes from their stories. At the end of the chapter, special attention is given to a synthesis of their leadership tips based on the themes. This synthesis of leadership tips is a good reminder of the rationale behind this book, which is the development of the next generation of Filipina women leaders.

The themes concerning leadership discussed below are based on the nuanced stories of the Global FWN100™ awardees. A sample of statements from their rich stories provides the context for the themes and calls attention to the women's deep and nuanced understanding of their individual journeys.

Imelda Cuyugan described leaders as having personal characteristics that "demand respect and trust from people" and are based on "integrity," and their ability to "carry" themselves in meetings. Imelda continued: "it's easy to just be quick on your feet and speak, but I think it's always good to be thoughtful first, before you say something, especially on very, very important issues."

Astrid Tuminez made a distinction between success and significance. She implored leaders to leave a "legacy of significance" where "the most important thing is how we treat people on a day-to-day basis—whether we are able to inspire, and also execute on a day-to-day basis, where people can believe in us and know that we are authentic, that we are real, that we care."

Lucille Tenazas noted that women leaders from the Philippines are a "product of our culture," and generally do not "declare" themselves "as leaders." Lucille contrasted leaders "with a loud voice... [who] bang their fists on the table or the podium" with "soft leadership, which is much more nuanced and it's really about providing a vision and being a model." She added: "I feel like I belong to that category."

Lirio Sobreviñas-Covey argued that "an important leadership quality is to be real, to be authentic, and to respect the people whom you are leading. But in front of that, I think authenticity is the most important thing. It engenders people's respect for you and trust in you."

Leadership Themes

The themes suggest that the Global FWN100™ honorees practice a flexible and adaptive approach to leadership. As a possible metaphor, Annette M. David suggested *halo-halo*, a traditional snack made of shaved ice with many different and often unexpected toppings. *Halo-halo*, like the leadership of global Filipina women is quintessentially Filipino because it is a mixture of different things that create something new that is better than the sum of its ingredients, something unique and great. According to Evelia Religiosa, Filipinas are very adaptable and resilient. You can "throw them in the water and they will easily adjust to the water."

While some of the awardees' leadership practices are consistent with models described in the literature, especially Exemplary Leadership associated with Kouzes and Posner (2000) and Filipino Leadership associated with Cuyegkeng and Palma-Angeles (2011), these models do not fully reflect the reality of Filipina women leadership practices that have spanned geographic and cultural boundaries. Possible explanations include the impact of Philippine culture, especially the unique understandings of relationships, virtues, motivations, and global experiences.

The chapters in this book present a range of perspectives of global Filipina women on the meaning of leadership. Their status as "global" is variously based on their organizations' global focus (Mendenhall

2013), workforce composition (Adler 1997), new home base (Spreitzer 1997), organizational goals (Caligiuri 2006), and corporate services (Brake 1997, Gregersen 1998). Global Filipina women leaders appear to demonstrate flexible leadership, defined as the ability to adjust "one's leadership style, method, or approach in response to different or changing contextual demands in a way that facilitates group performance" (Kaiser and Overfield 2010, 106).

Although there is no 'typical' global Filipina leader, the women profiled here embrace and personify themes that they consider important and that appear to guide their leadership. These themes are:

1. Relationships in Filipino culture, as rooted in *kapwa*.
2. Character strengths, values and virtues in ethical decision-making.
3. Having a sense of purpose and meaning and responding to a call.
4. Knowing and transforming oneself.
5. Exceeding expectations.
6. Leading for impact.
7. Giving back.

Theme One: Relationships in Filipino Culture, as rooted in Kapwa

When asked what "family custom or tradition you would like to pass on to others," the Global FWN100™ gave the following answers: respect, humility, helping, caring, collaboration, generosity, solidarity, hospitality, reciprocity, connecting, eating together, and, in Tagalog, *kapwa* [shared humanity], *bayanihan* [cooperative undertaking], *malasakitan* [solicitude], and *pakikisama* [fellowship]. All of these terms suggest or describe aspects of relationships among people. For many of these Filipina women, relationships that begin with family are extended to *pagmamalasakit sa kapwa* [being solicitous].

Respect for family and others was mentioned frequently, especially respect for the elderly, demonstrated by *mano po* [the younger person holding the hand of the older person to the younger person's forehead to show respect]. The gesture also demonstrates humility. Global FWN100™ honorees discussed gaining the respect of peers (Maria Almia delos Santos), gaining the respect of students (Dawn Bohulano Mabalon), gaining the respect of others in the workplace (Bella Aurora Belmonte), gaining the respect that one rightfully deserves (Isabelita Manalastas-Watanabe), and maintaining respect while going head-to-head with a diverse set of colleagues (Jocelyn Ding).

Marife Zamora identified one of her functions as the head of an organization as "keeping the family together." Carmencita Padilla referred to her colleagues as "family" when explaining that community was a factor in her professional development. Nina Aguas defined Filipina leadership as working with compassion and using "the Filipina heart," along with the mind, in interpersonal relations.

All of the statements made by these women describe aspects of relationships, whether vertical, as in showing respect and appreciation, or horizontal, as in signifying reciprocal relationships.

Enriquez (1989) claimed that *kapwa* is the core concept from which other relational Filipino values emanate. According to Enriquez, *kapwa* helps explain Filipino interpersonal behavior based on differentiating insiders [*hindi ibang tao*] from outsiders [*ibang tao*] and the different levels of interaction associated with differentiating insiders from outsiders. Different levels of interaction include the degree of civility [*pakikitungo*], level of oneness [*pakikiisa*], and degree of sensitivity [*pakikiramdam*]. Enriquez posited that *kapwa* is the unity of the "self" and "others" and, unlike the English concept of "others" that is used in opposition to the "self," *kapwa* is a "recognition of shared identity, an inner self shared with others" (34). (See Guevarra [2005] for a more nuanced definition when *kapwa* becomes *pakikipagkapwa*.)

Kouzes and Posner (2003) stated that "leadership is a relationship" and that leadership is a reciprocal connection between those who choose to lead and those who decide to follow (1). Uhl-Bien's (2006) concept of "relational leadership" that locates leadership in a jointly constructed social process and Follett's (1949) concept of "reciprocal control," a form of control that is not coercive but rather "a coordinating of all functions, that is, a collective self-control" (226) are especially relevant to how leadership is understood by the

Global FWN100™ and are consistent with the Filipino value of *kapwa*. Filipina women's early childhood socialization tends to focus on the social relations that shape the individual's identity. Thus, being mindful of different levels of relationships needed to exercise relational leadership comes naturally to most Filipina women.

Roffey (1999) noted "Filipina business leaders saw their roles as including a sense of personal responsibility for the social and psychological well-being of their employees" (392).

Theme Two: Character Strengths, Values and Virtues in Ethical Decision-Making

The stories of the Global FWN100™ provide evidence of the role of character and values in the women's ethical decision making. The character and values are core traits, or specific virtues identified by these women. The term "virtue" was defined by Villegas (2011) as "a habit that endows a person with the strength of will to carry out, despite difficulties or obstacles, his obligation to do what is good and right" (x). Character strengths, values, and virtues are also central to *Theme Four* concerning knowing and transforming oneself. While present in all the narratives, the theme of ethical decision making as central to leadership was especially prominent in the accounts of the two global Filipina women who are officers in the U.S. military. Both women referred to different acronyms that spell out what value-based leadership means.

Amelia Duran Stanton stated that for her, "the acronym LDRSHIP reflects the key values of Loyalty, Duty, Respect, Selfless service, Honor, Integrity, and Personal courage." Shirley Raguindin offered an acronym she learned in a diversity leadership training program: "RESPECT for Resilience, Excellence, Strength, Passion, Empathy, Courage, and Tenacity."

Personal values provided the moral compass which informed several of the Global FWN100™ that it was time to leave a situation when personal principles were being compromised. Despite being heartbroken about leaving her high school students, Janet Stickmon reported she listened to her "conscience" when she quit working for an institution that she felt undermined her values.

The Time Capsule activity for the 2013 Global awardees made it possible to code the words they used to describe their leadership. Two hundred fourteen words were coded as character strengths, values, and virtues; they were then clustered into the categories of humanity, transcendence, wisdom and knowledge, courage, temperance, and justice. These clusters of values correspond to the Values in Action (VIA) classification that is the basis for positive psychology (Peterson and Seligman 2004).

A number of the Global FWN100™ awardees used words associated with humanity included family, community, love, kindness, care, nurturance, and social intelligence. Words related to transcendence included belief, fun, happiness, hope, faith, religiosity, spirituality, success, purposefulness, and prayer. Wisdom and knowledge words included advice, choice, interest in the world, seeing, love of learning, change, culture, and creativity.

According to Crossan, Mazutiz, and Siejts (2013) virtues are the mean or middle between two extremes. Thus, courage is the mean or middle way between too much courage (impulsive) or too little courage (risk avoidance). Leadership requires finding the mean that is neither an excess nor a deficiency of the virtue in question. "Deficiency" and "Excess," headings of columns in Table 1, are words for virtues identified by Crossan, Mazutiz, and Siejts (2013). The words used by the Global FWN100™ awardees associated with virtues are shown in the column identified as "BALANCE." Finding the balance or middle way associated with character strengths, values, and virtues was a topic interwoven in many of the women's stories of leadership, and especially in their stories of what it meant to be their very best. These values and virtues are inculcated early on by Filipino families, extended kin, and community.

Theme Three: Having a Sense of Purpose and Meaning and Responding to a Call

In their responses to the question about their life philosophy, the Global FWN100™ made extensive reference to responding to a "call" and the importance of having meaning in and passion for what one does. They used terms such as having a sense of limitless

TABLE I: Character strengths defined by deficiency and excess by Crossan, Mazutis, and Seijts, with the BALANCE defined by words used by the Global FWN100™ awardees.

VIRTUE	DEFICIENCY	BALANCE	EXCESS
Humanity	Unfeeling	Compassion	Indulgent
	Socially awkward	Social Intelligence	Manipulative
	Harsh	Loving-kindness	Obsequious
	Stingy	Generosity	Profligate
Transcendence	Hopeless	Hope	Foolishness
	Spiritlessness	Spirituality	Fundamentalism
	Ungrateful	Thankfulness	Suppliant Behavior
Wisdom	Apathy	Love of Learning	Obsessiveness
	Unoriginal	Creative	Impracticality
	Closed mindedness	Seeking Advice	Lack of judgment
Courage	Laziness	Stick-to-it-iveness	Zealot
	Apathy	Passion	Lust
	Inauthenticity	Integrity	Righteousness
Temperance	Sloth	Balance	Inflexible
	Boastful	Humility	Self-deprecation
		Modesty	
Justice	Lack of confidence	Leadership	Dictatorship
	Unjust	Justice	Undiscerning

Based on Crossan, Mazutis, and Seijts (2013, 574)

possibilities, dreaming the impossible dream, and challenging oneself beyond imagination. For some of the FWN Global 100™ it was their faith, religion, and spirituality that provided their sense of purpose.

Bella Aurora Belmonte wrote "I am visionary, passionate about the Lord, and live a principle-centered and purpose-driven life." She continued, "This philosophy...guided me not only in my personal life, but also in my business dealings, as well as in serving my church and community services throughout my life."

Tess Mauricio indicated that she firmly believes "God has a plan." Voicing the same sentiment, Carmencita David -Padilla explained that in God's plan "there is purpose for every person in this world," and that we "can help shape the future, but only plans that are shaped with the guidance of God will reach perfection."

Dawn Bohulano Mabalon stated that "Everything happens for a reason, and you must be always prepared and thankful for the blessings and challenges that *Bathala*/God/Goddess puts in your path."

Mary Ann Lucille L. Sering referred to the need to think in terms of not just a decade, but a hundred years, with all of her efforts geared toward the benefit of future generations. Imelda Nicolas spoke of "a spiritual journey where you will discover what you are capable of achieving." For Janet Susan Nepales, "Nothing is impossible if you put your heart and soul into it and walk with God."

Maria Almia delos Santos, a spiritual director at a hospice facility, spoke of staying attuned constantly to both the physical and spiritual needs and expressions of her clients. Lirio-Sobreviñas-Covey talked about how "life and work are closely intertwined." For Lirio: "Happiness and a sense of fulfillment in your chosen work are crucial to living a long and satisfying life. It is a tragedy to engage in work that one does not love."

Some leaders, like Regina Manzana-Sawhney, simply have a desire to make the world a better place combined with a strong sense of "Why not?" Loisa Cabuhat noted that "seeing the happy faces of my clients purchasing their first home made me realize that I can make a client's dream come true and this led me to a wonderful career." Isabelita Manalastas-Watanabe spoke of the need to "share with others the blessings you receive." Marife Zamora recalled that she imbibed from her parents "a very deep commitment to do something in the world—and that is to always do a good deed for others." Annette David argued for the necessity "to always begin with the need in mind. Give it your best shot, then let go and let destiny take over."

Meriam Reynosa offered her guiding principles: "Be a voice to the voiceless, be a champion for the most vulnerable, fight with tenacity, forever be humble, forgive when it seems impossible and love always with never-ending joy."

Librada C. Yamat stated: "Life is what you make it. Don't pray for an easy life, pray to be a stronger person." She further stated that she relied on "prayer to provide the inner strength to cope and face the challenges of life."

These statements expressed by the FWN Global 100™ honorees are consistent with the concept of "calling" that according to Hunter, Dik, and Banning (2010) "embraces a sense of purpose and meaning, referencing or recognizing God, passion, and/or giftedness as motivating sources." Although some of these leaders recognize a divine call to serve God or a transcendent summon, other leaders depend upon an internal search for meaning and purpose that comes through self-reflection and meditation. This non-transcendent call is what Astin, Astin, and Lindholm (2011) referred to as knowing oneself at a deeper level and what Levinson (1986) called a person's life dream. The discussion of call and purpose by the FWN Global 100™ Filipina women appears to be consistent with Kouzes and Possner's (2007) "inspired shared vision." Kouzes and Possner described a situation in which an individual commits to "envisioning the future by imagining exciting and ennobling possibilities and enlist others in a common vision by appealing to shared aspirations" (26).

Theme Four: Knowing and Transforming Oneself

References to self-awareness and personal transformation were present throughout the responses of the Global FWN100™, but were especially obvious in their discussion of "turning points" in their professional life, and of their education and career choices. These Filipina women obviously were aware of their personal interests and passions, strengths, styles, and identities. They made extensive use of words like self-awareness, self-examination, self-improvement, self-reliance, self-confidence, self-expression, self-respect, self-trust, and self-esteem.

All the awardees had the experience of overcoming barriers, often related to poverty, social class, and discrimination based on gender, skin color, sexual orientation, culture, and language.

Astrid Tuminez reported that she was "born in a village and then raised in the city slums of Iloilo." Astrid noted: "I left the Philippines because I was so poor and I knew my opportunities were elsewhere." Several of those who grew up in the U.S. talked about negative experiences with schooling in the U.S. Regina Manzana-Shawney recalled: "We were all the same until I was told I could not audition for

Annie as a child because I wasn't white." For Allyson Tintiangco-Cu-bales, "Experience in school was both traumatic and disengaging." Teaching history to American students, Dawn Bohulano Mabalon de-scribed the first week as "always a continual challenge to push students to think beyond racist, age-ist, and gendered stereotypes."

Isabelita Manalastas-Watanabe, who is based in Japan, bemoaned that much needs to be changed in Japan "for women to achieve an equal status with men, in the work place." She contended that Filipi-na women are stereotyped as entertainers, adding: "The Japanese na-tionals are many times surprised that a woman, and a Filipina at that, can be the *shacho* [president] of a company in Japan." This sentiment was echoed by Patricia Gallardo-Dwyer who is based in Hong Kong. Gallardo observed: "Boardrooms are (still) not used to having strong Asian women who are well-versed in business, management, and their craft; and are as ballsy as their male counterparts." Mary Jane Alve-ro-Al Mahdi averred: "Working in a multi-cultural male dominated in-dustry was not easy for me at the start of my career in the United Arab Emirates due to gender discrimination."

Bella Aurora Belmonte reported feeling that she was being discriminated against, or that her abilities were "underestimated because I was a woman of color, inexperienced, and young." She re-called being greeted with questions like "What are you doing here?" or "Where's your 'boss'?" Gloria T. Caoile's coworker asked her why she, a foreigner, had been promoted over her co-worker to which she responded, "BECAUSE I AM THE MOST QUALIFIED" (emphasis in the original). Whereupon Gloria immediately gave her coworker a digni-fied, educated lesson on work ethics, race/gender issues, and offered to transfer her to another department if she felt strongly about NOT accepting the choice of the Company President. Gloria T. Caoile re-called admonishing the woman: "Being different from does not mean less than."

For several of the Global FWN100™ awardees, the sudden deaths of a loved one was a major turning point in their lives. What characterized these women as leaders was their ability to move on. "The pain of losing my loved one is always and will be always in my heart," explained Ernestina de los Santos-Mac. However, she noted "leadership also means extricating oneself from a seemingly hopeless situation, getting up, and moving on." Although resilience is valued, several of the awardees were explicit in asserting that even more important than being able to endure hardship is the ability to transform oneself in response to the hardship.

The commitment to continuous learning, personal development, and improvement was a recurring theme. Examples included seeking out non-traditional education, specializing in a new field, and learning from failures. Patricia Gallardo-Dwyer, who incorporated sustainable practices in a luxury hotel market where clients tended to value their high-end lifestyle over the environment, offered an example of continuous learning. She described being compelled to become an expert in sustainable practices.

The high value placed on education as a means of personal transformation was reflected in numerous responses, including that of Maria Beebe, one of the editors, who called her Ph.D. her "clout" card. "I migrated to the U.S. in 1985," recalled Imelda Cuyugan "to pursue my masters in public administration and seek the American dream of pursuing a good education and to be a career woman." Emma Cuenca pursued her doctoral degree to develop the competencies necessary to produce new knowledge and translate it to clinical practice. Emma made this decision at the same time that she was diagnosed with cancer and explained she would "not allow cancer to take over" her life.

These Filipina women leaders are able to transcend and go beyond their circumstances of birth or disruptions—whether those were the results of immigration or race, gender, and cultural barriers or other background factors. They were able to claim their personal identity through being self-aware. Self-awareness is a "measure of the person's ability to be truly conscious of the components of the self and to observe it accurately and objectively" and is one element in the development of a person's identity for leadership (Hall 2008, 154). Hall argued that minority women have to be "super-people to attain good opportunities for a good job and advancement" (Hall 2008, 157). The message from these leaders is that life's rewards are within a person's control and that helplessness, dependency, apathy, anger, and self-hate that may arise from barriers can be mitigated. Strategies they used to mitigate negative circumstances included learning continuousy and, as explained in *Theme 2*, being mindful of one's values and strengthening one's character. This aspect of leadership excellence through internal dialogue also builds on the eight types of intelligence as defined by Gardner (1983), which includes intrapersonal intelligence gathered through introspection and self-reflection.

Theme Five: Exceeding Expectations

Where *Theme Four* focuses on personal changes and transforming the self, *Theme Five* focuses on a willingness to be the first Filipina woman in a given field, sometimes exceeding expectations for what is considered appropriate for a Filipina woman minority and using leadership roles to significantly change organizations and policies. Notable examples of Filipina women who were the first in their roles include Cora Manese Tellez, first Filipina woman to "break through the glass ceiling" with her appointment as president and CEO of a Fortune 100 company, Health Net; Cris Comerford, first Filipina woman to be appointed executive chef in the U.S. White House; Michele Bumgarner, first Filipina woman racecar driver in the Philippines and the United States; Carmen Zita-Lamagna, first Filipina woman to become a vice-chancellor of an American international university; Lirio Sobreviñas-Covey, first Filipina to be appointed a full professor in the Columbia University Faculty and to be awarded a multi-million research grant from the National Institutes of Health-National Institute for Drug Abuse; Loida Nicolas Lewis, first Filipina woman to pass the New York bar without having attended law school in the United States; Mary Jane Alvero-Al Mahdi, first Filipina woman to be appointed CEO of an international geosciences testing laboratory; Loisa Cabuhat, first Filipina woman to be recognized as the realtor of the year for a geographical area larger than a city in Guam; Kris Valderrama, first Filipina American woman elected to the Maryland legislature; Lorraine Rodero-Inouye, first Filipina woman elected mayor on the Big Island of Hawaii; Velma Veloria, first Filipina woman elected to the Washington State Legislature; Meriam Reynosa, first Filipina woman to serve as an electoral college delegate for the election of a US president; Rebecca Rottman Delgado, first Filipina woman elected to the San Francisco Democratic County Central Committee, the governing structure for a major political party in one of the largest cities in the United States; Thelma Garcia, first Filipina woman elected to the Alaska legislature; Hydra Mendoza, first Filipina woman elected to a leadership position on the Board of Education in San Francisco; and Chief Justice Tani Gorre Cantil-Sakauye, first Filipina American to serve as California's Chief Justice.

Similar to being the first Filipina to have certain roles, Global FWN100™ awardees have been responsible for initiating significant changes in policies and for initiating or expanding private sector businesses in new areas. Carmencita David-Padilla was responsible for defining newborn screening policy, and Mary Ann Lucille L. Sering refined climate change policy; then both helped make changes in the policy process for the region. Carmela Clendening was responsible for the development of policy and political strategy at the state and local levels for a Political Action Committee (PAC). Jocelyn Ding serves as Vice President, Enterprise Operations Google. Margaret Lapiz was instrumental in Kaiser Permanente's increased focus on training doctors for leadership roles.

Several Global FWN100™ awardees have started new enterprises in non traditional areas, including money remittances, health saving accounts and IT support for the financial sector. Isabelita Manalastas-Watanabe established and was director of Speed Money Transfer in Japan. Cora Manese Tellez founded Sterling Health Services Administration, a pioneer in the health savings accounts (HSA) industry that is now recognized as among the top HSA services in the U.S. Adela Sering-Fojas founded Seven Seven Software, an IT Consulting Firm serving the New York financial district, and is one of the pioneers in establishing the Business Process Outsourcing (BPO) industry in the Philippines.

Having begun her banking career in the early 1980s, Nina Aguas rose to become one of the first Filipina women executives in a multinational bank. She recalled the challenge of being a Filipina in the industry in the 1980s: "It was a very male dominated industry, so I felt that I had to speak up, so that my views would be considered. I found that my colleagues, especially those outside the Philippines, equated how vocal one was with competence, so I had to learn to speak up in order to get my ideas across." She continued: "We are raised to be respectful and ensure that we do not offend anyone; however, in a highly competitive work environment, we need to learn to go head-to-head with a diverse set of colleagues while maintaining grace and respect."

Exceeding expectations is a consequence of flexible leadership defined as "adjusting one's leadership style, method, or approach in response to different or changing contextual demands in a way that facilitates group performance" (Kaiser and Overfield 2010). Whether they were the first Filipina woman in their field or were responsible for leading organizations into new areas, they disrupted the status quo but in a respectul manner. While some of the Global FWN100™ awardees appeared to be almost unaware that they were pioneers, others appeared to relish doing what others had not even thought of doing before. One aspect of disrupting the status quo is disruptive thinking, thinking "what no one else is thinking"—or being the disruptive change, doing "what no one else is doing" (Williams 2011, 17). The idea is not just to improve the status quo, but also to change it, to think the unthinkable, to spark transformation (Williams 2011).

Theme Six: Leading for Impact

The Global FWN100™ awardees expressed a deep commitment to having an impact on the world and identified numerous areas of impact.

Imelda Nicolas has continued to provide oversight in the development of policies and programs to benefit Overseas Filipinos. Carmen Zita-Lamagna contributed to women's empowerment by expanding higher educational opportunities for women in Bangladesh. Women's empowerment was also the reason given by Mary Jane Alvero for inspiring women in the Middle East to break into male-dominated professions. Patricia Ann V. Paez continues to be engaged in foreign policy and diplomacy as ambassador to Poland and as non-resident ambassador to Latvia, Lithuania and Estonia. Maria Africa Beebe designed and implemented projects that improved access to quality higher education in Afghanistan through increased access to information and communication technologies, via the Internet and especially targeted at females. Annette M. David was responsible for developing policies and procedures for evidence-based health in Guam, while Emma Cuenca's research directly increased the use of evidence-based practice to improve health care. Rozita Villanueva Lee's social activism has resulted in the engagement of Asian Pacific Islanders in the U.S. political process. Genevieve Jopanda's work has served as a national and global model for eliminating Hepatitis B in at-risk populations. Maria Almia delos Santos developed next-generation models for hospice services based on compassionate team care for the dying and their families. Patricia Gallardo-Dwyer was able to integrate sustainability into business operations and promote operations that are mitigating the impacts of climate change. Cora Manese Tellez founded Sterling Health Services Administration (HSA). Their clients trust Sterling with over $100,000,000 in HSA funds.

Even though some of the Global FWN100™ awardees are leaders in the private for-profit sector, their responses to the question about global impact focused on metrics concerning people and the environment, not just on profits. Metrics beyond profits that focus on people and the planet have been identified as essential to transcendent leadership and were identified as a global imperative of the Global Economic Forum 2007 (Gardiner 2009).

Theme Seven: Giving Back

A significant motivating factor in the leadership of many of the Global FWN100™ was their desire to give back. They described giving back as a responsibility and that giving back should be extended to the next generation. The desire to give back extended beyond the local organization into the awardees' desire to affect the entire Philippines and the rest of the world.

Loida Nicolas Lewis funded the microfinance People's Alternative Livelihood Foundation of Sorsogon Inc. (PALFSI) that has helped 20,000 families lift themselves out of poverty through micro-lending. Another of Loida's initiatives is The Lewis College (TLC), which offers pre-K through high school and college level coursework, including a six-month government approved nursing assistant course. TLC won a regional competition in 2010 and is now recognized throughout the Bicol Region as a leader in information technology.

Adela Sering-Fojas initiated a scholarship program for the children of the staff of her company. She and her husband donated to the University of the Philippines's Engineering Department a computer laboratory that provides a creative and technical venue for students and is credited with enriching the talent pool in the Philippines. Margaret Lapiz established the Lapiz Family Scholarship Fund in 2003 in honor of her parents and the family's experience in pursuing the American dream.

Rosemer Enverga started a foundation to bring together the Filipino-Canadian Community to promote the spirit of charity. The foundation has sent more than $440,000 worth of medical equipment and supplies to different hospitals in the Philippines, has supported medical and dental missions that have provided services to thousands of poor and needy families, and has assisted in building 33 houses for poor families.

Patricia Zamora Riingen noted how gratified she was to work with a company that values giving back to the communities in which it operates. She reported that she has been able to "get support to fund and implement several corporate social responsibility programs," including programs for increasing financial literacy, building schools, providing scholarships and continuing education, and assisting with sustainable disaster relief in the Philippines and other parts of Asia.

Lirio Sobreviñas-Covey founded in Manila the Association for Adults with Autism, Philippines (AAAP). To fulfill the organization's first mission of educating Filipinos regarding autism, Lirio and the AAAP Board of Directors started in 2012 an annual symposium series dedicated to clinical, research, and policy issues on autism. Lirio also leads ongoing work on the first residential community in the Philippines for adults with autism.

One of the most commonly mentioned ways of giving back was through formal and informal femtoring. Several of the FWN awardees described their commitment to empowering others as their way of doing for others what others have done for them.

Giving back is consistent with diaspora philanthropy, where an individual or group "identifies with an original homeland (either theirs or a member of their family's such as a grandparent), and is in the diaspora whether through their choice or a circumstance beyond their control" (Lethlean 2003, 1). Giving back is also consistent with transnational philanthropy that "builds transnational relations that link together origin and settlement societies" (Opiniano 2002, 3). Projects that are supported by the Global FWN100™ awardees often are linked to hometown communities and alumni associations. Moreover, their choices about which organizations to support are strongly influenced by the organizations' causes.

Conclusion

This book takes the outstanding work of FWN to the next level by making the annual awards part of an ongoing sustainable effort, framing the experiences and views of the leaders within academic perspectives, and extracting leadership themes for the next-generation leaders. Each chapter ends with a compelling list of leadership tips, based on the experience and insight of each leader.

Table 2 highlights leadership tips for each of the leadership themes in the Filipina narratives. The links between the leadership tips and the themes make explicit the connection between culture and leadership. This explicit linkage of culture to leadership becomes part of a growing body of scholarship that goes beyond Western models. It joins Bordas's (2013, 14-16) analysis of Latino leadership principles, with themes including personalization, self-awareness, destiny, culture, inclusiveness, activism, celebration, and hope.

These leadership themes and tips show how a holistic interpretation of leadership embedded in the local as well as the global context can help diaspora communities develop their own internal and external dialogues to succeed as leaders. Globalization will continue to add and blend leadership perspectives of regions ranging from the

TABLE 2. Seven Leadership Themes with Sample Leadership Tips by Global Filipina Women Leaders

Theme	Leadership Tips
1. Relationships in Filipino culture, as rooted in *kapwa*	-Learn how to talk and relate to everyone equally. -Be a good listener. Living is a team sport. -Embrace the positive aspects of our Philippine culture. -Recognize that our success also depends on the success of those around us.
2. Character strengths, values and virtues in ethical decision-making	-Keep true to your core but remain open to other viewpoints and possibilities. -Have courage. Resolve to go forward even when risk is involved. -Keep promises and maintain a good reputation.
3. Having a sense of purpose and meaning and responding to a call	-Follow your heart. -You are here for a reason. Live with purpose and passion every day. -Work for something bigger than yourself. -Maintain a good connection to your ancestors and the Divine.
4. Knowing and transforming oneself	-Think positive. Dream big. -Believe in yourself. -Walk with confidence. -Look within and examine why you want to lead. -Choose a career that brings out the passion in you
5. Exceeding expectations	-Adapt to new challenges and keep excelling in every domain. -Whenever one aims for perfection one may find it is a moving target
6. Leading for impact	-Inspire your teams. -Serve the people. -Determine the measure of your success. -Beyond being a CEO, one should be seen as a management role model, an oracle, as well as an icon for those who wish to ascend to the top.
7. Giving back	-Share stories; they are important. -Bring others along; we must pass on the lessons we gained along the way and create pathways for others to work for their own successes. -Give back to society. Civic engagement happens in the present, not when you retire. -Give back to the next generation.

Americas and Europe to Africa and Asia. This book shows how Filipina women leaders are adding their own voices to this body of knowledge on leadership.

ACKNOWLEDGEMENTS

This book required a collaborative effort made possible by the following:

* Marily Mondejar, FWN Founder & CEO, for executive oversight in making this book a reality.

* Thirty–five contributing authors shared their leadership reflections, narratives, case studies, and leadership tips—whether *en route* to Dubai, Manila, New York, Shanghai or getting ready for parliamentary delegations or waiting for an *apo* [grandchild].

* Our external readers read the whole book and gave us their invaluable advice:

   Madanmohan Rao, Ph.D.—an author and consultant from Bangalore, research advisor at the Asian Media Information and Communication Centre (AMIC), and editor of five book series: *The Asia Pacific Internet Handbook*, *The Knowledge Management Chronicles*, *AfricaDotEdu*, *World of Proverbs*, and *The Global Citizen*. He is the research director of YourStory, a leading platform for startups and investors.

   Penelope Flores, Ph.D. —a Professor Emerita, San Francisco State University, Multicultural Education, Mathematics Education and Teacher Credential program. She is recognized in the U.S and internationally as an author, writer, and editor of prestigious academic journals and as a FilAm community leader. Penelope is an FWN 2012 awardee.

   James Beebe, Ph.D.—just finished the second edition of his book on rapid qualitative inquiry. James was a professor in the Doctoral Program in Leadership Studies at Gonzaga University for 17 years and, prior to that he retired as a U.S. Foreign Service Officer (USAID) after serving in Sudan, Philippines, Liberia, and South Africa.

* Our peer reviewers provided comments, recommendations for improvement, and suggestions for edits—Mary Ann M. Covarrubias, Penelope V. Flores, Rachel B. Goodrich, Charmaine Mesina, Gemma Nemenzo, Letty Quizon, Lilia Villanueva, Lirio Sobreviñas-Covey, and Raissa Alvero. Although we publicly acknowledge our reviewers, the identity of the reviewer was not shared with the author of that chapter.

* Lucille Tenazas, Henry Wolf Professor of Communication Design and Associate Dean of Art, Media and Technology at Parsons The New School of Design, for book cover design.

* Edwin Lozada of Carayan Press and President of Philippine American Writers and Artists (PAWA), Inc., was responsible for the superb and artistic layout design and provided professional, patient, and conscientious publishing advice throughout the process.

* Our anonymous donor through PAWA, Inc.

* Barbara Jane Reyes for graciously giving us permission to use lines of her poetry from her book *Diwata* (BOA Editions, 2010).

* Leah Laxamana served as research fellow and checked references, made comments, and stepped up as necessary. Even after she started work as an intern for Public Policy–Community Outreach with Twitter's philanthropy group, she continued to lend us her research skills.

* Elysia Dela Peña, graphic artist from Manila for her sketches and design.

* Global Networks colleagues read the introduction and synthesis and gave comments—Jerri Shepard, Ed.D. and Shonna Bartlett from Gonzaga University, Robert Bartlett, Ph.D. from Eastern Washington University, and Mark Beattie, Ph.D. from Washington State University.

* Prosy Abarquez-Delacruz, US FWN100, 2012, and Betty Ann Quirino, Global FWN100 2013, shared intellectual capital as we envisioned the book and spent social capital in following-up responses to the call for abstracts.

* The 2014 Women and Leadership colloquium convened by Dr. Susan R. Madsen, Orin R. Woodbury Professor of Leadership and Ethics, the intersectionalities working group headed by Faith Ngunjiri, Ph.D. Participation in the colloquium ensured that we kept abreast with the theory, practice and development of women and leadership.

* The following Global FWN100 (2013) who were not able to write full chapters but whose insights in the FWN magazine (October 2013 issue) and their time capsule recordings contributed to the analysis and identification of themes: Loisa Cabuhat, Carmela Clendening, Allyson Tintiangco-Cubales, Emma Cuenca, Imelda Cuyugan, Annette M. David, Jocelyn Ding, Rosemer Enverga, Patricia Gallardo-Dwyer, Genevieve Jopanda, Rozita Villanueva Lee, Maria Almia de los Santos, Carmen-Zita Lamagna, Margaret Lapiz, Dawn Bohulano Mabalon, Tess Mauricio, Hydra Mendoza-McDonnell, Bella Aurora Padua-Belmonte, Meriam Reynosa, Patricia Zamora Riingen, Rebecca Delgado Rottman, Regina Manzana-Sawhney, Mary Ann Lucille L. Sering, Cora Manese Tellez, Lucille Tenazas, and Librada C. Yamat.

* As we launched the Amazon edition, we're grateful to Al Perez, FWN's long-term volunteer graphic designer, Franklin M. Ricarte for the technical support, and FWN Fellow Noemi Baguinon, our page checker.

* The FWN Board, FWN Editorial Board and other kapwa global Filipinas who have inspired us and given us support in spirit, too numerous to mention here. *Maraming Salamat.*

Appendices

Appendix A
References

Introduction

Abinales, Patricio N. and Donna J. Amoroso. 2005. *State and Society in the Philippines (State & Society in East Asia)*. Lanham, MD: Rowman & Littlefield Publishers, Inc.

Aguilar, Filomeno Jr. 2002. "Beyond Stereotypes: Human Subjectivity in the Structuring of Global Migrations." In *Filipinos in Global Migrations: At Home in the World?*, edited by Filomeno J. Aguilar, 41-58. Quezon City: Philippine Migration Research Network and Philippine Social Science Council.

Aquino, Belinda A. 1993. "Filipino Women and Political Engagement." Manoa: University of Hawaii.

Bautista, Maria Cynthia Rose Banzon. 2002"Migrant Workers and their Environments: Insights from the Filipino Diaspora." University of Philipines, Manila.

Buss, Claude A. 1987. *Cory Aquino and the People of the Philippines*. Stanford, CA: The Portable Stanford.

Cheng, S. A. 2003. "Rethinking the Globalization of Domestic Service: Foreign Domestics, State Control and the Politics of Identity in Taiwan." *Gender & Society* 17 (2): 166-186.

Chin, Christine. 1998. *In Service and Servitude*. New York: Columbia University Press.

Choy, C. C. 2003. *Empire of Care: Nursing and Migration in Filipino American History*. Manila: Ateneo de Manila University Press.

Ciulla, Joanne B. 2006. "What we Learned Along the Way." *In The Quest for a General Theory of Leadership*, edited by George R. Goethals and Georgia L. J. Sorenson, 221-233. Cheltenham, UK and Northampton, MA, USA: Edward Elgar.

Constable, Nicole. 1997. "Sexuality and Discipline among Filipina Domestic Workers in Hong Kong." *American Ethnologist* 24 (3): 539-558.

Cuyegkeng, Ma Assunta C. and Antonette Palma-Angeles, eds. 2011. *Defining Filipino Leadership*. Philippines: Ateneo de Manila Press.

De Jesus, Melinda, ed. 2005. *Pinay Power: Peminist Critical Theory*. New York: Routledge Press.

Doronila, Maria Luis C. 1989. *The Limits of Educational Change: National Identity Formation in a Philippine Public Elementary School*. Quezon City, Philippines: University of the Philippines Press.

Enriquez, Virgilio G. 1989. *Kapwa Theory and Indigenous Pscyhology*. Philippines: Institute for the Study of Languages and Cultures in Asia and Africa.

Guevarra, Jaime P., ed. 2005. *Pakikipagkapwa [Sharing/Merging Oneself with Others]*. Cultural Heritage and Contemporary Change Series IIID, Southeast Asia, edited by George F. McLean. Vol. 4: The Council for Research in Values and Philosophy.

Hall, Douglas T. 2008. "Self-Awareness, Identity and Leader Development." In *Leader Development for Transforming Organizations: Growing Leaders for Tomorrow*, edited by David V. Day, Stephen J. Zaccaro and Stanley M. Halpin, 154-173. New Jersey: Taylor & Francis e-Library.

Hammond, Sue Annis. 2013. *The Thin Book of Appreciative Inquiry*. 3rd ed. Oregon: Thin Book Publishing Co.

Herrera, April Glory P. and Paas R., Jayvee. 2010. "A Study of Filipino National Identity and Nationalism in the Age of Globalization among the Youth of Baguio City." B.A., University of the Philippines, Baguio City.

International Labor Organization. 2013. *Domestic Workers Across the World: Global and Regional Statistics and the Extent of Legal Protection*.

Kaiser, Robert B. and Darren B. Overfield. 2010. "Assessing Flexible Leadership as a Mastery of Opposites." *Consulting Psychology Journal: Practice and Research* 62 (2): 105-118.

Mananzan, Sr Mary John. 2010. "The Babaylan in Me." In *Babaylan: Filipinos and the Call of the Indigenous*, edited by Leny Mendoza Strobel. First ed., 1-308: Ateneo de Davao University Research and Publications Office.

Mendenhall, Mark E., Joyce C. Osland, Allan Bird, Gary R. Oddou, Marth L. Maznevski, Michael J. Stevens, and Gunther K. Stahl, eds. 2013. *Global Leadership*. New York and London: Routledge Taylor and Francis Group.

Parreñas, Rhacel Salazar. 2001. *Servants of Globalization: Women, Migration and Domestic Work*. California: Stanford University Press.

Remo, Michelle V. 2012. "Stop Illegal Remittance Agents, BSP Urged: Informal Forex Channels a Problem in the Region." *Philippine Daily Inquirer*.

Reyes, Melanie M. 2008. *Migration and Filipino Children Left-Behind: A Literature Review*. Miriam College/UNICEF.

Reyes, Barbara Jane. 2010. *Diwata. Poems by Barbara Jane Reyes*. American Poets Continuum Series, No. 123. Rochester, New York: Boa Editons Ltd.

Roffey, Bet. 1999. "Filipina Managers and Entrepreneurs: What Leadership Models Apply?" *Asian Studies Review* 23 (3): 375-405.

San Juan, Epifanio Jr. 2011. "Sisa's Vengeance: Rizal and the Mother of all Insurgencies." *Kritika Kultura* (17): 23-56.

Saplala, J. E. G. "Revisiting and Reliving our Filipino Virtues." Silliman University, http://teachingpsychology.files.wordpress.com/2011/11/1_revisiting_and_reliving_our_filipino_virtues_by_jay_saplala.pdf.

Scalabrini Migration Center. 2013. *Country Migration Report: The Philippines 2013*. Philippines: International Organization for Migration (IOM).

Shah, Nasra, Hanan Badr, and Makhdoom Shah. 2011. "Foreign Live-in Domestic Workers as Caretakers of Older Kuwaiti Men and Women: Socio-Demographic and Health Correlates." *Ageing & Society*: 1-22.

Stoney, Sierra and Batalova, Jeane. 2013 "The Migration Information Source–Filipino Immigrants in the United States." Migration Policy Institute. Migration Policy Institute, http://migrationpolicy.org/article/filipino-immigrants-united-states.

Strobel, Leny Mendoza, ed. 2010. *Babaylan: Filipinos and the Call of the Indigenous.* Davao, Philippines: Ateneo de Davao University Research and Publications Office.

Udani, Zenon Arthur S. and Caterina F. Lorenzo-Molo. 2012. "When Servant Becomes Leader: The Corazon C. Aquino Success Story as a Beacon for Business Leaders."

Uhl-Bien, Mary. 2006. "Relational Leadership Theory: Exploring the Social Processes of Leadership and Organizing." *The Leadership Quarterly* 17 (6): 654-676. World Economic Forum. 2013. *The Global Gender Gap Report.*

AGUAS, NINA

Aguas, Nina D. 2004. "Teaching Micro-Lenders the Way of Global Banking." Philippine Daily Inquirer, April 12, B9.

Bangko Sentral ng Pilipinas. 2012. Report on the State of Financial Inclusion in the Philippines.

Detjen, Jodi. 2014. "How Women in Banking can Rise to the Top." American Banker, May 22.

Dumlao, Tina Arceo. 2001. "After 98 Years, Citibank Puts a Woman at the Top." Philippine Daily Inquirer, July 16, C1.

Grant Thornton International Business Report. 2013. Women in Senior Management: Setting the Stage for Growth.

ASMUNDSON, RUTH UY

Cruz, Fr Francisco CM. 2006. "The Ruth Cause." *Adamson University News.*

Dunning, Bob. 2003. "Davis was Certainly Lucky to have Vigfus." *The Davis Enterprise Newspaper*, April 29.

Fetterly, Doug. 2008. "Ruth Asmundson: More than a Mayor." *Davis Life Magazine*, August.

Lactao, Sid Jr. 2009. "The Story of Ruth Uy Asmundson: From Gamu to Mayor in California." Isabela: 67 Unknown Facts: What we did not Learn in School.

Macapagal-Arroyo, Gloria. "Quote from Malacañang Palace." Quote, Philippines.

Strayer, Rachel. 2010. "Ruth Uy Asmundson M.S.'68 Retires as the First Filipina. Mayor of a U.S. City." *Wilkes Magazine*, Fall. Wilkes University.

Wolk, Lois. 2010. Testimonial Delivered at Retirement. Davis, California

BEEBE, MARIA AFRICA

Beekun, Rafik. "Effective Leadership Steps for Strategy Implementation in Islamic Organisations.", accessed July 31, 2014, http://makkah.files.wordpress. com/2006/12 /effective-leadership-tools-for-strategy-implementation-in-islamic-organiza tions.pdf.

Beekun, Rafik I. and Jamal A. Badawi. 1999. *Leadership: An Islamic Perspective.* 1st ed. Beltsville, MD: Amana Publications.

Bothe, Michael. & Fischer-Lescano, Andrea. 2002. "Protego Et Obligo. Afghanistan and the Paradox of Sovereignty." *German Law Journal* 3 (9).

Dupree, Louis. 1973. *Afghanistan.* Princeton, NJ: Princeton University Press.

Ghani, Ashraf and Claire Lockhart. 2008. *Fixing Failed States: A Framework for Rebuilding a Fractured World.* New York, NY: Oxford University Press.

Hill, Susan E. Kogler. 2010. "Team Leadership." In *Leadership Theory and Practice,* edited by Peter Northouse. 5th ed. Los Angeles, CA: Sage.

House, Robert J., Paul J. Hanges, Mansour Javidan, Peter W. Dorfman, and Vipin Gupta, eds. 2004. *Culture, Leadership and Organizations: The GLOBE Study of 62 Societies.* Thousand Oaks, CA: Sage.

Kanter, Rosabeth Moss. 1994. "Collaborative Advantage: The Art of Alliances." *Harvard Business Review*: 96-108.

Khalilzad, Zalmay and Daniel Byman. 2000 Winter. "Afghanistan: The Consolidation of a Rogue State." *The Washington Quarterly* 23 (1).

Khan, Adalat. 2007. "Islamic Leadership Principles." *American Chronicle.*

Khan, Mohammad W. 1998. "Prophetic Principles of Success." *Minaret,* 8-9.

Kouzes, James M. and Barry Z. Posner. 1995. *The Leadership Challenge.* 2nd ed. San Francisco, CA: Jossey Bass Publishers.

Mandell, Myrna P. 2003. "Types of Collaborations and Why the Differences really Matter." *The Public Manager* 31 (4).

Morgeson, Frederick P., D. Scott DeRue, and Elizabeth P. Karam. 2010. "Leadership in Teams: A Functional Approach to Understanding Leadership Structures and Processes." *Journal of Management* (36): 5-39.

Morgeson, Frederick P., D. Scott DeRue, and Elizabeth P. Karam. 2010. "Leadership in Teams: A Functional Approach to Understanding Leadership Structures and Processes." *Journal of Management* 36 (1): 5-39. doi:10.1177/0149206309347376.

Rice, Condoleeza. 2006, January 16. *New Direction for U.S. Foreign Assistance*: U.S. Department of State.

Rubin, Barnett. 2002. *The Fragmentation of Afghanistan: State Formation and the Collapse of the International System.* 2nd ed. US: Yale University Press.

Schon, Donald A. 1971. *Beyond the Stable State.* New York: Norton.

Unus, Iqbal and Beekun, Rafik I. "Leadership Lessons from the Qur'an: The Story of Dhul-Qarnayn.", accessed July 31, 2014, http://theislamicworkplace.com /2007/11/24/leadership-lessons-from-the-quran-the-story-of-dhul-qarnayn/.

BENITEZ, SUZIE

Benitez, Suzie M. 2000. *Perform 2, Developing a Professional Image. A Student's Handbook*. Assumption College.

—. 1999. Perform. *Women in Adjustment. A Student's Handbook*. Assumption College.

Covey, Stephen R. 1990. *Principle Centered Leadership*. NY: Simon and Schuster.

Krass, Peter. 1998. *The Book of Leadership Wisdom*. John Wiley & Sons, Inc.

Santos, Isabel A. 2004. *Bayanihan, the National Folk Dance Company of the Philippines. A Memory of Six Continents*, edited by Priscilla G. Cabanatan. Manila: Anvil Publishing.

Scott, Steven K. 2004. *Mentored by a Millionaire*. John Wiley & Sons Inc.

CUSTODIO, KRISTINE

DeVenny, Lynne J. 2010. *From File Clerk to Paralegal in Six Months*. Practical Paralegalism.

Estrin, Chere. 2007. *Who's Afraid of the Big, Bad Wolf?*. The Estrin Report.

Flatten, Amanda. "LAT's 2008 Paralegal of the Year and Runners-Up Flourish through Networking Ties." Paralegal Today. http://paralegaltoday.com/issue_ar chive/features/feature1_so08.htm.

Platt, Suzy. 1993. *Respectfully Quoted: A Dictionary of Quotations* [Desiderata by Max Ehrmann]. USA: Barnes & Noble Books.

San Diego Daily Transcript. "San Diego Paralegals - Kristine Custodio." San Diego Source.http://www.sddt.com/microsite/paralegals09/winner.cfm?w=6T FV478N.

Sipe, Charles. 2012. *Interview with Kristine M. Custodio, President of the San Diego Paralegal Association*. Vol. Interview.

DELEN, SONIA

Barbara, Annis and John Gray. 2013. *Work with Me: The 8 Blind Spots between Men and Women in Business*. New York, NY: Palgrave Macmillan.

Sandberg, Sheryl. 2013. *Lean in: Women, Work, and the Will to Lead*. New York, NY: Knopf.

Shambaugh, Rebecca. 2007. *It's Not a Glass Ceiling, it's a Sticky Floor: Free Yourself from the Hidden Behaviors Sabotaging Your Career Success*. New York, NY: McGraw-Hill.

DURAN-STANTON, AMELIA

Covey, Stephen. 1989. *The 7 Habits of Highly Effective People: Powerful Lessons in Personal Change*. New York: Fireside.

Klaus, Peggy. 1993. *Brag! the Art of Tooting Your Own Horn without Blowing it*. New York: Warner Business Books.

Platt, Suzy. 1993. *Respectfully Quoted: A Dictionary of Quotations* [Desiderata by Max Ehrmann]. USA: Barnes & Noble Books.

Powell, Colin. 1995. *My American Journey*. New York: Random House.

Rice, Condoleeza. 2010. *Extraordinary, Ordinary People: A Memoir of Family*. New York: Random House.

Sandberg, Sheryl. 2013. *Lean in: Women, Work, and the Will to Lead*. New York: Alfred A. Knopf.

Tarr-Whelan, Linda. 2009. *Women Lead the Way: Your Guide to Stepping Up to Leadership and Changing the World*. San Francisco: Berrett-Koehler Publishers, Inc.

ENRILE, ANNALISA

Adrian, Molly, Janice Zeman, Cynthia Erdley, Ludmila Lisa, and Leslie Sim. 2011. "Emotional Dysregulation and Interpersonal Difficulties as Risk Factors for Nonsuicidal Self-Injury in Adolescent Girls." *Journal of Abnormal Child Psychology* 39 (3): 389-400.

Brah, Avtar and Ann Phoenix. 2004. "Ain't I A Woman? Revisiting Intersectionality." *Journal of International Women's Studies* 5 (3): 75.

Eaton, D. K., L. Kann, S. Kinchen, S. Shanklin, K. H. Flint, J. Hawkins, and H. Wechsler. 2012. *Youth Risk Behavior Surveillance-United States, 2011 Morbidity and Mortality Weekly Report. Surveillance Summaries*. Washington, DC: Centers for Disease Control and Prevention.

Enrile, Annalisa V. and Jollene Levid. 2009. "GAB[Riela] Net[Work]: A Case Study of Transnational Sisterhood and Organizing." *Amerasia Journal* 35 (1): 92.

Kerkvliet, Benedict J. 2002. *The Huk Rebellion: A Study of Peasant Revolt in the Philippines*. Rowman & Littlefield Publishers.

Le Espiritu, Yen. 2003. *Home Bound: Filipino American Lives Across Cultures, Communities, and Countries*. University of California Press.

Lindio-McGovern, Ligaya. 2013. *Globalization, Labor Export and Resistance: A Study of Filipino Migrant Domestic Workers in Global Cities*. Vol. 32 Routledge.

Lorde, Audre. 1995. "Age, Race, Class, and Sex." *Sister Outsider* 16 (9).

—. "Conference Keynote Address: Sisterhood and Survival." The Black Scholar, 1986.

Maramba, Asuncion D. 1997. *Six Young Filipino Martyrs*. Philippines: Anvil Books.

Maramba, Dina C. and Kevin L. Nadal. 2013. "The State of Filipino/a American Faculty: Implications for Higher Education and Filipino American College Students." San Diego, Filipino American National Historical Society.

Marques, Joan. 2009. "Sisterhood in Short Supply in the Workplace: It's often the Women Who Hold Back their Female Colleagues." *Human Resource Management International Digest* 17 (5): 28.

Mohanty, Chandra T. 2003. *Feminism without Borders: Decolonizing Theory, Practicing Solidarity*. New Delhi, India: Zubaan.

Morgan, Robin, ed. 2007. *Sisterhood is Forever: The Women's Anthology for a New Millennium*. New York: Washington Square.

—. 1970. *Sisterhood is Powerful: An Anthology of Writings from the Women's Liberation Movement*. New York: Random House.

Oppenheim, James. "Bread and Roses." *The American Magazine*.

Tatum, Beverly Daniel. 2003. *"Why are all the Black Kids Sitting Together in the Cafeteria?": And Other Conversations about Race*. Revised ed. New York, NY: Basic Books.

Tintiangco-Cubales, Allyson, Roderick Daus-Magbual, and Arlene Daus-Magbual. 2010. "Pin@y Educational Partnerships A Counter-Pipeline to Create Critical Educators." *AAPI Nexus: Asian Americans & Pacific Islanders Policy, Practice and Community* 8 (1): 75-102.

Uris, Leon. 2014. *Mila 18*. Open Road Media.

Varkey, Prathibha, Aminah Jatoi, Amy Williams, Anita Mayer, Marcia Ko, Julia Files, Janis Blair, and Sharonne Hayes. 2012. "The Positive Impact of a Facilitated Peer Mentoring Program on Academic Skills of Women Faculty." *BMC Medical Education* 12 (1): 14.

Wiseman, Rosalind. 2009. *Queen Bees and Wannabes: Helping Your Daughter Survive Cliques, Gossip, Boyfriends, and the New Realities of Girl World*. Random House LLC.

Wolf, Diane L. 1997. "Family Secrets: Transnational Struggles among Children of Filipino Immigrants." *Sociological Perspectives* 40 (3): 457-482.

FLORES, PENELOPE

The Holy Bible. 1973. Translated by Committee on Bible Translation. New Interna-

"Rizal Forscherin." 2014. *Rhine-Neckar Zeitung Newspaper*, April 12.

Bernays, Anne and Pamela Painter. 2004. *What if? Writing Exercises for Fiction Writers*. 2nd ed. London: Pearson/Longman.

Brainard, Cecilia Manguerra and Orosa, Marily Ysip, ed. 2004. *Behind the Walls: Life of Convent Girls*. Manila: Anvil Press.

Brainard, Cecilia Manguerra, ed. 2012. *Magnificat: Mama Mary's Pilgrim Sites*. Manila: Anvil Press.

Flores, Penelope V. 2004. *Journal of the American Association for Philippine Psychology* 1 (1).

—. 2008. *Goodbye-Vientiane: Untold Stories of Filipinos in Lao*s. 1st ed. San Francisco, CA: Philippine American Writers and Artists, Inc.

—. 2010. *Goodbye-Vientiane: Untold Stories of Filipinos in Lao*s. 2nd ed. San Francisco, CA: Philippine American Writers and Artists, Inc.

—. 2002. *Reflections: Readings for the Young and Old*. San Francisco: Philippine American Writers and Artists, Inc.

Flores, Penelope V. and Allen Gaborro, eds. 2004. *Whisper of the Bamboo: An Anthology of Philippine American Writers and Artists*. San Francisco, CA: Philippine American Writers and Artists, Inc.

Flores, Penelope V. and Larry Hufford. 1997. *Journal of Interdisciplinary Education* 1 (1).

Flores, Penelope V., Larry Hufford, and Clay Starlin. 1998. "Journal of Interdisciplinary Education." *Journal of Interdisciplinary Education* 5 (1).

Flores, Penelope V. and Araceli N. Resus. 2012. *The Philippine Jeepney: A Metaphor for Understanding the Filipino American Family*. 1st ed. San Francisco, CA: Philippine American Writers and Artists, Inc.

Guerrero, Leon Maria. 2011. *A Biography of Jose Rizal*. Manila: National Historical Commission of the Philippines.

Lozada, Edwin, ed. 2008. *Field of Mirrors: An Anthology of Philippine American Writers*. San Francisco, CA: Philippine American Writers and Artists, Inc.

Villarica, Jose P. and Marcela Dayao Villarica. 1956. *Balagtas' Florante at Laura': A Parallel English Translation*. Manila: Alemar.

Viola, Maximo. 1990. "Mis Viajes Con El Dr. Jose Rizal." In *Rizal's Travels*. Manila: National Historical Commission of the Philippines.

Gillet, Mira

Connectivism and Open Online Learning in K-20 Education (COOL K-20). Video. Anonymous YouTube: 2013.

"Final Team Project, Description - Designing a New Learning Environment." NovoEd., https://venture-lab.org/education/exercises/64.

Peace Game Workshop on Open Ongoing Connectivist (WOOC) Massive Open Online Courses (MOOC). Video. Anonymous 2013.

Peace Game: Global Challenges. Facebook Group.

Paterson, Jeff. 2013. *John Hunter, Creator of the World Peace Game, on Experiences and New Book*.

LIM, LENORE

de la Paz, Christiane L. "Lenore Lim's Liberation of Colors." Artes de las Filipi-nas.2014,http://www.artesdelasfilipinas.com/page/10/archives.php?page_id=142.

Endaya, Imelda Cajipe. 2011. *Lenore RS Lim -Full Circle, A Retrospective Exhibition 1991 – 2010.* Cultural Center of the Philippines.

Sharpe, Paul. 2005. "Introduction." In *Profound Afterglow: The Prints of Lenore RS Lim*, edited by Clint White and Ruben D. F. Defeo. Subic, Philippines: Cacho Hermanos Inc.

MANAAY, SOLEDAD

Gundling, Ernest, Terry Hogan, and Karen Cvitkovich. 2011. *What is Global Leadership? 10 Key Behaviors that Define Great Global Leaders.* Boston, MA: Nicholas Brealey Publishing.

Hofstede, Geert, Gert Jan Hofstede, and Michael Minkov. 2010. *Cultures and Organizations, Software of the Mind: Intercultural Cooperation and its Importance for Survival.* New York, NY: Mc Graw Hill.

Munroe, Robert L. and Ruth H. Munroe. 1997. "A Comparative Anthropological Perspective." In *Handbook of Cross-Cultural Psychology: Theory and Method*, edited by John W. Berry, Ype H. Poortinga and Janak Pandey, 171-214. Needham Heights, MA: Allyn & Bacon.

Sam, David L. and John W. Berry. 2010. "Acculturation when Individual and Groups of Different Cultural Backgrounds Meet." *Perspectives on Psychological Science 5* (4): 472-481.

MANGAHAS, ELENA

Barrios, Joy. 2006 . *Mula Sa Mga Pakpak ng Entablado – Poetika ng Dulaang Kababaihan.* The University of the Philippines Press.

Henson, Maria Rosa. 1996 . *Comfort Woman, Slave of Destiny.* Pasig: Philippines Center for Investigative Journalism.

Holthe, Tess Uriza. 2002 .*When The Elephants Dance.* New York, NY: Crown Publishers.

Strobel, Leny Mendoza. 2010 . *Babaylan - Filipinos and the Call of the Indigenous.* Ateneo de Davao University – Research and Publication Office.

MONDEJAR, MARILY

Drath, Wilfred H. and Charles J. Palus. 1994. *Making Common Sense: Leadership as Meaning-Making in a Community of Practice.* San Diego, CA: Center for Creative Leadership.

Holt, Douglas B. 2004. *How Brands Become Icons: The Principles of Cultural Branding.* 1st ed. Boston, MA: Harvard Business Review Press.

Kouzes, James M. and Barry Z. Posner. 2007. *The Leadership Challenge.* 4th ed. San Francisco, CA: Jossey-Bass.

Moss, Cheryl

Eljera, Bert. 2014. "Fil-Am Judge Picks Up Two Key Endorsements in Poll." *Inquirer. Net.*

Gracian, Balthasar. 1993. *The Art of Worldly Wisdom.* Shambhala.

Peralta, Joseph L. 2008. "Cheryl Moss District Court Judge for the Family Division, Las Vegas, NV." *Asian Journal Publications*, A8.

Supreme Court of Nevada, Administrative Office of the Courts. 2012. *Annual Report of the Nevada Judiciary Fiscal Year 2012.* Carson City, Nevada: Supreme Court of Nevada, Administrative Office of the Courts.

Nicolas, Imelda

Brainard, Cecilia Manguerra and Marily Ysip-Orosa, eds. 2005. *Behind the Walls, Life of Convent Girls.* Manila: Anvil.

InciteGov, ed. 2008. *Crossover Leadership in Asia: Staying Whole in Two Halves from Civil Society to Goverment.*

Kalaw-Tirol. Lorna, ed. 2000. *From America to Africa, Voices of Filipino Women Overseas.* FAI Resource Management.

Manlapaz, Edna Zapanta, Teresita Villacorta, and Imelda Nicolas, eds. 2011. *Our Story: A Collection of Personal Memories by SCAns.*

Mislang, Ma Carmen. 2008. "Imelda "Mely" M. Nicolas." In *Cross-Over Leadership in Asia: Staying in Two Halves, from Civil Society to Government*, edited by InciteGov.

Padilla, Carmencita

"Republic Act no 9288." accessed April 19, 2014, http://www.newbornscreening.ph.

Donne, John. "Meditation XVII." Literature Network. accessed April 19, 2014, http://www.online-literature.com/donne/409.

Padilla, Carmencita D., Juanita A. Basilio, and Y. Oliveros. 2009. "Newborn Screening: Research to Policy." *Acta Medica Philippina* 43 (2): 6.

Padilla, Carmencita D. and Carmelita F. Domingo. 2002. "Implementation of New born Screening in the Philippines." *Philippine Journal of Pediatrics* 51: 2-10.

Padilla, Carmencita D., Danuta Krotoski, and Bradford Therrell. 2010. "Newborn Screening Progress in Developing Countries—Overcoming Internal Barriers." *Seminars in Perinatology* 34 (2): 145.

Pascual, Rory. 2005. "Screening Babies Featuring Carmencita D. Padilla." *Woman Today*, April 27, 33.

Rodis, Rodel. 2010. "First Quarter Storm Remembered." *Inquirer Global Nation*, February 4.

Tagiwalo, J. "Who were the Communards?" The Philippine Collegian. accessed April 19, 2014, http://www.philippinecollegian.org/who-were-the-communards.

Wilson, James Maxwell Glover and Gunner Jungner. 1968. "Principles and Practice of Screening for Disease." *Public Health Papers* 34.

RODRIGUEZ-AMAYA, DELIA

Rodriguez-Amaya, Delia B. 1997. *Carotenoids and Food Preparation: The Retention of Provitamin A Carotenoids in Prepared, Processed and Stored Foods. Opportunities for Micronutrient Interventions.* Arlington: United States Agency for International Development.

—. 1989. "Critical Review of Provitamin A Determination in Plant Foods." *Journal of Micronutrient Analysis* 5 (3): 191.

—. 1999. *A Guide to Carotenoid Analysis in Foods.* Washington, DC: International Life Sciences Institute (ILSI) Press.

—. 2010. "Quantitative Analysis, in Vitro Assessment of Bioavailability and Antioxidant Activity of Food Carotenoids—A Review." *Journal of Food Composition and Analysis* 23 (7): 726.

Rodriguez-Amaya, Delia B. and Mieko Kimura. 2004. *HarvestPlus Handbook for Carotenoid Analysis.* Washington, DC: International Food Policy Research Institute (IFPRI).

STICKMON, JANET

Andrews, Matthew M. 2005. "(Re)Examining (Multi)Racial Identity: Black-Filipino Multiracials in the San Francisco-Bay Area." *The Berkeley McNair Research Journal*: 27.

Daniel, G. Reginald. 2002. *More than Black?: Multiracial Identity and the New Racial Order.* Philadelphia, PA: Temple University Press.

Firman, John and Ann Gila. 2002. *Psychosynthesis: A Psychology of the Spirit.* Albany, NY: State University of New York Press,.

Gladwell, Malcolm. 2000. *The Tipping Point: How Little Things can make a Big Difference.* New York: Little, Brown & Company.

Guevarra, Rudy P. Jr. 2012. *Becoming Mexipino: Multiethnic Identities and Communities in San Diego.* New Brunswick, NJ: Rutgers University Press.

—. 2003. "Burritos and Bagoong: Mexipinos and Multiethnic Identity in San Diego, California." In *Crossing Lines: Race and Mixed Race Across Geohistorical Divide*, edited by Marc Coronado, Rudy P. Jr Guevarra, Jeffrey Moniz and Laura Furlan Szanto. Santa Barbara: Multiethnic Student Outreach, University of California.

Romo, Rebecca. "Blaxican Identity: An Exploratory Study of Multiracial Blacks/Chicana/os in California." San Jose, CA, National Association for Chicana and Chicano Studies Annual Conference, April 1, 2008.

Stickmon, Janet. 2014. ""Barack Obama: Embracing Multiplicity—Being a Catalyst for Change." In *Race, Gender, and the Obama Phenomenon: Toward a More Perfect Union*, edited by G. Reginald Daniel and Hettie Williams, 62. Jackson, MS: University Press of Mississippi.

Wilkerson, Isabel. 2010. *The Warmth of Other Sons: The Epic Story of America's Great Migration*. New York: Random House.

TUMINEZ, ASTRID S.

Ali Ahlam, Shabiya. 2014. *How Important are Diversity and Inclusion to our Society?*. Vol. Interview.

Tucker, Joseph D. and Astrid S. Tuminez. 2011. "Reframing Conceptual Approaches to Interpret Sex Worker Health." *Journal of Infectious Diseases* 204 (SUPPL 5): S1206-S1210.

Tuminez, Astrid S. 2012. *Rising to the Top? A Report on Women's Leadership in Asia*. Lee Kuan Yew School of Public Policy and Asia Society.

Tuminez, Astrid S. 2002. "Coming Home." In *Silent Notes Taken*, edited by Glen Nelson, 112-138. New York: Mormon Artists Group.

—. 2003. "Nationalism, Ethnic Pressures, and the Breakup of the USSR." *Journal of Cold War Studies* 5 (2): 81-136.

—. 2010. "Owed some Protection." *South China Morning Post*, 4 December, 13.

—. 2011. "The Problem that has been Named." *Global-is-Asian no. 11*, July-September, 34-37.

—. 2008. "Rebellion, Terrorism, Peace: America's Unfinished Business with the Muslims of the Philippines." *Brown Journal of World Affairs* 15 (1): 211-224.

—. 2012. "Rising Asia is Letting its Women Fall Behind." *South China Morning Post*, 20 April, 17.

—. 2000. *Russian Nationalism since 1856. Ideology and the Making of Foreign Policy*. Lanham, MD: Rowman and Littlefield.

—. 2007. "This Land is our Land: Moro Ancestral Domain and its Implications for Peace and Development in the Southern Philippines." *SAIS Review of International Affairs* 27 (2): 77-91.

Tuminez, Astrid S. and Mark Hong. 2012. "Russia in Southeast Asia: A New "Asian Moment?"." In *ASEAN-RUSSIA Foundation and Future Prospects*, edited by Victor Sumsky, Mark Hong and Amy Lu, 43. Singapore: ISEAS Publishing

ZAMORA, MARIFE

"Convergys Philippines: Celebrating a Decade of Excellence." 2013. *Business World S5* XXVII (90): 1-4.

"Marife Zamora: Sharing a Passion for Success." 2013. *Traversing the Orient*, July-August, 72.

Sandberg, Sheryl. 2013. *Lean in: Women, Work, and the Will to Lead.* New York, NY: Knopf.

SYNTHESIS

Adler, Nancy J. 1997. "Global Leadership: Women Leaders." *MIR: Management International Review* 37: 171-196.

Astin, A. W., H. S. Astin, and J. A. Lindholm. 2011. *Cultivating the Spirit: How College can Enhance Students' Inner Lives.'* 1st ed. San Francisco, CA: Jossey-Bass.

Bordas, Juana. 2013. *The Power of Latino Leadership: Culture, Inclusion, and Contribution.* BK Business. San Francisco, CA: Berrett-Koehler Publishers.

Brake, Terence. 1997. *The Global Leader: Critical Factors for Creating the World Class Organization.* Chicago: Irwin Professional Publishing.

Caligiuri, Paula. 2006. "Developing Global Leaders." *Human Resource Management Review* (16): 219-228.

Crossan, Mary, Dana Mazutis, and Gerard Seijts. 2013. "In Search of Virtue: The Role of Virtues, Values and Character Strengths in Ethical Decision-Making." *Journal of Business Ethics* (113): 567-581.

Cuyegkeng, Ma Assunta C. and Antonette Palma-Angeles, eds. 2011. *Defining Filipino Leadership.* Philippines: Ateneo de Manila Press.

Enriquez, Virgilio G. 1989. *Kapwa Theory and Indigenous Psychology and National Consciousness. Study of Languages and Cultures of Asia & Africa.* Vol. 23 Institute for the Study of Languages and Cultures of Asia and Africa.

Follett, Mary P. 1949. *Freedom and Co-Ordination: Lectures in Business Organization by Mary Parker Follett.* London: Management Publications Trust, Ltd.

Gardiner, John Jacob Zucker. 2009. "Transcendent Leadership: Board Metrics for Profits, People, and Planet." Prague, Czech Republic, Annual Meeting of the International Leadership Association, November 12.

Gardner, Howard. 1983. *Frames of Mind: The Theory of Multiple Intelligences.* 1st ed. New York, NY: Basic Books.

Gregersen, Hal B., Allen J. Morrison, and J. Stewart Black. 1998. "Developing Leaders for the Global Frontier." *Sloan Management Review* (Fall): 21-32.

Leksander, Susan. 2007. *Psychosynthesis and Multiracial Clients: Diversity and Integration of Multiple Selves*. San Francisco, CA: California Institute of Integral Studies.

Nobles, Wade. 2006. *Seeking the Sakhu: Foundational Writings for an African Psychology*. Chicago: Third World Press.

Guevarra, Jaime P. 2005. "Pakikipagkapwa [Sharing/Merging with Others]." In *Filipino Cultural Traits: Claro R. Ceniza Lectures*, edited by Rolando M. Gripaldo, 9-20. Washington, DC: The Council for Research in Values and Philosophy.

Hall, Douglas T. 2008. "Self-Awareness, Identity and Leader Development." In *Leader Development for Transforming Organizations: Growing Leaders for Tomorrow*, edited by David V. Day, Stephen J. Zaccaro and Stanley M. Halpin, 154-173. New Jersey: Taylor & Francis e-Library.

Hunter, I., B. J. Dik, and J. H. Banning. 2010. "College Students' Perceptions of Calling in Work and Life: A Qualitative Analysis." *Journal of Vocational Behavior* (76): 178-186.

Kaiser, Robert B. and Darren B. Overfield. 2010. "Assessing Flexible Leadership as a Mastery of Opposites." *Consulting Psychology Journal: Practice and Research* 62 (2): 105-118.

Kouzes, James M. Kouzes and Barry Z. Posner. 2003. *The Leadership Challenge*. The Leadership Practices Inventory (Book 53). 3rd ed. San Francisco, CA: Jossey-Bass.

Kouzes, James M. and Barry Z. Posner. 2000. *Five Practices of Exemplary Leadership*. San Francisco, CA: Jossey-Bass Pfeiffer.

Kouzes, James M. and Barry Z. Posner. 2007. *The Leadership Challenge*. 4th ed. San Francisco, CA: Jossey-Bass.

Lethlean, Esther. "Diaspora: The New Philanthropy?" Queensland University Technology., accessed 7/28, 2014, http://eprints.qut.edu.au/49983/.

Levinson, Daniel J. 1986. "A Conception of Adult Development." *American Psychologist* 41 (1): 3-13.

Mendenhall, Mark E., Joyce C. Osland, Allan Bird, Gary R. Oddou, Marth L. Maznevski, Michael J. Stevens, and Gunther K. Stahl, eds. 2013. *Global Leadership*. New York and London: Routledge Taylor and Francis Group.

Opiniano, J. 2002. "The Dynamics of Transnational Philanthropy by Migrant Workers to their Communities of Origin: The Case of Pozorrubio, Philippines." University of Cape Town, South Africa, Fifth International Society for Third-Sector Research.

Peterson, Christopher and Martin Seligman. 2004. *Character Strengths and Virtues: A Handbook and Classification*. Washington, DC: American Psychological Association / Oxford University Press.

Roffey, Bet. 1999. "Filipina Managers and Entrepreneurs: What Leadership Models Apply?" *Asian Studies Review* 23 (3): 375-405.

Spreitzer, Gretchen M., McCall Jr., Morgan W., and Joan D. Mahoney. 1997. "Early Identification of International Executive Potential." *Journal of Applied Psychology* 82 (1): 6-29.

Uhl-Bien, Mary. 2006. "Relational Leadership Theory: Exploring the Social Processes of Leadership and Organizing." *The Leadership Quarterly* 17 (6): 654-676.

Villegas, Bernardo M. 2011. *The Book of Virtues & Values*. Philippines: Center for Research and Communication, University of Asia and the Pacific.

Williams, Luke. 2010. *Disrupt: Think the Unthinkable to Spark Transformation in Your Business*. 1st ed. New Jersey: FT Press.

Apendix B
ADDITIONAL RESOURCES

Center for Creative Leadership.360 by design Facilitator's guide. Retrieved from <http://www.ccl.org/leadership/pdf/assessments/360BDfacguide.pdf>
The guide provides information on conducting CCL's 360 By Design assessment and facilitating a feedback workshop and one-one-one sessions with participants. 360 By Design is an assessment tool that uses feedback to identify the highest valued competencies for an organization in order to support the professional development and success of its participants.

Filipina Women's Network. 2007. Interviews with FWN100 2007 awardees.
The Filipina Women's Network interviews its Top 100 Most Influential Filipina Women awardees as part of its time capsule project with the objective of documenting the contributions of Filipina women to society to inspire future generations.

Filipina Women's Network. 2013. Interviews with FWN global 100 2013 awardees.
The Filipina Women's Network interviews its Top 100 Most Influential Filipina Women awardees as part of its time capsule project with the objective of documenting the contributions of Filipina women to society to inspire future generations.

Filipina Women's Network. 2103. FWN Global 100: The 100 Most Influential Filipina Women in the World.

Filipina Women's Network has published the Filipina Leadership Summit magazine from 2005-present. The magazine serves as a program and resource for attend ees. The 2013 issue showcases the first group of the FWN Global 100 Most Influential Women in the World.

Institute for Intercultural Communication. 2014.
Retrieved from <http://www.intercultural.org/tools.php>
Provides a list of selected intercultural training and assessment tool.

Kozai Group. The global competencies inventory (GCI). Retrieved from <http://kozaigroup.com/inventories/the-global-competencies-inventory-gci/> Global Competencies Inventory measures three facets of intercultural adapt ability in identifying personal characteristics related to successful performance in contexts where cultural norms and behaviors vary from one's own. This tool is generally used for purposes such as professional development, team building and succession planning.

Najafi Global Mindset Institute. Global mindset inventory's three capitals.
Retrieved from <http://globalmindset.thunderbird.edu/home/global-mindset-inventory/three-capitals>
The Global Mindset Inventory is an assessment tool for identifying one's capacity to lead and influence individuals and companies in a global context, particularly those who are from a different culture.

Ronald E. Dolan, ed. 1991. Philippines: A Country Study. Washington: GPO for the Library of Congress, 1991. Retrieved from http://countrystudies.us/philippines/

Via Institute on Character. Do you know your 24 character strengths?
Retrieved from <http://www.viacharacter.org/www/the-survey.>
The VIA survey was created to help individuals identify the make-up of their character strengths that are classified under six virtue categories. The survey can be taken online and is free of charge.

Appendix C
FWN Award Categories

Behind the Scenes Leaders

This award category recognizes Filipina women who may not have the big title or corner office, but is a driving force behind the success of a social cause or life issue, a community organization's project or initiative; or her employer's organizational business unit or department. Someone who has gone beyond the call of duty to devote time, energy, and resources to advocate for those who need a voice, or support the organization she represents or works for.

Builders

Builders have demonstrated exceptional business impact at a large workplace environment; displaying deep passion for a cause through collaborative initiatives or alliances with nonprofit organizations on behalf of her own organization; demonstrates high potential and skill with measurable results at a government agency, or organization in the public and private sectors. "Buildership" is about building better organizations, leading broken organizations to adjust, repair, and re-align.

Emerging Leaders

This award category recognizes Filipina women below age 35 who are making their mark in a leadership role, are on the pathway to principalship and building capacity across a system. Emerging Leaders have powerful mindsets and skill sets that drive achievement for their organizations.

Founders and Pioneers

This award honors Filipina women in their capacities as the chief executive, president, executive director or founder of a company, community organization, non-profit, or business venture that they helped start, build or significantly grow. This award category is for the trailblazers who have marshaled resources and applied innovative practices, processes and/or technologies in a new and groundbreaking way to address a significant business or organizational opportunity.

Innovators and Thought Leaders

This award recognizes women who have broken new ground in the global workplace, have delivered new and unique applications of emerging technology transforming the way people think, in the fields of sports, literature, the arts and pop culture, or have improved the lives of others by helping develop a product or service in the fields of science, technology, engineering, arts, or mathematics. This award category is also for someone who have either launched a new enterprise, a learning function, or completely overhauled an existing development or community initiative that has sparked a following.

538

Keepers of the Flame

Sustaining Pinay Power. As the excitement dies down and reality sets in, many will drop out and other will pick up the torch. The Keepers of the Flame are the caretakers, ensuring that the Pinay Power Vision is kept alive.

Nicole

This award honors Filipina women whose words, actions, and activism, inspire others to act and revolutionize society's way of understanding traditional beliefs and customs thus leaving behind a Filipino global imprint. "Nicole," who sparked an international dialogue about women's rights, national sovereignty, and international law, as she steadfastly pursued justice against her rapists, inspires this category.

Policymakers and Visionaries

This award recognizes Filipina women leaders who have demonstrated exceptional acumen combined with a forward-looking vision in the development or influencing of policies, campaigns or laws that impact business, industry, and society. Leaders who enrich the lives, careers and businesses of others; someone who shares the benefits of their wealth, experience, and knowledge; actions that significantly change how we think and live.

APPENDIX C
List of FWN Awardees
(2007-2013)

100 Most Influential Filipina Women in the U.S. (US FWN100™)

Behind the Scenes Leaders

2007

Asia Yulo-Blume
Aurora Cavosora Daly
Cheely Ann Sy
Cora Basa Cortez Tomalinas
Denielle Palomares
Edna Austria Rodis
Evangeline Canonizado-Buell
Flor Alcantara-Reyes
Kai Delen-Briones
Laarni San Juan
Lolita Kintanar
Lorna Lardizabal Dietz
Maria Jocelyn Bernal
Perla Gange Ibarrientos
Rosalinda Medina Rupel
Susie Quesada

2009

Aileen Suzara
Belle Santos
Cherie Querol Moreno
Daisy Magalit Rodriguez
Dolly Pangan-Specht
Elsie Rose
Helen Marte Bautista
Jian Zapata
Kathleen Davenport
Lorrie V. Reynoso
Lottie T. Buhain
Lovette Rosales Llantos
Lydia Castillo Fontan
Lyna Larcia-Calvario
Mady Rivera
Maria Concepcion Banatao

2009 *(cont.)*

Naomi Tacuyan Underwood
Nerissa M. Fernandez
Nida L. Recabo
Priscilla Magante Quinn
Roselyn Estepa Ibañez
Shirley Orille Brazis
Sunny Dykwel
Tess Ricafort Alarcon

2011

Bennie Lou Quevedo
Cherina Viloria Tinio
Evelyn Javier-Centeno
Evelyn Luluquisen
Francine Villarmia-Kahawai
Gloria Ramil Omania
Gretheline Bolandrina
Henni Espinosa
Julicta Zarate Hudson

2011 *(cont.)*

Mary Ann C. Ubaldo
Pearl Parmelee
Rosario "Puchi" Carrion
  Di Ricco

2012

Angie Louie
Edcelyn Pujol
JoAnn Fields
Marian Catedral-King
Maritessa Bravo Ares
Pureza Belza
Theresa Noriega-Lum
Yong Chavez

Builders and Emerging Leaders

2007

Arlene Marie A. "Bambi" Lorica
Bettina Santos Yap
Claire Oliveros
Edna M.Casteel
Genevieve Jopanda
Jennifer Briones Tjiong
Laura Izon Powell
Laureen Dumadag Laglagaron
Lorna Mae DeVera
Lyna Larcia-Calvario
May Nazareno
Melinda Poliarco
Milagros "Mitos" G. Santisteban
Nieves Cortez
Paz Gomez
Polly Cortez
Rachel Buenviaje
Rebecca Samson
Regina "Ging" E. Reyes
Rose-Ann K. Ubarra
Shirley Raguindin
Sonia T. Delen
Susan Afan
Sylvia Lichauco
Thelma Boac
Theresa Tantay Wilson
Zenei T. Cortez

2009

Ana Julaton
Cielo Martinez
Cynthia Aloot
Denise Castañeda Miles
Gel Santos Relos
Isabelita M. Abele
Jannah Arivan Manansala
Jennifer Ong
Katherine Abriam-Yago
Katrina R. Abarcar
Maria (Mimi) Amutan
Mivic Hirose
Raquel Cruz Bono
Raquel R. Redondiez
Rebecca Delgado Rottman
Rowena Verdau-Beduya
Stephanie Ong-Stillman
Valerie Pozon-de Leon

2011

Cynthia Rapaido
Diana Reyes
Estela Matriano
Esther Misa Chavez
Genevieve Herreria
Gloria B. Gil

2011 (cont.)

Kathleen Quinn DuBois
Keesa Ocampo
Leah Beth O. Naholowaa
Leia Lorica
Maria Africa Beebe
Melanie A. Caoile
Mila M. Josue
Odette Alcazaren Keeley
Selenna Franco-Cefre

2012

Belinda Muñoz
Cora Aragon Soriano
Cynthia A. Bonta
Eleanore Fernandez
Esther Lee
Jacqueline Dumlao Yu
Lili Tarachand
Nadia Catarata Jurani
Natalie C. Aliga
Olivia Finina De Jesus
Prosy Abarquez-Delacruz
Rita Dela Cruz
Rocio Nuyda
Sheryll Casuga
Stefanie Medious
Theresa Chua

Founders & Pioneers

2007

Celia Ruiz-Tomlinson
Connie S. Uy
Cora Alisuag
Ellen M. Abellera
Erlinda Sayson Limcaco
Gina Lopez Alexander
Gloria T. Caoile
Joy Bruce
Linda Maria Nietes-Little
Loida Nicolas Lewis
Ludy Payumo Corrales
Luzviminda Sapin Micabalo
Marietta Aster Nagrampa Almazan
Mary Carmen Madrid-Crost
Nimfa Yamsuan Gamez
Patricia Aldaba Lim-Yusah

2007 (cont.)

Rozita Villanueva Lee
Sony Robles Florendo
Tessie Guillermo
Virna S. Tintiangco

2009

Alice Bulos
Adelamar Alcantara
Analisa Balares
Carina Castañeda
Cora Oriel
Delle Sering Fojas
Ethel Luzario
Evelyn Silangcruz Bunoan
Fe Martinez

2009 (cont.)

Fe Punzalan
Fely Guzman
Imelda Ortega Anderson
Judy Arteche-Carr
Maria Maryles Casto
Mivic Hirose
Mona Lisa Yuchengco
Nanette D. Alcaro
Nelsie Parrado
Nini RB Bautista de Garcia
Norma Calderon-Panahon
Patricia Espiritu Halagao
Rosie Abriam
Ruthe Catolico Ashley
Sherri Burke
Zenaida Cunanan

Founders & Pioneers

2011

Alma Onrubia
Chateau Gardecki
Christina Rodriguez
 Laskowski
Dellie Punla
Geri Ferrer-Chan
Herna Cruz-Louie
Janelle So
Josefina R. Enriquez
Jossie Alegre

2011

Joy Dalauidao-Hermsen
Lillian Pardo
Maria Benel Se-Liban
Marjan Philhour
Perla Paredes Daly
Rhoda Yabes Alvarez
Soledad Manaay
Tess Mauricio
Vellie Sandalo Dietrich-Hall

2012

Betty O. Buccat
Conchita Bathan
Constance Valencia
 Santos
Elaine R. Serina
Josie Jones
Kristine Custodio
Victoria J. Santos

Innovators & Thought Leaders

2007

Angelita Castro-Kelly
Carissa Villacorta
Charmaine Clamor
Connie Mariano
Diana J. Galindo
Edith Mijares Ardiente
Elena Mangahas
Elenita Fe Mendoza Strobel
Gemma Nemenzo
Jane Hofileña
Leila Benitez-McCollum
Lilia Villanueva
Malu Rivera-Peoples
Marisa Marquez
Mutya San Agustin

2009

Brenda Buenviaje
Cora Manese Tellez
Esminia "Mia" Luluquisen
Hazel Sanchez
Jei Africa
Lenore RS Lim
Marlina Feleo Gonzales
Marissa Aroy
Nana Luz Khilnani
Norma P. Edar
Ma Rowena Verdan-Beduya
Robyn Rodriguez Canham
Sokie Paulin

2011

Angel Velasco Shaw
Celia Pangilinan-Donahue
Christina Dunham
Evelyn Dilsaver
France Viana
Gemma Bulos
Minerva Malabrigo Tantoco

2012

A. Fajilan
Cris Comerford
Janet Nepales
Maricel Quiroz
Penélope V. Flores
Vivian Zalvidea Araullo

Nicole

2007
M. Evelina Galang

2009
Jessica Cox

2012
Nilda Guanzon Valmores
Paulita Lasola Malay

2013
Annalisa Enrile

Policymakers and Visionaries

2007

Christina Arvin Baal
Eleonor G. Castillo
Grace Walker
Gwen de Vera
Irene Bueno
Kris Valderrama
Kymberly Marcos Pine

2007 *(cont.)*

Lillian Galedo
Lourdes Tancinco
Marissa Castro-Salvati
Miriam B. Redmiller
Mona Pasquil
Norma Doctor Sparks
Rida T. R. Cabanilla

2007 *(cont.)*

Ruth Asmundson Uy
Sonia Aranza
Tani Gorre Can-
 til-Sakauye
Vanessa Barcelona
Velma Veloria
Vida Benavides

Policymakers and Visionaries

2009

Carmelyn Malalis
Carmen Lagdameo Stull
Faith Bautista
Hydra B. Mendoza
Gertrude Quiroz Gregorio
Joanne F. del Rosario
Joselyn Geaga-Rosenthal
Lorraine Rodero Inouye
Lynn Finnegan
Marissa Garcia Bailey
Myrna L. De Vera

2009

Noella Tabladillo
Rose Zimmerman
Dr. Rozzana Verder-Aliga
Stephanie Ong Stillman

2011

Agnes Briones Ubalde
Amy Agbayani
Arlie Ricasa
Cheryl Nora Moss
Katherine M. Eldemar

2011 *(cont.)*

Mae Cendana Torlakson
Melissa Roxas
Monique Lhuillier
Pat Gacoscos
Rosa Mena Moran

2012

Alicia Fortaleza
Rosita Galang
Zenda Garcia-Lat

Keepers of the Flame

2007

Al Perez
Arlene Marie "Bambi" Lorica
Elena Mangahas
Franklin M. Ricarte
Genevieve Herreria
Maria Roseni "Nini" M. Alvero
Marily Mondejar
Maya Ong Escudero
Nida Recabo
Rowena Mendoza Sanchez
Sonia T. Delen
Thelma Boac

2009

Al Perez
Arlene Marie "Bambi" Lorica
Elena Mangahas
Ellen Abellera
Franklin M. Ricarte
Gloria T. Caoile
Jocelyn Bernal
Josephine "Jopin" Romero
Lilia V. Villanueva
Marily Mondejar
Mutya San Agustin Shaw
Shirley S. Raguindin
Sonia T. Delen
Thelma Boac

2011

Al Perez
Arlene Marie "Bambi" Lorica
Franklin M. Ricarte

2011 *(cont.)*

Gloria T. Caoile
Josephine "Jopin" Romero
Lilia V. Villanueva
Mutya San Agustin Shaw
Shirley S. Raguindin
Susie Quesada
Thelma Boac

2012

Al Perez
Arlene Marie "Bambi" Lorica
Cherina Tinio
Cynthia Rapaido
Elena Mangahas
Esther Chavez
Franklin M. Ricarte
Gloria T. Caoile
Josephine "Jopin" T. Romero
Judy Arteche Carr
Lilia V. Villanueva
Mutya San Agustin Shaw
Shirley S. Raguindin
Sonia T. Delen
Susie Quesada
Thelma Boac

2013

Al Perez
Arlene Marie "Bambi" Lorica
Alicia Fortaleza
Cynthia Rapaido
Edcelyn Pujol
Elena Mangahas

2013 *(cont.)*

Franklin M. Ricarte
Gloria T. Caoile
Marily Mondejar
Maria Roseni "Nini" M. Alvero
Maya Ong Escudero
Mutya San Agustin Shaw
Shirley S. Raguindin
Sonia T. Delen
Susie Quesada
Thelma Boac

2014

Arlene Marie "Bambi" Lorica
Alicia Fortaleza
Delle Sering Fojas
Edcelyn Pujol
Elena Mangahas
Franklin M. Ricarte
Gizelle Covarrubias Robinson
Gloria T. Caoile
Marily Mondejar
Maria Roseni "Nini" M. Alvero
Maya Ong Escudero
Mutya San Agustin Shaw
Shirley S. Raguindin
Sonia T. Delen
Susie Quesada
Thelma Boac

2013 Awards – 100 Most Influential Filipina Women in the World (Global FWN100™)

Behind the Scenes Leaders

Bessie Badilla
Elizabeth Ann Quirino
Emma Cuenca

Genevieve Jopanda
Loisa Cabuhat

Maria Beebe
Regina Manzana-Sawhney

Builders

Carmela Clendening
Imelda M. Nicolas

Jocelyn Ding
Nina D. Aguas

Rebecca Delgado Rottman

Emerging Leaders

Ariel Batungbacal
Christina Luna

Meriam Reynosa
Michelle Bumgarner

Patricia Gallardo-Dwyer

Founders & Pioneers

Allyson Tintiangco-Cubales
Bella Aurora Padua-Belmonte
Dawn Bohulano Mabalon
Delle Sering-Fojas
Ernestina de los Santos-Mac
Evelia V. Religioso
Isabelita Manalastas-Watanabe

Joselyn Geaga-Rosenthal
Julieta Gabiola
Librada Yamat
Loida Nicolas Lewis
Lydia Cruz
Maria Almia de los Santos

Mariedel Leviste
Marife Zamora
Norma Fulinara Placido
Patricia Zamora Riingen
Rosemer Enverga
Tess Mauricio

Innovators and Thought Leaders

Amelia Duran-Stanton
Annette M. David
Carmencita David-Padilla
Janet C. Mendoza Stickmon

Janet Susan R. Nepales
Lirio Sobrevinas Covey
Lucille Lozada Tenazas
Mary Ann Lucille L. Sering

Mary Jane Alvero-Al Mahdi
Mira Soriano Gillet
Rozita Villanueva Lee
Suzie Moya Benitez

Policymakers & Visionaries

Astrid S. Tuminez
Cora Manese Tellez
Eleanor Valentin

Hydra Mendoza-McDonnell
Imelda Cuyugan
Gloria T. Caoile

Kris Valderrama
Margaret Lapiz
Patricia V. Paez

Appendix D

Historical Timeline of the Philippines

—900
End of prehistory.
Laguna Copperplate Inscription, the earliest known Philippine document, is written in the Manila area in Kawi script.

—1400
Birth of the Baybayin, Hanunoo, Tagbanwa, and Buhid scripts from Brahmi.

—1521
March 28: Magellan reaches the Philippines March 31: The first mass on Philippine soil is celebrated. April 27: Magellan is killed by Lapu-Lapu in the battle of Mactan.

—1565
February 13: Miguel López de Legazpi arrives in the Philippines with four ships and 380 men'
May 8: Legazpi established the first permanent Spanish settlement in the country. First Philippine Spanish Treaty of Peace is drawn where Filipinos recognized Spanish sovereignty and gets protection in return. Christianity is introduced.

—1573 *to* 1811
Roughly between 1556 and 1813, Spain engaged in the Galleon Trade between Manila and Acapulco. The galleons were built in the shipyards of Cavite, outside Manila, by Filipino craftsmen. The trade was funded by Chinese traders, manned by Filipino sailors and "supervised" by Mexico City officials. In this time frame, Spain recruited Mexicans to serve as soldiers in Manila. Likewise, they drafted Filipinos to serve as soldiers in Mexico. Once drafted, the trip across the ocean sometimes came with a "one way" ticket.

—1587
First Filipinos ("Luzonians") to set foot in North America arrive in Morro Bay, (San Luis Obispo) California on board the Manila-built galleon ship Nuestra Senora de Esperanza under the command of Spanish Captain Pedro de Unamuno.

—1600s
Filipinos and Chinese reach Mexico aboard Spanish galleons on trade route between Manila, Philippines and Acapulco, Mexico.

—1600 *to* 1906
First wave of Filipino immigration to North and South America

—1700s
Filipino seamen jump off of Spanish galleon ships and create towns in the Louisiana bayous.

—1780
Real Sociedad Economica de los Amigos del Pais de Filipinas (Royal Economic Society of Friends of the Philippines) introduced in the Philippines to offer local and foreign scholarships and professorships to Filipinos, and financed trips of scientists from Spain to the Philippines.

—1781
Antonio Miranda Rodriguez chosen a member of the first group of settlers to establish the city of Los Angeles, California. He and his daughter fell sick with smallpox while en route, and remained in Baja California for an extended time to recuperate. When they finally arrived in Alta

California, it was discovered that Miranda Rodriguez was a skilled gunsmith. He was reassigned in 1782 to the Presidio of Santa Barbara as an armorer.

—1814
During the War of 1812, Filipinos from Manila Village (near New Orleans) were among the "Baratarians" who fought against the British under the command of Jean Lafitte in the Battle of New Orleans.

—1870
Filipino mestizos studying in New Orleans form the first Filipino Association in the United States, the "Sociedad de Beneficencia de los Hispanos Filipinos."

—1880
Manila is connected to Hongkong through telegraphic cable by Eastern Telecom.

—1898
First hoisting of the Filipino flag, and Battle of Imus beginning the successful series of battles against Spanish sovereignty.
Philippine Independence is declared in Kawit. Philippine National Anthem played for the first time.

—1899-1902
The Philippine American War becomes America's first colonial war. One quarter of the population of Luzon, Philippines dies in the three-year conflict.

—1901
600 trained U.S. teachers arrive on USS Thomas.

—1903
Governor Taft enunciates the policy of The Philippines for the Filipinos.
The Pensionado Act allows Filipino students to study in the U.S.
Forty Filipino men are contracted to come to North American to lay telephone cable from Seattle to Alaska. Most remain.

—1903 *to* 1934
Second wave of Filipino immigration to U.S. Called the *manong* generation, these Filipinos were U.S. nationals who arrived for various reasons but most were laborers, mostly from Ilocos and the Visayas. The Philippine Independence Act of 1934 restricted immigration to 50 persons a year, thus ending this wave of immigration.

—1946
The United States recognizes Philippine Independence, July 4, 1946, through Treaty of Manila. Republic of the Philippines reclaims legacies from the Generation of 1898 including Philippine Flag and National Anthem. During the 1946 parade Emilio Aguinaldo marches with Filipino veterans of the War of Independence, carrying the flag he designed and originally unfurled after he declared Philippine Independence on June 12, 1898. Manuel Roxas elected President.

—1946 *to* 1965
The third wave of immigration followed the end of WWII, where Filipinos who served in the war were given the option of becoming U.S. citizens. The War Brides Act and the Fiancee Act allowed over 16,000 Filipinas into the U.S.

—1965 *to* present
The fourth wave of immigration began in 1965, and most of the immigrants were professionals. Due to a shortage of qualified nurses, many Filipinas went to the U.S. and stayed.

Appendix E

Suggestions for Workshop Activities
to Enrich the Book Reading Experience
as Stand-Alone Activities
or as Part of a Leaderhip Course

1. **Activity:** Leaders you admire.
   Objective: To seek leadership characteristics through personal experience

Activity Description: Divide the group into small groups. Ask participants to share a story about the best or most influential leader they have read about in the book. After each story, identify leadership characteristics by asking the question: "What was it that made this person such an effective leader?" Then as a group, identify the traits that all the leaders seemed to share.

<http://www.workshopexercises.com>

2. **Activity:** Stand by your quote.
   Objective: To introduce leadership discussion and awareness

Activity Description: Place thoughtful leadership quotes from the women authors on the walls, making sure the print is readable. Ask the participants to walk around the room reading each of the quotes. Then have them stand by one quote that resonates well with their personal views on what makes a good leader (there can be more than one person standing by a quote). When all participants have selected a quote, have each explain to the group why her chosen quote is important to them--share a leadership insight.

<http://www.workshopexercises.com>

3. **Activity:** Character strengths.
   Objective: To learn your character strengths

Activity Description: Great leaders have identified and clarified their core working values. They understand how each of their core values translates into leadership behavior. Take the VIA survey to know your character strengths. Which character strengths do you share with any of the 3 or 4 women leaders? Are these character strengths unique to Filipino culture? Or to American culture?

<http://www.viacharacter.org/www/Character-Strengths/Personality-Assessment#nav>

4. **Activity:** Leadership tips.
   Objective: To find ways to strengthen leadership ability

Activity Description: Choose 2-3 chapters from the book. Compare and contrast the leadership story and the leadership tips and their implications for your own leadership experience. Make a list of intentional simple, on-the-job self-improvement strategies. For example, list ways of building meaningful work relationships. List ways of motivating others.

5. **ACTIVITY:** This I Believe Essay.
   OBJECTIVE: To describe the core values that guide your daily lives.

Activity Description: Follow the instructions for submitting an essay to 'This I Believe'. http://thisibelieve.org/guidelines/ Write and submit your own statement of personal belief. Reflect how you approach new challenges through your interpretation of the individual chapter readings.

Variation: Choose one of the women leaders and write a "This I Believe" essay from the woman's perspective--pretend you are that woman writing the essay. You may interview the author if possible.

6. **ACTIVITY:** Leadership theory and practice.
   OBJECTIVE: To define your own leadership theory and practice

Activity Description: From two or more of the chapters, share which leadership theory or practice you found most valid to your work-life and explain why. If none of the theories or explanations spoke to your personal experience, feel free to challenge the theory and propose your own explanation.

7. **ACTIVITY:** Reflected best self.
   OBJECTIVE: To compose a portrait of you when you are at your best.

Activity Description: (1) Solicit feedback about your best-self from others—classmates, work or community service colleagues, clients, personal friends, mentors, family members. Give them at least 2 weeks to respond. (2) While waiting for their responses, you should engage in a deep personal reflection about the times when you were at your best, write three short stories that stand out as times when you were at your best, then identify patterns or commonalities that arise across those stories. (3) Review your best-self feedback from others and look for themes. (4) Revise the portrait of who you are at your best, incorporating feedback from others with your own reflections. Your revised portrait should be a written description of the essence of your best-self. What are your key insights? What are the action implications for you, as you think about a) being at your best more often, and b) making your best-self even better? Which of the women authors is most like your best self? *Checkout:*
<http://positiveorgs.bus.umich.edu/cpo-tools/reflected-best-self-exe-cise-2nd-edition/>
or
<http://faculty.som.yale.edu/amywrzesniewski/documents/ReflectedBest SelfExerciseIntroduction2014Careers.pdf>

MARIA AFRICA BEEBE, PH.D.
Chief Editor

Maria is a sociolinguist interested in intercultural communication and has an M.A. in Anthropology and Ph.D. in Education from Stanford University. Her 25 years of global development work and research interests led her to launch Global Networks, a Portland, OR-based consulting, research, and education not-for-profit that works at the intersection of technology, content, and pedagogy. Her research interests include critical discourse analysis, women's leadership, and ICT for development. She co-edited the book *AfricaDotEdu: IT Opportunities and Higher Education in Africa*. She read papers at international conferences; including a paper on MOOCs, m-Learning and ICT Smart Hubs at the World Summit on Information Society in Geneva in 2013. Maria had academic appointments at Washington State University and Oregon State University while working on international development programs. She is a visiting researcher at Portland State University.

MAYA ONG ESCUDERO
Managing Editor

Along with her husband Nick Selby and children Ben and Ruth, Maya is an active supporter of youth leadership training in sports, the arts, and community activism.

CORA MANESE TELLEZ
Preface

Cora founded Sterling Health Services Administration (HAS) in 2004 and is its President and CEO. Sterling leads in the health benefits and healthcare financing by putting employers and consumers in control of healthcare spending and in touch with resources to help them manage their money and their health. The company serves clients throughout the U.S. Before 2004, Cora was the President of a division of HealthNet, President of Prudential's western health care operations, CEO of the Bay Region Blue Shield of California, and Regional Manager for Kaiser Permanente of Hawaii. Cora received her M.A. in public administration from California State University. She is a Phi Beta Kappa graduate of Mills College where she received a BA degree and then served as college Trustee. Cora serves on several boards of directors. She was instrumental in starting Asian Community Mental Health and Filipinos for Social Justice. She has been honored for professional and community service by numerous organization including Women Healthcare Executives, Asian Pacific Fund, Bay Area Tumor Institute, among others.

NINA D. AGUAS
A Filipina Leans In

Nina is perhaps best known as a leading Filipina banker who has held key positions at Citigroup within Asia-Pacific and ANZ Asia-Pacific, and in New York, and is currently President and CEO of the Philippine Bank of Communications. Beyond the walls of her CEO suite, however, she is an art lover and painter, a traveler with much wanderlust, and an accomplished home cook. To her husband Mario, she is a supportive wife and partner, and together they share a rich spiritual life. To her five children, she is a best friend, healer of broken bones and broken hearts, and disciplinarian—combining tough love with direct conversations. To her friends she is known for her generosity of spirit and infectious laughter. To her colleagues, she is a partner and mentor, bringing people of different skills and dispositions together and leading them to succeed. At the end of the day, she is just like any other woman: she loves dressing up and has an incurable weakness for shoes and handbags.

Mary Jane Alvero Al-Mahdi
Crossing Borders in Pursuit of Excellence

Mary is a Chemical Engineer and CEO of Geoscience Testing Laboratory (GTL). She has spent 22 years of her life living and working in the United Arab Emirates (UAE). She heads a multimillion-dollar and a multi-disciplinary company with over 450 employees, 4 branches, and 20 site laboratories. The prestigious Burj Khalifa, Downtown Dubai, and the Dubai Metro are examples of their impressive projects. Mary is a quintessential woman leader: an achiever, an influencer, a community volunteer, and a mother. As a visionary, she rose from the ranks through sheer hard work and determination steering GTL to greater success. Combining education and Filipina charm, she serves as a role model for Filipinas and women in UAE and elsewhere. In 2008, she was the first Filipina to win the prestigious Emirates Business Women's Award, the first runner-up in the Professional Category, and along with an elite group has been lauded by the UAE government for their professional excellence, exemplary work, and leadership. She is married to an Emirati national and they have two children.

Mayor Ruth Uy Asmundson, Ph.D.
From Barefoot in the Barrio to...

Ruth was born and raised in Isabela, Philippines. She graduated with a B.S. in Chemistry in 1964 from Adamson University, Manila, and with a Fulbright scholarship, obtained an M.S. in Chemistry in 1968 from Wilkes University, Wilkes-Barre, PA and a Ph.D. in Agricultural Chemistry in 1972 from UC Davis, CA. While in graduate school, she met the then Mayor of Davis, Vigfus Asmundson when she danced *Binasuan*. He was charmed by her grace and asked her for a date. On their third date, he asked her to marry him. She said "Yes." Her Fulbright scholarship required her to go back to Manila where she became a professor and chair of the graduate school in chemistry at Adamson University. Vigfus visited Ruth in Manila and again asked her to marry him and for the second time Ruth said yes. They have four daughters and raised two nephews. She was elected and served for 10 years on the Davis Board of Education and two terms as mayor of Davis. She is Ambassador to Davis Sister Cities and Special Assistant to UC Davis Vice Provost for University Outreach and International Programs.

Suzie Moya Benitez
Creating Initiatives for Change

Trustee/Executive Director, Bayanihan Folk Arts Foundation and Associate Vice President Campus life, Philippine Women's University (PWU), and Trustee, Philippine Women's College, Davao, Suzie toured the world as a Bayanihan dancer and Karilagan international model. She studied Foreign Service (Assumption College), Public Administration and Governance & Development Communications (UP), Strategic Business Economics (University of Asia & the Pacific), Development Management (AIM), and Social Development (PWU). Yet her love for the performing arts led to a career in arts and culture. She brought Filipino music and dance to the grassroots and the global scene through 'Teaching and Touching Lives.' Under her deft direction, Bayanihan has taken courageous steps towards innovation and change, becoming an 8th time world dance grand prize winner. She lectures on professional image and communications for financial institutions, is chair for Asia in the Federation for International Dance Festivals, and serves as international juror in Europe and Asia. Suzie and her late husband Noel are blessed with 3 children—Marco, Marielle and Marton.

MICHELE BUMGARNER
For the Love of Racing

Michelle is the first Filipina to reach the top level of open-wheel motorsports, racing of vehicles with the wheels outside the car's main body and in most cases one seat. Known throughout the Philippines as the Asian Karting Queen, Michele has blazed a trail in the karting world winning championships, breaking barriers, and representing her country on the international motorsports stage. She made her debut into single-seat racing with the National Karting Series in the Philippines in 1999 at the age of ten. She was the first female winner in the Asian Formula 3 Series and the youngest female participant in 2006. Michele became the first female champion of the Rock Island Grand Prix in Rock Island, Illinois, the world's largest street karting race and made her Pro Mazda debut at Sebring in 2008. She is now racing on the Mazda Road to Indy, the ladder system for drivers seeking to compete in the Verizon Indy Car Series and of course, the greatest spectacle in racing, The Indianapolis 500. Michele blogs for Top Gear Philippines <http://www.topgear.com.ph/author/michele-bumgarner>

Gloria Caoile
Stepping Up

Gloria has dedicated her life to empowering people who need the most help and ensuring their voices are heard. She is National Political Director of the Asian Pacific American Labor Alliance, a constituency group of the AFL-CIO. She served for over 30 years with the American Federation of State, County, and Municipal Employees (AFSCME), a 1.3 million-member union, where she fought for the rights of others to make a difference in their lives. She remains active in AFSCME special projects such as leading disaster response and relief teams. At one point, Gloria was the highest-ranking Asian Pacific-American woman in the labor movement. She has been a stalwart supporter of the Asian American and Pacific Islander community in the U.S. and devoted to developing the next generation of women. She is a recipient of distinguished awards including the Philippines' Presidential Merit of Honor, St. Scholastica's College Pax Award, and FWN100 Most Influential Women. She finds the greatest meaning from her private family life. She lives in Las Vegas, NV with her husband and loves being a grandmother.

CRIS COMERFORD
Chef to the Chiefs

Cris has been the executive chef for the White House since 2005 and is the first woman and person of ethnic minority origin to hold the position. She was hired as assistant chef in 1995 and appointed as head of the White House kitchen by the First Lady Laura Bush and retained by the Obama administration. Her love for cooking was nurtured by her mother, whom she assisted in the kitchen as a child. Cris has over 26 years of culinary experience including studying food technology at the University of the Philippines and working at various restaurants and hotels in Chicago, Washington, D.C., and Vienna, Austria. She is a member of the exclusive Le Club des Chefs des Chefs, a global association of chefs of heads of state. Cris has teamed up with the First Lady Obama's *Let's Move Initiative* to help promote healthy and nourishing food. Aside from being known for her food's vibrant colors and flavors, Cris is also a dedicated mentor, church deacon, wife, and mother.   <http://www.letsmove.gov>

Kristine M. Custodio, ACP
Chronicles of a Meeting Queen: ...

Kristine is a Senior Paralegal/Business Development Director for Butterfield Schechter & Van Clief LLP. She did her paralegal studies at the University of California, San Diego (UCSD) in 2004, became a Certified Paralegal in 2006, and received her Advanced Certified Paralegal designations in Discovery (2009) and Trial Practice (2010). In 2006, she obtained her Human Resource Management certificate from UCSD while serving as an administrator for her family's adult residential facility for developmentally disabled adults. Her many elected and appointed positions include: Vice President of Policy for the California Alliance of Paralegal Associations (2014), member of National Association of Legal Assistants-Paralegals (NALA) Continuing Education Council (2014), Rancho Peñasquitos Town Council (2103), Commissioner for the City of San Diego's Citizens Equal Opportunity Commission (2013), ethics chair for the Professional Development Committee (2009), and UCSD's Lambda Epsilon Chi, the National Honor Society in Paralegal/Legal Assistant Studies (2011).

CARMENCITA M. DAVID-PADILLA, M.D.
Guided Path: My Career in Medicine...

Carmencita is Professor of Pediatrics, College of Medicine, University of the Philippines (UP). She concurrently holds 3 positions: Executive Director of the Philippine Genome Center, UP System; Director, Newborn Screening Reference Center, National Institutes of Health, UP Manila; and Interim Director, Institute of Health Innovation and Translational Medicine of the Philippine California Advanced Research Institutes. Among her awards are: UPAA Distinguished Award in Health Education (2014), Most Outstanding Pediatrician (2013), Outstanding Science Administrator Award (2012), Outstanding Health Research Award (2010), and Academician of the National Academy of Science and Technology (2008). She has more than 100 publications. She crafted the Newborn Screening Act of 2004 and now lobbies for passage of the Rare Diseases Act of the Philippines. Dr. Padilla has an MA in Health Policy Studies from the UP College of Public Health (2005). She completed her pediatric residency at the Philippine General Hospital and a fellowship in Clinical Genetics at the Royal Alexandra Hospital for Children, Sydney, Australia.

SONIA T. DELEN-FITZIMMONS
From the Boondocks to the Boardroom

Sonia is known for her business acumen and support for many global causes. She is a Senior Vice President for Bank of America Merrill Lynch in San Francisco. She was the Executive Producer of the documentary *Harana*. Sonia sits on boards of FWN, Philippine International Aid, the University of the Philippines Alumni Association of San Francisco, and the Apl. de.ap Foundation International. She co-founded 'Kulinarya' an amateur and professional chefs competition to raise awareness about Filipino cuisine. As

an entrepreneur, she co-founded AcuGlobal Endeavors, an international trading and licensing company that exchanges goods and services in Asia. In 2010, Sonia received the Presidential Citation from President Gloria Macapagal-Arroyo for her decades of service in the Fil-Am community in the San Francisco Bay Area, and for raising funds for those affected by Typhoon Ketsana. Sonia appears on the FWN You Tube Channel's mentoring program. Sonia enjoys golf, classical music, and opera. She is married to Christopher Fitzsimmons and they have three sons—David, Justin, and Matthew.

ERNESTINA DELOS SANTOS-MAC, M.D.
Leadership by Inspiration

Determined to extricate herself from poverty, Ernie devised a plan to fulfill her dream of a better life. Her plan was simple and based on getting a good education. Since elementary school, she single-mindedly pursued her plan to obtain the best possible education. She hurdled obstacles posed by 'non-believers' who frowned on women who wanted to obtain college education. Her sacrifices included living in a depressed area in San Andres Bukid, Manila and walking every day to the University of Santo Tomas campus. Another obstacle was her father's opposition to her plan to take the test needed for medical jobs in the U.S. However, an uncle gave her the money to take the qualifying exam. Living in the U.S. for more than 40 years transformed the indigent girl from Bicol to a lady whose heart bleeds when she sees the woeful plight of the poor. She made a lifetime commitment to help the less fortunate through charitable activities benefiting poor people in the Philippines and in Michigan.

Amelia Duran-Stanton, Ph.D.
Standing on the Shoulder of Filipina...

Amelia is an Inspector General and a Physician Assistant (PA) with the U.S. Army Medical Command. Her military and medical career began in basic combat training in 1992. She was an enlisted patient administrator and then became a PA officer. She holds a Doctor of Science in PA Studies-Clinical Orthopaedics (DScPAS-CO), a Ph.D. in Postsecondary and Adult Education, a Masters in PA Studies, and a Bachelor in Business Administration. She was deployed to Kosovo, Iraq, and Afghanistan. Her awards include the Meritorious Service Medal, Army Commendation Award, Global War on Terrorism Service Medal, Global War on Terrorism Expeditionary Medal, Combat Medical Badge, and Expert Field Medical Badge. She is a member of the Order of Military Medical Merit, an Iron Majors recipient, a Distinguished Fellow of the American Academy of PA, and the first PA recipient of the Army Medical Specialist Corps New Horizon Research Award. She is an active mentor for researchers, PAs, and soldiers. She is married to Ralph Stanton, Jr. and they have two children, Sofia and Antonio.

ANNALISA ENRILE, PH.D.
We Speak their Names

Annalisa is Clinical Associate Professor at the University of Southern California (USC) School of Social Work. Her areas of research focus around transnational communities, particularly in the areas of adolescents and families, immigration, community based practice models, and gender/diversity issues. She is the Chair of the Community Organization, Planning Administration Concentration at USC and Chair of the MSW Foundation Behavior Sequence. She has worked with a number of community-based social service and women's organizations, including Search to Involve Pilipino Americans, the Board of Directors of the Mariposa Center for Change, and the YWCA. As a Fulbright Fellow, she created global immersion programs in the Philippines, bringing together student learning, activism, and feminist empowerment. She earned her BA in Sociology, her Masters in Social Work, and her Ph.D. in Social Welfare at the University of California, Los Angeles (UCLA). She dedicates her work to the strong women of her family--her mother, Eliza Enrile; her grandmother, Milagring Vicente; and her niece, Harley.

Penelope V. Flores, Ph.D.
Ad Astra per Aspira: ...

Penelope is Professor Emerita, San Francisco State University, Multicultural Education, Mathematics Education, and Teacher Credential program. She is an author, writer, and editor of academic journals. She earned her Ph.D. in Comparative and International Education at the University of Chicago, Masters in Educational Leadership at the University of Pennyslvania and B.Sc. in Education from the Philippine Normal University. She states: "I am a teacher of teachers in a post-modern world where the rights of ethnic minorities and women are continually challenged. The singularity of preparing credentialed teachers is an event of great importance to me because everything that follows it is altered forever." She served on the Boards of the Illinois and California Humanities Councils. She was a consultant to UNESCO, USAID, AED, UNDP, and to Ministries of Education in Nepal, Indonesia, & Ethiopia. She read papers at the World Council for Curriculum and Instruction conferences. As co-founder & past president of PAWA, she created the Manuel G. Flores Prize Fund to support FilAm writers.

JULIETA GABIOLA, M.D.
ABCs for Global Health

Dr. "Jette" is a Clinical Associate Professor of Medicine at Stanford University. Her clinical focus includes women's health services, essential hypertension, diabetes, and global health. Dr. Jette earned her BSN from Far Eastern University in the Philippines and her MD from Rush University. She completed her internship and residency at Stanford University, worked with Kaiser Permanente Medical Center, VA Medical Center, and ran a private practice in Utah. Her awards recognized her academic excellence, outstanding contributions in teaching, and her volunteerism. She is passionate about community work and has done significant work mentoring and developing medical students including authoring a textbook for aspiring medical professionals. She is the Founder of ABC's for Global Health, a nonprofit to develop community-centered solutions to prevent chronic diseases and promote healthy lifestyles—an outcome of years of medical mission trips she led in the Philippines. Dr. Jette is a proud mother to two children. She reached the summit of Mt. Kilimanjaro and is an avid scuba diver.

Mira Gillet
Grit: Leadership through Social Media...

Mira is a second-generation Filipina American. She lives in the San Francisco Bay Area with her husband Charles and their two beautiful children, Eva and Charlie. Mira was born in Daly City and grew up in Fremont, CA in a multi-generational household with her mother, Lally Soriano; father, Eliezer B. Soriano; twin sisters, Karen and Liza; and her grandparents. Mira is a California-credentialed teacher with a Masters of Education in Learning and Technology. She is trained in Design Thinking through Hasso Plattner Institute of Design at Stanford and has a Professional Certification in Project Management from Stanford University. Mira has a background in Graphic Design with a specialization in reading and working with dyslexic learners. She volunteers at the Marine Science Institute. She is also the Director of Design Thinking at Workshop Education and the founder and director of Peace Game online.

LENORE RS LIM
Full Circle

Lenore is an extraordinary printmaker who has led an extraordinary life. She is a pioneer and leader in printmaking. She received the Presidential Award, the Pamana ng Pilipino Award for Filipinos overseas in 2004 and the Outstanding Professional Award for Fine Arts from the University of the Philippines Alumni Association in 2005 for her accomplishments in the arts. She enjoys a growing audience of collectors in the U.S., where she was awarded a prestigious Jackson Pollock-Lee Krasner Foundation Grant, among other honors. She represented the Philippines at the UN World Women Conference Exhibit in New York in 2000 and OPEN, the International Exhibition of Sculptures and Installations, in Venice, Italy in 2002. Her work is included in the U.S. Library of Congress and the private collection of Agnes Gund, Chairman and President Emerita of The Museum of Modern Art in Manhattan. Ms. Gund wrote the foreword to *Profound Afterglow: The Prints of Lenore RS Lim* (2005). She is the president and founder of the Lenore RS Lim Foundation for the Arts.

SOLEDAD MUESCO MANAAY, PH.D.
The Power of Dreams

Soledad holds a Ph.D. in International Psychology and a Master's Degree in Gerontology/Psychology. She visited several countries to expand her knowledge of multiculturalism and the business practices of corporations across cultures. She is the President of Xicepta Sciences, Inc., a manufacturer of wellness supplements and the CEO of Biologic Cosmetics, Inc., a manufacturer of molecular cosmetics. Her business philosophy includes shaping a corporate culture that is sensitive to and supportive of diversity and motivating exemplary performance and productivity through empathy, understanding, and compassion. She believes that global mobility and e-commerce necessitates a diversified and flexible leadership strategy. She believes that the cycle of poverty can be broken through empowerment so she focused her company's corporate social responsibility function on education. Dr. Manaay is the author of two books for young adults. She is married to Dr. John S. Hayden, MD, PhD, who is also her business partner. She has a daughter from her previous marriage, Solitaire Patriz Manaay Miguel, and a silky terrier pet, Bebe.

ELENA MANGAHAS
Filipinas Rising

Elena Mangahas is a graduate of the University of the Philippines where she was also active in theater production with its repertory company. Elena currently serves as Chairperson for the Filipina Women's Network and serves on other boards. Her interests include historic preservation and goodwill relations. She received numerous awards that credit her for community work and mobilizing efforts. Her twenty years with the County as an employment specialist give her the advantage of working with various populations and creating programs that promote their economic independence. The work of FWN is near and dear to her heart because it represents her desire to insure that the significant contibutions of Filipinas are recognized in their adopted land.

ISABELITA MANALASTAS-WATANABE
Japan: A Love--Hate Relationship

Isabelita has studied, lived, and worked in Japan for more than half of her life. She started her Japan career as Deputy Director for Investment at the ASEAN-Japan Centre in Tokyo. She helped set up the Philippine National Bank's Japan presence, headed it, while also being Area Head for Asia and the Pacific. She was moved to Rome as First Senior Vice President and Area Head for Europe, Israel, and Africa, and resigned in June 2010, when she decided it was time to be with family. She became a full time wife and mother, but that was to last only a couple of months. Then she was back in the rat race, this time as the President of Speed Money Transfer Japan K.K. which she established. Lita lives in Tokyo with husband Fumio. Between the two of them and their children Anri, Chiori and JC, they speak 4 languages, have 3 nationalities, maintain 4 residences, and have a PhD degree (Sophia University), an M.A. (Tsukuba University), MBA (Wharton), a B.A. (UC San Diego), and a Diploma in Music (Cello, Toho Gakuen). They continue to live exciting, out of the ordinary lives as a family, and enjoy every moment. Lita continues to work 6/7, 12/24 as she has done during most of her professional life, but still manages to cook homemade meals, for an ever-appreciative husband who thinks Lita is a "genius" at being able to whip up a good meal in 15 minutes' time.

MARILY MONDEJAR
FWN and I

Marily, the CEO of the Filipina Women's Network (FWN) has dedicated the last decade to transforming how global Filipina women view themselves and how others perceive them. The transformed image is of women doing influential things. Her initiatives to bring about this transformation have included producing alternative and more positive search results on the Internet for the term "Filipina," embracing Eve Ensler's The Vagina Monologues and campaign to end domestic violence, and facilitating the creation of a pipeline of Filipina leaders with the skills to compete at all levels in all sectors. As the sixth of 13 children, Marily learned early how to get her voice heard by her family and carried this over throughout her career in roles such as a senior business leader, as a Board Member for organizations working on the Status of Women, and as a former Commissioner on the San Francisco Redistricting Task Force. Marily also draws from her experience as a survivor of an abusive relationship, a single mother, and a U.S. immigrant who started from scratch to promote networks for advancing the status of Filipina women globally. Marily has helped shift the language of mentorship to "femtorship," and the mindset of Filipinas from being a silent force in society to a catalyst in changing the face of power in America and worldwide. Her impact can be measured by the countless number of women she brought along with her and those they will in turn bring along with them to positions of leadership. San Francisco Mayor Ed Lee appointed Marily as Commissioner of the Community Investment and Infrastructure, the successor agency for the Redevelopment Commission responsible for $20 billion in assets to create jobs, affordable housing, commercial space, parks and open space areas.

JUDGE CHERYL NORA MOSS
Nevada's First Filipina ...

Judge Cheryl Nora Moss was born in Milwaukee, Wisconsin. She is a first generation Filipino-American and daughter of two medical doctors, Dr. Demetrio T. Nora and Dr. Rena Oquendo Magno Nora, who both graduated from the University of Santo Tomas (UST) Faculty of Medicine and Surgery, Philippines. Judge Moss has served in public office as the State of Nevada's first Filipino elected to a District Court. Judge Moss has two siblings, a brother who is an oncology surgeon in Los Angeles, California, and a sister who is a corporate executive in New York City. Judge Moss is married and her husband has been involved in the construction of City Center, Trump Tower Las Vegas, Red Rock Hotel & Casino, Hoover Dam Bypass, and The Las Vegas Springs Preserve. She has three dogs.

JANET SUSAN RODRIGUEZ NEPALES
Writing for Sainthood

Janet is the first and only Filipina member of the Hollywood Foreign Press Association that gives the Golden Globe Awards. Since 2007, she has sponsored the 'Janet Susan Rodriguez Nepales Journalism Awards' for deserving journalism students at her alma mater, Quezon City High School. She is a member of the International Women's Media Foundation, National Association of Professional Women, and LA Press Club. Janet won 1st prize in the Outstanding Entertainment category for the 2012 Philippine American Press Club's Plaridel Journalism Awards and 2nd prize in the Best Columnist/Critic-International Journalism category for the 2013 LA Press Club's Southern CA Journalism Awards. She is a columnist for the *Manila Bulletin* and *Philippine News*, a contributing editor at *Balikbayan Magazine*, and a correspondent for GMA-7. Awards she has received include the 2005 Celebrity Chronicle Journalist of the Year Award, the 2007 Asian PR-Wire Journalist of the Month Award, and the 2008 Quezon City Alumni Association Multi-Media Award. She graduated cum laude from the University of Santo Tomas.

IMELDA NICOLAS
Learnings from Several Lifetimes

Imelda is Chairperson of the Commission on Filipinos Overseas (CFO), a Cabinet-level position under the President of the Philippines. She chairs the Metropolis Asia Secretariat, is a member of the Metropolis International Steering Committee, and is on the Experts' Advisory Committee of the World Bank's Global Knowledge Partnership on Migration and Development. She teaches a course on International Migration and Development for the Metropolis Professional Development. She was Cabinet-level Sec. of the National Anti-Poverty Commision, former Chair of the National Commission on the Role of Filipino Women, Presidential Asst. for monitoring government funded infrastructures, Chair of the Women's Business Council of the Philippines, delegate to the APEC Business Advisory Council & head of the Philippine delegation at the Beijing UN Conference on Women in 1995. She was VP for Development at the New York-based TLC Beatrice International Holdings, Inc., & Managing Director at TLC Beatrice China. Secretary Nicolas graduated magna cum laude from St. Theresa's College & completed graduate courses in Arts History at Columbia University.

PATRICIA ANN V. PAEZ
Being a Woman Ambassador

Patricia is the Ambassador of the Philippines to Poland and non-resident Ambassador to Lithuania, Estonia, and Latvia. She is the first female Philippine ambassador to Poland since the Embassy reopened in 2009. Since she assumed her official duty in March 2013, the Philippine Embassy has participated in the Congress of Women sponsored by Poland's Ministry of Foreign Affairs and 40th anniversary of Poland-Philippines diplomatic relations with a feature on the Philippines in *Gazeta Wyborcza* and an interview in Poland's top-rated morning show about the status of women in the Philippines and the issue of human trafficking. She served two Presidents as Presidential Assistant for Foreign Affairs and as Executive Director of the Office of the Presidential Adviser for Foreign Affairs. She was assigned to the Philippine Embassy in Washington, D.C. She received the Presidential Order of Merit and the Gawad Mabini Award for her exemplary service in foreign policy and diplomacy. She graduated with a M.A. in International Relations from the Australian National University in Canberra and was a Fellow in Public Policy at the University of Maryland, U.S.

LOIDA NICOLAS-LEWIS
Ora et Labora: A Girl Named ...

Loida Nicolas Lewis served as Chair and CEO of LTC Beatrice International, a $2 billion multinational food company. She assumed leadership of the company after the death of her husband, the African-American financier Reginal F. Lewis. She provided successful, compassionate, faith based leadership of the company and after six years sold the company for a significant profit. Loida was recognized as the Top Business Woman in America in 1995. She currently heads a family investment firm. Previously she was General Attorney with the Immigration and Naturalization Service after winning a discrimination case against the INS. Her best-selling book *How to Get a Green Card* now is in its 10th edition. Loida is a philanthropist and a leader of the Filipino-American community. She founded The Lewis College (TLC) in Sorsogon in 1998. As noted in a recent *Philippine Daily Inquirer* article, she credits her father for her interest in politics and her entrepreneurial spirit. The article also noted that her two daughters graduated from Harvard and have successful careers.

Susie Quesada
Mommyla, Popsy and Me: ...

Susie is the President of Ramar Foods International, the leading manufacturer of Filipino and Asian frozen food in the U.S. Born and raised in the San Francisco Bay Area, Susie attended the University of California at Berkeley and graduated with a B.A. in Multicultural Literature and Education. She completed her Multiple Subject Credential at St. Mary's College and taught middle school in the public school system in California. She officially joined her family's business Ramar Foods International in 2005. With a background in education, her ability to work with many different personality types proved to be a strong asset when applied to the business world. She has served on the board of the Filipina Women's Network since 2012 and the Ramar Scholarship Foundation since 2010. She is also a member and VP for Education of the Toastmaster groups the Pittsburg Speakeasy and the RAMARkables. She currently resides in Walnut Creek, CA with her husband Dr. Christopher Woolf where they enjoy cycling, traveling, and spending time with their two cats and extended family.

Shirley Raguindin
Beating the Odds

Colonel Shirley S. Raguindin serves as Chief of National Guard Diversity to the Chief, National Guard Bureau (NGB), General Frank J. Grass. In her dual role she serves as Chief Diversity Officer as principal advisor to Director, Air National Guard (ANG). Lieutenant General Stanley E. Clarke III. She is responsible for the strategic direction, implementation, and alignment of ANG's integrated global diversity and inclusion initiatives to achieve the highest state of military readiness for over 458,000 Soldiers, Airmen, and civilians. Shirley was commissioned in 1986 as a distinguished graduate of the Air Force Reserve Officer Training Corps program from the University of Hawaii. She is the recipient of the Diversity Training University International Diversity Executive Leadership Award (2014), International Women's Outstanding Leadership Award (2013), and Diversity Officer LeadershipAward by Diversity Best Practices, Inc.

DELIA B.RODRIGUEZ-AMAYA, PH.D.
Uphill Road to Success in Science ...

Delia is the first woman president of the International Academy of Food Science and Technology. She was professor of Food Engineering, University of Campinas, Brazil (1977-2010) where she was Chair of the Department of Food Science, Coordinator of the Faculty Graduate Programs and Faculty Academic Council. She was advisor for 48 Masters and Doctoral theses. Her awards include: Presidential Award *Pamana ng Pilipino*, East-West Center Distinguished Alumni, Brazilian Society of Food Science and Technology's Andre Tosello Award, Philippine Association of Food Technologists' 50th Anniversary Recognition Award. Her research achievements include: more than 240 publications, invited lectures and 240 conference paper presentations in 25 countries. She is a visiting Professor at a new Brazilian federal university, scientific adviser of the International Foundation for Science, editor of *Current Opinion in Food Chemistry and Biochemistry*, and on the editorial board of five scientific journals. Her Ph.D. is in Agricultural Chemistry from the University of California Davis.

ADELA SERING-FOJAS
Pakikisama, Building Relationships...

Delle is the CEO and co-founder of Seven Seven Corporate Group, a comprehensive and integrated IT services company, offering services including onsite consulting and placement, software development, business process outsourcing, production and application support, and call center services. Her passion and the vision of her firm is to showcase the skills and talents of Filipino IT workers while creating thousands of jobs in Manila. She shares this vision with all of her employees. The company has evolved into an end-to-end, single source global provider of choice for IT-enabled services. Its success is attributed to collaborative partnerships, proven multinational and multi-industry track record, capacity expansion and value chain integration. Under Delle's leadership, Seven Seven has been consistently honored with DiversityBusiness.com's Top Business Award. Delle was selected for one of the Top 50 Asian-American Business Awards in 2011. Delle has initiated a scholarship program for the children of her company, and she and her husband donated a computer laboratory to the University of the Philippines.

LIRIO SOBREVIÑAS-COVEY, PH.D.
Letter to a Young Filipina

Lirio was class president and recipient of first academic honors each year starting in Grade 1. She was Student Council President in high school and college, and Treasurer of the National Union of Students. In 1964, she received a Ten Outstanding Students of the Philippines (TOS) award. Dr. Sobrevinas-Covey completed a B.S. in Commerce, Summa Cum Laude, from St. Theresa's College, Manila. She has lived in New York since 1965, where she completed a M.A. degree, a Ph.D. in Social and Personality Psychology, and a post-doctoral fellowship in Psychiatric Epidemiology. She is also a licensed Psychologist. Since 1987 she has worked at the New York State Institute and led the Smoking Cessation Clinic at Columbia University. Her areas of teaching and research include nicotine addiction, smoking cessation, major depression, attention deficit hyperactivity disorders, suicidal behavior, and research methods. She has extensive publications. She founded the Association for Adults with Autism Philippines (AAAP) in 2012 to focus on diagnostic, policy, and treatment issues affecting the lives of autism families.

JANET C. MENDOZA STICKMON
Blackapina

Janet is a teacher, performer, and author of *Crushing Soft Rubies* and *Midnight Peaches, Two O'clock Patience*. She has taught ethnic studies, social justice, and other subjects at the high school level and is a professor of Humanities at Napa Valley College where she teaches Filipina(o)-American Heritage, American Mind, and Introduction to Africana Studies. She founded and is a facilitator of the Broken Shackle Developmental Training Program, a program that promotes the use of healing techniques to help reduce the effects of internalized racism. Her books have been used in courses colleges across the country. As a spoken word artist she has performed at venues across the country. Through her literature and performances, she explores issues of love, motherhood, resilience, ancestral connection, and joy. She holds an M.A. in Ethnic Studies from San Francisco State University, an M.A. in Religion and Society from the Graduate Theological Union in Berkeley, and a B.S. in Civil Engineering from the University of California, Irvine.

ASTRID S. TUMINEZ, PH.D.
A Filipina in the Word, ...

Astrid joined Microsoft in 2012 as Regional Director, Legal and Corporate Affairs (Southeast Asia). She is an Adjunct Professor and former Vice-Dean at the Lee Kuan Yew School of Public Policy. At the U.S. Institute of Peace she was involved in peace negotiations between the Philippine government and the Moro Islamic Liberation Front. She was a research director at AIG Global Investments and Moscow office director of the Harvard Project on Strengthening Democratic Institutions. She is the author of *Russian Nationalism since 1856. Ideology and the Making of Foreign Policy* and "Rising to the Top? A Report on Women's Leadership in Asia." Astrid was a U.S. Institute of Peace Scholar, a Salzburg Freeman Fellow, a Harvard Kennedy School Fellow, and a Distinguished Alumna of Brigham Young University. She received fellowships from the Social Science Research Council and MacArthur Foundation, and serves on the boards of the Bank of the Philippine Islands and Singapore American School. She has a Master's in Soviet Studies from Harvard University and a Ph.D. in Political Science from MIT.

MARIFE ZAMORA
Leading an Industry: My Journey...

Marife is Chairperson of Convergys Philippines Services, a branch of Convergys Corporation (NYSE: CVG), a global leader in customer management. As the first country manager for Convergys she set up its first contact center in 2003. Since then Convergys Philippines has become the country's largest private employer. In 2011, she assumed responsibility for Convergys contact centers in the Philippines, India, United Kingdom, and Malaysia. Prior positions included serving as managing director for Headstrong Incorporated and IBM Philippines. She has provided leadership for numerous associations in the Philippines including the Philippine Software Association, Contact Center Association. American Chamber of Commerce, and the Integrity Initiative. Honors include the Asia CEO Awards 2011 Global Filipino Executive of the Year and the 'Go Negosyo' Woman STARpreneuer Award in the 2012 at the Women Entrepreneurship Summit. Marife attended the University of the Philippines and the Wharton School of the University of Pennsylvania.

Filipina Women's Network

Significant Milestones
2002 - 2013

2002 – First Filipina Summit @ Moscone Convention Center: CEO Panel

(L to R) Rica Echavez, Katherine Zarate, Celia Tomlinson, Dina Guingona, Laarni San Juan, Anna Villena, Cora Tellez, Evelyn Dilsaver, Elaine Serina, Tessie Guillermo, Cristina Dunham, Polly Cortez, Maya Ruiz, Marily Mondejar, Lisa Yuchengco

Photo Credit: Marily Mondejar's Photo Collection

Filipina Women Against Violence: The first all-Filipina women production of Eve Ensler's *The Vagina Monologues*. Cast and Crew with Eve Ensler at the Mark Hopkins Hotel, 2004.

Photo Credit: Nerissa Fernandez

570

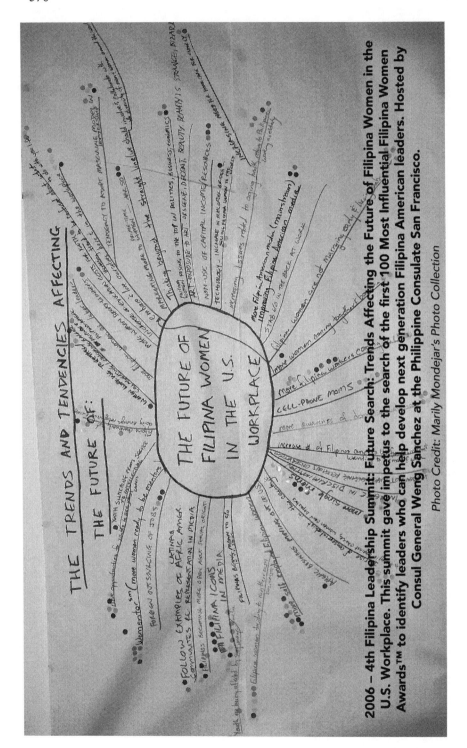

2006 – 4th Filipina Leadership Summit: Future Search: Trends Affecting the Future of Filipina Women in the U.S. Workplace. This summit gave impetus to the search of the first 100 Most Influential Filipina Women Awards™ to identify leaders who can help develop next generation Filipina American leaders. Hosted by Consul General Weng Sánchez at the Philippine Consulate San Francisco.

Photo Credit: Marily Mondejar's Photo Collection

Victoria Manalo Draves (4th from left, seated) attended the 4th Filipina Leadership Summit (2006). She was the first Asian-American diver who overcame ethnic prejudice to become the first woman to win springboard and platform gold medals in the 1948 U.S. Olympics. Vicki Manalo was the daughter of a Filipino father and an English mother, in a society in which mixed marriages were generally frowned on. Photo

Credit: *Marily Mondejar's Photo Collection*

US FWN100™ 2007 at the 5th Filipina Leadership Summit at the Hyatt Washington DC

Photo Credit: Gani Ricarte Photography

US FWN100™ 2009 at the 6th Filipina Leadership Summit at Claremont Hotel Berkeley, California

Photo Credit: Brenda Hartshorn

US FWN100™ 2011 at the 8th Filipina Leadership Summit at the Stanford Court, San Francisco, California

Photo Credit: Gani Ricarte Photography

US FWN100™ 2012 at the 9th Filipina Leadership Summit at the Stanford Court, San Francisco, California

Photo Credit: Meo Baaklini Photography

FWN expands search of influential Filipina women worldwide. Global FWN100™ 2011 at the 10th Filipina Leadership Summit at the Mark Hopkins Intercontinental Hotel, San Francisco, California

Photo Credit: Gani Ricarte Photography

Filipina Women's Network Magazine (2005-2013)

CREDIT: All the FWN Magazines designed by Al Perez

578

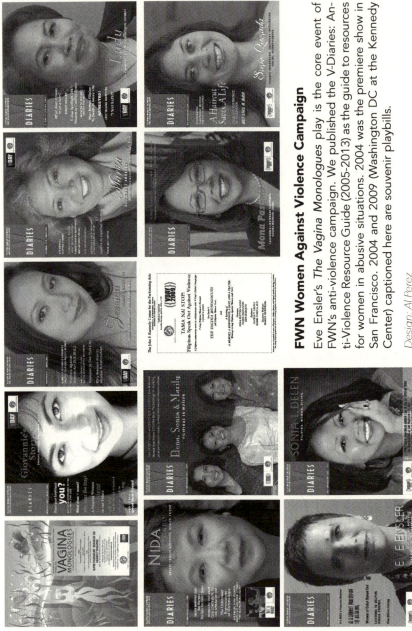

FWN Women Against Violence Campaign

Eve Ensler's *The Vagina Monologues* play is the core event of FWN's anti-violence campaign. We published the V-Diaries: Anti-Violence Resource Guide (2005-2013) as the guide to resources for women in abusive situations. 2004 was the premiere show in San Francisco. 2004 and 2009 (Washington DC at the Kennedy Center) captioned here are souvenir playbills.

Design: Al Perez

FWN Significant Events

(L to R) 2009 was a banner year: we launched the Filipina Salo Salo Adobo Crawl to support Filipino restaurants when the recession hit the U.S. and to highlight Filipino cuisine; premiered the *Sheroes Monologues*, a play about the women of the Philippine Revolution. Encouraging Filipina women to run for elected office started in 2006; 2010 saw more members active in politics. In 2012 we closed the FWN Time Capsule during the summit providing our next generation in 2112 a glimpse of Filipina women's achievements. Our founder, Marily Mondejar keynoted V-Day's 2013 One Billion Rising city-wide rally at San Francisco City Hall with Mayor Ed Lee, the Board of Supervisors, DA George Gascon, Police Chief Greg Suhr and over 4,000 activists. FWN responds to Typhoon Haiyan/Yolanda REBUILD Tacloban in 2014.

Salo Salo, Sheroes Monologues, Victory Party flyers designed by Al Perez, Tacloban flyer designed by Elisa Sunga Photo Credit: Marily Mondejar's Photo Collection,

Al Perez and **F.M. Ricarte,** rockstar volunteers, have been critical to the success of FWN the last 12 years. Al Perez designs the FWN marketing collaterals, including the FWN Magazine, the V-Diaries, Anti-Violence Resource Guide. Franklin designs the FWN websites and has been advisor and inspiration to the many initiatives of the FWN.

Photo Credit: Gani Ricarte Photography

About the Filipina Leadership Global Summit

Filipina Women's Network's annual meeting brings together Filipina women global leaders, influencers, thinkers and public figures for workshops, discussions, "kwentuhan" and private chats to ignite cooperation through public and private partnerships. The high-powered gathering is a vital part of FWN's Pinay Power 2020 Mission: A Filipina leader in every sector of the economy. Now on its 11th year, the 2014 summit will be held outside of the United States for the first time in the Philippines, our home country. The 2014 global summit's theme is "Disrupt: Be Proud. Be Loud. Leave No Doubt." The summit convenes sessions and learning journeys that reflect on the changes that sparked transformations in the lives of global Filipinas, and the disruptive strategies and unexpected solutions that influenced Filipina careers and businesses. More info: http://summit.filipinawomensnetwork.org

About the Global FWN100™ Awards

The Most Influential Filipina Women in the World Award™ recognizes Filipina women who are influencing the face of leadership in the global workplace, having reached status for outstanding work in their respective fields and are recognized for their leadership, achievement and contributions to society, femtorship and legacy. The awardees are asked to femtor a young Pinay through the FEMtorship initiative and bring her to the Filipina Summit. More info: http://summit.filipinawomensnetwork.org/100-most-influential-filipinas/

About FEMtorMatch™

FEMtorMatch™ is FWN's strategy for development of next generation of Filipina leaders through local and global partnerships between female mentors—FEMtors™ and female mentees—FEMtees™. FEMtorMatch™ provides structured one-on-one femtoring that harnesses the power of the Internet to broaden and deepen the reach of traditional femtoring. Thus, both FEMtors™ and FEMtees™ can reside anywhere in the world.

582

Board of Directors
Filipina Women's Network

DISRUPT book orders:

Philippine Launch: October 6, 2014 at the
11th Filipina Leadership Global Summit, Philippines

U.S.A. Launch: November 3, 2014
at the Charles Schwab Learning Center, San Francisco, California

Book tour schedule in the U.S. and selected cities overseas,
email Filipina@ffwn.org

Book orders: http://www.ffwn.org/event-876425

More info: 1.415.935.4396
• www.facebook.com/FilipinaWomensNetwork
• filipina@ffwn.org

Cover Design by Lucille Tenazas, Tenazas Design/NY

Made in the USA
Las Vegas, NV
18 September 2021